T0180905

Lecture Notes in Computer Science 12667

More information about this subseries at http://www.springer.com/series/7412

Alberto Del Bimbo · Rita Cucchiara ·
Stan Sclaroff · Giovanni Maria Farinella ·
Tao Mei · Marco Bertini ·
Hugo Jair Escalante · Roberto Vezzani (Eds.)

Pattern Recognition

ICPR International Workshops and Challenges

Virtual Event, January 10–15, 2021
Proceedings, Part VII

 Springer

Editors
Alberto Del Bimbo 🆔
Dipartimento di Ingegneria
dell'Informazione
University of Firenze
Firenze, Italy

Stan Sclaroff 🆔
Department of Computer Science
Boston University
Boston, MA, USA

Tao Mei
Cloud & AI, JD.COM
Beijing, China

Hugo Jair Escalante 🆔
Computational Sciences Department
National Institute of Astrophysics,
Optics and Electronics (INAOE)
Tonantzintla, Puebla, Mexico

Rita Cucchiara 🆔
Dipartimento di Ingegneria "Enzo Ferrari"
Università di Modena e Reggio Emilia
Modena, Italy

Giovanni Maria Farinella 🆔
Dipartimento di Matematica e Informatica
University of Catania
Catania, Italy

Marco Bertini 🆔
Dipartimento di Ingegneria
dell'Informazione
University of Firenze
Firenze, Italy

Roberto Vezzani 🆔
Dipartimento di Ingegneria "Enzo Ferrari"
Università di Modena e Reggio Emilia
Modena, Italy

ISSN 0302-9743 ISSN 1611-3349 (electronic)
Lecture Notes in Computer Science
ISBN 978-3-030-68786-1 ISBN 978-3-030-68787-8 (eBook)
https://doi.org/10.1007/978-3-030-68787-8

LNCS Sublibrary: SL6 – Image Processing, Computer Vision, Pattern Recognition, and Graphics

This Springer imprint is published by the registered company Springer Nature Switzerland AG
The registered company address is: Gewerbestrasse 11, 6330 Cham, Switzerland

Foreword by General Chairs

It is with great pleasure that we welcome you to the post-proceedings of the 25th International Conference on Pattern Recognition, ICPR2020 Virtual-Milano. ICPR2020 stands on the shoulders of generations of pioneering pattern recognition researchers. The first ICPR (then called IJCPR) convened in 1973 in Washington, DC, USA, under the leadership of Dr. King-Sun Fu as the General Chair. Since that time, the global community of pattern recognition researchers has continued to expand and thrive, growing evermore vibrant and vital. The motto of this year's conference was *Putting Artificial Intelligence to work on patterns*. Indeed, the deep learning revolution has its origins in the pattern recognition community – and the next generations of revolutionary insights and ideas continue with those presented at this 25th ICPR. Thus, it was our honor to help perpetuate this longstanding ICPR tradition to provide a lively meeting place and open exchange for the latest pathbreaking work in pattern recognition.

For the first time, the ICPR main conference employed a two-round review process similar to journal submissions, with new papers allowed to be submitted in either the first or the second round and papers submitted in the first round and not accepted allowed to be revised and re-submitted for second round review. In the first round, 1554 new submissions were received, out of which 554 (35.6%) were accepted and 579 (37.2%) were encouraged to be revised and resubmitted. In the second round, 1696 submissions were received (496 revised and 1200 new), out of which 305 (61.4%) of the revised submissions and 552 (46%) of the new submissions were accepted. Overall, there were 3250 submissions in total, and 1411 were accepted, out of which 144 (4.4%) were included in the main conference program as orals and 1263 (38.8%) as posters (4 papers were withdrawn after acceptance). We had the largest ICPR conference ever, with the most submitted papers and the most selective acceptance rates ever for ICPR, attesting both the increased interest in presenting research results at ICPR and the high scientific quality of work accepted for presentation at the conference.

We were honored to feature seven exceptional Keynotes in the program of the ICPR2020 main conference: David Doermann (Professor at the University at Buffalo), Pietro Perona (Professor at the California Institute of Technology and Amazon Fellow at Amazon Web Services), Mihaela van der Schaar (Professor at the University of Cambridge and a Turing Fellow at The Alan Turing Institute in London), Max Welling (Professor at the University of Amsterdam and VP of Technologies at Qualcomm), Ching Yee Suen (Professor at Concordia University) who was presented with the IAPR 2020 King-Sun Fu Prize, Maja Pantic (Professor at Imperial College UK and AI Scientific Research Lead at Facebook Research) who was presented with the IAPR 2020 Maria Petrou Prize, and Abhinav Gupta (Professor at Carnegie Mellon University and Research Manager at Facebook AI Research) who was presented with the IAPR 2020 J.K. Aggarwal Prize. Several best paper prizes were also announced and awarded, including the Piero Zamperoni Award for the best paper authored by a student, the BIRPA Best Industry Related Paper Award, and Best Paper Awards for each of the five tracks of the ICPR2020 main conference.

The five tracks of the ICPR2020 main conference were: (1) Artificial Intelligence, Machine Learning for Pattern Analysis, (2) Biometrics, Human Analysis and Behavior Understanding, (3) Computer Vision, Robotics and Intelligent Systems, (4) Document and Media Analysis, and (5) Image and Signal Processing. The best papers presented at the main conference had the opportunity for publication in expanded format in journal special issues of *IET Biometrics* (tracks 2 and 3), *Computer Vision and Image Understanding* (tracks 1 and 2), *Machine Vision and Applications* (tracks 2 and 3), *Multimedia Tools and Applications* (tracks 4 and 5), *Pattern Recognition Letters* (tracks 1, 2, 3 and 4), or *IEEE Trans. on Biometrics, Behavior, and Identity Science* (tracks 2 and 3).

In addition to the main conference, the ICPR2020 program offered workshops and tutorials, along with a broad range of cutting-edge industrial demos, challenge sessions, and panels. The virtual ICPR2020 conference was interactive, with real-time live-streamed sessions, including live talks, poster presentations, exhibitions, demos, Q&A, panels, meetups, and discussions – all hosted on the Underline virtual conference platform.

The ICPR2020 conference was originally scheduled to convene in Milano, which is one of the most beautiful cities of Italy for art, culture, lifestyle – and more. The city has so much to offer! With the need to go virtual, ICPR2020 included interactive **virtual tours** of Milano during the conference coffee breaks, which we hoped would introduce attendees to this wonderful city, and perhaps even entice them to visit Milano once international travel becomes possible again.

The success of such a large conference would not have been possible without the help of many people. We deeply appreciate the vision, commitment, and leadership of the ICPR2020 Program Chairs: Kim Boyer, Brian C. Lovell, Marcello Pelillo, Nicu Sebe, René Vidal, and Jingyi Yu. Our heartfelt gratitude also goes to the rest of the main conference organizing team, including the Track and Area Chairs, who all generously devoted their precious time in conducting the review process and in preparing the program, and the reviewers, who carefully evaluated the submitted papers and provided invaluable feedback to the authors. This time their effort was considerably higher given that many of them reviewed for both reviewing rounds. We also want to acknowledge the efforts of the conference committee, including the Challenge Chairs, Demo and Exhibit Chairs, Local Chairs, Financial Chairs, Publication Chair, Tutorial Chairs, Web Chairs, Women in ICPR Chairs, and Workshop Chairs. Many thanks, also, for the efforts of the dedicated staff who performed the crucially important work behind the scenes, including the members of the ICPR2020 Organizing Secretariat. Finally, we are grateful to the conference sponsors for their generous support of the ICPR2020 conference.

We hope everyone had an enjoyable and productive ICPR2020 conference.

Rita Cucchiara
Alberto Del Bimbo
Stan Sclaroff

Preface

The 25th International Conference on Pattern Recognition Workshops (ICPRW 2020) were held virtually in Milan, Italy and rescheduled to January 10 and January 11 of 2021 due to the Covid-19 pandemic. ICPRW 2020 included timely topics and applications of Computer Vision, Image and Sound Analysis, Pattern Recognition and Artificial Intelligence. We received 49 workshop proposals and 46 of them have been accepted, which is three times more than at ICPRW 2018. The workshop proceedings cover a wide range of areas including Machine Learning (8), Pattern Analysis (5), Healthcare (6), Human Behavior (5), Environment (5), Surveillance, Forensics and Biometrics (6), Robotics and Egovision (4), Cultural Heritage and Document Analysis (4), Retrieval (2), and Women at ICPR 2020 (1). Among them, 33 workshops are new to ICPRW. Specifically, the ICPRW 2020 volumes contain the following workshops (please refer to the corresponding workshop proceeding for details):

- CADL2020 – Workshop on Computational Aspects of Deep Learning.
- DLPR – Deep Learning for Pattern Recognition.
- EDL/AI – Explainable Deep Learning/AI.
- (Merged) IADS – Integrated Artificial Intelligence in Data Science, IWCR – IAPR workshop on Cognitive Robotics.
- ManifLearn – Manifold Learning in Machine Learning, From Euclid to Riemann.
- MOI2QDN – Metrification & Optimization of Input Image Quality in Deep Networks.
- IML – International Workshop on Industrial Machine Learning.
- MMDLCA – Multi-Modal Deep Learning: Challenges and Applications.
- IUC 2020 – Human and Vehicle Analysis for Intelligent Urban Computing.
- PATCAST – International Workshop on Pattern Forecasting.
- RRPR – Reproducible Research in Pattern Recognition.
- VAIB 2020 – Visual Observation and Analysis of Vertebrate and Insect Behavior.
- IMTA VII – Image Mining Theory & Applications.
- AIHA 2020 – Artificial Intelligence for Healthcare Applications.
- AIDP – Artificial Intelligence for Digital Pathology.
- (Merged) GOOD – Designing AI in support of Good Mental Health, CAIHA – Computational and Affective Intelligence in Healthcare Applications for Vulnerable Populations.
- CARE2020 – pattern recognition for positive teChnology And eldeRly wEllbeing.
- MADiMa 2020 – Multimedia Assisted Dietary Management.
- 3DHU 2020 – 3D Human Understanding.
- FBE2020 – Facial and Body Expressions, micro-expressions and behavior recognition.
- HCAU 2020 – Deep Learning for Human-Centric Activity Understanding.
- MPRSS - 6th IAPR Workshop on Multimodal Pattern Recognition for Social Signal Processing in Human Computer Interaction.

- CVAUI 2020 – Computer Vision for Analysis of Underwater Imagery.
- MAES – Machine Learning Advances Environmental Science.
- PRAConBE - Pattern Recognition and Automation in Construction & the Built Environment.
- PRRS 2020 – Pattern Recognition in Remote Sensing.
- WAAMI - Workshop on Analysis of Aerial Motion Imagery.
- DEEPRETAIL 2020 - Workshop on Deep Understanding Shopper Behaviours and Interactions in Intelligent Retail Environments 2020.
- MMForWild2020 – MultiMedia FORensics in the WILD 2020.
- FGVRID – Fine-Grained Visual Recognition and re-Identification.
- IWBDAF – Biometric Data Analysis and Forensics.
- RISS – Research & Innovation for Secure Societies.
- WMWB – TC4 Workshop on Mobile and Wearable Biometrics.
- EgoApp – Applications of Egocentric Vision.
- ETTAC 2020 – Eye Tracking Techniques, Applications and Challenges.
- PaMMO – Perception and Modelling for Manipulation of Objects.
- FAPER – Fine Art Pattern Extraction and Recognition.
- MANPU – coMics ANalysis, Processing and Understanding.
- PATRECH2020 – Pattern Recognition for Cultural Heritage.
- (Merged) CBIR – Content-Based Image Retrieval: where have we been, and where are we going, TAILOR – Texture AnalysIs, cLassificatiOn and Retrieval, VIQA – Video and Image Question Answering: building a bridge between visual content analysis and reasoning on textual data.
- W4PR - Women at ICPR.

We would like to thank all members of the workshops' Organizing Committee, the reviewers, and the authors for making this event successful. We also appreciate the support from all the invited speakers and participants. We wish to offer thanks in particular to the ICPR main conference general chairs: Rita Cucchiara, Alberto Del Bimbo, and Stan Sclaroff, and program chairs: Kim Boyer, Brian C. Lovell, Marcello Pelillo, Nicu Sebe, Rene Vidal, and Jingyi Yu. Finally, we are grateful to the publisher, Springer, for their cooperation in publishing the workshop proceedings in the series of Lecture Notes in Computer Science.

December 2020   Giovanni Maria Farinella
                                                                    Tao Mei

Challenges

Competitions are effective means for rapidly solving problems and advancing the state of the art. Organizers identify a problem of practical or scientific relevance and release it to the community. In this way the whole community can contribute to the solution of high-impact problems while having fun. This part of the proceedings compiles the best of the competitions track of the *25th International Conference on Pattern Recognition (ICPR)*.

Eight challenges were part of the track, covering a wide variety of fields and applications, all of this within the scope of ICPR. In every challenge organizers released data, and provided a platform for evaluation. The top-ranked participants were invited to submit papers for this volume. Likewise, organizers themselves wrote articles summarizing the design, organization and results of competitions. Submissions were subject to a standard review process carried out by the organizers of each competition. Papers associated with seven out the eight competitions are included in this volume, thus making it a representative compilation of what happened in the ICPR challenges.

We are immensely grateful to the organizers and participants of the ICPR 2020 challenges for their efforts and dedication to make the competition track a success. We hope the readers of this volume enjoy it as much as we have.

November 2020
Marco Bertini
Hugo Jair Escalante

ICPR Organization

General Chairs

Rita Cucchiara   Univ. of Modena and Reggio Emilia, Italy
Alberto Del Bimbo   Univ. of Florence, Italy
Stan Sclaroff   Boston Univ., USA

Program Chairs

Kim Boyer   Univ. at Albany, USA
Brian C. Lovell   Univ. of Queensland, Australia
Marcello Pelillo   Univ. Ca' Foscari Venezia, Italy
Nicu Sebe   Univ. of Trento, Italy
René Vidal   Johns Hopkins Univ., USA
Jingyi Yu   ShanghaiTech Univ., China

Workshop Chairs

Giovanni Maria Farinella   Univ. of Catania, Italy
Tao Mei   JD.COM, China

Challenge Chairs

Marco Bertini   Univ. of Florence, Italy
Hugo Jair Escalante   INAOE and CINVESTAV National Polytechnic
    Institute of Mexico, Mexico

Publication Chair

Roberto Vezzani   Univ. of Modena and Reggio Emilia, Italy

Tutorial Chairs

Vittorio Murino   Univ. of Verona, Italy
Sudeep Sarkar   Univ. of South Florida, USA

Women in ICPR Chairs

Alexandra Branzan Albu   Univ. of Victoria, Canada
Maria De Marsico   Univ. Roma La Sapienza, Italy

Demo and Exhibit Chairs

Lorenzo Baraldi   Univ. Modena Reggio Emilia, Italy
Bruce A. Maxwell   Colby College, USA
Lorenzo Seidenari   Univ. of Florence, Italy

Special Issue Initiative Chair

Michele Nappi   Univ. of Salerno, Italy

Web Chair

Andrea Ferracani   Univ. of Florence, Italy

Corporate Relations Chairs

Fabio Galasso   Univ. Roma La Sapienza, Italy
Matt Leotta   Kitware, Inc., USA
Zhongchao Shi   Lenovo Group Ltd., China

Local Chairs

Matteo Matteucci   Politecnico di Milano, Italy
Paolo Napoletano   Univ. of Milano-Bicocca, Italy

Financial Chairs

Cristiana Fiandra   The Office srl, Italy
Vittorio Murino   Univ. of Verona, Italy

Contents – Part VII

**PRAConBE - Pattern Recognition and Automation in Construction
and the Built Environment**

**PRRS 2020 - 11th IAPR Workshop on Pattern Recognition
in Remote Sensing**

**RISS 2020 - International Workshop on Research and Innovation
for Secure Societies**

PATCAST - International Workshop on Pattern Forecasting

International Workshop on Pattern Forecasting

Anticipating patterns has become a crucial activity in the last years, due to the combined availability of huge amount of data, techniques for exploiting noisy information, transferring knowledge across domains, and the need of forecasting services within many heterogeneous domains, from computer science to environmental sciences, from economics to robotics and from bioinformatics to social sciences and humanities. A growing spectrum of applications in self-driving cars, weather forecasting, financial market prediction, real-time epidemic forecasting, and social network modeling needs to be explored within a same venue. This first workshop aims therefore to identify commonalities, gather lessons learnt across domains, discuss modern and most successful techniques, and foster the exchange of new ideas, which may extend to other novel fields too.

The International Workshop on Pattern Forecasting addresses the general problem of forecasting patterns. This is not just limited to a specific domain, but rather intended as cross-fertilization of different disciplines. By doing so, it highlights possible general-purpose approaches which may be applied to a large span of data types, promoting and motivating further studies in specific directions. As an example, techniques for predicting the diffusion of epidemics are currently adopted to forecasting activities within social networks. We are convinced that many other hybridations are ready to be explored.

The workshop gathers contributions from researchers and practitioners from different domains, to share current best algorithms and practices, to foster discussion among diverse communities and to define common grounds for joint progress, within the general artificial intelligence and pattern recognition.

We have a number of invited talks by senior scientists from different domains and a final panel to gather the major challenges emerged in the day and the effective techniques. We have fructuous discussion on the relation between techniques and challenges and on the adoption of techniques beyond those fields where they have been originally designed.

We accept two papers for publication, which are thoroughly reviewed by 4 reviewers. In addition, we have 6 invited spotlight papers and an extensive poster session for stimulating collaborations among young researchers.

November 2020

Marco Cristani
Fabio Galasso
Kris Kitani
Siyu Tang

Organization

General Chairs

Marco Cristani   University of Verona, Italy
Fabio Galasso   Sapienza University of Rome, Italy
Kris Kitani   Carnegie Mellon University, USA
Siyu Tang   ETH Zürich, Switzerland

Adaptive Future Frame Prediction
with Ensemble Network

Wonjik Kim[1,2]($\boxtimes$) (ORCID), Masayuki Tanaka[1] (ORCID), Masatoshi Okutomi[1] (ORCID),
and Yoko Sasaki[2] (ORCID)

[1] Department of Systems and Control Engineering, School of Engineering,
Tokyo Institute of Technology, Meguto-ku, Tokyo 152-8550, Japan
wkim@ok.sc.e.titech.ac.jp, {mtanaka,mxo}@sc.e.titech.ac.jp
[2] Artificial Intelligence Research Center, National Institute of Advanced Industrial
Science and Technology, Koto-ku, Tokyo 135-0064, Japan
y-sasaki@aist.go.jp

Abstract. Future frame prediction in videos is a challenging problem because videos include complicated movements and large appearance changes. Learning-based future frame prediction approaches have been proposed in kinds of literature. A common limitation of the existing learning-based approaches is a mismatch of training data and test data. In the future frame prediction task, we can obtain the ground truth data by just waiting for a few frames. It means we can update the prediction model online in the test phase. Then, we propose an adaptive update framework for the future frame prediction task. The proposed adaptive updating framework consists of a pre-trained prediction network, a continuous-updating prediction network, and a weight estimation network. We also show that our pre-trained prediction model achieves comparable performance to the existing state-of-the-art approaches. We demonstrate that our approach outperforms existing methods especially for dynamically changing scenes.

Keywords: Deep neural network · Frame prediction · Online learning

1 Introduction

Videos contain rich information, including movement and deformation of objects, occlusions, illumination changes, and camera movements. We can use that information for many computer vision applications. Therefore, video analysis is actively researched to obtain such information [2,22]. After the deep neural networks provided a positive impact on the computer vision in image domain [11,14], neural networks in the video domain are actively studied [13,15]. Future frame prediction described in Fig. 1 is a branch of these research areas.

Video future frame prediction [9,20,23] is defined as estimating future frames from past frames. Video future frame prediction is a challenging task because

Electronic supplementary material The online version of this chapter (https://doi.org/10.1007/978-3-030-68787-8_1) contains supplementary material, which is available to authorized users.

A. Del Bimbo et al. (Eds.): ICPR 2020 Workshops, LNCS 12667, pp. 5–19, 2021.
https://doi.org/10.1007/978-3-030-68787-8_1

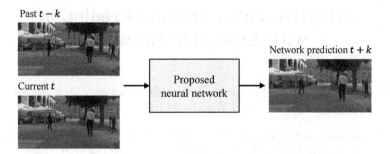

Fig. 1. Future frame prediction of 2in-1out. The neural network gets two frames and predicts the future frame according to the inputs. In particular, we can confirm the prediction effects in the red-highlighted region. (Color figure online)

videos include complicated appearance changes and complex motion dynamics of objects. The uniform linear motion assumption does not work for the video future prediction. Then, learning-based deep network approaches have been researched [9,20,23]. Existing future frame prediction algorithms based on the deep neural network can be classified in offline-supervised learning [9,20,23]. In offline-supervised learning, a network is trained in advance with training data. The limitation of offline-supervised learning is a mismatch of training data and real scenes. The performance of the pre-trained network for new environment scenes which is not included in the training data is very low. To overcome this limitation, we need to collect all possible scenes for the training data. However, it is infeasible to collect all possible scenes. One of the other approaches is adaptive online updating. If we can adaptively update the network model in the test phase, the prediction network can effectively work for new environment scenes. It is a big advantage of adaptive online updating. The problem of online updating is annotation. In the test phase, the annotation is required to obtain the ground truth. The annotation problem makes online updating difficult. However, in the future frame prediction task, we can easily obtain the ground truth data, even in the test phase, by just waiting for a few frames. Then, in this paper, we propose an adaptive online update framework for the future frame prediction. To the best of our knowledge, there is no existing research related to the adaptive online update framework for the future frame prediction.

The proposed adaptive online update framework consists of three subnetworks: a pre-trained prediction network, a continuous-updating prediction network, and a weight estimation network. The pre-trained prediction network is trained with the offline supervised learning manner as same as existing future frame prediction networks. The pre-trained prediction network model is fixed, while the continuous-updating prediction network model is updated in the test phase to adapt a huge variety of scenes. The continuous-updating prediction network is relatively unstable because it tries to adapt to the current environment. Therefore, we also simultaneously train the weight estimation network online manner. Then, the final results are generated by ensembling the outputs of the pre-trained prediction network and the continuous-updating prediction network based on the estimated weight.

The main contributions of our work are:

- We propose an adaptive future frame prediction framework using network ensemble. It is efficient for large-scale real scene prediction.
- We also propose the future prediction network model. We demonstrate that the performance of this network is comparable to those of the existing state-of-the-art network models.

We have published the proposed network, data, and reproduction code on the website[1].

2   Related Works

Online Learning. In the real world, data distribution is continuously changing. An online learning algorithm has to include a mechanism for handling the various scenarios in a dynamic environment. This fact indicates that the parameters need to be updated automatically. In an evolving data environment, the adaption algorithm is essential to process proper decision making.

According to [19], there are three major online learning trends: sliding window, forgetting factor, and classifier ensembles. The sliding window [12] is the most popular technique to handle the data flows. A window moves to include the latest data, then the model updates using the window. Therefore, the window size critically affects the model performance. The forgetting factor [8] incorporates a weight to maintain a balance in the streaming data. It classifies the data according to the importance and sets a weight. The importance can be determined with criteria such as age or relevance.

The other adaption algorithm is the classifier ensemble [4,17]. The classifier ensemble combines several models to obtain a final solution. Several models include an adaptive model for storing the latest information for the current environment. One of the main advantages of this approach is that it is more likely to be more accurate than a single classifier due to reduced error distribution. Another advantage is that the ensemble method can efficiently deal with repeated known environments. To use the benefits, we employed a classifier ensemble concept for constructing the adaptive future frame prediction network.

Future Frame Prediction. One of the popular approaches in future frame prediction is forecasting future frame pixel-values directly. Xingjian et al. [25] used long-short-term-memory (LSTM) for frame prediction. Lotter et al. [15] built a predictive recurrent neural network to mimic predictive coding in neuroscience. However, these approaches suffer from blurriness in prediction and fail to extract large scale transformation. This can be attributed to the difficulty of generating pixel values directly, and low-resolution data sets with no significant movement [5,21]. To address these problems, Wang et al. [23] focused on regions of interest to generate accurate predictions.

---

[1] http://www.ok.sc.e.titech.ac.jp/res/FFP/.

Another approach in future frame prediction is to estimate a future frame based on optical flows. Pintea et al. [20] assuming that similar motion is characterized by similar appearance, proposed a motion prediction method using optical flows. Liu et al. [13] designed a deep neural network that develops video frames from existing frames alternate to directly predicting pixel values. These approaches use optical flow estimation and warping function. Temporal consistency and spatial richness are guaranteed because the predicted pixels are derived from past frames. However, for the same reason, they fail if a place does not appear in past frames.

The other approach in future frame prediction is a multi-model composed of the above-mentioned approaches. Yan et al. [26] studied future frame prediction with a multi-model composed of the temporal and spatial sub-network. Kim et al. [9] detected key-points in input frames, and translated the frame according to key-points motion. Gao et al. [6] initially predicted the optical flow and made warp a past frame with predicted optical flow. Subsequently, they refined the warped image in pixel-wise to generate a final prediction. This approach refines the image warped with forecast optical flow. This helps to manage places unseen in past frames.

Among the approaches mentioned above, the multi-model methods showed effectiveness in various scenes. Therefore, we designed the future frame prediction network as a multi-model structure. Because the future frame prediction network is a multi-model structure, it can be expected to handle the dynamic and various online-updating environment.

3   Proposed Ensemble Network

Future frame prediction forecasts future frames from past frames. We consider a prediction task of 2in-1out that takes two frames $x_t, x_{t-k} \in \mathbb{R}^{W \times H \times 3}$ and predicts one future frame $x_{t+k} \in \mathbb{R}^{W \times H \times 3}$ in the same interval, where W, H, and 3 denote the width, height, and RGB channels of the frame respectively, and t and k are the current time, and the time interval respectively.

The entire process and network architecture are described in Sect. 3.1. In Sect. 3.1, the continuous-updating prediction network and weight estimation network which are online updating modules are also discussed in detail. Subsequently, the specification of the pre-trained prediction network which is a weight fixation module is explained in Sect. 3.2. Finally, network training is described in Sect. 3.3.

3.1   Overall Network Architecture

As mentioned in Sect. 1, the pre-trained future prediction network only works for similar scenes of the training data. We can adaptively update the prediction network while the continuous-updating prediction network tends to be unstable because the continuous-updating prediction network tries to adapt to the current scene. Therefore, we propose an adaptive ensemble network which is combined

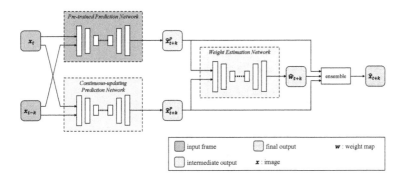

Fig. 2. Our proposed ensemble network for future frame prediction.

with the pre-trained and the continuous-updating prediction networks. The final prediction result is composed by combining the results of the pre-trained and the continuous-updating prediction networks based on the weight estimated by the weight estimation network as shown in Fig. 2.

Pre-trained Prediction Network. We train the pre-trained prediction network in advance with an offline learning manner. This approach is well studied in the deep learning research area. If test scenes are similar to the training data, the pre-trained prediction network can accurately predict the future frame. However, the pre-trained prediction network fails to predict untrained scenes. We use this pre-trained prediction network without updating weights in test phase.

Continuous-Updating Prediction Network. First, we train the continuous-updating prediction network with an offline learning manner as same as the pre-trained prediction network. If the network structure of the continuous-updating prediction network is identical to that of the pre-trained prediction network, the wights of the continuous-updating prediction network can be initialized by the weights of the pre-trained prediction network.

The point of the continuous-updating prediction network is an adaptive updating process. At time t, we already have the frames x_{t-2k}, x_{t-k}, and x_t. Then, we can update the weights of the continuous-updating prediction network, where the frames x_{t-2k} and x_{t-k} are used as inputs and the frame x_t can be used as the ground truth of the prediction. The loss to update the continuous-updating prediction network at the time t is

$$L_t^C(\boldsymbol{\theta}_C) = \mu\left(x_t, \boldsymbol{f}_C(x_{t-k}, x_{t-2k}; \boldsymbol{\theta}_C)\right), \tag{1}$$

where μ is the loss function, $\boldsymbol{f}_C$ represents the prediction network, and $\boldsymbol{\theta}_C$ is the parameters of the network. We call this updating process an online adaptive updating. We introduce an image quality measure μ for the loss function in Sect. 3.3.

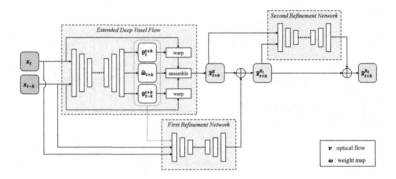

Fig. 3. Future frame prediction network architecture.

Weight Estimation Network. In our framework, we have two prediction networks; the pre-trained prediction network and the continuous-updating prediction network. Those two networks are good for different situations. Then, we blend two outputs of the networks. For the blending, we train a weight estimation network to obtain the blending coefficients.

$$\hat{\boldsymbol{x}}_{t+k} = \hat{\boldsymbol{w}}_{t+k} \otimes \hat{\boldsymbol{x}}_{t+k}^{P} + (1 - \hat{\boldsymbol{w}}_{t+k}) \otimes \hat{\boldsymbol{x}}_{t+k}^{C}, \tag{2}$$

where $\otimes$ represents elements-wise multiplication operator, and $\hat{\boldsymbol{x}}_{t+k}^{P}$, $\hat{\boldsymbol{x}}_{t+k}^{C}$, and $\hat{\boldsymbol{w}}_{t+k}$ are defined as

$$\hat{\boldsymbol{x}}_{t+k}^{P} = \boldsymbol{f}_P(\boldsymbol{x}_t, \boldsymbol{x}_{t-k}; \boldsymbol{\theta}_P), \tag{3}$$

$$\hat{\boldsymbol{x}}_{t+k}^{C} = \boldsymbol{f}_C(\boldsymbol{x}_t, \boldsymbol{x}_{t-k}; \boldsymbol{\theta}_C), \tag{4}$$

$$\hat{\boldsymbol{w}}_{t+k} = \boldsymbol{f}_W(\boldsymbol{x}_t, \boldsymbol{x}_{t-k}; \boldsymbol{\theta}_W). \tag{5}$$

Here, $\boldsymbol{f}_P$ represents the pre-trained prediction network, $\boldsymbol{\theta}_P$ is the parameters of the pre-trained prediction network, $\boldsymbol{f}_W$ represents the weight estimation network, and $\boldsymbol{\theta}_W$ is the parameters of the weight estimation network.

The pre-trained prediction network is fixed during the test phase, while the continuous-updating prediction network is updated in the test phase. Then, we need to train the weight estimation network by online updating.

In the early stage of the test phase or after a sudden scene change, the continuous-updating prediction network might be unstable. For those situations, the weight estimation network is trained to put a higher priority on the pre-trained prediction network. For the scene in which the training data does not include, the weight estimation network is trained to put a higher priority on the continuous-updating prediction network because the pre-trained prediction network fails to predict the scene.

3.2   Future Frame Prediction Network

The proposed online future frame prediction framework internally includes the future frame prediction network as shown in Fig. 2. We can independently design the network architectures for the pre-train prediction network and the continuous-updating prediction network. In this paper, we adopt to use the same network architecture for those two prediction networks for simplification of the network design. In addition, we can initialize the weight of the continuous-updating prediction network with those of the pre-trained prediction network if the network architectures of those two networks are the same. In this section, we describe common network architecture for those two prediction networks.

We design the prediction network architecture inspired by [6,13]. Our prediction network is composed of an extended deep voxel flow (EDVF) network with two refinement networks. The EDVF is an extended version of DVF [13]. In the original DVF, they assume that the optical flow from $t - k$ frame to $t + k$ frame is just twice the optical flow from t frame to $t + k$ frame. It means that they implicitly assume a linear uniform motion for the optical flow. In our EDVF, we separately estimate optical flow fields from $t - k$ frame to $t + k$ frame and from t frame to $t + k$ frame. Our EDVF is more general than the original DVF. Our EDVF network estimates optical flow fields $\hat{v}_{t-k}^{t+k}$, $\hat{v}_t^{t+k}$ and a weight map $\hat{\omega}_{t+k}$ from frames x_{t-k} and x_t as shown in Fig. 3. Then, the predicted frame $\hat{x}_{t+k}^E$ by the EDVF can be expressed as

$$\hat{x}_{t+k}^E = \hat{\omega}_{t+k} \otimes S(x_t; \hat{v}_t^{t+k}) + (1 - \hat{\omega}_{t+k})S(x_{t-k}; \hat{v}_{t-k}^{t+k}), \tag{6}$$

where $S(x; v)$ represents warping the frame x based on the optical flow field v.

Even if the EDVF can perfectly estimate the optical flow field, the EDVF cannot handle the occlusion and the appearance changes. Therefore, in our prediction network, two refinement networks follow the EDVF. Two refinement networks are the similar architecture of the hourglass-shaped network. The inputs of the first refinement network are the observed frames x_{t-k} and x_t, the estimated optical flow fields $\hat{v}_{t-k}^{t+k}$ and $\hat{v}_t^{t+k}$, and the estimated weight map $\hat{\omega}_{t+k}$. After the first refinement, the estimated frame $\hat{x}_{t+k}^{R_1}$ can be expressed as

$$\hat{x}_{t+k}^{R_1} = \hat{x}_{t+k}^E + g_{R_1}(x_{t-k}, x_t, \hat{v}_{t-k}^{+k}, \hat{v}_t^{t+k}, \hat{\omega}_{t+k}; \theta_{R_1}), \tag{7}$$

where g_{R_1} represents the first refinement network, and θ_{R_1} is the weights of the first refinement network. The inputs of the second refinement network are the output of the EDVF and the refinement result by the first refinement network. The final predicted frame can be obtained by adding the second refinement component as

$$\hat{x}_{t+k}^{R_2} = \hat{x}_{t+k}^{R_1} + g_{R_2}(\hat{x}_{t+k}^E, \hat{x}_{t+k}^{R_1}; \theta_{R_2}), \tag{8}$$

where g_{R_2} represents the first refinement network, and θ_{R_2} is the weights of the first refinement network.

3.3 Network Training

Before discussing the losses for the network training, we introduce an image quality measure. In the network-based restoration, a mean square error (MSE) in the pixel domain and in the gradient domain, a structural similarity (SSIM) [24], and a perceptual similarity [27] are used for the loss function. In this paper, we use the following image quality measure μ that consists of the above four metrics:

$$\mu(\hat{x}, x) = \rho_{\mathrm{MSEI}}||\hat{x} - x||_2^2 + \rho_{\mathrm{MSED}}||\nabla\hat{x} - \nabla x||_2^2$$
$$+ \rho_{\mathrm{SSIM}}(1 - \mathrm{SSIM}(\hat{x}, x)) + \rho_{\mathrm{Per}}||\Phi(\hat{x}) - \Phi(x)||_1, \qquad (9)$$

where x is a ground truth image, $\hat{x}$ is an image to be evaluated, ∇ is a vector differential operator, $||\cdot||_2$ represents L2-norm, $||\cdot||_1$ represents L1-norm, SSIM is a function to evaluate a structure similarity [24], $\Phi(\cdot)$ represents the Conv1-to-Conv5 of the AlexNet [11], and $\{\rho_{\mathrm{MSEI}}, \rho_{\mathrm{MSED}}, \rho_{\mathrm{SSIM}}, \rho_{\mathrm{Per}}\}$ is a set of hyper-parameters. We set $\{0.05, 0.001, 10, 10\}$ for the hyper-parameters of $\{\rho_{\mathrm{MSEI}}, \rho_{\mathrm{MSED}}, \rho_{\mathrm{SSIM}}, \rho_{\mathrm{Per}}\}$ in the Sect. 4.2, and $\{0.0001, 0, 10, 0\}$ for the hyper-parameters in the Sect. 4.3.

The pre-trained prediction network is the prediction network, as shown in Fig. 3, trained with the offline supervised manner in advance. For the loss function for that training, we evaluate the image quality measures of internal predictions $\{\hat{x}_{t+k}^E, \hat{x}_{t+k}^{R_1}\}$ and the final prediction $\hat{x}_{t+k}^{R_2}$. We also use the optical flow smoothness term assuming the optical flow is spatially smooth. The loss function for the pre-trained prediction network is

$$L_{\mathrm{Pre}} = \lambda_E \cdot \mu(\hat{x}_{t+k}^E, x_{t+k}) + \lambda_{R_1} \cdot \mu(\hat{x}_{t+k}^{R_1}, x_{t+k}) + \lambda_{R_2} \cdot \mu(\hat{x}_{t+k}^{R_2}, x_{t+k})$$
$$+ \lambda_{\mathrm{OF}}(||\nabla\hat{v}_{t-k}^{t+K}||_1 + ||\nabla\hat{v}_t^{t+K}||_1), \qquad (10)$$

where μ represents the image quality measure in Eq. 9, $\{\hat{v}_{t-k}^{t+K}, \hat{v}_t^{t+K}\}$ is the optical flow fields estimated by the EDVF, $\{\lambda_E, \lambda_{R_1}, \lambda_{R_2}, \lambda_{\mathrm{OF}}\}$ is a set of hyper-parameters. In this paper, we set $\{2, 3, 7, 0.1\}$ for the hyper-parameters of $\{\lambda_E, \lambda_{R_1}, \lambda_{R_2}, \lambda_{\mathrm{OF}}\}$. The pre-trained prediction network is randomly initialized, then trained with an end-to-end manner.

For online updating of the proposed framework as shown in Fig. 2, we use the following loss function:

$$L_{\mathrm{Ada}} = \mu(\hat{x}_t, x_t) + \lambda_C \cdot \mu(\hat{x}_t^C, x_t), \qquad (11)$$

where λ_C is a hyper-parameter. We set 0.1 for the hyper-parameter of λ_C.

Note that in the online update we predict t-frame from $(t - k)$- and $(t - 2k)$-frames. In the beginning, the weights of the continuous-updating prediction network are initialized by those of the pre-trained prediction network. The continuous-updating prediction network and the weight estimation network are updated with an end-to-end manner, while the weights of the pre-trained prediction network are fixed in the test phase.

4   Experiments

This section presents the benchmark data set, evaluation metrics, and previous studies for comparison. Previously, the frame interval had been generalized to k. Hereafter, k is set as 1 to address the next-frame prediction problem.

4.1   Experimental Environment

We used the KITTI Flow data set [16] for offline experiments. This data set contains high-resolution scenes with large movements, and frequent occlusions. Therefore, it is challenging for future frame prediction problems. There are 200 and 199 videos for training and testing respectively, consisting of 21 frames. All frames are center cropped into 640×320. The videos for training and testing were clipped in 3 frames to focus on the 2in-1out problem with $k = 1$. Therefore, $3,800$ and $3,789$ samples were generated for training and testing respectively.

For online-updating experiments, we used video clips "2011_09_26_drive_0013" and "2011_09_26_drive_0014" in KITTI RAW data [7] with frame size 768×256, and "Stuttgart_02" in Cityscapes demo video [3] with frame size 512×256. Owing to the data variety, we used videos from Miraikan [18] and the imitation store in AIST [1]. All frames of Miraikan and AIST store were 960×480.

We used Peak Signal-to-Noise Ratio (PSNR) and Structural Similarity Index Measure (SSIM) [24] metrics as performance evaluation of the methods. High PSNR and SSIM values indicate better performance. During SSIM and PSNR calculation, only 90% of the center of the image was used.

To compare with our pre-trained prediction network, existing high-performance network DVF [13] and DPG [6] were used. We also employed PredNet [15] and ConvLSTM [25]; however, we failed to tune those networks with several trials in different parameter settings. DVF [13] and DPG [6] were selected as comparison methods because they exhibit state-of-the-art performances in frame prediction. We implemented the DPG by ourselves because of scarcity of public domain code. We adapted the public code of the DVF to our experimental environment. All networks, including the proposed network, were trained in Adam [10] with $lr = 0.0001$ and $Epochs = 100$ in offline training. In online training, networks were updated 1 time by a set of three frames with a current input frame x_t as ground truth and past frames x_{t-1} and x_{t-2} as input. In the experiment of online updating, data from KITTI, Cityscape, AIST store, and Miraikan were progressed with switching, and online updating of the data was performed simultaneously with performance evaluation. For performance evaluations of future frame predictions in online-updating, we used DVF, DPG, and our future frame prediction network for the ensemble network components.

4.2   Performance of Future Frame Prediction Network Architecture

Table 1 summarizes the future frame prediction performances with the KITTI Flow data set. From Table 1, the our future frame prediction network performs the best in SSIM and PSNR. It achieved an SSIM of 0.718 and a PSNR of 22.1, whereas DPG [6] showed an SSIM of 0.706 and a PSNR of 21.6. The DVF [13] model achieved results inferior to those of our future frame prediction network and its SSIM and PSNR performances were com-

Table 1. Comparison of pre-trained prediction on KITTI Flow data set

Method	SSIM	PSNR
Repeat	0.577	17.6
PredNet [15]	0.162	9.58
ConvLSTM [25]	0.106	6.77
DVF [13]	0.712	21.7
DPG [6]	0.706	21.6
Ours	**0.718**	**22.1**

parable with those of DPG. The term "Repeat" means that the next frame is not predicted and current frame is responded as a prediction. Accordingly, a model showing a score higher than "Repeat" generates a significant prediction.

In Fig. 4, qualitative comparisons on KITTI Flow are depicted. All the frames predicted by DVF, DPG, and the our future frame prediction network are sharp and crisp. The our future frame prediction network predicted frames show minimal unnatural deformation, particularly in the red-highlighted region. However, the frames predicted by DVF and DPG include considerable unnatural deformation, particularly in the red-highlighted region. From the quantitative results in Table 1 and qualitative results in Fig. 4, the our future frame prediction network accurately predicted the flow and properly refined the future frame estimated by the predicted flow. More qualitative comparisons are shown in supplemental materials.

According to both quantitative and qualitative comparisons, we concluded that the future frame prediction network achieved the same level of performance as the existing state-of-the-art models.

4.3   Future Frame Prediction on Online-Updating

Table 2 shows the evaluation scores in the online-updating environment. The order of the scenes can be found in Fig. 5. The "Ours", "Pre-trained", "Continuous-updating", and "Ensemble" are meaning that proposed future frame prediction network, using the pre-trained prediction network only, using the continuous-updating prediction network only, and proposed ensemble network respectively. All networks in Table 2 use the network architectures and weights evaluated in Sect. 4.2. From the scores of SSIM and PSNR in Table 2, we can recognize that the proposed ensemble network using the future frame prediction network performs the best. No matter what network is used for the component, we can see that "Ensemble" achieves a higher score than "Continuous-updating", and "Continuous-updating" gets higher performance than "Pre-trained".

Figure 5 illustrates the SSIM and PSNR changes of "Pre-trained", "Continuous-updating", and "Ensemble" using the proposed future frame prediction network. A moving average was calculated on a window size 100 for

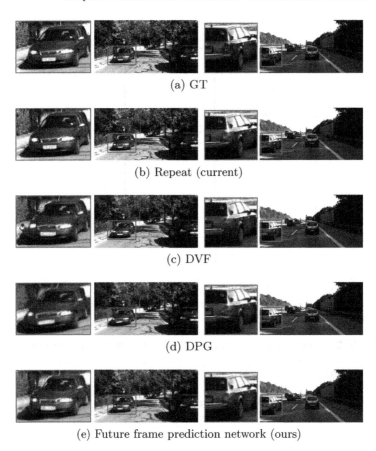

(a) GT

(b) Repeat (current)

(c) DVF

(d) DPG

(e) Future frame prediction network (ours)

Fig. 4. Comparison of future frame prediction on the KITTI Flow data set.

better visualization. From Fig. 5-(a) and Fig. 5-(b), we can observe that there is a similar tendency between all manners. However, "Ensemble" shows higher metric values than other manners. There is a period where "Pre-trained" shows lower SSIM and PSNR than "Repeat" around the frame 1200. It means that the "Pre-trained" failed to predict in the period. "Continuous" produces higher performance than "Ensemble" on the frame 1200, but lower than "Pre-trained" on the frame 1300. It shows a characteristic of "Continuous", which has low stability. Overall, the graphs for "Continuous" and "Ensemble" are almost the same. This is because the difference both SSIM and PSNR is small, as described in Table 2. However, "Ensemble" works to complement the part of "Continuous" that failed to predict, and visual examples are shown in Fig. 6.

The visual comparison of "Pre-trained", "Continuous-updating", and "Ensemble" using our future frame prediction network is shown in Fig. 6. In the left column, it can be seen that the prediction result of the "Pre-trained prediction network" is including unnatural deformation in the blue-highlighted

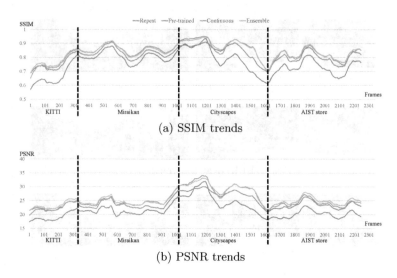

(a) SSIM trends

(b) PSNR trends

Fig. 5. Tendencies of SSIM/PSNR in online updating. The data flow from left to right. Only the trends of the second round data flow are shown in here. Entire trends are shown in supplemental materials.

Table 2. Comparison of methods toward online updating environment

	Repeat	Pre-trained			Continuous-updating			Ensemble (Ours)		
		DVF	DPG	Ours	DVF	DPG	Ours	DVF	DPG	Ours
SSIM	0.742	0.795	0.809	0.803	0.823	0.816	0.830	0.827	0.826	**0.833**
PSNR	21.8	24.1	24.4	24.4	25.3	25.0	25.6	25.7	25.7	**25.9**

region, and "Continuous-updating prediction network" is producing an aliasing-like error in the red-highlighted region. In the right column, we can see that the "Pre-trained prediction network" generates abnormal prediction, particularly in the blue-highlighted region. The "Continuous-updating prediction network" produces blurred prediction in both the blue- and red-highlighted region. However, problems appearing in the results of the "Pre-trained prediction network" and "Continuous-updating prediction network" are less observed in the "Proposed ensemble network." More qualitative comparisons are shown in supplemental materials.

The quantitative and qualitative evaluations indicate that the proposed ensemble network is more stable and high-performing in unknown environments. In addition, the proposed pre-trained prediction network is suitable for the component of ensemble network. Consequently, proposed ensemble network which is a combination of the proposed methods, shows the most effective performance.

The effectiveness of the proposed network was verified through Sect. 4.2 and 4.3. In the experiments, the frame interval is constant, but there are many variations in movement between frames. The employed data sets include all the walking, stopping, driving in the city, and driving on the highway. Therefore,

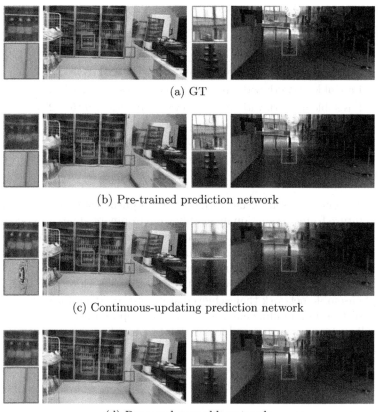

(a) GT

(b) Pre-trained prediction network

(c) Continuous-updating prediction network

(d) Proposed ensemble network

Fig. 6. Examples of frame prediction for online updating evaluation. (Color figure online)

when the overall performance is improved, the model can predict even in a large movement scene. In other words, the proposed networks keeps the effectiveness even if the frame interval is increased.

The proposed ensemble network with our future frame prediction network takes about 0.1 s to process KITTI RAW data [7] with the GeForce GTX 1070. However, it takes about 0.3 s to update the proposed ensemble network with the same GPU. The proposed ensemble network can be implemented by updating in parallel with prediction toward data flow. For example, the proposed network requires 0.1 s for KITTI RAW data [7] to predict and 0.3 s to update. Because KITTI RAW data [7] is 10 fps, the network can predict all frames and update every three frames. Table 3 shows the result of the parallel system at "2011_10_03_drive_0047" of KITTI RAW data [7]. According to Table 3, although it is better to update with every new frame, we can confirm the effect of the proposed ensemble method even with updating every several frames.

Table 3. Effectiveness of the ensemble network with updating in different frame intervals

Method	SSIM	PSNR
Our future frame prediction network (pre-trained)	0.834	24.2
Ensemble network with updating every frames	0.863	25.7
Ensemble network with updating every 3 frames	0.856	25.5
Ensemble network with updating every 5 frames	0.855	25.3

5 Conclusions

We proposed a novel ensemble network that accomplished state-of-the-art performance in future frame prediction in an online environment. The proposed ensemble network shows effectiveness toward unknown scenes that are not included in offline training data. From the experiments of online updating, we conclude that the design of the ensemble network is reasonable and effective.

We also proposed a future frame prediction network architecture used for the proposed ensemble network that achieved state-of-the-art performance in future frame prediction in an offline environment. The proposed network has improved the overall performance of ensemble network by providing pre-trained weight for initialization.

References

1. AIST. https://www.aist.go.jp/. Accessed 23 Jan 2020
2. Bovik, A.C.: The Essential Guide to Video Processing. Academic Press, Cambridge (2009)
3. Cordts, M., et al.: The cityscapes dataset for semantic urban scene understanding. In: Proceedings of the IEEE Conference on Computer Vision and Pattern Recognition (CVPR) (2016)
4. Ditzler, G., Rosen, G., Polikar, R.: Domain adaptation bounds for multiple expert systems under concept drift. In: 2014 International Joint Conference on Neural Networks (IJCNN), pp. 595–601. IEEE (2014)
5. Dollár, P., Wojek, C., Schiele, B., Perona, P.: Pedestrian detection: a benchmark. In: 2009 IEEE Conference on Computer Vision and Pattern Recognition, pp. 304–311. IEEE (2009)
6. Gao, H., Xu, H., Cai, Q.Z., Wang, R., Yu, F., Darrell, T.: Disentangling propagation and generation for video prediction. In: The IEEE International Conference on Computer Vision (ICCV) (October 2019)
7. Geiger, A., Lenz, P., Stiller, C., Urtasun, R.: Vision meets robotics: the KITTI dataset. Int. J. Robot. Res. (IJRR) **32**, 1231–1237 (2013)
8. Ghazikhani, A., Monsefi, R., Yazdi, H.S.: Online neural network model for nonstationary and imbalanced data stream classification. Int. J. Mach. Learn. Cybern. **5**(1), 51–62 (2014)
9. Kim, Y., Nam, S., Cho, I., Kim, S.J.: Unsupervised keypoint learning for guiding class-conditional video prediction. Adv. Neural Inf. Process. Syst. **32**, 3814–3824 (2019)

10. Kingma, D.P., Ba, J.: Adam: a method for stochastic optimization. arXiv preprint arXiv:1412.6980 (2014)
11. Krizhevsky, A., Sutskever, I., Hinton, G.E.: ImageNet classification with deep convolutional neural networks. Adv. Neural Inf. Process. Syst. **25**, 1097–1105 (2012)
12. Kuncheva, L.I., Žliobaitė, I.: On the window size for classification in changing environments. Intell. Data Anal. **13**(6), 861–872 (2009)
13. Liu, Z., Yeh, R.A., Tang, X., Liu, Y., Agarwala, A.: Video frame synthesis using deep voxel flow. In: Proceedings of the IEEE International Conference on Computer Vision, pp. 4463–4471 (2017)
14. Long, J., Shelhamer, E., Darrell, T.: Fully convolutional networks for semantic segmentation. In: Proceedings of the IEEE Conference on Computer Vision and Pattern Recognition, pp. 3431–3440 (2015)
15. Lotter, W., Kreiman, G., Cox, D.: Deep predictive coding networks for video prediction and unsupervised learning. arXiv preprint arXiv:1605.08104 (2016)
16. Menze, M., Geiger, A.: Object scene flow for autonomous vehicles. In: Proceedings of the IEEE Conference on Computer Vision and Pattern Recognition, pp. 3061–3070 (2015)
17. Minku, L.L., Yao, X.: DDD: a new ensemble approach for dealing with concept drift. IEEE Trans. Knowl. Data Eng. **24**(4), 619–633 (2011)
18. Miraikan. https://www.miraikan.jst.go.jp/. Accessed 23 Jan 2020
19. Pérez-Sánchez, B., Fontenla-Romero, O., Guijarro-Berdiñas, B.: A review of adaptive online learning for artificial neural networks. Artif. Intell. Rev. **49**(2), 281–299 (2018)
20. Pintea, S.L., van Gemert, J.C., Smeulders, A.W.M.: Déjà Vu. In: Fleet, D., Pajdla, T., Schiele, B., Tuytelaars, T. (eds.) ECCV 2014. LNCS, vol. 8691, pp. 172–187. Springer, Cham (2014). https://doi.org/10.1007/978-3-319-10578-9_12
21. Soomro, K., Zamir, A.R., Shah, M.: Ucf101: a dataset of 101 human actions classes from videos in the wild. arXiv preprint arXiv:1212.0402 (2012)
22. Tekalp, A.M., Tekalp, A.M.: Digital Video Processing, vol. 1. Prentice Hall PTR, Upper Saddle river (1995)
23. Wang, J., Wang, W., Gao, W.: Predicting diverse future frames with local transformation-guided masking. IEEE Trans. Circuits Syst. Video Technol. **29**(12), 3531–3543 (2018)
24. Wang, Z., Bovik, A.C., Sheikh, H.R., Simoncelli, E.P.: Image quality assessment: from error visibility to structural similarity. IEEE Trans. Image Process. **13**(4), 600–612 (2004)
25. Xingjian, S., Chen, Z., Wang, H., Yeung, D.Y., Wong, W.K., Woo, W.C.: Convolutional LSTM network: a machine learning approach for precipitation nowcasting. In: Advances in Neural Information Processing Systems, pp. 802–810 (2015)
26. Yan, J., Qin, G., Zhao, R., Liang, Y., Xu, Q.: Mixpred: video prediction beyond optical flow. IEEE Access **7**, 185654–185665 (2019)
27. Zhang, R., Isola, P., Efros, A.A., Shechtman, E., Wang, O.: The unreasonable effectiveness of deep features as a perceptual metric. In: CVPR (2018)

Rain-Code Fusion: Code-to-Code ConvLSTM Forecasting Spatiotemporal Precipitation

Takato Yasuno[✉], Akira Ishii, and Masazumi Amakata

Research Institute for Infrastructure Paradigm Shift, Yachiyo Engineering Co., Ltd.,
Asakusabashi 5-20-8, Taito-ku, Tokyo, Japan
{tk-yasuno,akri-ishii,amakata}@yachiyo-eng.co.jp

Abstract. Recently, flood damage has become a social problem owing to unexperienced weather conditions arising from climate change. An immediate response to heavy rain is important for the mitigation of economic losses and also for rapid recovery. Spatiotemporal precipitation forecasts may enhance the accuracy of dam inflow prediction, more than 6 h forward for flood damage mitigation. However, the ordinary ConvLSTM has the limitation of predictable range more than 3-timesteps in real-world precipitation forecasting owing to the irreducible bias between target prediction and ground-truth value. This paper proposes a rain-code approach for spatiotemporal precipitation code-to-code forecasting. We propose a novel rainy feature that represents a temporal rainy process using multi-frame fusion for the timestep reduction. We perform rain-code studies with various term ranges based on the standard ConvLSTM. We applied to a dam region within the Japanese rainy term hourly precipitation data, under 2006 to 2019 approximately 127 thousands hours, every year from May to October. We apply the radar analysis hourly data on the central broader region with an area of $136 \times 148 \text{ km}^2$. Finally we have provided sensitivity studies between the rain-code size and hourly accuracy within the several forecasting range.

Keywords: Spatiotemporal precipitation · 6 h forecasting · Rain-code fusion · Multi-frame feature · Code-to-code ConvLSTM

1 Introduction

1.1 Rain-Code Fusion Based Precipitation Forecasting

For the past decade, flood damage has become a social problem owing to unexperienced weather conditions arising from climate change. An immediate response to extreme rain and flood situation is important for the mitigation of casualties and economic losses and for faster recovery. The spatiotemporal precipitation forecast may influence the accuracy of dam inflow prediction more than 6 h forward for flood damage mitigation. In particular, in Japan, forecasting 6 h forward is critical and legally requested for the basic policy strengthening flood control function of an existing dam [1]. To prevent social losses due to incoming heavy rain and typhoons, we attempt to predict flood situations at least 6 h beforehand. The dam manager can inform downstream residents of the hazardous

© Springer Nature Switzerland AG 2021
A. Del Bimbo et al. (Eds.): ICPR 2020 Workshops, LNCS 12667, pp. 20–34, 2021.
https://doi.org/10.1007/978-3-030-68787-8_2

flood scenario via an announcement. Then, the elderly and children can escape to safety facilities. Therefore, forecasting precipitation 6 h forward is crucial for mitigating flood damage and ensuring safety of people downstream.

This paper proposes a rain-code approach for spatiotemporal precipitation forecasting. We propose a novel rainy feature fusion that represents a temporal rainy process including hourly multi-frames. We perform rain-code studies with various ranges based on spatiotemporal precipitation forecasting using the ConvLSTM. We applied to a dam region within the Japanese rainy term hourly precipitation data, under 2006 to 2019 approximately 127 thousands hours, every year from May to October. We can use the radar analysis hourly data on the central broader region with an area of 136×148 km^2, based on "rain-code" fusion that contains hourly multi-frames such as 3, 4, 6, and 12.

1.2 Related Works and Papers

Deep Learning Methods for Water Resources. Sit et al. [2] provided a comprehensive review, focusing on the application of deep-learning methods to the water sector, e.g., for monitoring, management, and governance of water resources. Their study provides guidance for the utilisation of deep-learning methods for water resources. There were 315 articles published from 2018 to the end of March2020, excluding editorials, and review papers. Surprisingly, among the reviewed papers, convolutional neural networks (CNNs) and long short-term memory networks (LSTMs) were the most widely investigated architectures. They pointed out their success of respective task in matrix prediction and sequence prediction, which are important in hydrologic modelling. In the field of weather forecasting, the CNNs and LSTMs are also used for quantitative precipitation estimation. Because the prediction of precipitation is generally a time-series problem, LSTM is commonly used. Wu et al. [3] designed a model combining a CNN and LSTM to improve the quantitative precipitation estimation accuracy. The proposed model uses multimodal data, including satellite data, rain gauge observations, and thermal infrared images. The CNN-LSTM model outperforms comparative models, such as the CNN, LSTM, and Multi-Layer Perceptron. Yan et al. [4] used a CNN model together with radar reflectance images to forecast the short-term precipitation for a local area in China. As a dataset, the radar reflection images and the corresponding precipitation values for one hour were collected. The model takes the images as inputs and returns the forecast value for one hour precipitation. Chen et al. [5] focused on precipitation nowcasting using a ConvLSTM model. The model uses radar echo data to forecast 30 or 60 min of precipitation. Thus, in the field of weather forecasting, CNNs and LSTM s have mainly been used for short-term precipitation "nowcasting," with a limited forecasting range of 30–60 min.

Spatiotemporal Sequence Precipitation Forecasting. Shi et al. surveyed the forecasting multi-step future of spatiotemporal systems according to past observations. They summarised and compared many machine-learning studies from a unified perspective [6]. These methods are classified two categories: classical methods and deep-learning methods. The former methods are subdivided into the feature-based methods, state-space models, and Gaussian processes. The latter methods include the deep temporal generative models, feedforward neural networks (FNNs), and recurrent neural networks

(RNNs). Remarkable methods for spatiotemporal precipitation forecasting have been developed, e.g., ConvLSTM [7], TrajGRU [8], and PredRNN [9, 10]. Although the state-of-art method is applicable to the benchmark moving MNIST and regularised generated movies, real-world weather prediction is limited to short-range forecasting (two or three timesteps) owing to the chaotic phenomena, non-stationary measurements, unexperienced anomaly weather even if we use the-state-of-the-art architectures.

In contrast, in the field of urban computing, e.g., air-quality forecasting [11] and traffic crowd prediction [12], the CNN and LSTM architectures allow 48- to 96-h forecasting and peak hour demand forecasting [13]. However, for precipitation forecasting in the case of uncertain extreme weather, it is difficult to accurately predict more than 6 h longer range forecasting beyond short-term nowcasting, for example 30, 60 min, and 2 h [5, 14]. Especially in Japan, the 6 h forecasting dam inflow are required practically [1]. To mitigate the flood damage, it is critical to extend the predictability of precipitation forecasting for predicting the dam inflow and controlling the outflow to the downstream region.

1.3 Stretch Predictability Using Code-to-Code Forecasting

Two problems are encountered in training the RNN algorithm: vanishing and exploding gradients [14]. An RNN model was proposed in the 1980s for modelling time series

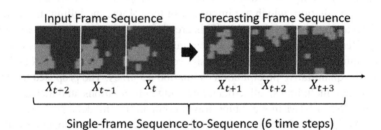

Fig. 1. Ordinary single-frame unit input and output for precipitation forecasting (This is the baseline model setting as the state-of-the-art **"Sequence-to-sequence"** ConvLSTM).

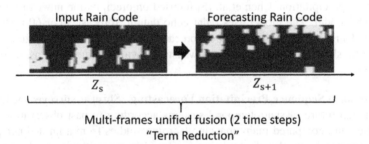

Fig. 2. Proposed rain-code based multi-frame input and output for precipitation forecasting (This is a proposed model setting **"Code-to-code"** ConvLSTM as general insight). This multi-frame composition per image results in the time step reduction for precipitation forecasting.

[15]. They suggested that we allow connections among hidden units associated with a time delay. Through these connections, the model can retain information about the past inputs, allowing it to discover temporal correlations between events that are possibly far from each other in the data (a crucial property for proper learning of time series) [16]. This crucial property of time series is similarly fitted to the property of the spatiotemporal sequence. In contrast to a simple location-fixed regular grid, the irregular moving coordinate, which is more complex, makes it more difficult to learn the information from the past inputs. In practice, standard RNNs are unable to store information about historical inputs for a long time, and the ability of the network to model the long-range dependence is limited [17]. Of course, numerous revised network strategies have been proposed, such as the stacked LSTM [18], memory cell with peephole connections, and the composite model to copy the weights of hidden-layer connections [19]. However, it is not yet completely solved to forecast long-range future outputs from the previous spatiotemporal inputs. This paper proposes a new insight "rain-code" feature based on the multi-frame inputs using a standard ConvLSTM algorithm. We present training results for rain-code based precipitation forecasting using real-world spatiotemporal data.

2 Precipitation Forecasting Method

2.1 Multi-frame Rain-Code Against Single-Frame Sequence

Rain-Code Fusion of Multi-Frame Feature. Figure 1 shows an ordinary single-frame based input feature and target output sequence for precipitation forecasting. For example, in case of an hourly unit sequence, the left-side images show the sequence for the past 3 h. The right-side images show the forward 3-h target sequence. This single-frame unit window contains the total 6-h timesteps. However, the ordinary ConvLSTM has the limitation of predictable range more than 3-timesteps in real-world precipitation forecasting, not simulated dataset as the MovingMNIST [7]. In contrast, Fig. 2 shows a proposed multi-frame-based input rain-code and target output rain-code for longer-term precipitation forecasting. In case of a 3-h multi-frame rain-code, the left-side rainy process feature is unified by the past 3-h 3-frame rain-code. The right-side process fusion is composed of the forward 3-h target 3-frame rain-code. From a new fusion, this multi-frame window contains only two rain-codes. A new dataset for the rain-code based ConvLSTM is created with a narrower multi-frame sliding window, it results in the forecasting term reduction from 6 to 2. The rain-code based training allows rainy process features with temporal 3 h to be learned simultaneously. This rain-code enable to represent the spatiotemporal relation with pair of 1–2 h, 2–3 h, and 1–3 h. When we predict 2-timestep forecasting using the three-frame rain-code, 6-h-forward precipitation forecasting is feasible.

2.2 Multi-frame-Based Forecasting Precipitation Method

Two-Timestep Forecasting Using Code-to-Code ConvLSTM. This paper proposes a rain-code based spatiotemporal precipitation forecasting. We introduce a new rainy feature fusion that represents a spatiotemporal rainy process including hourly multi-frames.

We perform multi-frame studies with various ranges based spatiotemporal precipitation forecasting using the standard ConvLSTM [7]. We build the 2-layer LSTM networks, and the Rectified Linear Unit (ReLU) activation function is used in each post-layer, as shown Fig. 3. The target size is 80×80 pixels, and the format is grayscale. The filter size of the hidden layer is 80. The loss function is the cross entropy. The gradient optimiser is RMSProp, and the weight of square gradient decay 0.95. The learning rate is 0.001. At the first timestep, the ConvLSTM layer uses the inputs of initialized hidden layer and memory cell, respectively. At the next timestep, the ConvLSTM layer computes with the inputs of previous hidden layer and memory cell, recurrently. Here, we note that batch-normalization is not effective though we tried it. In this study, we confirmed that it is feasible to predict the two-timestep forecasting precipitation dataset.

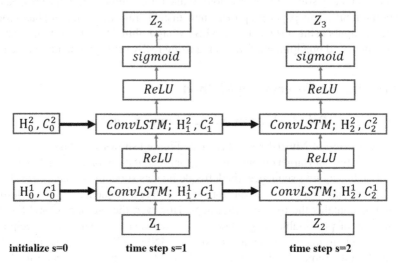

Fig. 3. Two-timestep Code-to-code ConvLSTM architecture using Rain-Code inputs and outputs.

2.3   Hourly Accuracy Indices for Rain-Code Forecasting

Rain-Code Multi-Frame Accuracy. We compute the root-mean-square error (RMSE) and the mean absolute error (MAE) of each 1- and 2-timestep rain-code based forecasting results using test data. These two indices are represented as follows.

$$\text{RMSE} = \frac{1}{SN^2} \sum_{s=1}^{S} \sum_{i=1}^{N} \sum_{j=1}^{N} \left[Z_s(i,j) - \hat{Z}_s(i,j) \right]^2 \tag{1}$$

$$\text{MAE} = \frac{1}{SN^2} \sum_{s=1}^{S} \sum_{i=1}^{N} \sum_{j=1}^{N} \left| Z_s(i,j) - \hat{Z}_s(i,j) \right| \tag{2}$$

Here, s stands for the timestep of rain-code, and $Z_s(i,j)$ indicates the ground truth of rain-code at timestep s, whose pixel location is the i-th row and j-th column. In contrast $\hat{Z}_s(i,j)$ denotes the predicted rain-code at timestep s, whose pixel location is (i,j).

Hourly Frame Accuracy. We compute each hourly frame based RMSE and MAE forecasting results using test data. These two indices are formulated as follows.

$$\text{RMSE}(h) = \frac{1}{SK^2} \sum_{s=1}^{S} \sum_{k=1}^{K} \sum_{m=1}^{K} \left[F_s^h(k, m) - \hat{F}_s^h(k, m) \right]^2, \text{h} = 1, \ldots, \text{H}. \quad (3)$$

$$\text{MAE}(h) = \frac{1}{SK^2} \sum_{s=1}^{S} \sum_{k=1}^{K} \sum_{m=1}^{K} \left| F_s^h(k, m) - \hat{F}_s^h(k, m) \right|, \text{h} = 1, \ldots, \text{H}. \quad (4)$$

Here, h stands for the hourly-frame within s-th rain-code, and $F_s^h(k, m)$ indicates the ground truth of h-th frame at rain-code with timestep s, whose pixel location is the k-th row and m-th column. On the other hand, $F_s^h(k, m)$ denotes the predicted hourly frame feature at rain-code with timestep s, whose pixel location is (k, m).

3 Applied Results

3.1 Training and Test Datasets for Matrix Prediction

We used the open-source Radar/Rain gauge Analysed Precipitation data [20], which have been provided by the Japan Meteorological Agency since 2006. They are updated every 10 min, with a spatial resolution of 1 km. The past data with a time interval of 30 min were displayed and downloaded. Figure 3 shows a display example of a real-time flood risk map for 15:10 JST, 30 September 2020. Additionally, the forecasts of hourly precipitation up to 6 h ahead are updated every 10 min, with a spatial resolution of 1 km. Forecasts of hourly precipitation from 7 to 15 h ahead are updated every hour, with a spatial resolution of 5 km.

We focused on one of the dams in the Kanto region with an area of approximately 100 km^2. We applied our method to this dam region of hourly precipitation data, under 2006 to 2019 approximately 127 thousands hours, every year from May to October whose term is the frequently rainy season in Japan. We downloaded and cropped the Radar Analysed Precipitation data on the dam central broader region with an area of 136 × 148 km^2, whose location is near the bottom left-side of Mount Fuji, as shown in Fig. 4. We aggregated 20 × 20 (400) grids for the beneficial feature enhancement.

Table 1 presents the percentile of hourly precipitation from 2006 to 2019 (a total of 14 years) in the study region with an area of 136 × 148 km^2. To enhance the precipitation intensity, we aggregated the 1-km unit mesh into a subgroup of 20 × 20 grids $(i, j = 1, \ldots, 20)$. For 81% of the 14 years, there was no precipitation; thus, this precipitation dataset was sparse. We excluded the empty of rainy term containing a zero-precipitation sequence, which was always 12 h long. We transformed the mini-max form $B_{ij} = \left(A_{ij} - \min\{A_{ij}\} \right) / \left(max\{A_{ij}\} - \min\{A_{ij}\} \right)$ so that it ranged from 0 to 1. To efficiently learn the model, we excluded almost zero precipitation always 12 h, whose grid precipitation is less than the threshold 1E+6 pixel counts. We set several thresholds and prepared a grayscale mask of dataset candidates; thus, we selected a practical level. Therefore, the rain-code dataset based on three frames contains the number of 37 thousands of the input and output features. The training data window includes three-frames based rain-codes ranging from 2006 May to 2018 October. The test dataset windows

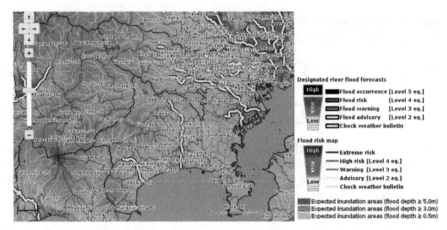

Fig. 4. Case study region in Kanto and an example of the real-time flood risk map (https://www.jma.go.jp/en/suigaimesh/flood.html).

Table 1. Percentile of hourly precipitation from 2006 to 2019 in the $136 \times 148 \text{ km}^2$ region, whose area was aggregated by a sub-group of 20×20 grids.

Percentile	Grid precipitation	Percentile	Grid precipitation
82%	0.008 mm/h	99.9%	15.25 mm/h
85%	0.10 mm/h	99.99%	32.18 mm/h
90%	0.40 mm/h	99.999%	50.65 mm/h
95%	0.92 mm/h	99.9999%	71.52 mm/h
97%	1.89 mm/h	99.99999%	93.80 mm/h
99%	4.70 mm/h	Maximum	106.37 mm/h

contains the last 30 windows with a 3-h input rain-code and 3-h output rain-code, whose 6 frames are multiplied by the 30 rain-code sets to obtain a 180-h test set that stands for 7.5 days until 2019 October.

3.2 Feasibility Study of Rain-Code Forecasting and Computing Accuracy

We implemented the training for the 3-h 1×3 frame-based rain-code. We set the number of mini-batches as 24 and performed the training for 10 epochs (approximately 1300 iterations). After 2.5 h, the loss reached a stable level. Using this trained ConvLSTM network, we computed RMSE using Eq. (3) at each frame.

Figure 5 shows a plot of hourly frame based accuracy RMSE of the 1- and 2-timestep rain-code based forecasting test results. Here, the number of test rain-code cases was 12. Each RMSE was computed in the range of 0–8, and the average RMSE among the 12 cases was approximately 4. Both an increasing error and a decreasing error occurred, because the test rain-code had variations in the precipitation region. The patterns of the rain-code features (precipitation process) within 3 h were classified, e.g., thin rain, decreasing rain, mid rain, increasing rain, and heavy rain. The prediction error was smaller for less rainy regions. The average frame based RMSEs forecasting results were almost constant level.

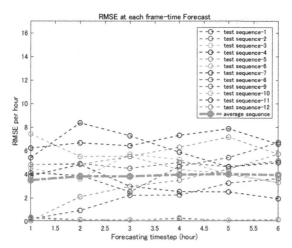

Fig. 5. Plot of the hourly frame based accuracy RMSE for the 1- and 2-timestep forecasting tests based on the 3-h rain-code.

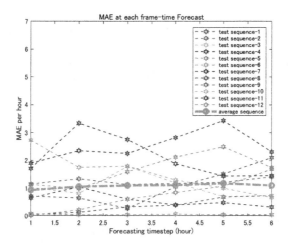

Fig. 6. Plot of the hourly frame based accuracy MAE for the 1- and 2-timestep forecasting tests based on the 3-h rain-code.

We computed MAE using Eq. (4) at each frame. Figure 6 shows a plot of the frame based MAE of the 1- and 2-timestep rain-code based forecasting test results. Each MAE was computed in the range of 0–3.5, and the average MAE among the 12 cases was approximately 1. Both an increasing error and a decreasing error occurred, owing to the variations in the precipitation region for each test rain-code. Similar to the RMSE results, the prediction error was smaller for less rainy regions. The average frame based MAEs for the 1- and 2-timestep forecasting results were almost constant level. Therefore, both the RMSE and MAE were stable.

4   Rain-Code Size Sensitivity Studies

4.1   Rain-Code Training Results and Accuracy Indices for Different Number of Frames

We computed the RMSE and MAE using Eqs. (1) (2) as the rain-code multi-frame based accuracy. Table 2 presents several training results and prediction error indices for different number of frames of the rain-code. We all trained the unified target size of 80×80; if the original rain-code size was different from the target size, we resized the rain-code to the unified size. However, we computed the prediction error indices resized back to the initial rain-code pixel size. Compared with four cases, the size of 2×2 frames rain-code outperform accuracy indices with both RMSE and MAE. This is because the rain-code was square rather than rectangular (as in the other cases); thus, the resized unified size operation and back to the original size influences a little information loss of rainy feature. A larger multi-frame size corresponded to a larger error of the rain-code based forecasting results. Unfortunately, a single-frame method as the baseline of Convolutional LSTM was impossible to predict the target 6 h precipitation forecasting, as far as we implemented it to the dataset of study region from 2009 to 2016.

Table 2. Training results and indices with different multi-frame sizes of the of rain-code.

Input Rain-Code multi-frame size	Target 6 h Predictability	Average RMSE(h)	Average MAE(h)	Training time
Single-frame **Baseline**	6 h **Not predictable**	—	—	—
3 (1 × 3 frames)	6 h Predictable	3.87	1.05	2 h 24 min (10 epoch)
4 (2 × 2 frames)	**8 h** **Predictable**	**3.68**	**1.02**	1 h 52 min (10 epoch)
6 (2 × 3 frames)	12 h Predictable	4.45	1.25	1 h 14 min (10 epoch)
12(3 × 4 frames)	24 h Predictable	6.96	2.43	1 h 12 min (20 epoch)

4.2   Rain-Code Based Forecasting Results and Accuracy Using 2 × 2 Frames

Figure 7 shows five test sets of prediction results at each line that contains the "ground truth" of rain-code (the left-side of two images) and the 2 time step rain-code based "forecasting result" (the right-side of two images), where each image is a rain-code feature composed by 4 h range of 2×2 frames. This square frame size is the most accurate case that outperform RMSE and MAE than other rectangle shape of multi-frame size, shown as Table 2.

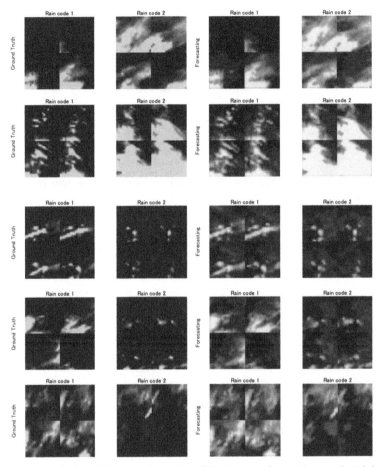

Fig. 7. Ground truth (left-side of two images) and 2 time step forecasting results (right-side of two images) using 2×2 frames 4 h rain-code.

Figure 8 shows a Plot of root mean square error (RMSE) of 1- and 2-time step rain-code based forecasting test results. Here, the number of test rain-code is 12 cases. Each RMSE is computed into the range from 0 to 10, and the average RMSE among 12 cases is around 3.5 level. In addition, Fig. 9 shows a Plot of mean absolute error (MAE) of 1- and 2-time step rain-code based forecasting test results. Each MAE is computed into the range from 0 to 7.5, and the average MAE among 12 cases is around 2 level.

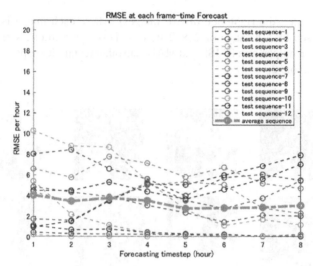

Fig. 8. Plot of RMSE hourly accuracy of 1- and 2-time step forecasting tests based on 2 × 2 frames 4 h rain-code.

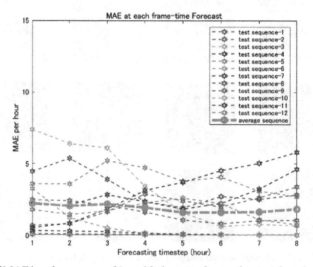

Fig. 9. Plot of MAE hourly accuracy of 1- and 2-time step forecasting tests based on 2 × 2 frames 4 h rain-code.

4.3   Rain-Code Based Forecasting Results and Accuracy Using 3 × 4 Frames with Padding 1 × 4 mask

Figure 10 shows five test sets of prediction results at each line that contains the "ground truth" of rain-code (the left-side of two images) and the 2 time step rain-code based "forecasting result" (the right-side of two images), where each image is a rain-code feature composed by 12 h range of 3 × 4 frames. Though this initial frame size is rectangle, but we added the padding 1×4 mask at the bottom in order to keep the ratio of row-column to be the square shape.

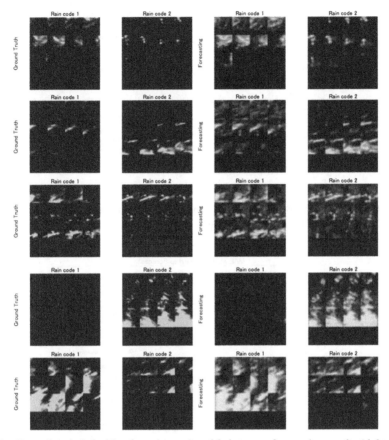

Fig. 10. Ground truth (left-side of two images) and 2 time step forecasting results (right-side of two images) using 3×4 frames 12 h rain-code with padding 1×4 mask at the bottom line.

Figure 11 shows a Plot of root mean square error (RMSE) of 1- and 2-time step rain-code based forecasting test results. Here, the number of test rain-code with 3×4 frame is 12 cases. Each RMSE is computed into the range from 0 to 30, and the average RMSE among 12 cases is around 10 level. In addition, Fig. 12 shows a Plot of mean absolute error (MAE) of 1- and 2-time step rain-code based forecasting test results. Each MAE is computed into the range from 0 to 20, and the average MAE among 12 cases is around 5 level.

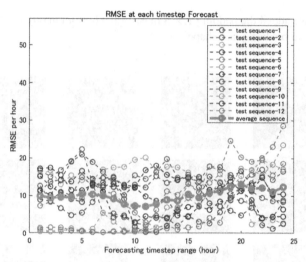

Fig. 11. Plot of RMSE hourly accuracy of 1- and 2-time step forecasting tests based on 3 × 4 frames 12 h rain-code with padding 1 × 4 mask.

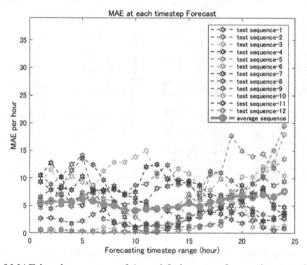

Fig. 12. Plot of MAE hourly accuracy of 1- and 2-time step forecasting tests based on 3 × 4 frames 12 h rain-code with padding 1 × 4 mask.

5　Concluding Remarks

5.1　Multi-frame Based Code-to-Code Spatiotemporal Forecasting

This paper proposed a rain-code based approach for spatiotemporal precipitation forecasting. We propose a novel rainy feature fusion that represents an unified multi-frame spatiotemporal relation for seemingly forecasting timestep reduction. We performed rain-code studies with various number of multi-frame using the algorithm of Code-to-code ConvLSTM for more than 6-h forward precipitation forecasting. We applied our method to a dam region focusing on the Japanese rainy term May to October approximately 37 thousands hourly precipitation data since 2006 to 2019. We used the radar analysis hourly data for the central broader region with an area of 136×148 km^2. Although the forecasting results were slightly blurred and within a region narrower than the ground-truth region, the rainy locations of precipitation has been accurate. We presented several training results and prediction error indices with various number of multi-frame of the rain-code. Compared with four cases, the size of 2×2 frames rain-code outperform accuracy indices with both RMSE and MAE. The rain-code based approach allowed to keep the hourly average accuracy almost constant level at precipitation forecasting using our proposed Code-to-code ConvLSTM.

5.2 Future Extend Forecasting Range for Dam Inflow Prediction

In this study, the ConvLSTM algorithm was used for rain-code based spatiotemporal forecasting. Although convolutional LSTM has limitations with regard to the forecasting timestep, we can perform two-timestep forecasting using the 2-layer ConvLSTM network. We will tackle to predict the dam inflow toward high water under heavy rain. As the input for dam inflow model, we will utilise the 6-h-forward precipitation for predicting the target dam inflow variable. This study focused on the rain-code of the multi-frame precipitation feature, but there are another important weather fusion, e.g., the sea surface temperature. Such weather movie data are usable for multi-frame-based spatiotemporal forecasting. Furthermore, with on-the-ground digital sensing, e.g., of the river water level at many locations, when we can set many sensors in multiple sub-region and temporally monitor condition, we believe that multi-frame based method allows the matrix of on-the-ground intensity codes to be used to extend the forecasting range by employing the code-to-code convolutional LSTM architecture.

Acknowledgements. We gratefully acknowledge the help provided by constructive comments of the anonymous referees. We thank Takuji Fukumoto and Shinichi Kuramoto (MathWorks Japan) for providing us with MATLAB resources.

References

1. Ministry of Land Infrastructure, Transport and Tourism: Basic policy strengthening flood control function of existing dam, 12 December 2019
2. Sit, M., Demiray, B., Xiang, Z., et al.: A Comprehensive Review of Deep Learning Applications in Hydrology and Water Resources. arXiv:2007.12269 (2020)
3. Wu, H., Yang, Q., Liu, J., et al.: A spatiotemporal deep fusion model for merging satellite and gauge precipitation in China. J. Hydrol. **584**, 124664 (2020)
4. Yan, Q., Ji, F., Miao, K., et al.: Convolutional residual attention: a deep learning approach for precipitation nowcasting. Adv., Meteorol (2020)
5. Chen, L., Cao, Y., Ma, L., et al.: A deep learning-based methodology for precipitation nowcasting with radar. Earth Space Sci. **7**(2), e2019EA000812 (2020)

6. Shi, X., Yeung, D.-Y.: Machine Learning for Spatiotemporal Sequence Forecasting: Survey. arXiv:1808.06865v1 (2018)
7. Shi, X., Chen, Z., Wang, H., Yeung, D.-Y., Wong, W.-K., Woo, W.-C.: Convolutional LSTM Network: A Machine Learning Approach for Precipitation Nowcasting. arXiv:1506.04214v2 (2015)
8. Shi, X., Gao, Z., Lausen, L., et al.: Deep learning for precipitation nowcasting: a benchmark and a new model. In: NIPS (2017)
9. Wang, Y., Long, M., Wang, J., et al.: PredRNN: recurrent neural networks for predictive learning using spatiotemporal LSTMs. In: NIPS (2017)
10. Wang, Y., Gao, Z., Long, M., et al.: PredRNN++: towards a resolution of the deep-in-time dilemma in spatiotemporal predictive learning. In: ICML (2018)
11. Alleon, A., Jauvion, G., Quennenhen, B., et al.: PlumeNet: Large-Scale Air Quality Forecasting Using A Convolutional LSTM Network. arXiv:2006.09204v1 (2020)
12. Liu, L., Zhang, R., Peng, J., et al.: Attentive Crowd Flow Machines. arXiv:1809.00101v1 (2018)
13. Wang, J., Zhu, W., Sun, Y., et al.: An Effective Dynamic Spatio-temporal Framework with Multi-Source Information for Traffic Prediction. arXiv:2005.05128v1 (2000)
14. Kim, S., Hong, S., Joh, M., et al.: DeepRain: ConvLSTM network for precipitqation prediction using multichannel radar data. In: 7th International Workshop on Climate Infomatics (2017)
15. Pascanu, R., Mikolov, T., Bengio, Y.: On the Difficulty of Training Recurrent Neural Networks. arXiv:1211.5063v2 (2013)
16. Rumelhart, D.E., Hinton, G.E., Williams, R.J.: Learning representations by backpropagating errors. Nature **323**(6088), 533–536 (1986)
17. Graves, A.: Generating Sequences with Recurrent Neural Networks. arXiv:1308.0850v5 (2014)
18. Gangopadhyay, T., Tan, S.-Y., Huang, G., et al.: Temporal attention and stacked LSTMs for multivariate time series prediction. In: NIPS (2018)
19. Srivastava, N., Mansimov, E., Salakhutdinov, R.: Unsupervised Learning of Video Representations using LSTMs. arXiv:1502.04681v3 (2016)
20. Japan Meteorological Agency: Radar/Rain gauge-Analysed Precipitation data. https://www.jma.go.jp/en/kaikotan/. Accessed 30 Sep 2020
21. Rajalingappaa, S.: Deep Learning for Computer Vision – Expert Techniques to Train Advanced Neural Networks using TensorFlow and Keras. Packt Publishing (2018)
22. Francois, C.: Deep Learning with Python. Manning Publications (2018)

PATRECH2020 - II International Workshop on Pattern Recognition for Cultural Heritage

PatReCH 2020 - 2nd International Workshop on Pattern Recognition for Cultural Heritage

Workshop Description

PatReCH is a forum for scholars who study Pattern Recognition applications for Cultural Heritage valorization and preservation. Pattern recognition is rapidly contaminating new areas of our life day by day. On the other hand, the management of Cultural Heritage is increasingly in need of new solutions to document, manage and visit (even virtually) the enormous number of artifacts and information that come from the past. The contamination of these two worlds is now a reality and creates the bounds of the main topics of this workshop. Currently, Pattern Recognition technologies are already employed in the fields of Cultural Heritage preservation and exploitation. From these fields two main issues arise:

- the information contained in digital representations of physical objects like scanned documents, scanned artifacts, maps, digital music, etc. are not easy to exploit and advanced patter recognition analysis is required.
- at the same time, the production of digital material such as augmented reality, Cultural Heritage games, robotics applications, etc. need innovative techniques and methodologies.

The above issues are leading PR researchers to develop new methodologies and applications, which are able to analyze the available data and learn mathematical models to generate new ones in a smart way (for augmented reality, serious games, etc.). The aim of this workshop is to bring together many experts in this multidisciplinary subject that involves different skills and knowledge, which span from the study of the cultural heritage to the development of PR/AI techniques for cultural heritage analysis, reconstruction and understanding.

The second edition of the International Workshop on Pattern Recognition for Cultural Heritage was virtually held in Milan, Italy, in conjunction with the 25th International Conference on Pattern Recognition (ICPR 2020).

The format of the workshop included the talk of the invited speaker Davide Tanasi (University of the South Florida), followed by technical presentation in oral and poster format. This year we received 35 submissions for reviews from authors belonging to 19 distinct countries. After an accurate and thorough peer-review, we selected 25 papers for presentation at the workshop. The review process focused on the quality of the papers, their scientific novelty, and the impact for Cultural Heritage valorization. The acceptance of the papers was the results of two different reviews. All the high-quality papers were accepted, and the acceptance rate was 69%. The accepted manuscripts included very interesting PR applications for Cultural Heritage which interested the workshop's audience. Finally, we would like to thank the PatReCH Program Committee, whose members made the workshop possible with their rigorous and timely review process.

Organization

Workshop Chairs

Dario Allegra	University of Catania, Italy
Francesco Colace	University of Salerno, Italy
Mario Molinara	University of Cassino and Southern Lazio, Italy
Alessandra Scotto di Freca	University of Cassino and Sotuhern Lazio, Italy
Filippo Stanco	University of Catania, Italy

Program Committee

Sebastiano Battiato	University of Catania, Italy
Alessandro Bria	University of Cassino and Sotuhern Lazio, Italy
Aladine Chetouani	PRISME, France
Carmen De Maio	University of Salerno, Italy
Massimo De Santo	University of Salerno, Italy
Claudio De Stefano	University of Cassino and Sotuhern Lazio, Italy
Pierluca Ferraro	University of Palermo, Italy
Francesco Fontanella	University of Cassino and Sotuhern Lazio, Italy
Giovanni Gallo	University of Catania, Italy
Luca Guarnera	University of Catania, Italy
Anna Gueli	University of Catania, Italy
Vicky Katsoni	University of Western Attica, Greece
Muhammad Khan	New York University, USA
Marco Lombardi	University of Salerno, Italy
Eva Savina Malinverni	Marche Polytechnic University, Italy
Claudio Marrocco	University of Cassino and Sotuhern Lazio, Italy
Filippo L. M. Milotta	University of Catania, Italy
Marco Morana	University of Palermo, Italy
Vincenzo Moscato	University of Naples, Italy
Francesco Moscato	University of Campania Luigi Vanvitelli, Italy
Henry Muccini	University of L'Aquila, Italy
Alessandro Ortis	University of Catania, Italy
David Picard	Ecole des Ponts ParisTech, France
Antonio Piccinno	University of Bari, Italy
Francesco Ragusa	University of Catania, Italy
Domenico Santaniello	University of Salerno, Italy
Roberto Scopigno	CNR-ISTI, Italy
Bogdan Smolka	Silesian University of Technology, Poland
Davide Tanasi	University of South Florida, USA
Alfredo Troiano	NetCom Engineering Spa, Italy

Using Graph Neural Networks
to Reconstruct Ancient Documents

Cecilia Ostertag[1,2]($\boxtimes$) and Marie Beurton-Aimar[2]

[1] L3i - EA 2118, La Rochelle, France
cecilia.ostertag1@univ-lr.fr
[2] LaBRI - CNRS 5800, Bordeaux, France
beurton@labri.fr

Abstract. In recent years, machine learning and deep learning approaches such as artificial neural networks have gained in popularity for the resolution of automatic puzzle resolution problems. Indeed, these methods are able to extract high-level representations from images, and then can be trained to separate matching image pieces from non-matching ones. These applications have many similarities to the problem of ancient document reconstruction from partially recovered fragments. In this work we present a solution based on a Graph Neural Network, using pairwise patch information to assign labels to edges representing the spatial relationships between pairs. This network classifies the relationship between a source and a target patch as being one of Up, Down, Left, Right or None. By doing so for all edges, our model outputs a new graph representing a reconstruction proposal. Finally, we show that our model is not only able to provide correct classifications at the edge-level, but also to generate partial or full reconstruction graphs from a set of patches.

Keywords: Deep learning · Graph Neural Networks · Document reconstruction · Cultural heritage

1 Introduction

The study of ancient documents and artifacts provides invaluable knowledge about previous civilizations. Indeed, they contain information about the economic, religious, and political organization at their time of writing. Unfortunately, the preservation conditions of such artifacts were often less than ideal, and nowadays archaeologists can only recover partial fragments of papers, papyri, and pottery shards. The restoration of old documents from recovered fragments is a daunting task, but it is necessary in order to decipher the writings. Recent image processing techniques can be applied to this problem, for example for text extraction [15] or object reconstruction [14]. In particular Convolutional Neural Networks, which are the best suited deep learning architectures for image inputs, can be used as an enhancement of traditional methods.

Here we consider that the task of ancient document reconstruction is analogous to puzzle resolution [8], with the added challenge that the shape of the pieces cannot be used to help the reconstruction, as the fragments' edges were eroded and distorted with time. We describe image reconstruction from patches

© Springer Nature Switzerland AG 2021
A. Del Bimbo et al. (Eds.): ICPR 2020 Workshops, LNCS 12667, pp. 39–53, 2021.
https://doi.org/10.1007/978-3-030-68787-8_3

as an edge classification problem, where all patches are represented by nodes in a graph. Instead of using a classical approach of pairwise comparisons followed by global reconstruction with a greedy algorithm, we use a Convolutional Graph Neural Network to test every pair of patches in a single pass. We also provide an interactive user interface for manual checking and correction of the assembly graphs predicted by our model.

2   Related Works

In 2010, Cho et al. [3] introduce a graphical model to solve the problem of puzzle reconstruction. Their approach uses the sum-of-squared color difference across junctions as a compatibility metric to evaluate pairwise patch assemblies, and a Markov network to specify constraints for the whole-image reconstruction. An other pairwise compatibility metric that was used in similar applications is the Mahalanobis Gradient Compatibility [9]. The work of [6] use a more complex compatibility metric, taking into account edge similarity and cosine similarity between patches' histograms. In 2015, Paikin et al. [11] present an optimized greedy algorithm for solving jigsaw puzzles with patches of unknown orientation and with missing pieces, where the key point is to find the best starting patch for the global assembly.

All of these works deal with puzzles representing natural images, which carry a lot of semantic information (foreground, background, objects, people,...) and a diversity of shapes and colors. In our case of ancient documents reconstruction, the images contain less information; mostly a low gradient of color across the whole image, some writings or inscriptions, and the texture of the document itself. Indeed, in the reconstruction examples given in all of these works, the areas that are the least correctly assembled are areas containing few semantic information, like the sky, the sea, or grass fields. A work by Paumard et al. [12] seemed closer to our cultural heritage problem, since the authors' goal is to reconstruct old paintings, or pictures of ancient objects, from patches, but their dataset is also mainly made of images with important semantic information.

In our previous work [10], based on [12] approach using a Siamese Convolutional Neural Network to test pairwise assemblies, we proposed a model able to predict for a pair of patches the direction of assembly (up, down, left, or right), or its absence. Then we greedily constructed a graph by choosing good candidates for each pair, according to a probability threshold. In case of multiple candidates, several graphs were created, to give the user multiple assembly proposals. The major drawback of our approach was the execution time of our greedy algorithm, and the exploding number of assembly proposals generated by our reconstruction pipeline.

In this work we apply the increasingly popular Graph Neural Network architecture to our old document reconstruction problem, in order to test in a single shot the entirety of pairwise alignments between patches. Graph Neural Networks [16] are used to work on non-Euclidean data. Here our original data is Euclidean, but we transform the set of image patches into a complete graph, hence the use of a Graph Network. In the context of classification, these networks can be used in different ways: node classification, edge classification, or graph classification, but always rely on node attributes to compute features. According to [16], Graph Neural Networks have mainly been applied to citation networks, bio-chemical graphs, and social networks, but to the best of our knowledge they haven't yet been used in the context of puzzle solving or document reconstruction.

3 Automatic Reconstruction Using a ConvGNN

3.1 Creation of a Ground Truth Dataset

Our image data consists in 5959 papyrus images, taken from the University of Michigan Library's papyrology collection, containing documents dating from 1000 BCE to 1000 CE [1]. This dataset was also used by [13] with the aim of finding fragments belonging to the same original papyrus. From this dataset, we removed 1865 images corresponding to reverse sides of some papyri. These images don't contain any textual information, so are of no importance for egyptologists, and would risk to worsen the training of our model because of this lack of information.

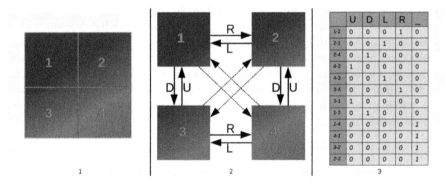

Fig. 1. Example of ground truth creation from an image split into 4 patches. 1: Original image. 2: Complete directed graph, Nodes are patches and Edges are spatial relationships. 3: One-hot labels for all edges. U=up, D=down, L=left, R=right, _=no relationship

We created our own dataset with ground truth by artificially splitting images from papyrus images into patches. Each image was first re-sized to 768×1280 pixels, then split into 15 non-overlapping patches of size 256×256. Then a graph representation of the image was created: this representation is a complete directed graph, where nodes are patches and edges represent the spatial relationship between two nodes. As per standard graph vocabulary, for a pair of nodes (s, t) linked by an edge e starting at node s and ending at node t, we call

s the source node and t the target node. Each node has as attribute an identifier and the pixel array corresponding to the patch image. Each edge has as attribute an identifier corresponding to the spatial relationship: up, down, left, right, and none. The edge attributes correspond to the five classes in our task, and can be encoded as one-hot vectors (see Fig. 1).

Given the nature of complete graphs, the class imbalance towards edges belonging to class "none" (see Table 1) would only increase with an increase of the number of patches per image. This is an important fact that we had to take into account during training.

Table 1. Number of samples per class, per image and for the entire dataset

Class	U	D	L	R	-
Samples per image	12	12	10	10	166
Samples total	49128	49128	40940	40940	679604

3.2 Model Architecture

Our model, that we named AssemblyGraphNet, is a Convolutional Graph Neural Network that uses node attributes information to predict edge labels. In order to do this, the model is actually made of two parts: a Global Model, and a Pairwise Comparison Model. The Pairwise Comparison Model (see Fig. 2) is a convolutional neural network which takes as input two connected nodes (source and target), and outputs a label for the edge connecting the source to its target. Here we defined five classes, corresponding to the alignment direction of the target patch in relation to the source patch. The classes are: up, down, left, right, and none.

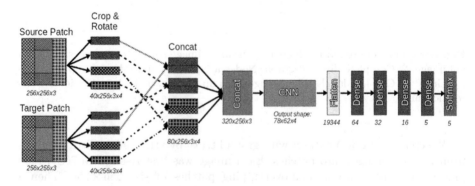

Fig. 2. Architecture of the pairwise comparison model part of our AssemblyGraphNet

As we focus on testing pairwise alignments in 4-connectivity, the first step of the network is to crop a 40-pixel-width stripe in each direction, for both patches. Then these stripes are concatenated according to the possible matching sites (for example, target-up with source-down). The four "assembly sites" are then concatenated together, and fed to a convolutional neural network (see Table 2) followed by four Dense layers of decreasing size. Finally, a Softmax layer outputs the probability that the edge corresponds to each of the five classes described previously. We note that we created our "assembly sites" using a concatenation operation, and not an averaging or an absolute difference, in order to benefit from the asymmetry inherent to this operation. Indeed, our goal is to check pairwise assembly in both directions, to obtain more information for the global reconstruction step.

Table 2. Architecture and parameters of the convolutional neural network used in the Pairwise Comparison Model

Layer	Output shape	Kernel size	Stride	Output nodes
BatchNorm	$320 \times 256 \times 3$			
Convolution	$318 \times 254 \times 4$	3	1	4
ReLU	$318 \times 254 \times 4$			
MaxPooling	$159 \times 127 \times 4$	2	2	
BatchNorm	$159 \times 127 \times 4$			
Convolution	$157 \times 125 \times 4$	3	1	4
ReLU	$157 \times 125 \times 4$			
MaxPooling	$78 \times 62 \times 4$	2	2	
BatchNorm	$78 \times 62 \times 4$			

The Global Model is the part that actually uses the graph representation of the image. The graph connectivity is represented by a matrix of size [2 × number of edges], where the first row is the identifiers of the source nodes and the second row is the identifiers of the target nodes. The RGB pixel values for all patches are stored in a node features matrix, and the edge labels are all initialized to [1,1,1,1,1] and stored into an edge features matrix. Using this connectivity matrix, two graph-level feature matrix of shape [number of edges × patch size × patch size × 3] are inferred from the node features matrix: one for the source nodes, and the other for the target nodes. The Pairwise Comparison Model is used on every source-target pair, while handling the first dimension of the matrix as if it were the dimension of a batch. The output of the Global Model is a new graph where the connectivity matrix and the node features matrix are not changed, but the edge feature matrix is replaced by the predicted edge labels (argmax of the Pairwise Comparison Model's output for each edge).

3.3   Experiments and Results

Our model was implemented using pytorch and torch-geometric [4], a pytorch library for graph neural networks. For memory and computation efficiency, the computations were made using float16 precision. The loss function is the categorical cross-entropy computed between the ground truth and predicted edge feature matrix, and the optimizer is Adam. We split our dataset into 3394 training images, 500 validation images, and 200 test images. During training the order of node pairs is shuffled for each image and at each iteration, to avoid an overfitting caused by the order of appearance of edges.

As we explained earlier, we have a huge class imbalance towards the fifth class, so to remedy this problem we decided to weight the loss for each class. A weight of 0.1 was assigned to the fifth class, and a weight of 0.8 for each of the remaining classes. During training and validation, we computed the balanced accuracy (average of recall obtained on each class) instead of the classic accuracy (percentage of correct predictions), to take into account class imbalance and have a score more representative of our model's ability to predict correct pairwise assemblies [2,7]. We also computed the F1-score for each class, as 1-versus-all binary classification results.

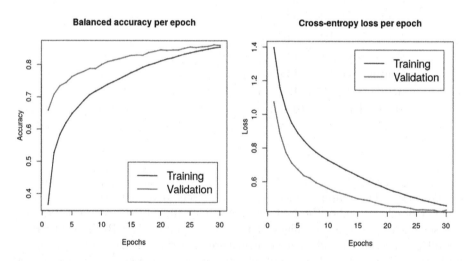

Fig. 3. Evolution of balanced accuracy and categorical cross-entropy loss during training

Our results (see Fig. 3 and Table 3) obtained after 30 epochs show that we reach a limit with a satisfying value of 86% balanced accuracy on the validation set. However, even though we used a weighted loss, the fifth class, corresponding to "no patch assembly" is the most correctly predicted. We can safely assume that a part of the features extracted by the Pairwise Comparison Model are related to the gradient of pixel values at the junction zones. This explains why the fifth class remains the best predicted class, given that it is easy to differentiate between a high gradient (corresponding to an absence of assembly) and a low gradient (corresponding to a possible assembly), but difficult to infer the direction of the match from such information.

Table 3. Value of loss, balanced accuracy, and per-class F1-score obtained after training for 30 epochs

	Loss	Acc	F1_1	F1_2	F1_3	F1_4	F1_5
Training	0.46	0.86	0.65	0.63	0.50	0.51	0.81
Validation	0.43	0.86	0.69	0.67	0.54	0.52	0.83
Test	0.42	0.85	0.69	0.68	0.53	0.52	0.81

Even though our results are convincing, they are based on the pairwise classification of patch pairs, and not on the actual whole-image reconstruction. The problem for evaluating the quality of image reconstructions is that with our model each node is susceptible to have multiple neighbour candidates in each direction. One solution is to filter automatically the results based on a threshold on the class-associated probabilities, and to consider every alignment probability inferior to this threshold as an occurrence of the "no patch assembly" class, but there is a risk to delete alignments correctly predicted but without enough confidence. Instead of this, we opted for an interactive visualization of the assembly proposal graphs, allowing the user to delete some "obviously wrong to the human eye" edges.

4   Interactive Visualization of Assembly Proposals

4.1   Graphical Interface

After running our AssemblyGraphNet on a set of patches, the resulting graph is saved in a text file, with all node features, and predicted edge labels with associated probabilities. To provide the user with a lightweight graphical interface, we use the Cytoscape.js graph library [5] to read and display the graph elements in an interactive way. To see correctly the reconstructed image, each node is attributed a 2D set of coordinates, and represented on the screen by the associated pixel values of the corresponding patch.

First the connected components are identified, then for each component, a node is arbitrarily chosen as the origin, and the coordinates of the rest of the nodes are iteratively computed using the spatial relationships to one-another, following a depth first search algorithm. We note that this can lead to several nodes being in the same position, and that the user needs to be careful to check if this happens. The connected components are separated from each other, to show clearly the partial image reconstructions.

The user can then choose between a compact representation, with edges and labels hidden, or an expanded representation showing node identifiers as well as edges with their label and associated probabilities. The user is able to move nodes around freely, to manually set a threshold for edge filtering, to select edges for deletion, and finally to refresh the node positions after modifications in the graph.

4.2 Examples of Image Reconstructions

Using images from our test set, we used our visualization tool to assess the quality of our assembly proposals. We started by inputting lists of 15 patches from the same image, and looking at reconstruction results for individual images.

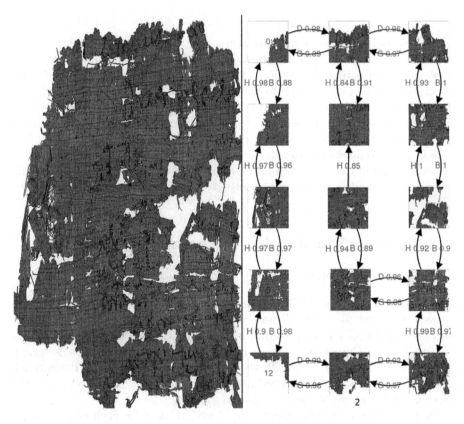

Fig. 4. Example of entirely correct image reconstruction. 1: Ground truth. 2: Assembly graph.

Figure 4 and Fig. 5 show assembly proposals, after filtering edges with a probability threshold of 0.8 for all classes. The assembly graph in Fig. 4 shows a case where we obtain a perfect reconstruction even if all edges were not correctly predicted, or not predicted with a satisfying probability. It also demonstrate the use of using a directed graph to test pairwise alignments both ways, as it means that we have twice the chance to have a correct prediction for each pair.

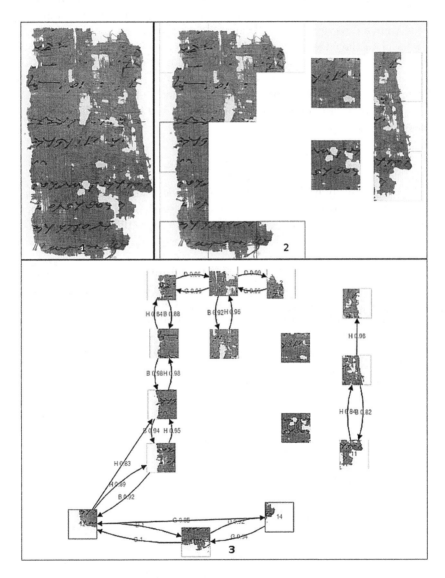

Fig. 5. Example of partial image reconstruction. 1: Ground truth. 2: Reconstructions. 3: Assembly graph. (Color figure online)

Figure 5 illustrates cases where only partial assemblies were found, either because of edge labels incorrectly predicted as "no patch assembly", or because of an edge filtering that was too drastic. In this assembly graph we have two nodes, highlighted by a blue border, that each have multiple candidates for the same alignment direction: patch 6 and 9 are both candidates to be above patch 12, and patch 12 and 13 are both candidates to be left to patch 14. However, it is easy for the user to filter out the incorrect edges, based simultaneously on the prediction probabilities, and on the existence of the reciprocal edge label in the target to source direction. Here for example the edge $12 \rightarrow 6$ has a probability of 0.83, inferior to the edge $12 \rightarrow 9$ with a probability of 0.89, but the relationship between patches 12 and 6 could also be removed on the basis that edge $6 \rightarrow 12$ with label "up" doesn't exist but edge $9 \rightarrow 12$ with label "up" does. The same reasoning can be applied to filter out edge 12 removed on the basis that edge $6 \rightarrow 12$ with label "up" doesn't exist but edge $9 \rightarrow 14$, and to finally obtain a better reconstruction.

4.3   Reconstructions from Multiple Images

After showing the ability of our model to provide accurate reconstructions of an image from the corresponding set of patches, we wanted to see if our model was capable to distinguish between patches coming from different images. To do this, we simply fed the network with a random list of patches coming from two test images.

Figure 6 and Fig. 7 are two examples, after filtering the probabilities at 0.8. The first figure shows a case where the two images are easily distinguished by the color of the papyrus, and the second where the differences are more subtle, being papyrus texture and scribe handwriting. Figure 6 also illustrate the importance of user input, as in this case a single edge was identified and removed by the user, instead of several edges including important ones if we had opted for automatic thresholding.

Looking at the assembly graph for these two examples, we can see that, with a 0.8 probability threshold, patches from different images are not mixed together. Moreover, even if the images are not wholly reconstructed, the user is provided with partial assemblies.

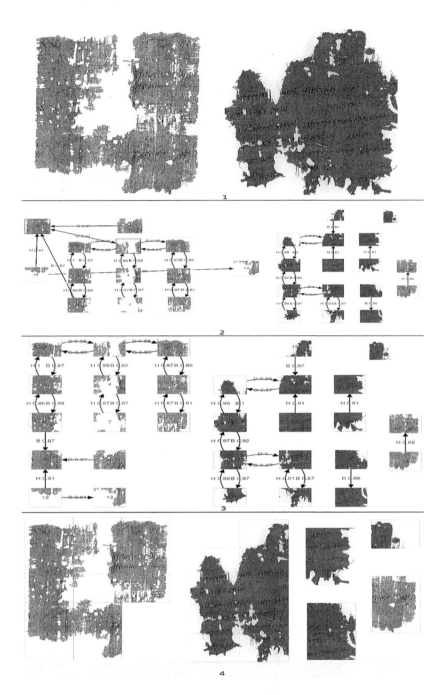

Fig. 6. Example of partial reconstructions from patches belonging to two images. 1: Ground truth. 2: Assembly graph before user intervention. 3: Assembly graph after user intervention (deletion of edge 4 → 9). 4: Reconstructions.

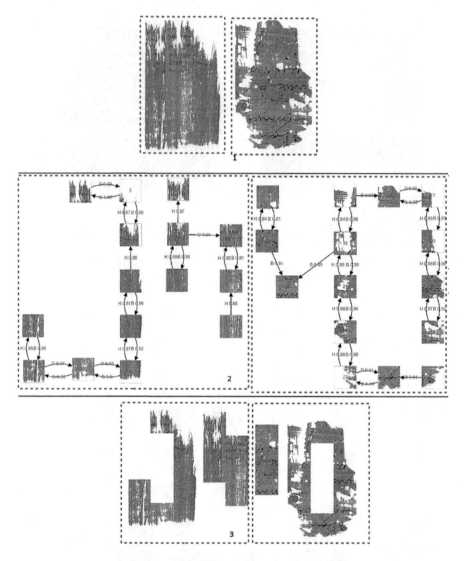

Fig. 7. Example of partial reconstructions from patches belonging to two images. 1: Ground truth. 2: Assembly graph, 3: Reconstructions.

5   Discussion and Conclusion

Our model AssemblyGraphNet gives an average of 86% correctly predicted spatial relationships between patch pairs for the validation set. This is a significant improvement over results obtained by Paumard et al. [12], who obtained 68.8% of correctly placed fragments for their dataset of pictures from the Metropolitan Museum of Art, composed mainly of paintings. Moreover, the authors of this article say that they obtain a perfect reconstruction only 28.8% of the time.

We don't have an objective means of estimating the number of perfect recon-structions that we can obtain, given that we rely on user intervention to filter the assembly graphs, but with our edge classification score we can assume that a larger number of perfect reconstructions can be obtained by using our model. Finally, in a situation where patches come from multiple images, the model pro-posed by Paumard et al. will not be able to separate the images during global reconstruction because they don't use a class to model the absence of assembly, contrarily to our AssemblyGraphNet.

By taking advantage of the Graph Neural Network architecture, our model is able to simultaneously predict the existence and, if need be, the direction of assembly between all pairs given a set of patches. Thus, the model outputs directly a whole-image reconstruction proposal. For the time being the model doesn't make use of a lot of graph properties, with the exception of the connec-tivity matrix allowing to process all node pairs at once. However this graphNN-based approach was used with the intent of reconstructing the whole images in several steps instead of a single step like we presented here, using a succession of convolution layers followed by graph coarsening layers [16] to assemble groups of small fragments into bigger fragments, that will be assembled together in the next layer, and so on.

Then, thanks to our interactive visualization interface, a user with some knowledge of the field can refine the assembly graph based on the probabilities associated to edge labels, or based on symmetric and neighbouring edges. More-over, if we consider only the inference, the execution time of our model is quicker than the execution of a greedy algorithm based on pairwise compatibility: on a GeForce RTX 2080 Ti, it takes an average of 0.8 ms to output an assembly graph from a set of 15 patches.

We also showed that our AssemblyGraphNet is not only able to predict spa-tial relationships between patches in an image, but is also able to distinguish between different images, based on information such as color, texture, and writ-ings. This result is important because it means that in a real-life application there will be no need for a preliminary step to group together fragments belonging to the same initial document, which is a problem tackled by [13].

At this time inputs of arbitrary shapes could be used with our model, with a padding to reconcile the input shape as a square or rectangle for the CNN architecture, but it would introduce noise. For example if we use zero-padding, then the gradient between two padded inputs would be small, even if the texture or color of the actual fragment were different. To tackle this problem, a strategy would be to introduce such input cases at training time. An other strategy would be to process the whole patches instead of the border regions only. Finally, the background (pixels corresponding to padded regions) versus foreground (pixels corresponding to the actual fragment) membership could be encoded into the network, so that during training the network learns to discard background-pixels information.

Here we consider that the correct orientation of every patch is known, so we will not test the possible rotation of patches. In practice, this assumption could only be made for patches containing writings, using the disposition of the symbols to find the correct rotation beforehand. In future works, we plan to work on solutions to take into account the possible rotation of patches, as well as erosion at the border of the fragments. We note that in this work the extraction of border stripes from the patches was done because of memory constraints (as explained before), but actually using the whole patches as input to a Siamese CNN would provide more information, and importantly information not limited to the junction zones between fragments, as these junctions might not correspond to anything if there was a lot of erosion.

Acknowledgements. This project has received funding from the European Research Council (ERC) under the European Union's Horizon 2020 research and innova.on programme (grant agreement No. 758907).

References

1. Papyrology Collection. https://www.lib.umich.edu/collections/collecting-areas/special-collections-and-archives/papyrology-collection
2. Brodersen, K.H., Ong, C.S., Stephan, K.E., Buhmann, J.M.: The balanced accuracy and its posterior distribution. In: 2010 20th International Conference on Pattern Recognition, pp. 3121–3124. IEEE (2010)
3. Cho, T.S., Avidan, S., Freeman, W.T.: A probabilistic image jigsaw puzzle solver. In: 2010 IEEE Computer Society Conference on Computer Vision and Pattern Recognition, pp. 183–190. IEEE (2010)
4. Fey, M., Lenssen, J.E.: Fast graph representation learning with PyTorch Geometric. In: ICLR Workshop on Representation Learning on Graphs and Manifolds (2019)
5. Franz, M., Lopes, C.T., Huck, G., Dong, Y., Sumer, O., Bader, G.D.: Cytoscape.js: a graph theory library for visualisation and analysis. Bioinformatics **32**(2), 309–311 (2016)
6. Jin, S.Y., Lee, S., Azis, N.A., Choi, H.J.: Jigsaw puzzle image retrieval via pairwise compatibility measurement. In: 2014 International Conference on Big Data and Smart Computing (BIGCOMP), pp. 123–127. IEEE (2014)
7. Kelleher, J.D., Mac Namee, B., D'arcy, A.: Fundamentals of Machine Learning for Predictive Data Analytics: Algorithms, Worked Examples, and Case Studies. MIT Press, Cambridge (2020)
8. Kleber, F., Sablatnig, R.: A survey of techniques for document and archaeology artefact reconstruction. In: 2009 10th International Conference on Document Analysis and Recognition, pp. 1061–1065. IEEE (2009)
9. Mondal, D., Wang, Y., Durocher, S.: Robust solvers for square jigsaw puzzles. In: 2013 International Conference on Computer and Robot Vision, pp. 249–256. IEEE (2013)
10. Ostertag, C., Beurton-Aimar, M.: Matching ostraca fragments using a Siamese neural network. Pattern Recogn. Lett. **131**, 336–340 (2020)
11. Paikin, G., Tal, A.: Solving multiple square jigsaw puzzles with missing pieces. In: Proceedings of the IEEE Conference on Computer Vision and Pattern Recognition, pp. 4832–4839 (2015)
12. Paumard, M.M., Picard, D., Tabia, H.: Jigsaw puzzle solving using local feature co-occurrences in deep neural networks. In: 2018 25th IEEE International Conference on Image Processing (ICIP), pp. 1018–1022. IEEE (2018)

13. Pirrone, A., Aimar, M.B., Journet, N.: Papy-S-Net: a Siamese network to match papyrus fragments. In: Proceedings of the 5th International Workshop on Historical Document Imaging and Processing, pp. 78–83 (2019)
14. Rasheed, N.A., Nordin, M.J.: A survey of classification and reconstruction methods for the 2D archaeological objects. In: 2015 International Symposium on Technology Management and Emerging Technologies (ISTMET), pp. 142–147. IEEE (2015)
15. Wadhwani, M., Kundu, D., Chakraborty, D., Chanda, B.: Text extraction and restoration of old handwritten documents. arXiv preprint arXiv:2001.08742 (2020)
16. Wu, Z., Pan, S., Chen, F., Long, G., Zhang, C., Philip, S.Y.: A comprehensive survey on graph neural networks. IEEE Trans. Neural Netw. Learn. Syst. **32**, 4–24 (2020)

AnCoins: Image-Based Automated Identification of Ancient Coins Through Transfer Learning Approaches

Chairi Kiourt$^{(\boxtimes)}$ ⓘ and Vasilis Evangelidis ⓘ

Athena-Research and Innovation Center in Information, Communication and Knowledge Technologies, Xanthi, Greece
{chairiq,vevangelidis}@athenarc.gr

Abstract. The identification of ancient coins is a time consuming and complex task with huge experience demands. The analysis of numismatic evidence through patterns detection executed by Machine Learning methods has started to be recognized as approaches that can provide archaeologists with a wide range of tools, which, especially in the fields of numismatics, can be used to ascertain distribution, continuity, change in engraving style and imitation. In this paper we introduce what we call the Ancient Coins (AnCoins-12) dataset. A set of images composed of 12 different classes of Greek ancient coins from the area of ancient Thrace, aiming for the automatic identification of their issuing authority. In this context we describe the methodology of data acquisition and dataset organization emphasizing the small number of images available in this field. In addition to that we apply deep learning approaches based on popular CNN architectures to classify the images of the new introduced dataset. Pre-trained CNNs, through transfer learning approaches, achieved a top-1 validation accuracy of 98.32% and top-5 validation accuracy of 99.99%. For a better diffusion of the results in the archaeological community, we introduce a responsive web-based application with an extension asset focusing in the identification of common characteristics in different coin types. We conclude the paper, by stressing some of the most importance key elements of the proposed approaches and by highlighting some future challenges.

Keywords: Numismatics · Transfer learning · Convolutional neural networks

1 Introduction

In recent years, Deep Learning (DL) has made remarkable achievements in various fields of Computer Vision (CV), especially in image classification, semantic segmentation and object recognition [1]. Within this framework the most challenging tasks come from images presenting difficult and very complex patterns. These are especially abundant in the field of Cultural Heritage (CH), where someone can find variety of content (data) with very complex patterns/motifs [2], but also with the restriction of limited amount of data. Therefore it is not strange that currently there is a large movement in Digital Archaeology (DA) to streamline processes of Machine Learning (ML) algorithms and

© Springer Nature Switzerland AG 2021
A. Del Bimbo et al. (Eds.): ICPR 2020 Workshops, LNCS 12667, pp. 54–67, 2021.
https://doi.org/10.1007/978-3-030-68787-8_4

improve current methods of pattern recognition in diverse categories of archaeological materials [2], especially numismatics [3–7].

The latter has proved to be a very fertile ground for the application of ML and CV approaches because the appearance of ancient coins of the same coin type, and area (origin), may vary due to several reasons, such as the period, the artistic depiction, the engraving style, the material or even the size of the coin. Another important factor that increases the difficulty of identifying a motif of an ancient coin, is its condition and damage that may has suffered due to the passage of time. In addition to that, the small amount of unique various images presenting such visual features is another limitation that increases the difficulty of creating a more accurate image classification model. All these difficulties can be translated as technical challenges in the field of ML and CV. Usually, most ancient coins are typically identified by expert numismatologists, trying to visually identify some features or patterns in the coins. This process is very difficult, time consuming and demands huge experience, while in many cases involves varying opinions. Based on the existing literature there is no any free automated ancient coins recognition system that would be used as a research and identification tool for archeologist or any related experts.

In this paper we focus on pattern detection and analysis of numismatic evidence by exploiting DL model with high accuracy which enhances the precision of mapping and understanding motifs in morphologically problematic ancient coins. Due to the fact that there was a small number of samples available for the training of the DL models, we have used crawling methods to create the required dataset. As with any such task, this effort is difficult without an "easy retrievable information" type of application. Therefore, we have also produced an easy-to-use system in the form of a web tool (AnCoins) for use by specialists (numismatologists or field archaeologists) but also by broader audiences (educators, students, visitors in museums etc.). A user-friendly web tool for coin recognition (a tangible output of the DL process) can be a large improvement over the current methods of managing images and coin recognition; something that will allow quick responses to requests for information by a variety of audiences. Further, it will improve efficiency in the field, by freeing archaeologists from manually looking up specialized books when trying to identify coins, especially in the case of a presence of significant visual information. In addition to that we introduce an approach for the identification of common characteristics in different coin types, as an additional asset of the web-based application.

Following this line of thought the interest in automatically extracting information is not just another ML practice but covers a real academic interest to accurately identify and thus define coins classes in area part of the ancient world with great circulation of coins. The high accuracy (even when a small number of images has been used) guarantees a more meaningful step towards understanding of this class of material culture [6].

The rest of this paper is organized as follows. The following section covers a brief background about the importance of numismatology as well as a brief literature review of related works. The third section describes the acquired dataset and the exploited methods. The fourth section provides the technological aspects for the training of the DL models. The fifth section presents the new novel web-based tool. The sixth section provides a discussion about the motifs recognition by the DL models and how they can be exploited to recognize coins in bad condition or to find relationships between different types of coins. The paper concludes by summarizing the key points of the proposed system and sets out future directions.

2 Background and Related Works

The value of coins as historical and archaeological evidence has been repeatedly debated since the early start of Archaeology as academic discipline [8]. Coins can be found in a multitude of places, they are numerous and varied, and they are not as easily destructible as other classes of material evidence. Indeed, coins, through their motifs, portraits and inscriptions (among other features) help to establish historical connotations, indicate specific minting rights, and help establish a better understanding of past societies. Coins designs describe a unique combination of images imprinted on both sides of a coins (obverse and reverse). The central motif (normally a heraldic emblem struck by a die mostly on the obverse side of the coin) would have authenticated the coins issuing authority (in this case the different city states or kingdoms in the case of the Hellenistic world) but also could reflect a cultural value (beyond its metal value) since the wide circulation of the silver and bronze coins upgraded them to tokens of origin. Simply put, coin finds can provide evidence where written sources are absent, by, telling us about distributions and power systems we did not otherwise know or demonstrating contacts between areas. This applies especially to Graceo Roman antiquity, when base-metal coinage was made and used on a large scale to support an even growing monetary economy. The gradual globalization of the Hellenistic and later Roman world allowed the wide diffusion of certain coin types in areas outside the Meditetterenean [9] world.

This is an active research field, where extensive work has been done over the last decade, focusing especially in the computational aspects. Kampel and Zaharieva in 2008 [4] for instance presented an approach that matches local features of different images to classify them by exploiting the SIFT, the Fast Approximated SIFT and the PCA-SIFT algorithms. The dataset consisted of 350 images for three different coins types (classes) and it was not available to public. In 2010 Arandjelovic achived an calsification acuracy of nearly 60% on Roman Imperial coins dataset which consisted of 65 classes with a total of 2236 images of 250×250 pixels [5]. The authors compared three different representations: hSIFT words, LBR and LDB kernel features, by highlighting the dominance of the LDB approach.

More recently, several works have tried to exploit characteristics in images to produce a more accurate image classification [10]. In this direction, one of the first approaches exploiting deep learning methods, especially CNNs, in ancient coins identification (Roman coins), introduced a novel approach for discovering coins characteristic landmarks in coins images [7]. This approach used salient regions in the coins to classify them. The dataset consisted of 4526 obverse-reverse image pairs. In 2017, Schlag and Arandicelovic used a modification of the VGG16 architecture to classify 83 different classes of ancient coins [11]. They achieved outstanding accuracies across different categories of classes. In 2019, Cooper and Aradjelovic showed that visual matching of coins approach is not practically efficient [12] and they argued that the understanding of the semantic content of a coin is a much more efficient approach. Also, they adopted a modified version of AlexNet [13] model which achieved a test accuracy of 0.79 (average of the 5 different classes). In 2020 a virtual restoration of ancient coins from images with Generative Adversarial Networks (GANs) was first introduced [14]. This approach exploited a dataset of 100,000 lots of ancient coins, while the empirical evaluation showed promising results.

In this paper, the area under study is the ancient Thrace, a large part of the Balkan peninsula that stretches from the shores of the Aegean to the banks of Danube, an area where different cultural groups (Greeks and different Thracian tribal groups) coexisted and culturally interacted [15]. From a numismatic point of view this is an area of unique importance [16] not only for the great circulation of coins [17] but also because of the presence of different variants of well-established coin types by local rulers and kings [9, 18]. Nevertheless, it should also be highlighted that the number of images presenting coins in good and bad quality is relatively low. In this context the proposed DL approaches (TL through popular CNN architecture) achieved a top-1 validation accuracy of 98.32% and top-5 validation accuracy of 99.99%, which can be considered as one of the most efficient in the literature. In addition to that we have introduced a novel web-based system not only for academic research or archaeological field work, but also and an easy-to-use system for the general public. Most importantly, this is a system free and accessible to everyone. An additional asset (on demand) which visualizes the learning features of the model and highlights them over the coin's images will hopefully help the field experts to identify coins even when these are in bad condition. The results show that coins with almost nonvisible characteristics (bad condition) are classified correctly, and the feature maps highlighted important local features over the coin's images.

3 TheAnCoins-12 Dataset

Within this research framework and towards the development of an ancient coins identification system, we created the AnCoins-12 dataset, consisted by coins circulating in the area of ancient Thrace. We have used a small corpus (dataset) of coins types, each characterized by a unique motif (in the obverse and in the reverse). The dataset represents a wide range of coins used in this area from the Archaic period (early 7th cent BC) to the Late Hellenistic period (1st BC). In addition to the well-known coinage of Greek city states like Thasos [19, 20], Abdera [21], Maroneia [22, 23], Ainos [24], Istrus [22] (pp. 226–228) and Chersonese [25] we have used coinage from Hellenistic institutions like the kingdom of Macedonia [26, 27], the kingdom of Thrace (Lysimachos) [28], Roman republican period local coins (Aesillas) [29] and coins issued pre and post mortem by Alexander and his successors. The dataset was comprised by selecting coins with wide distribution in the area and the interior of the Balkans. We tried to use coins of the same denomination (drachms or tetradrachms) but of a variety of materials and state of preservation. We have taken into account individual motifs (in obverse and reverse) that were copied and imitated by different issuing authorities such as standardized design of Hercules with the lion skin or Hellenistic coinage imitating designs of Alexander [30] or the Ianus head of Istrus who were struck was by numerous mints across the peninsula.

At this initial stage of research in order to access ancient coins for the development of image-dataset, we simply preferred to adopt an algorithm for retrieving images from the

Fig. 1. Preprocessed image samples of AnCoins-12 dataset.

internet via web-crawling methodologies by exploiting the Yandex.com search engine and by using a set of numismatically defined keyword combinations (for example: the name of the denomination (eg tetradrachm) + location/production site (eg Chersonese) + issuing authority + motif in the coin (eg Lion) etc.) as search terms. The collected images with this method were screened by a specialist in the archaeology of the area, who removed photos corresponding to wrong classes or disputed ones. In addition to that we preprocessed manually the images in order to keep only the one side of the coins (obverse or reverse), which remained almost the same over the time. Figure 1 depicts some image samples of the AnCoins-12 dataset. It is clear that what is collected represents a variety of coins (in each class) with different morphology and quality, focusing in better generalization outcomes. This highlights not only the difficulty of the introduced dataset (small number of images per class with high differentiation between images), but also real-life issues - difficulties in field archaeology excavations/research.

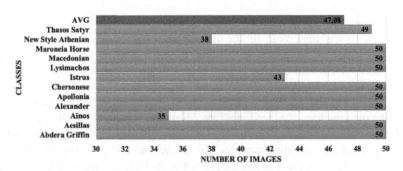

Fig. 2. Images distribution of AnCoins-12 dataset

The resulting AnCoins-12 dataset includes 565 images of 12 different classes (categories), with average about 47 images per class. The bar graph of Fig. 2 depicts the distribution of the images per class. At this point it should be highlighted that for some classes, as for example the coins from "Ainos", it was very difficult to find a great number unique images. For this reason, we have kept the upper limit for the other classes to 50 images, to develop more balanced dataset.

4 Experiments

In this section we present the deep learning-based classification approaches on the AnCoins-12 dataset. In particular, we exploited TL approaches, which in DL theory are popular techniques, in which a model developed and trained for a specific task is reused for another similar task under some parametrization (fine tuning) and a short re-training. This methodology is inspired by the ability of human to transfer knowledge across various tasks. Simply put, the previously acquired knowledge from learning how to solve a problem, is further exploited in solving similar new problems.

In fine tuning process, a pre-trained model is used without its top layers, which are replaced by new and more appropriate layers to the new task, and the model is re-trained with the new dataset. In Fig. 3 we present the underlying architecture, which has produced very good results in the domain of food recognition [31] and many other domains. The red colored block represents the input layer of the model (batch size, image-width, image-height, image-channels). Due to the poor quality of the collected images we have used $120 \times 120 \times 3$ tensor for each image for the training and evaluation of the models. The blue colored block depicts the pre-trained stack of layers of the considered popular architectures (pre-trained with ImagenNet), while the green colored block depicts the top layers which are selected according to the new task.

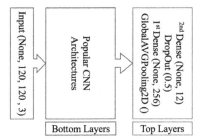

Fig. 3. Transfer learning based, models' architecture (Color figure online)

In this context, our experimental methodology relies on fine tuning approach exploiting widely used DL models, which were pre-trained with the ImageNet dataset [13], including the VGG16 [32], DenseNet121 [33], MobileNetV2 [34], ResNet50 [35], XceptionV3 [36], InceptionResNetV2 [37], as well as the EfficientNetB3 [38].

All the models were trained with 200 epochs and almost all started converging around the 50–60 first epochs. The top-1 accuracy of the training of each model was too high (intense blue columns in Fig. 4). In addition to that, the top-5 accuracy of almost all models was about 0.9999 (intense orange columns in Fig. 4). On the other hand, top-1 validation accuracies have shown several variations between the models (light blue columns in Fig. 4) by showing that the simpler the model, the better the outcomes. As

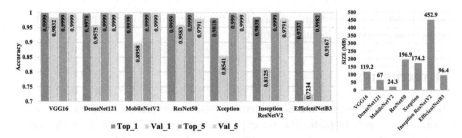

Fig. 4. The efficacy and the size of each model. (Color figure online)

it was expected top-5 validation accuracies (light orange columns in Fig. 4) were much better than the top-1 validation accuracies.

The size of an adopted model is very important when the target is the deployment of cross-platform systems, mainly focusing in mobile devices. For this reason, as can be seen in the green bar chart in Fig. 4, MobileNetV2 is the model with the smallest exported model size (in MB). The combination of the accuracy and the model size features, highlights that MobileNetV2 is the most appropriate solution to our approach. On the other hand, VGG16 can be considered as the most accurate model, which also had the smoothest training progresses, Fig. 5.

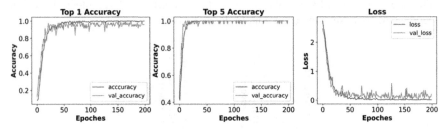

Fig. 5. VGG16 based approach, the most efficient one.

5   AnCoins Web-Based System

In this section we describe the responsive web-based system[1], that exploits the prediction capabilities of the MobileNetV2 model. The system is developed based on HTML5 technologies and can be considered as cross-platform system that can work in almost all OSs. The background algorithms of the prediction mechanism were based on TensorflowJS, thus the entire model is uploaded and managed in the browser.

The front-end of the system is responsive and self-adjustable based on the device's specifications, such as OS, screen size etc. For example, the "Choose File" button in desktops and laptops browsers, allows the user to upload a simple image through the file manager of the OS, in contrast to mobile devices where the system is automatically

---

[1] A demo and all additional resources of the system can be found at: https://tinyurl.com/yyjtajn3.

connected with the camera or the photo collection software of the device. The main screen of the front-end is split in 4 sections, as can be seen in the right-most image in Fig. 6. The section "A" provides some default samples images to test the systems. The section "B" provides the user with a feature for uploading or capturing a new image. The section "C" presents general status information about the processes of the model, while the section "D" shows the predictions of the model for an image, which are sorted from high to low accuracy. It should also be highlighted that the system requires internet access at least until the model is loaded in the browser.

Fig. 6. The web-based system, step by step usage example.

6   Discussion: Features Identification in Coins

For the implementation of the current project, we have chosen 8 sample images from 4 different classes of well distributed coins, 2 images per class. The 4 images present Coins in Good Condition (CGC) and other 4 Coins in Bad Condition (CBC). Each one of the classes presents its own unique motif (the heraldic griffin of Abdera, the prancing horse of Maroneia the head of Hercules in lion skin in the coins of Alexander, the heraldic lion of Chersonese and the double male head [Ianus] of Istrus). The aim of this research is to identify the learning features/capabilities of an adopted model and how can it act in coins of one class with multiple dissimilarities (due to variety of reasons, such as worn, bad state of preservation, local variant or imitation etc.), which is common issue in ancient coins. For this reason, we have adopted the SmoothGrad [39] and FasterScoreCAM (improved version of ScoreCAM [40]) algorithms, which exploit the class activation maps of the model in order to present visually learned features on images. These approaches are delivered as additional asset of the AnCoins web-based system on-demand, because they are computationally expensive.

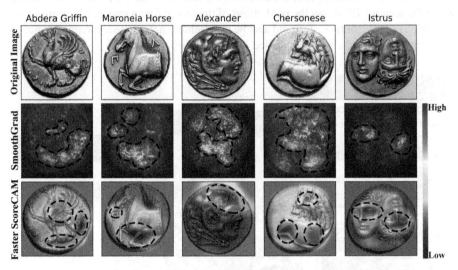

Fig. 7. Analyzing sample coins in good condition

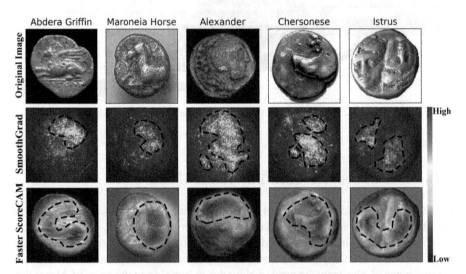

Fig. 8. Analyzing sample coins in bad condition

The Fig. 7 and Fig. 8 presents the results obtained by the visual explanation of the learned features of a CNN analysis, based on the aforementioned methods, for CGC and CBC, respectively. The highlighted areas with dashed lines in the heat-maps over the original images, present the important areas of the input data (image) that determined the class (category) of each individual image, based on the capabilities of the adopted DL model. The color gradients of the heat-maps range from intense blue to intense red and highlight the semantic importance of the features of the image (coin) from very-low to very-high, respectively.

The results indicate that despite semantic differences or variants of the motif, spatial arrangements and state of preservation (coins of poor condition) of the visual elements of the coin type the algorithm can contextualize the coins and recognize accurately the issuing authority. An accurate identification is carried out on the basis of pattern signatures defined by basic attributes, such as, the recognition of a central motif (eg the body and head of the heraldic lion of Chersonese or the double headed god in the coins of Istrus), as well as small variables (areas of interest) like for instance the wing and main body of the griffin in the case of Abdera or the body of the horse in the case of Maroneia.

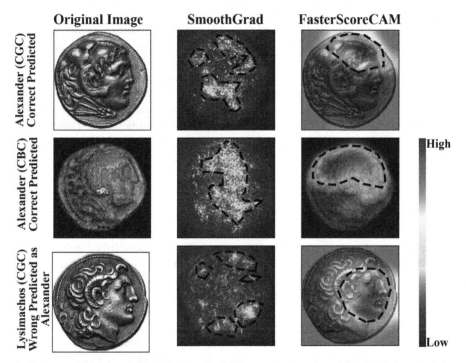

Fig. 9. Example of the relationship between different coins based on their visual characteristics

Even when no subtle elements are preserved (especially in the CBC), accurate recognition of coin type is feasible and can help towards accurate taxonomy and coins classification. If these pattern variables are accurately monitored and recognized, we can hypothesize that a highly regular patterned relationship exists between different-variants of coin types. The importance of accurate recognition of different classes of coins is especially seen when local imitations of well distributed coins are examined such as the coins of Alexander (with Hercules in lion skin on the obverse), Fig. 9. For example, when the system reads coin motifs that bear stylistic resemblances like the Hellenistic coins of Lysimachos which depict the head of Alexander with the horns of Ammon Zeus and the tetradrachms of Alexander III depicting the head of Hercules (or more accurately the head of Alexander being portrayed as the hero wearing the lion's skin as a helmet), the model gives false-positive results (Lysimachos coin predicted as Alexander coin with about 0.85 accuracy). Seeing this strictly from a computer science perspective can be considered as a problem (wrong classification), but in archaeology these common features identification in different classes of material culture (in this case coins), may lead to various research hypotheses about motif representation and symbolism.

An automatic identification of coin motifs (especially when combined with a easy to use web tool) is of great interest in the discipline of archaeology because it can help archaeologists (and especially field archaeologists) evaluate material in situ but also access inferences about connections between different levels of quality as is characteristically reflected in the case of local variants. In the field of archaeological investigation information retrieval by analyzing even the more subtle pattern differences can be a valuable tool in the assessment of the evidence. Furthermore, in recognizing and demonstrating the accuracy of a motif, and expressing this as a step of a functional coin classification method, we can (archaeologically) state different hypotheses relating the different datasets to processes at work in the ancient monetary system, such as: how accurate were the local imitations of well distributed coins? How consistent over time was the pattern motif of the coin? How rich in visual information were coins of small denominations or coins that were minted by local authorities? How close in style (engraving technique or die) were coins with stylistic resemblances? What this can tell us about the effort on the part of the die engraver to develop a design along specific artistic and symbolic lines?

7 Conclusions and Future Directions

Despite the small dataset available, there were several goals accomplished in this project. The first was to deploy a DL model with a high accuracy level. The proposed method can provide numismatologists and archaeologists with a recognition tool that captures a variety of patterns and automates recognition processes. While other similar methods are based on large number of images, the method we introduce can demonstrate significant results even trained with small datasets, which directly translates to better results for the end-users. The second goal was to provide enhanced experience in application development from initial recognition to sharing the result. This was accomplished with the use of the web-tool, a process that will continue in the future as the next phase of the project will be implemented. With the web-based system, archaeologists in the field but also museum visitors can quickly scan images and find additional information on coin type, which is much more convenient than manually looking up specialized books. The web-based system can be specifically designed to attract nonspecialized audience like students to take pictures of coins and instantly access information and later interactive learning experiences. In this case, the aim of incorporating image recognition in archaeological research is not only to provide general information regarding coins classification but also to help intuitively engage the audience with modern technology and classes of material culture [9].

Primarily the strengths of artificial intelligence is its ability to process huge amount of data and retrieve it in an efficient, precise and quickly generated way. Towards this direction the automatic identification of a motif from a single query coin photograph of its obverse and reverse can provide with reliable automated methods for quickly reconstructing archaeological materials classes and benefit from the application of web-based tools that will further audience understanding of the past.

In this paper, we tried to describe an outline for the recognition of ancient coins from the area of ancient Thrace based on image features. The achieved high accuracy of recognition rates indicates the feasibility of the approach, while the adaptation of the MobileNetV2 architecture for the deployment showed outstanding performance. In these directions it is highlighted that patterns in ancient coins cannot be considered as too complicated for the current popular architectures. Even the primary models of the DL area perform very well, in our case the VGG16 proved to be the most efficient. Based on the promising results we plan to extend the testing of the methods on larger collection of images consisted from diverse coin types, state of preservation and variety of coin condition (bad-medium-high quality of coins). Furthermore, we will extend our work towards the diffusion of data through web-based applications. In addition, we want to test the web platform created for mobile devices by following their impact and results in museum surveys. Producing an app which uses image recognition to identify displayed coins can be furthered enhanced by additional levels information concerning date, description or distribution.

Nevertheless, it should be considered that pattern recognition and classification using DL methods is a quite recent research topic in the field of numismatics. Early attempts have been mainly focused on monitoring obvious features rather than detecting unknown features that can mark different variants of known types.

In the case of AnCoins we believe that the quality of pattern extraction as well as the optimization of a given sample by the web tool can promise the possibility to reliably discriminate subtle archaeological features and filter out features that enhance a more cognitive approach to archaeology.

Acknowledgment. The present work was partially supported by the project "Computational Science and Technologies: Data, Content and Interaction/Technologies for Content Analysis in Culture", MIS code 5002437, co-financed by Greece and European Union in the framework of the Operational Programme "Competitiveness, Entrepreneurship and Innovation" 2014–2020.

We gratefully acknowledge the support of NVIDIA Corporation with the donation of the Titan Xp GPU used for the experiments of this research. We would also like to show our gratitude to the administrators of https://wildwinds.com/ who provided us with the permission to use the sample images in this paper.

References

1. Voulodimos, A., Doulamis, N., Doulamis, A., Protopapadakis, E.: Recent developments in deep learning for engineering applications. Comput. Intell. Neurosci. **2018**, 13 (2018)

2. Fiorucci, M., Khoroshiltseva, M., Pontil, M., Traviglia, A., Del Bue, A., James, S.: Machine learning for cultural heritage: a survey. Pattern Recogn. Lett. **133**, 102–108 (2020)
3. Zaharieva, M., Kampel, M., Zambanini, S.: Image based recognition of ancient coins. In: Kropatsch, W.G., Kampel, M., Hanbury, A. (eds.) CAIP 2007. LNCS, vol. 4673, pp. 547–554 (2007). Springer, Heidelberg. https://doi.org/10.1007/978-3-540-74272-2_68
4. Kampel, M., Zaharieva, M.: Recognizing ancient coins based on local features. In: Bebis, G., et al. (eds.) ISVC 2008. LNCS, vol. 5358, pp. 11–22. Springer, Heidelberg (2008). https://doi.org/10.1007/978-3-540-89639-5_2
5. Arandjelovic, O.: Automatic attribution of ancient Roman imperial coins. In: CVPR (2010)
6. Arandjelović, O.: Reading ancient coins: automatically identifying denarii using obverse legend seeded retrieval. In: Fitzgibbon, A., Lazebnik, S., Perona, P., Sato, Y., Schmid, C. (eds.) ECCV 2012. LNCS, vol. 7575, pp. 317–330. Springer, Heidelberg (2012). https://doi.org/10.1007/978-3-642-33765-9_23
7. Kim, J., Pavlovic, V.: Discovering characteristic landmarks on ancient coins using convolutional networks. In: 23rd International Conference on Pattern Recognition (ICPR), Cancun (2016)
8. Figueira, T.T.: The Power of Money: Coinage and Politics in the Athenian Empire. University of Pennsylvania Press, Philadelphia (1998)
9. Paunov, E.: Introduction to the Numismatics of Thrace, ca. 530 BCE–46 CE. In: Valeva, J., Nankov, E., Graninger, D. (eds.) A Companion to Ancient Thrace, pp. 267–291. Wiley, Chichester (2015)
10. Chai, Y., Lempitsky, V., Zisserman, A.: Symbiotic segmentation and part localization for fine-grained categorization. In: IEEE International Conference on Computer Vision, Sydney, NSW, pp. 321–328 (2013). https://doi.org/10.1109/ICCV.2013.47
11. Schlag, I., Arandjelovic, O.: Ancient Roman coin recognition in the wild using deep learning based recognition of artistically depicted face profiles. In: IEEE International Conference on Computer Vision Workshops (ICCVW), Venice, pp. 2898–2906 (2017). https://doi.org/10.1109/ICCVW.2017.342
12. Cooper, J., Arandjelović, O.: Understanding ancient coin images. In: Oneto, L., Navarin, N., Sperduti, A., Anguita, D. (eds.) INNSBDDL 2019. PINNS, vol. 1, pp. 330–340. Springer, Cham (2020). https://doi.org/10.1007/978-3-030-16841-4_34
13. Krizhevsky, A., Sutskever, I., Hinton, G.: ImageNet classification with deep convolutional neural networks. In: Proceedings of the 25th International Conference on Neural Information Processing Systems, Red Hook, NY, USA (2012)
14. Zachariou, M., Dimitriou, N., Arandjelovic, O.: Visual reconstruction of ancient coins using cycle-consistent generative adversarial networks. Science **2**(3), 55 (2020)
15. Theodossiev, N.: Ancient Thrace During the First Millennium BC. In: Tsetskhladze, G. (ed.) The Black Sea, Greece, Anatolia and Europe in the First Millennium BC (Colloquia Antiqua 1), pp. 1–60. Peeters, Leuven (2011)
16. Schönert-Geiss, E.: Bibliographie zur antiken Numismatik Thrakiens und Moesiens. Akademie Verlag, Griechisches Münzwerk), Berlin (1999)
17. Youroukova, Y.: Coins of the Ancient Thracians, (BAR Supplementary Series 4). British Archaeological Reports, Oxford (1976)
18. Peter, U.: Die Münzen der thrakischen Dynasten (5.–3. Jahrhundert v. Chr.): Hintergründe ihrer Prägung (Griechisches Münzwerk). Akademie Verlag, Berlin (1997)
19. de Callataÿ, F.: Les tétradrachmes hellénistiques au nom des thasiens et la circulation monétaire en thrace aux IIe et Ierr s. av. J.-C., Revue elge de numismatique et de sigillographie, vol. 154, pp. 31–54 (2008)
20. Picard, O.: Le monnayage de thasos. Νομισματικά Χρονικά **9**, 15–24 (1990)
21. Chryssantaki-Nagle, K.: L'histoire monétaire d'abdère en thrace (VIe s. av. J.-C.–IIe s. ap. J.-C.) (Meletemata 51). KERA, Athens (2007)

22. Psoma, S., Karadima, C., Terzopoulou, D.: The Coins from Maroneia and the Classical City at Molyvoti. A Contribution to the History of Aegean Thrace (Meletemata 62). KERA, Athens (2008)
23. Schonert-Geiss, E.: Die Munzpragung von Maroneia (Grieschisches Munzwerk, Schriften zur Geschichte und Kultur der Antike 26). Akademie Verlag, Berlin (1987)
24. May, J.: Ainos: Its History and Coinage, 474–341 B.C. Oxford University, Oxford (1950)
25. Tzvetkova, J.: Die Münzprägung der Thrakischen Chersones – Probleme der Chronologie und Periodisierung. In: Lazarenko, I. (ed.) Numismatic and Sphragistic Contributions to the History of the Western Black Sea Coast (International Conference Varna, 12–15 September 2001) (Acta Musei Varnaensis 2), Varna, pp. 17–31. Zograf, Varna (2004)
26. Gaebler, H.: Die antiken Münzen von Makedonia und Paeonia (Die antiken Münzen Nord-Griechenlands, Band III.2). Walter de Gruyter, Berlin (1935)
27. Price, M.J.: Coinage in the Name of Alexander the Great and Philip Arrhidaeus. A British Museum Catalogue, vol. I. The British Museum & Swiss Numismatic Society, London and Zürich (1991)
28. de Callataÿ, F.: L'histoire de guerres mithridatiques vue par les monnaies (Numismatica Lovaniensia 18). Département d'archéologie et d'histoire de l'art, Louvain-la-Neuve (1997)
29. Bauslaugh, R.A.: Silver Coinage with the Types of Aesillas the Questor. American Numismatic Society, New York (2000)
30. Gerassimov, T.: The Alexander Tetradrachms of Kabyle in Thrace. In: Ingolt, H. (ed.) The Centennial Publication of the American Numismatic Society, New York, pp. 273–277 (1958)
31. Kiourt, C., Pavlidis, G., Markantonatou, S.: Deep learning approaches in food recognition. In: Tsihrintzis, G., Jain, L. (eds.) Machine Learning Paradigms. LAIS, vol. 18, pp. 83–108. Springer, Cham (2020). https://doi.org/10.1007/978-3-030-49724-8_4
32. Simonyan, K., Zisserman, A.: Very deep convolutional networks for large-scale image recognition. In: 3rd International Conference on Learning Representations, San Diego, CA, USA (2015)
33. Huang, G., Liu, Z., Van Der Maaten, L., Weinberger, K.: Densely connected convolutional networks. In: 2017 IEEE Conference on Computer Vision and Pattern Recognition (CVPR) (2017)
34. Sandler, M., Howard, A., Zhu, M., Zhmoginov, A., Chen, L.: MobileNetV2: inverted residuals and linear bottlenecks. In: 2018 IEEE/CVF Conference on Computer Vision and Pattern Recognition (2018)
35. He, K., Zhang, X., Ren, S., Sun, J.: Deep residual learning for image recognition. In: 2016 IEEE Conference on Computer Vision and Pattern Recognition (CVPR) (2016)
36. Chollet, F.: Xception: deep learning with depthwise separable convolutions. In: Proceedings of the IEEE Conference on Computer Vision and Pattern Recognition (2017)
37. Szegedy, C., Ioffe, S., Vanhoucke, V., Alemi, A.: Inception-V4, inception-ResNet and the impact of residual connections on learning. In: Thirty-First AAAI Conference on Artificial Intelligence, San Francisco, California, USA (2017)
38. Tan, M., Le, V.Q.: EfficientNet: rethinking model scaling for convolutional neural networks. In: 36th International Conference on Machine Learning, Long Beach, California, USA (2019)
39. Smilkov, D., Thorat, N., Kim, B., Viégas, F., Wattenberg, M.: SmoothGrad: removing noise by adding noise. In: ICML Workshop on Visualization for Deep Learning (2017)
40. Wang, H., et al.: Score-CAM: score-weighted visual explanations for convolutional neural networks. In: Proceedings of the IEEE/CVF Conference on Computer Vision and Pattern Recognition (CVPR) Workshop (2020)

Subjective Assessments of Legibility in Ancient Manuscript Images - The SALAMI Dataset

Simon Brenner[(✉)] and Robert Sablatnig

Institute of Visual Computing and Human-Centered Technology,
TU Wien, 1040 Vienna, Austria
{sbrenner,sab}@cvl.tuwien.ac.at
https://cvl.tuwien.ac.at

Abstract. The research field concerned with the digital restoration of degraded written heritage lacks a quantitative metric for evaluating its results, which prevents the comparison of relevant methods on large datasets. Thus, we introduce a novel dataset of Subjective Assessments of Legibility in Ancient Manuscript Images (SALAMI) to serve as a ground truth for the development of quantitative evaluation metrics in the field of digital text restoration. This dataset consists of 250 images of 50 manuscript regions with corresponding spatial maps of mean legibility and uncertainty, which are based on a study conducted with 20 experts of philology and paleography. As this study is the first of its kind, the validity and reliability of its design and the results obtained are motivated statistically: we report a high intra- and inter-rater agreement and show that the bulk of variation in the scores is introduced by the image regions observed and not by controlled or uncontrolled properties of participants and test environments, thus concluding that the legibility scores measured are valid attributes of the underlying images.

Keywords: Dataset · Image Quality Assessment · Historic manuscripts · Human legibility

1 Introduction

Written heritage is a valuable resource for historians and linguists. However, the physical medium preserved may be in a condition that prohibits the direct accessing of the text. Addressing this problem, a research field dedicated to the digital restoration of such degraded sources based on specialized imaging techniques, such as multi- and hyperspectral imaging as well as x-ray fluorescence mapping, has ensued [1,6,8,9,11,21,25,28]. In general, corresponding approaches aim at producing output images in which a text of interest is maximally legible for a human observer.

Funded by the Austrian Science Fund (FWF): P29892.

A. Del Bimbo et al. (Eds.): ICPR 2020 Workshops, LNCS 12667, pp. 68–82, 2021.
https://doi.org/10.1007/978-3-030-68787-8_5

We note that an inherent problem of this research field is the absence of a suitable quantitative metric for this property of human legibility. Consequently, the evaluation of proposed approaches is commonly based on expert ratings, the demonstration on selected examples or case studies [6,11,21,25,28]. This practice is unfavorable for the research field: it does not allow for an automated evaluation on large public datasets, such that an objective comparison of different approaches is impeded.

Attempts to quantitatively assess the success of legibility enhancements have been made before: Arsene et al. quantify the success of dimensionality reduction methods via cluster separability metrics, however acknowledging that the resulting scores do not correlate well with human assessments [1]. Shaus et al. introduce the metric of "potential contrast" between user-defined foreground and background areas [29]. Giacometti et al. created a multispectral image dataset of manuscript patches before and after artificial degradation [8], which allows the quantitative assessment of digital restoration approaches by comparison with the non-degraded originals. The performance of Handwritten Character Recognition (HCR) systems on the enhanced images is used as a quantitative metric as well [13,18]; this approach addresses the property of readability more directly than the approaches mentioned before and is a reasonable choice when the purpose of text restoration lies in the subsequent processing with a HCR system, rather than in the preparation for a human observer. For restoration approaches producing binary images, evaluation is more straight-forward: for this purpose, multispectral image datasets with ground truth annotations have been published [10,12]. While the above-named approaches to quantitative evaluation are promising for their respective use cases, their correlation to legibility by human observers is yet to be shown.

For the development of general objective Image Quality Assessment (IQA) methods, the use of public databases containing subjectively rated images is a well-established practice [22,32]. A variety of such datasets have been published; they primarily aim at measuring the perceptual impacts of technical parameters such as image compression artefacts, transmission errors, or sensor quality [19, 23,24,30,32]. However, no such dataset exists for the assessment of text legibility in images.

This paper introduces a new dataset of manuscript images subjectively rated for legibility, designed for the development and validation of objective legibility assessment methods. The main contributions of this work are:

1. a methodology to conduct studies of subjective legibility assessment in manuscript images.
2. publication of a novel dataset that serves as a reference for the development of objective legibility assessment methods.

The remainder of the paper is structured as follows: Sect. 2 describes the methodology of the subjective IQA study carried out, while Sect. 3 details its technical and practical implementation. In Sect. 4 we analyze the results obtained, motivating the validity of our study design and the properties of the published dataset. Section 5 describes the published dataset in detail, and Sect. 6 concludes the paper with final observations and potentials for improvement.

2   Study Design

In the following, the design of the subjective IQA study carried out to establish the SALAMI dataset is described and motivated. The documents ITU-T P.910 [15] and ITU-R BT.500-13 [16] by the International Telecommunication Union provide guidelines for the implementation of subjective IQA studies that are commonly followed in the creation of respective datasets [4,7,19,27,32]. In the design of this study, we implement these guidelines wherever applicable.

2.1   Test Images

Our test image set is based on 50 manuscript regions of 60 × 60 mm, each of which is represented by 5 images. The regions are sampled from 48 different manuscripts and 8 language families. Slavonic (19), Latin (13) and Greek (12) texts make up the majority of the samples; additionally, two Ottoman texts and one each in Armenian, Georgian, German and Gothic are contained in the dataset. Depending on line height and layout, the regions contain 1–17 lines of text. In the following, the selection of manuscript regions and the creation of the final image set is described in detail, and choices made in the process are motivated.

The manuscript regions represented in the SALAMI dataset are drawn from a set of approximately 4600 pages of 67 historical manuscripts, of which the Computer Vision Lab (TU Wien) has acquired multispectral images in the course of consecutive research projects between 2007 and 2019[1]. The multispectral images were acquired using different imaging devices and protocols [5,12,14], with 6–12 wavebands per image. Rather than presenting whole manuscript pages to the participants, we reduce the image contents to square-shaped regions of 60mm side-length. This enables the presentation of a fixed region in sufficient magnification, avoiding the need for zooming and panning. The assessment task is thus simplified and accelerated, and the risk of overlooking small pieces of text is minimized. To limit the scope of this study, manuscript regions containing multiple layers of text (such as palimpsests or interlinear glosses) are excluded and must be considered in future work. In order to select 50 suitable regions from the entirety of available pages, a semi-automatic scheme of random selection and human redaction was employed. The scheme ensures that 1) the number of different manuscripts from which the samples are drawn is maximized, 2) the selected regions contain only a single layer of text and 3) the role of a human

---

[1] Projects financed by the Austrian Science Fund (FWF) with grant numbers P19608-G12 (2007–2010), P23133 (2011–2014) and P29892 (2017–2019), as well as a project financed by the Austrian Federal Ministry of Science, Research and Economy (2014–2016).

operator is reduced to deciding if a randomly selected region is suitable for the study (i.e., it contains exactly one layer of text) or not, thus minimizing bias.

The source multispectral images are cropped to the selected square regions and re-sampled to a standard resolution of 12 px/mm (or 304.8 ppi), resulting in an image size of 720×720 pixels. This standardization is done to eliminate image size and resolution as a source of variance. For each region, five processed variants are generated to serve as the actual test images. For the sake of simplicity and repeatability, those variants are produced by a principal component analysis on the multispectral layers[2]. Figure 1 shows an example. The inclusion of multiple versions of the same manuscript region enables a versatile use of the SALAMI dataset: additionally to absolute rating applications, it can be used for the development of systems in which relative comparisons between multiple images of the same content are paramount. With 5 variants for each of the 50 manuscript regions the SALAMI dataset contains 250 test images. According to preliminary tests, this number of images can be assessed in approximately one hour by a single participant.

(a)   (b)

Fig. 1. Test image generation: (a) multispectral source layers of a given manuscript region. (b) the principal components corresponding to the 5 largest eigenvalues constitute the published test images.

2.2 Test Method

Test methods most commonly used for performing IQA studies are based on degradation ratings, pair comparisons, or absolute ratings [15,16,20,22,30]. Degradation rating approaches assume the existence of an ideal reference image; this is advantageous for experiments, in which degradations of an optimal original are evaluated (such as with JPEG compression [30]). In our case, such an optimal reference does not exist, such that this class of methods is not applicable. Pair Comparisons between variants of the same content are shown to provide higher discriminatory power and lower variance than Absolute Ratings, especially when the perceptual differences between those variants are small [15,20,24]. However, the downsides of this approach are the high number of necessary comparisons $((n^2 - n)/2$ for n variants) and the lack of a common absolute scale among different contents. The latter problem is solvable when performing cross-content comparisons [22], however, it is not clear if such direct comparisons between different manuscript regions (which vary in preservational condition, size and

---

[2] PCA is frequently used as a standard procedure for dimensionality reduction and source separation in multispectral manuscript images [1,8,21].

Table 1. Left: available rating options. Right: options for participant self-evaluation.

	description	value
	80-100% readable	5
	60-80% readable	4
legibility score	40-60% readable	3
	20-40% readable	2
	0-20% readable	1
	[non-selected areas]	0

	description	value
	expert (primary research field)	3
language expertise	advanced (read and understand)	2
	basics (knows the script)	1
	unacquainted	0
	multiple times a week	3
SMI exposure	multiple times a month	2
	occasionally	1
	never	0
	professor	4
academic level	post-doc	3
	pre-doc	2
	student	1
	none	0

amount of text and alphabets) are meaningful. For this study, we opt for Absolute Ratings as a base design. Additionally to the above named reasons, this approach readily allows the following extension for a more detailed specification of legibility: instead of asking the participants to assign a single score to the whole test image, they are required to mark all visible text with rectangular bounding boxes, which are then rated individually (see Fig. 2). With this approach we obtain a spatial distribution of legibility instead of a single score per image.

2.3   Rating Scale

Following ITU recommendations [16], a five point rating scale is used. As we only want to assess text legibility and not any other quality of the image, we refrain from using the standard category labels given by ITU ('Excellent', 'Good', 'Fair',...); they could lead to misinterpretations of the task. Instead, we explicitly break down the property of legibility to the percentage of text within a given area that a participant deems clear enough to read. Dividing the available range into 5 equal intervals leads to the labels and corresponding numerical scores shown at the top of Table 1. With the phrasing of legibility in terms of percentages we obtain scores on a true interval scale, which can not be assumed for the usual qualitative category descriptions [33].

2.4   Test Environment

Traditionally, subjective IQA experiments are carried out under controlled laboratory conditions [15,16]. However, Ribeiro et al. [27] show that subjective ratings on the LIVE [30] dataset obtained in laboratory conditions can be accurately reproduced in crowd sourcing experiments conducted with Amazon Mechanical Turk. Ghadiyaram and Bovik [7] create an IQA dataset of 1162 mobile camera images rated by over 8100 participants online and report excellent internal consistency. Considering these results and our special requirements for the participants (see Sect. 2.6) that lead to a relative shortage of suitable volunteers, we decided to loosen the laboratory constraints and allow both participation in controlled conditions and on-line participation. A statistical comparison between the results of laboratory and online participation is given in Sect. 4. Participants were allowed to ask questions during the instruction and tutorial phases. Online participants could make use of this option via email or phone.

2.5   Order of Presentation

The test images are divided into five batches, where each batch contains one variant of each manuscript region. The assignment of the individual variants to the batches is done randomly, but equally for all participants. Within those batches, the images are randomly shuffled for each participant individually. In order to measure intra-rater variability, one randomly chosen image per batch is duplicated.

2.6   Participants

ITU-T P.910 recommends a minimum of 15 participants for any IQA study, while stating that four participants are the absolute minimum that allows a statistical assessment and there is no use in having more than 40 participants [15]. For the study we recruited 20 participants among researchers in the fields of philology and paleography, that have experience in reading original manuscripts. We looked for a mixture of university students, pre-doctoral researchers, post-doctoral researchers and professors.

3   Experiment Conduction

For an efficient and consistent conduction of the experiment we provide a web-based user interface for the assessment task, which is equally used by participants in laboratory conditions and online participants. During the primary test one image at a time is displayed on a medium gray background (50% brightness, following ITU-T P.910 recommendations [15]). The participant is required to mark text areas with approximate bounding boxes and individually rate them. For this rating, the estimated amount of legible text within the marked region is chosen from a list, according to Table 1. Figure 2 shows a screenshot of the primary test interface. Prior to performing the primary test, the participants must complete three preparatory stages:

1. **Self-assessment.** Participants are required to answer questions about their professional background: academic level, expertise in each of the language

families present in our dataset and frequency of exposure to scientific manuscript images (from here on referred to as *SMI exposure*) are queried. The available options for those questions are listed in the right part of Table 1.

2. **Instructions.** Participants are presented a sequence of pages, in which their task and the functionality of the user interface are explained, each supported by a demonstrative animation.

3. **Tutorial.** 5 images are assessed within the primary test interface without the answers being recorded. These images were manually selected to cover a variety of text coverage and readability levels.

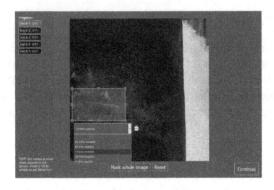

Fig. 2. A screenshot of the user interface for legibility assessment. The image is displayed on a neutral gray background. The participant is required to mark blocks of visible text with bounding boxes and give an estimation on how much of this text can be read.

All laboratory test sessions were conducted on the same workplace using a Samsung SyncMaster 2493HM LCD monitor with a screen diagonal of 24 inches at a resolution of 1920×1200 pixels, and a peak luminance of $400\,\text{cd/m}^2$. Viewing distance was not restricted, as this would not reflect a real situation of manuscript studying. All laboratory participants rated the full set of test images (including duplicates) in a single session. They were allowed to take breaks at any time; however, none of the participants used this option.

4 Evaluation

In total, 4718 assessments were obtained from 20 participants (excluding duplicates for intra-rater variability). Not every participant rated all of the 250 test images, as some of the online-participants terminated the test earlier. The median time required to assess a single image was 12.4 s (with quartiles $Q_1 = 7.5$ s and $Q_3 = 22.4$ s). As the participants were free to select arbitrary image areas for rating, those areas can not be directly related between participants. Instead, each assessment (a given image rated by a given participant) is interpreted as a score map which is zero in non-selected areas and a value in the range from 1 to 5 in selected areas, according to their rating. Intersection areas of overlapping bounding boxes receive their maximum score. The choice of the maximum (over a median or rounded mean) was motivated by the observation that laboratory participants deliberately placing one bounding box on top of another always intended to label small areas with higher legibility than their surroundings, and never the other way around. For the following analysis we partition the images in observational *units* of 2×2 mm (corresponding to 24×24 pixels). An elementary *observation* is defined as the rounded mean of scores assigned to the pixels of a given unit by a single participant; accordingly, an image assessed by one participant results in 900 observations. A first look at the relative frequencies of scores over all observations leads to the insight that the bulk of observations report background, i.e. units where no text is visible. Furthermore, the 2D histogram of unit-wise mean scores and standard deviations (Fig. 3a) shows a concentration of units with low scores and low standard deviations. This suggests that participants largely agree on the distinction between foreground and background. In order to prevent this mass of trivial background observations from biasing our analysis of intra- and inter-participant agreement, we exclude units that are labeled as background by more than half of the participants from all statistical considerations of this section.

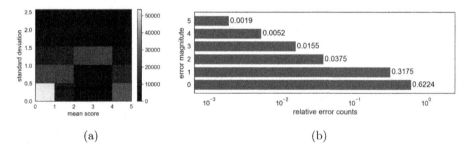

(a)   (b)

Fig. 3. (a) 2D histogram of mean scores and standard deviation of all units; (b) distribution of absolute intra-rater errors of all participants. The bar width shows the relative frequencies of error magnitudes on a logarithmic scale.

4.1 Participant Characteristics and Agreement

Participant screening was performed following the algorithm described in ITU-R BT.500 [16]. None of the participants were rejected.

Intra- and Inter-rater Variability. To assess intra-rater variability and thus the repeatability of the experiment, the absolute errors between units of duplicate presentations (see Sect. 2.5) are recorded. In accordance with the evaluation strategy given at the beginning of this section, only units with a score greater

Table 2. Left: intraclass correlation coefficients for all participants. Right: comparison
of ICCs of participants grouped by test environment and SMI exposure

variant	ICC	95% CI		ICC(2,1)	95% CI
ICC(2,1)	0.668	[0.64, 0.69]	lab participants	0.702	[0.65, 0.74]
ICC(3,1)	0.711	[0.71, 0.71]	online participants	0.664	[0.63, 0.69]
ICC(2,k)	0.976	[0.97, 0.98]	SMI exposure > 1x/week	0.690	[0.66, 0.72]
ICC(3,k)	0.980	[0.98, 0.98]	SMI exposure ≤ 1x/week	0.649	[0.57, 0.71]

than zero in at least one of the duplicate presentations are considered. The distributions of absolute errors is visualized in Fig. 3b on a logarithmic scale. The
mean absolute error across all duplicate observations is **0.469**.

The agreement of different raters (participants) on legibility scores was measured using Intraclass Correlation Coefficients (ICC). Following the definitions of
Shrout and Fleiss [31], we report the ICC variants ICC(2,1), ICC(3,1), ICC(2,k)
and ICC(3,k). While the variants ICC(2,x) view the set of participants as a
random sample from a larger population and thus express the reliability of the
proposed experimental design, variants ICC(3,x) express the reliability of the
specific dataset that is published, rated by the specific participants of this study.
On the other hand, ICC(x,1) estimate the reliability of a single participant, while
ICC(x,k) estimate the reliability of the average of k (in our case k = 20) participants [31]. The results are shown in Table 2 along with their 95% confidence
intervals.

Impact of the Test Environment and Expertise. As we work with a mixture of 7 laboratory sessions and 13 online sessions, it is worth assessing the
influence of the test environment on rater agreement; uncontrolled factors in the
online environment (such as monitor characteristics or insufficient understanding of the task) could lead to a greater divergence between participants. We thus
report ICC(2,1) for each of the groups separately; other ICC variants are omitted, as we want to address this question independent of a specific set/number of
participants. As shown at the right of Table 2, the ICC estimate is indeed higher
for the lab participants; however, note the large confidence intervals, where the
ICC estimate for online participants is within the 95% confidence interval of the
lab participants.

The first hypothesis related to participant expertise is that an increased professional exposure to scientific manuscript imagery improves inter-rater agreement. Again, ICC(2,1) are computed separately for participants who work with
such imagery multiple times a week and all participants with less exposure (we
refrained from a finer distinction due to a small number of participants in the
lower exposure categories). The bottom right of Table 2 shows the results. As
with the test environment, an effect on the ICC can be observed, but with largely
overlapping confidence intervals.

Secondly, we investigate if language expertise promotes agreement. For this, the observations on images containing Latin, Greek and Slavonic (which constitute the bulk of the test images) are treated separately. For each of those image sets, we partition the observations according to the expertise level of their raters in the respective language and compute ICC(2,1) scores. The resulting estimates along with their 95% confidence intervals are visualized in Fig. 4, where no general trend is observable.

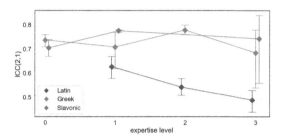

Fig. 4. Inter-rater agreement for different levels of expertise in Latin, Greek and Slavonic. Vertical bars show 95% confidence intervals. Missing values are due to an insufficient number of participants in the respective expertise category. (Color figure online)

4.2 Systematic Effects and Sources of Variation

After addressing the effects of participant and experimental parameters on inter-rater agreement, we now turn to the analysis of their systematic effects, i.e., their influences on mean scores. Furthermore, we compare these effects to uncontrolled variations between participants and, most importantly, to the variation introduced by the properties of the observed units. We concentrate on the following controlled parameters which gave reason to suspect linear relations (see Figs. 5a–5d): test environment, SMI exposure, academic level and *language fit*. The language fit of an observation is defined as the participant's skill level in the language associated with the observed unit. For the possible values of the above-mentioned parameters refer to Table 1. The sum of those influences plus an uncontrolled (random) source of variation constitutes the participant-wise variation of means shown in Fig. 5e.

In order to jointly model and investigate those participant-specific effects and the effects of observed units, we employ linear mixed effects models. In our initial model, legibility score is the dependent variable. Fixed effects are test environment, SMI experience, academic level and language fit. As further uncontrolled variations between participants are to be expected, we include the participant ID as a random intercept. A second random intercept is defined as the ID of the observed unit to model the dependence of an observation's score on the observed unit. The model was fitted in *R* [26] using the *lme4* package [2]. For each of the fixed effects a likelihood ratio test of the full model against a model without the respective effect was performed. We found that language fit

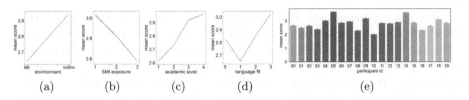

Fig. 5. Effects of participant parameters on mean scores: (a) test environment, (b) exposure to scientific manuscript images, (c) academic level, (d) language fit, i.e., for a given observation, the expertise of the participant in the language of the observed manuscript patch. In (e) the mean score for each participant is shown.

affects legibility scores by an increase of **0.05** per skill level, at a $p < 0.001$ confidence level. For the other fixed effects, p values are above 0.05. The random effects 'unit ID' and 'participant ID' contribute a variance of **2.133** and **0.136**, respectively; the residual variance is **0.803**.

4.3   Spatial Distribution of Variability

Finally, we investigate if the spatial distribution of units with a high variability in legibility scores follows a pattern. Qualitative inspection of standard deviation maps that are part of the published dataset (see Fig. 7c for an example) suggests that the highest variability is found near the boundaries of text areas and is thus caused by the variations in bounding box placement. To test this hypothesis, we define such critical border areas as the union of symmetric differences between pairs of similar bounding boxes from different participants; in this context, we consider bounding boxes as similar if their intersection-over-union ratio is greater than 0.9. The idea is illustrated in Fig. 6a. It was found that 7.56% of units fall under the definition of border areas given above. The distributions of standard deviations of border areas and other areas are shown in Fig. 6b. The mean standard deviation of border areas (**1.218**) is significantly higher than the mean standard deviation of other areas (**0.750**) at a $p < 0.001$ confidence level (according to a Mann-Whitney U test as the respective distributions are non-normal).

5   Dataset Description and Validity

As described in Sect. 2.1, the SALAMI dataset is based on 250 test images: 50 manuscript regions are represented by 5 processed variants each. Along with every test image, we publish a legibility map averaging the scores of all participants as well as a standard deviation map, showing the spatial distribution of uncertainty. See Fig. 7 for an example of such an image triplet. The test images and their legibility maps are ready to be used as a ground truth for developing computer vision methods for the localized estimation of legibility in manuscript images. Additionally to the estimation of absolute legibility from a single image,

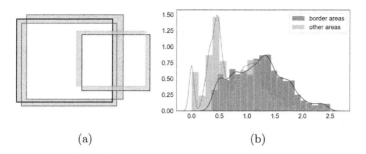

(a)   (b)

Fig. 6. (a) Definition of critical border areas. The differently colored rectangles are bounding boxes defined by different participants. The union of pairwise symmetric differences of similar bounding boxes (in terms of intersection over union) is shown in yellow. (b) Distribution of standard deviations for border areas versus other areas. (Color figure online)

the dataset also supports pairwise comparison or ranking applications due to the 5 variants per manuscript region contained in the dataset. The standard deviation maps can be used to exclude regions with a high uncertainty from training/evaluation, or for implementing weighted loss function depending on local uncertainty. Additionally to the pixel maps, the originally recorded data (.json encoded) are provided, along with well-documented python scripts that can be used to reproduce the legibility and score maps as well as the results described in Sect. 4. The dataset, code and documentation are available on **zenodo** [3]. As the SALAMI dataset is the first of its kind, we have to justify its validity as well as the appropriateness of the novel study design used to generate it. For this purpose we summarize the results of the statistical analyses obtained in Sect. 4.

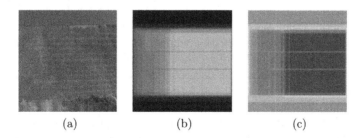

(a)   (b)   (c)

Fig. 7. An instance of the dataset: (a) test image; (b) mean score map; (c) standard deviation map.

Repeatability: Even with background areas excluded, 62.2% of absolute intra-rater errors are zero and the mean absolute error is 0.469.

Reliability: Table 2 summarizes the inter-rater agreement and thus reliability of the test method (ICC(2,x)) as well as the specific test results published in the form of our dataset (ICC(3,x)). According to the highly cited guidelines by Koo et al. [17], we can in either case expect moderate reliability from a single rater (ICC(x,1)) but excellent reliability from the average of 20 independent raters (ICC(x,k)). We have not found conclusive evidence for a negative impact of online participation or lack of participant skills/experience on the reliability.

Systematic Effects: The linear mixed effects model analysis does not show a statistically significant impact of SMI experience, test environment or academic level on the scores obtained. Only the property of language fit has a significant effect; however, we would not attribute any practical relevance to an increase of mean scores by 0.05 for each language skill level. Furthermore, it should be noted that the language skills of participants were acquired through self-assessment and not validated in any way.

Sources of Variation: The second and most important conclusion that can be drawn from the linear mixed effects model is that the identity of the observed unit contributes the majority of variance in the scores (2.133), while the identity of the participant only contributes a variance of 0.136. This is a good indicator that the measured legibility is an objective property of a given image area and not dominated by subjective preferences of the participants.

Spatial Distribution of Uncertainty: We show that uncertainty is varying spatially within test images and that especially border regions of text areas exhibit an increased variability in scores. This motivates the publishing of mean score maps along with standard deviation maps as an essential part of the dataset.

6   Conclusion

We have conducted a study with 20 experts of philology and paleography to create the first dataset of Subjective Assessments of Legibility in Ancient Manuscript Images, intended to serve as a ground truth for developing and validating computer vision-based methods for quantitative legibility assessment. Such methods, in turn, would elevate a whole research field centered around the digital restoration of written heritage; their development is the subject of future work. Additionally to creating the dataset itself, we describe a novel methodology to conduct similar studies in the future, demonstrating the validity of the results and the robustness against variations in test environment and participant properties. We have collected qualitative comments of the participating experts regarding their perspective on the study design, which revealed potentials for improvement in future work. Specifically, the following issues were pointed out:

- Line height has an impact on readability. This property of the assessed images is not considered in our analysis.
- The study only assesses the percentage of text that is readable; however, another relevant dimension would be the time/effort required to read a text.
- Manuscript experts tend to dynamically 'play' with the images (i.e., vary contrast, brightness, scale, etc.) in order to decipher texts. This was not permitted in our test design, potentially biasing the results.

References

1. Arsene, C.T.C., Church, S., Dickinson, M.: High performance software in multi-dimensional reduction methods for image processing with application to ancient manuscripts. Manuscr. Cult. **11**, 73–96 (2018)
2. Bates, D., Mächler, M., Bolker, B., Walker, S.: Fitting linear mixed-effects models using lme4. J. Stat. Softw. **67**(1), 1–48 (2015)
3. Brenner, S.: SALAMI 1.0 (2020). https://doi.org/10.5281/zenodo.4270352
4. De Simone, F., Naccari, M., Tagliasacchi, M., Dufaux, F., Tubaro, S., Ebrahimi, T.: Subjective assessment of H.264/AVC video sequences transmitted over a noisy channel. In: 2009 International Workshop on Quality of Multimedia Experience, QoMEx 2009, pp. 204–209 (2009)
5. Diem, M., Sablatnig, R.: Registration of ancient manuscript images using local descriptors. In: Digital Heritage, Proceedings of the 14th International Conference on Virtual Systems and Multimedia, pp. 188–192 (2008)
6. Easton, R.L., Christens-Barry, W.A., Knox, K.T.: Spectral image processing and analysis of the Archimedes Palimpsest. In: European Signal Processing Conference (Eusipco), pp. 1440–1444 (2011)
7. Ghadiyaram, D., Bovik, A.C.: Massive online crowdsourced study of subjective and objective picture quality. IEEE Trans. Image Process. **25**(1), 372–387 (2016)
8. Giacometti, A., et al.: The value of critical destruction: evaluating multispectral image processing methods for the analysis of primary historical texts. Digit. Scholarsh. Humanit. **32**(1), 101–122 (2017)
9. Glaser, L., Deckers, D.: The basics of fast-scanning XRF element mapping for iron-gall ink palimpsests. Manuscr. Cult. **7**, 104–112 (2013)
10. Hedjam, R., Nafchi, H.Z., Moghaddam, R.F., Kalacska, M., Cheriet, M.: ICDAR 2015 contest on multispectral text extraction (MS-TEx 2015). In: Proceedings of the International Conference on Document Analysis and Recognition, ICDAR 2015, pp. 1181–1185 (November 2015)
11. Hollaus, F., Diem, M., Fiel, S., Kleber, F., Sablatnig, R.: Investigation of ancient manuscripts based on multispectral imaging. In: DocEng 2015 - Proceedings of the 2015 ACM Symposium on Document Engineering, no. 1, pp. 93–96 (2015)
12. Hollaus, F., Brenner, S., Sablatnig, R.: CNN based binarization of multispectral document images. In: Proceedings of the International Conference on Document Analysis and Recognition, ICDAR, pp. 533–538 (2019)
13. Hollaus, F., Diem, M., Sablatnig, R.: Improving OCR accuracy by applying enhancement techniques on multispectral images. In: Proceedings - International Conference on Pattern Recognition, pp. 3080–3085 (2014)
14. Hollaus, F., Gau, M., Sablatnig, R.: Multispectral image acquisition of ancient manuscripts. In: Ioannides, M., Fritsch, D., Leissner, J., Davies, R., Remondino, F., Caffo, R. (eds.) EuroMed 2012. LNCS, vol. 7616, pp. 30–39. Springer, Heidelberg (2012). https://doi.org/10.1007/978-3-642-34234-9_4
15. International Telecommunication Union: Subjective video quality assessment methods for multimedia applications P.910. ITU-T (April 2008)
16. International Telecommunication Union: Methodology for the subjective assessment of the quality of television pictures ITU-R BT.500-13. ITU-R (January 2012)
17. Koo, T.K., Li, M.Y.: A guideline of selecting and reporting intraclass correlation coefficients for reliability research. J. Chiropr. Med. **15**(2), 155–163 (2016)
18. Likforman-Sulem, L., Darbon, J., Smith, E.H.: Enhancement of historical printed document images by combining total variation regularization and non-local means filtering. Image Vis. Comput. **29**(5), 351–363 (2011)

19. Lin, H., Hosu, V., Saupe, D.: KADID-10k: a large-scale artificially distorted IQA database. In: 2019 Eleventh International Conference on Quality of Multimedia Experience (QoMEX), pp. 1–3 (2019)

20. Mantiuk, R.K., Tomaszewska, A., Mantiuk, R.: Comparison of four subjective methods for image quality assessment. Comput. Graph. Forum **31**(8), 2478–2491 (2012)

21. Mindermann, S.: Hyperspectral imaging for readability enhancement of historic manuscripts. Master's thesis, TU München (2018)

22. Perez-Ortiz, M., Mikhailiuk, A., Zerman, E., Hulusic, V., Valenzise, G., Mantiuk, R.K.: From pairwise comparisons and rating to a unified quality scale. IEEE Trans. Image Process. **29**, 1139–1151 (2019)

23. Ponomarenko, N., et al.: Image database TID2013: peculiarities, results and perspectives. Signal Process.: Image Commun. **30**, 57–77 (2015)

24. Ponomarenko, N., et al.: TID2008 - a database for evaluation of full-reference visual quality assessment metrics. Adv. Mod. Radioelectron. **10**(4), 30–45 (2009)

25. Pouyet, E., et al.: Revealing the biography of a hidden medieval manuscript using synchrotron and conventional imaging techniques. Anal. Chimica Acta **982**, 20–30 (2017)

26. R Development Core Team: R: A Language and Environment for Statistical Computing. R Foundation for Statistical Computing, Vienna, Austria (2008). http://www.R-project.org. ISBN 3-900051-07-0

27. Ribeiro, F., Florencio, D., Nascimento, V.: Crowdsourcing subjective image quality evaluation. In: Proceedings - International Conference on Image Processing, ICIP, pp. 3097–3100 (2011)

28. Salerno, E., Tonazzini, A., Bedini, L.: Digital image analysis to enhance underwritten text in the Archimedes palimpsest. Int. J. Doc. Anal. Recognit. **9**(2–4), 79–87 (2007)

29. Shaus, A., Faigenbaum-Golovin, S., Sober, B., Turkel, E.: Potential contrast - a new image quality measure. Electron. Imaging **2017**(12), 52–58 (2017)

30. Sheikh, H.R., Sabir, M.F., Bovik, A.C.: A statistical evaluation of recent full reference image quality assessment algorithms. IEEE Trans. Image Process. **15**(11), 3441–3452 (2006)

31. Shrout, P.E., Fleiss, J.L.: Intraclass correlations: uses in assessing rater reliability. Psychol. Bull. **86**(2), 420–428 (1979)

32. Virtanen, T., Nuutinen, M., Vaahteranoksa, M., Oittinen, P., Häkkinen, J.: CID2013: a database for evaluating no-reference image quality assessment algorithms. IEEE Trans. Image Process. **24**(1), 390–402 (2015)

33. Ye, P., Doermann, D.: Combining preference and absolute judgements in a crowdsourced setting. In: Proceedings of International Conference on Machine Learning, pp. 1–7 (2013)

Can OpenPose Be Used as a 3D Registration Method for 3D Scans of Cultural Heritage Artifacts

Tomislav Pribanić$^{(\boxtimes)}$, David Bojanić , Kristijan Bartol,
and Tomislav Petković

Faculty of Electrical Engineering and Computing,
University of Zagreb, Zagreb, Croatia
{tomislav.pribanic,david.bojanic,kristijan.bartol}@fer.hr,
tomislav.petkovic.jr@fer.hr

Abstract. 3D scanning of artifacts is an important tool for studying and preservation of a culture heritage. Systems for 3D reconstruction are constantly developing but due to the shape and size of artifacts it is usually necessary to perform 3D scanning from several different positions in space. This brings up the problem of 3D registration which is a process of aligning different point clouds. Software-based 3D registration methods typically require identifying the sufficient number of point correspondence pairs between different point clouds. These correspondences are frequently found manually and/or by introducing a specially designed objects in the scene. On the other hand, in this work we explore whether OpenPose, a well-known deep learning model, can be used to find corresponded point pairs between different views and eventually assure a successful 3D registration. OpenPose is trained to find patterns and keypoints on images containing people. We acknowledge that many artifacts are indeed human like postures and we test our ideas on finding correspondences using OpenPose. Furthermore, if an artifact is nothing like human like appearance, we demonstrate a method introducing in 3D scene a simple human like image, and in turn allowing OpenPose to facilitate 3D registration between 3D scans from different views. The proposed 3D registration pipeline is easily applicable to many existing 3D scanning solutions of artifacts.

Keywords: Cultural heritage artifacts · 3D scanning · 3D registration · OpenPose

1 Introduction

An important tool for studying and preservation of cultural heritage is 3D scanning of the material [1]. In general, 3D scanning can be divided in long, medium and close-range scanning. The common characteristic of all three of them is that a single view 3D scan is typically insufficient due to the size and complexity of the

© Springer Nature Switzerland AG 2021
A. Del Bimbo et al. (Eds.): ICPR 2020 Workshops, LNCS 12667, pp. 83–96, 2021.
https://doi.org/10.1007/978-3-030-68787-8_6

scanned object. Scanning the object from the multiple views demands aligning multiple 3D point clouds into a common coordinate system. The task is known as 3D registration [2]. Two main approaches here are hardware and software based registration techniques. The latter is evidently preferred since it simplifies the 3D system design and its cost. However, many software methods are subtle to insufficient object texture, object symmetry, too small overlap between scanned views etc. [3]. Consequently, in practice it is common to introduce in the scene particularly designed registration objects/points which should be at minimum: firstly, easily recognizable on the image; secondly, reconstructable on at least consecutive (neighboring) scans; and thirdly, the correspondent pairs of the same point registration point on the neighboring image need to be robustly determined. Unfortunately, the above mentioned three demands are not always easily meet. In turn, the manual intervention of the operator on the 3D point clouds and/or 2D images is still needed in practice, in order to facilitate a correct 3D registration.

In this work we recall the fact and bring to the attention that many archaeological artifacts have a human like shape and appearance. In addition, human body shape has been a subject of numerous research within computer vision and deep learning communities, starting with, for example, detecting humans on the image, human gesture, 2D/3D human pose, human body segmentation and so forth. One of the most prominent works in those areas is OpenPose system, designed to detect keypoints on 2D images of multiple people [4]. OpenPose is a deep learning model trained on datasets with humans in different poses and scenarios [5] and it is currently considered as state of the art for the detection of human body keypoints on 2D images. In this work we propose a key insight that OpenPose, by providing keypoints on the images, can be readily used for 3D registration of human shape like 3D scanned archeological artifacts. Moreover, in the failure cases when OpenPose cannot find keypoints, we propose an introduction of simple 2D image in the 3D scene which can be successfully processed by OpenPose and, in turn, allow an efficient 3D registration even if the archeological artifact itself is nothing like 3D human shape.

In summary our main contributions are as follows: i) proposing when scanning archeological artifact with humans in the scene, we can then take advantage of OpenPose to find necessary correspondences for 3D registration. There is no need to introduce any specially designed objects, or even hardware, which serve merely purpose to 3D register point clouds. ii) Even if the scanned 3D scene is without objects that is OpenPose currently trained to find, by simply introducing an image of human in 3D scene we acquire enough data for 3D registration.

The remainder of this work is structured as follows. We first briefly recall work about 3D scanning and 3D registration, including both traditional computer vision approaches and some newer deep learning ideas. Next, we describe our method in more detail. That is followed by the experiments and discussion. At last, the main concluding remarks are stated.

2   Related Work

2.1   Traditional Approaches

3D reconstruction has been a long-standing research topic in computer vision community. A camera-based 3D system takes advantage of photogrammetric approach to extract 3D from 2D images [6]. Different ideas have been explored, frequently collectively called under the name Shape from X where "X" can be shading, texture, (de)focus, silhouettes, photometric stereo [7] etc. In theory, monocular cues (single image 3D reconstruction) can be used, but in reality binocular cues, such as stereo camera approach, have been proven to be more robust. The main prerequisite with stereo is to find the corresponding image points on two or more images, based on which a 3D position can be triangulated. If the process of correspondence search is meant to be automatic, it requires an efficient algorithm to detect and describe so called keypoints (silent) on the images. Many such keypoints detectors/descriptors have been proposed [8] and later provided as further input to, for example, Structure from Motion (SfM) [9] and Surface Localization and Mapping (SLAM) tasks [10]. Unfortunately, keypoints detection will fail if a scene does not have a sufficient texture which may easily be the case when reconstructing archeological artifacts. As a remedy, a powerful solution can be found in structured light (SL) approach [11]. SL along with Time-of-flight (ToF) principle [12], is the most notable example of active stereo method where an additional source of light, a video projector, is used in order to allow a dense and robust 3D reconstruction, even in the case of no texture present in the scene. In comparison to ToF and for close range applications, SL provides is generally a more accurate and dense solution. As a consequence, a large body of commercially available scanners are structured light based, including those used for scanning of archeological artifacts [13].

3D Registration. Regardless of the reconstruction technique, for a complete object reconstruction, multiple view 3D reconstructions are needed, introducing then the task of 3D registration [3] which aligns two point clouds originating from two different views. Alignment requires rotating and translating one point cloud wrt to another point cloud by some rotation matrix R and translation vector t, respectively. A straightforward hardware solution is to use a robotic arm and/or a turntable which readily provide necessary data to align point clouds [14], at the evident expense of increasing the system cost. On the contrary, software-based solutions ask finding a minimum three pairs of corresponding points on the views which are sufficient to find rotation matrix and translation vector. To that end and not surprisingly, proposed solutions for 2D keypoint detection and descriptions have been modified for 3D registration task too. Moreover, some of the 2D keypoint variants have been readily extended in 3D domain. An intermediate registration solution would be using the software and hardware based approaches. For example in [15], the authors present a structured light scanner on the tablet and utilize data from accelerometer and magnetometer to easy up the registration problem. In either case the alignment procedure is typically done in two steps: a rough alignment and a fine alignment. In the former case the goal is only to approximately align two point clouds [16], in order to subsequently apply a fine alignment method which would otherwise almost certainly fail, if the point clouds had not been initially aligned. For a fine alignment the well-known iterative closest point (ICP) has been basically a standard with its many variants [17] and implementations in open source software packages [18].

2.2 Deep Learning Approaches

Deep Learning 3D Reconstruction. In parallel with a classical computer vision approaches, topics of 3D reconstruction and 3D registration have been tremendously researched within the machine learning framework as well. Particularly in the last decade where the efficient machine (deep) learning training platforms (e.g., GPU cards, cloud services) have become widely available, along with the huge amounts of databases, essential for deep learning. Besides standard 2D vision tasks, such as image classification [19], semantic segmentation [20], object detection [21], and image captioning, a deep learning has extended to 3D domain as well which gave a rise to 3D shape analyses [22]. When working with 3D objects one of the key issues is to learn a good (vector) representation [23] of the object's original point cloud which should allow to reconstruct back the original point cloud from its learned representation. In addition, that (vector) representation should be predictable from 2D images. Unfortunately, to learn the mapping from 2D images to 3D world is very challenging, usually providing rather sparse and approximate 3D representation [24]. Particularly, if the training phase did not take place on the entire point cloud, but rather just on some of it reduced version, e.g. on a regular grid such as voxel grid, or even some of its improvements [25], which has been a traditional approach when working with 3D data. Alternatively, 3D data can be represented on graphs and manifolds [26] but that usually makes representation and processing rather complex compared to working directly with point clouds. The work that is usually attributed as pioneer work allowing a deep learning on the unorder data set, i.e., the entire point cloud, is PointNet [27]. PointNet has demonstrated nice results for 3D object part segmentation and 3D classification.

Deep Learning 3D Registration. However, learning a point cloud representation for 3D registration task is even more difficult. PointNetLK [28] is an attempt to extend PointNet for 3D registration. Similarly, Deep Closest Point is another deep learning variant for 3D registration [29]. However, both approaches are trained and tested on essentially noise free 3D data (Modelnet [30]). Perhaps even more importantly the point clouds were complete with 100% overlap, or at least the template point cloud was a full model. These are quite unrealistic assumptions for many practical applications. Instead of learning registration parameters directly, an alternative is to learn local descriptors for each individual point cloud [31]. Afterwards, those descriptors can be compared and if correct matches between different point clouds are found, the registration parameters can be computed too. Descriptors can be learned directly on 3D data or in 2D domain [32]. In general, even if only category specific descriptors are trained [33], learning to detect and describe in 2D domain represents somewhat of a less challenge compared to 3D domain. One of the reasons could be simply the existence of abundant training data in 2D domain compared to 3D domain. Annotated images with humans are relatively easy to find in comparison to any kind of 3D database. One of the most notable work on detecting keypoints on humans is OpenPose model [4]. Current version estimates 2D human pose with up to 135 keypoints.

As pointed out in [4], OpenPose has been extensively used in the research of numerous other applications, for example, person re-identification, GAN-based video retargeting of human faces and bodies, human-computer Interaction, 3D pose estimation, and 3D human mesh model generation. However, to the best of authors knowledge this is the first work where OpenPose is investigated with the intent to register to 3D scans of archaeological artifacts.

3   Method Description

3.1   3D Scanning System Components

In our work we use SL system consisted of a single projector and a camera. In terms of patterns projection, we take advantage of multiple phase shifting (MPS) strategy [11] which is generally considered as one of the most robust and accurate pattern SL projection strategies in the case of static scenes. Therefore, after projecting a sequence of MPS patterns and processing the acquired images on the camera, our 3D scanning system yields 3D point cloud for a particular view in space. We repeat the procedure from several different views in the space in order to cover (almost) entire object surface. However, the core of our idea about 3D registration is agnostic with respect to the actual type of 3D system used. In principle any 3D system with at least moderate output accuracy would suffice.

We compute registration parameters pairwise, i.e. for each two consecutive scanned views and subsequently combine all the registered pairs into a joint 3D scan.

3.2   Providing Data for a Coarse 3D Registration - OpenPose

We follow the usual pipeline in 3D registration where first a coarse 3D registration is found. To that end, we provide a camera image into OpenPose model. OpenPose has several trained models in terms of number of keypoints it can output. In this work body_25 model was utilized to estimate human 2D pose (Table 1), accordingly 25 different keypoints on the body are estimated on one camera image per scanning view. As it will be shown in the result section, we demonstrate an experiment where keypoints can be found directly on the scanned object of interest. Alternatively, if the scanned object has no human like shape, we propose a simple solution by introducing in the scene an arbitrary human picture on which OpenPose can easily find keypoints. In either case, on a pair of consecutive scanning views and their camera images, we use OpenPose to find the correspondent 2D keypoints x_1 and x_2, for the first and second scanning view, respectively. The 3D scanner provides immediately the corresponding 3D positions X_1 and X_2, that are related with the following expression:

$$X_2 = R \cdot X_1 + t \tag{1}$$

Where R and t are registration parameters needed to roughly align two scanned point clouds. The former one is rotation matrix $R \in SO(3)$ and having 3 degrees of freedom, similarly, the latter one is a translation vector $t \in R^3$, having 3 degrees of freedom too. The computational procedure for R and t acknowledges the existence of noise for both X_1 and X_2. Thus, the problem is typically formulated as finding the least square solution during minimization of the expression:

$$\frac{1}{N} \cdot \sum_{i=1}^{N} \|R \cdot X_1 + t - X_2\|^2 \tag{2}$$

where N is the number of the corresponded OpenPose found and reconstructed keypoints between two scanned views. By translating each set of points X_1 and X_2 by their correspondent means $\overline{X_1}$ and $\overline{X_2}$, respectively, it can be shown that solution for R and t can be found through the singular value decomposition of a dispersion matrix $D = U \cdot S \cdot V^T$:

$$D = \sum_{i=1}^{N} \left(X_1 - \overline{X_1}\right) \cdot \left(X_2 - \overline{X_2}\right)^T \tag{3}$$

$$R = V \cdot U^T, \quad t = \overline{X_2} - R \cdot \overline{X_1}$$

3.3   Providing Data for a Fine 3D Registration - ICP

Once a given pair of 3D views is roughly registered using data from (3), we proceed with the next step in the 3D registration pipeline, a refinement of initially computed values R and t. As already pointed out ICP is usually a method for choice for the refinement step. Essentially it operates using the same equations shown above with the slight but crucial modification. It includes the matching function:

$$\frac{1}{N} \cdot \sum_{i=1}^{N} \|R \cdot X_1 + t - X_{2f(x_1)}\|^2 \tag{4}$$

where $f(X_1)$ is a matching function that finds for a point X_2 its putative match X_1. After the matches are determined, the registration parameters (R, t) are computed as shown and one of the point clouds is aligned closer to the

Table 1. Positions and list of keypoints on the human body detected by OpenPose for body_25 model.

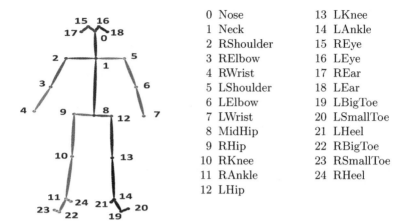

0 Nose	13 LKnee
1 Neck	14 LAnkle
2 RShoulder	15 REye
3 RElbow	16 LEye
4 RWrist	17 REar
5 LShoulder	18 LEar
6 LElbow	19 LBigToe
7 LWrist	20 LSmallToe
8 MidHip	21 LHeel
9 RHip	22 RBigToe
10 RKnee	23 RSmallToe
11 RAnkle	24 RHeel
12 LHip	

other one. Next another set of matches is searched, new (R, t) are found, and therefore, ICP iterates to hopefully a convergent solution. Actually, a lot trick of trades revolves around the ICP stopping criteria and even more importantly how to choose a strategy to find putative matches between iterations [17]. We use in this work one of the simplest ideas where we simply look for the nearest neighbor (NN) in another point cloud:

$$f(X_{1i}) = \min_{j} \| R \cdot X_1 + t - X_{2jf(x_1)} \|^2 \tag{5}$$

where given some point i from the first point cloud we look for a point j in the second point cloud at the minimum Euclidean distance. Additionally, if the NN is not closer than some threshold distance (in our experiments set to $20mm$) we discard it from the computation of registration parameters. More comprehensive ICP strategies may involve point to plane distance matching criteria, apply different subsamplings before matching even starts, in order to match a diverse set of points, etc., but in our work we tested our ideas using the simplest approach possible.

4   Results and Discussion

The following experiment considered the head bust sculpture (Fig. 1). Evidently, applying a standard 25 body model only on the head is clearly not the best solution since only a few points could be expected to be found in the area of a face. An alternative would be to apply detection for facial keypoints as well (OpenPose has that option too). However, OpenPose performed quite poorly on detecting facial keypoints, for this particular example. Regardless of some artistic features clearly present on the sculpture, most humans would still recognize this sculpture as a human head and relatively easy find a number of keypoints on it. Therefore, we can only suspect that types of images OpenPose was trained on, it had different features which prevents OpenPose to generalize on the cases as shown. But since the shown example is relatively mild example of what archeological artifacts may look like when it comes to head busts, we propose another solution. Figure 1 (top row, in the upper right part of images) shows an arbitrary chosen image of a male person which was introduced in 3D scene, along the subject of 3D reconstruction, and on whom OpenPose has found keypoints. We have scanned the head bust from number of views in the space and it turned out that OpenPose managed to find robustly on each view almost all of 25 keypoints (recall that 3 are minimum to acquire a rough registration). Figure 1, second row, is an example showing two point clouds, from two consecutive scanned views. After the coarse alignment using the OpenPose found keypoints and their 3D positions supplied by 3D SL scanner, alignment was successfully refined with ICP (Fig. 1 bottom row).

Our second experiment explored an idea on the reconstruction and registration of a female mannequin which we believe can be for the purpose of experiment regarded as a possible, human shape and size like, archeological artifact. We have 3D scanned it from several views, four of which are shown on Fig. 2. The top row shows camera views along with OpenPose found keypoints which are 3D reconstructed and used for a coarse registration. The second row shows individual 3D point clouds. The bottom row shows several views around the mannequin after the coarse registration have been refined with ICP. 3D scanning system resolution was kept at the minimum in order to test idea using as few points as possible. Besides, the visualization shows 3D point clouds, raw data only. No mesh creation or any kind of postprocessing was done on either individual point cloud or the registered point clouds.

The traditional approach to 3D registration, in order to at least solve the coarse registration, would include manually assigning the point correspondence on each and every point cloud which could be time consuming. Alternatively, a specially designed control points are introduced in the 3D scene which then needs to be both reconstructed and identified on every view scanned (image taken) which may not be always practical, especially with the fragile archeological artifacts. On the other hand, our experiments suggest that is doable to use OpenPose during the 3D registration if either the subject of scanning resembles human like shape (Fig. 2) or by simple introducing a human image in the scene (Fig. 1). We also note that both examples, just as many archeological artifacts, do not have a rich texture on their surface. In turn, applying some classical keypoint detectors/descriptors is likely to fail due to insufficient textures.

For completeness we briefly mention that regarding the registration of point clouds at different scales it is possible to compute a scale factor as well [34], as an additional parameter. However, for 3D registrations of rigid body surfaces a scale typically should not change. One plausible situation where the information about scale would be needed is the registration of real size object surfaces against previously stored a full 3D computer model which may be at different scale. In

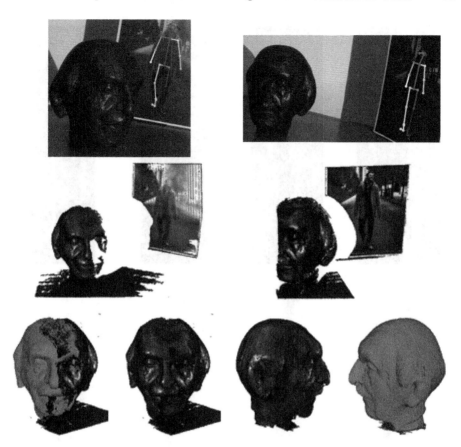

Fig. 1. 3D scanning and registration of a head bust sculpture. Top row: camera images from two different views. Middle row: The respective 3D point clouds from two different views. Bottom row: aligned point clouds in the common mesh. The first two meshes on the left represents the aligned point clouds from above rows and where on the left most mesh, the left point cloud is shown with grey texture for better visualization. The two right most meshes are examples after the alignment from several views around the sculpture.

that case a scale is either known in advance or can be relatively easily estimated, given some correspondent pairs of points on the 3D computer model and the actually reconstructed surface parts. Once at least a rough scale estimate is known, that should suffice for a coarse type of registration.

4.1   Limitations

The limitations of the proposed approach originate primarily from the fact that OpenPose model is apparently trained on such dataset with humans mostly in the upright position. Figure 3 a) is an example where several photographs of

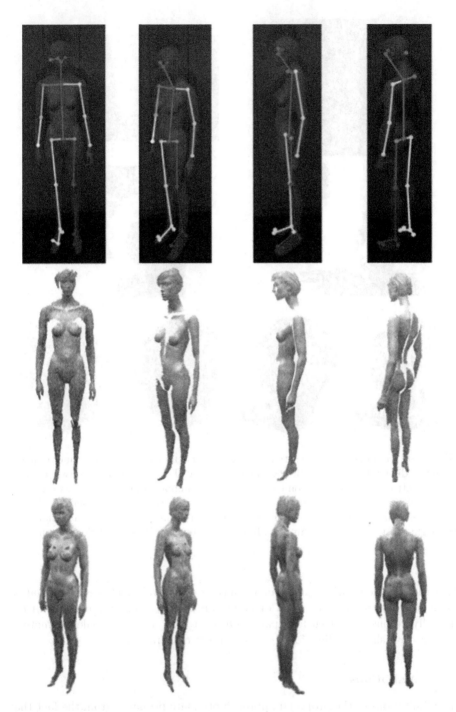

Fig. 2. 3D scanning and registration of female mannequin acting as 'archeological artifact' (please see text for more details)

human were positioned around the head bust sculpture and ones which were horizontal (female person standing on one leg) OpenPose failed to find keypoints. Moreover, sometimes shadows, in the form of human contour, can create problems as well. Figure 3 b) represents a situation where next to the head bust sculpture, a small toy was positioned. This toy can be understood either as primary interest of scanning or just a helper object which would give us OpenPose keypoints for a coarse registration. In both cases, the shadows in the background would need to be discarded during the automatic procedure of extracting the relevant points for a coarse 3D registration.

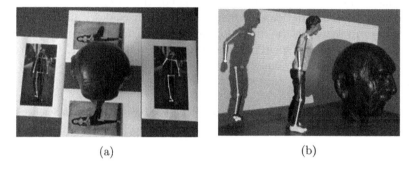

(a)   (b)

Fig. 3. a) OpenPose failure case of not detecting keypoints on all humans present in the image. b) OpenPose detecting a desired points keypoints on a toy model, but also undesired ones on the shadow in the background.

In part of our experiments, when we used an image of human as registration tool (Fig. 1), all correspondent points taken for a coarse registration are coplanar, whereas in another part of experiments we have used spatially spread points (Fig. 2). We recall that the minimum of 3 distinct noncolinear points are needed and such 3 points are in that case evidently always coplanar. More than 3 points spread equally in 3D space should assure greater stability and accuracy. However, 2D image keypoints provided by OpenPose represents 2D image projections of internal (joint) points and 3D scanner provides locations of surface points. For instance, consider a left knee keypoint from frontal and lateral view (Fig. 2 top row: first and third image, respectively). Obviously, they do not correspond to the same 3D surface point. Fortunately, for a coarse registration that would still suffice. Consequently, and in contrast to the intuitive expectations, a coarse registration using coplanar set of points (Fig. 1) may even provide more accurate rough registration result, since the correspondence discrepancy between the OpenPose keypoint locations and image locations which are actually reconstructed should be less. This is partially the reason while scanning the head sculpture we have opted to detected keypoints on the planar object such as simply an image of the human (Fig. 1 top row) rather than 3D object such as toy (Fig. 3 b)).

5   Conclusion

We have brought to the attention the importance of having a convenient app-roach for a registration of archeological artifacts 3D scans. To that end we have introduced a well-known deep learning model OpenPose which is currently the state of the art in detecting 2D human pose on the images and has been used in many applications. More specifically, we have examined the possibility of apply-ing OpenPose keypoints output as a toll for a coarse registration of 3D scans. Our experiments have shown that OpenPose is a liable alternative for 3D regis-tration, both in cases when the subject of interest has a human like appearance, and we have shown an approach when that is not the case.

The mentioned restrictions of OpenPose in the discussion, and for the par-ticular usage in scanning the archeological artifacts, may also suggest a future research direction where OpenPose model (or some similar) would be re-trained for detecting keypoints on one or more object categories of archeological arti-facts.

Acknowledgment. This work has been fully supported by the Croatian Science Foun-dation under the project IP-2018-01-8118.

References

1. Levoy, M., et al.: The digital Michelangelo project: 3D scanning of large statues. In: SIGGRAPH (2000)
2. Salvi, J., Matabosch, C., Fofi, D., Forest, J.: A review of recent range image reg-istration methods with accuracy evaluation. Image Vis. Comput. **25**(5), 578–596 (2007)
3. Tam, G.K.L., et al.: Registration of 3D point clouds and meshes: a survey from rigid to nonrigid. Trans. Vis. Comput. Graph. **19**(7), 1199–1217 (2013)
4. Cao, Z., Hidalgo Martinez, G., Simon, T., Wei, S., Sheikh, Y.A.: OpenPose: real-time multi-person 2D pose estimation using part affinity fields. IEEE Trans. Pat-tern Anal. Mach. Intell. **43**(1), 172–186 (2019)
5. CMU Panoptic Studio Dataset. http://domedb.perception.cs.cmu.edu/. Accessed 10 Oct 2020
6. Brown, M., Song, M.: Overview of three-dimensional shape measurement using optical methods. Opt. Eng. **39**(1), 10–22 (2000)
7. Barsky, S., Maria, P.: The 4-source photometric stereo technique for three-dimensional surfaces in the presence of highlights and shadows. IEEE Trans. Pat-tern Anal. Mach. Intell. **25**(10), 1239–1252 (2003)
8. Mukherjee, D., Wu, Q.M.J., Wang, G.: A comparative experimental study of image feature detectors and descriptors. Mach. Vis. Appl. **26**(4), 443–466 (2015). https://doi.org/10.1007/s00138-015-0679-9
9. Schonberger, J.L., Frahm, J.M.: Structure-from-motion revisited. In: Proceedings of the IEEE Computer Society Conference on Computer Vision and Pattern Recog-nition (2016)
10. Mur-Artal, R., Montiel, J., Tardos, J.: ORB-SLAM: a versatile and accurate monocular SLAM system. IEEE Trans. Robot. **31**, 1147–1163 (2015)

11. Salvi, J., Fernandez, S., Pribanic, T., Llado, X.: A state of the art in structured light patterns for surface profilometry. Pattern Recogn. **43**(8), 2666–2680 (2010)
12. Horaud, R., Hansard, M., Evangelidis, G., Ménier, C.: An overview of depth cameras and range scanners based on time-of-flight technologies. Mach. Vis. Appl. **27**(7), 1005–1020 (2016). https://doi.org/10.1007/s00138-016-0784-4
13. 3D scanning for cultural heritage conversation. https://www.factum-arte.com/pag/701/3D-Scanning-for-Cultural-Heritage-Conservation. Accessed Oct 2020
14. Martins, A.F., Bessant, M., Manukyan, L., Milinkovitch, M.C.: R2 OBBIE-3D, a fast robotic high-resolution system for quantitative phenotyping of surface geometry and colour-texture. PLoS One **10**(6), 1–18 (2015)
15. Pribanic, T., Petković, T., Donlić, M.: 3D registration based on the direction sensor measurements. Pattern Recogn. **88**, 532–546 (2019)
16. Díez, Y., Roure, F., Lladó, X., Salvi, J.: A qualitative review on 3D coarse registration methods. ACM Comput. Surv. **47**(3), 45:1–45:36 (2015)
17. Rusinkiewicz, S., Levoy, M.: Efficient variants of the ICP algorithm. In: Proceedings Third International Conference on 3-D Digital Imaging and Modeling, pp. 145–152 (2001)
18. Point Cloud Library (PCL). http://www.pointclouds.org/. Accessed 10 Oct 2020
19. He, K., Zhang, X., Ren, S., Sun, J.: Identity mappings in deep residual networks. In: Leibe, B., Matas, J., Sebe, N., Welling, M. (eds.) ECCV 2016. LNCS, vol. 9908, pp. 630–645. Springer, Cham (2016). https://doi.org/10.1007/978-3-319-46493-0_38
20. Yu, F., Koltun, V.: Multi-scale context aggregation by dilated convolutions. In: ICLR (2016)
21. Ren, S., He, K., Girshick, R., Sun, J.: Faster R-CNN: towards real-time object detection with region proposal networks. In: NIPS (2015)
22. Verma, N., Boyer, E., Verbeek, J.: FeaStNet: feature-steered graph convolutions for 3D shape analysis. In: CVPR, pp. 2598–2606 (2018)
23. Girdhar, R., Fouhey, D.F., Rodriguez, M., Gupta, A.: Learning a predictable and generative vector representation for objects. In: Leibe, B., Matas, J., Sebe, N., Welling, M. (eds.) ECCV 2016. LNCS, vol. 9910, pp. 484–499. Springer, Cham (2016). https://doi.org/10.1007/978-3-319-46466-4_29
24. Choy, C.B., Xu, D., Gwak, J.Y., Chen, K., Savarese, S.: 3D-R2N2: a unified approach for single and multi-view 3D object reconstruction. In: Leibe, B., Matas, J., Sebe, N., Welling, M. (eds.) ECCV 2016. LNCS, vol. 9912, pp. 628–644. Springer, Cham (2016). https://doi.org/10.1007/978-3-319-46484-8_38
25. Riegler, G., Ulusoy, A.O., Geiger, A.: OctNet: learning deep 3D representations at high resolutions. In: CVPR (2017)
26. Bronstein, M.M., Bruna, J., LeCun, Y., Szlam, A., Vandergheynst, P.: Geometric deep learning: going beyond Euclidean data. IEEE Sig. Process. Mag. **34**, 18–42 (2017)
27. Qi, C.R., Su, H., Mo, K.,Guibas, L.J.: PointNet: deep learning on point sets for 3D classification and segmentation. In: CVPR (2017)
28. Aoki, Y., Goforth, H., Srivatsan, R.A., Lucey, S.: PointNetLK: robust & efficient point cloud registration using PointNet. In: CVPR (2019)
29. Wang, Y., Solomon, J.M.: Deep closest point: learning representations for point cloud registration. In: IEEE International Conference on Computer Vision, ICCV 2019 (2019)
30. Wu, Z., Song, S., Khosla, A., Zhang, L., Tang, X., Xiao, J.: 3D shapenets: a deep representation for volumetric shape modeling. In: CVPR 2015 (2015)
31. Zeng, A., Song, S., Nießner, M., Fisher, M., Xiao, J., Funkhouser, T.: 3DMatch: learning local geometric descriptors from RGB-D reconstructions. In: CVPR (2017)

32. Altwaijry, H., Veit, A., Belongie, S.: Learning to detect and match keypoints with deep architectures. In: British Machine Vision Conference (2016)
33. Suwajanakorn, S., Snavely, N., Tompson, J., Norouzi, M.: Discovery of latent 3D keypoints via end-to-end geometric reasoning. In: Proceedings of the 32nd International Conference on Neural Information Processing Systems, NIPS 2018 (2018)
34. Challis, J.H.: A procedure for determining rigid body transformation parameters. J. Biomech. **28**(6), 733–737 (1995)

Survey on Deep Learning-Based Kuzushiji Recognition

Kazuya Ueki[(⊠)] and Tomoka Kojima

School of Information Science, Meisei University, 2-1-1 Hodokubo,
Hino-city, Tokyo 191-8506, Japan
kazuya.ueki@meisei-u.ac.jp

Abstract. Owing to the overwhelming accuracy of the deep learning method demonstrated at the 2012 image classification competition, deep learning has been successfully applied to a variety of other tasks. The high-precision detection and recognition of Kuzushiji, a Japanese cursive script used for transcribing historical documents, has been made possible through the use of deep learning. In recent years, competitions on Kuzushiji recognition have been held, and many researchers have proposed various recognition methods. This study examines recent research trends, current problems, and future prospects in Kuzushiji recognition using deep learning.

Keywords: Kuzushiji recognition · Handwritten character recognition · Survey · Deep learning

1 Introduction

Kuzushiji has been commonly used in Japan for more than a thousand years. However, since the 1900s, schools have no longer been teaching Kuzushiji, and only a few thousand people in Japan can currently read and understand it. Hiragana characters[1] have a root Kanji[2] called a Jibo[3], leading to various shapes for a single character; training is required to read characters that differ from modern Hiragana. For this reason, many researchers have been working on Kuzushiji recognition using machine learning techniques. Recently, with the advent of deep learning, research on Kuzushiji recognition has accelerated and the accuracy of the methods has significantly improved. In this paper, we present a survey and analysis of recent methods of Kuzushiji recognition based on deep learning.

---

[1] Hiragana is one of the three different character sets used in Japanese writing. Each Hiragana character represents a particular syllable. There are 46 basic characters.

[2] Kanji is another one of the three character sets used in the Japanese language. Along with syllabaries, Kanji is made up of ideographic characters, and each letter symbolizes a specific meaning. Most Kanji characters were imported from China, although some were developed in Japan. Although there are approximately 50,000 Kanji characters, only approximately 2,500 are actually used in daily life in Japan.

[3] A Jibo is a root Kanji character of Hiragana. For example, the character "あ" is derived from different Jibos including "安" and "阿".

© Springer Nature Switzerland AG 2021
A. Del Bimbo et al. (Eds.): ICPR 2020 Workshops, LNCS 12667, pp. 97–111, 2021.
https://doi.org/10.1007/978-3-030-68787-8_7

2   Representative Research on Kuzushiji Recognition

Many studies on Kuzushiji recognition were conducted prior to the introduction of deep learning. The "Historical Character Recognition Project" [1], which was initiated in 1999, reported the development of a system to support the transcription of ancient documents. In this project, to develop a historical document research support system, the authors studied a character database, corpus, character segmentation, character recognition, intellectual transcription support system, and a digital dictionary. Specifically, they developed a computerized historical character dictionary using stroke information [2] as well as Japanese off-line hand-written optical character recognition (OCR) technology, and implemented a Kuzushiji recognition system for 67,739 categories by combining on-line and off-line recognition methods [3]. Other methods, such as [4,5], which is a recognition method using self-organizing maps, and [6], which is a recognition method using a neocognitron, have also been proposed.

Since the introduction of deep learning, further research on Kuzushiji recognition has become increasingly active, and various methods have been proposed. During the early introductory stage of deep learning, most recognition methods [7,8] were based on approximately 50 different Hiragana images with recognition rates of 75% to 90%. There were also studies in which more than 1,000 characters including Hiragana, and Katakana[4] and Kanji, were recognized [9], along with the results of character recognition in documents of the Taiwan Governor's Office, which dealt with more than 3,000 characters [10]. In these studies, the problems of large numbers of classes, an unbalanced number of data between classes, and a variation of characters were solved through a data augmentation commonly used in deep learning training.

In addition, a network that outputs a three-character string has also been proposed as a method for recognizing consecutive characters [11]. This method uses single-character and binary classifiers to distinguish between characters; the character strings are then recognized using bidirectional long short-term memory (BLSTM). The authors reported that the recognition rate of a single character was approximately 92%; however, the recognition rate of three characters was only approximately 76%. Similarly, a method for recognizing a string of three consecutive characters using a sliding window and BLSTM was proposed [12]. The authors used the tendency in which the maximum output probability of a neural network is not particularly high for a misaligned character image but is high for an accurately aligned image, and increased the recognition rate to 86% by integrating multiple results. In addition, a deep learning method for recognizing a series of Kuzushiji phrases using an image from "The Tale of Genji" was proposed [13]. An end-to-end method with an attention mechanism was applied to recognize consecutive Kuzushiji characters within phrases. This method can recognize phrases written in Hiragana (47 different characters) with

---

[4] In the same way as Hiragana, Katakana is one of the three different character sets used in Japanese. Katakana is also a phonetic syllabary, in which each letter represents the sound of a syllable. There are also 46 basic characters.

78.92% accuracy, and phrases containing both Kanji (63 different characters) and Hiragana with 59.80% accuracy.

In recent years, research on Kuzushiji recognition has become increasingly active since the Kuzushiji dataset first became publicly available [14]. With the development of this database, a PRMU algorithm contest described in Sect. 4.1 and a Kaggle competition introduced in Sect. 4.2 were held, and many researchers have started to work on Kuzushiji recognition. The preparation, progress, and results of a Kuzushiji recognition competition, knowledge obtained from the competition, and the value of utilizing machine learning competitions have also been reported [15,16]. In these reports, the results of the Kuzushiji recognition competition showed that existing object detection algorithms such as a Faster R-CNN [17] and cascade R-CNN [18] are also effective for Kuzushiji detection. At the forefront of Kuzushiji recognition, end-to-end approaches for actual transcriptions are becoming the mainstream. As a representative method, an end-to-end method, KuroNet, was proposed to recognize whole pages of text using the U-Net architecture [19,20]. The authors demonstrated that KuroNet can handle long-range contexts, large vocabularies, and non-standardized character layouts by predicting the location and identity of all characters given a page of text without any preprocessing. To recognize multiple lines of historical documents, a document reading system inspired by human eye movements was proposed, and the results of evaluations of the PRMU algorithm contest database described in Sect. 4.1 [21] and the Kaggle competition database described in Sect. 4.2 [22] were reported. In addition, a two-dimensional context box proposal network used to detect Kuzushiji in historical documents was proposed [23]. The authors employed VGG16 to extract features from an input image and BLSTM [24] for exploring the vertical and horizontal dimensions, and then predicted the bounding boxes from the output of the two-dimensional context.

In a study on the practical aspects of transcription, a new type of OCR technology was proposed to reduce the labor of a high-load transcription [25]. This technology is not a fully automated process but aims to save labor by dividing tasks between experts and non-experts and applying an automatic processing. The authors stated that a translation can be made quickly and accurately by not aiming at a decoding accuracy of 100% using only the OCR of automatic processing, but by leaving the characters with a low degree of certainty as a "■ (geta)" (geta) and entrusting the evaluation to experts in the following process. A method for automatically determining which characters should be held for evaluation using a machine learning technique was also proposed [26,27]. This method can automatically identify difficult-to-recognize characters or characters that were not used during training based on the confidence level obtained from the neural network.

A study on an interface of a Kuzushiji recognition system also introduced a system that can operate on a Raspberry Pi without problems and with almost the same processing time and accuracy as in previous studies; there was also no need for a high-performance computer [28].

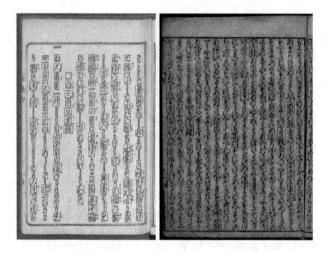

Fig. 1. Example images of Kuzushiji dataset

As another area of focus, a framework for assisting humans in reading Japanese historical manuscripts, formulated as a constraint satisfaction problem, and a system for transcribing Kuzushiji and its graphical user interface have also been introduced [29, 30].

An interactive system was also been proposed to assist in the transcription of digitized Japanese historical woodblock-printed books [31]. This system includes a layout analysis, character segmentation, transcription, and the generation of a character image database. The procedures for applying the system consist of two major phases. During the first phase, the system automatically produces provisional character segmentation data, and users interactively edit and transcribe the data into text data for storage in the character image database. During the second phase, the system conducts automatic character segmentation and transcription using the database generated during the first phase. By repeating the first and second phases with a variety of materials, the contents of the character image database can be enhanced and the performance of the system in terms of character segmentation and transcription will increase.

3   Datasets

3.1   Kuzushiji Dataset

The Kuzushiji dataset[5] consists of 6,151 pages of image data of 44 classical books held by National Institute of Japanese Literature and published by ROIS-DS Center for Open Data in the Humanities (CODH). Example images included in the Kuzushiji dataset are shown in Fig. 1. This Kuzushiji database comprises bounding boxes for characters, including 4,328 character types and 1,086,326

---

[5] http://codh.rois.ac.jp/char-shape/.

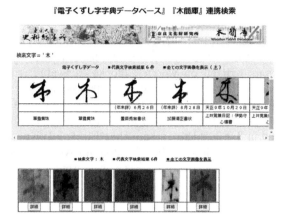

Fig. 2. "Electronic Kuzushiji dictionary database" and "wooden tablet database" collaborative search function

characters. There is a large bias in the number of data depending on the class: The class with the largest number of images is "の" (character code, U+306B), which has 41,293 images; many classes have extremely few images, and 790 classes only have 1 image.

Kuzushiji-MNIST, Kuzushiji-49, and Kuzushiji-Kanji were also provided as a subset of the above dataset[6] [32]. These datasets not only serve as a benchmark for advanced classification algorithms, they can also be used in more creative areas such as generative modeling, adversarial examples, few-shot learning, transfer learning, and domain adaptation. Kuzushiji-MNIST has 70,000 28×28 grayscale images with 10 Hiragana character classes. Kuzushiji-49 is an imbalanced dataset that has 49 classes (28×28 grayscale, 270,912 images) containing 48 Hiragana characters and one Hiragana iteration mark. Kuzushiji-Kanji is an imbalanced dataset with a total of 3,832 Kanji characters (64×64 grayscale, 140,426 images), ranging from 1,766 examples to only a single example per class.

3.2 Electronic Kuzushiji Dictionary Database

The Electronic Kuzushiji Dictionary Database[7] is a database of glyphs and fonts collected from ancient documents and records in the Historiographical Institute of the University of Tokyo; it contains approximately 6,000 different characters, 2,600 different vocabularies, and 280,000 character image files. This database contains character forms from various periods from the Nara period (8th century) to the Edo period (18th century).

---

[6] https://github.com/rois-codh/kmnist.
[7] https://wwwap.hi.u-tokyo.ac.jp/ships/shipscontroller.

3.3   Wooden Tablet Database

The Nara National Research Institute for Cultural Properties has developed and published a database that collects images of glyphs and fonts allowing the recognition of inscriptions written on wooden blocks excavated from underground sites. The database contains approximately 24,000 characters, 1,500 character types, and 35,000 character images. It contains information from the Asuka-Nara period, which is not often included in the Electronic Kuzushiji Dictionary Database described in 3.2. For this reason, the "Electronic Kuzushiji Dictionary Database" and "wooden tablet database" collaborative search function[8] shown in Fig. 2, which integrates the two databases, was provided for convenience.

4   Benchmarks

4.1   PRMU Algorithm Contest

The tasks used in the 2017 and 2019 PRMU Algorithm Contest[9] required recognizing Kuzushiji contained in the designated region of an image of a classical Japanese book and outputting the Unicode of each character. In this contest, a total of 46 types of Hiragana characters that do not include Katakana or Kanji needed to be recognized. The 2017 contest had three tasks for three different difficulty levels, levels 1, 2, and 3, depending on the number of characters contained in the rectangle. The participants were required to recognize single segmented characters in level 1, three consecutive characters in the vertical direction in level 2, and three or more characters in the vertical and horizontal directions in level 3. In the 2019 contest, the task was to recognize three consecutive characters in the vertical direction as in level 2 in 2017.

Herein, we introduce the tasks of the 2017 contest and the methods used by the best performing teams [33]. The dataset applied in 2017 was constructed from 2,222 scanned pages of 15 historical books provided by CODH. One of the 15 books was used as the test data because it contained many fragmented and noisy patterns, as well as various backgrounds. The dataset for level 1 consisted of 228,334 single Hiragana images, and test data of 47,950 were selected from the dataset. To improve the accuracy, multiple models were trained and a voting-based ensemble method was employed to integrate the results of many different models. The level 2 dataset consists of 92,813 images of three consecutive characters, and a test set of 13,648 images was selected from the dataset. A combined architecture of a CNN , BLSTM, and connectionist temporal classification (CTC) was employed [34], and a sequence error rate (SER) of 31.60% was achieved. In the level 3 dataset, there are 12,583 images from which a test set of 1,340 images were selected. The authors employed a combination of vertical line segmentation and multiple line concatenation before applying a deep

---

[8] http://clioapi.hi.u-tokyo.ac.jp/ships/ZClient/W34/z_srch.php.
[9] A contest held annually by the Pattern Recognition and Media Understanding (PRMU) for the purpose of revitalizing research group activities.

convolutional recurrent network. The SER is 82.57%, and there is still a significant need for improvement.

Another report evaluated a historical document recognition system inspired by human eye movements using the dataset from the 2017 PRMU algorithm contest [21]. This system includes two modules: a CNN for feature extraction and an LSTM decoder with an attention model for generating the target characters. The authors achieved SERs of 9.87% and 53.81% at levels 2 and 3 of the dataset, respectively.

Now, we introduce the methods of the first through third place teams in the 2019 contest. The dataset used in 2019 was also composed of 48 Hiragana character images cropped from the books in the Kuzushiji dataset provided by CODH. Single-character images and images containing three consecutive characters in the vertical direction were provided as data for training. A total of 388,146 single-character images were applied, and 119,997 images with three consecutive characters were used for training and 16,387 were used for testing.

The first place team adopted a method dividing the characters into three images through a preprocessing, inputting each image into the CNN to extract the features, and recognizing three consecutive characters using two layers of a bidirectional gated recurrent unit (GRU) [35][10]. They achieved a rate of 90.63% through a combination of three backbone models (SE-ResNeXt, DenseNet, and Inception-v4). As data augmentation methods, in addition to a random crop and a random shift, the division position was randomly shifted up and down slightly during training for robustness to the division position.

The second place team used a CNN, BLSTM, and CTC in the first step and output three characters by majority voting during the second step. In the first step, a CNN (six layers) was used to extract the features, BLSTM (two layers) was used to convert the features into sequential data, and CTC was used to output the text. To improve the accuracy, data augmentation such as a random rotation, random zoom, parallel shift, random noise, and random erasing [36] were used.

The third place team employed an algorithm that applies multi-label image classification. In the first step, a multi-label estimation was conducted using an image classification model, and three characters were estimated in no particular order. During the second step, Grad-CAM [37] identified and aligned the region of interest for each candidate character and output three consecutive characters.

4.2 Kaggle Competition

A Kaggle competition called "Opening the door to a thousand years of Japanese culture" was held from July 19 to October 14, 2019. Whereas the PRMU algorithm competition involved a recognition of single-character images or images containing a few characters, the Kaggle competition tackled the more challenging task of automatically detecting the position of characters on a page of a classical book and correctly recognizing the type of characters. Of the 44 books in the

---

[10] https://github.com/katsura-jp/alcon23.

Table 1. Explanation and program implementation of the winning method in the Kaggle competition

Rank	F value	URL
1	0.950	Explanation: https://www.kaggle.com/c/kuzushiji-recognition/discussion/112788
		Implementation: https://github.com/tascj/kaggle-kuzushiji-recognition
2	0.950	Explanation: https://www.kaggle.com/c/kuzushiji-recognition/discussion/112712
		Implementation: https://github.com/lopuhin/kaggle-kuzushiji-2019
3	0.944	Explanation: https://www.kaggle.com/c/kuzushiji-recognition/discussion/113049
		Implementation: https://github.com/knjcode/kaggle-kuzushiji-recognition-2019
4	0.942	Explanation: https://www.kaggle.com/c/kuzushiji-recognition/discussion/114764
		Implementation: https://github.com/linhuifj/kaggle-kuzushiji-recognition
5	0.940	Explanation: https://www.kaggle.com/c/kuzushiji-recognition/discussion/112771
		Implementation: https://github.com/see−/kuzushiji-recognition
7	0.934	Explanation: https://www.kaggle.com/c/kuzushiji-recognition/discussion/112899
		Implementation: https://www.kaggle.com/kmat2019/centernet-keypoint-detector
8	0.920	Explanation: https://www.kaggle.com/c/kuzushiji-recognition/discussion/113419
		Implementation: https://github.com/t-hanya/kuzushiji-recognition
9	0.910	Explanation: https://www.kaggle.com/c/kuzushiji-recognition/discussion/112807
		Implementation: https://github.com/mv-lab/kuzushiji-recognition
13	0.901	Explanation: https://www.kaggle.com/c/kuzushiji-recognition/discussion/113518
		Implementation: https://github.com/jday96314/Kuzushiji
15	0.900	Explanation: https://www.kaggle.com/c/kuzushiji-recognition/discussion/114120
		Implementation: https://github.com/statsu1990/kuzushiji-recognition

Kuzushiji dataset described in Sect. 3.1, 28 books released before the competition were used as training data, and 15 books released after the competition were used as the test data[11]. The F value, which is the harmonic mean of the precision (the percentage of correct responses among the characters output by the system) and the recall (the percentage of correct responses among the characters in the test data), was used for evaluation. For approximately 3 months, many international researchers worked on this competition and achieved a practical level of accuracy (F value of greater than 0.9). There were two typical methods, namely, a single-stage method that applies detection and recognition simultaneously, and a two-stage method that conducts character detection and recognition in stages. Most of the top teams adopted the two-stage method. The two-stage method applied detectors such as a Faster R-CNN and CenterNet [38] to detect character regions, and models such as ResNet [39] to recognize individual characters. As shown in Table 1, the method descriptions and implementations of the top teams were published. We now describe the methods of the top winning teams.

The Chinese team took first place using a straightforward method with a Cascade R-CNN. Cascade R-CNN can improve the accuracy of object detection by connecting a Faster R-CNN in multiple stages. High-Resolution Net (HRNet) [40] was used as the backbone network of the Cascade R-CNN. HRNet utilizes multi-resolution feature maps and can retain high-resolution feature representations without a loss. The team was able to achieve a high accuracy while maintaining greater simplicity than the methods used by the other teams because the

---

[11] One book was eliminated from the competition.

latest techniques were applied, including a Cascade R-CNN and HRNet, which showed the highest levels of accuracy.

The second place team, from Russia, used a two-stage method of detection and classification. A Faster R-CNN with a ResNet152 backbone was used for detection. ResNet and ResNeXt [41] were used to estimate the type of characters. Various efforts have been made to improve the accuracy of recognition. For example, because books of test data are different from books of training data, pseudo labels have also been used to adapt to the environment of an unknown book (author). Moreover, a new character class, called a detection error character class, was added to eliminate the detection error at the classification stage. Finally, the gradient boosting methods LightGBM [42] and XGBoost [43] were also used to further improve the accuracy.

The third place team, from Japan, adopted a two-stage method of character detection using a Faster R-CNN and character-type classification using EfficientNet [44]. The team employed several types of data augmentation to increase the number of training data, as shown below. First, because color and grayscale images were mixed in the training data, they used a random grayscale, which randomly converts images into monochrome during training. In addition, the training data were augmented using techniques such as combining multiple images by applying mixup [45] and random image cropping and patching (RICAP) [46], and adding some noise to the image by random erasing. Because Furigana[12] is not a recognition target, post-processing such as the creation of a false positive predictor is used for its removal.

The fourth place team, from China, adopted a different method than the other groups; they used a hybrid task cascade (HTC) [47] for character detection followed by a connectionist text proposal network (CTPN) [48] for line-by-line character recognition. One-line images were resized to 32×800, and then fed to a model that recognizes a single line of text. A convolutional recurrent neural network (CRNN) model was used for line recognition and had a structure with 200 outputs. A six-gram language model was trained using the KenLM toolkit [49], and a beam search was applied to decode the CTC output of the model. The positional accuracy of the CTC output was improved using multitask learning [50], which added an attention loss. For the data augmentation methods, contrast limited adaptive histogram equalization, random brightness, random contrast, random scale, and random distortion were used. A dropout and cutout were applied as the regularization methods. Although many other teams reported that language models are ineffective, this team reported a slight increase in accuracy.

The fifth place team, from Germany, reported that the one-stage method using CenterNet is consistently more accurate, unlike the two-stage method of the other top teams. Although, it is common for object detection tasks to deal with approximately 80 classes of objects, such as the MS COCO dataset, this team showed that detection can be achieved without problems even if the number of classes is large. They made several modifications to CenterNet, such as

---

[12] Furigana is made up of phonetic symbols occasionally written next to difficult or rare Kanji to show their pronunciation.

creating it from scratch, avoiding the use of an HourglassNet, and using the ResNet50 and ResNet101 structures with a feature pyramid network. They also reported that the use of high-resolution images such as 1536×1536 did not show any improvement.

The seventh place team, from Japan, adopted a two-stage method of character region detection using CenterNet followed by ResNet-based character recognition. For the data augmentation, flipping, cropping, brightness, and contrast were used to create the detector, and cropping, brightness, contrast, and a pseudo-label were used to create a classifier. The authors attempted to build their own model instead of using a predefined approach. In general, although predefined models have been designed to provide local features at a high resolution and a wide field of view at a low resolution, it was not necessary to provide a wide field of view at a significantly low resolution for the Kuzushiji detection task. The team reported that the success of this model was due to the fact that they built their own task-specific model with a high degree of freedom.

The eighth place team, also from Japan, adopted a two-stage method of character detection using CenterNet (ResNet18, UNet) and character classification using MobileNetV3 [51]. The character detection was made by maintaining the aspect ratio to prevent a separation of characters, and bounding box voting [52] was used to reduce the number of undetected characters. Because the appearance of the characters varies significantly depending on the book applied, the team augmented the data, such as through a grid distortion, elastic transform, and random erasing, to increase the visual variation.

The nineth place team adopted a simple two-stage method using CenterNet with HourglassNet as the backbone for detection and ResNet18 for classification. Because the detection accuracy was insufficient, multiple results were combined. For character classification, the team treated characters with less than 5 data as pseudo-labels, NaN, because 276 of the characters were not in the training data.

The 13th place team used a Faster R-CNN to detect and classify the character regions, but did not share the network for the detection and classification. A wide ResNet-34 was used as the backbone of the network for both character detection and character recognition. The team tried to apply deeper networks, such as ResNet-50 and ResNet-101, but reported that the wider and shallower networks achieve a better accuracy. They also reported that the use of color images slightly improves the accuracy of detection but worsens the accuracy of the character recognition. Although they attempted to use a language model to correct incorrect labels, it was ineffective.

The 15th place team, from Japan, used a two-stage method of detection and classification. First, they applied a grayscale conversion, Gaussian filter, gamma correction, and Ben's pre-processing of the images. A two-stage CenterNet with HourglassNet as a backbone was applied for character detection. In the first stage of CenterNet, the bounding box was estimated, and the outside of the outermost bounding box was removed. In the second stage of CenterNet, the bounding box was estimated again, and the results of the first and second stages were combined. Random erasing, horizontal movement, and a brightness adjustment were used to augment the data when creating the detection model. For character classification, the results of three types of ResNet-based models also trained using pseudo labels were combined and output. Horizontal movement, rotation, zoom, and random erasing were used for data augmentation when creating the character classification model.

Summarizing the methods of the top teams explained here, we can see that it is important to make use of recently proposed detection and classification models. However, it is impossible to determine whether a one-stage or two-stage method achieves better results. For the detection method, models such as YOLO [53], which are frequently used in object detection, did not perform well, whereas Faster R-CNN and CenterNet were successful. As the reason for this, there is almost no overlap of characters in the image, which differs from conventional object detection. Some teams reported an improved accuracy using the latest models with strong backbones, whereas others reported that their own methods were more successful.

5   Activities Related to Kuzushiji Recognition

The "Japanese Culture and AI Symposium 2019"[13] was held in November 2019. This symposium introduced leading research being conducted on Kuzushiji globally, and the participants discussed the past and present studies with an aim toward future research using AI for the reading and understanding of Kuzushiji.

In the "Cloud Honkoku (Cloud Transcription)" project, a system that allows correcting the transcriptions of other participants was implemented. By cooperating with the Kuzushiji learning application using KuLA and AI technology, the methods developed by the participants were simplified and made more efficient. The transcribed results can also be used as training data.

CODH provides several online services such as the KuroNet Kuzushiji character recognition service, KogumaNet Kuzushiji character recognition service, and International Image Interoperability Framework (IIIF)[14] compatible Kuzushiji character recognition viewer. The KuroNet Kuzushiji recognition service[15] provides a multi-character Kuzushiji OCR function for IIIF-compliant images. With this service, we do not need to upload images to the server, but can test our own images. The IIIF-compatible character recognition viewer provides a single-character OCR function for IIIF-compliant images. As an advantage of using this viewer, it can be applied immediately while viewing an image, allowing not only the top candidate but also other candidates to be viewed.

In the future, it is expected that Kuzushiji transcription will be further enabled by individuals in various fields, such as those involved in machine learning, the humanities, and the actual application of this historical script.

---

[13] http://codh.rois.ac.jp/symposium/japanese-culture-ai-2019/.

[14] A set of technology standards intended to make it easier for researchers, students, and the public at large to view, manipulate, compare, and annotate digital images on the web. https://iiif.io/.

[15] http://codh.rois.ac.jp/kuronet/.

6   Future Studies on Kuzushiji Recognition

In Japan, historical materials have been preserved for more than a thousand years; pre-modern books and historical documents and records have been estimated to number approximately three million and one billion, respectively. However, most historical materials have not been transcribed. Currently, because the Kuzushiji database provided by CODH is mainly limited to documents after the Edo period, it is difficult to automatically transcribe books written prior to this period. To address this issue, it will be necessary to combine multiple books of various periods owned by multiple institutions and rebuild a large-scale Kuzushiji database. Looking back further into history, the rules for Kuzushiji increase, and thus it is expected that there will be many character types and character forms that cannot be found in the database. Therefore, we need a framework for handling unknown character types and character forms that do not exist in the training data. In addition, as one of the problems in character classification, the number of data for each character class is imbalanced, and it is impossible to accurately recognize characters in a class with an extremely small number of data.

In addition, the quality of the images differs significantly from one book to the next, and the writing styles are completely different depending on the author, which also makes character recognition difficult to achieve. To this end, it is important to increase the number and variation of training data, to incorporate techniques such as domain adaptation, and improve the database itself.

There is room for further studies on not only individual character-by-character recognition, but also word/phrase/sentence-level recognition based on the surrounding characters and context. In the Kaggle competition, although many teams added contextual information, such as the use of language models, the accuracy did not significantly improve because there are problems specific to Kuzushiji that differ from those of modern languages. Therefore, we believe it will be necessary to not only improve machine learning techniques such as deep learning, but also learn rules based on specialized knowledge regarding Kuzushiji.

Based on the current state of transcription, it is important to design an interface that not only allows a complete and automatic recognition of characters, but also allows the user to work effortlessly. It is desirable to have various functions, such as a visualization of characters with uncertain estimation results, and output alternative candidate characters.

7   Conclusion

In this paper, we introduced recent techniques and problems in Kuzushiji recognition using deep learning. The introduction of deep learning has dramatically improved the detection and recognition rate of Kuzushiji. In particular, the inclusion of Kuzushiji recognition in the PRMU algorithm contest and Kaggle competition has attracted the attention of numerous researchers, who have contributed to significant improvements in accuracy. However, there are still many old manuscripts that need to be transcribed, and there are still many issues to be addressed. To solve these problems, in addition to improving algorithms such as machine learning, it is necessary to further promote the development of a Kuzushiji database and cooperation among individuals in different fields.

References

1. Yamada, S., et al.: Historical character recognition (HCR) project report (2). IPSJ SIG Comput. Hum. (CH) **50**(2), 9–16 (2001). (in Japanese)
2. Yamada, S., Waizumi, Y., Kato, N., Shibayama, M.: Development of a digital dictionary of historical characters with search function of similar characters. IPSJ SIG Comput. Hum. (CH) **54**(7), 43–50 (2002). (in Japanese)
3. Onuma, M., Zhu, B., Yamada, S., Shibayama, M., Nakagawa, M.: Development of cursive character pattern recognition for accessing a digital dictionary to support decoding of historical documents. IEICE Technical Report, vol. 106, no. 606, PRMU2006-270, pp. 91–96 (2007). (in Japanese)
4. Horiuchi, T., Kato, S.: A study on Japanese historical character recognition using modular neural networks. Int. J. Innov. Comput. Inf. Control **7**(8), 5003–5014 (2011)
5. Kato, S., Asano, R.: A study on historical character recognition by using SOM template. In: Proceedings of 30th Fuzzy System Symposium, pp. 242–245 (2014). (in Japanese)
6. Hayasaka, T., Ohno, W., Kato, Y.: Recognition of obsolete script in pre-modern Japanese texts by Neocognitron. J. Toyota Coll. Technol. **48**, 5–12 (2015). (in Japanese)
7. Hayasaka, T., Ohno, W., Kato, Y., Yamamoto, K.: Recognition of hentaigana by deep learning and trial production of WWW application. In: Proceedings of IPSJ Symposium of Humanities and Computer Symposium, pp. 7–12 (2016). (in Japanese)
8. Ueda, K., Sonogashira, M., Iiyama, M.: Old Japanese character recognition by convolutional neural net and character aspect ratio. ELCAS J. **3**, 88–90 (2018). (in Japanese)
9. Kojima, T., Ueki, K.: Utilization and analysis of deep learning for Kuzushiji translation. J. Japan Soc. Precis. Eng. **85**(12), 1081–1086 (2019). (in Japanese)
10. Yang, Z., Doman, K., Yamada, M., Mekada, Y.: Character recognition of modern Japanese official documents using CNN for imblanced learning data. In: Proceedings of 2019 International Workshop on Advanced Image Technology (IWAIT), no. 74 (2019)
11. Nagai, A.: Recognizing three character string of old Japanese cursive by convolutional neural networks. In: Proceedings of Information Processing Society of Japan (IPSJ) Symposium, pp. 213–218 (2017). (in Japanese)
12. Ueki, K., Kojima, T., Mutou, R., Nezhad, R.S., Hagiwara, Y.: Recognition of Japanese connected cursive characters using multiple softmax outputs. In: Proceedings of International Conference on Multimedia Information Processing and Retrieval (2020)
13. Hu, X., Inamoto, M., Konagaya, A.: Recognition of Kuzushi-ji with deep learning method: a case study of Kiritsubo chapter in the tale of Genji. In: The 33rd Annual Conference of the Japanese Society for Artificial Intelligence (2019)

14. Kitamoto, A., Clanuwat, T., Miyazaki, T., Yayamoto, K.: Analysis of character data: potential and impact of Kuzushiji recognition by machine learning. J. Inst. Electron. Inf. Commun. Eng. **102**(6), 563–568 (2019). (in Japanese)
15. Kitamoto, A., Clanuwat, T., Lamb, A., Bober-Irizar, M.: Progress and results of kaggle machine learning competition for Kuzushiji recognition. In: Proceedings of the Computers and the Humanities Symposium, pp. 223–230 (2019). (in Japanese)
16. Kitamoto, A., Clanuwat, T., Bober-Irizar, M.: Kaggle Kuzushiji recognition competition - challenges of hosting a world-wide competition in the digital humanities. J. Japanese Soc. Artif. Intell. **35**(3), 366–376 (2020). (in Japanese)
17. Ren, S., He, K., Girshick, R., Sun, J.: Faster R-CNN: Towards Real-Time Object Detection with Region Proposal Networks. arXiv:1506.01497 (2015)
18. Cai, Z., Vasconcelos, N.: Cascade R-CNN: High Quality Object Detection and Instance Segmentation. arXiv:1906.09756 (2019)
19. Clanuwat, T., Lamb, A., Kitamoto, A.: KuroNet: pre-modern Japanese Kuzushiji character recognition with deep learning. In: Proceedings of International Conference on Document Analysis and Recognition (ICDAR2019) (2019)
20. Lamb, A., Clanuwat, T., Kitamoto, A.: KuroNet: regularized residual U-nets for end-to-end Kuzushiji character recognition. In: Proceedings of SN Computer Science (2020)
21. Le, A.D., Clanuwat, T., Kitamoto, A.: A human-inspired recognition system for premodern Japanese historical documents. arXiv:1905.05377 (2019)
22. Le, A.D.: Automated Transcription for Pre-Modern Japanese Kuzushiji Documents by Random Lines Erasure and Curriculum Learning. arXiv:2005.02669 (2020)
23. Le, A.D.: Detecting Kuzushiji characters from historical documents by two-dimensional context box proposal network. Future Data Secur. Eng. 731–738
24. Graves, A., Schmidhuber, J.: Framewise phoneme classification with bidirectional LSTM and other neural network architectures. Neural Netw. **18**(5–6), 602–610 (2005)
25. Yamamoto, S., Tomejiro, O.: Labor saving for reprinting Japanese rare classical books. J. Inf. Process. Manag. **58**(11), 819–827 (2016). (in Japanese)
26. Ueki, K., Kojima, T.: Feasibility study of deep learning based Japanese cursive character recognition. IIEEJ Trans. Image Electron. Vis. Comput. **8**(1), 10–16 (2020)
27. Ueki, K., Kojima, T.: Japanese cursive character recognition for efficient transcription. In: Proceedings of the International Conference on Pattern Recognition Applications and Methods (2020)
28. Takeuchi, M.: Development of embedded system for recognizing Kuzushiji by deep learning. In: Proceedings of the 33rd Annual Conference of the Japanese Society for Artificial Intelligence (2019). (in Japanese)
29. Sando, K., Suzuki, T., Aiba, A.: A constraint solving web service for recognizing historical Japanese KANA texts. In: Proceedings of the 10th International Conference on Agents and Artificial Intelligence (ICAART) (2018)
30. Yamazaki, A., Suzuki, T., Sando, K., Aiba, A.: A handwritten Japanese historical kana reprint support system. In: Proceedings of the 18th ACM Symposium on Document Engineering (2018)
31. Panichkriangkrai, C., Li, L., Kaneko, T., Akama, R., Hachimura, K.: Character segmentation and transcription system for historical Japanese books with a self-proliferating character image database. Int. J. Doc. Anal. Recogn. (IJDAR) **20**, 241–257 (2017)
32. Clanuwat, T., Bober-Irizar, M., Kitamoto, A., Lamb, A., Yamamoto, K., Ha, D.: Deep learning for classical Japanese literature. arXiv:1812.01718 (2018)

33. Nguyen, H.T., Ly, N.T., Nguyen, K.C., Nguyen, C.T., Nakagawa, M.: Attempts to recognize anomalously deformed Kana in Japanese historical documents. In: Proceedings of the International Workshop on Historical Document Imaging and Processing (HIP 2017) (2017)

34. Graves, A., Fernandez, S., Gomez, F., Schmidhuber, J.: Connectionist temporal classification: labelling unsegmented sequence data with recurrent neural networks. In: Proceedings of the International Conference on Machine Learning, pp. 369–376 (2006)

35. Cho, K., et al.: Learning phrase representations using RNN encoder-decoder for statistical machine translation. In: Proceedings of the Conference on Empirical Methods in Natural Language Processing (EMNLP), pp. 1724–1734 (2014)

36. Zhong, Z., Zheng, L., Kang, G., Li, S., Yang, Y.: Random Erasing Data Augmentation. arXiv:1708.04896 (2017)

37. Selvaraju, R.R., Cogswell, M., Das, A., Vedantam, R., Parikh, D., Batra, D.: Grad-CAM: Visual Explanations from Deep Networks via Gradientbased Localization. arXiv:1610.02391 (2016)

38. Duan, K., Bai, S., Xie, L., Qi, H., Huang, Q., Tian, Q.: CenterNet: Keypoint Triplets for Object Detection. arXiv:1904.08189 (2019)

39. He, K., Zhang, X., Ren, S., Sun, J.: Deep Residual Learning for Image Recognition. arXiv:1512.03385 (2015)

40. Wang, J., et al.: Deep high-resolution representation learning for visual recognition. IEEE Trans. Pattern Anal. Mach. Intell. (2020)

41. Xie, S., Girshick, R., Dollár, P., Tu, Z., He, K.: Aggregated residual transformation for deep neural networks. In: Proceedings of IEEE Conference on Computer Vision and Pattern Recognition (CVPR) (2017)

42. Ke, G., et al.: LightGBM: a highly efficient gradient boosting decision tree. Adv. Neural Inf. Process. Syst. (NIPS) **30**, 3148–3156 (2017)

43. Chen, T., Guestrin, C.: XGBoost: A Scalable Tree Boosting System. arXiv:1603.02754 (2016)

44. Tan, M., Le, Q.V.: EfficientNet: Rethinking Model Scaling for Convolutional Neural Networks. arxiv:1905.11946 (2019)

45. Zhang, H., Cisse, M., Dauphin, Y.N., Lopez-Paz, D.: mixup: Beyond Empirical Risk Minimization. arXiv:1710.09412 (2017)

46. Takahashi, R., Matsubara, T., Uehara, K.: Data Augmentation using Random Image Cropping and Patching for Deep CNNs. arXiv:1811.09030 (2018)

47. Chen, K., et al.: Hybrid task cascade for instance segmentation. In: Proceedings of IEEE Conference on Computer Vision and Pattern Recognition (CVPR), pp. 4974–4983 (2019)

48. Tian, Z., Huang, W., He, T., He, P., Qiao, Y.: Detecting Text in Natural Image with Connectionist Text Proposal Network. arXiv:1609.03605 (2016)

49. Heafield, K.: KenLM: faster and smaller language model queries. In: Proceedings of the Sixth Workshop on Statistical Machine Translation, pp. 187–197 (2011)

50. Kim, S., Hori, T., Watanabe, S.: Joint CTC-attention based end-to-end speech recognition using multi-task learning. In: Proceedings of the IEEE International Conference on Acoustics, Speech and Signal Processing (ICASSP) (2017)

51. Howard, A., et al.: Searching for MobileNetV3. arXiv:1905.02244 (2019)

52. Gidaris, S., Komodakis, N.: Object detection via a multi-region & semantic segmentation-aware CNN model. arXiv:1505.01749 (2015)

53. Redmon, J., Divvala, S., Girshick, R., Farhadi, A.: You Only Look Once: Unified, Real-Time Object Detection. arXiv:1506.02640 (2015)

Stylistic Classification of Historical Violins: A Deep Learning Approach

Piercarlo Dondi[1,2(✉)] ⓘ, Luca Lombardi[1] ⓘ, Marco Malagodi[2,3] ⓘ,
and Maurizio Licchelli[2,4] ⓘ

[1] Department of Electrical, Computer and Biomedical Engineering,
University of Pavia, Via Ferrata 5, 27100 Pavia, Italy
{piercarlo.dondi,luca.lombardi}@unipv.it
[2] CISRiC - Arvedi Laboratory of Non-invasive Diagnostics, University of Pavia,
Via Bell'Aspa 3, 26100 Cremona, Italy
[3] Department of Musicology and Cultural Heritage, University of Pavia,
Corso Garibaldi 178, 26100 Cremona, Italy
marco.malagodi@unipv.it
[4] Department of Chemistry, University of Pavia, via Taramelli 12, 27100 Pavia, Italy
maurizio.licchelli@unipv.it

Abstract. Stylistic study of artworks is a well-known problem in the
Cultural Heritage field. Traditional artworks, such as statues and paintings, have been extensively studied by art experts, producing standard
methodologies to analyze and recognize the style of an artist. In this context, the case of historical violins is peculiar. Even if the main stylistic
features of a violin are known, only few experts are capable to attribute a
violin to its maker with a high degree of certainty. This paper presents a
study about the use of deep learning to discriminate a violin style. Firstly,
we collected images of 17th–18th century violins held, or in temporary
loan, at "Museo del Violino" of Cremona (Italy) to be used as reference dataset. Then, we tested the performances of three state-of-the-art
CNNs (VGG16, ResNet50 and InceptionV3) on a binary classification
(Stradivari vs. NotStradivari). The best performing model was able to
achieve 77.27% accuracy and 0.72 F1 score. A promising result, keeping
in mind the limited amount of data and the complexity of the task, even
for human experts. Finally, we compared the regions of interest identified
by the network with the regions of interest identified in a previous eye
tracking study conducted on expert luthiers, to highlight similarity and
differences between the two behaviors.

Keywords: Deep learning · CNN · Transfer learning · Data
augmentation · Cultural Heritage · Historical violins

1 Introduction

Stylistic study of artworks is a well-known problem in the Cultural Heritage field.
Statues and paintings have been extensively studied by art experts, producing

This work was partially granted by "Fondazione Arvedi-Buschini" of Cremona, Italy.

A. Del Bimbo et al. (Eds.): ICPR 2020 Workshops, LNCS 12667, pp. 112–125, 2021.
https://doi.org/10.1007/978-3-030-68787-8_8

standard methodologies to analyze and recognize the style of an artist. In this context, the case of historical violins is peculiar. Until few decades ago, they were not considered artworks to be study and preserved in museums, but only exceptional instruments to be played in concerts and exhibitions. Therefore, the number of studies dedicated to historical violins is still relatively limited, especially when compared to those dedicated to other more traditional works of art.

Even if the main stylistic features of a violin are known, only few experts are able to recognize with certainty the maker of a historical violin simply observing it. To try to understand what and where are the most meaningful areas of a violins, in one of our previous works we conducted an eye-tracking study on 34 luthiers, who were asked to attribute to their makers a series of violins looking at a sequence of images [5]. The obtained results showed that experts tend to focus their attention always on a small set of specific areas of the violins, even when they are not able to correctly attribute the instrument. With the present work we want to verify if it is possible to train a convolutional neural network (CNN) to perform a stylistic recognition of a violin, and if the most meaningful areas chosen by the network are similar to those mainly used by the luthiers.

Of course, to properly train a deep learning classifier, a large number of samples for each class are needed. Unfortunately, in our case, the availability of data is limited. Historical violins are objects very light and easy to carry. During centuries, they have been moved and played all around the world, thus, many of them are now lost. For very prolific authors, like Antonio Stradivari (who he is thought to have made more than 900 violins!), many instruments survived until today, but it is the exception, not the rule. For other important violin makers, such as Amati, Bergonzi or Ruggeri, only few instruments remain. Moreover, even when the instruments exist, the access to them can be limited or even not possible. In fact, many historical violins are not held in museums, but are part of private collections, and the owners do not always allow to perform analyses or to use their data for scientific studies.

In the last years, we had the possibility to analyze several instruments held or in temporary loan at the "Museo del Violino" of Cremona (Italy), performing various kind of non-invasive examinations such as UVIFL photography, XRF and FTIR spectroscopy, tomography and magnetic resonance, with the goal to monitor their state of conservation and to characterize the used materials and varnishes [6,11,16]. During the analytical campaign, we have also collected a complete photographic documentation of each of the studied instrument. For this work, among the data that can be publicly shared, we have selected a collection of images of violins made by some of the most famous makers of 17th–18th century, including Stradivari, Amati and Guarneri. Since for most of the luthiers we have only one or two samples, we focused our study on a binary classification (Stradivari vs. NotStradivari).

It is important to stress that our final goal is not to perform an expertise, that clearly require many more examinations, such as dentrocronology or complex physico-chemical analyses; but instead we want to teach a computer to recognize the artistic style of violins as well as it was done for paintings.

The main contributions of this paper are three: (i) the creation of a labeled dataset containing images of 17th—18th century violins; (ii) a study of the potentiality of deep learning to discriminate a violin maker style, testing the performances of various state-of-the art CNNs as feature extractors; (iii) a comparison between the computer and the luthiers' behaviour, confronting the regions of interest chosen by the best performing network with the global heatmaps generated by the luhtiers' gaze.

The paper is structured as follow: Sect. 2 provides an overview of previous works related to artwork style recognition and analysis; Sect. 3 illustrates the dataset and the pre-processing operations; Sect. 4 describes our architecture and the chosen hyper-parameters; Sect. 5 presents and discusses the experimental results; finally, Sect. 6 draws the conclusions and proposes the possible next steps.

2   Related Works

Automatic stylistic analysis of artworks is a challenging task widely studied by image processing and machine learning researchers. Historically, most of the works in this field focus on paintings, where both traditional and deep learning approaches have been proposed.

Notable examples of classic image processing solutions are: the identification of different styles in Chinese ink paintings using 2D multi-resolution hidden Markov models [13]; the recognition of the style of some famous painters (Cezanne, Monet, Pissarro, Seurat, Sisley, and Van Gogh) using a combination of supervised and unsupervised machine learning algorithms [14]; the identification of seven different fine-art styles (Renaissance, Baroque, Impressionism, Cubism, Abstract, Expressionism, and Pop art) using discriminative and generative Bag-of-Words algorithms [1]; the application of multiple types of Fisher vector features to deal with artist classification, style classification, artist influence and style influence in paintings [17]; and a stochastic analysis conducted to compare the works of Leonardo da Vinci and Picasso [19].

Of course, in recent years, the rapid explosion of deep learning paved the way to new remarkable results. Famous works include the style transfer neural network created by Gatys et al. [9] able to combine the content of a photo with the style of an artwork, and "The Next Rembrandt" project, where the Microsoft researchers were able to train a deep learning algorithm to create a "new" Rembrandt painting, starting from images and 3D scans of the works of the famous Dutch painter [15].

Tan et al. presented one of the first studies about the use of a CNN for large-scale style, genre, and artist classification of paintings, proving the potentiality of transfer learning in this field [24]. While Elgammal et al. presented an analysis of the performances of three widely known CNNs (AlexNet, VGGNet and ResNet) when classifying twenty different painting styles [8]. Cetinic et al.

tested different CNN fine-tuning strategies for five different classification tasks, namely the recognition of artist, genre, style, timeframe and nationality [2]; then, they fine-tuned CNN models pre-trained for style classification to predict values of Wölfflin's features, five key style visual principles [3]. Other interesting approaches for fine-arts classifications include PigeoNET, a variation of AlexNet, used for recognize artists by their artworks [25], and a two-stage deep learning method, where in the first stage a CNN classifies separately five patches of the image, and, in the second one, the outputs of the CNN are fused and used as input for a shallow network that completes the classification [18].

General solutions for image style recognition, not specifically designed for artworks but for any kind of pictures, have been proposed, too. Karayev et al. presented one of the first works in this context, proving that a CNN pre-trained on Imagenet can be fine-tuned for style recognition achieving better results than methods that use hand-tuned features [12]. More recently, Sun et al. adopted an interesting approach for the same task, designing a two pathways CNN architecture, where one focuses on texture features and the other on objects features [22].

However, despite the great number of studies on art style analysis, to the best of the authors knowledge, no other works have been previously done about the application of deep learning methods for the stylistic recognition of violins.

3   Dataset

The goal of this study is to check the capability of a CNN to discriminate a violin maker style. Since stylistic differences can be subtle even for experts, we wanted to limit, as much as possible, any bias due to different ambient conditions, cameras, or post-production retouches. Thus, we considered only images rigorously acquired under the same ambient conditions and in the same photographic set. More precisely, we used a Nikon D4 camera 50 mm lens, following a standard acquisition protocol for this kind of instruments [7]. For each violin we have taken pictures of the four main views (front, back, left, and right side) and details of the body and of the head (see a sample set in Fig. 1). These are the most common views adopted for historical violins documentation (e.g., in museum catalogues and dedicated books), used as reference by experts. All the images have been rescaled at 150×224 pixels. We plan a future open access release of the dataset. Since the distribution of high-resolution images of the instruments of the museum is strictly forbidden, we used for our experiments only low-resolution ones.

The dataset includes images of nineteen historical violins of 17th–18th century, eight made by Antonio Stradivari, and eleven made by famous coeval luthiers. Stradivari had a very long life (over 90 years), and, of course, his style changes during time. The chosen selection is small, but representative, since it comprehends samples of early, middle, and late works. Regarding the other instruments, they are works of some of the most important makers of the period, including Girolamo and Nicola Amati, Guarneri del Gesù, Andrea and Giuseppe Guarneri, Carlo Bergonzi and Francesco Ruggeri. Even if there are only few violins for each maker, overall, this subset is a good representation of the various

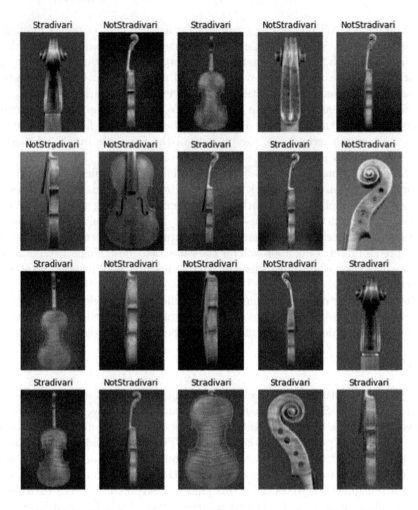

Fig. 1. Some sample images of both classes from the dataset.

luthier schools of the time. Even if available, we have excluded rare violins that show unique features, such as inlays or painted decorations, that can be easily identified and can introduce unwanted features. In total there are 96 images for the class "Stradivari" and 124 for the class "NotStradivari", thus, they are quite balanced in size. For each instrument there are twelve images, with the only exception of one "NotStradivari" violin for which only the photos of the body were available.

To properly train the network, we increased the size of the dataset applying a data augmentation step. We considered random variations in contrast and brightness, plus horizontal and vertical flips. More precisely, for contrast and brightness, we used the formula $I_{out} = \alpha I_{in} + \beta$, varying α between $[0.5, 1.5]$ and β between $[-50, 50]$.

4   Network Architecture

Early studies proved that transfer learning, starting from a CNN pre-trained on ImageNet [4], is particularly effective for the task of art style recognition [12,24]. For this study, we adopted a similar approach. We used a pre-trained CNN for feature extraction, followed by a fully connected binary classifier. Our architecture is summarized in Fig. 2: the fully connected (FC) layer has 1024 units, ReLu as activation function and a L2 kernel regularization; dropout is set at 0.5; the prediction layer has 1 unit and uses a Sigmoid as activation function (more commonly adopted for binary classification respect to Softmax). We set the batch size to 20, and the Binary Cross Entropy as loss function. We tested three different optimizers, Adam, Statistic Gradient Descent (SGD) and Root Mean Square Propagation (RMSprop) at three different learning rates $(10^{-2}; 10^{-3}; 10^{-4})$.

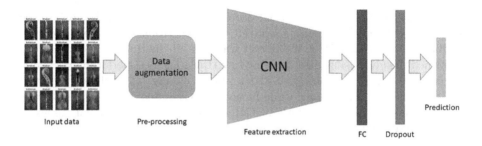

Fig. 2. High level scheme of the adopted network.

For feature extraction, we considered three of the most used CNNs: VGG16 [21], ResNet50 [10] and InceptionV3 [23]. For InceptionV3, we chose as output layer the last 7×7 convolution, since preliminary experiments showed that the features extracted by the standard 3×3 last layer were too small for our scenario. The network was trained in two steps: firstly, we trained only the fully connected layers for 10 epochs, maintaining freezed all the convolutional layers; then, we performed a fine-tuning for other 30 epochs unfreezing only the last convolutional layer. We tested fine-tuning unfreezing more layers, but the results were very unstable, probably due to the limited number of samples in the dataset.

5   Experimental Results

Firstly, we tested the various network configurations. The dataset was randomly split with the following ratio: 60% train, 20% validation and 20% test. Each split has the same ratio between the two classes and at least two samples for each of the possible view. The split was done before data augmentation, that was applied only to training and validation set (obtaining 1584 and 528 images respectively). We classified the single views separately, and not multiple views of the same violin together. This means that different images of the same instrument can appear in training, validation, and test split. This can be seen as a violation of the independence between training and test, but, in our scenario, completely separate violin images can produce involuntary biases. The style of a maker can change during time, thus, ideally, multiple samples for each period would be needed to obtain a proper characterization, a condition difficult to satisfy in this scenario. For example, completely removing a violin from the training set of the Stradivari class can lead to an overfit towards features common only to the remaining ones. Fortunately, as can be seen in Fig. 1, each view is very different from the others, thus, they can be considered as independent images, with the only exception of detail of the same view (e.g., the entire back side of the instrument and the backplate) that are always maintained together in the same split. Of course, this approximation can be overcome in the future, when more samples for author will be available, if not for all the makers, at least for Stradivari, considering his vast production.

Table 1 shows the results achieved on test set by the various configurations described in Sect. 4. Those reported are the average performances in term of accuracy, recall, precision, and F1 score after five repetitions, each time randomly shuffling the dataset splits in a different way. For all the three networks, Adam performed the best, using a low learning rate (LR). The best performing network was VGG16 (77.27% accuracy, 0.72 F1 score), closely followed by ResNet50 (75% accuracy, 0.70 F1 score), while InceptionV3 was unable to go over 68.18% accuracy and 0.68 F1 score. Both VGG16 and ResNet50 show similar values of precision and recall, with the former higher than the latter, while for InceptionV3 it is the opposite.

With this first experiment, we identified the most promising configurations using the entire dataset. As second step, we considered separately the two main parts of the violin, the body, and the head. This is a reasonable alternative way to train a network for a violin attribution, since these two regions of the instrument are very different and present specific characteristics. For this test, we split the dataset only in train and validation, since there are not enough images, even after data augmentation, for also having a meaningful test split. We tested each of the three networks using their best configurations (see Table 1). The experiment was repeated five times, each time randomly splitting the dataset in a different way, but always maintaining the same ratio between the train and validation split (70%–30%).

Figure 3 shows the learning curve for accuracy and loss during one sample execution. Of course, with a so small dataset, the training quickly overfits and reaches a perfect accuracy, while the validation accuracy is far more unstable. However, the loss curves show a good fit, both train and validation curve slow down to a point of stability.

Tables 2 and 3 show the obtained average results in term of accuracy, recall, precision, and F1 score, for the body and the head, respectively. The results for the body are lower than those obtained using the entire dataset, but the networks rating remains the same, with VGG16 first, slightly better than Resnet50, and InceptionV3 last. On the contrary, on the head, all the networks performed better

Table 1. First experiment: performance of the various networks on test set. The best result for each network is highlighted in green.

Model	Optimizer	LR	Accuracy	Recall	Precision	F1
VGG16	Adam	10^{-2}	0.5682	0.2105	0.5000	0.2963
VGG16	Adam	10^{-3}	0.7273	0.4738	0.8182	0.6001
VGG16	Adam	10^{-4}	0.7727	0.6842	0.7647	0.7222
VGG16	RMSprop	10^{-2}	0.6136	0.6316	0.5455	0.5854
VGG16	RMSprop	10^{-3}	0.7273	0.6316	0.7059	0.6667
VGG16	RMSprop	10^{-4}	0.6818	0.6316	0.6471	0.6393
VGG16	SGD	10^{-2}	0.5682	0.5681	0.5681	0.5681
VGG16	SGD	10^{-3}	0.7045	0.5789	0.6875	0.6285
VGG16	SGD	10^{-4}	0.6591	0.5263	0.6250	0.5714
ResNet50	Adam	10^{-2}	0.5682	0.6842	0.5000	0.5778
ResNet50	Adam	10^{-3}	0.7045	0.7895	0.6250	0.6842
ResNet50	Adam	10^{-4}	0.7500	0.6842	0.7222	0.7027
ResNet50	RMSprop	10^{-2}	0.6816	0.8421	0.5926	0.6557
ResNet50	RMSprop	10^{-3}	0.7045	0.8421	0.6154	0.7111
ResNet50	RMSprop	10^{-4}	0.7273	0.6842	0.6842	0.6842
ResNet50	SGD	10^{-2}	0.5682	0.5682	0.5682	0.5682
ResNet50	SGD	10^{-3}	0.7045	0.4737	0.7500	0.5807
ResNet50	SGD	10^{-4}	0.7500	0.5263	0.8333	0.6451
InceptionV3	Adam	10^{-2}	0.6136	0.6316	0.5455	0.5854
InceptionV3	Adam	10^{-3}	0.6818	0.7895	0.6000	0.6818
InceptionV3	Adam	10^{-4}	0.5682	0.6842	0.5000	0.5778
InceptionV3	RMSprop	10^{-2}	0.5909	0.5789	0.5238	0.5500
InceptionV3	RMSprop	10^{-3}	0.6136	0.7895	0.5357	0.6383
InceptionV3	RMSprop	10^{-4}	0.6591	0.3158	0.7500	0.4445
InceptionV3	SGD	10^{-2}	0.5909	0.2632	0.5556	0.3572
InceptionV3	SGD	10^{-3}	0.5227	0.7368	0.4667	0.5714
InceptionV3	SGD	10^{-4}	0.4545	0.6842	0.4194	0.5200

than in the first experiment, and also InceptionV3 was able to reach the same outcomes of VGG16 and ResNet50. This discrepancy can be explained by the fact that the body of the violin has many more details than the head, thus, it is more difficult to analyze.

Overall, considering all the results, VGG16 was the best performing network, closely followed by ResNet50, while InceptionV3 proved to be useful only for the head. The obtained performances are good considering the limited amount of sample data and the complexity of the problem, even for experienced humans. In fact, in our previous study [5], when 34 luthiers were asked to perform a similar task, namely, to attribute to their author five violins observing images

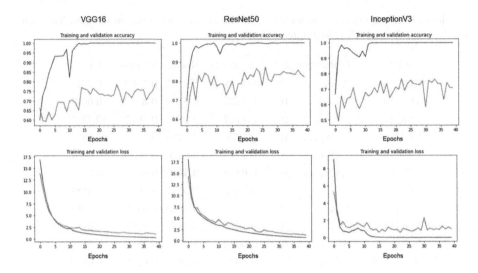

Fig. 3. Second experiment: learning curves of accuracy and loss for the three networks (training in blue and validation in orange). (Color figure online)

Table 2. Second experiment: average performance for the three best models on validation set using only images of the body.

Model	Accuracy	Recall	Precision	F1 score
VGG16	0.7585	0.6260	0.7625	0.6859
ResNet50	0.7401	0.6466	0.7310	0.6825
InceptionV3	0.6715	0.6467	0.6201	0.6253

of different views, only 14 were able to correctly classify at least four out of five instruments.

As final experiment, we compared the behavior of the best trained model (VGG16) with the gaze behavior of 34 expert luthiers, while analyzing the same images. As reference, we used six images of Stradivari "Cremonese" 1715 previously used in our eye tracking study [5].

The network was able to correctly attribute each image to Antonio Stradivari. Using the Grad-CAM algorithm [20], we generated the activation maps for each

Table 3. Second experiment: average performance for the three best models on validation set using only images of the head.

Model	Accuracy	Recall	Precision	F1 score
VGG16	0.7646	0.7383	0.7597	0.7392
ResNet50	0.7704	0.7036	0.7743	0.7341
InceptionV3	0.7667	0.6667	0.7951	0.7233

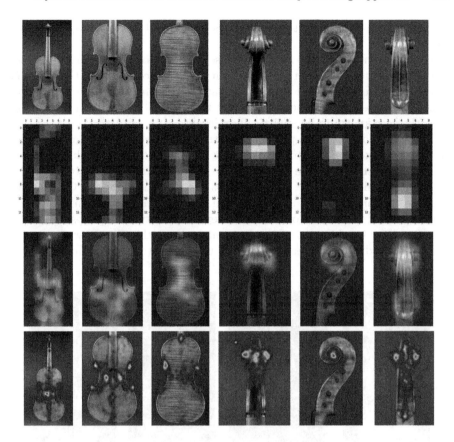

Fig. 4. Heatmaps comparison on six different views of Stradivari "Cremonese" (1715). From left to right: front side, sound table, back plate, front side of the head, right side of the head, back of the head. From top to bottom: first row, original images; second row, Grad-CAM [20] class activation maps of VGG16; third row, Grad-CAM class activation maps overlapped to the correspondent images; fourth row, global heatmaps of luthiers' gaze [5].

image to highlight the most meaningful areas for the network. Figure 4 shows the comparison between the heatmaps produced by Grad-CAM and the global heatmaps obtained by the analysis of luthiers' gaze. A global heatmap is built using all the fixations made by all the testers and provides a qualitative graphical representation of the most observed regions of the image. A fixation is a period of time in which the eyes are relatively still, so that the visual system can acquire detailed information about what is being looked at.

On the front image, the network focused on the entire sound table and partially on the top part of the head. These areas are similar to those identified by the luthiers, even if the network consider a larger region, while the luthiers' gaze was more focused. It is interesting to notice that the network learned to completely avoid the fingerboard. This is a correct behavior since the neck of many historical violins was substituted and does not present any meaningful stylistic feature.

On the sound table, the network focused on the bottom part of the f-holes, on the central area between them, and on the lower corners. On the contrary, luthiers' gaze focused more on the top part of the f-holes and on all the four corners. However, it must be noticed that the network chose (even if partially) areas that are known to be stylistically relevant.

The result on the back plate is the strangest of the six, the main regions chosen by the network are totally different from those checked by luthiers.

Finally, the images of the head show the most similar outcomes. In particular, for the front and right side, the heatmaps are quite overlapping. On the back side, the network focused slightly more on the bottom region than on the top, while the luthiers did the opposite. However, these two heatmaps are not so different, since on this part of the instrument the luthiers' gaze was generally well distributed with no area significantly most observed than the others.

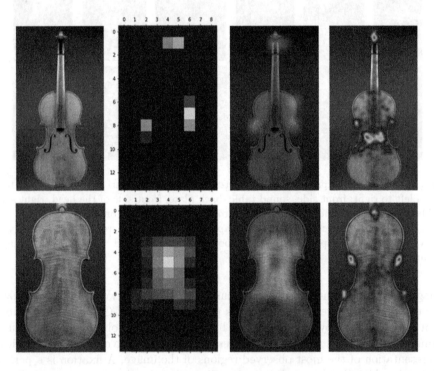

Fig. 5. Heatmaps comparison on front view (first row) and back plate (second row) of Stradivari "Clisbee" (1669). From left to right: original images; Grad-CAM [20] class activation maps of VGG16; Grad-CAM class activation maps overlapped to the correspondent images; global heatmaps of luthiers' gaze [5].

A particular result was obtained on the front view of Stradivari "Clisbee" 1669 (Fig. 5, top row). As in the previous case, the network was able to properly classify the violin, but this time the activation areas are few and focused only on top corners and on the head, a subset of the regions observed by the luthiers. This can be an indication that the network is potentially able to perform a correct classification using only a reduced number of features. This is not so different by an expert behavior. The global heatmap is an overall visualization of the most observed regions by all the luthiers, but some of them focused only of few of the regions highlighted. Also in this case we compared the heatmaps of the back plate (Fig. 5, bottom row). As for the "Cremonese" the regions chosen by the network were mainly focused on center and very different respect to those observed by the luthiers, but even in this case the network achieved a correct classification. This is an indication that on the back plate there are meaningful regions different by those commonly used by experts, but probably equally effective.

6   Conclusions

In this work we have presented a study about the application of deep learning for stylistic recognition of historical violins. The experiments have been conducted on a small dataset containing images of important violins of 17th–18th century, with promising results. In a binary classification (Stradivari vs. NotStradivari), the best performing model was able to achieve 77.27% accuracy (0.72 F1 score) considering images of the entire instrument, 75.85% (0.68 F1 score) considering only the body and 77.04% (0.73 F1 score) considering only the head. This is a good outcome, keeping in mind the limited amount of data available and the complexity of the task.

Finally, a comparison between the heatmaps produced by the trained network and the heatmap generated by the gaze of expert luthiers showed that the network was able to choose regions of interest that are similar to those chosen by human experts in the majority of the cases, and to properly identify areas that are considered stylistically meaningful.

The next step involves the collection of a larger dataset, to better evaluate the performance of the network. We are in contact with other museums and institutions to have the possibility to use the data of other important instruments and makers. Given enough data our goal is to develop an effective multi-author classifier. We also plan to use images acquired under different conditions to test a more challenging scenario.

Acknowledges. We would like to thank "Fondazione Museo del Violino Antonio Stradivari", "Friends of Stradivari" and "Cultural District of Violin Making of Cremona".

References

1. Arora, R.S., Elgammal, A.: Towards automated classification of fine-art painting style: a comparative study. In: Proceedings of the 21st International Conference on Pattern Recognition (ICPR2012), pp. 3541–3544 (2012)

2. Cetinic, E., Lipic, T., Grgic, S.: Fine-tuning convolutional neural networks for fine art classification. Expert Syst. Appl. **114**, 107–118 (2018). https://doi.org/10.1016/j.eswa.2018.07.026

3. Cetinic, E., Lipic, T., Grgic, S.: Learning the principles of art history with convolutional neural networks. Pattern Recogn. Lett. **129**, 56–62 (2020). https://doi.org/10.1016/j.patrec.2019.11.008

4. Deng, J., Dong, W., Socher, R., Li, L.J., Li, K., Fei-Fei, L.: Imagenet: a large-scale hierarchical image database. In: 2009 IEEE Conference on Computer Vision and Pattern Recognition, pp. 248–255 (2009). https://doi.org/10.1109/CVPR.2009.5206848

5. Dondi, P., Lombardi, L., Porta, M., Rovetta, T., Invernizzi, C., Malagodi, M.: What do luthiers look at? An eye tracking study on the identification of meaningful areas in historical violins. Multimedia Tools Appl. **78**(14), 19115–19139 (2019). https://doi.org/10.1007/s11042-019-7276-2

6. Dondi, P., Lombardi, L., Invernizzi, C., Rovetta, T., Malagodi, M., Licchelli, M.: Automatic analysis of UV-induced fluorescence imagery of historical violins. J. Comput. Cult. Herit. **10**(2), 12:1–12:13 (2017). https://doi.org/10.1145/3051472

7. Dondi, P., Lombardi, L., Malagodi, M., Licchelli, M., Rovetta, T., Invernizzi, C.: An interactive tool for speed up the analysis of UV images of stradivari violins. In: Murino, V., Puppo, E., Sona, D., Cristani, M., Sansone, C. (eds.) ICIAP 2015. LNCS, vol. 9281, pp. 103–110. Springer, Cham (2015). https://doi.org/10.1007/978-3-319-23222-5_13

8. Elgammal, A., Mazzone, M., Liu, B., Kim, D., Elhoseiny, M.: The shape of art history in the eyes of the machine. arXiv preprint arXiv:1801.07729 (2018)

9. Gatys, L.A., Ecker, A.S., Bethge, M.: Image style transfer using convolutional neural networks. In: Proceedings of the IEEE Conference on Computer Vision and Pattern Recognition (CVPR), June 2016

10. He, K., Zhang, X., Ren, S., Sun, J.: Deep residual learning for image recognition. In: Proceedings of the IEEE Conference on Computer Vision and Pattern Recognition, pp. 770–778 (2016). https://doi.org/10.1109/CVPR.2016.90

11. Invernizzi, C., Fiocco, G., Iwanicka, M., Kowalska, M., Targowski, P., Blümich, B., Rehorn, C., Gabrielli, V., Bersani, D., Licchelli, M., Malagodi, M.: Non-invasive mobile technology to study the stratigraphy of ancient cremonese violins: OCT, NMR-MOUSE, XRF and reflection FT-IR spectroscopy. Microchem. J. **155**, 104754 (2020). https://doi.org/10.1016/j.microc.2020.104754

12. Karayev, S., et al.: Recognizing image style. In: Proceedings of the British Machine Vision Conference. BMVA Press (2014). https://doi.org/10.5244/C.28.122

13. Li, J., Wang, J.Z.: Studying digital imagery of ancient paintings by mixtures of stochastic models. IEEE Trans. Image Process. **13**(3), 340–353 (2004). https://doi.org/10.1109/TIP.2003.821349

14. Lombardi, T.E.: The Classification of Style in Fine-Art Painting. Citeseer (2005)

15. Microsoft, ING, TUDelft, Mauritshuis: The Next Rembrandt project. https://www.nextrembrandt.com/. Accessed 15 Oct 2020

16. Poggialini, F., et al.: Stratigraphic analysis of historical wooden samples from ancient bowed string instruments by laser induced breakdown spectroscopy. J. Cultural Heritage **44**, 275–284 (2020). https://doi.org/10.1016/j.culher.2020.01.011

17. Puthenputhussery, A., Liu, Q., Liu, C.: Color multi-fusion fisher vector feature for fine art painting categorization and influence analysis. In: 2016 IEEE Winter Conference on Applications of Computer Vision (WACV), pp. 1–9. IEEE (2016)

18. Sandoval, C., Pirogova, E., Lech, M.: Two-stage deep learning approach to the classification of fine-art paintings. IEEE Access **7**, 41770–41781 (2019). https://doi.org/10.1109/ACCESS.2019.2907986

19. Sargentis, G., Dimitriadis, P., Koutsoyiannis, D., et al.: Aesthetical issues of leonardo da vinci's and pablo picasso's paintings with stochastic evaluation. Heritage **3**(2), 283–305 (2020). https://doi.org/10.3390/heritage3020017

20. Selvaraju, R.R., Cogswell, M., Das, A., Vedantam, R., Parikh, D., Batra, D.: Gradcam: visual explanations from deep networks via gradient-based localization. In: 2017 IEEE International Conference on Computer Vision (ICCV), pp. 618–626 (2017). https://doi.org/10.1109/ICCV.2017.74

21. Simonyan, K., Zisserman, A.: Very deep convolutional networks for large-scale image recognition. arXiv preprint arXiv:1409.1556 (2014)

22. Sun, T., Wang, Y., Yang, J., Hu, X.: Convolution neural networks with two pathways for image style recognition. IEEE Trans. Image Process. **26**(9), 4102–4113 (2017). https://doi.org/10.1109/TIP.2017.2710631

23. Szegedy, C., Vanhoucke, V., Ioffe, S., Shlens, J., Wojna, Z.: Rethinking the inception architecture for computer vision. In: Proceedings of the IEEE Conference on Computer Vision and Pattern Recognition, pp. 2818–2826 (2016). https://doi.org/10.1109/CVPR.2016.308

24. Tan, W.R., Chan, C.S., Aguirre, H.E., Tanaka, K.: Ceci n'est pas une pipe: a deep convolutional network for fine-art paintings classification. In: 2016 IEEE International Conference on Image Processing (ICIP), pp. 3703–3707 (2016). https://doi.org/10.1109/ICIP.2016.7533051

25. van Noord, N., Hendriks, E., Postma, E.: Toward discovery of the artist's style: learning to recognize artists by their artworks. IEEE Sig. Process. Mag. **32**(4), 46–54 (2015). https://doi.org/10.1109/MSP.2015.2406955

Text Line Extraction Using Fully Convolutional Network and Energy Minimization

Berat Kurar Barakat[1]($\boxtimes$) (ID), Ahmad Droby[1], Reem Alaasam[1], Boraq Madi[1],
Irina Rabaev[2], and Jihad El-Sana[1]

[1] Ben-Gurion University of the Negev, Beersheba, Israel
{berat,drobya,rym,borak}@post.bgu.ac.il
[2] Shamoon College of Engineering, Ashdod, Israel
irinar@ac.sce.ac.il

Abstract. Text lines are important parts of handwritten document images and easier to analyze by further applications. Despite recent progress in text line detection, text line extraction from a handwritten document remains an unsolved task. This paper proposes to use a fully convolutional network for text line detection and energy minimization for text line extraction. Detected text lines are represented by blob lines that strike through the text lines. These blob lines assist an energy function for text line extraction. The detection stage can locate arbitrarily oriented text lines. Furthermore, the extraction stage is capable of finding out the pixels of text lines with various heights and interline proximity independent of their orientations. Besides, it can finely split the touching and overlapping text lines without an orientation assumption. We evaluate the proposed method on VML-AHTE, VML-MOC, and Diva-HisDB datasets. The VML-AHTE dataset contains overlapping, touching and close text lines with rich diacritics. The VML-MOC dataset is very challenging by its multiply oriented and skewed text lines. The Diva-HisDB dataset exhibits distinct text line heights and touching text lines. The results demonstrate the effectiveness of the method despite various types of challenges, yet using the same parameters in all the experiments.

Keywords: Historical documents analysis · Text line segmentation · Text line detection · Text line extraction · Handwritten document

1 Introduction

Segmentation in computer vision is the task of dividing an image into parts that are easier to analyse. Text lines of a handwritten document image are widely used for word segmentation, text recognition and spotting, manuscripts alignment and writer recognition. Text lines need to be provided to these applications either by their locations or by complete set of their pixels. The task of identifying the location of each text line is called detection, whereas the task of determining the pixels of each text line is called extraction. Much research in the recent years has focused on text line detection [3,14,24]. However, detection defines the text

© Springer Nature Switzerland AG 2021
A. Del Bimbo et al. (Eds.): ICPR 2020 Workshops, LNCS 12667, pp. 126–140, 2021.
https://doi.org/10.1007/978-3-030-68787-8_9

lines loosely by baselines or main body blobs. On the other hand, extraction is a harder task which defines text lines precisely by pixel labels or bounding polygons.

The challenges in text line extraction arise due to variations in text line heights and orientations, presence of overlapping and touching text lines, and diacritical marks within close interline proximity. It has been generally demonstrated that deep learning based methods are effective at detecting text lines with various orientations [14,22,25,30]. However, only few of the recent researches [8,30] have addressed the problem of extraction given the detection, yet with the assumption of horizontal text lines.

This paper proposes a text line extraction method (FCN+EM) which uses Fully Convolutional Network (FCN) to detect text lines in the form of blob lines (Fig. 1(b)), followed by an Energy Minimization (EM) function assisted by these blob lines to extract the text lines (Fig. 1(c)). FCN is capable of handling curved and arbitrarily oriented text lines. However, extraction is problematic due to the Sayre's paradox [27] which states that exact boundaries of handwritten text can be defined only after its recognition and handwritten text can be recognized only after extraction of its boundaries. Nevertheless, humans are good at understanding boundaries of text lines written in a language they do not know. Therefore, we consider EM framework to formulate the text line extraction in compliance with the human visual perception, with the aid of the Gestalt proximity principle for grouping [17]. The proposed EM formulation for text line extraction is free of an orientation assumption and can be used with touching and overlapping text lines with disjoint strokes and close interline proximity (Fig. 1(a)).

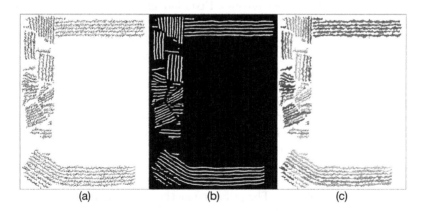

(a)   (b)   (c)

Fig. 1. Given a handwritten document image (a), FCN learns to detect blob lines that strike through text lines (b). EM with the assistance of detected blob lines extracts the pixel labels of text lines which are in turn enclosed by bounding polygons (c).

The proposed extraction method (FCN+EM) is evaluated on Visual Media Lab Arabic Handwritten Text line Extraction (VML-AHTE) dataset, Multiply Oriented and Curved (VML-MOC) dataset [5], and DIVA Historical Manuscript

Database (DIVA-HisDB) [28]. VML-AHTE dataset is characterized by touching and overlapping text lines with close proximity and rich diacritics. VML-MOC dataset contains arbitrarily oriented and curved text lines. DIVA-HisDB dataset exhibit varying text line heights and touching text lines.

The rest of the paper is organized as follows. Related work is discussed in Sect. 2, and the datasets are described in Sect. 3. Later, the method is presented in Sect. 4. The experimental evaluation and the results are then provided in Sect. 5. Finally, Sect. 6 draws conclusions and outlines future work.

2   Related Work

A text line is a set of image elements, such as pixels or connected components. Text line components in a document image can be represented using basic geometric primitives such as points, lines, polylines, polygons or blobs. Text line representation is given as an input to other document image processing algorithms, and, therefore, important to be complete and correct.

There are two main approaches to represent text lines: text line detection and text line extraction. Text line detection detects the lines, polylines or blobs that represent the locations of spatially aligned set of text line elements. Detected line or polyline is called a baseline [14,24] if it joins the lower part of the character main bodies, and a separator path [8,26] if it follows the space between two consecutive text lines. Detected blobs [3] that cover the character main bodies in a text line are called text line blobs.

Text line extraction determines the constituting pixels or the polygons around the spatially aligned text line elements. Pixel labeling assigns the same label to all the pixels of a text line [9,26,30]. Bounding polygon is used to enclose all the elements of a text line together with its neighbourhood background pixels [11, 15]. Most of the extraction methods assume horizontally parallel text lines with constant heights, whereas some methods [2,5] are more generic.

Recent deep learning methods estimate x-height of text lines using FCN and apply Line Adjacency Graphs (LAG) to post-process FCN output to split touching lines [20,21]. Renton *et al.* [24,25] also use FCN to predict x-height of text lines. Kurar *et al.* [3] applied FCN for challenging manuscript images with multi-skewed, multi-directed and curved handwritten text lines. However these methods either do only text line detection or their extraction phase is not appropriate for unstructured text lines because their assumption of horizontal and constant height text lines. The proposed method assumes the both, detection and extraction phases to be for complex layout.

ICDAR 2009 [12] and ICDAR 2013 [29] datasets are commonly used for evaluating text line extraction methods and ICDAR 2017 [10] dataset is used for evaluating text line detection methods. DIVA-HisDB dataset [28] is used for both types of evaluations: detection and extraction. Therefore, we select to use DIVA-HisDB [28] as it provides ground truth for detection and extraction. However, this dataset is not enough representative of all the segmentation problems to evaluate a generic method. Hence, we also evaluated the proposed method on publicly available VML-MOC [5] dataset that contains multiply oriented and curved text lines with heterogeneous heights, and on VML-AHTE dataset that contains crowded diacritics.

3   Datasets

We evaluated the proposed method on three publicly available handwritten datasets. We suppose that these datasets demonstrate the generality of our method. As VML-AHTE dataset contains lines with crowded diacritics, VML-MOC dataset contains multiply oriented and curved lines, and Diva-HisDB dataset contains consecutively touching multiple lines. In this section we present these datasets.

3.1   VML-AHTE

VML-AHTE dataset is a collection of 30 binary document images selected from several manuscripts (Fig. 2). It is a newly published dataset and available online for downloading[1]. The dataset is split into 20 train pages and 10 test pages. Its ground truth is provided in three formats: bounding polygons in PAGE xml [23] format, color pixel labels and DIVA pixel labels [28].

Touching letters   Overlapping letters   Rich diacritics

Fig. 2. Some samples of challenges in VML-AHTE dataset.

3.2   Diva-HisDB

DIVA-HisDB dataset [28] contains 150 pages from 3 medieval manuscripts: CB55, CSG18 and CSG863 (Fig. 3). Each book has 20 train pages and 10 test pages. Among them, CB55 is characterized by a vast number of touching characters. Ground truth is provided in three formats: baselines and bounding polygons in PAGE xml [23] format and DIVA pixel labels [28].

---

[1] https://www.cs.bgu.ac.il/~berat/data/ahte_dataset.

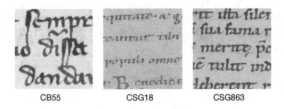

CB55   CSG18   CSG863

Fig. 3. Diva-HisDB dataset contains 3 manuscripts: CB55, CSG18 and CSG863. Notice the touching characters among multiple consecutive text lines in CB55.

3.3 VML-MOC

VML-MOC dataset [5] is a multiply oriented and curved handwritten text lines dataset that is publicly available[2]. These text lines are side notes added by various scholars over the years on the page margins, in arbitrary orientations and curvy forms due to space constraints (Fig. 4). The dataset contains 30 binary document images and divided into 20 train pages and 10 test pages. The ground truth is provided in three formats: bounding polygons in PAGE xml [23] format, color pixel labels and DIVA pixel labels [28].

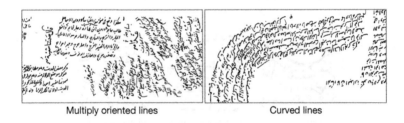

Multiply oriented lines   Curved lines

Fig. 4. VML-MOC dataset purely contains binarized side notes with arbitrary orientations and curvy forms.

4   Method

We present a method (FCN+EM) for text line detection together with extraction, and show its effectiveness on handwritten document images. In the first phase, the method uses an FCN to densely predict the pixels of the blob lines that strike through the text lines (Fig. 1(b)). In the second phase, we use an EM framework to extract the pixel labels of text lines with the assistance of detected blob lines (Fig. 1(c)). In the rest of this section we give a detailed of description FCN, EM and how they are used for text line detection and text line extraction.

---

[2] https://www.cs.bgu.ac.il/~berat/data/moc_dataset.

4.1 Text Line Detection Using FCN

Fully Convolutional Network (FCN) is an end-to-end semantic segmentation algorithm that extracts the features and learns the classifier function simultaneously. FCN inputs the original images and their pixel level annotations for learning the hypothesis function that can predict whether a pixel belongs to a text line label or not. A crucial decision have to be made about the representation of text line detection. Text line detection labels can be represented as baselines or blob lines.

We use blob line labeling that connects the characters in the same line while disregarding diacritics and touching components among the text lines. Blob line labeling for VML-AHTE and DIVA-HisDB datasets is automatically generated using the skeletons of bounding polygons provided by their ground truth (Fig. 5(d)). Blob line labeling for VML-MOC dataset is manually drawn using a sharp rectangular brush with a diameter of 12 pixels (Fig. 5(b)).

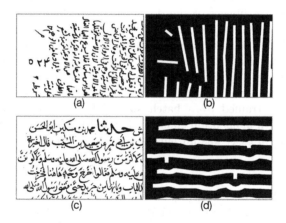

Fig. 5. Sample patches from document images of VML-MOC (a) and VML-AHTE (c). Blob line labeling for VML-AHTE and DIVA-HisDB is generated automatically (d). Blob line labeling for VML-AHTE is manually drawn using a paint brush with a diameter of 12 pixels (b).

FCN Architecture. The FCN architecture (Fig. 6) we used is based on the FCN8 proposed for semantic segmentation [19]. Particularly FCN8 architecture was selected because it has been successful in page layout analysis of handwritten documents [4]. It consists of an encoder and a decoder. The encoder downsamples the input image and the filters can see coarser information with larger receptive field. Consequently the decoder adds final layer of encoder to the lower layers with finer information, then upsamples the combined layer back to the input size. Default input size is 224×224, which does not cover more than 2 to 3 text lines. To include more context, we changed the input size to 350×350 pixels. We also changed the number of output channels to 2, which is the number of classes: blob line or not.

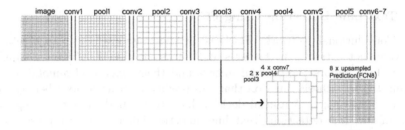

Fig. 6. The FCN architecture used for text line detection. Vertical lines show the convolutional layers. Grids show the relative coarseness of the pooling and prediction layers. FCN8 upsamples 4 times the final layer, upsamples twice the pool4 layer, and combine them with pool3 layer. Finally, FCN8 upsamples the combination to the input size.

FCN Training. For training, we randomly crop $50,000$ patches of size 350×350 from inverted binary images of the documents and their corresponding labels from the blob line label images (Fig. 5(b)). We adopted this patch size due to memory limitation. Using full pages for training and prediction is not feasible on non-specialized systems without resizing the pages to a more manageable size. Resizing the pages will result in details loss, which usually reduces the accuracy of segmentation results.

The FCN was trained by a batch size of 12, using Stochastic Gradient Descent (SGD) with momentum equals to 0.9 and learning rate equals to 0.001. The encoder part of FCN was initialized with its publicly available pre-trained weights.

FCN Testing. During the testing, a sliding window of size 350×350 was used for prediction, but only the inner window of size 250×250 was considered to eliminate the edge effect. Page was padded with black pixels at its right and bottom sides if its size is not an integer multiple of the sliding window size, in addition to padding it at 4 sides for considering only the central part of the sliding window.

4.2   Text Line Extraction Using EM

We adapt the energy minimization (EM) framework [6] that uses graph cuts to approximate the minima of arbitrary functions. These functions can be formulated in terms of image elements such pixels or connected components. In this section we formulate a general function for text line extraction using text line detection. Then, we adapt this general function to be used with connected components for text line extraction.

EM Formulation. Let $\mathcal{L}$ be the set of binary blob lines, and $\mathcal{E}$ be the set of elements in the binary document image. Energy minimization finds a labeling f that assigns each element $e \in \mathcal{E}$ to a label $l_e \in \mathcal{L}$, where energy function $\mathbf{E}(f)$ has the minimum.

$$\mathbf{E}(f) = \sum_{e \in \mathcal{E}} D(e, \ell_e) + \sum_{\{e,e'\} \in \mathcal{N}} d(e, e') \cdot \delta(\ell_e \neq \ell_{e'}) \tag{1}$$

The term D is the data cost, d is the smoothness cost, and δ is an indicator function. Data cost is the cost of assigning element e to label l_e. $D(e, \ell_e)$ is defined to be the Euclidean distance between the centroid of the element e and the nearest neighbour pixel in blob line l_e for the centroid of the element e. Smoothness cost is the cost of assigning neighbouring elements to different labels. Let $\mathcal{N}$ be the set of nearest element pairs. Then $\forall \{e, e'\} \in \mathcal{N}$,

$$d(e, e') = \exp(-\beta \cdot d_e(e, e')) \tag{2}$$

where $d_e(e, e')$ is the Euclidean distance between the centroids of the elements e and e', and β is defined as

$$\beta = (2\langle d_e(e, e')\rangle)^{-1} \tag{3}$$

$\langle \cdot \rangle$ denotes expectation over all pairs of neighbouring elements [7] in a document page image. $\delta(\ell_e \neq \ell_{e'})$ is equal to 1 if the condition inside the parentheses holds and 0 otherwise.

EM Adaptation to Connected Components. The presented method extracts text lines using results of the text line detection procedure by FCN. Extraction level representation labels each pixel of the text lines in a document image. The major difficulty in pixel labeling lies in the computational cost. A typical document image in the experimented datasets includes around $14,000,000$ pixels. Due to this reason, we adapt the energy function (Eq. 1) to be used with connected components for extraction of text lines.

Data cost of the adapted function measures how appropriate a label is for the component e, given the blob lines $\mathcal{L}$. Actually, the data cost alone would be equal to clustering the components with their nearest neighbour blob line. However, simply nearest neighbour clustering would be deficient to correctly label the free components that are disconnected from the blob lines (Fig. 7).

A free component tends to exist closer to the components of a line it belongs to, but can be a nearest neighbour of a blob line that it does not belong to. This is because the proximity grouping strength decays exponentially with Euclidean distance [18]. This phenomenon is formulated using the smoothness cost (Eq. 2). Semantically this means that closer components have a higher probability to have the same label than distant components. Hence, the competition between data cost and smoothness cost dictates free components to be labeled spatially coherent with their neighbouring components.

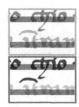  

Fig. 7. Segmented samples that show the necessity of smoothness cost for text line extraction. Samples in the first row are true and achieved with smoothness cost. Samples in the second row are false and caused by the lack of a smoothness cost. Notice that smoothness cost pulls the diacritics to the components they belong to, in spite of their proximity to the wrong blob line.

5   Experiments

We experiment with three datasets that are different in terms of the text line segmentation challenges they contain. VML-AHTE dataset exhibits crowded diacritics and cramped text lines, whereas DIVA-HisDB dataset contains consequently touching text lines. Completely different than them VML-MOC exhibits challenges caused by arbitrarily skewed and curved text lines. The performance is measured using the line segmentation evaluation metrics of ICDAR 2013 [13] and ICDAR 2017 [1].

5.1   ICDAR 2013 Line Segmentation Evaluation Metrics

ICDAR 2013 metrics calculate recognition accuracy (RA), detection rate (DR) and F-measure (FM) values. Given a set of image points I, let R_i be the set of points inside the ith result region, G_j be the set of points inside the jth ground truth region, and $T(p)$ is a function that counts the points inside the set p, then the $MatchScore(i,j)$ is calculated by Eq. 4

$$MatchScore(i,j) = \frac{T(Gj \cap Ri)}{T(Gj \cup Ri)} \qquad (4)$$

The evaluator considers a region pair (i,j) as a one-to-one match if the $MatchScore(i,j)$ is equal or above the threshold, which we set to 90. Let N_1 and N_2 be the number of ground truth and output elements, respectively, and let M be the number of one-to-one matches. The evaluator calculates the DR, RA and FM as follows:

$$DR = \frac{M}{N_1} \qquad (5)$$

$$RA = \frac{M}{N_2} \tag{6}$$

$$FM = \frac{2 \times DR \times RA}{DR + RA} \tag{7}$$

5.2   ICDAR 2017 Line Segmentation Evaluation Metrics

ICDAR 2017 metrics are based on the Intersection over Union (IU). IU scores for each possible pair of Ground Truth (GT) polygons and Prediction (P) polygons are computed as follows:

$$IU = \frac{IP}{UP} \tag{8}$$

IP denotes the number of intersecting foreground pixels among the pair of polygons. UP denotes number of foreground pixels in the union of foreground pixels of the pair of polygons. The pairs with maximum IU score are selected as the matching pairs of GT polygons and P polygons. Then, pixel IU and line IU are calculated among these matching pairs. For each matching pair, line TP, line FP and line FN are given by: Line TP is the number of foreground pixels that are correctly predicted in the matching pair. Line FP is the number of foreground pixels that are falsely predicted in the matching pair. Line FN is the number of false negative foreground pixels in the matching pair. Accordingly pixel IU is:

$$\text{Pixel } IU = \frac{TP}{TP + FP + FN} \tag{9}$$

where TP is the global sum of line TPs, FP is the global sum of line FPs, and FN is the global sum of line FNs.

Line IU is measured at line level. For each matching pair, line precision and line recall are:

$$\text{Line precision} = \frac{\text{line } TP}{\text{line } TP + \text{line } FP} \tag{10}$$

$$\text{Line recall} = \frac{\text{line } TP}{\text{line } TP + \text{line } FN} \tag{11}$$

Accordingly, line IU is:

$$\text{Line } IU = \frac{CL}{CL + ML + EL} \tag{12}$$

where CL is the number of correct lines, ML is the number of missed lines, and EL is the number of extra lines.

For each matching pair: A line is correct if both, the line precision and the line recall are above the threshold value. A line is missed if the line recall is below the threshold value. A line is extra if the line precision is below the threshold value.

5.3   Results on VML-AHTE Dataset

Since VML-AHTE and VML-MOC datasets are recently published datasets we
run two other supervised methods. First method is a holistic method that can
extract text lines in one phase and is based on instance segmentation using
MRCNN [16]. Second method is based on running the EM framework using the
blob line labels from the ground truth and we refer to it Human+EM. On VML-
AHTE dataset, FCN+EM outperforms all the other methods in terms of all
the metrics except Line IU. It can successfully split the touching text lines and
assign the disjoint strokes to the correct text lines (Table 1).

Table 1. Results on VML-AHTE dataset

	Line IU	Pixel IU	DR	RA	FM
FCN+EM	94.52	**90.01**	**95.55**	**92.8**	**94.3**
MRCNN	93.08	86.97	84.43	58.89	68.77
Human+EM	**97.83**	89.61	88.14	87.78	87.96

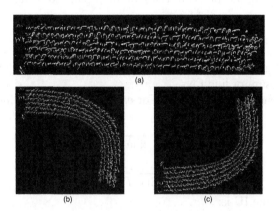

Fig. 8. Example of generated curved lines: (a) shows the original straight lines section,
(b) is the result of warping (a) by 90° in the middle to generated the curved lines, and
(c) is the mirrored image of (b) in the vertical direction.

5.4   Results on VML-MOC Dataset

The VML-MOC dataset contains both types, straight text lines and curved text
lines. Number of straight text lines is substantially greater than the number of
curved text lines. This imbalance causes the FCN to overfit on the straight text
lines. This in turn leads to fragmented blob lines when predicting over the curved

text lines. Therefore, to compensate this imbalance, we generated images containing artificially curved text lines. We selected the document image parts with straight lines and warp these images 90° from their middle. Furthermore, each one of those warped lines was mirrored in the horizontal and vertical directions resulting in curved lines in four directions. Figure 8 illustrates this procedure. The FCN+EM that is trained with augmented curved text lines (FCN+EM+Aug) outperforms the FCN+EM that is trained only with the training set (Table 2). But FCN+EM+Aug still underperforms a learning free algorithm [5].

Table 2. Results on VML-MOC dataset

	Line IU	Pixel IU	DR	RA	FM
FCN+EM	25.04	48.71	26.45	17.73	31.09
FCN+EM+Aug	35.12	60.97	84.43	58.89	68.77
[5]	60.99	80.96	–	–	–
Human+EM	**96.62**	**99.01**	**90.41**	**91.74**	**91.03**

5.5   Results on DIVA-HisDB Dataset

We compare the results with the results of Task-3 from ICDAR 2017 competition on layout analysis for medieval manuscripts [28]. Task-3's scope of interest is only the main text lines but not the interlinear glosses. We removed these glosses prior to all our experiments using the ground truth. It should be noticed that Task-3 participants removed these glosses using their own algorithms.

Table 3 presents a comparison of our methods with the participants of ICDAR 2017 competition on layout analysis for challenging medieval manuscripts for text line extraction. The FCN+EM can obtain a perfect Line IU score on the books CSG863 and CB55. Its Pixel IU is on par with the best preforming method in the competition.

Table 3. Comparison with the Task-3 results of the ICDAR2017 competition on layout analysis for challenging medieval manuscripts [28].

	CB55		CSG18		CSG863	
	LIU	PIU	LIU	PIU	LIU	PIU
FCN+EM	**100**	**97.64**	**97.65**	**97.79**	**100**	97.18
System-2	84.29	80.23	69.57	75.31	90.64	93.68
System-6	5.67	30.53	39.17	54.52	25.96	46.09
System-8	99.33	93.75	94.90	94.47	96.75	90.81
System-9+4.1	98.04	96.67	96.91	96.93	98.62	**97.54**

5.6   Discussion

An observable pattern in the results is the parallel flow of line IU values and pixel IU values while RA values are fluctuating in comparison to DR values. Clearly, such counter-intuitive behaviour of a metric is not preferable in terms of interpretability of the results. On the other hand, ICDAR 2017 evaluator can not handle the cases where a text line consists of multiple polygons. Such case arises from MRCNN results. MRCNN segments a text line instance correctly but represents it as multiple polygons with the same label. Evaluating MRCNN results in their raw form yields to low values unfairly (Fig. 9). Because ICDAR 2017 evaluator calculates an IU score for each possible pair of ground truth polygons and prediction polygons then selects the pairs with maximum IU score as the matching pairs. Consequently, a text line represented by multiple polygons is considered only by its largest polygon.

| Input image | MRCNN predicted blobs |

Fig. 9. MRCNN method correctly predicts text line pixels but its results are not fairly evaluated due to disconnected polygons.

6   Conclusion

This paper presents a supervised text line segmentation method FCN+EM. The FCN detect the blob lines that strike through the text lines and the EM extracts the pixels of text lines with the guidance of the detected blob lines. FCN+EM does not make any assumption about the text line orientation or text line height. The algorithm is very effective in detecting cramped, crowded and touching text lines. It has a superior performance on VML-AHTE and DIVA-HisDB datasets but comparable results on VML-MOC dataset.

Acknowledgment. The authors would like to thank Gunes Cevik for annotating the ground truth. This work has been partially supported by the Frankel Center for Computer Science.

References

1. Alberti, M., Bouillon, M., Ingold, R., Liwicki, M.: Open evaluation tool for layout analysis of document images. In: 2017 14th IAPR International Conference on Document Analysis and Recognition (ICDAR), vol. 4, pp. 43–47. IEEE (2017)

2. Aldavert, D., Rusiñol, M.: Manuscript text line detection and segmentation using second-order derivatives. In: 2018 13th IAPR International Workshop on Document Analysis Systems (DAS), pp. 293–298. IEEE (2018)
3. Barakat, B., Droby, A., Kassis, M., El-Sana, J.: Text line segmentation for challenging handwritten document images using fully convolutional network. In: 2018 16th International Conference on Frontiers in Handwriting Recognition (ICFHR), pp. 374–379. IEEE (2018)
4. Barakat, B., El-Sana, J.: Binarization free layout analysis for Arabic historical documents using fully convolutional networks. In: 2nd International Workshop on Arabic Script Analysis and Recognition (ASAR), pp. 26–30. IEEE (2018)
5. Barakat, B.K., Cohen, R., El-Sana, J., Rabaev, I.: VML-MOC: segmenting a multiply oriented and curved handwritten text line dataset. In: 2019 International Conference on Document Analysis and Recognition Workshops (ICDARW), vol. 6, pp. 13–18. IEEE (2019)
6. Boykov, Y., Veksler, O., Zabih, R.: Fast approximate energy minimization via graph cuts. IEEE Trans. Pattern Anal. Mach. Intell. **23**(11), 1222–1239 (2001)
7. Boykov, Y.Y., Jolly, M.P.: Interactive graph cuts for optimal boundary & region segmentation of objects in ND images. In: Proceedings Eighth IEEE International Conference on Computer Vision, ICCV 2001, vol. 1, pp. 105–112. IEEE (2001)
8. Campos, V.B., Gómez, V.R., Rossi, A.H.T., Ruiz, E.V.: Text line extraction based on distance map features and dynamic programming. In: 2018 16th International Conference on Frontiers in Handwriting Recognition (ICFHR), pp. 357–362. IEEE (2018)
9. Cohen, R., Dinstein, I., El-Sana, J., Kedem, K.: Using scale-space anisotropic smoothing for text line extraction in historical documents. In: Campilho, A., Kamel, M. (eds.) ICIAR 2014. LNCS, vol. 8814, pp. 349–358. Springer, Cham (2014). https://doi.org/10.1007/978-3-319-11758-4_38
10. Diem, M., Kleber, F., Fiel, S., Grüning, T., Gatos, B.: cBAD: ICDAR2017 competition on baseline detection. In: 2017 14th IAPR International Conference on Document Analysis and Recognition (ICDAR), vol. 1, pp. 1355–1360. IEEE (2017)
11. Fischer, A., Baechler, M., Garz, A., Liwicki, M., Ingold, R.: A combined system for text line extraction and handwriting recognition in historical documents. In: 2014 11th IAPR International Workshop on Document Analysis Systems, pp. 71–75. IEEE (2014)
12. Gatos, B., Stamatopoulos, N., Louloudis, G.: ICDAR2009 handwriting segmentation contest. Int. J. Doc. Anal. Recogn. (IJDAR) **14**(1), 25–33 (2011)
13. Gatos, B., Stamatopoulos, N., Louloudis, G.: ICFHR 2010 handwriting segmentation contest. In: 2010 12th International Conference on Frontiers in Handwriting Recognition, pp. 737–742. IEEE (2010)
14. Grüning, T., Leifert, G., Strauß, T., Michael, J., Labahn, R.: A two-stage method for text line detection in historical documents. Int. J. Doc. Anal. Recogn. (IJDAR) **22**(3), 285–302 (2019). https://doi.org/10.1007/s10032-019-00332-1
15. Gruuening, T., Leifert, G., Strauss, T., Labahn, R.: A robust and binarization-free approach for text line detection in historical documents. In: 2017 14th IAPR International Conference on Document Analysis and Recognition (ICDAR), vol. 1, pp. 236–241. IEEE (2017)
16. He, K., Gkioxari, G., Dollár, P., Girshick, R.: Mask R-CNN. In: Proceedings of the IEEE International Conference on Computer Vision, pp. 2961–2969 (2017)
17. Koffka, K.: Principles of Gestalt Psychology, vol. 44. Routledge, Abingdon (2013)

18. Kubovy, M., Van Den Berg, M.: The whole is equal to the sum of its parts: a probabilistic model of grouping by proximity and similarity in regular patterns. Psychol. Rev. **115**(1), 131 (2008)
19. Long, J., Shelhamer, E., Darrell, T.: Fully convolutional networks for semantic segmentation. In: Proceedings of the IEEE Conference on Computer Vision and Pattern Recognition, pp. 3431–3440 (2015)
20. Moysset, B., Kermorvant, C., Wolf, C., Louradour, J.: Paragraph text segmentation into lines with recurrent neural networks. In: 2015 13th International Conference on Document Analysis and Recognition (ICDAR), pp. 456–460. IEEE (2015)
21. Moysset, B., Louradour, J., Kermorvant, C., Wolf, C.: Learning text-line localization with shared and local regression neural networks. In: 2016 15th International Conference on Frontiers in Handwriting Recognition (ICFHR), pp. 1–6. IEEE (2016)
22. Oliveira, S.A., Seguin, B., Kaplan, F.: dhSegment: a generic deep-learning approach for document segmentation. In: 2018 16th International Conference on Frontiers in Handwriting Recognition (ICFHR), pp. 7–12. IEEE (2018)
23. Pletschacher, S., Antonacopoulos, A.: The page (page analysis and ground-truth elements) format framework. In: 2010 20th International Conference on Pattern Recognition, pp. 257–260. IEEE (2010)
24. Renton, G., Chatelain, C., Adam, S., Kermorvant, C., Paquet, T.: Handwritten text line segmentation using fully convolutional network. In: 2017 14th IAPR International Conference on Document Analysis and Recognition (ICDAR), vol. 5, pp. 5–9. IEEE (2017)
25. Renton, G., Soullard, Y., Chatelain, C., Adam, S., Kermorvant, C., Paquet, T.: Fully convolutional network with dilated convolutions for handwritten text line segmentation. Int. J. Doc. Anal. Recogn. (IJDAR) **21**(3), 177–186 (2018). https://doi.org/10.1007/s10032-018-0304-3
26. Saabni, R., Asi, A., El-Sana, J.: Text line extraction for historical document images. Pattern Recogn. Lett. **35**, 23–33 (2014)
27. Sayre, K.M.: Machine recognition of handwritten words: a project report. Pattern Recogn. **5**(3), 213–228 (1973)
28. Simistira, F., et al.: ICDAR2017 competition on layout analysis for challenging medieval manuscripts. In: 2017 14th IAPR International Conference on Document Analysis and Recognition (ICDAR), vol. 1, pp. 1361–1370. IEEE (2017)
29. Stamatopoulos, N., Gatos, B., Louloudis, G., Pal, U., Alaei, A.: ICDAR 2013 handwriting segmentation contest. In: 2013 12th International Conference on Document Analysis and Recognition, pp. 1402–1406. IEEE (2013)
30. Vo, Q.N., Lee, G.: Dense prediction for text line segmentation in handwritten document images. In: 2016 IEEE International Conference on Image Processing (ICIP), pp. 3264–3268. IEEE (2016)

Handwriting Classification of Byzantine Codices via Geometric Transformations Induced by Curvature Deformations

Dimitris Arabadjis[(⊠)] [iD], Constantin Papaodysseus [iD], Athanasios Rafail Mamatsis, and Eirini Mamatsi

School of Electrical and Computer Engineering, National Technical University of Athens, 9 Iroon Polytechniou St., 15780 Athens, Greece

alphad.d@gmail.com, cpapaod@cs.ntua.gr, mamatsis@mail.ntua.gr

Abstract. In the present paper, we propose a methodology of general applicability for matching, comparing and grouping planar shapes, under a unified framework. This is achieved by interpreting shapes' grouping as a result of the hypothesis that shapes of the same class come from the same implicit family of curves. In order to render the analysis independent of the functional form of the curves families' implicit function, we have formalized the shapes' comparison in terms of the implicit curvature function. The implementation of the methodology targets towards automatic writer identification and the corresponding information system has been applied to the identification of the writer of Byzantine codices that preserve Iliad. The shapes in hand are the alphabet symbols appearing in the documents' images to be classified. The realizations of each alphabet symbol are compared pairwise, modulo affine transformations. The statistical compatibility of these comparisons inside the same document and between different documents determines the likelihood of attributing different documents to the same hand. By maximizing the joint likelihood for all alphabet symbols, common in all documents we determine the most probable classification of the given documents into writing hands. Application of the methodology to 25 images of Byzantine codices' pages indicated that these pages have been written by 4 hands in full accordance with experts' opinion and knowledge.

Keywords: Historical documents' writer identification · Handwriting identification · 2D affine registration · Curvature deformation · Shapes classification

1 Introduction

The goal of the present work is the automatic classification of important historical documents according to their writer. This is a problem belonging to the field of automatic handwriting identification and the approach proposed here is based on modeling and determining geometric correspondences between the shapes of the alphabet symbols appearing in the considered historical documents.

© Springer Nature Switzerland AG 2021
A. Del Bimbo et al. (Eds.): ICPR 2020 Workshops, LNCS 12667, pp. 141–155, 2021.
https://doi.org/10.1007/978-3-030-68787-8_10

Ancient documents and, specifically, Byzantine/Medieval codices constitute a primary source of information, which is of fundamental importance to History, Archaeology and Classical Studies. In general, knowledge of the hand that wrote a specific document is a central element for the reconstruction and the study of the document's content. However, as a rule, ancient documents are unsigned, undated, while they have frequently suffered a considerable/serious wear. Therefore, it is very difficult to date ancient documents objectively, although their dating is crucial. Up to Medieval Period and even in more recent ages, writing or reproducing a document was a skill usually limited to a relatively small number of dedicated individuals. In addition, the time interval during which a professional or dedicated writer was active, usually did not exceed 25–30 years. Thus, if one may prove that a group of documents has been written by the same hand, then dating of all these documents may become far easier.

Consequently, the development of an Information System that performs automatic identification of the writer of an ancient document and classification of any set of ancient documents according to their writer, may assist in reconstructing and dating their content in an objective manner. In addition, such a system may prove very powerful in the effort to establish weather a set of documents includes only genuine ones or not.

1.1   Relation of the Proposed Methodology with State of the Art

From the application specific point of view, the proposed methodology should be classified, in terms of the bibliography, as an "off-line, character based, writer identification system" but its technical approach fundamentally differs from the existing systems in this class. Specifically, most of the existing methodologies are based on classification of properly selected features that may encode curvature free patterns [1], junction patterns [2], texture features [3], allograph prototypes [4] or cohesion of the writing style [5]. The classification of the documents into writers is based either in machine learning techniques [6, 7] or in special purpose classifiers mainly dependent on an efficient estimation of a single density function for the selected features characteristic for each writer. The efficiency of such approaches mainly depends on the specificity of the selected features. Thus, in many cases, these features have very loose causal relation with the geometric form of the writing style so as to absorb intentional changes in the writing style, at the same time trying to capture unintentionally repetitive patterns. On the other hand, the proposed writer identification approach is based on modeling and determining purely geometric correspondences between the alphabet symbols' shapes themselves and not between some features of them.

Specifically, the main technical features of the proposed methodology are summarized as follows:

- it does not adopt any error functional for the shapes deformation representation,
- it treats the shapes' matching via a matching error derived by the shapes deformation rules, thus being intrinsically compatible with them and
- it treats the shapes classification by deriving a classification error intrinsically compatible with the matching process results' stationarity.

These are also the main features that differentiate the proposed approach from the state of the art in the shapes matching research subject. Namely, implicit representation of planar curves has been adopted by a number of approaches in the shapes matching problem. Characteristic examples are the shapes classification approaches of [8–11], which employ implicit representations of curves in order to enrich the feature vectors that drive the proposed classification procedures with characteristics that bare certain desirable grouping identities (Euclidean, scale and parameterization invariance, etc.). On the other hand, diffeomorphic image registration methods [12–15] intrinsically incorporate implicit shapes representations in the matching procedure. However, the deformation fields that map one family of shapes to another are univocally determined from stationary points of the corresponding images registration problem. Hence, no geometric restrictions can be imposed while mapping between shapes families. As a consequence, invariant transformations and invariance with respect to the functional form of the implicit function cannot be incorporated in the matching procedure.

Such a requirement for mutual consistency between matching error optimization and shapes representation led to a class of methods, [16–20], that fix a representation of the shapes, consistent with the selected matching error and then the shapes representation is transported along geodesics of the metric space that the matching error induces. Moreover, coupling of the shapes' deformations with specific metrics allowed for computing Karcher means of shapes [21] and, consequently, for adapting classification methods so as to group shapes, without incorporating feature vector representations [22]. Although, very efficient for mapping between shapes, these methods do not allow for deriving classification conditions, since one cannot represent inside these shape spaces congruence classes of a certain shape.

On the contrary, the shapes classification is inherent in the proposed approach and the deformation from one shape to the other is modeled so as to split between deformation of a shape's congruence class and deformation of a shape inside its class. This allows for deriving compatibility conditions for a tested grouping of shapes straight from the deformations that map the shapes of the group, one to each other.

2 The Introduced Methodology for Matching and Comparing Letters' Shapes

2.1 Fundamental Entities and Hypotheses

The data upon which the proposed methodology will be developed are the shapes of the alphabet symbols. We note that this choice requires off-line pre-processing of the documents, in order to extract the various alphabet symbols' realizations appearing on them. However, this off-line preprocessing leads to a very detailed and powerful representation of the handwriting style, since it is based on all the fundamental units of writing. The available data for the documents consist of high quality images (average resolution 300 pixels/cm). First, the letter symbols are cropped semi-automatically. Then, automatic segmentation of letters' body is performed on the basis of the cropped images' intensity distributions (see Fig. 1).

On this basis, the problem of classifying an ensemble of documents to a proper set of writers is reduced to a) the determination of substantial differences between the shapes

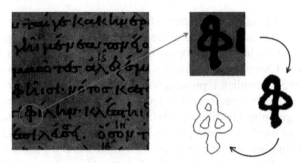

Fig. 1. Documents' pre-processing: Detection of the darker flat areas in the image → semi-automatic crop of the letters → binary image segmentation → extraction of 1-pixel contour set with finite curvature

of the alphabet symbols common in them and b) the formation of closed subsets of alphabet symbols realizations manifesting statistically significant similarity/uniformity. For expressing these two tasks quantitatively, suppose for a moment that a class of curves includes distorted elements of the same family of implicitly described curves. Then, the deformation of each curve of this class may be decomposed in a) a deformation that respects the family's implicit functional form and b) a deformation associated with the alteration of the functional form. Our goal is to identify and suppress these two types of deformations sequentially, so as to obtain a single curve, which best represents all curves of the class.

Intending to match and classify alphabet symbols modulo affine transformations, we identify them as the deformations that retain the functional forms of the implicit families of the alphabet symbols' shapes. Translation and rotation will be suppressed indirectly, by formalizing the letters' shapes matching and similarity in terms of their curvature, while matching scaling factors will be determined via a corresponding shapes alignment procedure.

2.2 Geometrical Setting of the Letters Similarity Problem

Consider a collection of realizations of the same alphabet symbol and form a class of shapes under the hypothesis that these realizations come from the same implicit family of curves, formed by the level-sets of a function $f : \mathbb{R}^2 \to \mathbb{R}$. Then, optimal alignment of the shape χ_1 of an alphabet symbol realization inside this family of curves should minimize total geodesic distance between the aligned shape χ_1 and a certain level-set χ of f. Namely, the geodesic distance between a point p of χ_1 and the level-set $\chi : f|_\chi = f_\chi$ corresponds to the integral $\sigma(\mathrm{p}, \chi) = \int_{f(\mathrm{p})}^{f_\chi} \frac{df}{\nabla f}$. Letting also the contour of the shape χ_1 to be parametrized by its curve length γ, the total geodesic distance between χ_1 and χ is expressed via the integral $S(\chi_1, \chi) = \int_{\chi_1} \sigma(\mathrm{p}(\gamma), \chi) d\gamma$.

This integral actually corresponds to the area of the domain $\Omega(\chi_1, \chi)$ bounded by the contours χ_1 and χ. The variation of this integral with respect to χ can be calculated using Cartan's formula as $\delta S(\chi_1, \chi) = \int_{\Omega(\chi_1, \chi)} (\nabla \cdot \delta\chi) d\Omega$. Here $\delta\chi$ represents an arbitrary variation of χ with $\|\delta\chi\| = 1$ and, since χ is a level-set of f, it is deformed only along ∇f. Consequently, $\sup\limits_{\|\delta\chi\|=1} \delta S(\chi_1, \chi) = \int_{\Omega(\chi_1,\chi)} |\nabla \cdot (\nabla f/\|\nabla f\|)| d\Omega$, thus expressing the variation of the area enclosed by the mismatch of χ_1 with the level-sets of f in terms of their curvature

$$C[f] \equiv \nabla \cdot (n[f]), n[f] \equiv \nabla f/\|\nabla f\|$$

On the other hand, minimization of $\int_{\Omega(\chi_1,\chi)} |C[f]| d\Omega$ is implied by minimization of $\int_{\Omega(\chi_1,\chi)} (C[f])^2 d\Omega$, which by Stokes' theorem reads

$$\int_{\Omega(\chi_1,\chi)} (C[f])^2 d\Omega = 2 \int_{\chi_1} \left| C[f]|_{p(\gamma)} - C[f]|_{\chi} \right| d\gamma \tag{1}$$

In this way, we have formally connected the probability of the hypothesis that a realization of an alphabet symbol comes from a certain implicit family of curves with a deformation of the curvature $C[f]$ of this implicit family. Namely, a letter shape χ_1 is optimally aligned inside a given implicit family of curves $f(x, y) = $ constant if the curvature functional, $C[f]$, exhibits on χ_1 minimal deviation from the isocontours of f.

2.3 Derivation of the Implicit Curvature Deformation Rule

The curvature deformation that we should take into consideration are the ones induced by transformations of the Euclidean domain. In general a reversible transformation $\rho : (x, y) \mapsto (\tilde{x}, \tilde{y})$ that retains smoothness induces a modification $f \to \tilde{f}$ of the functional form of f such that $\tilde{f}(\tilde{x}, \tilde{y}) = f(x, y)$. In turn, this modification results to a modifications of the curvature $C[f] \to C[\tilde{f}]$ that reads $C[\tilde{f}](\tilde{x}, \tilde{y}) = (J^{-1}\nabla) \cdot \left(\frac{J^{-1}\nabla f}{\|J^{-1}\nabla f\|} \right)$, where J stands for the Jacobian of the transformation. Although, from this relation there is no straightforward connection between $C[f]$ and $C[\tilde{f}]$, we could recover such a connection by asking that transformation ρ is infinitesimally generated. Namely, we ask for a transformation $\rho : (x, y, t) \mapsto (\tilde{x}(t), \tilde{y}(t))$, such that $q \equiv \partial_t \rho$ is continuous. Such a transformation induces a t-parametrized modification of the functional form of f such that

$$\tilde{f}(\tilde{x}, \tilde{y}, t) = \tilde{f}|_{t=0} = f(x, y) \tag{2}$$

Then, the corresponding curvature deformation obeys the PDE

$$\frac{\partial}{\partial t}\tilde{c} = \tilde{c}\left(\tilde{n} \cdot \left(\frac{\partial q}{\partial \rho}\tilde{n}\right) - 2\tilde{\tau} \cdot \left(\frac{\partial q}{\partial \rho}\tilde{\tau}\right)\right) - \tilde{\tau} \cdot \left(\tilde{\tau} \cdot \frac{\partial}{\partial \rho}\left(\frac{\partial q}{\partial \rho}\right)\tilde{n}\right)$$

where $\tilde{c} \equiv C[\tilde{f}](\tilde{x}, \tilde{y}, t)$, $\frac{\partial}{\partial \rho} \equiv \left(\frac{\partial}{\partial \tilde{x}}, \frac{\partial}{\partial \tilde{y}}\right)$, $\tilde{n} = n[\tilde{f}](\tilde{x}, \tilde{y}, t)$ and $\tilde{\tau}$ is the unit vector that results by rotating $\tilde{n}$ by $\pi/2$.

This PDE describes the curvature deformation under any infinitesimally generated diffeomorphism of the Euclidean plane. In the case of letter shapes, we can limit our analysis to affine transformations, since handwriting is a procedure learned so that it is performed on planar surfaces. In this case, the matrix $A \equiv \frac{\partial q}{\partial \rho}$ is constant with respect to ρ and reads $A = \begin{bmatrix} \dot{\lambda}_x & \dot{\phi} \\ -\dot{\phi} & \dot{\lambda}_y \end{bmatrix}$, where $\dot{\lambda}_x$ and $\dot{\lambda}_y$ correspond to the x and y scaling factors' infinitesimals, respectively and $\dot{\phi}$ corresponds to the infinitesimal of rotation angle. Then, the curvature deformation PDE reads $\partial_t \tilde{c} = \tilde{c}(\tilde{n} \cdot (A\tilde{n}) - 2\tilde{\tau} \cdot (A\tilde{\tau}))$, which, after substitution of A, leads to the curvature deformation rule

$$\tilde{c} = e^{\frac{1}{2}(\lambda_x + \lambda_y)} C[f] \exp \int_{\Delta(t)} \frac{3\tilde{f}_{\tilde{x}}^2 - \tilde{f}_{\tilde{y}}^2}{2} \frac{1}{\|\nabla \tilde{f}\|^2} (d\lambda_x - d\lambda_y) \tag{3}$$

where $\Delta(t)$ is the transformation's integral path, $\tilde{f}_{\tilde{x}} = \frac{\partial \tilde{f}}{\partial \tilde{x}}, \tilde{f}_{\tilde{y}} = \frac{\partial \tilde{f}}{\partial \tilde{y}}$. We should note here the compatibility of this deformation rule with the expected curvature invariance under Euclidean transformations, since (3) is independent to $\dot{\phi}$. Moreover, path integral of (3) may be calculated if one considers the deformation PDE of $\tilde{n}$,

$$\tilde{\tau} \cdot \frac{\partial \tilde{n}}{\partial t} = -\tilde{\tau} \cdot (A\tilde{n}) \tag{4}$$

which, after substitution of A and absorption of rigid body rotation, leads to an explicit formula for the integrand of (3). Also, since A is constant with respect to ρ, without any loss of generality, we can consider A to be also constant with respect to t. In this case, the path integral of (3) gets an explicit expression, which, in turn, allows for obtaining a corresponding explicit formula for the deformation of the implicit curvature

$$\tilde{c} = e^{-\lambda_x - \lambda_y} C[f] \|\nabla f\|^3 / \left(\left(e^{-\lambda_x} f_x\right)^2 + \left(e^{-\lambda_y} f_y\right)^2 \right)^{3/2} \tag{5}$$

2.4 Optimal Affine Registration of the Letters' Shapes

Consider two shapes χ_1, χ_2 of the same alphabet symbol χ and their corresponding contours Γ_1 and Γ_2. In order to match Γ_2 to Γ_1 we let χ_1 define the family of curves with implicit representation

$$f_{\chi_1} = \text{DT}(\chi_1 \backslash \Gamma_1) - \text{DT}(\neg \chi_1)$$

where DT is the Euclidean Distance Transform of a binary shape. We should stress here that the whole methodology does not require a specific functional form for the implicit family of curves but for the implementation of the methodology, we should fix a functional form for it. Euclidean Distance Transform has been selected, since congruent points of its level-sets bare the same unit normal vector $n[f]$ and thus the same curvature deformation ratio, as it is implied by (5).

Using the curvature deformation formula (5) we can explicitly determine the optimal x and y scaling factors, e^{λ_x} and e^{λ_y} respectively. Namely, as (1) indicates, we seek for a pair of congruent points on Γ_1 and Γ_2, whose curvature ratio, via (5), induces scaling factors which minimize

$$\int_{\Gamma_2} \left| C[f_{\chi_1}]\big|_{\Gamma_2} - C[f_{\chi_1}]\big|_{\Gamma_1} \right| d\Gamma$$

This, search should be performed for all relative cyclic permutations of the points of Γ_1 and Γ_2, since the whole curves comparison procedure is performed modulo rotation.

Having determined the optimal scaling factors of Γ_2 so as to optimally match Γ_1, indirectly, with respect to the isocontours of f_{χ_1}, we should then determine the optimal Euclidean transform of the resized Γ_2 that allows for an actual alignment of it with Γ_1 (see Fig. 2). However, the dimensionality of this problem has already been vastly reduced, since the optimal correspondence between the points of Γ_1 and Γ_2 has been determined during the optimal scaling search. So the optimal translation and rotation of the scaled Γ_2 so as to match Γ_1 is reduced to a corresponding Least Squares optimization problem with an exact solution in terms of the points' cross-covariance matrix.

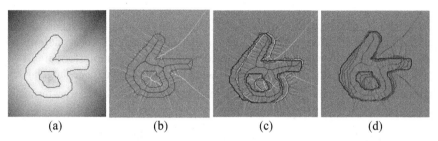

(a)   (b)   (c)   (d)

Fig. 2. The procedure of matching a pair of shapes **(a)** The contour Γ_1 (in red) together with the function f_{χ_1}. **(b)** The implicit curvature $C[f_{\chi_1}]$ of the level sets of f_{χ_1}. **(c)** The curvature deformation caused by inclusion of a 2nd member χ_2 in the same family (Γ_1 is in blue, Γ_2 is in red, curvature deformation of $C[f_{\chi_1}]$ is depicted in grayscale). **(d)** Affine registration of Γ_2 inside the family of isocontours of f_{χ_1}. The optimally transformed Γ_2 is depicted in green, while the grayscale background depicts the minimized curvature deformation. (Color figure online)

2.5 Evaluation of the Joint Implicit Family Hypothesis

Having dealt with optimal affine registration of one shape inside an implicit family of curves, we can proceed in evaluating the hypothesis that a collection of shapes forms a class of deformed members of the same implicit family of curves. In order to do so, we should consider a deformation rule that maintains the determined optimal affine registration invariant. Namely, we should consider a deformation $\rho_\perp : (x, y, s) \mapsto (\tilde{x}(s), \tilde{y}(s))$ such that $\partial_s \rho_\perp \cdot \partial_t \rho = 0$, i.e. a vector flow normal to the one of the optimal affine registration. Such, a vector flow results to a curvature deformation PDE of the form $\partial_s \tilde{c} = \tilde{c}(\tilde{n} \cdot (A\tilde{\tau}) + 2\tilde{\tau} \cdot (A\tilde{n}))$ or equivalently to a curvature deformation rule

$$\tilde{c} = \tilde{c}|_{s=0} \exp \int_{\Delta_\perp(s)} \left(\frac{3}{2} \sin 2\tilde{\theta} (\dot{\lambda}_y - \dot{\lambda}_x) - \dot{\phi} \right) ds \qquad (6)$$

where $\tilde{\theta} \equiv \text{atan2}\left(\tilde{f}_{\tilde{y}}, \tilde{f}_{\tilde{x}}\right)$ and $\Delta_\perp(s)$ is the transformation's integral path. Again, path integral of (6) may be calculated if one considers the corresponding deformation PDE of $\tilde{n}$, given in (4), which now takes the form $\tilde{\tau} \cdot \frac{\partial \tilde{n}}{\partial s} = -\tilde{\tau} \cdot (A\tilde{\tau})$. After substitution of A, this PDE reads

$$-2\partial_s\tilde{\theta} = \left(\dot{\lambda}_y + \dot{\lambda}_x\right) + \left(\dot{\lambda}_y - \dot{\lambda}_x\right)\cos 2\tilde{\theta} \tag{7}$$

Again, constancy of A with respect to ρ allows for considering it to be also constant with respect to s, thus allowing for computing explicit solutions for (6) and (7). Namely, substitution of (7) in the path integral of (6) leads to its explicit calculation, thus offering a closed form for the corresponding curvature deformation, which reads

$$\tilde{c} = \tilde{c}|_{s=0} \left(\frac{\left(\dot{\lambda}_y + \dot{\lambda}_x\right) + \left(\dot{\lambda}_y - \dot{\lambda}_x\right)\cos 2\tilde{\theta}}{\left(\dot{\lambda}_y + \dot{\lambda}_x\right) + \left(\dot{\lambda}_y - \dot{\lambda}_x\right)\cos 2\tilde{\theta}|_{s=0}} \right)^{3/2} \tag{8}$$

We should denote here that the factor $e^{-s\dot{\phi}}$, induced by the rotation elements of A, has been eliminated in the aforementioned formula, since the matching process described in Sects. 2.3 and 2.4 is formulated and performed modulo Euclidean transformations.

On the other hand, Eq. (7) bares itself a closed form solution that relates angular deviations between $\tilde{n}\left[\tilde{f}\right]$ and $n[f]$ with the path length, s, of the considered transformation. Namely,

$$s\sqrt{\dot{\lambda}_y\dot{\lambda}_x} = \left[\text{atan}\left(\tan\tilde{\theta}\sqrt{\dot{\lambda}_x/\dot{\lambda}_y} \right) \right]_s^0 \tag{9}$$

Deformation rules (8) and (9), together with the scaling factors determined via optimal affine registration allow for calculating a deformation path length s congruent to each curvature correspondence $C[f_{\chi 1}]$ $C[f_{\chi 2}]$ between two implicit families of shapes. By integrating these deformation path lengths for all congruent points of the contours Γ_1, Γ_2 of the shapes χ_1, χ_2 we obtain the area $\delta E(\chi_1, \chi_2)$ covered while deforming Γ_1 and Γ_2 along $\rho_\perp$, up to coincidence of their congruent points (Fig. 3).

$$\delta E(\chi_1, \chi_2) = \frac{1}{\int_V dV} \int_V \left(\frac{C[f_{\chi 1}]}{C[f_{\chi 2}]} \right)^{\frac{3}{2}} \left(\frac{C[f_{\chi 2}]}{m[f_{\chi 1}]} - \frac{C[f_{\chi 1}]}{m[f_{\chi 2}]} \right) dV \tag{10}$$

where $V = \left(\chi_1 \backslash \chi_2\right) \cup \left(\chi_2 \backslash \chi_1\right)$ and $m[f_\chi] \equiv \dot{\lambda}_y \cos^2\tilde{\theta}_\chi + \dot{\lambda}_x \sin^2\tilde{\theta}_\chi$.

This measure is in a one to one correspondence with the domain of the probability that χ_1 and χ_2, modulo affine transformations, correspond to the same implicit family of curves. Hence, δE is the quantity set at the center of the statistical analysis of the hypothesis that a collection of realizations of the same letter has been written by the same writer.

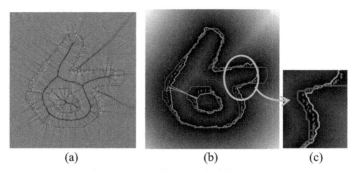

(a)   (b)   (c)

Fig. 3. Evaluation of the hypothesis that a pair of realizations of an alphabet symbol have been written by the same writer. In all figures the aligned realizations' contours correspond to the blue and green lines, while the red points lie at the locus of stationary points of the integrand of (10). (a) The background depicts the target curvature deformation. (b), (c) The background depicts the integrand of (10), i.e. the probability density that the two realizations come from the same implicit family of curves. (Color figure online)

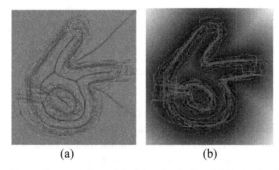

(a)   (b)

Fig. 4. The locus of the stationary points of the joint similarity of all letter "epsilon" realizations of the same document, computed by overlaying all pairwise comparisons of the realizations' shapes. The underlying image intensities depict (a) the succession of the curvature deformations and (b) the succession of the integrands of the matching error δE, defined in (10), both computed for all pairwise comparisons of the letter's realizations.

3   Statistical Classification of Documents into Writers

Classification of a document to a writer is based on the maximization of the joint probability of the following hypothesis

Classification Hypothesis: *If a document* D_2 *has been written by the same hand with another document* D_1, *then for any symbol* χ *that appears in both* D_1 *and* D_2 *the population mean value of* $\delta E(\chi_1, \chi_2)$ *when* $\chi_1, \chi_2 \in D_1$ *should be equal to the population mean value of* $\delta E(\chi_1, \chi_2)$ *when* $(\chi_1, \chi_2) \in D_1 \times D_2$.

This null hypothesis is quantified by computing the mean values and standard deviations of δE for all pairwise comparisons inside D_1 (Fig. 4) and between D_1 and D_2:

$$\delta M_1^\chi \equiv \underset{\chi_1,\chi_2 \in D_1}{\text{mean}} \{\delta E(\chi_1,\chi_2)\} \qquad \delta S_1^\chi \equiv \underset{\chi_1,\chi_2 \in D_1}{\text{std}} \{\delta E(\chi_1,\chi_2)\}$$

$$\delta M_{1,2}^\chi \equiv \underset{(\chi_1,\chi_2) \in D_1 \times D_2}{\text{mean}} \{\delta E(\chi_1,\chi_2)\} \qquad \delta S_{1,2}^\chi \equiv \underset{(\chi_1,\chi_2) \in D_1 \times D_2}{\text{std}} \{\delta E(\chi_1,\chi_2)\}$$

and, on this basis by evaluating the quantity

$$T^\chi(D_1, D_2) = \frac{\delta M_1^\chi - \delta M_{1,2}^\chi}{\sqrt{\left(\delta S_1^\chi\right)^2 / N_1^\chi + \left(\delta S_{1,2}^\chi\right)^2 / N_{1,2}^\chi}} \tag{11}$$

which follows a Student distribution. In (11), the cardinal numbers N_1^χ and $N_{1,2}^\chi$ read

$$N_1^\chi = \frac{1}{2}|\{\chi \in D_1\}|(|\{\chi \in D_2\}| - 1) \qquad N_{1,2}^\chi = |\{\chi \in D_2\}||\{\chi \in D_2\}|$$

The classification hypothesis states that the realizations of any symbol χ retain their mean dissimilarity between two documents D_1, D_2, written by the same hand. Then, the joint probability distribution of the classification hypothesis, evaluated for all symbols χ, common in D_1 and D_2, reflects to the probability of attributing D_1 and D_2 to the same writer. The likelihood that corresponds to the aforementioned probability is

$$\xi(D_1, D_2) = \left(\prod_\chi \text{Student}\left(T^\chi(D_1, D_2)\right)\right)^{1/\#\chi} \tag{12}$$

Although, the "classification hypothesis" quantifies the likelihood that a pair of documents has been written by the same hand, it does not offer an immediate condition for accepting/rejecting the common writer hypothesis for these documents. In order to determine conditions for taking such a decision we consider the case of a set of alphabet symbols realizations that resulted from merging a pair of documents. If the realizations of the constituent documents become inseparable after their merge, then we will consider the merge as acceptable, otherwise the merge is unverified. Unverified merges are acceptable only if they correspond to a composition of acceptable merges. The condition for accepting pairwise documents' merges is stated below:

Acceptable Merge of a Pair of Documents: If for a pair of documents, D_1 and D_2, it holds that $D_2 = \arg \min_{D \neq D_1} \xi(D_1, D)$, then merge the alphabet symbols' realizations of D_1 and D_2, forming $D_{1,2}$. For each alphabet symbol χ of $D_{1,2}$ compute

$$\widetilde{T}^\chi(D_1, D_2) = \frac{\delta \widetilde{M}_{1,2}^\chi \sqrt{\widetilde{N}_{1,2}^\chi}}{\delta \widetilde{S}_{1,2}^\chi}, \qquad \begin{array}{l} \delta \widetilde{M}_{1,2}^\chi \equiv \underset{\chi_1,\chi_2 \in D_{1,2}}{\text{mean}} \{\delta E(\chi_1,\chi_2)\} \\[2mm] \delta \widetilde{S}_{1,2}^\chi \equiv \underset{\chi_1,\chi_2 \in D_{1,2}}{\text{std}} \{\delta E(\chi_1,\chi_2)\} \end{array}$$

and, on this basis evaluate the total likelihood for merging D_1 and D_2 as

$$\widetilde{\xi}(D_1, D_2) = \left(\prod_\chi \text{Student}\left(\widetilde{T}^\chi(D_1, D_2)\right)\right)^{1/\#\chi}$$

If $\tilde{\xi}(D_1, D_2) \geq \min(\xi(D_1, D_2), \xi(D_2, D_1))$ the merge of D_1 with D_2 is acceptable.

In fact, this condition states that each document merges with its "closest" one if the likelihood of the single writer hypothesis increases, when the two documents are merged. By composing the acceptable merges sequentially we determine the proposed classification for the considered documents. In Fig. 5 we visualize the first 4 levels of application of the pairwise merging condition for the documents of the considered data set (see Table 1). By composing the determined pairwise merges we obtain the proposed classification of the documents into 4 writers.

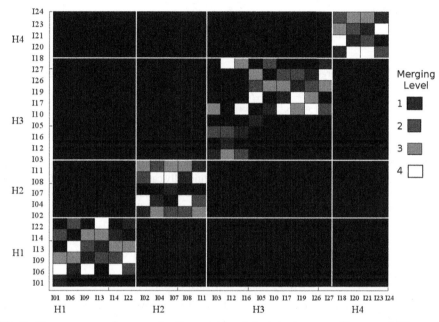

Fig. 5. The sequence of merges for the considered documents pages. The pages' IDs are in correspondence with the ones of Table 1 and they are ordered with respect to the determined writing hands. Each pair of documents merge is colored according to the level of composition at which the merging is verified. One can note that the determined grouping of the considered documents' pages into 4 writing hands has been established from the 2nd iteration of the merging procedure (Color figure online)

4   Identification of the Writer of Important Historical Documents

The developed methodology has been applied to the very important problem of the automatic classification of Byzantine codices according to their writer. The introduced approach has been applied to 25 images of pages of Byzantine codices, selected by Professor Christopher Blackwell of Furman University.

We would like to emphasize that the authors did not employ any reference manuscript, they had no idea about the number of distinct hands who had written the considered pages and they did not have any related information whatsoever at their disposal. The only data available was the pages' images denoted only with the IDs that appear in the column "Codices' pages' IDs" of Table 1. The developed system classified the 25 Byzantine codices' pages in 4 different writers, designated as H1, H2, H3 and H4 (see Table 1 – column "Hand").

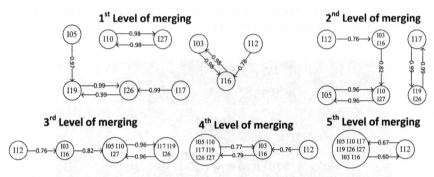

Fig. 6. The merging procedure that formed the group of H3. The arrows indicate the determined acceptable merges at each iteration of the pairwise merging procedure. In terms of the definition of an "acceptable merge" the source of each arrow is the document D_1 and the target of each arrow points to its "closest" document D_2, which additionally can be merged with D_1 forming an inseparable ensemble. The value assigned to each arrow corresponds to the value of the likelihood $\xi(D_1, D_2)$ that the writer of the source document has also written the target one.

Table 1. Byzantine Codices' classification into hands

Codices' pages' IDs	Writing Hand	Original Codex
I01, I06, I09, I13, I14, I22	H1	Escorialensis 4 (West F, Escorialensis Ω.I.12)
I02, I04, I07, I08, I11	H2	Venetus A, Marcianus Graecus Z. 454
I05, I10, I17, I19, I26, I27	H3	Escorialensis 3 (West E, Escorialensis Y.I.1)
I03, I12, I16	H3	Venetus B, Marcianus Graecus Z. 453
I18, I20, I21, I23, I24	H4	Marcianus Graecus Z. 458

Professor Blackwell, has verified that the automatic classification of the 25 pages is fully compatible with their classification according to the Byzantine Codices they belong to (see "Original Codex" column in Table 1). Moreover, Prof. Blackwell recovered that these manuscripts are of central importance in paleography, since they all preserve Homeric Iliad. Finally, Prof. Blackwell indicated that the classification of "Escorialencis 3" and "Venetus B" pages to the same writer, H3, is in accordance with the hypothesis of Allen [23] and Maniaci [24] that these two codices have been written by the same hand, a hypothesis which was stated and supported using qualitative stylistic arguments and intuition. The developed automatic handwriting classification system allowed for a quantitative unbiased evaluation of this hypothesis. Namely, classification results support that the common writer hypothesis for "Escorialencis 3" and "Venetus B" holds with probability equivalent to the one of the hypothesis that the pages of each codex actually belong to its writer. In Fig. 6 we visualize the way that the merge of these documents is determined, page by page, together with the common writer hypothesis likelihoods, $\xi(D_1, D_2)$. From this figure it becomes evident that the grouping of these documents emerges from the 2nd iteration of the merging procedure, where the merged pages "I03" and "I06" of "Venetus B" relate with the merged pages "I10" and "I27" of "Escorialencis 3" forming an acceptable merge.

In addition we have tested the classification performance of efficient methodologies of shapes comparison in the case of the considered byzantine codices. Specifically, we have chosen the method of "Inner Distance shape context" (IDSC) [25] and the method of [26] for improving the classification results offered by the IDSC and we have repeated the codices' classification experiment on the basis of this similarity measure, instead of δE (10). In Fig. 7 we visualize the first 4 levels of application of the pairwise merging condition for the considered codices' pages, where it becomes evident that, from the 2nd iteration of the merging procedure, H3 and H4 mix together and with the other two "hands", thus leading to misclassification of the codices' pages.

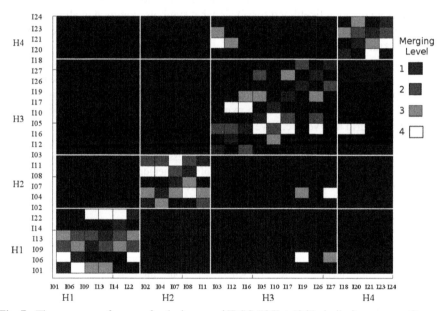

Fig. 7. The sequence of merges for the improved IDSC ([25] + [26]) similarity measure. One can note that the determined grouping violates the ground-truth classification from the 2nd iteration of the merging procedure.

5 Conclusion

The technical elements of this work, constitute a general methodology for matching, comparing and grouping planar shapes under a unified framework. Specifically, the shapes' grouping is interpreted as the procedure of turning collections of shapes into classes under the hypothesis that these shapes come from the same implicit family of curves, formed by the level-sets of a function $f : \mathbb{R}^2 \to \mathbb{R}$. In order to render the analysis purely geometric and independent to the specific functional form of f, we have formulated the shapes' comparison in terms of the curvature of the level-sets of f. Namely, we have derived the PDE that governs the curvature deformations, as well as explicit formulas for the change of curvature under affine transformations. On this basis, we have determined those geometric transformations that respect (Sect. 2.4) and those that violate (Sect. 2.5) the common implicit family of curves hypothesis. The second type of transformations offers the geometric measure, upon which we evaluate the probability that two shapes' classes can be merged into a single class.

The methodology has been implemented so as to deal with automatic writer identification and the corresponding system has been applied to the identification of the writer of Byzantine codices that preserve Iliad. The processed shapes are the realizations of the alphabet symbols extracted from the documents' images. The realizations of each alphabet symbol are compared pairwise, modulo affine transformations. The statistical compatibility of these comparisons inside the same document and between different documents determines the likelihood of attributing different documents to the same hand. By maximizing the joint likelihood for all alphabet symbols, common in all documents' images we have established the most probable classification of the given documents' according to their writer.

Specifically, application of the methodology to 25 images of Byzantine codices' pages indicated that these pages have been written by 4 hands in full accordance with experts' opinion and knowledge. Moreover, the classification of these pages into hands offered an objective verification of an experts' hypothesis that 2 Byzantine codices, preserved in Madrid and Venice, have been written by the same writer.

Acknowledgements. The authors are thankful to the Professor Christopher Blackwell of Furman University for setting up the experimental validation of the writer identification performance of the developed methodology with scientific precision. Moreover, the selections that Prof. Blackwell made concerning the processed manuscripts has offered additional value to the experimental results; hence, we are really thankful to him for this provision.

This research is co-financed by Greece and the European Union (European Social Fund- ESF) through the Operational Programme «Human Resources Development, Education and Lifelong Learning» in the context of the project "Reinforcement of Postdoctoral Researchers - 2nd Cycle" (MIS-5033021), implemented by the State Scholarships Foundation (IKΥ).

Ευρωπαϊκή Ένωση
European Social Fund

**Operational Programme
Human Resources Development,
Education and Lifelong Learning**

Co-financed by Greece and the European Union

References

1. He, S., Schomaker, L.: Writer identification using curvature-free features. Pattern Recogn. **63**, 451–464 (2017)

2. He, S., Wiering, M., Schomaker, L.: Junction detection in handwritten documents and its applicationto writer identification. Pattern Recogn. **48**, 4036–4048 (2015)
3. Hannad, Y., Siddiqi, I., El Youssfi Kettani, M.: Writer identification using texture descriptors of handwritten fragments. Expert Syst. Appl. **47**(4), 14–22 (2016)
4. Schomaker, L., Bulacu, M.: Automatic writer identification using connected-component contours and edge-based features of uppercase western script. IEEE Trans. Pattern Anal. Mach. Intell. **26**(6), 787–798 (2004)
5. Tan, G.X., Viard-Gaudin, C., Kot, A.C.: Automatic writer identification framework for online handwritten documents using character prototypes. Pattern Recogn. **42**(12), 3313–3323 (2009)
6. Wolf, L., et al.: Identifying join candidates in cairo genizah. Int. J. Comput. Vis. **94**(1), 118–135 (2011)
7. Schlapbach, A., Bunke, H.: A writer identification and verification system using HMM based recognizers. Pattern Anal. Appl. **10**(1), 33–43 (2007)
8. Gorelick, L., Galun, M., Sharon, E., Basri, R., Brandt, A.: Shape representation and classification using the poisson equation. IEEE Trans. PAMI **28**(12), 1991–2005 (2006)
9. Hamsici, O.C., Martinez, A.M.: Rotation invariant kernels and their application to shape analysis. IEEE Trans. Pattern Anal. Mach. Intell. **31**(10), 1985–1999 (2009)
10. Manay, S., Cremers, D., Hong, B.-W., Yezzi, A.J., Soatto, S.: Integral invariants for shape matching. IEEE Trans. Pattern Anal. Mach. Intell. **28**(10), 1602–1618 (2006)
11. Hong, B.-W., Soatto, S.: Shape matching using integral invariants. IEEE Trans. Pattern Anal. Mach. Intell. **37**(1), 1602–1618 (2015)
12. Huang, X., Paragios, N., Metaxas, D.N.: Shape registration in implicit spaces using information theory and free form deformations. IEEE Trans. PAMI **28**(8), 1303–1318 (2006)
13. Beg, M.F., Miller, M.I., Trouve, A., Younes, L.: Computing large deformation metric mappings via geodesic flows of diffeomorphisms. Int. J. Comput. Vis. **61**(2), 139–157 (2005)
14. Lorenzi, M., Pennec, X.: Geodesics, parallel transport & one-parameter sub-groups for diffeomorphic image registration. Int. J. Comput. Vis. **105**(2), 111–127 (2013)
15. Zhang, M., Fletcher, P.T.: Fast diffeomorphic image registration via fourier-approximated lie algebras. Int. J. Comput. Vis. **127**(1), 61–73 (2018). https://doi.org/10.1007/s11263-018-1099-x
16. Wirth, B., Bar, L., Rumpf, M., Sapiro, G.: A continuum mechanical approach to geodesics in shape space. Int. J. Comput. Vis. **93**(3), 293–318 (2011)
17. Mio, W., Bowers, J.C., Liu, X.: Shape of elastic strings in euclidean space. Int. J. Comput. Vis. **82**, 96–112 (2009)
18. Klassen, E., Srivastava, A., Mio, W., Joshi, S.H.: Analysis of planar shapes using geodesic paths on shape spaces. IEEE Trans. Pattern Anal. Mach. Intell. **26**(3), 372–383 (2004)
19. Bryner, D., Klassen, E., Le, H., Srivastava, A.: 2D affine and projective shape analysis. IEEE Trans. Pattern Anal. Mach. Intell. **36**(5), 998–1011 (2014)
20. Younes, L., Michor, P.W., Shah, J., Mumford, D.: A metric on shape space with explicit geodesics. Rend. Lincei Mat. Appl. **19**, 25–57 (2008)
21. Bauer, M., Bruveris, M., Harms, P., Moeller – Andersen, J.: A numerical framework for sobolev metrics on the space of curves. SIAM J. Imaging Sci. **10**(1), 47–73 (2017)
22. Jin, L., Wen, Z., Hu, Z.: Topology-preserving nonlinear shape registration on the shape manifold. Multimed. Tools Appl. (2020, in Press)
23. Allen, T.W.: Homeri Ilias, vol. 2. Oxford (1931)
24. Maniaci, M.: Problemi di 'mise en page' dei manoscritti con comment a cornice: L'esempio di alcuni testimoni dell' Iliade. Segno e testo **4**, 211–297 (2006)
25. Ling, H., Jacobs, D.W.: Shape classification using the inner-distance. IEEE Trans. PAMI **29**(2), 286–299 (2007)
26. Bai, X., Yang, X., Latecki, L.J., Liu, W., Tu, Z.: Learning context-sensitive shape similarity by graph transduction. IEEE Trans. PAMI **32**(5), 861–874 (2010)

Visual Programming-Based Interactive Analysis of Ancient Documents: The Case of Magical Signs in Jewish Manuscripts

Parth Sarthi Pandey[1(✉)], Vinodh Rajan[1], H. Siegfried Stiehl[1], and Michael Kohs[2]

[1] iXMan_Lab, Research Group Image Processing, Department of Informatics, Universität Hamburg, Hamburg, Germany
{6pandey,sampath,stiehl}@informatik.uni-hamburg.de
[2] Center for the Study of Manuscript Cultures, Universität Hamburg, Hamburg, Germany
michael.kohs@uni-hamburg.de

Abstract. This paper presents an interactive system for experimental ancient document analysis applied to the specific use case of the computational analysis of magical signs, called *Brillenbuchstaben* or *charaktêres*, in digitized Jewish manuscripts. It draws upon known theories as well as methods from open source toolboxes and embeds them into a visual programming-based user interface. Its general design is particularly aimed at the needs of Humanities scholars and thus enables them to computationally analyze these signs without requiring any prior programming experience. In the light of this, the web-based system has been designed to be e.g. interoperable, modular, flexible, transparent and readily accessible by tech-unsavvy users regardless of their background. The paper further discusses a paradigmatic user study conducted with domain experts to evaluate this system and presents first results from those evaluations.

Keywords: Ancient document analysis · Interactive software tools · User experience

1 Introduction

Magic has been an integral part of human civilization. This is evidenced by examples of astrology, alchemy, healing, and shamanism having been found in most human cultures [12]. All cultures are packed with stories of magic and about

Parts of the research for this paper were undertaken at SFB 950 'Manuscript Cultures in Asia, Africa and Europe', funded by the German Research Foundation (Deutsche Forschungsgemeinschaft, DFG) and within the scope of the Centre for the Study of Manuscript Cultures (CSMC), Universität Hamburg. We are also indebted to Christopher Hahn for his pioneering work as referenced and Dieter Jessen for his support in setting up the iXMan_Lab hardware.

A. Del Bimbo et al. (Eds.): ICPR 2020 Workshops, LNCS 12667, pp. 156–170, 2021.
https://doi.org/10.1007/978-3-030-68787-8_11

magic, and Jewish culture is no exception. For instance, given the abundance of manuscripts, possibly thousands of them, with magical signs stretching over cultures and eras awaiting digitization, various Jewish manuscripts are known that contain recipes for curses and love potions written in Hebrew along with some magical signs scribbled in and around the text. These magical signs are called *Brillenbuchstaben* in German or *charaktêres* in general [7]. These *charaktêres* are interesting because their semantics have not been deciphered yet, although it has been acknowledged that they are not arbitrary [2, 7].

Digital Humanities (DH) is a domain that involves collaborative, transdisciplinary, and computationally-driven research in the field of Humanities by provision of beneficial digital tools and versatile innovative methods [4]. Digital Humanities as a research field has gained momentum in recent years and several attempts are being made to bridge the gaps between Informatics and Humanities. This paper ventures into designing and evaluating a Digital Humanities tool, which facilitates the interactive application of image analysis algorithms from open-source toolboxes to digitized manuscripts through Visual Programming. The research question that guides the development of the tool can be formulated as:

How can we enable scholars in the Humanities working on charaktêres (as just one use case) to perform computational analyses with minimal effort?

The general outline of the paper is as follows. Section 2 presents an introduction to *charaktêres* along with their visual properties. It further gives some background on the general topic of computational analysis of manuscripts. Section 3 elaborates on the system design including user requirements and the approach taken. Section 4 presents the use case of computational analysis of *charaktêres* focusing on the interactive design and deployment of the required toolchains. Section 5 delves into the user evaluation conducted with domain experts to evaluate the usability and usefulness of the system. Finally Sect. 6 concludes the paper with a summary and suggestions for future work.

2 Background and Related Work

2.1 Introduction to *charaktêres*

Gordon [7] defines a magical sign as any sign which looks more or less like an alphabetic sign or a simple ideogram, but one that does not belong to any of the alphabets used in that specific magical text, or to any known system of meaningful symbols. The magical signs termed *charaktêres* appear in Jewish magic, too. The signs usually do not appear in isolation but along with some Hebrew text and other scribbling.

Bohak [2, pp. 36–37] discusses three distinct magical recipes (love spells) with their time of creation separated by at least 200 years. They vary in their texts but the representation of the *charaktêres* is almost similar. This establishes that the scribes copied the *charaktêres* carefully and accurately because they attributed a meaning or even efficacy and power to them.

Magical signs are an important aspect of the Jewish magical culture and the lack of understanding of their meaning is to be acknowledged. Computational analysis, therefore, is expected to be adjuvant in finding the subtle and unobtrusive patterns (if present) within the countless occurrences of *charaktêres* in order to decipher, if not at least categorize, them.

2.2   Visual Properties

Winkler [14, p. 150] described *charaktêres* to be composed of bars, crosses, stars, triangles, etc. and characterized by appended circles. Gordon [6, pp. 27–30], on the other hand, gives a more elaborate definition and states that they are derived from 31 basal signs, namely 26 Greek and Latin characters and five other simple shapes.

Hahn [8] considers them to be consisting of *lines, curves* and *annuli* as elements of an assumed visual vocabulary. Lines and curves are defined by two endpoints. Annuli are often connected to the end of a line, but can also exist unconnected. Where lines or curves intersect or touch, they form a *junction*. Lines and curves that do neither terminate in a junction nor an annulus, are terminated by a *line end*. This definition reduces the *charaktêres* to a set of visual features that can be individually detected through standard image processing methods. Figure 1 shows a typical *charaktêr* with lines and curves highlighted in red and the annuli with small blue circles. A sample from a a typical manuscript page can be seen in Fig. 2.

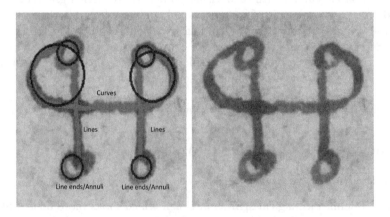

Fig. 1. Visual properties of *charaktêres* (source: Bibliothèque de Genève, Comites Latentes 145, p. 186. (www.e-codices.ch)) [8]

2.3   Computational Analysis

Computational analysis of manuscripts is an active and multidisciplinary research field e.g. in the ICDAR community, e.g. [ICDAR 2019]. Researchers

Fig. 2. Sample from a manuscript (source: Bibliothèque de Genève, Comites Latentes 145, p. 548. (www.e-codices.ch))

have been applying algorithms in order to e.g. improve the quality of digitized manuscripts, spot patterns in historical writings, or identify scribes for long - a survey of which is too broad and clearly beyond the scope of this paper. However, to our best knowledge, no published papers exist on computational analysis of *charaktêres* as yet (except for the special case of computerized scroll unfolding and display [1]).

Hahn's unpublished work [8] is the most relevant to our research since he at first presents a proof-of-concept for computational analysis of *charaktêres* in digitized manuscripts. He proposes several toolchains consisting of sets of digital image processing methods like binarization, edge detection, and skeletonization, etc. in order to i) detect visual properties like lines, curves, junctions and annuli, and ii) represent them as graphs.

However, due to the nature of a proof-of-concept demonstrating the feasibility of computational analysis of magical signs, little attention was paid to the issue of UI/UX of the resulting prototype. The system developed clearly did not focus on usability as one of its goals, as it involves tedious initial software setup, running multiple command line scripts and a clunky UI. Hence, researchers sans a sufficient level of programming experience failed to capitalize on it.

As it can be seen in Fig. 3, the user interface does not allow for functions like easy experimentation by changing parameters or modifying the specific processing chain. Therefore, there was a need for a working system with an interface that requires minimal technical assistance and can also be easily used by non-programmers (i.e. scholars in the Humanities working with signs).

Fig. 3. User interface of Hahn's prototype [8]

3   System Design

3.1   User Requirements

Taking Hahn's work as baseline, we conducted brainstorming sessions with stakeholders from both the Humanities and Informatics in order to both derive a set of requirements and to tailor a system according to scholarly needs. E.g. it was agreed that the computational analysis of *charaktêres* can be reduced to the detection and representation of lines, circles and junctions. Furthermore, the target system should support the lay user in comprehensible algorithm parametrization, replicable experimentation and provision of working systems for real-world use cases. This is to be seen as the first step and prerequisite for a later implementation of an automated retrieval and classification of *charaktêres* in digitzed manuscripts.

Four major requirements came to surface during the requirement analysis:

- Accessibility - web-based or local installation with minimum effort (even by a technical novice)
- Transparency - flexible toolchains and complete clarity on the parameters with liberty to modify them
- Reproducibility - easy sharing of analysis processes that can be replicated and modified along with lab log for a stable parameter regime of individual methods and toolchains
- Metadata Information - information on the properties of the image like source, resolution, width, scale, etc.

3.2   Approach

As the new system was targeted for a non-technical audience, a modular and extendable system with ease of use was the fundamental goal. In this context, visual programming is a software development paradigm based on graphical user interaction. It provides intuitive interfaces to develop personalized solutions which are specifically designed to make programming more accessible and exciting to a novice [11].

Rajan and Stiehl [10] present a visual programming based R&D environment, called *Advanced Manuscript Analysis Portal (AMAP)*, dedicated to cater to the needs of non-programming-savvy users of digital image processing and pattern recognition. It visualizes different methods as blocks that can be attached to digital images via tangible interaction on a large-area multi-touch table. The parameters of these blocks can be set interactively in real-time. Any change to a parameter or addition/removal of blocks in a chain receives an immediate response. While it may not include all the programming constructs such as conditionals and branching (as of now), it does simulate a fairly simple linear program with the ability to perform batch processing and parameterization through loops.

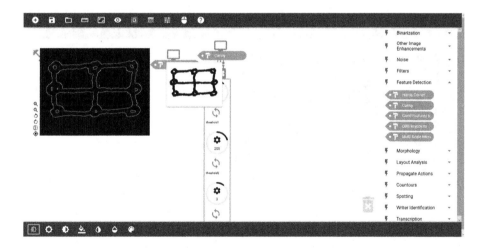

Fig. 4. AMAP workspace

Figure 4 shows a screenshot of a sample workspace. The manuscript researchers can interactively experiment with this system by attaching/detaching blocks of different functionalities to their images, setting and updating parameters and observing the changes [10]. All these general features made the AMAP platform a well-accessible tool for computational analysis of *charaktêres*. The system implemented on AMAP fulfills the user requirements discussed in Sect. 3.1 as follows.

Accessibility. Accessibility is taken care of, as the system developed on the AMAP environment is hosted online and can be accessed 24/7 via the URL https://bv.informatik.uni-hamburg.de/amap/.

Along with this, the source-code for both front-end and back-end of the AMAP platform is made publicly available on GitHub[1] for both transparency and encouraging contributions of further computational methods to the platform.

Transparency. The new visual programming based system presents each image processing method as a block that can be attached to images either individually or in conjunction with other such blocks. This allows the end-users to customize their own toolchain and use the methods in whichever sequence they need. All the free parameters of the methods are also allowed to be modified without any restriction. In case the user is unsure about which value of the parameter would suit them best, they can simply loop blocks and pick the best result.

As a trivial example, Fig. 5 shows a workspace where the threshold parameter for OpenCV binarization is looped between values 0 to 135 with a step size of 1. All possible results are stacked on the top left corner which could be spread and individually observed as shown in the figure.

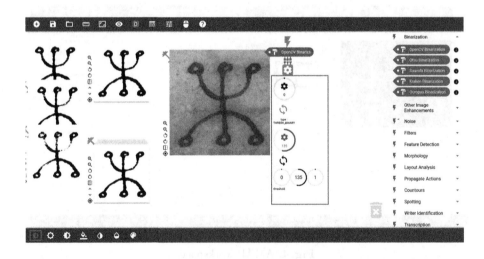

Fig. 5. Looping parameters

Reproducibility. *Saving Workspace* - a button on the top left of the user interface called "Save Workspace" allows the user to save the current session in the form of a JSON file. This file can be downloaded and later opened to recreate

---

[1] http://www.github.com/virtualvinodh/AMAP; under GPLv3 License.

the exact session. This process saves all the methods applied to the image along with their particular parameter settings.

Figure 6 shows a screenshot of the user interface when the workspace is being saved. A confirmation message from the browser can be seen at the bottom end of the web page.

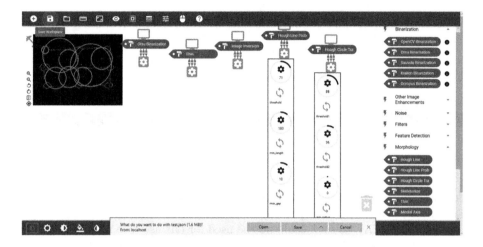

Fig. 6. Saving workspace

Docker Container - Another great benefit of using the AMAP environment is its support for Docker containers. Containers allow a developer to pack all the dependencies (e.g. libraries) of an application together and deploy it as one package. This ensures the application will run on any other machine without a need to install all the dependencies separately. Docker containers prove immensely helpful in avoiding versioning issues and making the system more reliable.

Metadata Information. Figure 7 is a screenshot of the user interface indicating options to extract the metadata of an image from the toolbar on the top of the page. The "Show Scale & Tilt" option displays the scale, tilt, and height & width in pixels on the top of the image. The values can be confirmed or independently checked via "Ruler" and "Protractor" options. As the names suggest, the ruler can be used to measure the length, width or any other distance on the image in pixels and the protractor can measure the angles of e.g. lines.

4   Analyzing *charaktê*res with AMAP

The imperative motive of this research is to provide a web-based research platform where researchers from Humanities - with minimal or no knowledge of programming - are empowered to apply algorithms to the analysis of *charaktêres*,

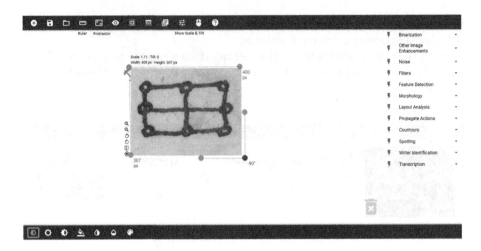

Fig. 7. Functions to extract metadata

ideally teaming up with experts from Informatics during evolving experimentation. In this context, AMAP perfectly matches our use case needs.

However, AMAP as such could not be used for our use case related research. Though it provides the necessary platform, it lacked the specific algorithms required for analyzing the *charaktêres*. Thus, in order to utilize AMAP, we had to extend it by several problem-specific methods such as Line Detection, Circle Detection, Skeletonization etc.

Additionally, using AMAP also encouraged us to think of the analysis as a modular workflow problem, wherein individual methods can be swapped for other methods and different workflows can be experimented to obtain the required end-result.

The *charaktêres*, as mentioned earlier, can be considered as a composition of lines, circles and junctions. However, as a proof-of-concept we deal here with only the detection of various lines and circles present in them. The detection of junctions is to be taken up as future work due to its complexity.

As such, using AMAP, a toolchain for detecting lines and circles can be developed by using different blocks. Figure 8 shows an example which starts with Otsu's binarization followed by skeletonization. The image is inverted after that using the "Image Inversion" method. This is done because the thinning method returns an n-dimensional array as output and the Hough transform requires an 8-bit, single-channel binary source image as input. This is followed by the Hough circle transform. Detected lines are drawn in red color while circles are drawn in green. It can be seen that all four *annuli* of the *charaktêr* are detected along with both of the vertical lines.

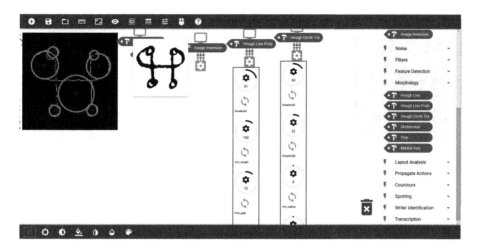

Fig. 8. Line and circle detection (Color figure online)

4.1 Interactive Exploration of Toolchains

The toolchains are completely flexible and the methods can be swapped or removed at any time. The users can take a basic toolchain and interactively explore its functionality and validity by testing different methods and setting a stable parameter regime in an incremental way up to a solution that works best for their particular use case.

The toolchain for line and circle detection discussed in the previous section is considered here as an example. A user can replace Otsu's binarization with OpenCV binarization that offers an option to modify the threshold, change the skeletonization method from "thin" to "medial axis", then invert the image and apply Hough circle detection. The results are shown in Fig. 9. As it can be seen, they are slightly more precise than what was discovered with the previous set of methods.

The user can also create a completely new toolchain as shown in Fig. 10. The methods being used here are OpenCV binarization, Canny edge detection, and Hough line transform.

Thus, an AMAP-based platform offers enough flexibility to the end users to experiment with the available plethora of methods and create customizable toolchains or workflows to support their activities. The process is as simple as dragging and dropping the method blocks and does not require any technical expertise. It is accessible via a browser and therefore does not require any software installation either. Being open-source, it also allows for new methods to be added to the platform as we added many for the analysis of *charaktêres*.

4.2 Limitations

The system presented in this paper does not yet provide a full-scale description and representation of *charaktêres* that could actually render their classification

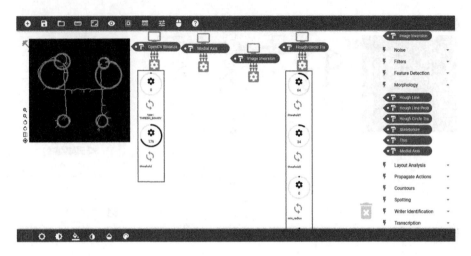

Fig. 9. Swapping methods (Color figure online)

possible - it is just the initial step to test the user-centric paradigm behind. Future work is required to automatically generate a fault-tolerant graph representation from the detected lines and circles that will enable classification and even identification of *charaktêres*.

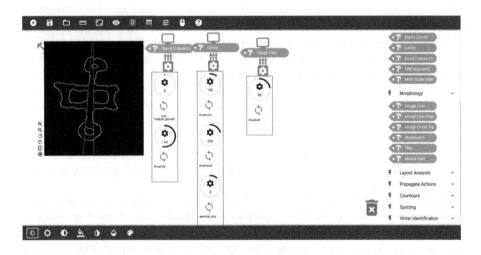

Fig. 10. Customized toolchain

5   User Evaluation

As discussed in Sect. 3.1, the prime motivation for designing the system presented in this paper was to provide a more interactive, workflow-supporting and dynamic platform to the manuscript researchers applying computational algorithms to their scholarly problems. An evaluation of such a system is, thus, of paramount importance to judge how successful the system was in facilitating the researchers in their work and in offering interactive ways to apply computational algorithms to manuscript analysis. To this end, we adopted the SUS and TAM approaches as described below in our paradigmatic study in the context of computational manuscript analysis.

5.1 Participants

We recruited six user study participants from the Centre for the Study of Manuscript Cultures (CSMC), University of Hamburg. Since scholars working specifically on *charaktêres* are a minority, we recruited participants who work with manuscripts in general. A computer scientist with experience in working with digitized manuscripts was also involved to get the point of view of a technical user. Thus, as yet the total number of participants in our initial study was seven. Due to practical constraints, the number of participants was quite limited and we could not select a diverse group with various levels of DH competency. A larger user study can be taken up as future work.

Almost all of the participants confirmed that manuscript analysis is *absolutely relevant* to their work and that they work with manuscripts *always* or *very often* (with the exception of the computer scientist). However, most of them stated that a computer-aided manuscript analysis was *somewhat* to *mildly relevant* for their work and none of them, barring two, have ever used a software for analyzing or studying a manuscript. All the participants regularly used computers but hardly ever for computer aided manuscript analysis.

5.2 Design

All the evaluation interviews were conducted in person. At a typical evaluation session, the participants were initially given an overview of the study and a short system demonstration. Following this, the participants were asked to perform five tasks on their own. Four of them clearly mentioned the steps to be taken while the fifth was just a set of instructions to perform a task, without specific steps instructing how to do it. As the evaluation primarily focuses on the interface and its usefulness and usability, the assigned tasks were designed to be simple and straight forward, focusing on the user interaction.

5.3 Methods and Results

We used the System Usability Scale (SUS) [3] and Technology Acceptance Model (TAM) [13] for evaluating usability and usefulness, respectively. SUS is simple, undemanding, and suits the system presented in this research well. The scale consists of 10 questions where odd-numbered questions are framed with a positive connotation and the even-numbered questions are posed in a negative sense. The questions are answered with respect to a five-point *Likert* scale [9].

Calculating SUS scores, at first, requires transposing the *Likert* scale rating to a discrete interval ranging from 1 to 5. The score for an individual question is calculated by subtracting 1 from the rating, if it is odd-numbered or subtracting the rating from 5, if it is even-numbered. The process normalizes any bias that might have been created by the connotations of the language in which these questions are framed. It leaves every question marked out of a maximum of 4. The individual scores of each question can then be added to get a final score out of 40. This score is further multiplied by 2.5 to obtain a score out of 100 which is interpreted as the cumulative SUS score of the system.

The minimum score attained by the system presented in this paper is 30 and the maximum is 80. Both the scores are out of the total of 100. The median SUS score of the system lies at 67.5 and the average at 61.78. In total, the system was rated to be consistent, easy-to-use and not overly complex. The graphical distribution of SUS scores per participants can be seen in Fig. 11.

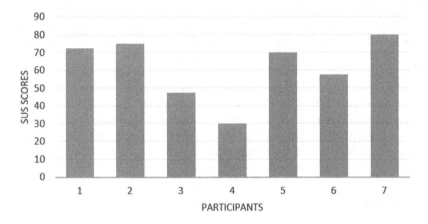

Fig. 11. Distribution of SUS scores

TAM is based on the concepts of i) *perceived usefulness*, that is "the degree to which a person believes that using a particular system would enhance his or her job performance" [5, p. 320], and ii) *perceived ease-of-use*, which is defined as "the degree to which a person believes that using a particular system would be free from effort [5, p. 320].

The questionnaire consists of 12 questions, 6 to measure the usefulness and 6 to measure the ease of use of the system. They are all rated on the *Likert* scale of base five, just like the usability questionnaire.

Only one of the participants in evaluations works on the analysis of *charaktêres* and just two more work on manuscripts where an automated computational analysis might be of help. The rest of the participants work in different fields and did not have any opportunities in their day-to-day tasks to make use of such a system. Therefore, the first section of the questionnaire related to usefulness expectedly received low ratings. The average minimum rating of the first six questions is 1 but the median turns out to be a grade better at 2.

However, the system was overwhelmingly rated high on ease-of-use with median score of 4. Most participants found the system to be clear, understandable, flexible, and easy to use.

In an additional question, the participants were asked to rate the visual interface on a five-point scale. It received the best scores with a median rating of 4 out of 5.

Finally, the participants were asked to record their views about the system in a free format interview. Some of the positive comments shared by them are:

"I like the layout of the interface, I think it is very easy to understand. It is not very complicated, not too many (confusing) functions".

"Visually logical 'sandbox' layout, no need for a chronological order of using functions as in a normal image processing software".

Some criticism was also voiced in the form of:

"not intuitive - when to double click and when to click just once. not very 'snappy' but 'laggy'. wastebin not intuitive. no explanation of parameters".

"Works better on touch-screens".

In addition, some of the recommendations were given as follows:

"I think it would be helpful if one could use it also for bigger images, so that a whole page of a manuscript can be analysed".

"Deleting operations seems rather complicated and not very intuitive. They get attached to each other easily and it's difficult to separate them".

6   Conclusion and Future Work

The goal of our research was to design and provide an interactive, intuitive and easy-to-use platform for the computational analysis of ancient documents with focus on *charaktêres*. As shown, the tool developed on the visual programming based AMAP environment clearly serves the purpose. However, as yet it still lacks methods for a complete visual feature detection or representation and subsequent magical sign recognition, a void which can easily be filled via open source toolboxes like DIVAservices[2] in specific and OpenCV in general.

Several suggestions for future work on the user interface came from the user evaluation as well. The most popular demand is to have explanatory descriptions of the parameters of each method and their effect - a general demand in our community. Some others are to make the click and drag functionality smoother, have pre-defined toolchains encompassing multiple methods like binarization followed by thinning, etc., arrow based resizing of the image, returning detailed error messages to the UI and implementing ways to declutter the workspace.

In summary, our research is the first step towards integrating visual programming in the field of computational analysis of digitized manuscripts for the sake of joint experimentation and provision of workflow-supporting tools.

---

[2] https://diuf.unifr.ch/main/hisdoc/divaservices.

Several more methods from open-source toolboxes can be readily added to the platform to facilitate improved computational analysis for a broad range of use cases. Although our particular research focused on analyzing *charaktêres*, AMAP may easily be configured for other research problems in manuscript analysis like handwriting identification and manuscript dating.

References

1. Barfod, G.H., Larsen, J.M., Lichtenberger, A., Raja, R.: Revealing text in a complexly rolled silver scroll from jerash with computed tomography and advanced imaging software. Sci. Rep. **5**, 17765 (2015)
2. Bohak, G.: The charaktêres in ancient and medieval Jewish magic. Acta Classica Univ. Sci. Debreceniensis **47**, 25–44 (2011)
3. Brooke, J., et al.: SUS - a quick and dirty usability scale. Usabil. Eval. Ind. **189**(194), 4–7 (1996)
4. Burdick, A., Drucker, J., Lunenfeld, P., Presner, T., Schnapp, J.: Digital Humanities. The MIT Press, Cambridge (2012)
5. Davis, F.D.: Perceived usefulness, perceived ease of use, and user acceptance of information technology. MIS Q. **15**, 319–340 (1989)
6. Gordon, R.: 'Signa nova et inaudita': the theory and practice of invented signs (charaktêres) in Graeco-Egyptian magical texts. MHNH: Rev. Int. Invest. sobre Magia Astrol. Antiguas (11), 15–44 (2011)
7. Gordon, R.: Charaktêres between antiquity and renaissance: transmission and reinvention. In: Dasen, V., Spieser, J.M. (eds.) Les savoirs magiques et leur transmission de l'Antiquité à la Renaissance, pp. 253–300 (2014)
8. Hahn, T.C.: Computational analysis of Charaktêres in digitized manuscripts: a proof of concept. Master's thesis, University of Hamburg (2019, unpublished)
9. Likert, R.: A technique for the measurement of attitudes. Arch. Psychol. (1932)
10. Rajan, V., Stiehl, H.S.: AMAP: a visual programming language based system to support document image analysis. In: Proceedings of Mensch und Computer 2019, pp. 881–884 (2019)
11. Repenning, A.: Moving beyond syntax: lessons from 20 years of blocks programing in AgentSheets. J. Vis. Lang. Sentient Syst. **3**(1), 68–89 (2017)
12. Stratton, K.B.: Naming the Witch: Magic, Ideology, and Stereotype in the Ancient World. Columbia University Press, New York (2007)
13. Szajna, B.: Empirical evaluation of the revised technology acceptance model. Manage. Sci. **42**(1), 85–92 (1996)
14. Winkler, H.A.: Siegel und Charaktere in der muhammedanischen Zauberei. de Gruyter, Berlin (2015). [1930]

Quaternion Generative Adversarial Networks for Inscription Detection in Byzantine Monuments

Giorgos Sfikas[1]([⊠]), Angelos P. Giotis[1], George Retsinas[2], and Christophoros Nikou[1]

[1] Department of Computer Science and Engineering,
University of Ioannina, Ioannina, Greece
{sfikas,agiotis,cnikou}@cse.uoi.gr
[2] School of Electrical and Computer Engineering,
National Technical University of Athens, Athens, Greece
gretsinas@central.ntua.gr

Abstract. In this work, we introduce and discuss Quaternion Generative Adversarial Networks, a variant of generative adversarial networks that uses quaternion-valued inputs, weights and intermediate network representations. Quaternionic representation has the advantage of treating cross-channel information carried by multichannel signals (e.g. color images) holistically, while quaternionic convolution has been shown to be less resource-demanding. Standard convolutional and deconvolutional layers are replaced by their quaternionic variants, in both generator and discriminator nets, while activations and loss functions are adapted accordingly. We have succesfully tested the model on the task of detecting byzantine inscriptions in the wild, where the proposed model is on par with a vanilla conditional generative adversarial network, but is significantly less expensive in terms of model size (requires 4× less parameters). Code is available at https://github.com/sfikas/quaternion-gan.

Keywords: Quaternions · Generative Adversarial Networks · Byzantine inscriptions · Text detection

1 Introduction

Digitization and online accessibility in cultural institutions such as museums, libraries and archives can achieve much greater visibility to the public when the digitized content is organized in meaningful entities. For example, text in natural images generally conveys rich semantic information about the scene and the enclosed objects, which might be of great use in real scenarios where the digitized raw image information is not directly exploitable for searching and browsing.

One of the most prominent trends in content-based image retrieval applications is to discriminate which part of the image includes useful information, as opposed to background objects, occlusion and task-irrelevant parts [20]. Such tasks may concern image analysis, understanding, indexing or classification of

© Springer Nature Switzerland AG 2021
A. Del Bimbo et al. (Eds.): ICPR 2020 Workshops, LNCS 12667, pp. 171–184, 2021.
https://doi.org/10.1007/978-3-030-68787-8_12

objects according to some inherent property. In the particular case of text understanding applications, the main goal is to retrieve regions that contain solely textual cues, either as holistic region information or as textual parts at line, word or even character level.

Text detection is a challenging task due to the variety of text appearance, the unconstrained locations of text within the natural image, degradations of text components over hundreds of years, as well as the complexity of each scene. To address these challenges, standard convolutional neural networks (CNNs) have been the main attraction over the last five years for text detection [8, 23]. However, the effectiveness of CNNs is usually limited by the homogeneity of the dataset images used for training as well as the particular loss function that is to be minimized for the specific task at hand. Generative Adversarial Networks (GANs) [5] offer a more flexible framework that can in effect learn the appropriate loss function to satisfy the task at hand. GANs setup an adversarial learning paradigm where the game dynamics of two players-networks lead to a model that, in its convolutional variant is the state of the art in numerous vision tasks today.

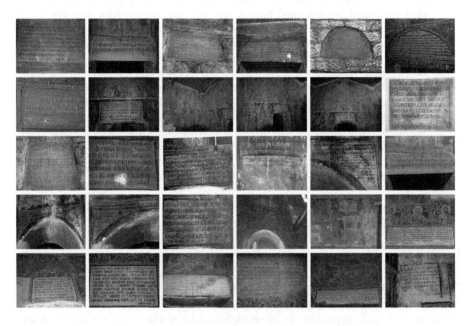

Fig. 1. Sample images of our inscription dataset.

With the current work, we discuss a novel neural network variant that brings together the concepts of GANs with that of Quaternionic convolution and deconvolution, and build a model that can effectively perform text detection in a context where the content of interest is "donor" inscriptions found in byzantine monuments [9,21] (see Fig. 1 and 2). Quaternions are a form of non-real numbers that can be understood as 4-dimensional generalizations of complex numbers, with one real part and three independent imaginary parts. The use of non-real numbers as neuron and parameter values has been proposed as far as 1991, with an adaptation of backpropagation for complex numbers [10]. Similar developments for quaternions have followed suit [14]. The more recently proposed quaternion convolutional neural networks (QCNNs) [18,26] a special form of convolution that makes use of quaternion product rules, effectively treating multichannel information holistically. Furthermore, QCNNs have been shown to be much more economical (i.e. less resource-demanding) networks than their non-quaternionic counterparts, with four times smaller parameter set size [17,18]. Motivated by the promising properties of quaternionic neural networks, we propose using quaternionic operations with adversarial networks. In particular, the contribution of this work concerns the introduction of quaternionic convolution to the conditional convolutional generative adversarial paradigm, where we replace the encoder-decoder architecture with quaternionic layer versions, and otherwise adapt network architecture where necessary. In order to setup our numerical and qualitative experiments, we test the proposed model for inscription localization in the wild. In terms of numerical results, we conclude that the proposed model attains comparable evaluation scores to its non-quaternionic counterpart, while being less resource demanding.

The remainder of this paper is structured in the following manner. In Sect. 2, we review related work. In Sect. 3, we present the basics of quaternion algebra, and in Sect. 4, we move to quaternionic convolution and its use with convolutional neural networks. In Sect. 5, we discuss the proposed model and we present the dataset, task and numerical experiments employed in Sect. 6. Finally, with Sect. 7, we close the paper and discuss future work.

2   Related Work

The automatic detection of text can be categorized into two main families. The first direction includes identifying text of scanned document images whereas the second contains text captured by natural images (indoor or outdoor images with text of more complex shapes, cuneiform tablet images or inscriptions) which is further subject to various geometric distortions, illumination and environmental conditions. The latter category is also known as text detection in the wild or scene text detection [19]. In the first category, text detection in printed documents is usually tackled by OCR techniques [25], while in handwritten document images, the problem is formulated as a keyword search in a segmentation free scenario [4].

In the text detection-in-the-wild paradigm, conditions such as wide variety of colors and fonts, orientations and languages are present. Moreover, scene elements might have similar appearance to text components, and finally, images may be distorted with blurriness, or contain degradations due to low camera resolution during digitization process, capturing angle and partial occlusions. Under such adverse situations deep learning based methods have shown great effectiveness in detecting text. Recent deep approaches for text detection in the wild, inspired by object detection frameworks, can be categorized into *bounding-box regression based*, *segmentation-based* and *hybrid* approaches.

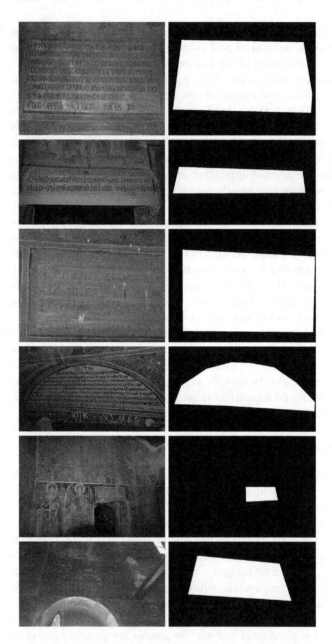

Fig. 2. Example ground-truth annotation for selected samples from our inscription dataset.

Bounding-box regression based methods for text detection [11] regard text as an object and aim to predict the candidate bounding boxes directly. Segmentation-based methods in [24] enforce text detection as a semantic segmentation task, aiming to classify text regions at pixel level and then obtain bounding boxes containing text during post-processing. Hybrid methods [12] rely on a segmentation step to predict score maps of text which in turn yield text bounding-boxes as a result of regression. Similarly to [24], our method localizes text in a holistic manner, by performing text detection as a semantic segmentation problem to produce global pixel-wise prediction maps.

While CNNs are at the top of the dominant problem-solvers in image recognition tasks, such as the text detection in the wild case explored in this work, traditional real-valued CNNs encode local relations of the input features from R, G, B channels of each pixel along with structural relations composed by groups of pixels, independently. On the contrary, our proposed quaternionic conditional adversarial network treats text detection as a semantic segmentation task, performing at input RGB channels holistically with the use of quaternions, so as to obtain a binary output of white text pixels. To our knowledge, GANs have not been used yet for text detection in the wild [19]. Moreover, the quaternionic representation of the conditional variant of the generative adversarial networks is a first attempt to discriminate a text region by its non-text counterpart with less computational load.

Recent works on quaternion CNNs [18,26] indicate that the lower number of parameters required for the multidimensional representation of a single pixel in R,G,B channels leads to better image classification results than traditional CNNs. The authors claim that the performance boost is also due to the specific quaternion algebra. Such a boost is further explored in [16], where instead of a real-valued dot product, a vector product operation allows quaternion CNNs to capture internal latent relations by sharing quaternion weights during the product operation, and in turn by creating relations within the product's elements.

3   Elements of Quaternions

Quaternions, introduced in the mid-19th century, form an algebraic structure known as a skew-field, that is characterized by all the properties of a field except that of multiplication commutativity. We denote the quaternion skew-field as $\mathbb{H}$. Quaternions are four-dimensional, in the sense of $\mathbb{H}$ being isomorphic to $\mathbb{R}^4$, and each $q \in \mathbb{H}$ can be written as:

$$q = a + b\boldsymbol{i} + c\boldsymbol{j} + d\boldsymbol{k}, \tag{1}$$

where $a, b, c, d \in \mathbb{R}$ and $\boldsymbol{i}, \boldsymbol{j}, \boldsymbol{k}$ are independent imaginary units. Hence, analogous to the representation of complex numbers, which bear one real and one imaginary part, quaternions have one real and three independent imaginary parts. Alternatively, quaternions can be represented as the sum of a scalar (their real part) and a three-dimensional vector (their imaginary part). Formally we can write:

$$q = S(q) + V(q), \tag{2}$$

where $S(q) = a$ and $V(q) = bi+cj+dk$. Further generalizing the related $i^2 = -1$ formula for complex numbers, for quaternions we have:

$$i^2 = j^2 = k^2 = ijk = -1,$$

$$ij = -ji = k, jk = -kj = i, ki = -ik = j. \tag{3}$$

Quaternion conjugacy is defined as:

$$\bar{q} = a - bi - cj - dk, \tag{4}$$

while quaternion magnitude is defined as:

$$|q| = \sqrt{q\bar{q}} = \sqrt{\bar{q}q} = \sqrt{a^2 + b^2 + c^2 + d^2}. \tag{5}$$

As a consequence of the properties of a skew-field and Eq. (3), we have the following multiplication rule for quaternions:

$$pq = (a_p a_q - b_p b_q - c_p c_q - d_p d_q) \tag{6}$$
$$+ (a_p b_q + b_p a_q + c_p d_q - d_p c_q)i \tag{7}$$
$$+ (a_p c_q - b_p d_q + c_p a_q + d_p b_q)j \tag{8}$$
$$+ (a_p d_q + b_p c_q - c_p b_q + d_p a_q)k, \tag{9}$$

where $p = a_p + b_p i + c_p j + d_p k$ and $q = a_q + b_q i + c_q j + d_q k$. Following the notation of Eq. (2), we can write the above rule also as:

$$pq = S(p)S(q) - V(p) \cdot V(q) + S(p)V(q) + S(q)V(p) + V(p) \times V(q), \tag{10}$$

where $\cdot$ and $\times$ denote the dot and cross product respectively. Interestingly, note that when p, q are pure (i.e., they have zero respective real parts), the quaternion product boils down to a cross product. The above formulae are also referred to as a Hamilton product [17] in the literature.

4   Quaternionic Convolutional Neural Networks

Quaternionic Convolutional Neural Networks have been recently introduced as variants of the widely used Convolutional Neural Networks that have quaternionic model parameters, inputs, activations, pre-activations and outputs. This creates issues with a number of network components and concepts, including the definition of convolution, whether standard activation functions are usable and how back-propagation is handled. In theory, multiple proposals for a convolution operation could be considered [2]. Two quaternionic extensions of convolution have been succesfully employed in two recent works [18,26]. In all cases, a quaternionic kernel $g \in \mathbb{H}^{K \times K}$ acts on an input feature map $f \in \mathbb{H}^{M \times N}$ to generate the output map $g \in \mathbb{H}^{M+K-1 \times N+K-1}$. The two extensions differ in the choice of elementary operation used in each case.

In [26], a convolution extension that is based on the equation used to apply quaternionic rotation is employed (i.e. $w \rightarrow qw\bar{q}$, where q is a pure unit quaternion). In particular, they define quaternionic convolution $g = f * w$ as:

$$g_{kk'} = \sum_{l=1}^{K} \sum_{l'=1}^{K} s_{ll'}^{-1} w_{ll'} f_{(k+l)(k'+l')} \bar{w}_{ll'}, \tag{11}$$

where $f = [f_{ij}]$ denotes the input feature map, $w = [w_{ij}]$ is the convolution kernel, and $s_{ll'} = |w_{ll'}|$.

In [18], which is the convolution version that we test in this work, convolution is more simply defined as:

$$g_{kk'} = \sum_{l=1}^{K} \sum_{l'=1}^{K} w_{ll'} f_{(k+l)(k'+l')}, \tag{12}$$

where the definition is analogous to standard convolution, with the difference that elements are quaternionic and the kernel multiplies the signal from the left on each summation term. Strided convolution, deconvolution and padding are also defined analogously to real-valued convolution.

Concerning activation functions, the most straightforward option is to use standard activations that are used in real-valued networks (e.g. sigmoid, ReLU, etc.) and use them on each quaternion real and imaginary part separately, as if they were separate real channels. This type of activations are referred to in the literature as split-activation functions. In this work, we use split-activation versions of leaky Rectified linear unit (ReLU) and the sigmoid function.

5   Proposed Model

The proposed model is made up of the well-known pair of the generator and discriminator networks that are used in standard GANs. The vanilla (non-conditional) GAN objective function [13] is, in its original form as follows:

$$L_{\text{GAN}} = E_x \log D(x) + E_z \log(1 - D(G(z))), \tag{13}$$

where $G(\cdot)$ and $D(\cdot)$ denote the generator and discriminator network respectively. x are samples of the training set, while z denotes random noise that is used as input to the generator. For the discriminator, the aim is to maximize this function, while for the generator the aim is to minimize it. These competing terms result in a two-player game, of which we require to obtain a parameter set that would correspond to a Nash equilibrium.

We employ a supervised variant that is referred to as a conditional GAN (cGAN) architecture, made popular with the pix2pix model [7]. Formally, the objective function is written as:

$$L_{\text{cGAN}} = E_x[log D(y)] + E_x[log(1 - D(G(x)))]] + \lambda E_{x,y}[\|y - G(x)\|_1] \tag{14}$$

where we can comment on a number of differences comparing with the standard GAN formula of Eq. (13). In particular, no random noise variable z exists, and on the contrary the generator takes as input a sample x to produce a target y. In that sense, the cGAN is supervised; a cGAN learns a mapping from input x to target y. Also, a second L_1 regularizing term is employed, penalizing the difference of the produced $G(x)$ to the desired target y. A regularizing term λ controls trade-off of the two terms.

In this work, x is a quaternion-valued image, formally $x \in \mathbb{H}^{H \times W}$, where H and W are image height and width in pixels. In particular x is assumed to be a dataset image, and estimate $G(x)$ is a detection heatmap that ranges in $[0, 1]$. A pixel value of $G(x)$ that is close to 1 means a high probability that this pixel is part of a text inscription, and vice-versa. Ground truth target y is binary, with values in $\{0, 1\}$ (see Fig. 2). In order to form each quaternion-valued input x, we assign each of its three colour channels (Red, Green, Blue) to each of the quaternion imaginary axes. Hence, we assign $Red \to i$, $Green \to j$, $Blue \to k$. The real part is left to be equal to zero, or in other words all values of x are pure quaternions.

The generator is constructed as a U-net-like model [22] with two symmetric groups of layers, arranged to an encoder and a decoder part. The encoder is composed of strided quaternionic convolutional layers that produce quaternionic feature maps of progressively lower resolution in comparison to the original input image size. The decoder mirrors the encoder layers, by using a quaternionic deconvolutional layer for each forward convolution layer of the encoder, and upsampling feature maps progressively to the original resolution. Furthermore, U-net-like skip connections connect corresponding encoder - decoder layers. We use 4 quaternionic convolutional layers for the encoder, and 4 quaternionic deconvolutional layers for the decoder. Dropout layers top layers 5 and 6. Convolutions are strided with stride $= 2$, kernel sizes $= 4 \times 4$, and output number of channels equal to $16, 32, 64, 64$ for layers 1 to 4 respectively. Deconvolutional layers share the same characteristics, mirroring the encoder architecture, with added skip connections. All layers, except the final layer, are topped by split-activation leaky ReLU functions with parameter $= 0.2$. These act on each quaternionic pixel value x as:

$$lReLU_q(x) = lReLU_r(x_a) + lReLU_r(x_b)i + lReLU_r(x_c)j + lReLU_r(x_d)k \quad (15)$$

where $lReLU_r$ is the well-known real-valued leaky ReLU function and we assume $x = x_a + x_b i + x_c j + x_d k$. The generator implements a mapping $\mathbb{H}^{H \times W} \to [0, 1]^{H \times W}$, from a quaternion-valued image to a real image. All intermediate layers map quaternion-valued feature maps again to quaternion-valued feature maps, save for the final activation. We define the final activation simply as the sum:

$$qsum(x) = x_a + x_b + x_c + x_d. \quad (16)$$

which ensures a real-valued output.

The discriminator is constructed as a cascade of strided quaternionic convolutions, with strides and size identical to those used for the generator encoder.

It implements a mapping $\mathbb{H}^{H \times W} \rightarrow [0, 1]$, where the output represents the degree in which the network believes that the input is fake or genuine. Inputs to the discriminator are constructed as concatenations of color inscription images to the estimated target. In particular, we map *Detection estimate* $\rightarrow$ *real part*, *Red* $\rightarrow$ i, *Green* $\rightarrow$ j, *Blue* $\rightarrow$ k. As the output is real while the input is quaternionic, in the final layer we use the activation of Eq. (16), before applying a sigmoid function on top of it. The discriminator is made up of 6 quaternionic convolutional layers. Output number of channels equal to $16, 32, 64, 64, 128, 1$ respectively for the 6 convolutional layers.

Note also that the setup of the generator and discirminator is such that inputs and outputs can be of variable size. Indeed, the generator is a fully convolutional network, with parameters and layers that are independent of input and feature map size. The discriminator leads to feature maps that are reduced to a single probability value, again regardless of the input image and annotation dimensions.

6   Experimental Results

6.1   Dataset

The dataset is comprised of a total of 67 images containing inscriptions written in Greek, and found in Byzantine churches and monasteries in the region of Epirus, located in Northwestern Greece [9, 21]. Our inscriptions are donor's inscriptions, typically made up of a few lines of text and containing information about who donated funds and other resources required to build the monument where the inscription is located. The photographed images were captured with a Samsung GT-I9505 and a Nikon Coolpix L810 camera. All images were then resized so as their width was at most 1024 pixels, keeping their aspect ratio fixed. We have chosen to partition the set to a training and test set according to a 80%/20% rule, which resulted to training and test sets of 55 and 12 images respectively.

6.2   Experiments

Concerning training, we have used the Adam optimizer with parameters $\beta_1 = 0.5$, $\beta_2 = 0.999$. No data augmentation is used. The trade-off parameter λ was set to 10 and base learning rates were set to 10^{-4} for the discriminator and 5×10^{-4} for the generator. Furthermore, a learning rate scheduling strategy was used, where learning rate is divided by 10 for both networks if test binary cross-entropy deteriorates continuously for 2 consecutive epochs. Batch size was set to 1, as our model was setup to accept inputs of variant size.

We have used two evaluation measures: a) binary cross-entropy (BCE) of the test images and b) Intersection over Union (IoU). Test BCE is applied in an analogous manner to the corresponding loss component discussed in Sect. 5, and effectively tests for correct per-pixel binary classification. The IoU measure is applied after computing a binarized version of the estimate detection map, with a threshold of 0.5 (Pascal VOC challenge [3]). Subsequently, IoU is computed between this binarized estimate and the ground truth.

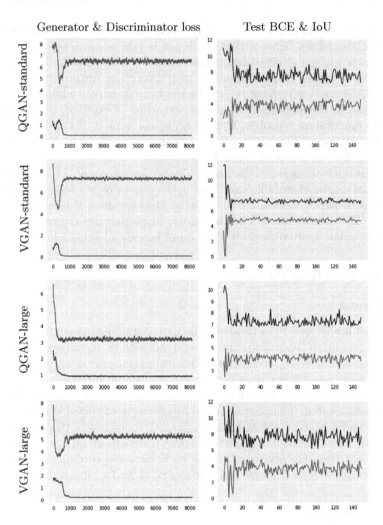

Fig. 3. Generator loss, Discriminator loss, Test BCE loss and IoU score plots for all models tested in this work. From top row to bottom, we show results for QGAN-standard, VGAN-standard, QGAN-large, VGAN-large. Left column shows Generator and Discriminator loss (red and blue respectively, lower is better for both), and right column shows test BCE and IoU (black and green respectively. Lower BCE is better, higher IoU is better). Generator and Discriminator losses are smoothed with a 100-point uniform convolution kernel and plotted per iteration, test BCE and IoU are plotted per epoch. IoU score is shown multiplied 10× for better visualization.

In Fig. 3, we show plots for the generator and discriminator loss calculated per training iteration, and test BCE loss and IoU calculated as an average over test images and at the end of each epoch. QGAN and VGAN are compared, as well as two considered model sizes. Standard size corresponds to the model described previously in Sect. 5. Large size corresponds to QGAN and VGAN models that have double the number of channels per convolutional or deconvolutional layer.

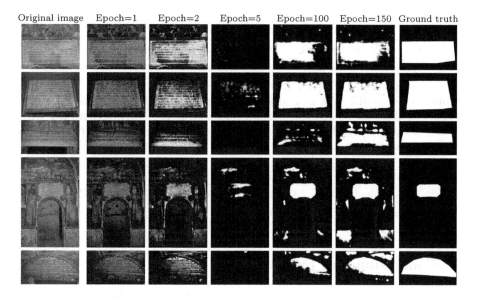

Fig. 4. Sample results of proposed model on test images.

We show results for test images as a function of current epoch training in Fig. 4.

We compare each Quaternionic GAN model with its vanilla (non- quaternionic) counterpart, by considering a network with the same amount of neurons. For each quaternionic neuron of the QGAN, we need to create four neurons for the corresponding VGAN, due to the isomorphism between $\mathbb{H}$ and $\mathfrak{R}^4$. As shown before [17], computation of the quaternionic (Hamilton) product and consequently quaternionic convolution requires considerably less storage. Judging from the results shown in Fig. 3 and Table 1, we can conclude that in all cases performance of the proposed QGAN is comparable with its corresponding non-quaternionic model, and definitely with scores on the same order of magnitude. IoU scores seems somewhat worse, though BCE results are more inconclusive, with QGAN faring slightly better than VGAN with respect to the "Standard" model size. What is definitely noteworthy though, is that QGAN is a considerably less expensive network (in Table 2 we show the number of total network parameters for each version of the QGANs and VGANs considered). The number of weights, translated in practice in required storage, is only 25% of the non-quaternionic versions. This means that the proposed QGAN can achieve similar results with the standard GAN, using four times less parameters.

Table 1. Numerical results for two variants of the proposed model (QGAN) versus its non-quaternionic counterpart with the same number of neurons (VGAN). Test BCE figures (lower is better) are shown and corresponding IoU scores in parenthesis (higher is better).

Model/Network type	Standard	Large
Quaternionic GAN	6.54(45.4%)	6.91(44.9%)
Vanilla GAN	7.4(51.9%)	6.45(52.0%)

Table 2. Comparative table of model sizes, measured in numbers of trainable weights. Number of quaternionic and real weights are shown respectively. In parenthesis, the number of equivalent real weights is shown, in order to ease storage size requirements comparison for the two variants.

Model/Network type	Standard	Large
Quaternionic GAN	$381,426$ $(1,525,704)$	$1,516,514$ $(6,066,056)$
Vanilla GAN	$6,053,826$	$24,166,274$

7   Conclusion and Future Work

We have presented a new variant of Generative Adversarial Networks that uses quaternion-valued neurons and weights, as well as suitable quaternionic variants of convolutional and deconvolutional layers. The proposed model is a conditional GAN, with the generator accepting a color input image and outputing a detection heatmap. We have applied the new model on the task of inscription detection, where we have used a set of byzantine monument text inscriptions as our targets. Quaternion-valued networks such as the proposed one can inherently deal with representing color intercorrelation. The inscriptions themselves are not characterized by color variance; however, the elements that are not part of the inscription very often do (murals, paintings). The proposed network showed that it can be as effective as a real-valued GAN, while being much less expensive in terms of model size. This can be a very important factor, especially in use cases where the resource budget is very constrained (e.g. neural networks running on mobile phones, etc.).

As future work, we plan to conduct more extensive sets of experiments, testing multiple architectures as well as other GAN variants, or experiment with spatially-constrained adjustments to the loss function [15]. Alternative features may also be considered, such as QFT-based cues [6]. Extensive augmentation is another technique that we can plan to explore, especially using perspective transforms to simulate alternate viewpoints, or experimenting with learning-based augmentation [1].

Acknowledgement. We would like to thank Dr. Christos Stavrakos, Dr. Katerina Kontopanagou, Dr. Fanny Lyttari and Ioannis Theodorakopoulos for supplying us with the Byzantine inscription images used for our experiments.

We also gratefully acknowledge the support of NVIDIA Corporation with the donation of the Titan XP GPU used for this research.

This research has been partially co-financed by the EU and Greek national funds through the Operational Program Competitiveness, Entrepreneurship and Innovation, under the call OPEN INNOVATION IN CULTURE, project *Bessarion* (T6YBΠ-00214).

References

1. Dimitrakopoulos, P., Sfikas, G., Nikou, C.: ISING-GAN: annotated data augmentation with a spatially constrained generative adversarial network. In: 2020 IEEE 17th International Symposium on Biomedical Imaging (ISBI), pp. 1600–1603. IEEE (2020)
2. Ell, T.A., Sangwine, S.J.: Hypercomplex fourier transforms of color images. IEEE Trans. Image Process. **16**(1), 22–35 (2007)
3. Everingham, M., Van Gool, L., Williams, C.K.I., Winn, J., Zisserman, A.: The pascal visual object classes (VOC) challenge. Int. J. Comput. Vision **88**, 303–338 (2010)
4. Giotis, A.P., Sfikas, G., Gatos, B., Nikou, C.: A survey of document image word spotting techniques. Pattern Recogn. **68**, 310–332 (2017)
5. Goodfellow, I., et al.: Generative adversarial nets. In: Advances in Neural Information Processing Systems (NIPS), pp. 2672–2680 (2014)
6. Hui, W., Xiao-Hui, W., Yue, Z., Jie, Y.: Color texture segmentation using quaternion-gabor filters. In: 2006 International Conference on Image Processing, pp. 745–748. IEEE (2006)
7. Isola, P., Zhu, J.Y., Zhou, T., Efros, A.A.: Image-to-image translation with conditional adversarial networks. arXiv preprint arXiv:1611.07004 (2016)
8. Jaderberg, M., Simonyan, K., Vedaldi, A., Zisserman, A.: Reading text in the wild with convolutional neural networks. Int. J. Comput. Vision **116**(1), 1–20 (2016)
9. Kordatos, E., Exarchos, D., Stavrakos, C., Moropoulou, A., Matikas, T.: Infrared thermographic inspection of murals and characterization of degradation in historic monuments. Constr. Build. Mater. **48**, 1261–1265 (2013)
10. Leung, H., Haykin, S.: The complex backpropagation algorithm. IEEE Trans. Signal Process. **39**(9), 2101–2104 (1991)
11. Liao, M., Shi, B., Bai, X.: Textboxes++: a single-shot oriented scene text detector. IEEE Trans. Image Process. **27**(8), 3676–3690 (2018)
12. Liao, M., Zhu, Z., Shi, B., song Xia, G., Bai, X.: Rotation-sensitive regression for oriented scene text detection (2018)
13. Lucic, M., Kurach, K., Michalski, M., Gelly, S., Bousquet, O.: Are GANs created equal? A large-scale study. In: Advances in Neural Information Processing Systems (NIPS), pp. 700–709 (2018)
14. Nitta, T.: A quaternary version of the back-propagation algorithm. In: Proceedings of ICNN 1995-International Conference on Neural Networks, vol. 5, pp. 2753–2756. IEEE (1995)
15. Papadimitriou, K., Sfikas, G., Nikou, C.: Tomographic image reconstruction with a spatially varying gamma mixture prior. J. Math. Imaging Vis. **60**(8), 1355–1365 (2018)

16. Parcollet, T., Morchid, M., Linarès, G.: Quaternion convolutional neural networks for heterogeneous image processing. In: ICASSP 2019-2019 IEEE International Conference on Acoustics, Speech and Signal Processing (ICASSP), pp. 8514–8518. IEEE (2019)

17. Parcollet, T., Morchid, M., Linares, G.: A survey of quaternion neural networks. Artif. Intell. Rev. **53**(4), 2957–2982 (2020)

18. Parcollet, T., et al.: Quaternion convolutional neural networks for end-to-end automatic speech recognition. arXiv preprint arXiv:1806.07789 (2018)

19. Raisi, Z., Naiel, M.A., Fieguth, P., Wardell, S., Zelek, J.: Text detection and recognition in the wild: a review (2020)

20. Ren, S., He, K., Girshick, R., Sun, J.: Faster R-CNN: towards real-time object detection with region proposal networks (2016)

21. Rhoby, A.: Text as art? Byzantine inscriptions and their display. In: Writing Matters: Presenting and Perceiving Monumental Inscriptions in Antiquity and the Middle Ages, pp. 265–283. de Gruyter, Berlin (2017)

22. Ronneberger, O., Fischer, P., Brox, T.: U-Net: convolutional networks for biomedical image segmentation. In: Navab, N., Hornegger, J., Wells, W.M., Frangi, A.F. (eds.) MICCAI 2015. LNCS, vol. 9351, pp. 234–241. Springer, Cham (2015). https://doi.org/10.1007/978-3-319-24574-4_28

23. Su, F., Ding, W., Wang, L., Shan, S., Xu, H.: Text proposals based on windowed maximally stable extremal region for scene text detection. In: 2017 14th IAPR International Conference on Document Analysis and Recognition (ICDAR), vol. 1, pp. 376–381 (2017)

24. Yao, C., Bai, X., Sang, N., Zhou, X., Zhou, S., Cao, Z.: Scene text detection via holistic, multi-channel prediction (2016)

25. Ye, Q., Doermann, D.: Text detection and recognition in imagery: a survey. IEEE Trans. Pattern Anal. Mach. Intell. **37**(07), 1480–1500 (2015)

26. Zhu, X., Xu, Y., Xu, H., Chen, C.: Quaternion convolutional neural networks. In: Proceedings of the European Conference on Computer Vision (ECCV), pp. 631–647 (2018)

Transfer Learning Methods for Extracting, Classifying and Searching Large Collections of Historical Images and Their Captions

Cindy Roullet[✉], David Fredrick[✉], John Gauch[✉],
Rhodora G. Vennarucci[✉], and William Loder[✉]

University of Arkansas, Fayetteville, AR 72701, USA
{ceroulle,dfredric,jgauch,rhodorav,wtloder}@uark.edu
http://computer-science-and-computer-engineering.uark.edu/,
http://fulbright.uark.edu/departments/world-languages/

Abstract. This paper is about the creation of an interactive software tool and dataset useful for exploring the unindexed 11-volume set, *Pompei: Pitture e Mosaici* (PPM), a valuable resource containing over 20,000 annotated historical images of the archaeological site of Pompeii, Italy. The tool includes functionalities such as a word search, and an images and captions similarity search. Searches for similarity are conducted using transfer learning on the data retrieved from the scanned version of PPM. Image processing, convolutional neural networks and natural language processing also had to come into play to extract, classify, and archive the text and image data from the digitized version of the books.

Keywords: Image processing · Information retrieval · Transfer learning · Pompeii · Interactive software tool · Text/Graphics separation · Digital culture heritage · Dataset · Scanned documents · Convolutional neural networks · Similarity calculation · Noise removal · Term frequency · Clustering

1 Introduction

Pompei: Pitture e Mosaici (PPM) is a collection of books that inventories black and white and color photographs and illustrations of Pompeii's art accompanied by extensive captions. The set of volumes contains over 20,000 historical annotated images of the archaeological site, which makes it a very valuable, but unfortunately hard to exploit, resource. Academics use it for finding specific evidence or seeing what exists in individual structures, but it is very difficult to take a large-scale analytical approach to the data in the volumes as they exist.

Our work is aimed at creating a system to ease the usability of PPM, and is also part of a larger Virtual Pompeii Project. We used image processing and Optical Character Recognition (OCR) to extract and collect data from the digitized form of PPM. We created an annotated database with the acquired data. We also performed analysis on the data using machine learning methods such

© Springer Nature Switzerland AG 2021
A. Del Bimbo et al. (Eds.): ICPR 2020 Workshops, LNCS 12667, pp. 185–199, 2021.
https://doi.org/10.1007/978-3-030-68787-8_13

as feature extractions with Convolutional Neural Networks (CNN) and Natural Language Processing (NLP), classification with the retraining of a CNN and K-Nearest Neighbors (KNN). From the analysis' results, we developed an interactive software search tool allowing users to explore and make relevant connections between art and the built environment in Pompeii, using data from PPM in a new way.

This paper presents the steps of how we created the software interactive search tool. Section 2 reviews the related work. Section 3 describes the steps of information retrieval leading to the dataset creation. Section 4 presents data analysis and manipulation of the images and text from PPM retrieved from Sect. 3. Section 5 describes the integration of Sects. 3 and 4 into the creation of the interactive software research tool. Finally, Sect. 6 draws conclusions and outlines future work.

2   Related Work

In this section we review some of the related work focused on cultural data analysis. Related work in other domains are mentioned throughout the paper.

2.1   Applications and Data Analysis Methods with Historical Data

Thanks to the increased digitization of historical documents all over the world, we are able to present and explore historical artifacts in innovative ways with new technologies. Deep Learning methods have given us many opportunities. Transfer learning technologies have been used in recognizing Batik fabrics from Indonesia [6], generating labels for non-annotated historical images [4], and digitally archiving historical documents [18]. Architecture style recognition and classification of building facades in India [8] has also been possible with transfer learning. Image segmentation has been used to automatically recognize artistic influence of paintings [2]. The RANSAC algorithm has been tested as a support for analysis and interpretation of old paintings [19]. Reorganizing museums by similar objects instead of themes [1] using text similarity has been explored and tested in Europe. Deep learning methods have been utilized to recreate paintings and to restore damaged ones [7]. These are some of the few innovative applications that Deep Learning facilitates. With the help of interactive interfaces we are able to present data retrieved with this new technology through applications.

Not only do these interactive tools allow information to be shared among more people, they also present opportunities to improve the technology. Applications using CNNs trained on data can collect user inputs and enhance the tool as the more users interact with them; for instance, when users manually add labels to unlabelled data or upload their own images to databases [8]. Interactive tools can also generate information from one form to another thereby making it accessible to sight or hearing impaired users (audio file, image, text) [5]. Utilizing mobile apps for quick and easy access to cultural heritage information such as monument recognition [10] or artwork recognition [3] is also a field in development.

3   Information Retrieval

This section describes the information retrieval process and dataset creation from the images and captions contained in the scanned version of PPM, and is divided into 3 parts, image extraction, caption extraction, and image-caption indexing.

3.1   Image Extractions

To extract and collect the PPM's images, we used the exact same methods described in a previous paper [11]. Figure 1 summarizes the different steps to collect the coordinates of the images. We used this process to extract the images from volumes 1–10 but volume 11 contains significantly more color images. Most of these colored images have a very bright background that the adaptive threshold has trouble differentiating from the background of the page because the adaptive threshold function works with the grayscale, and the page background is not a perfect white [11]. Additionally, the scans sometimes have a yellow tint to them according to how hard the books were pressed against the scanning machine.

3.1.1   A New Module: Yellow Tint Overlay Subtraction

To reduce manual labor, we worked to improve automatization of the method from [11] by adding a module that calculates mathematically the yellow tint overlay to subtract it from the pages. This cleans every scan leaving the background of each page more white, while at the same time improving the color on the images themselves. The module also adds colored pixels as foreground pixels to be segmented from the background to further improve the results. To

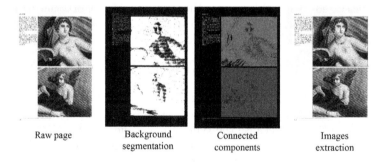

| Raw page | Background segmentation | Connected components | Images extraction |

Fig. 1. From left to right, the images representing the steps to extract the coordinate of the bounding box for each image on the pages. It starts with a raw page, to the background/foreground segmentation to the connected component, to the coordinates extraction. The background segmentation was done using an adaptive threshold function followed by a median noise reduction. The connected components use 8 neighbors and are combined with a previous average blur to increase connections disrupted from the median blur. The red box frames on the image extraction page are the representation of the coordinates used to save the images. (Color figure online)

recreate the noise overlay from the scan we used a bi-linear interpolation which is a weighted average of the RGB values from the four corners of the page. As seen in Fig. 2(a), no page in PPM has writing and/or images in the corners.

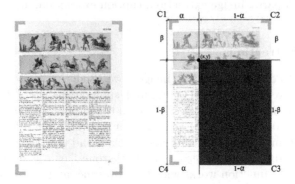

Fig. 2. Two scanned pages from PPM with L-shaped corners highlighted representing the area of the page used to calculate the four colors to interpolate the noise tint overlay.(b) has an explanatory diagram of the α and β calculation. The overlay pixel (x,y) is at the intersection of the horizontal and vertical line. The corners' weights are calculated proportionally to the opposite area of the four respective corners C1, C2, C3 and C4. The area to calculate C1's weight has been grayed out. (Color figure online)

As first step, we calculate four values for each corner as the average of each L-shaped area that can be seen in Fig. 2(a). We call these values C1, C2, C3, and C4. We now assume that the noise overlay is composed of a combination of those four colors.

Each color's weight is proportional to the opposite area of the corner color. This is illustrated in Fig. 2(b) where the color C1 is proportional to the area grayed out. Meaning that the weight of C1 would be equal to (1-α)*(1-β). Therefore we can define the overlay pixels as:

$$pix_{overlay}(x,y) = C1(1-\alpha)(1\beta) + C2(\alpha)(1-\beta) + C3(\alpha)(\beta) + C4(1-\alpha)(\beta) \quad (3.1)$$

Alpha and beta are normalized by the size of the image and represent the percentage of width and height respectively. Calculating the specific overlay for each page was essential because the type of noise and amount of pixels present differ depending on how the person scanning the page handled the book. This module significantly improved the detecting the image borders.

3.1.2 Evaluation

The overlay subtraction was not applied to volumes 1–10 since the initial results had already been processed and saved at a 98.7% accuracy, making the reapplication of the algorithm with the new module unnecessary. The remaining problems in the images extraction are the same ones as described in [11]. However, the new module of overlay subtraction introduced new problems.

Table 1. Results table of the coordinate extraction of images in volumes 1–11 of PPM, except for volume 7, which had at this time not been scanned.

Meta info		Number of images				Errors
Volume	Images	Cropped correctly	Missed	Cropped too small	Cropped too big	
1	1,660	1,653	0	5	2	7
2	1,623	1,620	0	3	0	3
3	1,993	1,982	2	9	0	11
4	2,028	1,995	3	27	3	33
5	1,710	1,687	7	14	2	23
6	1,972	1,910	9	51	2	62
8	2,084	2,019	10	55	0	65
9	1,969	1,927	6	35	1	42
10	820	815	0	5	0	5
11	1,331	1,282	18	28	3	49
Total	17,190	16,890	55	232	13	300

For very white images, the yellow overlay actually helped their detection because without it the image color blended with the background. In this case, the improvement of the process created an error that did not exist before. These cases did not counteract the overall positive improvement of the results; it is a compromise we lived with. Table 1, summarizes the extraction results of Volume 1 through 11 (Volume 7 not scanned yet).

3.2 Text Extraction

Once we successfully gathered all the images from PPM, we had to collect the captions of each image and link them together.

3.2.1 Image Indexes

The images in PPM are indexed with a small number, located at the image's top or bottom corner. This number associates the image to a caption indexed with the same number, sometimes located on a separate page (usually no more than 5 pages apart). Running OCR on the page or focused on the number did not show good results. However, the PPM volumes are organized by regions in Pompeii (Regio I-IX), and within each volume, the content is structured by city blocks within that region and properties within the block. An unindexed map introduces the discussion of each property, and every image index restarts at 1 after the map is displayed, indicating that the images of frescoes, mosaics, artifacts, and architecture that follow belong to the property depicted in the map. Therefore, we went through each image in order of appearance and indexed them with a counter that restarts when a map is presented. This way, we assigned the image index numbers to their appropriate captions and saved it in our database.

We knew which images were maps from our preliminary work where we retrained the last layer of a pre-trained Inception V3 [14] to classify images of PPM. The retrained CNN automatically classified the images in volume 2 into 6 categories: ruins, frescoes, schemas, mosaics, ruins with frescoes present, and maps. In classifying maps, our retrained CNN had an error rate of 0.3%, a precision of 99.4%, a recall of 97.8%, and an accuracy of 99.7%.

3.2.2   Caption Extraction

After entering the image's name, type (maps or not map), and potential index number into the database, we began to collect the captions and their indexes.

We pre-processed the pages for OCR by transforming them into grayscale images, shifting all the near-white pixels to be absolutely white, and the rest to be zero, which made sure the letters were black. We also applied an erosion to enhance the letters' thicknesses. We encountered a problem when the OCR algorithm tried to make up text from the images, which required us to save a version of the page containing only text based on the image cropping algorithm from Sect. 3.1. In this way, we collected the OCR of every page.

To extract the caption text from the OCR page files, we went through each line of the file to detect a string pattern of a caption's beginning. Each time a string of this type was detected, we collected the index and text of that caption that we saved into a separate file and in the database.

To link the collected caption data to its corresponding image, we implemented an algorithm that goes through the image indexes and looks for a corresponding caption index on the image's page. If no matching caption index is present on the page, it looks for the closest matching one in the vicinity of five pages before and after the image page. The results are then saved in the database.

3.2.3   Evaluation Tool

In order to correct occasional errors in caption indexing, we created an additional interactive tool that displays an image and its corresponding caption that allows the user to label the assignment as "correct" or "incorrect". Incorrect assignments can then be manually corrected. The tool displays one image with its automatically assigned index, its automatically assigned caption text, and the PPM page on the side. It allows a human corrector to rapidly go through all the images and check manually if the assignment is correct (see Fig. 3). The tool does not include the functionality to type in the correct index, but this is something that we plan on adding later. The cases not yet handled are: captions indexes with multiple numbers for the same caption text, indexes with letters, indexes with OCR noise or with undetected images, and captions that continue on the following page. Out of 1,623 images (including 67 maps), we collected 78 images with missing captions and 108 images with incorrect assignments. For images that are not maps in volume 2, 88% (corresponding to 1,370 images) are confirmed to have a correct caption and index. This is the data we used for further analysis.

Fig. 3. Screenshot of the evaluation tool utilized to check if image indexes match caption indexes

4 Data Analysis

We have collected all the images data from PPM and 1,370 captions correctly linked to their image from Volume 2. We put aside the captions incorrectly collected due to OCR errors and the incorrect image-caption index pairs. This section describes the analysis we performed with this data.

4.1 Image Similarity

After various experiments, such as the one briefly described in Sect. 3.2.1, we decided to look into calculating the degrees of similarities between PPM images using Transfer Learning [15]. This way, we collected the features vector describing each image of PPM from a pre-trained CNN to transfer into another model. We first used the Inception V3 pre-trained on 1,000 classes from the ImageNet dataset, meaning that all the weights of the CNN were already adjusted to detect over 1,000 types of various images. We ran it through our PPM images from Volume 2 and it provided us with a 1,000 long feature vector for each image. Once we had this data, we implemented a K-Nearest Neighbors (KNN)[16] algorithm to classify the images into 10 classes.

Figure 4 and 5 show a sample of each class that the KNN created with the features from Inception V3. The following list is a description of each category as one could observe:

- 0: 183 images, mostly images of ruins, black and white.
- 1: 52 images, frescoes containing square structures.
- 2: 69 images, long walls with rectangular shapes (either vertical or horizontal).
- 3: 386 images, maps and schemes, and complex shapes.
- 4: 47 images, close-ups black and white, flying people or animals.
- 5: 62 images, closeups with round shapes.
- 6: 79 images, people and animal representations.
- 7: 30 images, animals, and angels.
- 8: 274 images, big walls.
- 9: 259 images, big spaces.

From observing the classification results, we concluded that these feature vectors were relevant to be used as a descriptor vector for further analysis of the images. Hence, we prepared the feature vectors to be used inside the research tool by calculating a matrix containing how close each vector was to one another using the cosine similarity [9].

4.2 Caption Similarity

Regarding the caption similarity, we wanted to extract a feature vector for each caption. A necessary step was to use Natural Language Processing. First, we got rid of line breaks and dashes that were in the caption text file from the OCR process. Indeed, the captions in the books are laid out in columns which forced the writers to cut a lot of the words with dashes to create line breaks.

To create feature vectors for each caption we used the Latent Dirichlet Allocation (LDA) method [17]. In our case, the LDA model would generate a predefined number of topics from PPM, represented by a distribution of words. Then each caption would be represented by a distribution of these topics, i.e. its feature vector. To prepare the corpus for the LDA model generation, we split the corpus into single words that we lowercased (Tokenization). Then we removed the numerical values, words shorter than three characters and Italian stop-words (the most common words in the language). Then we reduced all the words to their root form (Stemming). After these steps and a designated number of topics, we can generate and save an LDA model. Selecting the number of topics to use is tricky and requires the performance of various iterations. We collected three different models to observe: 10 topics, 50 topics, and 100 topics. In the stemming step, we wanted to make sure the cardinal coordinates information (North, South, West, East) would be taken into account in the feature vector.

Indeed, the captions often include detailed spatial information to specify where the image is located on a wall in a room in a house. For instance, a caption might indicate that an image was located in the middle horizontal zone of the left vertical track of the northern wall of room X in house X. In this example, the northern wall would be described as "parete N" in the caption; however, by default, the stemming process cuts the word's ending and any word shorter than three letters. Therefore, "parete N" would become "par", and we would lose the cardinal information. To avoid this, we pre-processed the text and moved the cardinal letter to the beginning of the word. For instance, "parete N" would be transformed into "Nparete" which would be stemmed to be "npar".

The captions also sometimes contain a fresco's style designation, classifying it as one of the four main styles of Roman wall painting, appearing in the text as "stile I", "stile II", etc. To retain the style information in the feature, we changed the wording to "Istile," which gets transformed into "istil". To check that the cardinal information and style information was indeed taken into account in the topic creation, we created a model with 10 topics and observed the word distribution of each. The topics generated did have predominating words containing cardinal and style information. It implies that we could potentially detect captions describing images similar to one another containing location information

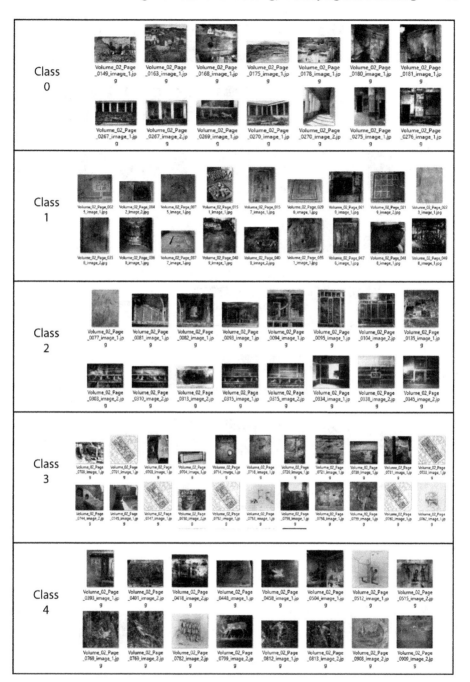

Fig. 4. Sample of images for the classes 0 to 4 collected from the KNN clustering.

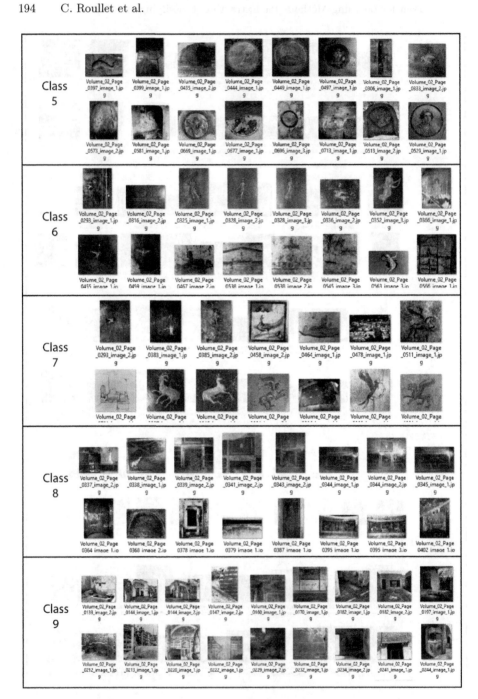

Fig. 5. Sample of images for the classes 5 to 9 collected from the KNN clustering.

in the houses of Pompeii in their feature vectors. We could also possibly answer questions such as such as whether bird representations are often located on the southern part of walls.

As was done with the images, we also used the feature vectors of the captions from the LDA model to calculate a distance matrix of each vector to one another using the cosine similarity.

5   Research Tool

This section describes how we have integrated into an interactive software tool all the data we have collected in Sects. 3 and 4. Currently, the tool uses data from volume 2 of PPM, but it will be extended to include all 11 volumes in the future.

5.1   Word Lookup

To do a similarity search on an image or a caption of PPM, a user must first pick a pair of image/captions. To pull up an image/caption pair, we implemented a word search functionality that recovers captions containing a search query. The user has the option to conduct this query search in two different ways, both of which use frequency-based methods.

5.1.1   Query Search

We made it possible for a user to do a search query with multiple terms using a method of their choice. The tool will either calculate the Term Frequency (TF) score or the Term Frequency and Inverse Dense Frequency (TF-IDF) score [17] of the captions relative to the query words. The TF measure, will calculate a score for each caption according to the words in the query, then the tool will return the captions with the highest TF scores. This method serves its purpose, but it does tend to prioritize captions with fewer words. TF-IDF makes it possible to analyze a word with respect to the entire corpus of PPM and not only to its caption. A TF-IDF score is calculated in the form of a vector for each caption and for the query. The results returned are the captions with a TF-IDF score closest to the query's TF-IDF score. To calculate the closeness between the query and the captions, the user has the choice to pick between the Euclidian distance or the cosine similarity [9]. The Euclidean distance is recommended for queries with a single word, otherwise, the cosine similarity will return the captions in order of appearance in the book. Cosine similarity is more relevant when the vectors are of a greater length than one.

5.2   Similarity Calculation

Once a user has picked a pair of an artifact image/caption, they are able to click on it to unlock the functionality of looking for a similar image, a similar caption, or a combination of both.

5.2.1 Image Similarity

With the image similarity, the user can choose either the CNN inception V3 [14] or Inception ResNet v2 [13] for the feature vectors to be used. Once they pick how many results (10 by default) they want to visualize, and the CNN features they want to use, the tool displays image/caption pairs ranked by how similar they are to one another. Figure 6 is an example of similarity results using Inception ResNet v2. The results are returned almost immediately because the distance matrix has been calculated beforehand as described in Sect. 3. Although we shrunk the images down in size to increase the tool's speed, loading the images, which are large, can still slow it down. Figure 6 is a screenshot from the search tool, after an image similarity search query using the Inception ResNet v2.

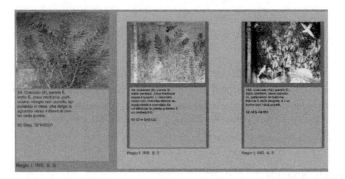

Fig. 6. Example of an image similarity search result with the search tool. The image/caption pair on the far left is the one used for the similarity search. the two image/caption pairs on the right are the top 2 results from an image similarity search using Inception ResNet v2.

5.2.2 Caption Similarity

Caption similarity works like the image similarity except that the user can choose the number of topics distributed from the LDA model to be used for the feature vectors. The user has the choice of 10, 50, or 100 topics. Figure 7 illustrates the results of a caption similarity search. Like Sect. 5.2.1, the results are returned fast because the distance matrices have been pre-calculated. There is no significant decrease in speed of response going from 10-50-100 topics either. Figure 7 is a screenshot from the search tool, after a caption similarity search query using an LDA model with 100 topics. The query was made with the same image/caption pair as Fig. 6.

5.2.3 Combination Similarity

We wanted to allow the user the additional option of returning results that take into account the similarity of the image and the caption at the same time. An image similarity search returns results with similar images without considering

Fig. 7. Example of a caption similarity search result with the search tool. The image/caption pair on the far left is the one used for the similarity search. the two image/caption pairs on the right are the top 2 results from a caption similarity search using an LDA model with 100 topics.

the information in the caption. Vice versa, a caption similarity search does not take into consideration the similarity of their corresponding image. Therefore, we added a slider to our interface which corresponds to image/caption weights similarity. Putting the slider at 50% would return results where the similarity with the image matters as much as the similarity with the caption.

We have previously calculated the distance matrices between each feature vector. For a given image feature vector, we have the distances between that vector and all the other image feature vectors. We also have that information for the caption feature vectors. This information can be merged into a single vector using weights. This final vector contains the final score to consider for returning the similarity search results.

$$\vec{d_{combination}} = w_{image} * \vec{d_{image}} + w_{caption} * \vec{d_{caption}} \tag{5.1}$$

$\vec{d_{image}}$ is the vector of distances between the feature vector of the picked image for the similarity search and all the other image feature vectors of PPM. $\vec{d_{caption}}$ is the vector of distances between the feature vector of the picked caption for the similarity search and all the other caption feature vectors of PPM. w_{image} is the weight for the image distance chosen by the user. $w_{caption}$ is the weight for the caption distance chosen by the user. The user defines the weights by moving a slider handle along a bar.

6   Conclusions and Future Work

In this paper we have presented a process to exploit and analyze the content of PPM. We were able to extract images and captions from digitized versions of the books using image processing and natural language processing. We used transfer learning employing convolution neural networks to extract image features. We used generative statistical models (LDA) to extract caption features. With these images and caption features, we performed similarity searches between captions and images of PPM that were integrated in an interactive software tool.

Our tool has the capability to return pairs of caption/images from Volume 2 of PPM using a word search input. From a chosen pair, the user can perform three different type of searches: image similarity search, caption similarity search, or a combination of image and caption similarity search. This allows users to explore the PPM data by looking up words and research relevant connections between decorations with similarity searches.

In the future, we plan to add the images from the other volumes of PPM in the search tool since all previous work and analysis has been based solely on the images and captions from Volume 2.

We will also design an experimental framework to evaluate the current state of the search tool and its features using methods such as the "two alternative forced choice" method (2AFC) [12] with archaeology experts. Other evaluations will include observation of the user workflow when using the tool for specific tasks or activities along with a higher level questionnaire. This will allow us to see in which contexts caption similarity is more useful than image similarity search and vice versa.

PPM provides us with spatial information on the images that we plan on adding as search feature. The user will then be able to search according to spatial proximity as well as spatial similarity. In addition, this tool has potential to evolve beyond currently planned functionality as the project progresses.

References

1. Aletras, N., Stevenson, M., Clough, P.: Computing similarity between items in a digital library of cultural heritage. J. Comput. Cult. Heritage (JOCCH) 5(4), 1–19 (2013)
2. Arnold, T., Tilton, L.: Enriching historic photography with structured data using image region segmentation. In: Proceedings of the 1st International Workshop on Artificial Intelligence for Historical Image Enrichment and Access, pp. 1–10 (2020)
3. Becattini, F., Ferracani, A., Landucci, L., Pezzatini, D., Uricchio, T., Del Bimbo, A.: Imaging novecento. A mobile app for automatic recognition of artworks and transfer of artistic styles. In: Ioannides, M., et al. (eds.) EuroMed 2016. LNCS, vol. 10058, pp. 781–791. Springer, Cham (2016). https://doi.org/10.1007/978-3-319-48496-9_62
4. Belhi, A., Bouras, A., Foufou, S.: Leveraging known data for missing label prediction in cultural heritage context. Appl. Sci. 8(10), 1768 (2018)
5. Díaz-Rodríguez, N., Pisoni, G.: Accessible cultural heritage through explainable artificial intelligence. In: 11th Workshop on Personalized Access to Cultural Heritage (2020)
6. Gultom, Y., Arymurthy, A.M., Masikome, R.J.: Batik classification using deep convolutional network transfer learning. J. Ilmu Komputer dan Inf. 11(2), 59–66 (2018)
7. Jboor, N.H., et al.: Towards an inpainting framework for visual cultural heritage. In: 2019 IEEE Jordan International Joint Conference on Electrical Engineering and Information Technology (JEEIT), pp. 602–607. IEEE (2019)

8. Kulkarni, U., et al.: Classification of cultural heritage sites using transfer learning. In: 2019 IEEE Fifth International Conference on Multimedia Big Data (BigMM), pp. 391–397. IEEE (2019)
9. Liu, Y., et al.: A many-objective evolutionary algorithm using a one-by-one selection strategy. IEEE Trans. Cybern. **47**(9), 2689–2702 (2017)
10. Palma, V: Towards deep learning for architecture: amonument recognition mobile app. In: International Archives of the Photogrammetry, Remote Sensing & Spatial Information Sciences (2019)
11. Roullet, C., et al.: An automated technique to recognize and extract images from scanned archaeological documents. In: 2019 International Conference on Document Analysis and Recognition Workshops (ICDARW), vol. 1, pp. 20–25. IEEE (2019)
12. Schulman, A.J., Mitchell, R.R.: Operating characteristics from yes-no and forced-choice procedures. J. Acoust. Soc. Am. **40**(2), 473–477 (1966)
13. Szegedy, C., et al.: Inception-v4, inception-resnet and the impact of residual connections on learning. arXiv preprint arXiv: 1602.07261 (2016)
14. Szegedy, C., et al.: Rethinking the inception architecture for computer vision. In: Proceedings of the IEEE Conference on Computer Vision and Pattern Recognition, pp. 2818–2826 (2016)
15. Tan, C., Sun, F., Kong, T., Zhang, W., Yang, C., Liu, C.: A survey on deep transfer learning. In: Kůrková, V., Manolopoulos, Y., Hammer, B., Iliadis, L., Maglogiannis, I. (eds.) ICANN 2018. LNCS, vol. 11141, pp. 270–279. Springer, Cham (2018). https://doi.org/10.1007/978-3-030-01424-7_27
16. Trstenjak, B., Mikac, S., Donko, D.: KNN with TF-IDF based framework for text categorization. Proc. Eng. **69**, 1356–1364 (2014)
17. Wang, J., et al.: Text similarity calculation method based on hybrid model of LDA and TF-IDF. In: Proceedings of the 2019 3rd International Conference on Computer Science and Artificial Intelligence, pp. 1–8 (2019)
18. Wevers, M., Smits, T.: The visual digital turn: using neural networks to study historical images. Digit. Scholarsh. Hum. **35**(1), 194–207 (2020)
19. Zohar, M., Shimshoni, I., Khateb, F.: GIScience Integrated with Computer Vision for the Interpretation and Analysis of Old Paintings. In: GISTAM, pp. 233–239 (2020)

Deep Learning Spatial-Spectral Processing of Hyperspectral Images for Pigment Mapping of Cultural Heritage Artifacts

Di Bai[1]([✉])[ID], David W. Messinger[1][ID], and David Howell[2][ID]

[1] Rochester Institute of Technology, Rochester, NY 14623, USA
db3641@rit.edu, messinger@cis.rit.edu
[2] University of Oxford, Oxford, UK
david.howell.dh51@gmail.com

Abstract. In 2015, the Gough Map was imaged using a hyperspectral imaging system while in the collection at the Bodleian Library, University of Oxford. It is one of the earliest surviving maps of Britain. Hyperspectral image (HSI) classification has been widely used to identify materials in remotely sensed images. Recently, hyperspectral imaging has been applied to historical artifact studies. The collection of the HSI data of the Gough Map was aimed at pigment mapping for towns and writing with different spatial patterns and spectral (color) features. We developed a spatial-spectral deep learning framework called 3D-SE-ResNet to automatically classify pigments in large HSI of cultural heritage artifacts with limited reference (labelled) data and have applied it to the Gough Map. With much less effort and much higher efficiency, this is a breakthrough in object identification and classification in cultural heritage studies that leverages the spectral and spatial information contained in this imagery, providing codicological information to cartographic historians.

Keywords: Cultural heritage artifacts · Medieval maps · 3D-SE-Resnet · 3D deep learning · Hyperspectral image classification

1 Introduction

The Gough Map is a medieval map of Great Britain dating from the 15th century [8,13,19]. As shown in Fig. 1(a), the map is colored in green indicating the rivers, ocean and coastal areas. The red symbols indicate towns and the red and black writing indicate the names of towns or rivers [8,13,19]. Examples of different towns and writing are shown in Fig. 1(b). Previous study had shown that the Gough Map was broadly revised after its creation [8,19] and consequently we find three kinds of red towns and two kinds of black writing. The map was imaged using a visible-near infrared hyperspectral system at the Bodleian Library, Oxford University in 2015, with the aim of faded text

© Springer Nature Switzerland AG 2021
A. Del Bimbo et al. (Eds.): ICPR 2020 Workshops, LNCS 12667, pp. 200–214, 2021.
https://doi.org/10.1007/978-3-030-68787-8_14

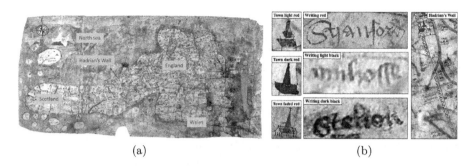

(a)   (b)

Fig. 1. The Gough Map. (a) RGB Gough Map with names of different regions. (b) Several magnified views in the "zoom" window. Towns, some writings and distances are indicated in red; Ocean, coastal areas and rivers are colored in green. The map was drawn on a combination of sheepskin (right 3/4 of map) and lambskin (left 1/4 of map). The magnified views indicate three kinds of red towns (light, dark and faded red), red writing, two kinds of black writings and Hadrian's Wall. (Color figure online)

enhancement for reading and pigment mapping (classification) for codicological studies, i.e., understanding the techniques and materials used in its creation and potentially its creation and revision timeline. Pigment mapping is essential for historians to identify and classify objects in cultural heritage artifacts. The goal of this research is to segment pixels into different classes, such as the towns, writing and Hadrian's Wall across the entire Gough Map. This is a pixel level classification method which also classify different objects (towns, writings, etc.) into different categories. We achieved this using a deep learning method with a very limited amount of reference data.

Pigment analysis of historical artifacts includes material identification and pigment mapping (classification). Manually pixel labelling was time consuming and not accurate, so that researchers used different imaging systems, such as laser-induced breakdown spectroscopy [15], infrared imaging [6] and X-ray fluorescence imaging [7] to identify different materials in historical artifacts. However, these methods could only provide pixel level identification instead of an image with spatial patterns. Hyperspectral images (HSIs) provide both the spatial and spectral information of the Gough Map for the first time. Compared to RGB images, HSIs have hundreds of continuous spectral bands (typically over the visible and infrared spectral range, e.g. 400–1000) in the same spatial area. HSIs provide more spectral information to accurately identify different pigments or materials [2–5,7,10]. In this research, a novel spatial-spectral deep learning framework called 3D-SE-ResNet is developed for HSI classification of historical artifacts, specifically the Gough Map. This is the first attempt using deep learning methods to pigment mapping of HSIs of historical artifacts. Learning both spatial and spectral features, it classifies the red pigments in the towns, Hadrian's Wall and red & black pigments in the writing accurately with a limited amount of reference data. It also outperforms all the other methods on HSI classification of the Gough Map.

HSI classification can be widely used in different applications, such as pigment analysis [5] and terrain classification [9]. Researchers usually first reduce the dimensionality of the data using principal component analysis (PCA) to compress the spectral information, and then feed the first three principal components into a neural network [9,21]. This feature extraction procedure will lose some spectral-spatial information since the HSI data has been compressed and transformed to another space. Alternatively, instead of dimensionality reduction, some researchers have adopted 3D-CNN (using 3D filter banks) to extract spectral-spatial features directly from raw HSI data, such as spectral–spatial residual network (SSRN) [23], fast dense spectral–spatial convolution network (FDSSC) [20] and fully dense multiscale fusion network (FDMFN) [16].

2   Dataset and Methodology

The size of the Gough Map is about $115\,cm \times 56\,cm$. To ensure full coverage with sufficient spatial resolution, the collection was done in six overlapping HSI "chips", each covering an area of approximately $71.5\,cm \times 23.5\,cm$ at a spatial resolution of 68 pixels/cm vertically and 77 pixels/cm horizontally. The size of each chip is $1600(pixels) \times 5512(pixels) \times 334(bands)$. The spectral range is $400\,nm$ and $1000\,nm$, including the visible and near infrared (Vis-NIR).

2.1   Labelled Reference Data of the Gough Map

As shown in Fig. 2, we labelled the Gough Map into seven classes, including (1) light red town (indicated in red), (2) dark red town (violet), (3) faded red town (green), (4) red writing (blue), (5) light black writing (yellow), (6) dark black writing (magenta) and (7) Hadrian's Wall (cyan). Specifically, class 3 (faded red town) is mainly in the faded regions of the map (on the right side), class 6 (dark black writings) is in the top right region of the map and class 7 (Hadrian's Wall) pixels are in the middle left of the map.

Notice that class 1, 4 and 7 are different objects (different spatial patterns) with similar spectral (color) features. Class 1–3 are similar objects ("towns" with similar spatial patterns, as shown in Fig. 1(b)) with different spectral (color) features. Historical artifacts such as medieval maps usually contain objects with different spatial and spectral features, so that it is necessary to consider both spectral and spatial information of the objects in historical artifacts during pigment mapping (classification).

2.2   Input and Output (I/O) of the Neural Network

In order to decrease the computation time and memory usage, we cut each chip into two overlapping sub-chips $(1600 \times 3000 \times 334)$ and spatially down sample it by 1/4 to $400 \times 750 \times 334$. Sufficient spatial resolution is still maintained

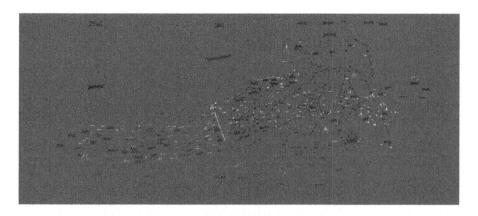

Fig. 2. Seven different classes of labelled reference data of the Gough Map.

to identify the spatial features on the map. To extract and learn both spatial and spectral features from the HSI, we extract 3D spatial-spectral volumes of $w \times w \times b$ for each pixel in the data as input, where w is the spatial input size and b indicates the number of spectral bands. The corresponding label is the label of the pixel in the center. Now each pixel is represented by its neighboring $w \times w \times b$ 3D spatial-spectral volume instead of only its spectrum (color) information. For example, from a HSI, we randomly choose a number of $7 \times 7 \times 334(bands)$ small chips as training data and put them into the neural network. The label of the central pixel is the output label of the network. As a pixel level classification method, all the pixels in the towns, writing and Hadrian's Wall of the Gough Map will be represented as a 3D spatial-spectral volume and assigned a label between one and seven.

2.3   3D-SE-ResNet Architecture

3D-SE-ResNet is a 3D residual neural network (ResNet) with 3D squeeze and excitation (SE) blocks. This neural network can learn both spatial and spectral features from HSIs.

In general, a residual unit is shown below:

$$x_{i+1} = x_i + F_{res}(x_i, w_i) \tag{1}$$

where x_i and x_{i+1} are the input and output vectors of the corresponding layers, F_{res} is the learned residual mapping and w_i is its associated weight. The key idea of the ResNet is to evaluate the residual function F_{res} with respect to the input x_i, which results in x_I as:

$$x_I = x_i + \sum_{i=k}^{I-1} F_{res}(x_k, w_k) \tag{2}$$

therefore, the feature x_I of any layers can be derived as the x_I of an early input plus the summarized residual functions $\sum_{i=k}^{I-1} F_{res}(x_k, w_k)$.

In this research, we first extend the 2D-ResNet into 3D-ResNet by adding a third dimension to the filters, e.g. by converting a 2D filter to a 3D filter. Specifically, we would use two kinds of filter banks to learn both spectral features and spatial features. The filter size of the spectral feature learning blocks is $1 \times 1 \times 7$ and the filter size of the spatial feature learning blocks is $3 \times 3 \times 1$. The reason for using different filters sizes is because we have to treat the spatial and spectral features differently due to the different nature (size and shape) of features in the spatial and spectral domains.

Then, we incorporated 3D Squeeze-and-Excitation blocks into the 3D-ResNet to learn the weight of the filters (channels) during the training process. The squeeze and excitation network (SE-Nets) was originally created for training RGB images [11]. Given a transformation $Y = F(X)$, where X and Y are both four dimensional vector: $X \in R^{W' * H' * D' * C'}$ and $Y \in R^{W * H * D * C}$. X is the input, Y is the feature after a convolution or several convolutions. W' and H' indicate the spatial dimensions of X, D' is the depth (spectral) dimension and C' indicates the channel of X. Similarly, W, H, D, C represent corresponding information of Y. In this transformation, F is a standard convolutional operator, $K = [k_1, k_1, ..., k_c]$ is a set of kernels, where k_c represents the parameters of the c-th filter. Now we write the outputs of F as $Y = [y_1, y_1, ..., y_c]$, where

$$y_c = k_c * X = \sum_{S=1}^{C'} k_c^s * x^s \tag{3}$$

y_c is the result of the convolution between $k_c = [k_c^1, k_c^2, ..., k_c^{C'}]$ and $X = [x^1, x^2, ..., x^{C'}]$. In this case, k_c^m is a 3D kernel representing a single channel of k_c which convolutes with the corresponding channel of X. Since the output y_c is a summation of all channels, as a result, the channel dependencies are embedded in k_c. Squeeze and excitation blocks increases the network's sensitivity to informative features and exploit subsequent transformations.

An example of the 3D-SE-ResNet and its blocks are shown in Fig. 3. From each HSI chip of the Gough Map, we extract $7 \times 7 \times 334(bands)$ small chips as input. There are in total 104,011 pixels of towns, writings and Hadrian's Wall in the Gough Map after spatially subsampling. If we select 5% of the data as training data, 10% as validation data and the rest of it as test data, we will have about $5227 \times 7 \times 334(bands)$ training data, $10375 \times 7 \times 334(bands)$ validation data and $88409 \times 7 \times 334(bands)$ test data.

As shown in Fig. 3(a), the framework includes two 3D-SE-ResNet spectral feature learning blocks, two 3D-SE-ResNet spatial feature learning blocks, an average pooling layer, and a fully connected (FC) layer. The spectral feature learning block is shown in Fig. 3(b) and the spatial feature learning block is shown in Fig. 3(c). Both blocks use bottleneck layers (the $1 \times 1 \times 1$ filter banks) to increase the efficiency of the network. Notice the different kernel sizes between

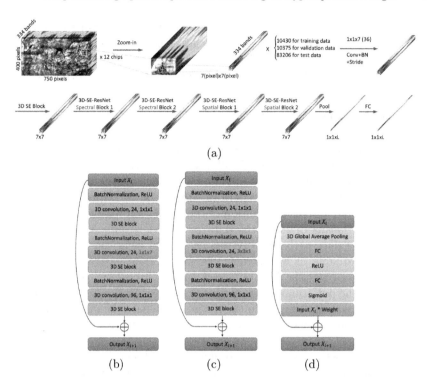

Fig. 3. The framework of 3D-SE-ResNet for HSI classification. (a) including two spectral residual blocks and two spatial residual blocks. An average pooling layer and a fully connected layer; (b) The spectral feature extraction block of 3D-SE-ResNet; (c) The spatial feature extraction block of 3D-SE-ResNet; (d) The 3D-SE block of 3D-SE-ResNet.

(a) and (b). As an example, we used $1 \times 1 \times 7$ filter banks for spectral feature learning blocks and $3 \times 3 \times 1$ filter banks for spatial feature learning blocks. In all of the convolutional layers in each block, we use padding to keep the sizes of output cubes unchanged.

Within each 3D-SE-ResNet feature learning block in Fig. 3(b) and Fig. 3(c), 3D squeeze and excitation blocks (Fig. 3(d)) are added after each convolution layer. By giving a weight and bias to each channel (filter), the SE blocks increase the framework's sensitivity to informative features. As shown in Fig. 3(d), a 3D global average pooling layer is added to squeeze global spatial (spectral) information into a channel descriptor and channel-wise statistics is generated. Then a ReLU [17] and a Sigmoid activation function are utilized to learn the nonlinearity between the channels. Meanwhile, we add two fully-connected layers around ReLU to perform a bottleneck, so that we will limit the complexity of the framework.

After the 3D-SE-ResNet feature learning blocks, an average pooling layer is added to transform a $7 \times 7 \times L$ feature volume to a $1 \times 1 \times L$ feature vector.

Then, a fully connected layer is added to adapt the framework to the dataset according to the number of classes (seven classes here) and generates an output vector. In addition, batch-normalization (BN), dropout and early stopping are used as to control overfitting and improve the classification performance.

3   Experimental Results

In this section, we will show both qualitative and quantitative results of the experiments. We computed (1) overall accuracy (OA), (2) average accuracy (AA), (3) per class accuracy, (4) kappa, and recorded training time. In all experiments, k-fold cross validation was performed to avoid overlapping training data and then mean and standard deviation of the prediction were calculated. K-fold cross validation means dividing the data set into k groups and taking one of them as training data each time. K was calculated from the amount of training data. For example, if we extract 10% of the data as training data, then $k = 1/10\% = 10$, if we take 5% training data, k will be $1/5\% = 20$. To qualitatively evaluate the performance, we mapped the classification results back to the Gough Map for visualization. To quantitatively evaluate the performance of the framework, we consider parameters from both a dataset aspect and a framework aspect.

From the dataset aspect, these parameters are chosen based on typical HSI pixel level classification methods using deep learning techniques [12,18,20,22]. Here we compared:

1. Different amounts of training data: 1%, 5%, 10%, etc. From the reference data, we randomly selected $x\%$ of each class across the entire map as training data, $y\%$ as validation date and the rest as test data.
2. Different spatial input sizes: we extracted 3D data volume with different spatial input sizes, $e.g.$, $3 \times 3 \times bands$, $5 \times 5 \times bands$ and $7 \times 7 \times bands$, etc.
3. Different spectral input sizes: The original HSI has 334 spectral bands, which results in (1) long computation time, (2) high memory usage and (3) low signal to noise ratio (SNR). To decrease the spectral bands, we binned the data in the spectral domain by taking an average every w bands. For example, if $w = 3$, after binning the data, there will be 111 spectral bands.

From the framework aspect, we compared:

1. Different learning rates: such as 0.01, 0.001 and 0.0001, etc.
2. Different number of kernels per layer: such as 8, 16 and 24, etc.
3. Different number of 3D-SE-ResNet blocks: such as 2, 4 and 6, etc. Here, two blocks mean one spectral feature extraction block and one spatial feature extraction block, including about 70 layers in total. In addition, four blocks: 110 layers, six blocks: 150 layers and eight blocks: 190 layers in total.
4. Other deep learning frameworks.

3.1 Experimental Results from the Dataset Aspect

We first computed the accuracy of prediction with different amount of training data and kept all the other parameters constant, for example: (1) selecting 10% of the reference data as validation data; (2) spectral bin: 12; (3) spatial input size: $7 \times 7 \times bands$; (4) learning rate: 0.0001; (5) number of filters per layer: 32; (6) number of 3D-SE-ResNet blocks: 4;

The results are shown in Table 1. Notice that both OA and AA increase as the amount of training data increases. With 5% training data, the overall accuracy is 90.49%, but the average accuracy is 83.92% due to the accuracy of Hadrian's Wall at 67.52%. But as we add more training data (from 1% to 5%), there is a large improvement (from 1.92% to 67.52%) on its accuracy. Since there are very few pixels in Hadrian's Wall (1158 pixels/104011 pixels total) compared to other classes and its spectrum is very similar to class 4 (red writings), it is hard to separate it from the other classes. To visualize the classification results, we map the predictions back to the Gough Map. As shown in Fig. 4(b), even with 5% training data, we can still easily identify the towns, writing and Hadrian's Wall in it. From the perspective of "object" level detection (which is important for codicological studies), the result is acceptable.

Table 1. Classification results with different amount of training data.

Training data/All data	1%	5%	10%	20%	30%
OA (%)	82.38 ± 1.49	90.49 ± 0.54	93.88 ± 0.4	96.43 ± 0.26	97.64 ± 0.54
AA (%)	65.33 ± 1.77	83.92 ± 1.4	90.2 ± 0.87	94.34 ± 0.75	96.49 ± 0.53
Kappa × 100	76.07 ± 2.09	87.16 ± 0.71	91.75 ± 0.53	95.18 ± 0.35	96.83 ± 0.73
1 light red town	64.49 ± 8.56	74.31 ± 6	85.51 ± 4.83	89.68 ± 3.56	95.52 ± 1.25
2 dark red town	74.29 ± 10.18	88.76 ± 4.46	92.75 ± 3.05	97.25 ± 0.57	98.24 ± 0.76
3 faded red town	55.23 ± 7.34	76.58 ± 3.91	86.61 ± 3.68	93.25 ± 1.09	96.27 ± 1.98
4 red writing	93.87 ± 1.78	96.35 ± 1.1	97.59 ± 0.73	98.41 ± 0.29	98.33 ± 1.04
5 writing light bk	79.74 ± 2.42	90.23 ± 1.89	92.86 ± 1.61	95.64 ± 1.24	97.26 ± 0.26
6 writing dark bk	87.79 ± 1.87	93.68 ± 1.34	94.4 ± 1.66	96.63 ± 0.87	97.48 ± 0.15
7 Hadrian's Wall	1.92 ± 3.25	67.52 ± 7.46	81.71 ± 6.32	89.54 ± 3.34	92.35 ± 0.2

Specifically in the zoom in window shown in Fig. 4(c), even though pixel level accuracy is just 67.52% with 5% training data, the wall can still be easily identified. From the perspective of "object" level detection, the framework makes a good prediction. In this research, we care about the detection and classification for different towns, writing and Hadrian's Wall at an object level. If pixel level accuracy is necessary, the 3D-SE-ResNet can still achieve high prediction accuracy with a bit more training data (10%–20%) as shown in Table 1. Even though the training set is commonly composed of more samples with the respect to the validation and test sets, in this research, we could still achieve good performance with a significantly small amount of training data. This is due to the powerful deep learning framework 3D-SE-ResNet, which is able to extract and learn subtle features between different classes.

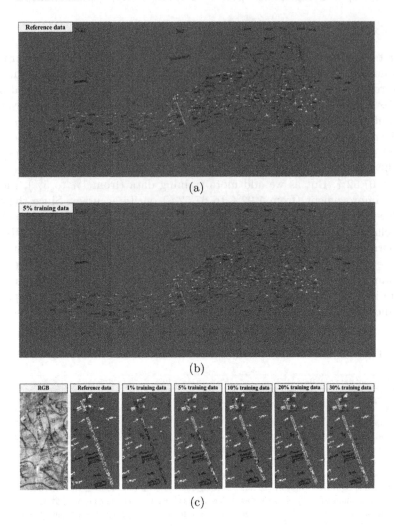

Fig. 4. The Gough Map classification results of with different amount of training data. (a) Labelled reference data of the map. (b) Classification results with 5% training data. (c) Zoom-in window of high resolution RGB image of Hadrian's Wall (Class 7) and classification results of it using 1%, 5%, 10%, 20% and 30% of reference data as training data.

We computed the prediction accuracy with different spatial input sizes including: $3 \times 3 \times bands$, $5 \times 5 \times bands$, $7 \times 7 \times bands$, $9 \times 9 \times bands$ and $11 \times 11 \times bands$. Here we took 20% training data and kept all the other parameters the same. As shown in Table 2, OA and AA increase as the spatial input size increases. This is because the neural network is able to extract and learn more spatial and spectral information from a larger volume. When the spatial input size is over $7 \times 7 \times bands$, the prediction is robust and stable.

Table 2. Classification results with different spatial input sizes.

Spatial input size	3 × 3	5 × 5	7 × 7	9 × 9	11 × 11
OA (%)	86.25 ± 0.4	93.48 ± 0.12	96.55 ± 0.06	97.11 ± 0.05	97.42 ± 0.28
AA (%)	75.8 ± 1.05	89.8 ± 0.72	94.63 ± 0.96	96.34 ± 0.23	96.83 ± 0.36
Kappa × 100	81.42 ± 0.58	91.21 ± 0.14	95.36 ± 0.07	96.11 ± 0.07	96.52 ± 0.39

We then computed the prediction accuracy with different spectral input sizes, including spectral bin number at: $w = 1, 3, 6, 12, 24, 36$ with 20% training data. As shown in Table 3, when spectral bin at 6 or 12, both OA and AA reach the highest value. This is because too many spectral bands will result in low SNR and too few spectral bands ($w = 36$) will lose necessary spectral information.

Table 3. Classification results with different spectral bins.

Spectral bin	1	3	6	12	24	36
OA (%)	96 ± 0.57	96.2 ± 0.4	96.59 ± 0.45	96.54 ± 0.28	95.84 ± 0.27	95.21 ± 0.49
AA (%)	92.74 ± 1.56	94.51 ± 0.75	94.96 ± 0.24	94.75 ± 0.43	94.1 ± 0.4	92.99 ± 0.35
Kappa × 100	94.59 ± 0.78	94.89 ± 0.52	95.4 ± 0.59	95.33 ± 0.37	94.4 ± 0.36	93.54 ± 0.65

3.2 Experimental Results from Framework Aspect

We first fine-tuned the learning rate of the neural network, including, 0.01, 0.001, 0.0001 and 0.00001. As shown in Table 4, a learning rate at 0.0001 achieves the best results of OA and AA. This is because larger learning rates (such as 0.01) would not enable the network to converge to the best result. Small learning rates (0.00001) would take a much longer time to converge even though it resulted in similar OA or AA as 0.0001.

Table 4. Classification results with different learning rate.

Learning rate	0.01	0.001	0.0001	0.00001
OA (%)	83.9 ± 0.65	94.3 ± 0.66	96.46 ± 0.34	96.16 ± 0.2
AA (%)	68.17 ± 4.89	90.96 ± 1.29	94.74 ± 0.41	94.01 ± 0.52
Kappa × 100	78.1 ± 0.92	92.31 ± 0.89	95.24 ± 0.45	94.83 ± 0.27
Training time (s)	917 ± 275	1196 ± 207	2295 ± 938	6430 ± 853
Training epochs	22 ± 6	28 ± 5	52 ± 16	147 ± 16
Training time/epoch (s)	42 ± 3	43 ± 4	43 ± 4	44 ± 4

We then evaluated different numbers of kernels per layer including 8, 16, 24, 32, 40, 48. As shown in Table 5, both OA and AA increase with more filters and

24 filters per layer have provided robust prediction accuracy. Too many filters are not necessary because it makes the neural network too complicated and results in a longer training time.

Table 5. Classification results with different number of filters per layer.

# of filters/layer	8	16	24	32	40	48
OA (%)	92.92 ± 0.66	95.49 ± 0.4	96.22 ± 0.53	96.64 ± 0.44	96.74 ± 0.29	96.83 ± 0.34
AA (%)	85.53 ± 3.39	93.18 ± 0.83	94.33 ± 0.44	94.46 ± 1.05	95.31 ± 0.23	95.32 ± 0.4
Kappa × 100	90.43 ± 0.9	93.92 ± 0.54	94.9 ± 0.7	95.47 ± 0.59	95.61 ± 0.38	95.72 ± 0.45
Training time (s)	4171 ± 686	2321 ± 400	1909 ± 246	2069 ± 290	2211 ± 456	2631 ± 437
Training epochs	108 ± 14	59 ± 9	48 ± 9	51 ± 7	52 ± 13	58 ± 8
Training time/epoch (s)	39 ± 3	39 ± 3	40 ± 3	41 ± 2	43 ± 2	45 ± 2

We also tested if the number of 3D-SE-ResNet blocks may affect the prediction accuracy. As shown in Table 6, more blocks did not increase the accuracy but resulted in a longer training time per epoch. Two blocks have already achieved sufficient prediction accuracy.

Table 6. Classification results with different number of blocks.

# of 3D-SE-Resnet blocks	2	4	6	8
OA (%)	96.46 ± 0.27	96.49 ± 0.51	96.27 ± 0.3	96.29 ± 0.39
AA (%)	94.59 ± 0.48	94.59 ± 1.01	94.76 ± 0.23	95.3 ± 0.57
Kappa × 100	95.23 ± 0.37	95.26 ± 0.68	94.97 ± 0.39	95.01 ± 0.52
Training time (s)	1447 ± 205	1818 ± 375	2306 ± 435	3349 ± 775
Training epochs	49 ± 7	44 ± 9	43 ± 8	51 ± 12
Training time/epoch (s)	29 ± 1	42 ± 1	53 ± 2	65 ± 2

The 3D-SE-ResNet was designed to learn both spatial and spectral information from the HSIs. We tested if only learning spatial or spectral features may affect the results. As shown in Table 7, the AA of learning both features is higher than the other two. For example, 5% training data results in an AA of 83.92% with both blocks. However learning spectral features only achieves an AA at 79.1% and learning spatial features only achieves an AA at 68.84%. This is because the pigments in the towns, writing and Hadrian's Wall have both spatial and spectral differences.

We also compared the 3D-SE-ResNet with other HSI classification methods, including the baseline 3D-CNN [12], PCA based CNN framework [14], semantic segmentation method: the U-Net [18], Spectral-Spatial Residual Network (SSRN) [22] and Fast Dense Spectral-Spatial Convolutional Network (FDSSC) [20]. As shown in Table 8, 3D-SE-ResNet outperforms other methods with different amounts of training data. With 5% training data, the 3D-SE-ResNet results

Table 7. Average accuracy of 3D-SE-ResNet, 3D-SE-ResNet (spectral block only) and 3D-SE-ResNet (spatial block only).

Neural network	1%	5%	10%	20%	30%
3D-SE-ResNet	**65.33 ± 1.77**	**83.92 ± 1.4**	**90.2 ± 0.87**	**94.34 ± 0.75**	**96.49 ± 0.53**
3D-SE-ResNet (spectral)	65.78 ± 1.22	79.1 ± 1.9	84.08 ± 1.13	89.87 ± 1.38	91.05 ± 2.01
3D-SE-ResNet (spatial)	51.95 ± 2.81	68.84 ± 3.41	77.42 ± 3.11	83.84 ± 2.59	92.12 ± 1.11

Table 8. AA of different methods for the Gough Map.

Neural network	1%	5%	10%	20%	30%
3D-SE-ResNet	**65.33 ± 1.77**	**83.92 ± 1.4**	**90.2 ± 0.87**	**94.34 ± 0.75**	**96.49 ± 0.53**
Unet	63.12 ± 2.94	81.63 ± 1.52	86.49 ± 1.08	90.2 ± 0.27	91.01 ± 0.34
PCA + CNN	45.47 ± 1.53	63.04 ± 1.42	70.64 ± 1.28	78.27 ± 1.18	84.62 ± 1.01
3D-CNN	49.8 ± 1.97	65.88 ± 1.29	72.86 ± 0.54	80.23 ± 0.59	84.6 ± 0.21
FDSSC	63.19 ± 1.47	79.41 ± 1.8	85.72 ± 1.76	91.3 ± 1.27	95.18 ± 0.61
SSRN	64.09 ± 3.18	81.31 ± 1.55	89.37 ± 0.7	93.79 ± 1.1	96.71 ± 0.27

in an AA of 83.92% compared to the U-Net at 81.63%, PCA based CNN at 63.04%, 3D-CNN at 65.88%, FDSSC at 79.41% and SSRN at 81.31%.

The proposed 3D-SE-ResNet is a novel pigment classification framework that can be generalized to classify other HSIs of maps or other cultural heritage artifacts. For example, in [1], the author also applied the 3D-SE-ResNet to another medieval map called the Selden Map of China and three benchmark remote sensing HSIs including the Indian Pines, Kennedy Space Center and University of Pavia. Specifically, the HSI of the Selden Map of China was also collected at the Bodleian Library, Oxford University. As shown in Fig. 5, the Selden Map had 18 different classes with more complicated spatial patterns and spectral features.

In short, the results showed that the 3D-SE-ResNet achieved a pixel level accuracy at 87.57% with only 5% of the reference data, but from object level, all 18 different classes can be easily identified. We also found that when the spatial input size was over $9 \times 9 \times bands$, the classification result was the best. Compared to the Gough Map's minimum spatial input size ($7 \times 7 \times bands$), the Selden Map needed a bigger spatial input size due to the difficulty of separating more classes and more complicated spatial features. The hyper-parameters fine-tuning were similar to the Gough Map, but it required more filters per layer (here 32 filters/layer) to achieve a robust performance.

The results showed that the 3D-SE-ResNet is a robust and efficient framework that is able to classify HSIs of cultural heritage artifacts with limited amount of training data. It also achieved the state-of-the-art accuracy on three HSI benchmarks. More details are welcome to be reviewed in [1].

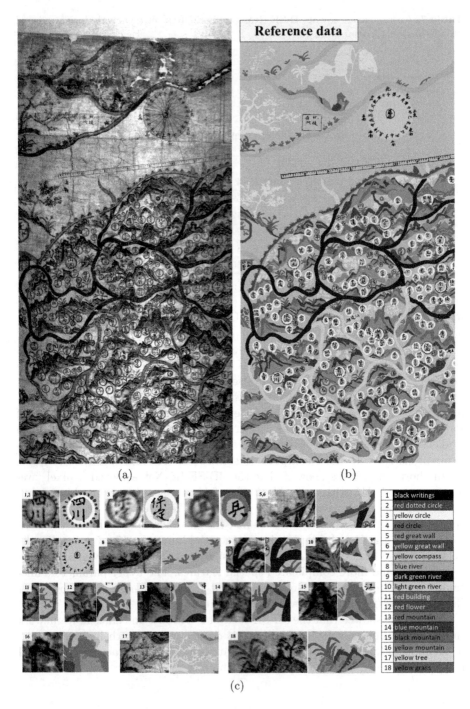

Fig. 5. The Selden Map (a) RGB image, (b) labelled reference image (18 classes) and (c) Zoom windows of RGB with reference image.

4 Conclusions

In this research, we present a novel deep learning approach for analysis of HSIs for pigment mapping of large cultural heritage artifacts, specifically the Gough Map, one of the earliest surviving maps of Britain in geographically recognizable form. With a limited amount of labelled reference data, the 3D-SE-ResNet leverages both spatial and spectral information from HSIs and classify the towns, writings and Hadrian's Wall in the Gough Map accurately in both object level and pixel level. This framework enables investigation of large HSIs classification with high accuracy.

The results show that with only 5% of the reference data, the 3D-SE-ResNet is able to identify towns, writings and Hadrian's Wall at a high object level accuracy. From both a dataset aspect and the framework aspect, this research provides ways of fine-tuning the network and discusses the significance of learning both spectral features and spatial features in the 3D-SE-ResNet framework. After comparing with other methods, the proposed 3D-SE-ResNet achieves higher OA and AA than all the other methods applied to the Gough Map.

This robust and efficient methodology can not only be applied to the Gough Map, but also be generalized to a novel pigment classification method for other artifacts and remotely sensed HSIs. Specifically, historical geographers and cartographic historians will benefit from this work when working on pigment mapping of cultural heritage artifacts. Specifically this new method provides a non-invasive way to study the cultural heritage artifacts without damaging the object, meanwhile accurate information is obtained. This research will consequently contribute to the codicological study of historical artifacts.

References

1. Bai, D.: A hyperspectral image classification approach to pigment mapping of historical artifacts using deep learning methods. Ph.D. dissertation, Rochester Institute of Technology (2019)
2. Bai, D., Messinger, D.W., Howell, D.: Hyperspectral analysis of cultural heritage artifacts: pigment material diversity in the Gough map of Britain. Opt. Eng. **56**(8), 081805–081805 (2017)
3. Bai, D., Messinger, D.W., Howell, D.: A pigment analysis tool for hyperspectral images of cultural heritage artifacts. In: SPIE Defense+ Security, p. 101981A. International Society for Optics and Photonics (2017)
4. Bai, D., Messinger, D.W., Howell, D.: Pigment diversity estimation for hyperspectral images of the Selden Map of China. In: Algorithms and Technologies for Multispectral, Hyperspectral, and Ultraspectral Imagery XXIV, vol. 10644, p. 1064415. International Society for Optics and Photonics (2018)
5. Bai, D., Messinger, D.W., Howell, D.: A hyperspectral imaging spectral unmixing and classification approach to pigment mapping in the Gough and Selden Maps. J. Am. Inst. Conserv. (2019). https://doi.org/10.1080/01971360.2019.1574436
6. Casini, A., Lotti, F., Picollo, M., Stefani, L., Buzzegoli, E.: Image spectroscopy mapping technique for noninvasive analysis of paintings. Stud. Conserv. **44**(1), 39–48 (1999)

7. Delaney, J.K., Thoury, M., Zeibel, J.G., Ricciardi, P., Morales, K.M., Dooley, K.A.: Visible and infrared imaging spectroscopy of paintings and improved reflectography. Heritage Sci. **4**(1), 6 (2016)
8. Delano-Smith, C., et al.: New light on the Medieval Gough Map of Britain. Imago Mundi **69**(1), 1–36 (2016)
9. Devaram, R.R., Allegra, D., Gallo, G., Stanco, F.: Hyperspectral image classification via convolutional neural network based on dilation layers. In: Ricci, E., Rota Bulò, S., Snoek, C., Lanz, O., Messelodi, S., Sebe, N. (eds.) ICIAP 2019. LNCS, vol. 11751, pp. 378–387. Springer, Cham (2019). https://doi.org/10.1007/978-3-030-30642-7_34
10. Fischer, C., Kakoulli, I.: Multispectral and hyperspectral imaging technologies in conservation: current research and potential applications. Stud. Conserv. **51**(sup1), 3–16 (2006)
11. Hu, J., Shen, L., Sun, G.: Squeeze-and-excitation networks. arXiv preprint arXiv:1709.01507 (2017)
12. Li, Y., Zhang, H., Shen, Q.: Spectral-spatial classification of hyperspectral imagery with 3D convolutional neural network. Remote Sens. **9**(1), 67 (2017)
13. Lilley, K.D., Lloyd, C.D., Campbell, B.M.S.: Mapping the realm: a new look at the Gough map of Britain cartographic veracity in medieval mapping: analyzing geographical variation in the Gough map of great Britain. Imago Mundi **61**(1), 1–28 (2009)
14. Makantasis, K., Karantzalos, K., Doulamis, A., Doulamis, N.: Deep supervised learning for hyperspectral data classification through convolutional neural networks. In: 2015 IEEE International Geoscience and Remote Sensing Symposium (IGARSS), pp. 4959–4962. IEEE (2015)
15. Melessanaki, K., Papadakis, V., Balas, C., Anglos, D.: Laser induced breakdown spectroscopy and hyper-spectral imaging analysis of pigments on an illuminated manuscript. Spectrochim. Acta Part B Atomic Spectrosc. **56**(12), 2337–2346 (2001)
16. Meng, Z., Li, L., Jiao, L., Feng, Z., Tang, X., Liang, M.: Fully dense multiscale fusion network for hyperspectral image classification. Remote Sens. **11**(22), 2718 (2019)
17. Nair, V., Hinton, G.E.: Rectified linear units improve restricted Boltzmann machines. In: Proceedings of the 27th International Conference on Machine Learning (ICML 2010), pp. 807–814 (2010)
18. Ronneberger, O., Fischer, P., Brox, T.: U-Net: convolutional networks for biomedical image segmentation. In: Navab, N., Hornegger, J., Wells, W.M., Frangi, A.F. (eds.) MICCAI 2015. LNCS, vol. 9351, pp. 234–241. Springer, Cham (2015). https://doi.org/10.1007/978-3-319-24574-4_28
19. Solopova, E.: The making and re-making of the Gough map of Britain: manuscript evidence and historical context. Imago Mundi **64**(2), 155–168 (2012)
20. Wang, W., Dou, S., Jiang, Z., Sun, L.: A fast dense spectral-spatial convolution network framework for hyperspectral images classification. Remote Sens. **10**(7), 1068 (2018)
21. Yue, J., Zhao, W., Mao, S., Liu, H.: Spectral-spatial classification of hyperspectral images using deep convolutional neural networks. Remote Sens. Lett. **6**(6), 468–477 (2015)
22. Zhong, Z., Li, J., Luo, Z., Chapman, M.: Spectral-spatial residual network for hyperspectral image classification: a 3-D deep learning framework. IEEE Trans. Geosci. Remote Sens. **56**(2), 847–858 (2017)
23. Zhong, Z., Li, J., Ma, L., Jiang, H., Zhao, H.: Deep residual networks for hyperspectral image classification. Institute of Electrical and Electronics Engineers (2017)

Abstracting Stone Walls for Visualization and Analysis

Giovanni Gallo[1]([⊠]), Francesca Buscemi[2], Michele Ferro[1], Marianna Figuera[3], and Paolo Marco Riela[1]

[1] Dipartimento di Matematica e Informatica, Università di Catania, viale A.Doria 6, 95125 Catania, Italy
giovanni.gallo@unict.it
[2] CNR, Istituto di Scienze del Patrimonio Culturale, Via Biblioteca 4, 95124 Catania, Italy
francesca.buscemi@cnr.it
[3] Dipartimento di Scienze Umanistiche, Università di Catania, via Biblioteca 4, 95124 Catania, Italy
marianna.figuera@unict.it

Abstract. An innovative abstraction technique to represent both mathematically and visually some geometric properties of the facing stones in a wall is presented. The technique has been developed within the W.A.L.(L) Project, an interdisciplinary effort to apply Machine Learning techniques to support and integrate archaeological research. More precisely the paper introduces an original way to "abstract" the complex and irregular 3D shapes of stones in a wall with suitable ellipsoids. A wall is first digitized into a unique 3D point cloud and it is successively segmented into the sub-meshes of its stones. Each stone mesh is then "summarized" by the inertial ellipsoid relative to the point cloud of its vertices. A wall is in this way turned into a "population" of ellipsoid shapes statistical properties of which may be processed with Machine Learning algorithms to identify typologies of the walls under study. The paper also reports two simple case studies to assess the effectiveness of the proposed approach.

Keywords: Data visualization · Data abstraction · Quantitative archaeology

1 Introduction

Integration of visual abstract representation with quantitative methods is today a well-established practice in Data Science. This paper proposes a simple, yet original technique to represent a stone wall. It has been developed within a CNR project aimed to apply methods of quantitative analysis to Prehistoric and Protohistoric architecture in Crete (Greece)[1].

---

[1] W.A.L.(L), *Wall-facing Automatic images identification Laboratory. A quantitative analysis method for the study of ancient architecture.* International Archaeological Joint Laboratories (2020–2021).

© Springer Nature Switzerland AG 2021
A. Del Bimbo et al. (Eds.): ICPR 2020 Workshops, LNCS 12667, pp. 215–222, 2021.
https://doi.org/10.1007/978-3-030-68787-8_15

Quantifying is in the nature of Archaeology and already since 50es statistics have entered this discipline that is familiar with tools such as spatial analysis, graphical representation, inference, cluster analysis, regression/correlation analysis [1, 2]. Quantitative methods are today firmly part of the archaeological discourse [3] up to the notion of Quantitative Archaeology [4] and the annual organisation by the CAA of an International Conference on Computer Applications and Quantitative Methods in Archaeology.

The growth of digital data in archaeology furtherly modified the "quantitative idiom" [5], allowing sophisticated data analysis. Advanced tools like unsupervised classification and Machine Learning, that until a few years ago were only available to statisticians, are now more widely adopted by archaeologists [6].

Nevertheless, archaeologists share a strong indication to develop methods sensitive to the unique problems of archaeological inference [1, 3, 7], in combination with primarily intuitive aspects of traditional archaeology.

On this base, the foreseen workflow of the W.A.L.(L) Project presented below led off from specific archaeological questions and from an on field analysis of the structures to be investigated (step 1).

	STEPS	PROBLEMS OF ACCURACY POTENTIALLY AFFECTING THE RESULTS (TO BE EVALUATED AND DECLARED)
1)	Identification of architectural features estimated as peculiar and significant with relation to the investigated structures, to be mathematically analysed	
2)	Photogrammetric survey of the selected walls;	Resolution of the photographs (side dimension of pixels and number of pixels for cm^2)
3)	Realization of a 3D photogrammetric model;	Resolution of the 3D model (number of photographs, number and edge size of the mesh triangles)
4)	Manual segmentation of the model (each stone is cut and mathematically analysed)	3D model resolution and operator-dependency factors
5)	Transformation of the model into an abstract mathematic model, composed by inertial ellipsoids	3D model resolution
6)	Elaboration of a conceptual model for a DB aimed to query the virtual models	
7)	Creation of a tool for the dialogue between a 3D visualizer and the DB.	

Fig. 1. Workflow of the W.A.L.(L) Project

The continuous intersection of the tasks respectively of archaeologists and computer scientists in the workflow means a strong confrontation between the different specialists of the research group - with their "foreign languages" - always relying on the consciousness that "meaning comes only from a body of theory" [5].

That is why, as an archaeologist, I feel intrigued by the experiment of abstraction of architecture we present in this paper and by being involved in an historical-content-free discourse, where doesn't matter if a wall is a Minoan or a Modern one, because of the abstract, axiomatic, formal language of mathematics is at the service of theoretical questions about which information is meaningful and how we can obtain it (F.B.).

The W.A.L.(L) Project foresees the integration of the geometric information discussed here within a relational DB specifically focused on the management of ancient architecture. In the last decade the digital analysis of architectural heritage has widely developed, bringing attention to the need to support the quantitative information with the qualitative ones, produced by interpretation of data acquired [8]. An important point is the treatment of 3D data and their connection with databases, as well as the semantic classification [9].

The correct interpretation and contextualization of the data is linked to a right conceptualization [10], which essential reference points are the CIDOC-CRM and, for our specific purpose, the recent extension CRMBA for the documentation of archaeological buildings [11]. The creation of a similar DB involves certain methodological key-issues: type and complexity of the objects, the strategic involvement of specialists, and the importance to normalize the terminology, using further existing vocabulary as the *Art and Architecture Thesaurus* (AAT) developed by the Getty Institute.

The added value of the DB for our project is the management and query of all the data related to masonries and wall facing stones, which are the fulcrum of the conceptual model. A complete data analysis will be made possible through the management of the background information (e.g. finding area, site, stratigraphic relationships, chronology, etc.), the peculiar features (e.g. material, typology, degree of working, petrographic analysis, etc.), as well as the previous documentation (excavation diaries, paper notebooks, photographs, drawings, maps, etc.), management of which involves the concept of archaeological legacy data and their reuse in a responsible way [12] (Ma.F.).

Researching and developing automated tools to assist the archaeological research is by now a relevant sub-field of Computer Graphics and Vision. [13] Although much theoretical work is yet to be done [14], "to abstract", i.e. to draw away unnecessary information from the raw data to make understanding and conjecturing easier, is a common practice in many research fields. Principal Component Analysis is one of the most applied techniques to automatically achieve "abstraction" in an automated way. It has been applied to several high dimensional data to reduce complexity and to provide a parametric space for the classification of the observation (see for example [15]). The technique proposed here inscribes itself in this line of application, but to simpler 3D data as in [16]. In particular the paper proposes an original way to "abstract" the complex and irregular 3D shapes of stones in a wall with suitable ellipsoids. More precisely, a stone is first digitized into a 3D point cloud and then it is "summarized" by the inertial ellipsoid relative to such a cloud. The point cloud is considered as a rigid body and each vertex in the cloud is a material point of a unitary mass. Inertial ellipsoids, introduced in Mechanics by L. Poinsot in 1834 [17], are an established method of this discipline [18]. The substitution of the original stone shape with the abstract shape of an ellipsoid requires a relevant caveat: the proposed technique is not aimed to assess the static properties of a wall but only to illustrate and make more readable its layout. This is so because the point cloud of each stone refers only to the wall facing, i.e. to the "exposed" part of it.

The visual representation of the wall as an aggregate of ellipsoids is a valuable tool to more clearly read the layout of the wall and may help the expert to gain insights, formulate hypotheses about construction habits, dating or comparisons with other walls. More: the parameters of the inertial ellipsoids (size and orientation) summarize well the high/middle scale geometric properties of stones. A wall may hence be treated as a "population" made by such ellipsoids and its statistical properties may be used to identify typologies of the walls under study. Analysis of these data with Machine Learning algorithms will be considered in further studies.

This paper substantiates the above claims by reporting the results obtained with two case studies of walls from Donnafugata (from about 1900 A.D.) and Mongialino (from about 1500 A.D.) in Sicily. The paper is organized as follows: first, the pipeline from the image acquisition to the 3d model construction, to the computation of the inertial ellipsoids is described. In a successive section the results from the application of the method to two case studies are reported. In the conclusion the proposed technique is framed within a more ambitious program about the use of Data Science technique in archaeological studies (G.G.).

2   The Proposed Technique

The technique presented in this paper is part of a more general processing pipeline that could be summarized as follows (see Fig. 1):

Step 1. Photogrammetric survey of the selected walls;
Step 2. Realization of a 3D photogrammetric model of a whole wall section;
Step 3. Manual segmentation of the 3D model into separate sub-meshes for each stone of the wall;
Step 4. Transformation of stone sub-meshes into corresponding inertial ellipsoid;
Step 5. Data mining over the DB of the intrinsic (size) and extrinsic (orientation) geometric properties of the ellipsoids;

This Section offers an overview of the whole process with greater focus on Step 4 and Step 5.

Data Collection and 3D Reconstruction. The technique starts with a photographic survey of the wall fragment under study. 3D reconstruction may be done with off-the-shelf tools. In our experiments Meshroom from AliceVision has been used [19]. A highly detailed model is obtained in this way (average edge mesh in 0.2–0.8 cm range).

Cleaning and Decimating Data. The reconstructed wall mesh is imported into Blender 2.9.1 3D software [20] to be cleaned and aligned to a global reference. For the scope of this paper, only moderate spatial resolution is needed; for this reason the mesh is decimated to a resolution of average edge mesh in 0.8–1.5 cm range.

Segmentation into Stone Sub-meshes. The lighter mesh obtained insofar is segmented into a collection of sub-meshes, one for each visible stone of the wall. No available automatic technique can, up today, produce a reliable segmentation of the stones due to the large irregularity of their shape and layout: a human operator is needed at this step. Intra- and inter-operator variability have been checked and no significant differences have been found. A wall is now a collection of sub-meshes. The mortar is not considered.

Analysis of Stone Sub-meshes. Further abstraction is obtained computing numerical information for each sub-mesh. The computations are done within Blender with a Python script. Vertices are considered as material points of unitary mass, and their ensemble is assumed to be a rigid body. The following information are at first computed:

- Coordinates of the center mass of the sub-mesh M_x, M_y, M_z.
- Variance of the vertex coordinates of the sub-mesh around the center mass: V_x, V_y, V_z.
- Mean normal of the faces of the sub-mesh $N_m = (n_{m,x}, n_{m,y}, n_{m,z})$.
- Variance of the normal of the faces of the sub-mesh: V_{nx}, V_{ny}, V_{nz}.
- Inertial symmetric 3x3 tensor T of each sub-mesh.
- Eigenvalues Ev_x, Ev_y, Ev_z and eigenvectors rotation matrix Rot of T.

Visualization of Inertial Ellipsoids. A new object collection is created in the Blender scene including a 3D ellipsoid for each stone sub-mesh. The lengths of the axes of each ellipsoid are proportional respectively to $Ev_x^{-1/2}$, $Ev_y^{-1/2}$, $Ev_z^{-1/2}$. Each ellipsoid is centered at its (M_x, M_y, M_z) and rotated by Rot.

The material of each ellipsoid may be assigned random or may color-code other information. For sake of demonstration of this possibility the $n_{m,y}$ indicator has been color coded in the experiments reported below, other choices are of course possible. Eventually the ellipsoidal simplification of the wall is presented to the expert and can be used for visual inspection and reasoning.

Statistical Data exploration. All the information gathered insofar is saved into a .csv file suitable for further statistical analysis. The analysis may be oriented to two main tasks: a) classification of stones into several categories; b) characterization of the wall through the distribution of the indicators of its stone population.

Both directions are promising and research in this direction is still in progress. As for single stone classification it should be noted that, since the processing is done on a middle/low resolution model, lack of finer details makes this task difficult. The initial results about the wall characterization are, on the other hand, promising.

(G.G., Mi.F., P.M.R.).

3   Two Case Studies

The two selected case studies are one wall fragment near to the Donnafugata Castle and one wall fragment inside the Mongialino Castle. Both walls have facing sizes of about 1.2×1.6 m. The first is a typical wall of the Ragusa district in Sicily dated about early 1900 A.D. The second one has been built about 1600 A.D. (Fig. 2).

Resulting abstractions with inertial ellipsoids are shown in Fig. 3. Both gray colored and color-coded ellipsoids are shown. The color coding refers, for sake of demonstration, to the $n_{m,y}$ indicator, i.e. the magnitude of the normal mean facing the observer.

The abstract visual representations capture the geometric layout of the walls and enhance the structural differences between the two walls, proving that the proposed method may offer a great help to the expert in formulating hypotheses and assessing properties.

Besides providing visual help the proposed method produces valuable numerical data for statistical analysis. Although the research about this issue is currently in progress the two case studies reported here offer some evidence of the potential use of the proposed

Fig. 2. (a1), (b1) Donnafugata and Mongialino locations; (a2), (b2) photos of the two walls; (a3), (b3) the segmented walls in false random colors. (Color figure online)

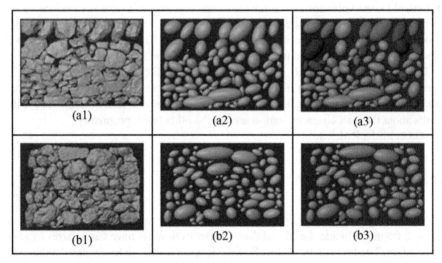

Fig. 3. (a1), (b1) 3D models of the two walls; (a2), (b2) inertial ellipsoids representation; (a3), (b3) color coded ellipsoid: degree of blue means greater values of the $n_{m,y}$ indicator. (Color figure online)

approach. In particular Fig. 4 shows the distribution over the two populations of the indicators $V = V_x * V_y * V_z$, $R = V_{Nx} * V_{ny} * V_{nz}$ and of the $n_{m,y}$ indicator. The V variable is a good indicator of the size of the corresponding stone. Similarly the R variable provides a rough estimate for the degree of roughness of the stone. The indicator finally provides an approximate estimate of the "overhanging" degree of the triangular faces in the corresponding mesh.

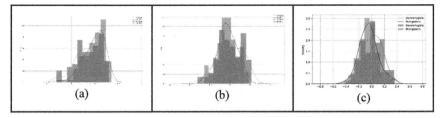

Fig. 4. (a) Histogram and density plot of the indicator $V = V_x * V_y * V_z$; bimodality of Donnafugata stones (cyan) vs unimodality of Mongialino stones (green) is manifest; (b) histogram and density plot of the indicator $R = V_{nx} * V_{ny} * V_{nz}$; (c) histogram and density plot of the indicator $n_{m,y}$ shows the more uniform layout of Mongialino stones vs Donnafugata stones. (Color figure online)

The histograms visually show some difference between distributions of the above indicators over the two populations under study. Chi square test has proven significant only for the indicators V ($p < 0.01$) and R ($p < 0.01$).

A visually evident difference between the two distributions of both the variables V and R is the bi-modality of the Donnafugata data versus the unimodality of the other sample. This could be read in qualitative terms as an evidence that while in Donnafugata stones are of two classes (larger and more polished and smaller rougher ones) the wall fragment from Mongialino is made of more homogeneous stones in size and roughness. (G.G., Mi.F., P.M.R.).

4 Conclusions and Future Work

The method presented in this paper is a promising experiment at an early stage of the workflow foreseen by the W.A.L.(L) Project. While abstraction allows to obtain and visualize information about the essential properties of the stones in the wall facings (i.e. dimensions and orientation), further features have to be taken into account under a quantitative perspective (shape; coursing and positioning; finishing of the stones). The use of photogrammetric models purposely realized to fit this goal constitute a strength from the point of view of innovation in ancient architecture analysis, but also entail several challenges, from issues of accuracy, to the resolution and manageability of the 3D models, to specific problems posed by Iron Age architecture, highly irregular and therefore poorly predictive (F.B.).

Further work will include semi-automatic assistance for stone segmentation, the extraction and integration of further features and their integration in the DB discussed in the Introduction and the application of Machine Learning methods to assist the specialist in the archaeological issues of interest (G.G.).

References

1. VanPool, T.L., Leonard, R.D.: Quantitative Analysis in Archaeology, Hoboken (2011)
2. Shennan, S.: Quantifying Archaeology, Edimburg (1988)
3. Renfrew, C., Bahn, P.G.: Archaeology: Theories, Methods and Practices, London (1996)

4. Nakoinz, O.: History and perspective of quantitative archaeology. In: Digital Archaeology. Quantitative Approaches Spatial Statistics and Socioecological Modelling. Proceedings of International Colloquium on Digital Archaeology, Bern 4–6 February 2019. https://doi.org/10.5281/zenodo.2628304

5. Aldenderfer, M.: Quantitative methods in archaeology: a review of recent trends and developments. J. Archaeol. Res. **6**(2), 91–120 (1998). https://doi.org/10.1007/BF02446161

6. Hinz, M., Laabs, J., Castiello, M.E.: Archaeology that counts: international colloquium on digital archaeology, Workshop Report, in Pages Magazine, vol. 7, no. 1, p. 37 (2019)

7. Kintigh, K.: Quantitative methods designed for archaeological problems. In: Quantitative Research in Archaeology: Progress and Prospects, Newbury Park, pp. 89–113 (1987)

8. De Luca, L., Busayarat, C., Stefani, C., Véron, P., Florenzano, M.: A semantic-based platform for the digital analysis of architectural heritage. Comput. Graph. **35**, 227–241 (2011). https://doi.org/10.1016/j.cag.2010.11.009

9. Manferdini, A.M., Remondino, F., Baldissini, S., Gaiani, M., Benedetti, B.: Modeling and semantic classification of archaeological finds for management and visualization in 3D archaeological databases. In: Proceedings of the 14th International Conference on Virtual Systems and Multimedia, pp. 221–228 (2008)

10. Noardo, F.: Architectural heritage ontology - concepts and some practical issues. In: Proceedings of the 2nd International Conference on Geographical Information Systems Theory, Applications and Management, GISTAM, Rome, vol. 1, pp. 168–179 (2016). https://doi.org/10.5220/0005830901680179

11. Ronzino, P., Niccolucci, F., Felicetti, A., Doerr, M.: CRMBA a CRM extension for the documentation of standing buildings. Int. J. Digit. Libr. **17**(1), 71–78 (2015). https://doi.org/10.1007/s00799-015-0160-4

12. Wilkinson, M.D., et al.: The FAIR guiding principles for scientific data management and stewardship. Sci. Data **3**, 160018 (2016). https://doi.org/10.1038/sdata.2016.18

13. Stanco, F., Battiato, S., Gallo, G.: Digital imaging for cultural heritage preservation: analysis, restoration and reconstruction of ancient artworks. CRC Press, Boco Raton (2011). ISBN: 978-1-4398217-3-2

14. Allegra, D., et al.: Low cost handheld 3D scanning for architectural elements acquisition. In: Proceedings of "Smart Tools and Apps for Graphics - Eurographics Italian Chapter Conference 2016, pp. 127–131 (2016). ISBN: 978-3-03868-026-0. https://doi.org/10.2312/stag.20161372

15. Viola, I., Isenberg, T.: Pondering the concept of abstraction in (illustrative) visualization. IEEE Trans. Vis. Comput. Graph. **24**(9), 2573–2588 (2018)

16. Catanuto, G., et al.: Breast shape analysis with curvature estimates and principal component analysis for cosmetic and reconstructive breast surgery. Aesthetic Surg. J. **39**(2), 164–173 (2019). ISSN: 1527330X https://doi.org/10.1093/asj/sjy070

17. Poinsot, L.: Outlines of a New Theory of Rotatory Motion. R. Newby, Cambridge (1834)

18. Landau, L.D., Lifshitz, E.M.: Mechanics, 3rd edn. Butterworth-Heinemann, London (1976)

19. Alice Vision: Metashape. https://alicevision.org/. Accessed 18 Oct 2020

20. Blender: https://www.blender.org/. Accessed 18 Oct 2020

PapyRow: A Dataset of Row Images from Ancient Greek Papyri for Writers Identification

Nicole Dalia Cilia[1]([⊠]), Claudio De Stefano[1], Francesco Fontanella[1],
Isabelle Marthot-Santaniello[2], and Alessandra Scotto di Freca[1]

[1] University of Cassino and Southern Lazio, Via di Biasio 43, Cassino, Italy
{nicoledalia.cilia,destefano,f.fontanella,a.scotto}@unicas.it
[2] Universität Basel, Basel, Switzerland
i.marthot-santaniello@unibas.ch

Abstract. Papyrology is the discipline that studies texts written on ancient papyri. An important problem faced by papyrologists and, in general by paleographers, is to identify the writers, also known as scribes, who contributed to the drawing up of a manuscript. Traditionally, paleographers perform qualitative evaluations to distinguish the writers, and in recent years, these techniques have been combined with computer-based tools to automatically measure quantities such as height and width of letters, distances between characters, inclination angles, number and types of abbreviations, etc. Recently-emerged approaches in digital paleography combine powerful machine learning algorithms with high-quality digital images. Some of these approaches have been used for feature extraction, other to classify writers with machine learning algorithms or deep learning systems. However, traditional techniques require a preliminary feature engineering step that involves an expert in the field. For this reason, publishing a well-labeled dataset is always a challenge and a stimulus for the academic world as researchers can test their methods and then compare their results from the same starting point. In this paper, we propose a new dataset of handwriting on papyri for the task of writer identification. This dataset is derived directly from GRK-Papyri dataset and the samples are obtained with some enhancement image operation. This paper presents not only the details of the dataset but also the operation of resizing, rotation, background smoothing, and rows segmentation in order to overcome the difficulties posed by the image degradation of this dataset. It is prepared and made freely available for non-commercial research along with their confirmed ground-truth information related to the task of writer identification.

Keywords: Greek papyri · Row extraction · Dataset · Writer identification

This work was supported in part by the Italian Ministry of University and Research, grant "Dipartimenti di Eccellenza 2018–2022", and the Swiss National Science Foundation as part of the project n PZ00P1-174149 "Reuniting fragments, identifying scribes and characterizing scripts: the Digital paleography of Greek and Coptic papyri".

A. Del Bimbo et al. (Eds.): ICPR 2020 Workshops, LNCS 12667, pp. 223–234, 2021.
https://doi.org/10.1007/978-3-030-68787-8_16

1   Introduction

The large majority of databases publicly available for writer identification tasks, are composed of contemporary handwritings [12,14,17,19–21]. Historical documents, however, present specific difficulties (limited amount of data, complex material, degradation) that digital technologies must be able to cope with, in order to be successfully applied by Historians to actual research problems.

An exception in this context is represented by the Historical-WI dataset [13], containing about 3600 handwritten pages selected from manuscripts ranging from the thirteenth to the sixteenth century, which were produced by 720 different scribes. The main problem in the use of these data is that most of the documents were automatically selected by an algorithm made by computer scientists and not by manuscript experts: therefore, it is not tailored to answer actual research questions (see [22], p. 726).

Moreover, as discussed in [27], when computerized writer identification approaches are tried on historical texts, it is required that the handwriting samples are previously associated with the corresponding writers, in order to verify the correctness of the automatic classification results: such labeling often relies on the judgement of ancient writings specialists (epigraphers, paleographers) or forensic experts, which are all subjective and often not in accordance among them.

Recently-emerged approaches in digital paleography combine powerful machine learning algorithms with high-quality digital images. Machine-learning-based approaches have received increasing attention from researchers, thanks to their ability to handle complex and difficult image classification tasks for writer identification [3,7,11,30]. Some of these methodologies have been used for feature selection [4] and extraction [16,18], others for image segmentation in lines in order to improve or enlarge the dataset [23–25], or for studying the most appropriate dataset size [5,8]. Finally, in recent years deep learning systems are not only tested for identifying sundry elements of interest inside document pages, but also with a specific focus on writer recognition problems [2,6,9,10].

Ancient texts from antiquity survived only in rare cases, the wide majority as carved inscriptions on stone, in more specific contexts as impressions on clay tablets and writings on potsherds (ostraca[1]).

Papyri from Egypt stand as an exception: thanks to the dryness of the climate, an unparalleled quantity of texts reached out to us, literary pieces as well as documents from daily life. Papyri written in Ancient Greek cover a millennium of Egypt History, from Alexander the Great at the end of the fourth century BCE to the Arab conquest in the middle of the seventh century CE. There are already more than 70,000 published texts and hundreds of thousands still waiting for publication in museums and libraries, not to mention newly excavated material each year [28]. Therefore, papyri offer a unique opportunity

---

[1] An ostracon (Greek term, whose plural is ostraca) is a piece of pottery on which an inscription is engraved. Usually these pieces are fragments of broken pottery vessels, on which inscriptions were subsequently made.

to analyse ancient handwritings but with specific constraints: by definition a papyrus leaf, made of strips cut in the plant stem, is a brownish, complex background. The state of preservation is usually bad (breaks, holes, mud, erasure of ink) and the amount of text is limited, not to be compared with hundred-page long medieval manuscripts. Furthermore, the majority of papyri was acquired by collections in the antiquities market, so without archaeological context and often voluntarily broken into pieces to increase their sale value. Scholars have to reconstruct original documents as well as piece up ancient archives. Being able to identify the same writer over several fragments allow substantial progress in our understanding of Egypt ancient History.

For all these reasons, publishing a well-labeled dataset is always a challenge and a stimulus for the academic world, as researchers can test their methodologies and then compare their results from the same starting point. In this paper, we propose a new dataset of handwriting on Ancient Greek papyri for the task of writer identification. This dataset is derived directly from GRK-Papyri dataset [22] and the samples are obtained through complex image enhancement operations. Moreover, it is made of objectively attributed documents thanks to inner evidence, the subscription - signature - of their writers: reference data are therefore available to verify the actual classification results.

The samples have been selected to reflect real investigations from scholars, thus representing a severe test bed for writer identification algorithms: they come from the same kind of documents, the same period of time and the same geographic area but the images are from various collections (museums, libraries) and therefore vary greatly (see below, in Sect. 2). What is at stake is to be able to differentiate the handwriting of an individual from the ones of his contemporaries in a writing context as homogeneous as possible. If this extreme case gives successful results, then heterogeneous cases (different handwriting styles, periods, locations) and homogeneous data (same digitization process) should yield even better results.

The remainder of the paper is organized as follows: after a description of the original dataset GRK-Papyri in Sect. 2 and its extension, we present the operation of background smoothing in Sect. 3.1, resizing in Sect. 3.2, rotation in Sect. 3.3, and rows segmentation in Sect. 3.4, in order to overcome the difficulties posed by the image degradation of this dataset. Finally, in Sect. 4 we present the obtained row dataset, which is freely available for non-commercial research along with the confirmed ground-truth information related to the task of writer identification.

2   Description of the Original Dataset

The reference dataset used in this work is composed of images depicting Greek papyri dating back to the 6th century. Writer identification is ensured by the presence of notary subscriptions, whose analysis can be found in [29] and in a forthcoming article on Notaries in Aphrodito by Isabelle Marthot-Santaniello. Images have been checked, selected, cataloged and cropped (see [22]) to keep

Table 1. Distribution of papyri by authors

Authors	Number of papyri
Amais, Anouphis, Daueit, Kyros2, Victor2	1
Ieremias, Kollouthos, Konstantinos, Psates	2
Philotheos	3
Andreas, Apa Rhasios	4
Dioscorus, Hermauos, Kyros3, Menas, Theodosios	5
Isak	8
Kyros1	9
Pilatos, Victor1	10
Dios	15
Abraamios	21

only the part written by the notary and not by potential parties and witnesses. Almost all the documents used are part of the richest archive of the Byzantine period belonging to Dioscorus of Aphrodito, which collects more than 700 texts (see [26] and [15]). All the images of this archive are accessible in [1]. The only exception is for the writer Menas, who lived in the same period and practises the same profession but living in Hermopolis, a city roughly 150 km north of Aphrodito. His dossier is about to be published by Isabelle Marthot-Santaniello while the images are provided by BNUS, Strasbourg (Menas 1 and 2) and the British Library (Menas 3, 4 and 5).

The basis of the present dataset is the GRK-Papyri, used for the task of identifying the writers and composed of 50 images distributed unequally among the 10 writers present [22]. Other papyri have been added to this starting set, increasing the number of papyri of the above writer, as well as introducing new writers. Summarizing, a number of papyri images equal to 122 was reached for a total number of 23 writers, further increasing the imbalance in the number of documents per author. It is useful to note that not all the images contain the same amount of text: in fact some of them include few fragments of text, while others contain larger sequences of lines.

Table 1 reports detailed information on the distribution of papyri by writers. Metadata on each papyrus image (publication name of the papyrus, reference on the writer attribution, copyright) will be available in a dedicated section of d-scribes.org.

The papyri appear to be very degraded by time: in fact for most of them there are missing pieces or holes that extend almost everywhere, causing the loss of the writing trace (see Fig. 1).

In addition to the characteristics already listed, there are also different contrasts, different lighting conditions and in some cases even reflections due to the presence of glass used to preserve them. Moreover, there are both color and

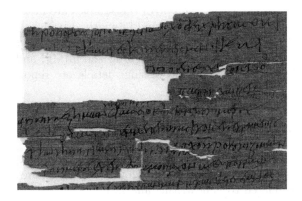

Fig. 1. Examples of original papyri.

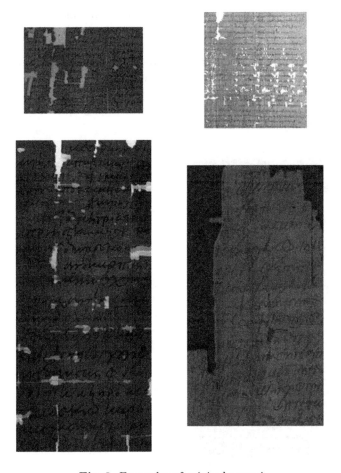

Fig. 2. Examples of original papyri.

grayscale images (as shown in Fig. 2). All the samples are in JPG format, with a resolution that varies both in height and in width.

To achieve the goal of enhancing image quality, we applied a procedure based on the use of standard tools, such as LabelImg and GIMP, and python scripts with specific libraries for images processing: details are reported in the next Section.

3 Image Enhancement

Given the heavy degradation of images in this dataset, applying image enhancement techniques is needed in order to improve the performance of any computational method related to handwriting analysis.

3.1 Background Smoothing

The first step tries to uniform as much as possible the image background. For this purpose, it was necessary to fill all the holes in the image with the same color as the papyrus; this operation allows the elimination of any unwanted colors, which could adversely affect the following phases of image enhancement. This procedure, carried out for both color and grayscale images, was performed using the GIMP program (GNU Image Manipulation Program) which allows us to perform manipulations on digital images in a very simple and fast way. The result obtained is showed in the Fig. 3.

Fig. 3. An example of unwanted colors elimination.

3.2   Line Resizing

The next phase consists of various operations that allow us to adequately prepare images for the labeling, i.e. for the selection and the extraction of individual lines in each papyrus, to be assigned to the actual writer. As previously mentioned, each image has its own dimension, which is different from that of all the other images. However, in order to be processed and compared properly, all the lines must have similar dimensions: therefore it was necessary to resize all the lines to an appropriate size.

For each papyrus image, the heights of the individual lines were taken and a resize was made in proportion to the maximum line height identified among all the papyri images. Once the new height relative to an image has been identified, the new width is calculated in such a way as to preserve the original aspect ratio (ratio between width and height).

3.3   Image Rotation

Before proceeding with the labeling phase, some rotations were made (with the GIMP program) on papyrus images whose text was too skewed (see Fig. 4). The rotation was necessary for using the LabelImg tool, through which it is possible to correctly label the lines of the papyri. Among all the available images, only few of them required this rotation. Furthermore, color images were converted in grayscale ones, using Python libraries (see Fig. 5): thus, all the images included in our dataset are in grayscale format.

Fig. 4. An example of an image before and after rotation.

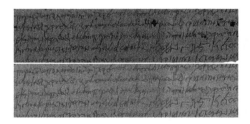

Fig. 5. An example of an image before and after grayscale conversion.

3.4   Row Labeling

The row labeling operation was manually performed with LabelImg tool, taking care of not including part of the image where there is no writing. The tool allows us to create rectangles (bounding box) surrounding the rows to be selected (see Fig. 6). Following this operation, LabelImg generates a file with XML extension, containing all the details of the bounding boxes such as, for example, the start and end coordinates of every one.

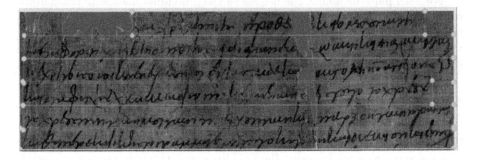

Fig. 6. Image divided into bounding box rows.

Using both the information included in this XLM file and the python libraries, it is possible to cut out each selected element and save it separately: the result of this process is a sequence of images, each containing a single row, for each original papyrus image. Moreover, since the images obtained according to the above process exhibit a very large width variation, two different procedures were designed for generating images of similar width, namely Pre-processing 1 end Pre-processing 2.

- Pre-processing 1: in this case the line image with the lowest width among all the available ones was identified (this width value is equal to 1232 pixels in our case) and all the other images were divided according to this width. This implies that, the final part of a line image may be discarded if its width is lower than the above value (see Fig. 7).
- Pre-processing 2: in this second option all the lines have been cut assuming a predetermined threshold value for the width (500 pixels). The result is a larger number of line images, possibly reducing the loss of useful writing (see Fig. 8).

4   Description of the Final Dataset and Conclusion

In this paper, we have proposed a new dataset of handwriting on Ancient Greek papyri for the task of writer identification: the PapyRow Dataset. The samples,

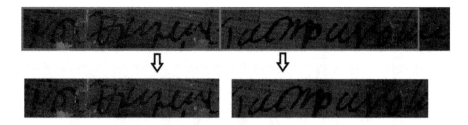

Fig. 7. Image cutting according to pre-processing 1.

Fig. 8. Image cutting according to pre-processing 2.

derived directly from the extended GRK-Papyri dataset, are obtained with some enhancement image operation. In particular, as the papyri appear to be very degraded by time, with missing pieces, holes, different contrasts and different lighting conditions, we have employed a background smoothing. Moreover, since image dimensions were very different, they have been resized preserving the original aspect ratio, but allowing the line height to be very similar across all images. Image rotation have been also applied for correcting too skewed images and a format conversion have been performed on color images to obtain a database composed of all grayscale images.

Finally, we have used a rows segmentation procedure to generate the Papy-Row Dataset. This dataset, including 6498 samples, is freely available for non-commercial research along with the confirmed ground-truth information related to the task of writer identification, at link: http://webuser.unicas.it/fontanella/papyri/.

The distribution of the samples among all the writers is reported in the histogram of Fig. 9.

The row segmentation have been performed for two main reasons: on one hand, for increasing the number of samples available for the training phase of the considered classifiers and, on the other hand, to discard the parts of the original images that contain no text.

Moreover, as previously noticed, not all the images contain the same amount of text: in fact some of them include few fragments of text, while others contain larger sequences of lines.

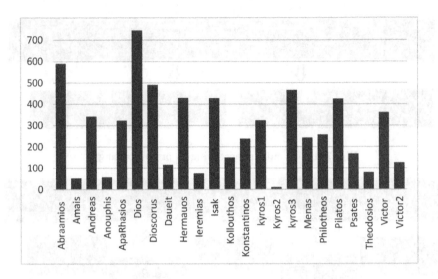

Fig. 9. Sample distribution among all the writers.

References

1. Bipab (ed.): The Bank of Papyrus Images of Byzantine Aphrodite BIPAb (00). http://bipab.aphrodito.info/
2. Bria, A., et al.: Deep transfer learning for writer identification in medieval books. In: 2018 IEEE International Conference on Metrology for Archaeology and Cultural Heritage, pp. 455–460 (2018)
3. Bulacu, M., Schomaker, L.: Text-independent writer identification and verification using textural and allographic features. IEEE Trans. Pattern Anal. Mach. Intell. **29**(4), 701–717 (2007)
4. Cilia, N., De Stefano, C., Fontanella, F., di Freca, A.S.: A ranking-based feature selection approach for handwritten character recognition. Pattern Recogn. Lett. **121**, 77–86 (2018)
5. Cilia, N.D., De Stefano, C., Fontanella, F., Molinara, M., Scotto di Freca, A.: Minimizing training data for reliable writer identification in medieval manuscripts. In: Cristani, M., Prati, A., Lanz, O., Messelodi, S., Sebe, N. (eds.) ICIAP 2019. LNCS, vol. 11808, pp. 198–208. Springer, Cham (2019). https://doi.org/10.1007/978-3-030-30754-7_20
6. Cilia, N.D., De Stefano, C., Fontanella, F., Molinara, M., Scotto di Freca, A.: An end-to-end deep learning system for medieval writer identification. Pattern Recogn. Lett. **129**, 137–143 (2020)
7. Cilia, N.D., De Stefano, C., Fontanella, F., Molinara, M., Scotto di Freca, A.: An experimental comparison between deep learning and classical machine learning approaches for writer identification in medieval documents. J. Imaging **6**(9), 89 (2020)
8. Cilia, N.D., De Stefano, C., Fontanella, F., Molinara, M., Scotto di Freca, A.: What is the minimum training data size to reliably identify writers in medieval manuscripts? Pattern Recogn. Lett. **129**, 198–204 (2020)

9. Cilia, N.D., De Stefano, C., Fontanella, F., Marrocco, C., Molinara, M., Scotto di Freca, A.: A page-based reject option for writer identification in medieval books. In: Cristani, M., Prati, A., Lanz, O., Messelodi, S., Sebe, N. (eds.) ICIAP 2019. LNCS, vol. 11808, pp. 187–197. Springer, Cham (2019). https://doi.org/10.1007/978-3-030-30754-7_19

10. Cilia, N.D., De Stefano, C., Fontanella, F., Marrocco, C., Molinara, M., Scotto Di Freca, A.: A two-step system based on deep transfer learning for writer identification in medieval books. In: Vento, M., Percannella, G. (eds.) CAIP 2019. LNCS, vol. 11679, pp. 305–316. Springer, Cham (2019). https://doi.org/10.1007/978-3-030-29891-3_27

11. Dahllof, M.: Scribe attribution for early medieval handwriting by means of letter extraction and classification and a voting procedure for larger pieces. In: Proceedings of the 22nd International Conference on Pattern Recognition, pp. 1910–1915. IEEE Computer Society (2014). https://doi.org/10.1109/ICPR.2014.334

12. Djeddi, C., Al-Maadeed, S., Gattal, A., Siddiqi, I., Ennaji, A., El Abed, H.: ICFHR 2016 competition on multi-script writer demographics classification using "QUWI" database. ICFHR Proc. IEEE **01**, 602–606 (2016)

13. Fiel, S., et al.: ICDAR 2017 competition on historical document writer identification (historical-WI). In: Proceedings of the 2017 International Conference on Document Analysis and Recognition (ICDAR), pp. 1377–1382 (2017)

14. Fornes, A., Dutta, A., Gordo, A., J., L.: The ICDAR 2011 music scores competition: staff removal and writer identification. In: Proceedings of the 2011 International Conference on Document Analysis and Recognition, ICDAR, pp. 1511–1515 (2011)

15. Fournet, J. (ed.): Les archives de Dioscore d'Aphrodité cent ans après leur découverte, histoire et culture dans l'Égypte byzantine. Actes du Colloque de Strasbourg. Études d'archéologie et d'histoire ancienne, Paris (2008)

16. Joutel, G., Eglin, V., Bres, S., Emptoz, H.: Curvelets based feature extraction of handwritten shapes for ancient manuscripts classification. In: Document Recognition and Retrieval XIV, San Jose, California, USA, 30 January - 1 February 2007, pp. 65000D 1–12 (2007)

17. Kleber, F., Fiel, S., Diem, M., R., S.: CVL-database: an off-line database for writer retrieval, writer identification and word spotting. In: Proceedings of the 2013 International Conference on Document Analysis and Recognition, ICDAR pp. 560–564 (2013)

18. Liang, Y., Fairhurst, M.C., Guest, R.M., Erbilek, M.: Automatic handwriting feature extraction, analysis and visualization in the context of digital palaeography. IJPRAI **30**(4), 1653001 (2016). 1–26

19. Louloudis, G., Gatos, B., N., S.: ICFHR 2012 competition on writer identification challenge 1: Latin/Greek documents. In: Frontiers in Handwriting Recognition (ICFHR), pp. 829–834 (2012)

20. Louloudis, G., Gatos, B., Stamatopoulos, N., Papandreou, A.: ICDAR 2013 competition on writer identification. In: Proceedings of the 2013 International Conference on Document Analysis and Recognition, ICDAR, pp. 1397–1401 (2013)

21. Louloudis, G., Stamatopoulos, N., Gatos, B.: ICDAR 2011 writer identification contest. In: Proceedings of the 2011 International Conference on Document Analysis and Recognition, ICDAR, pp. 1475–1479 (2011)

22. Mohammed, H.A., Marthot-Santaniello, I., Märgner, V.: GRK-papyri: a dataset of Greek handwriting on papyri for the task of writer identification. In: Proceedings of the 2019 International Conference on Document Analysis and Recognition (ICDAR), pp. 726–731 (2019)

23. Papavassiliou, V., Stafylakis, T., Katsouros, V., Carayannis, G.: Handwritten document image segmentation into text lines and words. Pattern Recogn. **43**(1), 369–377 (2010)

24. Pintus, R., Yang, Y., Gobbetti, E., Rushmeier, H.E.: A TALISMAN: automatic text and line segmentation of historical manuscripts. In: 2014 Eurographics Workshop on Graphics and Cultural Heritage, GCH 2014, Darmstadt, Germany, 6–8 October 2014, pp. 35–44 (2014)

25. Pintus, R., Yang, Y., Rushmeier, H.E.: ATHENA: automatic text height extraction for the analysis of text lines in old handwritten manuscripts. JOCCH **8**(1), 1:1–1:25 (2015)

26. Ruffini, G. (ed.): Life in an Egyptian Village in Late Antiquity: Aphrodito Before and After the Islamic Conquest. Cambridge University Press, Cambridge, New York (2018)

27. Shaus, A., Gerber, Y., Faigenbaum-Golovin, S., Sober, B., Piasetzky, E., Finkelstein, I.: Forensic document examination and algorithmic handwriting analysis of Judahite biblical period inscriptions reveal significant literacy level. PLoS One **15**(9), e0237962 (2020)

28. Van Minnen, P. (ed.): The future of papyrology. In: Bagnall, R.S. (ed.) The Oxford Handbook of Papyrology. Oxford University Press, Oxford (2009)

29. Worp, K., Diethart, J. (eds.): Notarsunterschriften im Byzantinischen Ägypten (1986)

30. Yosef, I.B., Beckman, I., Kedem, K., Dinstein, I.: Binarization, character extraction, and writer identification of historical Hebrew calligraphy documents. IJDAR **9**(2–4), 89–99 (2007)

Stone-by-Stone Segmentation for Monitoring Large Historical Monuments Using Deep Neural Networks

Koubouratou Idjaton[1]([✉])(iD), Xavier Desquesnes[1], Sylvie Treuillet[1], and Xavier Brunetaud[2]

[1] Université d'Orléans, INSA CVL, PRISME EA 4229, 45072 Orléans, France
{koubouratou.idjaton,sylvie.treuillet}@univ-orleans.fr
[2] Université d'Orléans, INSA CVL, LaMé, Orléans, France

Abstract. Monitoring and restoration of cultural heritage buildings require the definition of an accurate health record. A critical step is the labeling of the exhaustive constitutive elements of the building. Stone-by-stone segmentation is a major part. Traditionally it is done by visual inspection and manual drawing on a 2D orthomosaic. This is an increasingly complex, time-consuming and resource-intensive task.

In this paper, algorithms to perform stone-by-stone segmentation automatically on large cultural heritage building are presented. Two advanced convolutional neural networks are tested and compared to conventional edge detection or thresholding methods on image dataset from Loire Valley's châteaux: Château de Chambord and Château de Chaumont-sur-Loire, two castles of Renaissance style. The results show the applicability of the methods to the historical buildings of the Renaissance style.

Keywords: Cultural heritage · Orthomosaic · Semantic segmentation · Transfer learning · Image processing

1 Introduction

In 2019, château de Chambord, a well-known Loire Valley's châteaux, has celebrated its five hundred year anniversary. Built often between middle-age and Renaissance era, castles are architectural symbols and represent an important part of cultural heritage in Europe. The Renaissance-style castle marks the transition from military architecture to pleasure architecture, as evidenced by the large windows, numerous fireplaces and an improved sanitary comfort. Stone remained the chosen material for these prestigious buildings. The Loire Valley's châteaux generally owe their white color to tuffeau, a limestone whose properties allowed creations of extreme finesse, the ornamentation typical of Renaissance architecture in particular. This extraordinarily fine limestone formed from 90 million-year-old marine sediments. Its high porosity (45% to 50%) and softness

© Springer Nature Switzerland AG 2021
A. Del Bimbo et al. (Eds.): ICPR 2020 Workshops, LNCS 12667, pp. 235–248, 2021.
https://doi.org/10.1007/978-3-030-68787-8_17

compared with other kinds of limestone make it easy to work. In general, the stone blocks were graded in sizes ranging from 48 to 55 cm long, 22 to 33 cm high and 15 to 28 cm width.

Unfortunately, as it is a porous and soft limestone, tuffeau is very sensitive to humidity variations and presents degradations in time. The most damaging degradation is scaling in forms of spalling and flaking: cracks develop parallel to the surface of the stone at few millimeters or centimeters depth, forming plates that eventually fall, leaving a powdery surface [12]. To document and study surface degradations, it is necessary to produce mappings at the stone level, and therefore to segment the masonry joints [13]. This segmentation can be done manually for small areas, but covering the whole masonry of a large castle would be too laborious and time-consuming. Cultural heritage experts are therefore looking for an automatic segmentation method.

This segmentation task is challenging because the masonry of the Loire Valley's châteaux was designed to provide very smooth and homogeneous facade by limiting the visual contrast of joints through colors very similar to those of the stones. Moreover, tuffeau stones vary in color from white or cream to yellowish depending on the layers in the quarry. These hue differences are reinforced by the variation in lighting in outdoor shots, so that applying a direct threshold method (such as Otsu or Canny) does not provide a perfect segmentation. We have previously proposed an improved Canny-based methods [11].

In this paper, we experiment two different state-of-art deep learning methods for semantic segmentation and compare them with conventional edge detection and thresholding methods. For training the deep learning model, we introduce a new manually labeled dataset from orthomosaic maps of the château de Chambord facades. These deep learning methods are compared with two usual thresholding methods. We also show that our trained model can perform good segmentation on other Renaissance-style historical building.

The rest of the paper is organized as follows: Sect. 2 presents the related work, Sect. 3 describes the different the methods that have been implemented. In Sect. 4, we present the dataset, the experiments and discuss the results. Finally, in Sect. 5, we conclude and give some future work.

2   Related Work

Recent advancement in digital technologies encourages researchers to take advantage of different data (high resolution images, terrestrial laser scanner, LiDAR, 3D point cloud) for the development of new digital tools to ease the surveying and maintenance task for cultural heritage experts. Several previous researches have been performed using 3D point cloud from LiDAR or terrestrial laser scanner (TLS). From LiDAR 3D data in [24,25], authors create structural models and performs automatic morphologic analysis of quasi-periodic masonry walls. Authors in [26,31] use terrestrial laser scanning 3D data for the monitoring of ashlar masonry wall of historic buildings. Terrestrial laser scanner 3D data serves also for the generation of accurate models from dense clouds and their reduction to models with simplified geometries. These offer the possibility to detect the size and the anomalies of the wall systems; together with the possibility of identifying the lay of the individual drywall blocks and also the signs of cracks and collapses are explored [17] as well for classification of common building materials using machine learning [32].

Fig. 1. Orthomosaic of the south facade of the château de Chambord

Moreover, 3D point cloud has received particular attention; it has served to realize the recognition of deteriorated regions [16]; detect the state of corrosion damage on historic buildings [14] and perform texture detection for the classification of historic monuments [7,10,18] (see [23] for a review of 3D modeling techniques with their limitations and potentialities).

However, less research has covered the specific task of stone-by-stone segmentation. Authors in [30] use 3D point cloud data for automatic detection and classification of defects in the digitised ashlar masonry wall. The classification method is based on the use of supervised machine learning algorithms, assisted by experts. The segmentation algorithm is based on the 2D Continuous Wavelet Transform for segmentation of 3D point cloud of rubble stone [29].

Although 3D point cloud from LiDAR and terrestrial laser scanner data have been largely exploited, they constraint experts to acquire new tools and perform complementary data acquisition campaign in order to provide these new types of data on the buildings. In fact, most often the cultural heritage building has been documented with 2D images and photogrammetry data like orthomosaic map (example in Fig. 1). On these large images, complete visual inspection and manual labeling of individual stone can be very time and resource intensive.

Furthermore, 3D point cloud data are not appropriate to the stone-by-stone segmentation task as the walls of Château de Chambord are made of smooth cut stones. The architectural style of the Loire castles is particularly characterized by a research of uniformity between stones surfaces and joints. These latter thus presents only a very slight relief, sometimes imperceptible and a shade close to that of stones surfaces. Moreover, the previous restoration operations to replace damaged parts of some stones have been made with the aim of hiding stone connections as much as possible, thus adding new joints thinner and the same shade as the stones have been prioritized.

Authors in [19] performed a semi-automatic stone segmentation in 2D image to extract features for the classification of buildings. They use the probabilistic Hough transform to find straight segments on some boundaries of the stones. The geometric properties of these segments provide enough information for the classification task. This approach, in addition to being semi-automatic, does not provide enough straight segments to detect all the joints and straight segments do not hold sufficient details to get the shape of the stones boundaries to achieve the stone-by-stone segmentation accurately. We have previously shown the feasibility to exploit 2D orthomosaics to perform a more accurate automatic stone-by-stone segmentation [11]. The objective is a binary segmentation separating the surface of the stones and the sealing mortar lap.

Recently, deep convolutional neural networks (CNN) offered efficient performances in several applications of pattern recognition for object detection [6], image classification [8], and image segmentation [1,5,15]. CNN for semantic segmentation, also known as pixel wise segmentation, are well adapted to our purpose as they provide a label for each pixel depending on whether they belong to a sealing lap or a stone surface. These learning methods are also known to be more robust to the wide variations of brightness present in our images. The following section describes orthomosaic map images used in our dataset and the methods tested.

3   Methods

3.1   Orthomosaic Map

Orthomosaics are convenient photo representations widely used for the surveillance of large historic buildings since it's a good media for annotating and localizing the alterations. Orthomosaic map is created out from a set of color photos, captured on site, that have been geometrically corrected (orthorectified) and stitched together, so that the scale is uniform and accurate to measure true distances. It allows to visualize a whole section of a building such as a whole facade or tower as a detailed and accurate map. For example, the outer surrounding walls of the castle in Chambord are about 600 m long and 8.5 m high for the lower part (Fig. 1). About 1595 images were captured with a Canon 5D ProMark cameras equipped with different focal lengths (from 24 to 200 mm) to produce orthomosaic maps for all facades and towers using the free open source photogrammetric software MicMac [21]. To put it simply, the 3D reconstruction of the castle was first computed from images in a fully automated way using Structure-from-Motion (SfM) method. For matching methods to be successful, the images must be captured with a large overlap (80%) as perpendicular to the wall as possible from the ground level in order to limit perspective distortion. More than ten million points have been calculated from the short focal length images (34 to 35 mm), and twenty-five million more by gradually adding the longer focal length images. Deviations in the 3D structure are compensated by evenly distributed ground control points. At the end, the average error on the control points is about 1 cm (less than one pixel residual in the images). The relief on the walls and the position and orientation of the cameras given by SfM were then used to rectified and stitched the images together. More details on this topic can be found in [22]. The dataset used in this study and detailed in Sect. 4.1 is extracted from the orthomosaic maps of the castle outer surrounding walls.

3.2   Edge Detection and Thresholding Methods

Canny edge detector is a popular edge detection algorithm for image segmentation tasks. It uses multi-step detection to find a wide range of edges in an image [2]. A critical parameters are the hysteresis, it uses two thresholds (upper and lower). In order to automatically fix threshold values on our dataset images, we use the binarization threshold provided by a Sobel detector [28] the high hysteresis threshold is equal to the binarization threshold and the low threshold is fixed at 0.4 times the binarization threshold. In a previous work [11], it has been demonstrated that a combination produces a more precise result and helps reduce false edge detection due to noise on the stone surface.

Another popular method of automatic thresholding is the one proposed by OTSU [20]. A threshold value is automatically defined from the histogram of a grayscale image to give the best segmentation into two classes, maximizing separability while maintaining intra-class variability. Despite its simplicity, this method gives fairly good results on a wide range of cases.

Both thresholding methods are applied to images after grayscale conversion based on a weighted sum of the three color channels.

3.3   Deep Learning Methods

SegNet is a deep fully convolutional neural network for semantic segmentation [1]. The network is based on an encoder-decoder achitecture. It contains an encoder network and a corresponding decoder network following by a pixel classification layer (Fig. 2). The encoder network is made of convolutional layers from the VGG16 network [27]. It contains 13 convolution layers arrange in blocks. Each block of convolution is followed by a max pooling layer. The max pooling is performed with a 2×2 kernel and the indices of the max pooling are stored. The mutiple pooling carried out in the encoder network cause a significant reduction in the spatial resolution. The decoder address this using upsampling. The decoder network is made of corresponding layers to each encoder layer. Upsampling is performed using the previously stored indices from each max pooling. It followed by convolutions layers. Finally, a pixel classification layer using Kclass

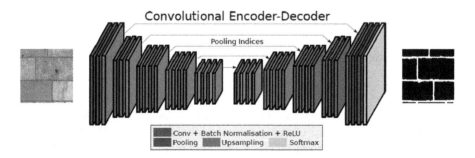

Fig. 2. SegNet: encoder-decoder network architecture [1]

softmax classifier, where K corresponds to the number of classes, is performed to predict the class of each pixel independently.

Deeplab exists in different versions. In this work we use Deeplabv3+, the lastest and best performing version [4]. DeepLabv3+ is an encoder-decoder with atrous separable convolution network architecture (Fig. 3). The encoder network is made of convolutional layers from the ResNet-18 network [9]. It contains 18 convolution layers and encodes multiscale contextual information by applying atrous convolution at multiple scales.

To address the reduction in the spatial resolution after the encoding, atrous convolution of the last encoder layer feature map is performed plus a 1×1 convolutions to reduce the number of channels. Atrous convolution serves to effectively enlarge the field of view of filters to incorporate larger context without increasing the number of parameters or the amount of computation [3]. The output of the 1×1 convolutions are concatenated with the corresponding feature map size from the encoder network. Followed by 3×3 convolutions and upsampling to get the original image size.

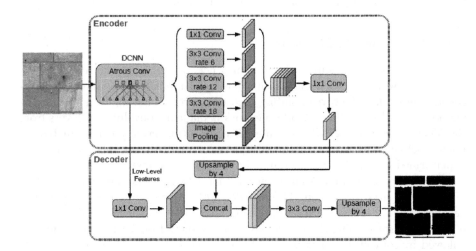

Fig. 3. DeepLabv3+: encoder-decoder with atrous separable convolution network architecture [4]

4   Experimental Results

4.1   Dataset

The dataset is made of 245 sub-images with the size of 256×256 extracted from the orthomosaic map of the outer surrounding walls of the Château de Chambord (Fig. 1). The ground truth is provided by manual labeling performed by experts. An advantage of a pixel-wise convolutional neural network is that this sub-division does not prevent the generalization of segmentation to the whole orthomosaic map.

We applied various data augmentation techniques to our dataset (two type of brightness changes, two types of contrast changes, flipping and blurring). In the choice of the different techniques applied, we take into consideration a domain-dependent integrity of the image as joints are relatively horizontally or vertically oriented. However, as the image acquisition might be done in different lighting conditions, so techniques like brightness and contrast variation has been performed more.

These techniques are applied to each sub-image. For example, for a sub-image I, two type of contrast changes are applied. The first type of contrast change consists of mapping each color channel pixel intensity in the range $[0:3;0:9]$. The second type of contrast change converts I into HSV color space and scale pixel value of I by a factor of the uniform distribution $[-2;4]$. Then two types of brightness changes are executed. The first consists of adding a value from the range $[-0:6;-0:1]$ to the brightness value of each pixel of I after conversion into HSV color space to obtain a darker version of I. The second consists of adding a value from the range $[0:1;0:6]$ to the brightness value of each pixel of I to obtain a brighter version of I. After that, the image I goes through an affine reflexion on X axis or Y axis. Finally, a blurring process is applied on I using Gaussian filter.

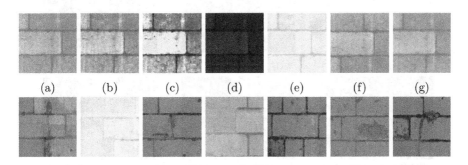

Fig. 4. Example of images and applied transformations: **First row:** (a) Original image I. (b) I after first contrast change. (c) I after second contrast change. (d) I after first brightness change. (e) I after second brightness change. (f) I after affine reflexion on X axis or Y axis. (g) I after blurring using Gaussian filter. **Second row:** Some challenging images in the dataset.

We obtain an augmented dataset of 1715 images with the size of 256×256 (some example in Fig. 4). Figure 4 presents the dataset use for the training. The dataset has been separated into 70% for training, 15% for validation and 15% for testing. The network training is performed using transfer learning. The transfer learning technique performed is Finetuning of two networks: SegNet and Deeplabv3+, on orthomosaic subimages as inputs. The network is trained once on a sample of images from the orthomosaic images of Château de Chambord. Then, the model obtained is tested on different sample of orthomosaic images of Château de Chambord and on orthomosaic images from the Château de Chaumont-sur-Loire.

The testing is performed on a workstation with one NVIDIA Quadro P5000 graphics card of 16 GB memory, the RAM of 64 GB and the CPU Xeon E5-2620 v4. From the result, it is a clear fact that the use of deep CNN architecture allows us to obtain better results.

4.2   Comparative Tests

We compare SegNet and DeepLab v3+, two state-of-art CNN for semantic segmentation, with OTSU thresholding method and our previous Canny-based method [11]. The different methods are applied to sub-images from the orthomosaic maps of the outer surrounding walls of the castle. For quantitative evaluation, we present Precision, Recall and F-measure values.

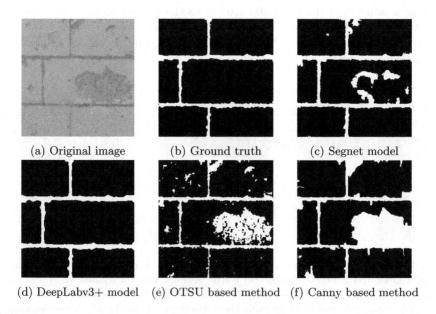

(a) Original image   (b) Ground truth   (c) Segnet model

(d) DeepLabv3+ model   (e) OTSU based method   (f) Canny based method

Fig. 5. Stone segmentation on a noisy sub-image. (a) Original image; (b) Ground truth; (c) Segnet model segmentation result; (d) DeepLabv3+ model segmentation result; (e) OTSU based method segmentation result; (f) Canny based method segmentation result.

The results presented in the Table 1 concern all the test database with large lighting variations. Indeed, the image acquisition might be done on several days in different weather conditions. It is usual to get a shadow on part of the image, different brightness and different contrast in the same image. Sometimes the photogrametry process performed to obtain the orthomosaic generates some error like blurred images. Another source of complexity is the alterations on the walls.

In these conditions, we observe that deep learning methods perform much better than edge detection and thresholding methods. The SegNet model reaches a precision of 96.1% and the DeepLabv3+ model 97.8%.

Table 1. Comparison of segmentation methods on images with lighting variation

Methods	Precision	Recall	F-measure
Canny based method	0.535	0.308	0.390
OTSU based method	0.526	0.306	0.387
SegNet model	0.961	0.897	0.927
DeepLabv3+ model	0.978	0.982	0.980

For complementary test, we compared in Table 2 the four same methods tested on the previous sub dataset used in [11]. This subset corresponds to approximatively the third of the wall shown in Fig. 1 and presents a relative homogeneity in brightness. We can observe that the classic methods present an equivalent precision with the deep learning on this subset. Recall is lower for Otsu but our Canny based method gives comparable performance to SegNet. This demonstrates the greater sensitivity of the classic methods to lighting variations. On challenging images as shown in Fig. 5, we can clearly appreciate deep CNN models have advantages over edge detection and thresholding methods (More examples in Fig. 7).

Overall, DeepLabv3+ shows the best performance in Tables 1 and 2.

Table 2. Comparison of segmentation methods on images without lighting variation

Methods	Precision	Recall	F-measure
Canny based method	0.967	0.871	0.917
OTSU based method	0.964	0.743	0.839
SegNet model	0.962	0.860	0.908
DeepLabv3+ model	0.957	0.924	0.940

In Tables 3 and 4, we present the confusion matrices obtained on the overall dataset. For the SegNet model, we observe that only 3.6% of pixels part of stone surface has been misclassified as joint pixels, and 10.4% of pixels part of the joint has been misclassified as stone surface. The noise in image and the joint polishing after a maintenance to make them indistinguishable might be some factors that can explain this misclassifications. The model architecture might also contribute to enhance this as some details of a sub-image are lost as the different layers of convolutions of the encoder are processed.

Table 3. Confusion matrix for segnet model trained

	Joint	Stone surface
Joint	0.896	0.104
Stone surface	0.036	0.964

In Table 4, we can notice that DeepLabv3+ gives better results with only 2.1% and 1.8% of miscclassified pixels for stone surface and joint classes respectively. The better performance might be explained by the residual capability of the DeepLab architecture, since previous layers outputs are recollect into the following layers.

Table 4. Confusion matrix for deeplabv3+ model trained

	Joint	Stone surface
Joint	0.982	0.018
Stone surface	0.021	0.978

To observe the capability of our trained DeepLabv3+ model to segment images from a different Renaissance-style castle, we test it on orthomosaic map of château de Chaumont-sur-Loire without supplementary training. Figure 6 shows the results. The model performance seems really encouraging to achieve automatic stone-by-stone segmentation on different cultural heritage buildings.

(a) Original image

(b) DeepLabv3+ model segmentation

Fig. 6. DeepLabv3+ model segmentation on château de Chaumont-sur-Loire.

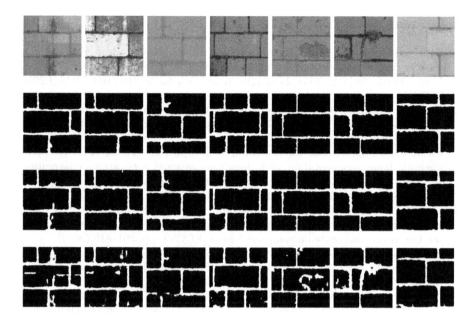

Fig. 7. Stone segmentation on some challenging samples. **First row:** Original image; **Second row:** Ground truth realized by experts; **Third row:** DeepLabv3+ model segmentation result; **Fourth row:** Segnet model segmentation result.

5   Conclusion and Future Work

As the years passed and life happened, surveying and maintenance of cultural heritage buildings becomes increasingly resource consuming. The evaluation of the health status in order to perform the maintenance involves the conception of a health record. Stone segmentation is a critical step in establishing the health record.

In this work we have introduced the use of deep convolutional network to perform the stone-by-stone segmentation task on 2D orthomosaic map of large historical buildings. We demonstrate that it allows us to obtain better performance compared to classic edge detection and thresholding methods. We show our approach can be general and applicable to other large historical building like château de Chaumont-sur-Loire.

In future work, we will primarily focus on the segmentation of regions of alterations on the orthomosaic map based on the stone-by-stone segmentation results obtained in this paper in order to achieve a fully automated analysis of cultural heritage building with high accuracy stone precision.

References

1. Badrinarayanan, V., Kendall, A., Cipolla, R.: SegNet: a deep convolutional encoder-decoder architecture for image segmentation. IEEE Trans. Pattern Anal. Mach. Intell. **39**(12), 2481–2495 (2017). https://doi.org/10.1109/TPAMI.2016. 2644615
2. Canny, J.: A computational approach to edge detection. IEEE Trans. Pattern Anal. Mach. Intell. **PAMI–8**, 679–698 (1986). https://doi.org/10.1109/TPAMI. 1986.4767851
3. Chen, L.C., Papandreou, G., Kokkinos, I., Murphy, K., Yuille, A.L.: DeepLab: semantic image segmentation with deep convolutional nets, atrous convolution, and fully connected CRFs. IEEE Trans. Pattern Anal. Mach. Intell. **40**(4), 834–848 (2018). https://doi.org/10.1109/tpami.2017.2699184
4. Chen, L.C., Zhu, Y., Papandreou, G., Schroff, F., Adam, H.: Encoder-decoder with atrous separable convolution for semantic image segmentation. In: Proceedings of the European conference on computer vision (ECCV), pp. 801–818 (2018)
5. Garcia-Garcia, A., Orts-Escolano, S., Oprea, S., Villena-Martinez, V., Garcia-Rodriguez, J.: A review on deep learning techniques applied to semantic segmentation. arXiv preprint arXiv:1704.06857 (2017)
6. Girshick, R.: Fast R-CNN. In: 2015 IEEE International Conference on Computer Vision (ICCV), pp. 1440–1448, December 2015. https://doi.org/10.1109/ICCV. 2015.169
7. Grilli, E., Dininno, D., Petrucci, G., Remondino, F.: From 2D to 3D supervised segmentation and classification for cultural heritage applications. Int. Arch. Photogr. Remote Sens. Spat. Inf. Sci. **42**(2) (2018)
8. He, K., Zhang, X., Ren, S., Sun, J.: Deep residual learning for image recognition. In: The IEEE Conference on Computer Vision and Pattern Recognition (CVPR), June 2016
9. He, K., Zhang, X., Ren, S., Sun, J.: Deep residual learning for image recognition. In: Proceedings of the IEEE Conference on Computer Vision and Pattern Recognition, pp. 770–778 (2016)
10. Hess, M.R., Petrovic, V., Kuester, F.: Interactive classification of construction materials: feedback driven framework for annotation and analysis of 3D point clouds. ISPRS - Int. Arch. Photogr. Remote Sens. Spat. Inf. Sci. **XLII–2/W5**, 343–347 (2017). https://doi.org/10.5194/isprs-archives-XLII-2-W5-343-2017
11. Idjaton, K., Desquesnes, X., Treuillet, S., Brunetaud, X.: Segmentation automatique d'images pour le diagnostic de monuments historiques. In: Colloque GRETSI (Groupement de Recherche en Traitement du Signal et des Images) (2019)
12. Janvier-Badosa, S., Beck, K., Brunetaud, X., Guirimand-Dufour, A., Al-Mukhtar, M.: Gypsum and spalling decay mechanism of tuffeau limestone. Environ. Earth Sci. **74**(3), 2209–2221 (2015). https://doi.org/10.1007/s12665-015-4212-2
13. Janvier-Badosa, S., Brunetaud, X., Beck, K., Al-Mukhtar, M.: Kinetics of stone degradation of the castle of chambord in France. Int. J. Archit. Heritage **10**(1), 96–105 (2016)
14. Kapsalas, P., Zervakis, M., Maravelaki-Kalaitzaki, P., Delegou, E., Moropoulou, A.: Machine vision schemes towards detecting and estimating the state of corrosion. In: Pattern Recognition and Signal Processing in Archaeometry: Mathematical and Computational Solutions for Archaeology, pp. 146–165. IGI Global (2012)
15. Long, J., Shelhamer, E., Darrell, T.: Fully convolutional networks for semantic segmentation. In: 2015 IEEE Conference on Computer Vision and Pattern Recognition (CVPR), pp. 3431–3440 (2015). https://doi.org/10.1109/CVPR.2015.7298965

16. Manferdini, A.M., Baroncini, V., Corsi, C.: An integrated and automated segmentation approach to deteriorated regions recognition on 3D reality-based models of cultural heritage artifacts. J. Cult. Heritage (2012). https://doi.org/10.1016/j.culher.2012.01.014

17. Marson, C., Sammartano, G., Spanò, A., Valluzzi, M.R.: Lidar data analyses for assessing the conservation status of the so-called baths-church in Hierapolis of Phrygia (TR). ISPRS - Int. Arch. Photogr. Remote Sens. Spat. Inf. Sci. **XLII–2/W11**, 823–830 (2019). https://doi.org/10.5194/isprs-archives-XLII-2-W11-823-2019

18. Murtiyoso, A., Grussenmeyer, P.: Point cloud segmentation and semantic annotation aided by GIS data for heritage complexes. In: ISPRS Annals of the Photogrammetry, Remote Sensing and Spatial Information Sciences, vol. 42, pp. 523–528. Copernicus GmbH (2019). https://doi.org/10.5194/isprs-archives-XLII-2-W9-523-2019

19. Oses, N., Dornaika, F.: Image-based delineation of built heritage masonry for automatic classification. In: Kamel, M., Campilho, A. (eds.) ICIAR 2013. LNCS, vol. 7950, pp. 782–789. Springer, Heidelberg (2013). https://doi.org/10.1007/978-3-642-39094-4_90

20. Otsu, N.: A threshold selection method from gray-level histograms. IEEE Trans. Syst. Man Cybern. **9**(1), 62–66 (1979)

21. Pierrot, D.M.: Producing orthomosaic with a free open source software (micmac), application to the archeological survey of meremptah's tomb (2014)

22. Pinte, A., Héno, R., Pierrot-Deseilligny, M., Brunetaud, X., Janvier-Badosa, S., Janvier, R.: Orthoimages of the outer walls and towers of the château de Chambord. ISPRS Ann. Photogr. Remote Sens. Spat. Inf. Sci. **II–5/W3**, 243–250 (2015). https://doi.org/10.5194/isprsannals-II-5-W3-243-2015

23. Remondino, F.: Heritage recording and 3D modeling with photogrammetry and 3D scanning. Remote Sens. **3**(6), 1104–1138 (2011). https://doi.org/10.3390/rs3061104

24. Riveiro, B., Conde-Carnero, B., González-Jorge, H., Arias, P., Caamaño, J.: Automatic creation of structural models from point cloud data: the case of masonry structures. ISPRS Ann. Photogr. Remote Sens. Spat. Inf. Sci. **2** (2015)

25. Riveiro, B., Lourenço, P.B., Oliveira, D.V., González-Jorge, H., Arias, P.: Automatic morphologic analysis of quasi-periodic masonry walls from LiDAR. Comput. Aided Civ. Infrastr. Eng. **31**(4), 305–319 (2016). https://doi.org/10.1111/mice.12145

26. Sánchez-Aparicio, L.J., Del Pozo, S., Ramos, L.F., Arce, A., Fernandes, F.M.: Heritage site preservation with combined radiometric and geometric analysis of TLS data. Autom. Constr. **85**, 24–39 (2018). https://doi.org/10.1016/j.autcon.2017.09.023

27. Simonyan, K., Zisserman, A.: Very deep convolutional networks for large-scale image recognition. arXiv preprint arXiv:1409.1556 (2014)

28. Sobel, I.: An Isotropic 3× 3 Gradient Operator, Machine Vision for Three-dimensional Scenes, p. 376379. Freeman, H., Academic Press (1990)

29. Valero, E., Bosché, F., Forster, A.: Automatic segmentation of 3D point clouds of rubble masonry walls, and its application to building surveying, repair and maintenance. Autom. Constr. (2018). https://doi.org/10.1016/j.autcon.2018.08.018

30. Valero, E., Forster, A., Bosché, F., Hyslop, E., Wilson, L., Turmel, A.: Automated defect detection and classification in ashlar masonry walls using machine learning. Autom. Constr. (2019). https://doi.org/10.1016/j.autcon.2019.102846

31. Valero, E., Forster, A., Bosché, F., Renier, C., Hyslop, E., Wilson, L.: High level-of-detail BIM and machine learning for automated masonry wall defect surveying (2018). https://doi.org/10.22260/ISARC2018/0101
32. Yuan, L., Guo, J., Wang, Q.: Automatic classification of common building materials from 3D terrestrial laser scan data. Autom. Constr. (2020). https://doi.org/10.1016/j.autcon.2019.103017

A Convolutional Recurrent Neural Network for the Handwritten Text Recognition of Historical Greek Manuscripts

K. Markou[1], L. Tsochatzidis[1], K. Zagoris[2], A. Papazoglou[1], X. Karagiannis[1], S. Symeonidis[1], and I. Pratikakis[1(✉)]

[1] Department of Electrical and Computer Engineering,
Democritus University of Thrace, 67100 Xanthi, Greece
`ipratika@ee.duth.gr`
[2] Department of Computer Science, Neapolis University Pafos, Pafos, Cyprus
`k.zagoris@nup.ac.cy`

Abstract. In this paper, a Convolutional Recurrent Neural Network architecture for offline handwriting recognition is proposed. Specifically, a Convolutional Neural Network is used as an encoder for the input which is a textline image, while a Bidirectional Long Short-Term Memory (BLSTM) network followed by a fully connected neural network acts as the decoder for the prediction of a sequence of characters. This work was motivated by the need to transcribe historical Greek manuscripts that entail several challenges which have been extensively analysed. The proposed architecture has been tested for standard datasets, namely the IAM and RIMES, as well as for a newly created dataset, namely EPARCHOS, which contains historical Greek manuscripts and has been made publicly available for research purposes. Our experimental work relies upon a detailed ablation study which shows that the proposed architecture outperforms state-of-the-art approaches.

Keywords: Offline handwriting recognition · Recurrent Neural Networks · Historical documents

1 Introduction

The potential to access our written past, which stimulates the interest of not only researchers but also the general public, makes Handwritten Text Recognition (HTR) a highly appealing technology, among the ones appearing in the document image analysis research area. The complexity of an HTR task draws upon the content type, which is mostly unconstrained and coupled with the variability of different hands as well as the high computational load, which is most of the times required.

HTR can be realised by systems which address either online or offline recognition. In the former case, a time series of coordinates is captured that represent

© Springer Nature Switzerland AG 2021
A. Del Bimbo et al. (Eds.): ICPR 2020 Workshops, LNCS 12667, pp. 249–262, 2021.
https://doi.org/10.1007/978-3-030-68787-8_18

the imprint of the movement of the hand writing in a surface. In the latter case, only a test image is available, which ranges from a whole document to a textline or a word. In this paper, our research focus on an unconstrained offline handwriting recognition context, where the input image is a textline.

Neural networks have become a key component in current handwritting recognition systems [16]. Many of the recent offline HTR systems use the line-level recognition way to train a neural network with a certain architecture for which the most common is a combination of Convolutional Neural Networks (CNNs) and Recurrent Neural Networks (RNNs) [5]. While the CNN uses a limited amount of context, the RNN comes in place to enhance the training performance using sequential data [17], thus enabling information storage in its internal states from previous input cases. The only shortcoming with RNNs concerns the exploding and vanishing gradient effect. To this end, Long Short-Term Memory (LSTM) cells [10] have been introduced, which has proved to be an appealing solution, due to their powerful learning capacity. In general, the LSTM architecture allows the network to store information for a longer amount of time through its internal gates. In our work, we are using a slightly different type of LSTM, called Bidirectional LSTM network, which analyzes the information both ways (right-to-left and left-to-right) [16].

The proposed architecture contains two fully connected linear layers (FCL) after the CNNs and the BLSTMs. In this way, the mapping between hidden units and the output becomes deeper [14]. Overall, we build a network that contains CNNs, that are good at reducing frequency variations, BLSTMs that are good at temporal modeling and FCLs that are appropriate for mapping features to an improved separable space [14].

The remainder of this paper is structured as follows: in Sect. 2 we present the related work, Sect. 3 is dedicated to the description of the proposed methodology and Sect. 4 presents the experimental work which relies upon an ablation study of the proposed architecture using standard datasets as well as a newly created dataset that contains historical Greek handwritten manuscripts. Finally, in Sect. 5 conclusions are drawn.

2   Related Work

HTR is inherently modelled as a problem of sequential data, for which relevant deep learning networks, like the Recurrent Neural Networks (RNN), have been used to address the relevant challenges. In particular, for offline handwriting text recognition, several methods have been proposed which use LSTMs in different configurations, such as 1D-LSTM, Bidirectional LSTM and Multi-directional LSTM [3,16]. Also, for boosting classification performance, a unified approach has been followed, by introducing the recurrent property achieved by RNN in certain traditional CNN structure, where the RNN takes the CNN output as input and returns sequential predictions for distinct timesteps [10,11,16]. It has also been reported in the literature that adding FCLs after an LSTM the results can be improved, due to the reduction in variation of the hidden states [14].

Besides the network structure itself, a key role hold configurations such as, regularization methods (dropout, batch normalization) and the data augmentation strategy, often realized as random distortions of existing samples. Combinations of such configurations have been adopted in state-of-the-art works [10,11,16]. Regarding training, the Connectionist Temporal Classification (CTC) loss function [3] is a widely adopted choice to quantify the correlation between ground-truth and produced sequences.

The most recent works which have set the base of our work, also used in our comparative study, are the following: Shi et al. [15] proposed a novel neural network architecture, which integrates feature extraction, sequence modeling and transcription into a unified framework. This architecture is based on a Convolutional RNN model, with a CNN encoder and a RNN decoder. Their model is end-to-end trainable, it handles sequences of arbitrary lengths and it is not confined to any predefined lexicon. In a similar spirit, Puigcerver [11] has used Convolutional 1-D LSTMs to deal with textline HTR. Finally, Dutta et al. [2] proposed a CNN-RNN hybrid architecture (residual convolutional blocks and BLSTMs), focusing on three points: (i) efficient intialization of network using synthetic data for pre-training, (ii) an image normalization for slant correction and (iii) specific data transformation and distortion for learning important variances.

3   Proposed Methodology

The proposed neural network architecture, namely CRNN-FCNN is a combination of the works introduced by Puigcerver [11] and Sainath et al. [14], which addressed problems in transcription of handwritten documents and speech recognition, respectively. It comprises three distinct components, including (i) a convolutional stage that processes a textline document image as input, consisting of consecutive CNN blocks that produce a sequence of features; (ii) a Recurrent stage which is fed by the outcome of the convolutional part and consists of a set of BLSTMs that produce per image predictions; (iii) two fully connected layers which translate the BLSTMs outcome into a sequence of labels. An overview of the proposed network architecture is illustrated in Fig. 1, while a detailed description about the convolutional and recurrent stage along with details about the training stage, are given in the following.

3.1   Architecture

1. *Convolutional stage:* The first stage consists of a typical feed-forward convolutional network, which aims to extract features from the input image. This model uses 5 consecutive convolutional blocks. Each one of these blocks has a convolutional layer with kernel size 3 × 3 pixels, stride equal to 1 and a batch normalization layer. The leaky rectified linear function is used for neuron activation (LeakyReLU) that allows for a small, non-zero gradient when the unit is saturated and not active [7]. The first three blocks additionally

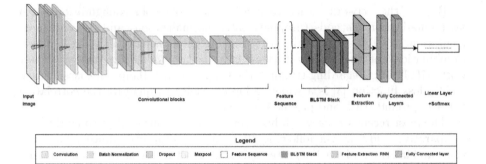

Fig. 1. The proposed CRNN-FCNN architecture

incorporate a Maximum Pooling layer (with non-overlapping kernels of size 2×2), in order to reduce the dimensionality of the input image. A dropout layer (with probability 0.2) is included in the last three blocks, to improve the generalization ability of high-level features. In Table 1, the configuration of each convolutional block is given. Finally, a number of feature maps are extracted from each image. For the subsequent processing, the average of each column of the feature maps is calculated, to acquire a feature vector for each time step.

Table 1. Configuration of the convolutional blocks in the proposed neural network architecture

Configurations	Values
Convolutional filters	16-32-48-64-80
Dropout	0-0-0-0.2-0.2-0.2
Maxpool (2×2)	Yes-Yes-Yes-No-No
Batch Normalisation	True-True-True-True-True

2. *Recurrent stage:* As a decoder, a stack of recurrent blocks is applied, formed by 1-D Bidirectional LSTM (BLSTM) layers, that sequentially process the extracted feature vectors, corresponding to columns of the feature maps. The BLSTM layers process the information bidirectionally (right-to-left and left-to-right) leading to a separate feature vector for each direction (two in total). The feature vectors of each direction are then concatenated to form a single vector representation. In each recurrent block a dropout layer is incorporated with probability 0.5.
3. *Fully-connected layers:* After the recurrent stage, two fully-connected layers are added. In the case of LSTMs, mapping between recursive information that floats through the network and the output of every time-step does not contain

any hidden non-linear layers. To deal with datasets which have a relatively large character set (as in the case of historical Greek manuscripts), we used two fully connected hidden layers with 512 hidden units.

3.2 Training

Training of the model is performed using the Connectionist Temporal Classification (CTC) loss function [3], minimized using RmsProp [13]. The learning rate is set to 0.003. Additionally, early stopping is applied, terminating the training process, when the Character Error Rate (CER) on the validation set does not improve for 20 consecutive epochs.

4 Experimental Results

The main motivation for the proposed work has been the need to transcribe Historical Greek manuscripts, which have particularities that make the HTR task much more challenging. In view of this, our comparative study relies upon a newly created historical dataset, called 'EPARCHOS', which has been made publicly available for research purposes [9]. To prove the generic character of the proposed approach, our method is also tested against two standard modern handwritten datasets, namely, the IAM and RIMES datasets. In the following, we provide a description of the datasets used in our experimental work with a particular focus on the challenging aspects which appear in the 'EPARCHOS' dataset.

4.1 Datasets

Historical Greek 'EPARCHOS' Dataset. This particular dataset originates from a Greek handwritten codex that dates from around 1500–1530. This is the subset of the codex British Museum Addit. 6791, written by two hands, one by Antonius Eparchos and the other by Camillos Zanettus (ff. 104r-174v) and delivers texts by Hierocles (In Aureum carmen), Matthaeus Blastares (Collectio alphabetica) and, notably, texts by Michael Psellos (De omnifaria doctrina). In particular, the writing which appears in the dataset delivers the most important abbreviations, logograms and conjunctions, which are cited in virtually every Greek minuscule handwritten codex from the years of the manuscript transliteration and the prevalence of the minuscule script (9th century) to the post-Byzantine years. This dataset consists of 9285 lines of text containing 18809 words (6787 unique words) that are distributed over 120 scanned handwritten text pages, created by 2 writers. The dataset is separated into training, validation and testing partitions of 1435 (63%), 381 (17%) and 456 (20%) textlines, respectively. Every textline has an average of 477×37 pixels and the characters that compose the dataset are 312. An example page is shown in Fig. 2.

In the following, after a comprehensive study of the dataset, we list several particularities that originate from the writing, coupled by visual examples:

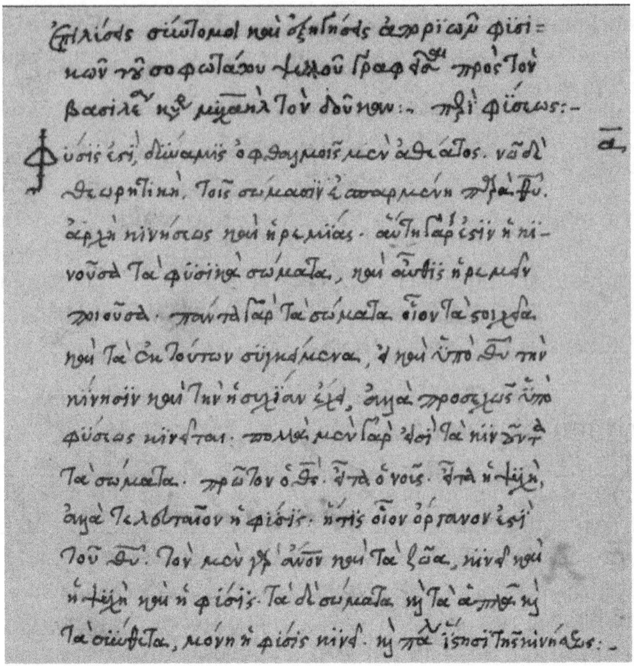

Fig. 2. 'EPARCHOS' dataset: example document image

- Abbreviations: They are typical in the writing of 'EPARCHOS' dataset. Those are used in a variety of grammatical context including those related to endings of inflected and uninflected words (Fig. 3 and 4). For the sake of clarity, it should be noted that the abbreviation learning by our system relies upon the correspondence between the abbreviation symbol and the ground truth character combination as shown in Fig. 3.
- Floating characters: This particular case is mostly appearing in the case of word endings. For the sake of clarity, we give examples where the floating part of the word is indicated by a rectangle while the remainder part of the word is underlined. In these examples, we also encounter two potential cases. The first, concerns uninflected words (Fig. 5a) and the second concerns inflected words (Fig. 5b). For both cases, the textline image along with the ground truth are given.
- Minuscule writing: A noticeable particularity is related to the use of a lower-case letter instead of an upper-case one after a 'full stop' character. This is due to the particular period of time, where in principle there were no capital letters and this type of writing is called "Minuscule". A representative example is shown in Fig. 6 where specific regions in a textline that relate to the under discussion particularity are underlined in both the image and the ground truth.

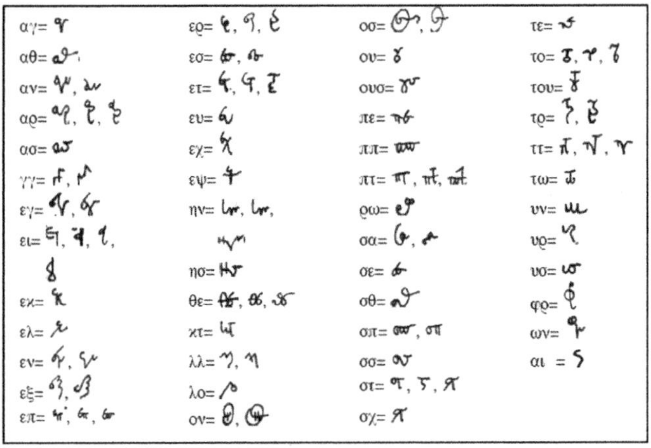

α'γ'= ૪	εϱ= ૬, ૧, ૮	οο= ⊙, ૭	τε= ⌇
αθ= ⌐	εο= ૭, ᠕	ου= ૪	το= ૪, ૪, ૪
αν= ૧, ᠕	ετ= ૬, ૧, ૪	ουο= ૪	του= ૪
αϱ= ૧, ૮, ૮	ευ= ૬	πε= ᠕	τϱ= ૧, ૪
αο= ⌐	εγ= ૪	ππ= ᠕	ττ= ૪, ૧, ૪
γ'γ'= ૪, ᠕	εψ= ૪	πτ= ᠕, ᠕, ᠕	τω= ૪
εγ= ૪, ૪	ην= ᠕, ᠕,	ϱω= ૪	υν= ᠕
ει= ૧, ૪, ૮,	᠕	οα= ૬, ᠕	υϱ= ૪
૪	ηο= ᠕	οε= ૪	υο= ᠕
εκ= ૪	θε= ᠕, ᠕, ᠕	οθ= ⌐	ϙο= ૪
ελ= ᠕	κτ= ᠕	οπ= ᠕, οπ	ων= ૪
εν= ૪, ૪	λλ= ᠕, ᠕	οο= ᠕	αι = ૪
εξ= ᠕, ᠕	λο= ᠕	οτ= ᠕, ૪, ᠕	
επ= ૪, ᠕, ᠕	ου= ૪, ᠕	ογ= ᠕	

Fig. 3. Abbreviations

– Polytonic orthography: It is typical in all Byzantine manuscripts the use of the polytonic system, as shown in the example document image in Fig. 2. A particularity appearing in this polytonic system are the characters ϋ and ϊ, which were used in this form in order to be distinguished from the dipthong letters (see Fig. 7). The problem with these characters concerns its transcription which is not unique but it relies upon the context. In particular, either the character is transcribed as shown or it is transcribed as character without the specific diacritic marks (diaeresis).

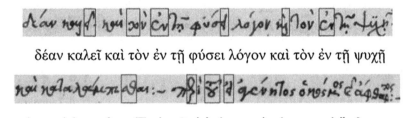

δέαν καλεῖ καὶ τὸν ἐν τῇ φύσει λόγον καὶ τὸν ἐν τῇ ψυχῇ

καὶ καταλάμπεσθαι:- Περὶ τοῦ εἰ ἀγένητος ὁ κόσμος καὶ ἄφθαρτος:-

Fig. 4. Example textlines with abbreviations

Standard Handwritten Document Datasets - IAM, RIMES. For a concise comparative study with the state-of-the-art, we have made experiments with two other standard handwritten document image datasets, namely, IAM and RIMES. The IAM dataset [8] includes handwritten documents in modern English by 657 writers resulting in 1539 scanned handwritten text pages, that contain 10841 different words distributed over 9285 lines of text. It is separated

τὰ σύνθετα, μόνη ἡ φύσις κινεῖ. καὶ πάλιν ἵστησι τῆς κινήσεως:-

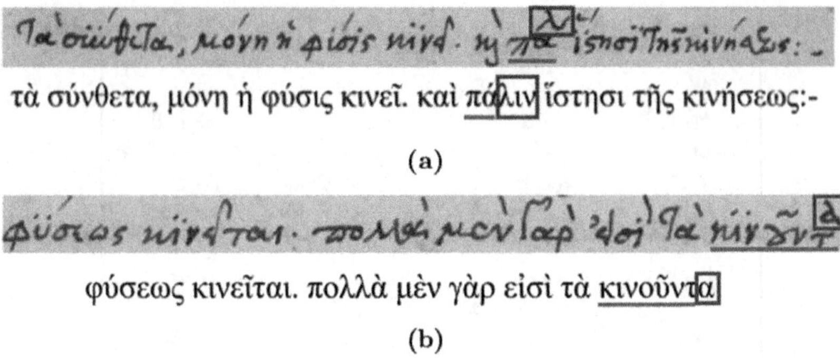

(a)

φύσεως κινεῖται. πολλὰ μὲν γὰρ εἰσὶ τὰ κινοῦντα

(b)

Fig. 5. Floating ending of (a) an uninflected and (b) an inflected word

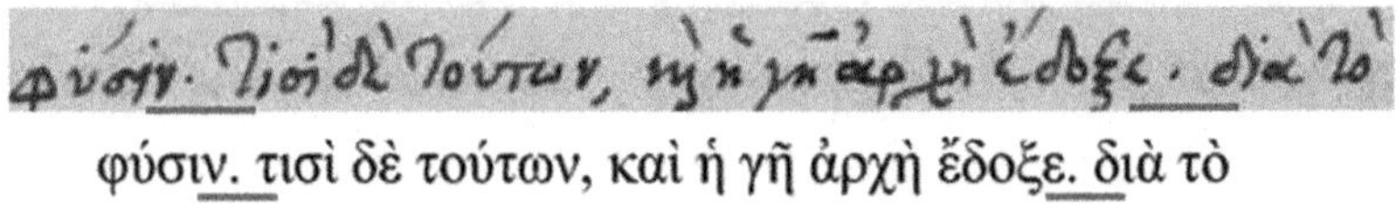

φύσιν. τισὶ δὲ τούτων, καὶ ἡ γῆ ἀρχὴ ἔδοξε. διὰ τὸ

Fig. 6. Example of "Minuscule" writing

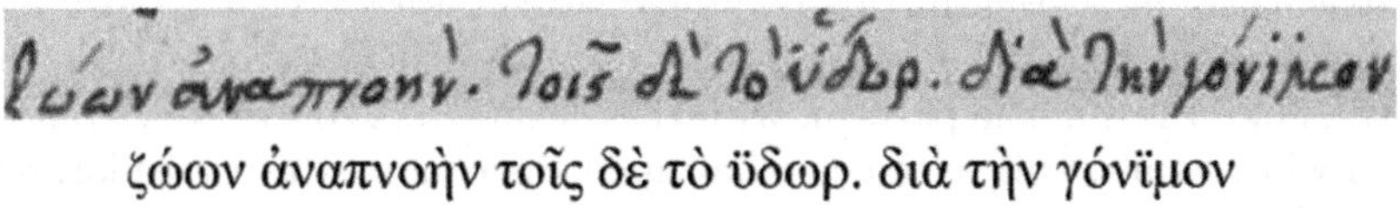

ζώων ἀναπνοὴν τοῖς δὲ τὸ ὕδωρ. διὰ τὴν γόνιμον

Fig. 7. Characters ÿ and ï

into training, validation and testing partitions of 6161 (60%), 966 (10%) and 2915 (30%) textlines, respectively. Every line has an average of 1751 × 124 pixels. The characters that are observed throughout these pages are 79, plus the white space.

The RIMES dataset [4] contains handwritten documents in modern French, which are presented in partitions of 10,203 (85%), 1130 (10%) and 778 (5%) textlines for training, validation and testing, respectively. Every line has an average of 1658 × 113 pixels and the characters that compose the dataset are 99.

4.2   Ablation Study

The proposed neural network architecture (CRNN-FCNN) which is described in Sect. 3 has been tested for its performance in handwritten text recognition at the aforementioned datasets using a concise ablation study wherein alternative configurations of the network have been extensively examined. Furthermore, a comparison against the state of the art has also been performed.

Table 2 presents the recognition results in the case of different configurations including the case of (i) applying random distortions (rotation, scaling, shearing,

Table 2. Text recognition performance of the proposed CRNN-FCNN architecture for different configurations tested in EPARCHOS, IAM and RIMES datasets

System	CER (%)		WER (%)	
	Val.	Test	Val.	Test
(a) EPARCHOS				
CRNN-FCNN	7.50	11.29	23.86	30.10
CRNN-FCNN + Distortions	7.07	10.64	21.99	28.72
CRNN-FCNN + Distortions + BN	7.51	11.53	24.90	32.19
CRNN-FCNN + Distortions + BN + Dropout	**6.63**	**9.87**	**21.99**	**27.19**
(b) IAM				
CRNN-FCNN	4.78	7.86	16.37	23.85
CRNN-FCNN + Distortions	4.13	6.38	14.50	20.54
CRNN-FCNN + Distortions + BN	4.27	6.48	15.35	20.82
CRNN-FCNN + Distortions + Dropout + BN	**3.86**	**6.14**	**13.51**	**20.04**
(c) RIMES				
CRNN-FCNN	4.56	3.93	14.14	13.37
CRNN-FCNN + Distortions	4.04	3.48	12.52	11.81
CRNN-FCNN + Distortions + BN	4.14	3.51	12.90	12.37
CRNN-FCNN + Distortions + Dropout + BN	**3.90**	**3.34**	**12.17**	**11.23**

erosion, dilation) on the input image to reduce overfitting; (ii) adding batch normalization to configuration (i) which helps with the reduction of the error rates when applied with random distortions on the input images; (iii) applying dropout to configuration (ii) for some of the convolutional blocks of the network (see Table 1). As shown in Table 2, the configuration (iii) has achieved the best performance among all others in all datasets both in terms of Character Error Rate (CER) and Word Error Rate (WER).

Concerning the number of fully-connected layers as well as the number of corresponding neurons we performed a testing with different options where the results are presented in Table 3. In 'EPARCHOS' dataset, this particular selection plays an important role due to the large number of characters (classes) that exist in historical Greek manuscripts. As shown in Table 3 the best option is attributed to the configuration of two hidden layers with 512 hidden units for each layer with a performance of 11.29% CER and 30.10% WER. It is worth to mention that the network operates with the minimum amount of configurations (no distortions, dropout and batch normalization).

In Table 4, comparative results are given taking into account the proposed network (CRNN-FCNN) and the network presented in [11], which has set the base for our own approach. At this point, it is worth to mention that the experimental results achieved by the approach in [11] have been produced by using the PyLaia toolkit [12] in order for each dataset used, to consider the same training,

Table 3. Text recognition performance of the proposed CRNN-FCNN architecture for different configurations of the FCNN component

		1-hidden layer	2-hidden layers
(a) 512 hidden units			
CER (%)	Val.	8.03	**7.50**
	Test	12.49	**11.29**
WER (%)	Val.	25.63	**23.86**
	Test	33.17	**30.10**
(b) 1024 hidden units			
CER (%)	Val.	**7.51**	8.31
	Test	**11.49**	12.55
WER (%)	Val.	**24.58**	26.60
	Test	**31.31**	34.39

validation and testing portion of the dataset. As shown in Table 4, the proposed approach outperforms the approach in [11] for all three datasets, namely the newly created historical Greek dataset EPARCHOS, and the standard modern handwritten document datasets, IAM and RIMES.

Table 4. Text recognition performance of the proposed CRNN-FCNN architecture against the architecture of Puigcerver [11].

		Puigcerver [11]	Proposed method
(a) EPARCHOS			
CER (%)	Val.	6.81	**6.63**
	Test	10.37	**9.87**
WER (%)	Val.	22.06	**21.99**
	Test	28.51	**27.19**
(b) IAM			
CER (%)	Val.	4.25	**3.86**
	Test	6.49	**6.14**
WER (%)	Val.	14.97	**13.51**
	Test	20.91	**20.04**
(c) RIMES			
CER (%)	Val.	4.14	**3.90**
	Test	3.76	**3.34**
WER (%)	Val.	12.40	**12.17**
	Test	12.60	**11.23**

Furthermore, our comparative study has been performed against other state-of-the-art methods, for both the standard IAM and RIMES datasets. As shown in Table 5, the proposed method compares favourably with the other state-of-the-art methods, with a superior achievement in the case of RIMES dataset.

Table 5. Text recognition performance of the proposed CRNN-FCNN architecture against state-of-the-art for IAM and RIMES datasets

Methods	CER	WER
(a) IAM		
Chen et al. [1]	11.15	34.55
Dutta et al. [2]	**5.70**	**17.82**
Krishnan et al. [6]	9.87	32.89
Pham et al. [10]	10.80	35.10
Puigcerver [11]	6.49	20.91
Proposed method	6.14	20.04
(b) RIMES		
Chen et al. [1]	8.29	30.54
Dutta et al. [2]	5.07	14.70
Pham et al. [10]	6.80	28.50
Puigcerver [11]	3.76	12.60
Proposed method	**3.34**	**11.23**

4.3   Error Analysis in the 'EPARCHOS' Dataset

During evaluation with the 'EPARCHOS' dataset, several error types have been observed which motivated us to proceed in a detailed error analysis which shows that these errors are directly related to the particularities of the dataset that have been discussed in Sect. 4.1.

Merged / Splitted Words. This type of error concerns a potential confusion about the spaces between words. In the example given in Fig. 8(a)-(b), there are words that are shown as being erroneously merged or splitted, respectively, based on the degree of closeness between each other.

Confusion with the Intonation in the Polytonic System. This error is caused due to the complicated intonation system that dominates in the EPAR-CHOS dataset which results in confusing intonations. An erroneous resulting intonation is shown in (Fig. 9).

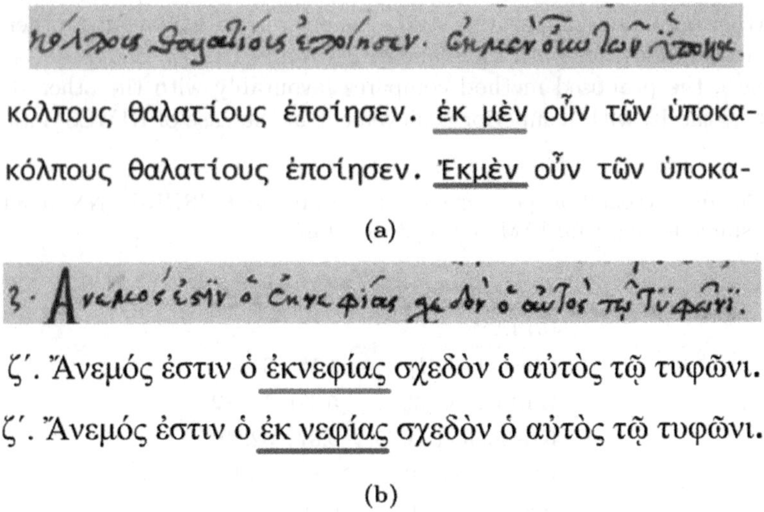

κόλπους θαλατίους ἐποίησεν. ἐκ μὲν οὖν τῶν ὑποκα-

κόλπους θαλατίους ἐποίησεν. Ἐκμὲν οὖν τῶν ὑποκα-

(a)

ζ'. Ἄνεμός ἐστιν ὁ ἐκνεφίας σχεδὸν ὁ αὐτὸς τῷ τυφῶνι.

ζ'. Ἄνεμός ἐστιν ὁ ἐκ νεφίας σχεδὸν ὁ αὐτὸς τῷ τυφῶνι.

(b)

Fig. 8. Error with (a) merged and (b) splitted words

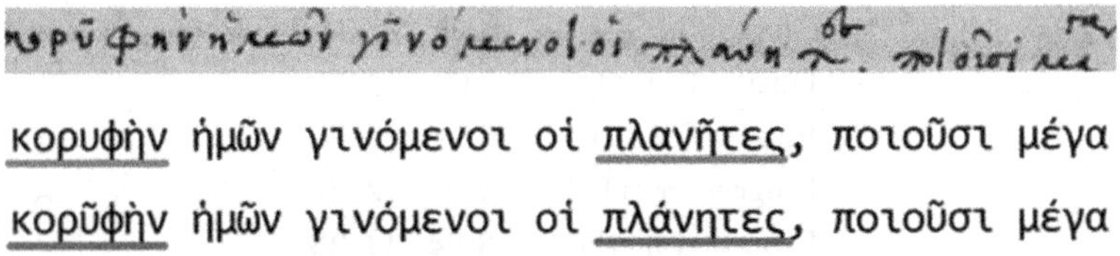

κορυφὴν ἡμῶν γινόμενοι οἱ πλανῆτες, ποιοῦσι μέγα

κορῦφὴν ἡμῶν γινόμενοι οἱ πλάνητες, ποιοῦσι μέγα

Fig. 9. Intonation error at the polytonic system

Incorrect Character Recognition of Capital Letters After Full Stops.
This error is linked to the particularity of the "EPARCHOS" dataset, that relates
to the "Minuscule" writing of that era, where lower-case letters are used after a
'full stop' (Fig. 10).

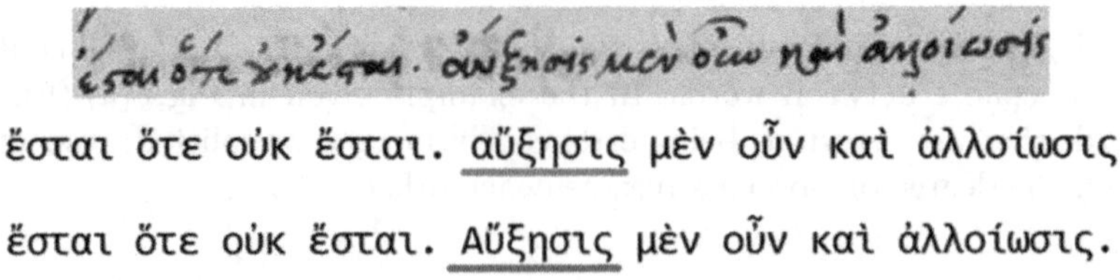

ἔσται ὅτε οὐκ ἔσται. αὔξησις μὲν οὖν καὶ ἀλλοίωσις

ἔσται ὅτε οὐκ ἔσται. Αὔξησις μὲν οὖν καὶ ἀλλοίωσις.

Fig. 10. Incorrect character recognition of capital letters after full stops

5 Conclusions

The proposed Convolutional Recurrent Neural Network architecture for offline handwriting recognition, namely CRNN-FCNN, has proven to deal effectively with Handwritten Text Recognition with a particular emphasis on historical Greek manuscripts. This has been drawn after a consistent evaluation methodology, which took into account an ablation study that was performed for three datasets and among the state-of-the-art methods. Last but not least, it is worth mentioning the use of a newly created dataset for historical Greek manuscripts, which has been made publicly available for research purposes.

Acknowledgement. This research has been co-financed by the European Union and Greek national funds through the Operational Program Competitiveness, Entrepreneurship and Innovation, under the call RESEARCH-CREATE-INNOVATE (project code: T1EDK-01939). We would also like to thank NVIDIA Corporation, which kindly donated the Titan X GPU, that has been used for this research.

References

1. Chen, Z., Wu, Y., Yin, F., Liu, C.: Simultaneous script identification and handwriting recognition via multi-task learning of recurrent neural networks. In: 14th IAPR International Conference on Document Analysis and Recognition, ICDAR 2017, Kyoto, Japan, 9–15 November 2017, pp. 525–530. IEEE (2017)
2. Dutta, K., Krishnan, P., Mathew, M., Jawahar, C.V.: Improving CNN-RNN hybrid networks for handwriting recognition. In: 16th International Conference on Frontiers in Handwriting Recognition, ICFHR 2018, Niagara Falls, NY, USA, 5–8 August 2018, pp. 80–85. IEEE Computer Society (2018)
3. Graves, A., Fernández, S., Gomez, F.J., Schmidhuber, J.: Connectionist temporal classification: labelling unsegmented sequence data with recurrent neural networks. In: Cohen, W.W., Moore, A.W. (eds.) Machine Learning, Proceedings of the Twenty-Third International Conference (ICML 2006), Pittsburgh, Pennsylvania, USA, 25–29 June 2006. ACM International Conference Proceeding Series, vol. 148, pp. 369–376. ACM (2006)
4. Grosicki, E., Carré, M., Brodin, J., Geoffrois, E.: Results of the RIMES evaluation campaign for handwritten mail processing. In: 10th International Conference on Document Analysis and Recognition, ICDAR 2009, Barcelona, Spain, 26–29 July 2009, pp. 941–945. IEEE Computer Society (2009)
5. Ingle, R.R., Fujii, Y., Deselaers, T., Baccash, J., Popat, A.C.: A scalable handwritten text recognition system. In: 2019 International Conference on Document Analysis and Recognition, ICDAR 2019, Sydney, Australia, 20–25 September 2019, pp. 17–24. IEEE (2019)
6. Krishnan, P., Dutta, K., Jawahar, C.V.: Word spotting and recognition using deep embedding. In: 13th IAPR International Workshop on Document Analysis Systems, DAS 2018, Vienna, Austria, 24–27 April 2018, pp. 1–6. IEEE Computer Society (2018)
7. Maas, A.L., Hannun, A.Y., Ng, A.Y.: Rectifier nonlinearities improve neural network acoustic models. In: Proceedings of ICML, vol. 30, p. 3 (2013)
8. Marti, U., Bunke, H.: The iam-database: an english sentence database for offline handwriting recognition. IJDAR **5**(1), 39–46 (2002)

9. Papazoglou, A., Pratikakis, I., Markou, K., Tsochatzidis, L.: Eparchos - historical Greek handwritten document dataset (version 1.0) [data set] (2020). https://doi.org/10.5281/zenodo.4095301

10. Pham, V., Bluche, T., Kermorvant, C., Louradour, J.: Dropout improves recurrent neural networks for handwriting recognition. In: 14th International Conference on Frontiers in Handwriting Recognition, ICFHR 2014, Crete, Greece, 1–4 September 2014, pp. 285–290. IEEE Computer Society (2014)

11. Puigcerver, J.: Are multidimensional recurrent layers really necessary for handwritten text recognition? In: 14th IAPR International Conference on Document Analysis and Recognition, ICDAR 2017, Kyoto, Japan, 9–15 November 2017, pp. 67–72. IEEE (2017)

12. Puigcerver, J.: PyLaia Toolkit (2017). https://github.com/jpuigcerver/PyLaia. Accessed 7 Apr 2020

13. Ruder, S.: An overview of gradient descent optimization algorithms. CoRR abs/1609.04747 (2016)

14. Sainath, T.N., Vinyals, O., Senior, A.W., Sak, H.: Convolutional, long short-term memory, fully connected deep neural networks. In: 2015 IEEE International Conference on Acoustics, Speech and Signal Processing, ICASSP 2015, South Brisbane, Queensland, Australia, 19–24 April 2015. pp. 4580–4584. IEEE (2015)

15. Shi, B., Bai, X., Yao, C.: An end-to-end trainable neural network for image-based sequence recognition and its application to scene text recognition. IEEE Trans. Pattern Anal. Mach. Intell. 39(11), 2298–2304 (2017)

16. Voigtlaender, P., Doetsch, P., Ney, H.: Handwriting recognition with large multidimensional long short-term memory recurrent neural networks. In: 15th International Conference on Frontiers in Handwriting Recognition, ICFHR 2016, Shenzhen, China, 23–26 October 2016, pp. 228–233. IEEE Computer Society (2016)

17. Yu, Y., Si, X., Hu, C., Zhang, J.: A review of recurrent neural networks: LSTM cells and network architectures. Neural Comput. 31(7), 1235–1270 (2019)

MCCNet: Multi-Color Cascade Network with Weight Transfer for Single Image Depth Prediction on Outdoor Relief Images

Aufaclav Zatu Kusuma Frisky[1,2]([✉]) [iD], Andi Putranto[3],
Sebastian Zambanini[1] [iD], and Robert Sablatnig[1] [iD]

[1] Computer Vision Lab, Institute of Visual Computing and Human-Centered Technology, Faculty of Informatics, TU Wien, Vienna, Austria
aufaclav@cvl.tuwien.ac.at
[2] Department of Computer Science and Electronics, Faculty of Mathematics and Natural Sciences, Universitas Gadjah Mada, Yogyakarta, Indonesia
[3] Department of Archaeology, Faculty of Cultural Science, Universitas Gadjah Mada, Yogyakarta, Indonesia

Abstract. Single image depth prediction is considerably difficult since depth cannot be estimated from pixel correspondences. Thus, prior knowledge, such as registered pixel and depth information from the user is required. Another problem rises when targeting a specific domain requirement as the number of freely available training datasets is limited. Due to color problem in relief images, we present a new outdoor Registered Relief Depth (RRD) Prambanan dataset, consisting of outdoor images of Prambanan temple relief with registered depth information supervised by archaeologists and computer scientists. In order to solve the problem, we also propose a new depth predictor, called Multi-Color Cascade Network (MCCNet), with weight transfer. Applied on the new RRD Prambanan dataset, our method performs better in different materials than the baseline with 2.53 mm RMSE. In the NYU Depth V2 dataset, our method's performance is better than the baselines and in line with other state-of-the-art works.

Keywords: Multi-color · Cascade · Single image · Depth prediction · Cultural heritage · Relief · Weight transfer

1 Introduction

Cultural heritage preservation gets more attention, along with awareness of the need to maintain outdoor artifacts. The most used preservation action is a documentation of the current state of the object of interest for future use. Furthermore, an accurate representation of objects, in any size and shape, becomes a primary scientific interest for as long as the specialists feel the need for studying

© Springer Nature Switzerland AG 2021
A. Del Bimbo et al. (Eds.): ICPR 2020 Workshops, LNCS 12667, pp. 263–278, 2021.
https://doi.org/10.1007/978-3-030-68787-8_19

without harming those objects. These days, 3D scanners are prevalently used for digital archiving of cultural heritage artifacts [12]. However, 3D scanning of scenes and multiple objects is time-consuming and depends on the scanner performance. The use of these scanners is subject to high maintenance setup when used outdoor. This situation is exacerbated by the absence of electricity sources and objects at locations that are difficult to reach. Coupled with the high cost of scanning equipment, archaeologists aim for other alternative scanning devices.

If the object of interest has a distinctive surface, photogrammetric techniques are favored [26]. As we see in Fig. 1(a), reliefs also have a fairly unique surface. The quality of the models depends on the number, resolution, and the coverage of the captured images. Because of that, images from every perspective of the object need to be captured to obtain a perfect shape, which will be difficult for a bigger artifact or unreachable perspective [26]. There are a huge number of reliefs available in the Javanese wall temple, such as 2672 reliefs at Borobudur temples and more than 200 reliefs at Prambanan temples [35]. As photogrammetry requires multiple images to obtain 3D models, this method is not cost-effective for use in massive 3D reconstruction.

The 3D models reconstruction of one-side artifacts such as reliefs and other wall artifacts is 2.5D which does not require the backside of the object. This becomes the basis of our approach using a Single Image Reconstruction (SIR) method to be able to reconstruct the artifact from a single perspective. Recently, the SIR method has been introduced to produce depth maps from a single image [13]. From a practical viewpoint, SIR is beneficial compared to 3d scanning devices and Structure-from-Motion techniques, as 3D models can be obtained with minimal acquisition time. From these methods, it can be seen that estimating the depth, so-called Single Image Depth Prediction (SIDP), is one of the key steps to perform reconstruction using a single image. In 2014, Eigen et al. [8] use multi-depth networks, a coarse and fine architecture and concatenation step to get the final depth. The concatenation process used in their work has been proven to merge the extracted features. Because of the effectiveness of their works, Pan et al. [29] adopt their approach to reconstruct the relief of Borobudur temple. However, grayscale frontal view images are used as input which does not represent the color of the object. In the Prambanan temple, some of the reliefs have different materials and colors in one panel.

In Fig. 1(b), we can see the result of applying a pre-trained model from [14] to one of the Prambanan reliefs. Their method performs self-supervised depth estimation by training a network to predict the appearance of a target image from the viewpoint of another image. It can be seen that it fails to reconstruct the depth, which shows that features computed by a pre-trained CNN cannot be reused in these new problem domains. However, the only publicly available relief dataset only consists of one 3D model from photogrammetry or a low-cost scanner [39], and registered images with depth information are not provided. The color change from the environment can also not be ignored, since it can change the surface appearance in the image, especially for reliefs [32]. In order to help archaeologists in relief digitalization, this problem needs a solution which is time efficient and robust to color differences [10].

(a)   (b)   (c)

Fig. 1. (a) Example data from RRD Prambanan dataset. (b) Depth prediction using pretrained model [14] using (a) as test data. (c) Proposed method result.

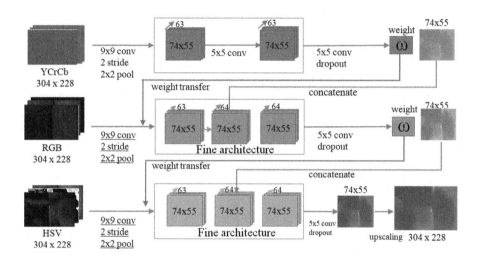

Fig. 2. Proposed Three-level MCCNet with weight transfer.

In another work, Larbi et al. [20] show the potential of multiple color spaces to enrich the information in neural network architectures. In this paper, we use three popular color space types, namely RGB, HSV, and YCbCr. The three types are used because they exhibit different characteristics to represent an image [24]. The RGB (Red, Green, and Blue) color model provides additive color information [24]. In this model, RGB describes how humans perceive color. Another type of color space used in this paper is HSV (Hue, Saturation, Value). HSV is different from RGB because it represents a non-linear transformation of the RGB color space. Therefore in the HSV color space, the color information (Hue and Saturation) is independent of the brightness (Value). The third color used is YCbCr. Unlike HSV, this color is a linear transformation from RGB but has the same construction as HSV. The Y value represents luminance which means it is constructed from the weighted sum of gamma-compressed RGB components, while Cb represents blue-difference and Cr represents red-difference. All these color spaces are represented by a combination of the pixel value in three different spaces. It can be assumed that a neural net utilizes a color space as a completely different input representation. Based on this, we propose a multi-level architecture to exploit the different color space representations to enhance the variance of training data.

Another problem that arises is that there are not enough open benchmark datasets available for training the associated algorithms and procedures, especially for archaeological artifacts. Most of the data available are only a minimal amount of 3D scans, which are then registered manually. Meanwhile, the data requirements for training data using deep learning methods are the main factors for successful prediction. Most existing methods use subsets of ShapeNet [5] for training and testing. Recently, Wiles and Zisserman [36] introduced two new synthetic datasets: Blobby objects and Sculptures. However, these datasets contain only a limited number of 3D samples, which is problematic for training deep networks that are dependent on the number of training data [27].

Finally, the contributions of this paper are three-fold. First, a new outdoor Registered Relief Depth (RRD) Prambanan temple is presented which had been supervised by an archaeologist in charge and adjusted to the need in the fieldwork. Second, a new Multi-Color Cascade Network (MCCNet) architecture for Single Image Depth Prediction inspired by [8] and [7] is proposed (Fig. 2). Third, a weight transfer to reduce the training time process in MCCNet architecture is utilized.

2   Related Work

Recovering the lost dimension from 2D images shares the goal of classic multi-view stereo and 3D reconstruction from a single image, which has been extensively investigated for many decades. The purpose is to regain the depth information using available features contained in 2D images. In particular, 3D reconstruction of 2D images is divided into three forms of input methods, namely: a single image, multiple images and an image sequence [16]. Single image reconstruction is very challenging because of the ambiguities in the 3D reconstruction. When the input is an image sequence, one can exploit the temporal correlation to facilitate the 3D reconstruction while ensuring that the reconstruction is smooth and consistent across all the frames of the video stream. Also, the input can depict one or multiple 3D objects belonging to known or unknown shape categories. It can also include additional information such as silhouettes, segmentation masks, and semantic labels as priors to guide the reconstruction.

The disadvantage of using a single image is that it is hard to determine the association between a point in the image and its depth. If two images are available, then the position of a 3D point can be found using triangulation by determining the intersection of the two projection rays. The key for this process is that the corresponding sets of points must contain some distinctive features which will be used in calibration at the beginning of the process. On the other hand, a single image input is more beneficial in a practical process for archaeologists. Therefore, the focus of this paper is to use a single image reconstruction to perform relief reconstruction.

Historically, single-image 3D reconstruction has been approached via shape-from-shading [31]. In other works, texture [25] and defocus [9] feature is used as a parameter to determine the depth, but these shape from shading methods are only applicable with visible parts of a surface using a single depth cue. At first, Saxena et al. [33] estimated depth from a single image by training an MRF on local and global image features. After that, Oswald et al. [28] improved the performance using interactive user input with the same depth estimation problem. In addition, Karsch et al. [19] presented object-level recognition to learn depth from a database of images and corresponding depth maps.

Most of the recent methods are trained convolutional networks using direct 3D supervision and demonstrated exciting and promising results on various tasks related to computer vision and graphics, for instance, 3D reconstruction [14, 37]. In order to improve the computational and memory efficiency, Hane et al. [17] performed hierarchical partitioning of the output space. Johnston et al. [18] used another approach by reconstructing high-resolution 3D shapes with an inverse discrete cosine transform decoder. In archaeology, the reconstruction of the cultural object using 2D images is used because of the flexibility [3]. Pollefeys et al. [30] present an approach that obtains virtual models. In recent work, Pan et al. [29] reconstruct a Borobudur relief using single image reconstruction based on the multi-depth approach from [7]. However, the data used in their paper does not involve material color changes, which appear in practical conditions. We present a new dataset based on the real conditions of reliefs and aim to solve the problem occurring in the data.

3 Proposed Method

Our main idea is to build a single robust image depth prediction for a real condition dataset. A new approach is developed to obtain depth information from a single image by directly extracting color information from an RGB image. In the following, we present our new RRD Prambanan dataset and describe our new methodology.

3.1 Dataset

The availability of data from the field is one of the obstacles to solve the problems faced in this paper. The limited number of artifacts causes a minimum amount of data available to the public. For example, Zolhofer et al. [39] focused on reconstructing several artifacts of the same color with no variation. Therefore, to be able to solve the problem of color differences that occur on reliefs, we made

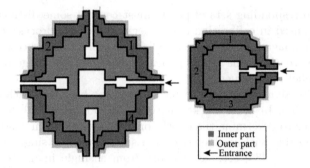

Fig. 3. Prambanan temple sketch from above. left = Shiva temple with four regions, Right = Vishnu and Brahma temple with three regions.

our own dataset which was taken and supervised by archaeologists in charge and tailored to their needs.

Our RRD Prambanan dataset[1] was taken from 41 reliefs scattered from three main temples inside the Prambanan temple location, namely Shiva, Brahma, and Vishnu. The relief images were taken using an Olympus EMD-10 mirrorless camera on a sunny day with a lux of around 10,000 to 20,000. The produced data are RGB relief images with a 3840 × 2160 pixel resolution (4k). For ground truth depth, the reliefs were scanned using an ASUS XTION scanner. After that, we manually selected 30 point pairs in both RGB and depth images and registered them using an projective transformation model. The data retrieval process and supervision are done by the Department of Archaeology, Universitas Gadjah Mada, and consisted of ten experts and five practitioners from Prambanan Center for Conservation of Culture (BPCB).

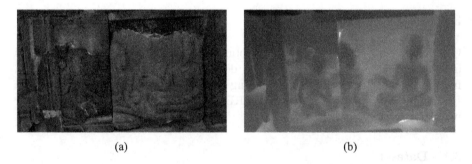

(a)   (b)

Fig. 4. (a) Image from RRD Prambanan Dataset (Brahma 4), (b) its registered depth.

---

[1] The dataset can be obtained by sending an email to aufaclav@ugm.ac.id or aufaclav@cvl.tuwien.ac.at.

The sketch of the temple area separation of Shiva, Brahma and Vishnu temple is depicted in Fig. 3. Each registered pair has additional location information provided. Finally, 41 RGB images of 3840×2160 pixel resolution registered with their depth have been generated for the RRD Prambanan dataset. For example, in Fig. 4(a), Brahma image 4 has the registered depth shown in Fig. 4(b) with additional information: Inner 1 bottom. It means that Brahma image number 4 is located in the inner part of the Brahma temple in region one bottom area (based on Fig. 3 sketches). Figure 5 depicts the different materials of the relief in the RRD Prambanan Dataset.

Fig. 5. Examples of different materials appearing in the RRD Prambanan Dataset. Left: cement material, middle: white candi stone, and right: black candi stone.

In order to estimate the accuracy of the registration process, we conducted a verification experiment using one pair of images (RGB and depth) from the dataset and additional RGB images. Hence, we have three images: two RGB images from different viewpoints, i_{m1} and i_{m2}, and one depth image d from the same relief. Then, we create a three-way transformation to get the final projective transformation matrix. First, we register d with i_{m1} to get transformation matrices T_1, then register i_{m1} to i_{m2} for T_2, and register i_{m2} to d for T_3. Finally we obtain the final projective transformation matrix $T_I = T_3 \cdot T_2 \cdot T_1$. After that, we apply this projective transformation matrix to d, obtain $\hat{d}$, and find the differences between them using RMSE. This way, we are able to estimate the systematic error of our registration process. Based on our experiment, we obtain a RMSE of 0.785 mm, which shows that our registration process has a relatively small error and is reliable to be used as ground-truth.

3.2 Multi-Color Cascade Network with Weight Transfer

Obtaining in-depth shape prediction is an essential way to solve depth prediction [38]. The work of Eigen et al. [7,8] and Pan et al. [29] use multi-depth levels. The concatenation process in their work has proven to increase accuracy; however, each step consumes a huge amount of time in the training phase. This problem inspires us to use this mechanism to merge the color spaces information as input and reduce the training time process. On the first level, the weights initialization starts with random numbers and we then train them using inputs from the first level. Instead of random initialization, the next level weights are using the previous level weights as an initial weight (weight transfer). Each level has its own training process and does not backpropagate using previous data. All inputs, function maps and output sizes are also shown in Fig. 2: one level network contains three feature extraction layers of convolution and max-pooling, followed by fully connected layers, except for the very first network, which contains only two feature extraction layers. The final output is at 1/4 resolution relative to the input from the original dataset. We perform linear upsampling at the end of the process to retrieve the original resolution. All hidden layers use rectified linear units for activation, and we use 0.01 learning rate. For the fully connected network, we used two fully connected layers with 4096 - 4096 - 1000 output units each, with dropout applied to the two hidden layers.

We aim to provide the properties of different color spaces in an explicit manner and conduct an approach by assuming that each of these color space types represents a different perspective. Generally, there exist three types of color spaces, namely color-based color space (RGB, normalized RGB), Hue-based color space (HSI, HSV, and HSL), and luminance-based color space (YCrCb, YIQ, and YUV) [15]. In order to limit the variation, we only use three popular color spaces from each cluster as a representative, which are RGB, HSV and YCrCb. We focus on creating and improving the new architecture instead of trying more different color spaces to improve accuracy and robustness. Features from each color space are extracted using a fine architecture layer and processed sequentially (see Fig. 2). For the training loss, we use the scale-invariant mean squared error:

$$D(y, y^*) = \frac{1}{n} \sum_{i=1}^{n} (log(y_i - y_i^* + \alpha(y, y^*)))^2 \qquad (1)$$

where y^* is the ground truth depth, y is the predicted depth, n is the number of pixels, and $\alpha(y, y^*) = \frac{1}{n} \sum_i log(y_i - y_i^*)$ is the value to minimize given (y, y^*).

4   Experiments and Results

First, we evaluate the optimal version that gives the best results within several steps of the experiment. After that, we compare our method with the state-of-the-art by applying it to the NYU Depth V2 dataset using official splits. This experiment aims to test the performance of methods that have been made using open dataset standards.

4.1   Optimal Network Architecture and Comparison on Prambanan RRD Dataset

First, we identify an architecture that can provide optimal results. In this phase, we use the Prambanan RRD dataset so that the results obtained can be directly applied without any further changes. In this experiment, there are three main steps that need to be checked: color space effect, the number of stack levels, and color space orders (see Fig. 6). In order to check the impact of different color spaces, we use a one stack level to check the effect between color space inputs in our architecture. We selected the three color spaces and applied them to the one stack level MCCNet. From Table 1, it can be seen that the results of the three color spaces are very similar even though the values of each channel are different. This proves that the architecture used can recognize object shapes and features of the image, although using different color spaces. At this step, 100 epochs are used.

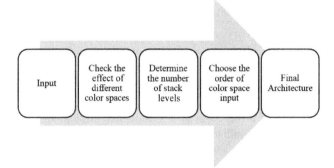

Fig. 6. Flow diagram for obtaining optimal architecture

Fig. 7. Results of the proposed method on the RRD Prambanan datasets. First row is RGB images, second is ground truth, and third is our results.

In our method, all hidden layers use rectified linear units as an activation function. After the fine architecture layer in each level, dropout is applied. In RRD Prambanan dataset, the 4k image is sliced into 304×228 tiles as input. Each image produces 108 non-overlapping slices which are augmented using AutoAugment [6] and Generative Adversarial Network [2]. From 41 relief images available from the dataset, we use 10 images for the test data, 21 images for the training purpose and the rest as the validation set.

Table 1. Results of color space evaluation for one level MCCNet applied to the RRD Prambanan Dataset. Note: RMSE = RMSE Linear in mm, Time = training time.

No.	Color space	RMSE	Time (hh:mm)
1	RGB	5.25	03:02
2	YCrCb	5.14	03:02
3	HSV	4.89	03:02

Second, a number of levels from one to four, are implemented. In this phase, we tried to find the most efficient number of levels. In Table 2, it can be seen that the result of three stack levels gives the best performance, and it converges after 410 epochs. The four-level architecture has a slightly higher error with a longer training time than three-level. Hence, the three-level architecture is used as our main method.

Table 2. Results of different levels of MCCNet applied to the RRD Prambanan Dataset. Note: RMSE = RMSE Linear in mm, Time = training time.

No.	Method	RMSE	Time (hh:mm)
1	1 level RGB	5.25	03:02
2	2 Level RGB	4.36	07:02
3	**3 Level RGB**	**3.26**	**15:02**
4	4 Level RGB	3.47	20:36
5	5 Level RGB	3.53	26:53
6	6 Level RGB	3.38	34:27

The third step aims to find the optimal color space input order and compare it with the baseline. It is found that the YCbCr-RGB-HSV combination produced the best results among all combinations. In this step, we applied the weight transfer mechanism to cut the training data. Basically, the weight transfer mechanism allows the system to transfer weights in each level. Compared to Table 2, the results in Table 3 using the three-level-architecture with weight transfer gives shorter training times. By adding this weight transfer mechanism, the results in Table 3 converge at 234 epochs. As a result, in Fig. 7, we can see the performance of our method in RRD Prambanan dataset. From these results, it can be seen that our method can infer the depth although there are slight color differences due to relief material and shadows contained in the image.

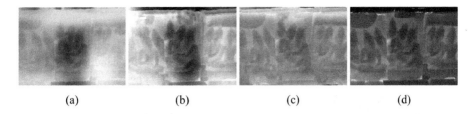

(a)   (b)   (c)   (d)

Fig. 8. Results using RRD Prambanan Dataset. (a) [8] (b) [7] (c) Proposed method
(d) Groundtruth.

For more details, Fig. 8, using Fig. 1 (a) as an input image, shows that our
approach can solve the material difference problem appearing in real conditions.
In addition, we also created three kinds of patches based on the material (Fig. 5).
Each material contains 30 patches. This experiment aims to find out more about
performance details that occur on specific different materials. Then, we calculate
the average RMSE on all these patches in Table 4. It can be concluded from the
results shown that different materials can cause depth problem because of the
color differences. The results also proved that our method provides a more coherent depth estimation in case of material and color changes than the baselines
methods.

Table 3. Results of MCCNet algorithm in RRD Prambanan Dataset compared with
other methods. Note: RMSE = RMSE Linear in mm, * = baseline, WT = weight
transfer, Time = training time.

No.	Method	RMSE	Time (hh:mm)
1	Eigen et al. [8]*	5.25	15:12
2	Eigen and Fergus [7]*	3.32	15:31
3	Godard et al. [14]*	2.93	25:18
4	YCrCb-HSV-RGB + WT	3.16	07:26
5	RGB-YCrCb-HSV + WT	2.84	07:15
6	**YCrCb-RGB-HSV + WT**	**2.53**	**07:19**

4.2   Comparison on NYU Depth V2 Dataset

In the second part, to examine the architecture performance using an open
dataset, we apply our MCCNet method to the NYU Depth V2 [34] dataset.
We use the official training data and augment it to 50.000 images (can be found
in [1]) and then test it using the 654 official test images. The input is cropped
into 304 × 228 tiles and transformed to the three different color spaces. In this
part, three-level MCCNet with YCrCb-RGB-HSV configuration is used.

Table 4. Average RMSE of 30 patches from three different materials.

Method	Cement	White candi stone	Black candi stone
Eigen et al. [8]	8.12	6.43	4.02
Eigen and Fergus [7]	5.74	4.36	3.25
Godard et al. [14]	4.23	3.34	2.73
Ours	**2.78**	**2.64**	**2.05**

Table 5. Results of the proposed method on NYU Depth V2 compared with other state-of-the-art methods.

	Higher better			Lower better		
	$\delta < 1.25$	$\delta < 1.25^2$	$\delta < 1.25^3$	RMSE linear	RMSE log	RMSE log inv.
Eigen et al. [8]	61.60%	88.90%	97.10%	0.874	0.284	0.219
Liu et al. [23]	66.20%	91.30%	97.90%	0.756	0.261	0.214
Eigen and Fergus [7]	77.10%	95.00%	98.80%	0.639	0.215	0.171
Cakrabarti et al. [4]	80.60%	95.80%	98.70%	0.620	0.205	0.166
Proposed	**79.40%**	**95.50%**	**99.10%**	**0.598**	**0.202**	**0.165**
Lee et al. [21]	81.50%	96.30%	99.10%	0.572	0.193	0.156
Fu et al. [11]	85.60%	96.10%	98.60%	0.547	0.188	0.158
Lee and Kim [22]	83.70%	97.10%	99.40%	0.538	0.180	0.148

Fig. 9. Results of proposed method on the NYU Depth V2 dataset. First row shows RGB images, second the ground truth, and third our results.

In Table 5, our results are compared to other state-of-the-art methods. This table also shows that our method outperforms other baseline methods in the public dataset, in this case, NYU Depth V2 dataset. Our proposed network also obtain a small difference error with Lee and Kim [22] works with 0.30% gap in $\delta < 1.25^3$ and also a narrow difference in three RMSE measurements. To see more detailed results, we present the performance results of our algorithm applied to NYU Depth V2 datasets in Fig. 9. The NYU Depth V2 dataset has a different color property than the RRD Prambanan dataset. In the RRD Prambanan dataset, the types of colors displayed on the material differences are similar. That is why it becomes a challenge to be able to detect the same depth with different material colors. However, the NYU Depth V2 dataset presents a different color data property. In the NYU Depth V2 dataset, the majority of objects contained in the image have quite significant different colors than the other objects in the same image, for example, the colors of the table are different from the walls of the room. Another challenge present in the dataset is that the RAW depth images have a lot of noise. However, it can be seen in Fig. 9 that our dataset can solve these problems. For this experiment, we use several error measurement methods, such as linear RMSE (2), RMSE log (3), threshold (4) and RMSE log invariant (1).

$$\text{RMSE Linear} = \sqrt{\frac{1}{|n|} \sum_{ys \in T} ||y_i - y_i^*||^2} \tag{2}$$

$$\text{RMSE log.} = \sqrt{\frac{1}{|n|} \sum_{ys \in T} ||log\ y_i - log\ y_i^*||^2} \tag{3}$$

$$\%\ of\ y_1\ s.t.\ max(\frac{y_i}{y_i^*}, \frac{y_i^*}{y_i}) = \delta < thr \tag{4}$$

5   Conclusion

In outdoor reliefs or artifacts, there are color differences caused by differences in material and changes in conditions caused by the environment. Due to the limited open-source data for real condition reliefs with these challenges, a new RRD Prambanan dataset that represents artifacts in the field has been presented. Making this dataset is also supervised by an archaeologist so that the results are in accordance with the needs in the field. To solve this, a new MCCNet with weight transfer architecture has been proposed. Our work can be used to solve color difference problems that occur in real condition applications and obtain a better results than the baseline.

To obtain the optimal architecture, we check several parameters such as differences in color space using one level MCCNet, checking the number of levels, and checking the order of each level. To check performance using common benchmark standards, we use the NYU Depth V2 Dataset with official splits. Our method shows competitive results with other state-of-the-art approaches on the NYU Depth V2 Dataset. Because the depth and color information are not directly related, for future research, we aim to investigate an approach to separate the color and depth information based on the surface information and process them separately.

Acknowledgment. This work is funded by a collaboration scheme between the Ministry of Research and Technology of the Republic of Indonesia and OeAD-GmbH within the Indonesian-Austrian Scholarship Program (IASP). This work is also supported by the Ministry of Education and Culture of the Republic of Indonesia and the Institute for Preservation of Cultural Heritage (BPCB) D.I. Yogyakarta by their permission to take the relief dataset.

References

1. Alhashim, I., Wonka, P.: High quality monocular depth estimation via transfer learning. arXiv e-prints arXiv:1812.11941, December 2018
2. Antoniou, A., Storkey, A., Edwards, H.: Augmenting image classifiers using data augmentation generative adversarial networks. In: 27th International Conference on Artificial Neural Networks, pp. 594–603, October 2018. https://doi.org/10.1007/978-3-030-01424-758
3. Bernardes, P., Magalhães, F., Ribeiro, J., Madeira, J., Martins, M.: Image-based 3D modelling in archaeology: application and evaluation. In: 22nd International Conference in Central Europe on Computer Graphics, Visualization and Computer Vision, June 2014
4. Chakrabarti, A., Shao, J., Shakhnarovich, G.: Depth from a single image by harmonizing overcomplete local network predictions. In: Advances in Neural Information Processing Systems 29, pp. 2658–2666. Curran Associates, Inc. (2016)
5. Chang, A.X., et al.: ShapeNet: an information-rich 3D model repository. CoRR abs/1512.03012 (2015)
6. Cubuk, E.D., Zoph, B., Mané, D., Vasudevan, V., Le, Q.V.: Autoaugment: learning augmentation policies from data. arXiv e-prints, abs/1805.09501. arXiv:1805.09501, August 2018
7. Eigen, D., Fergus, R.: Predicting depth, surface normals and semantic labels with a common multi-scale convolutional architecture. In: Proceedings of IEEE International Conference on Computer Vision (ICCV), pp. 2650–2658, December 2015. https://doi.org/10.1109/ICCV.2015.304
8. Eigen, D., Puhrsch, C., Fergus, R.: Depth map prediction from a single image using a multi-scale deep network. In: Advances in Neural Information Processing Systems 27, pp. 2366–2374. Curran Associates, Inc. (2014)
9. Favaro, P., Soatto, S.: A geometric approach to shape from defocus. IEEE Trans. Pattern Anal. Mach. Intell. **27**(3), 406–417 (2005)
10. Frisky, A.Z.K., Fajri, A., Brenner, S., Sablatnig, R.: Acquisition evaluation on outdoor scanning for archaeological artifact digitalization. In: Farinella, G.M., Radeva, P., Braz, J. (eds.) Proceedings of the 15th International Joint Conference on Computer Vision, Imaging and Computer Graphics Theory and Applications, VISIGRAPP 2020, Volume 5: VISAPP, Valletta, Malta, 27–29 February 2020, pp. 792–799. SCITEPRESS (2020). https://doi.org/10.5220/0008964907920799

11. Fu, H., Gong, M., Wang, C., Batmanghelich, K., Tao, D.: Deep ordinal regression network for monocular depth estimation. In: Proceedings of the IEEE Computer Society Conference on Computer Vision and Pattern Recognition (CVPR), vol. 2018, pp. 2002–2011, June 2018. https://doi.org/10.1109/CVPR.2018.00214

12. Georgopoulos, A., Ioannidis, C., Valanis, A.: Assessing the performance of a structured light scanner. Int. Arch. Photogram. Remote Sens. Spatial Inf. Sci. **XXXVIII**, 250–255 (2010)

13. Georgopoulos, A., Stathopoulou, E.K.: Data acquisition for 3D geometric recording: state of the art and recent innovations. In: Vincent, M.L., López-Menchero Bendicho, V.M., Ioannides, M., Levy, T.E. (eds.) Heritage and Archaeology in the Digital Age. QMHSS, pp. 1–26. Springer, Cham (2017). https://doi.org/10.1007/978-3-319-65370-9_1

14. Godard, C., Mac Aodha, O., Firman, M., Brostow, G.J.: Digging into self-supervised monocular depth prediction. In: The International Conference on Computer Vision (ICCV), pp. 3828–3838, October 2019

15. Gowda, S.N., Yuan, C.: ColorNet: investigating the importance of color spaces for image classification. In: Jawahar, C.V., Li, H., Mori, G., Schindler, K. (eds.) ACCV 2018. LNCS, vol. 11364, pp. 581–596. Springer, Cham (2019). https://doi.org/10.1007/978-3-030-20870-7_36

16. Han, X., Laga, H., Bennamoun, M.: Image-based 3D object reconstruction: state-of-the-art and trends in the deep learning era. IEEE Trans. Pattern Anal. Mach. Intell. 1–27 (2019)

17. Hane, C., Tulsiani, S., Malik, J.: Hierarchical surface prediction for 3D object reconstruction. In: 2017 International Conference on 3D Vision (3DV), pp. 412–420 (2017)

18. Johnston, A., Garg, R., Carneiro, G., Reid, I., van den Hengel, A.: Scaling CNNs for high resolution volumetric reconstruction from a single image. In: 2017 IEEE International Conference on Computer Vision Workshops (ICCVW), pp. 930–939 (2017)

19. Karsch, K., Liu, C., Kang, S.B.: Depth transfer: depth extraction from video using non-parametric sampling. IEEE Trans. Pattern Anal. Mach. Intell. **36**(11), 2144–2158 (2014)

20. Larbi, K., Ouarda, W., Drira, H., Ben Amor, B., Ben Amar, C.: DeepColorfASD: face anti spoofing solution using a multi channeled color spaces CNN. In: 2018 IEEE International Conference on Systems, Man, and Cybernetics (SMC), pp. 4011–4016, October 2018. https://doi.org/10.1109/SMC.2018.00680

21. Lee, J., Heo, M., Kim, K., Kim, C.: Single-image depth estimation based on Fourier domain analysis. In: 2018 IEEE/CVF Conference on Computer Vision and Pattern Recognition, pp. 330–339, June 2018. https://doi.org/10.1109/CVPR.2018.00042

22. Lee, J.H., Kim, C.S.: Monocular depth estimation using relative depth maps. In: The IEEE Conference on Computer Vision and Pattern Recognition (CVPR), pp. 9729–9738, June 2019

23. Liu, F., Shen, C., Lin, G.: Deep convolutional neural fields for depth estimation from a single image. In: 2015 IEEE Conference on Computer Vision and Pattern Recognition (CVPR), pp. 5162–5170, June 2015. https://doi.org/10.1109/CVPR.2015.7299152

24. Loesdau, M., Chabrier, S., Gabillon, A.: Hue and saturation in the RGB color space. In: Elmoataz, A., Lezoray, O., Nouboud, F., Mammass, D. (eds.) ICISP 2014. LNCS, vol. 8509, pp. 203–212. Springer, Cham (2014). https://doi.org/10.1007/978-3-319-07998-1_23

25. Loh, A.: The recovery of 3-D structure using visual texture patterns. Ph.D. thesis, University of Western Australia (2006)

26. Luhmann, T., Stuart, R., Kyle, S., Boehmn, J.: Close-Range photogrammetry and 3D imaging. De Gruyter, Berlin, Germany (2013)

27. Mikołajczyk, A., Grochowski, M.: Data augmentation for improving deep learning in image classification problem. In: 2018 International Interdisciplinary Ph.D. Workshop (IIPhDW), pp. 117–122 (2018)

28. Oswald, M.R., Töppe, E., Cremers, D.: Fast and globally optimal single view reconstruction of curved objects. In: 2012 IEEE Conference on Computer Vision and Pattern Recognition, pp. 534–541 (2012)

29. Pan, J., et al.: 3D reconstruction and transparent visualization of Indonesian cultural heritage from a single image. In: Eurographics Workshop on Graphics and Cultural Heritage, pp. 207–210. The Eurographics Association (2018). https://doi.org/10.2312/gch.20181363

30. Pollefeys, M., Van Gool, L., Vergauwen, M., Cornelis, K., Verbiest, F., Tops, J.: Image-based 3d acquisition of archaeological heritage and applications. In: Proceedings of the 2001 Conference on Virtual Reality, Archeology, and Cultural Heritage, VAST 01, pp. 255–262, January 2001. https://doi.org/10.1145/584993.585033

31. Zhang, R., Tsai, P.-S., Cryer, J.E., Shah, M.: Shape-from-shading: a survey. IEEE Trans. Pattern Anal. Mach. Intell. **21**(8), 690–706 (1999)

32. Sablier, M., Garrigues, P.: Cultural heritage and its environment: an issue of interest for environmental science and pollution research. Environ. Sci. Pollution Res. **21**(9), 5769–5773 (2014). https://doi.org/10.1007/s11356-013-2458-3

33. Saxena, A., Sun, M., Ng, A.Y.: Make3D: learning 3D scene structure from a single still image. IEEE Trans. Pattern Anal. Mach. Intell. **31**(5), 824–840 (2009). https://doi.org/10.1109/TPAMI.2008.132

34. Silberman, N., Hoiem, D., Kohli, P., Fergus, R.: Indoor segmentation and support inference from RGBD images. In: Fitzgibbon, A., Lazebnik, S., Perona, P., Sato, Y., Schmid, C. (eds.) ECCV 2012. LNCS, vol. 7576, pp. 746–760. Springer, Heidelberg (2012). https://doi.org/10.1007/978-3-642-33715-4_54

35. Snodgrass, A.: The Symbolism of the Stupa, 2nd edn. Cornell University Press (1985). http://www.jstor.org/stable/10.7591/j.ctv1nhnhr

36. Wiles, O., Zisserman, A.: SilNet: single- and multi-view reconstruction by learning from silhouettes. In: British Machine Vision Conference (2017)

37. Wu, S., Rupprecht, C., Vedaldi, A.: Unsupervised learning of probably symmetric deformable 3D objects from images in the wild. In: Proceedings of the IEEE/CVF Conference on Computer Vision and Pattern Recognition (CVPR), pp. 1–10, June 2020

38. Xu, H., Jiang, M.: Depth prediction from a single image based on non-parametric learning in the gradient domain. Optik **181**, 880–890 (2019). https://doi.org/10.1016/j.ijleo.2018.12.061

39. Zollhöfer, M., et al.: Shading-based refinement on volumetric signed distance functions. ACM Trans. Graph. **34**(4), 96:1–96:14 (2015). https://doi.org/10.1145/2766887

Simultaneous Detection of Regular Patterns in Ancient Manuscripts Using GAN-Based Deep Unsupervised Segmentation

Milad Omrani Tamrin$^{(\boxtimes)}$ and Mohamed Cheriet

École de technologie supérieure, 1100 Notre-Dame St W, Montreal, Qc, Canada
milad.omrani-tamrin.2@ens.etsmtl.ca, mohamed.cheriet@etsmtl.ca

Abstract. Document Information Retrieval has attracted researchers' attention when discovering secrets behind ancient manuscripts. To understand such documents, analyzing their layouts and segmenting their relevant features are fundamental tasks. Recent efforts represent unsupervised document segmentation, and its importance in ancient manuscripts has provided a unique opportunity to study the said problem. This paper proposes a novel collaborative deep learning architecture in an unsupervised mode that can generate synthetic data to avoid uncertainties regarding their degradations. Moreover, this approach utilizes the generated distribution to assign labels that are associated with superpixels. The unsupervised trained model is used to segment the page, ornaments, and characters simultaneously. Promising accuracies in the segmentation task were noted. Experiments with data from degraded documents show that the proposed method can synthesize noise-free documents and enhance associations better than the state-of-the-art methods. We also investigate the usage of overall generated samples, and their effectiveness in different unlabelled historical documents tasks.

Keywords: Ancient manuscripts · Degradations · Synthesize data · Unsupervised segmentation · Layout

1 Introduction

Ancient manuscripts play a vital source in cultural heritage as a fundamental role in history and social development. Since historical documents have deteriorated and aged, there are always difficulties in having a high level of acknowledgements rather than current analysis documents. Some ancient manuscripts have been available and copied on the online networks. However, it is quite challenging to find relevant and classified documents for users without having an electronic search-tool. Furthermore, to capture a categorized dataset manually, including different types of historical documents, is costly and would require high consumption of time to process. Such training recognition systems require

© Springer Nature Switzerland AG 2021
A. Del Bimbo et al. (Eds.): ICPR 2020 Workshops, LNCS 12667, pp. 279–291, 2021.
https://doi.org/10.1007/978-3-030-68787-8_20

a large amount of data [5]. Lately, the variety of manuscripts with different qualities has increased, which creates a more complex task. Besides, using heuristic image processing techniques to achieve artificial data is high maintenance [31]. The indexing technique is considered imperative to ensure having an automated search tool for document image classification. In contrast, the current approaches for document categorization depend on feature learning and hand-crafted features [4,6,7,9,16,21]. Recently, feature learning achieved state-of-the-art performance in Convolutional Neural Network (CNN). Despite CNN being recognized as state-of-the-art performance-based, it still found inaccuracy of recording document retrieval and text recognition. Besides, most of the feature learning methods are in supervised learning domains. Using such approaches requires large amount of label data to reach better results [1]. Preparing manually labelled data is time-consuming and needs expertise. Thus unsupervised approaches are good candidates to develop a robust textual information extraction such as page, ornaments, and texts without data annotation. Since having segmented data regarding ancient manuscripts is a binarization task, it is necessary to have sufficient data to train deep learning models without annotations. This task is counted as one of the critical steps seen as a limitation for the researchers in the deep learning domain [31]. Figure 1 demonstrates some samples of ancient manuscripts that have been damaged and eroded due to the passing of time. To handle the variance of such data, we propose to explore further the use of generative adversarial networks (GAN). Following recent work exploring generative

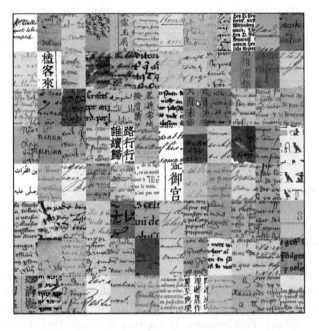

Fig. 1. Random samples of degraded manuscripts [29]

models in research settings with scarce data, [23] GAN shows promise in synthesizing new samples. This paper attempts to produce an artificial dataset using state of the art generative models for the ancient and degraded manuscripts to reconstruct the synthesized historical documents. The contribution of this paper is three-fold:

- We propose a joint augmentation, Deep convolutional GAN, which obtains a new state-of-the-art that increases the accuracy for synthesizing ancient manuscripts.
- We propose an appropriate unsupervised approach that leads to extracting the page, Ornament, and Characters of generated documents' to improve the segmentation performance.
- By a small amount of unlabeled data, we improved and validated the performance of generated data segmentation.

Section 2 review and study the related work. Section 3 pulls up the proposed approach in detail, including the generative framework and its advantages for synthesizing data in an unsupervised manner. The experimental result is presented in Sect. 4, and finally, Sect. 5 concludes the results obtained by the models and discuss their performance concerning our goal. To our knowledge, this work is the first use of Deep Convolutional Generative Adversarial networks (DCGANs) [26], which utilize an unsupervised segmentation model to synthesize the annotations of historical manuscripts.

2   Related Work

GAN is introduced by [15] to generate images that have been used in several problems, but we are briefly summarizing the relevance of our work. Document annotation introduced by [32] is a platform that helps users to annotate an image with labels. The process of annotating is time-consuming and requires some expertise. Later, the document image analysis community created a system that could augment data structure via XML. However, the system must know when asked about the dentition of document pages. Pix2Pix [18] and image to image transformation frameworks are also using source and target to function the mapping.

The idea of unsupervised segmentation was first introduced in W-Net [33] for semantic segmentation. In [12], an unsupervised medical image segmentation based on the local center of mass computation, was proposed. While the method if of interest, achieving those results using deep learning is a worthy challenge. As of late, the [22] generalized a fully convolutional network (FCN) to process the semantic segmentation task. The method was taken from pre-trained networks of a well-known structure called ImageNet [10] to do the downsampling and upsampling. In order to get a better prediction of segmentation, the last layer was combined. The U-Net [27] proposed another segmentation structure presented with a U-shaped architecture. The famous approach also had the

same structure as AutoEncoder. There was also competition in document analysis [11, 25, 30]. However, most of such methods were required to have labelled
data, including pre-training steps. In terms of unsupervised learning, Deep Belief
Networks (DBNs) [17] worked to learn from training distribution to reach the
common features. The model tries to maximize the latent likelihood of variables
during the training process. The problem of such models measures the latent
likelihood variables, which are limited. Additionally, [14] introduced a new approach that utilizes various rotations in the training data to distinguish the correct
labels.

3 Overview of Proposed Method

Our proposed framework is based on unsupervised learning combined with a
Deep Convolutional Generative Adversarial Networks (DCGAN) [26] model. Our
approach follows one of the fundamental elements of feature extraction with
different styles, including pages, ornaments, and characters, to efficiently have
a high volume of data in an unsupervised manner. Albeit, it is shown in Fig. 2
the proposed approach reveals an adversarial process to identify the different
features in reconstructing documents. The step of learning features is used in a
later segmentation step to improve classification performance.

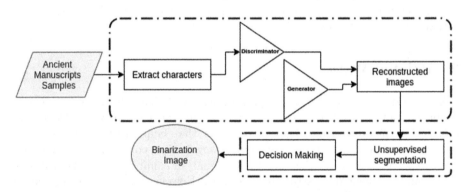

Fig. 2. Historical documents analysis diagram

3.1 Work Methodology

Our idea aims to develop an unsupervised segmentation model for reconstructing ancient manuscripts using DCGAN on different non labelled historical documents. Our effort is to achieve a rich performance of augmentation tasks. Additionally, we propose an unsupervised segmentation method using backpropagation to segment the document layouts. We offer an improved technique to assess
the effects on documents' anomalies. The generator and discriminator play an
adversarial game against each other to generate new samples from unlabeled
data.

The Deep Learning Frameworks. The original architecture of GANs [15] has two components, including Generator G, which tries to fool the second note called Discriminator D. The generator aims to produce fake images using random noises vector z via original images' latent space. Moreover, the Discriminator by assessing the output $D(G(z))$ and generated images $G(z)$ from the latent space of $\mathbf{z} \sim P_{\text{noise}}(\mathbf{z})$ decides whether the output is real image x from $p_{data}(x)$ or is fake from $p(z)$ that represents the distribution of sample z. Follow the Eq. 1 in DCGAN, where the G utilize the transposed technique to apply up-sampling of image size, the convNet tries o find the correlated area of images. The objective of training consists of two processes. In the first step, the discriminator updates parameters by maximizing the expected log-likelihood, and in the second step, while the discriminator parameters are updated, the generator generates fake images.

$$\min_{G} \max_{D} V(G, D) = \mathbb{E}_{\mathbf{x} \sim P_{\text{data}}(\mathbf{x})}[\log(D(\mathbf{x}))] + \mathbb{E}_{\mathbf{z} \sim P_{\text{noise}}(\mathbf{z})}[\log(1 - D(G(\mathbf{z})))]$$
(1)

We consider the information from two figures, where Fig. 3 illustrates the reduction of cost function during the training of 5000 epochs and Fig. 4 depicts the results which shows that the model has improved the quality of generated images. Such an adversarial game continues between these two notes by targeting identifying the generated ones from the original samples. The learning part from the generator is also done during backpropagation steps from the statistical distribution of the training dataset through the discriminator. The $p_g(x)$ also refers to the distribution of vectors from a generator that tries to maximize its loss. Contrary, the discriminator is trying to max the rewards $V(D, G)$ through training operations [8]. In this work, we use a developed version of GANs called DC-GANs. in the next step, we use the output of GANs as the input of segmentation. Besides, the unsupervised segmentation by backpropagation is applied [20]. As shown in the Fig. 5, a reconstructing degraded ancient manuscript's proposed learning architecture is presented.

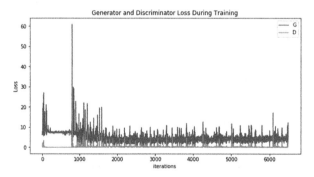

Fig. 3. Generator and Discriminator loss during 5k epochs

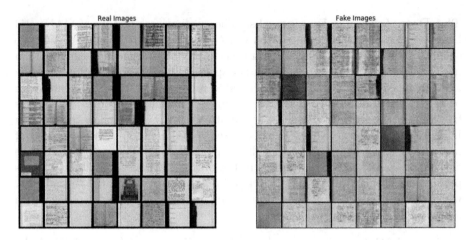

Fig. 4. Real vs fake images using DCGAN

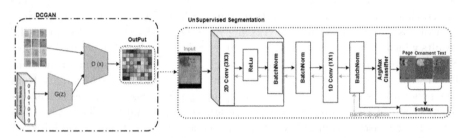

Fig. 5. Proposed Learning architecture

Restriction on Similar Features. The first challenge is to assign the pixels of common features to the same labels. We take the input images in colour, and then each pixel is normalized between [0,1]. The structure to get the feature map from the input image consists of a 2D Conv layers, ReLu activation, and batch normalization function. The method takes the map response by utilizing a linear classifier. $\{y_n = W_c x_n + b\}_{n+1}^{N} = 1$ where $W_c \in \mathbb{R}^{p \times q}$, $b_c \in \mathbb{R}^q$ and q represents the number of classes and p sets for the region's filters. Since the number of segments is unknown, we need to label the remaining clusters. The normalization procedure selects the maximum value in y'_n to achieve the most frequent cluster labels between the group of $\{1, ..., q\}$ clusters. Equation 2 demonstrates the ith cluster in y'_n.

$$C_i = y'_n \in \mathbb{R} | y'_{n,i} \geq y'_{n,j}, \forall j \tag{2}$$

Restraint on Clustering Label. To reach decent quality, we need to extract superpixels C_{max} in each input image. Then we constrain other pixels to their superpixel as a cluster label. The simple linear iterative clustering proposed in [2] is used to get the superpixels. The algorithm benefits from the k-means clustering

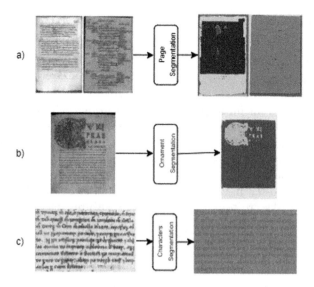

Fig. 6. Samples of generated data and segmented features, a) cBAD dataset b) DIBCO dataset, c) Irish dataset

approach to generate the superpixels. The motivation behind such a technique is that ancient manuscripts' datasets are usually highly imbalanced and contain no labels or masks for segmentation between foreground (page, ornaments, and layout) and background (stain and other natural noises). The aim of using a generating label is to design an automatic mask for documents. The objective is to qualify the capacity of good augmentation masks of the learned networks. In our scarce data setting, the Inception score may be of little use. In Fig. 6, we demonstrated some of the generated masks using our methods. It also reveals the network's dropout that sets out other values from random images of document masks to do the data transformation process. Any 3×3 pixel patch could then exhibit another historical document's characteristics and segment the natural noises of degraded documents.

3.2 Learning Networks

The case of document object detection in ancient manuscripts can be viewed as a binary classification task, where the author [19] would indicate the presence of anomaly within the entire document. Due to the two properties of DCGAN, the reconstructed images are fed into the unsupervised generating segments. While the training is done, the networks transfer the learned features to the unsupervised generation. Our full objective is described in Eq. 3:

$$L(G_x, D_{G(z)}, y'_n) = L_{DC-GAN}(D(x), D(G(z))) + L_{y'}(y'_n, c'_n) \qquad (3)$$

This objective would minimize the G's loss and maximize the $log D(G(z))$. Training is split up into two main parts, where at first, the DC-GAN would update the network weights, and in the second part, the network parameters would predict the superpixels that are considered labels.

4   Experiments

This paper explores an unsupervised feature learning where the model input is the synthesized data from DCGAN. We adopt a standard testing protocol using generated data by DCGAN as our input for the unsupervised segmentation model. Given our approach to the restricted data, we can see a better improvement in various corrupted document images. Since the dataset has not provided the ground-truth, we use Otsu's algorithm to obtain the binary masks. Three different tasks are tested to extract the features, including Page, Ornament, and characters. Three datasets are used to illustrate the performance of the proposed method. Since the *Pytorch* framework is used in our models, we had to fix tensors' dimensions to train our generative model. The below Eq. 4) normalized the height and width of samples where the *mean* is a sequence of means for each channel, and *std* represents the standard deviations for each channel.

$$image = \frac{image - mean}{std} \tag{4}$$

Once the normalization is done, all the train samples are resized. Table 1 demonstrates the comparison of segmentation between original data and simulated data. The results show that True positive, which is the number of correctly segmented pixels as foreground, is higher than the false positive, falsely segmented.

Table 1. Performance for feature extraction in %

Method	TruePositive	FalsePositive	F1-Score
Page Segment	0.44	0.08	0.55
Orn Segment	0.35	0.16	0.47

4.1   Page Segmentation

Historical documents have different boundary regions, which can lead to displeasing results for document image processing approaches. In this experiment, we used the cBAD dataset [11] to apply our model as real samples for DCGAN to generate fake images; later we used the proposed unsupervised segmentation. To apply the page segmentation and predict the relevant page pixels, the binary masks are essential. 600 complete images are used to train for 200 epochs. Such an approach is suitable for uncovering the pages of historical documents where the ground-truths are not provided. Figure 7 demonstrate the result of our approach.

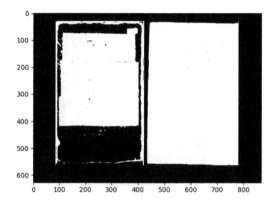

Fig. 7. Sample of generated data and segmented Page

4.2   Ornament Segmentation

Ornaments in historical documents play an essential role in discovering the symbols and signs of our ancestors. Therefore, to have a better understanding of such signs, large quantities of such images are considered to be an essential task. The data used to train our generator is gathered randomly from a different database, including 400 images. The model is trained with 5000 epochs to generate new ornaments. To apply the segmentation step, we trained with 10 epochs; later, we used Otsu to have a binary mask. Figure 8 demonstrates the result of our approach.

4.3   Character Segmentation

Characters are an essential part of manuscripts. They are the meaningful regions of documents. This experiment uses the Irish dataset to generate more images to overcome the lack of abnormal compilations within this domain. We used 149 images to train our DCGAN and generate fake samples. In the next chapter, to segment the characters and their regions, the proposed method proved great results by removing the degradation and separating the foreground from a noisy background. Figure 9 shows promising results with only 15 self-training epochs to achieve the segmented characters. To study the performance of binarization via learned representation and evaluate the proposed method for Character recognition, we use F-Measure (FM), pseudoFMeasure (Fps), PSNR and DRD standard metrics presented in [24]. Following the result in Table 2, we compare the quality of representation to other binarization techniques. Their architecture is based on different hyperparameters, which make the comparison difficult. However, our result is still significant.

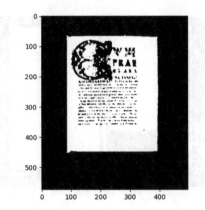

Fig. 8. Sample of generated data and segmented Ornament

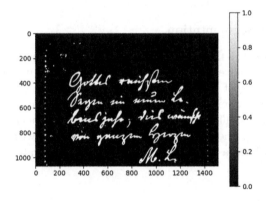

Fig. 9. Sample of generated data and segmented Character

Table 2. Comparison with other binarization technique

Method	FM	Fps	PSNR	DRD
Adak et al. [3]	73.45	75.94	14.62	26.24
Gattal et al. [13]	64.52	68.29	13.57	16.67
Saddami et al. [28]	46.35	51.39	11.79	24.56
Proposed method	**78.16**	**80.25**	**16.31**	**11.35**

5   Conclusion

We presented, in this paper, a novel deep generative segmentation approach to obtain the regular pattern in historical documents. We developed an augmentation method in order to generate synthetic data. The approach has combined two methods, including augmentation, to generate more data and unsupervised segmentation to detect patterns such as page, ornaments, and characters. The experimental results on three different benchmark datasets show that the model's performance is competitive regarding the state-of-the-art. Furthermore, the technique is able to overcome the lack of dataset with generating images and segment the layouts of generated images on three different ancient manuscript datasets. Future work will be devoted to a more detailed study of automatically extracting bounding boxes for our training set in a large quantity of different synthesized document types.

Acknowledgement. The authors thank the NSERC Discovery held by Prof. Cheriet for their financial support. We thank Ms. MG Jones, for assistance and comments that greatly improved the manuscript.

References

1. Abuelwafa, S., Pedersoli, M., Cheriet, M.: Unsupervised exemplar-based learning for improved document image classification. IEEE Access **7**, 133738–133748 (2019)
2. Achanta, R., Shaji, A., Smith, K., Lucchi, A., Fua, P., Süsstrunk, S.: Slic superpixels compared to state-of-the-art superpixel methods. IEEE Trans. Pattern Anal. Mach. Intelli. **34**(11), 2274–2282 (2012)
3. Adak, C., Chaudhuri, B.B., Blumenstein, M.: A study on idiosyncratic handwriting with impact on writer identification. In: 2018 16th International Conference on Frontiers in Handwriting Recognition (ICFHR), pp. 193–198. IEEE (2018)
4. Afzal, M.Z., Kölsch, A., Ahmed, S., Liwicki, M.: Cutting the error by half: investigation of very deep CNN and advanced training strategies for document image classification. In: 2017 14th IAPR International Conference on Document Analysis and Recognition (ICDAR), vol. 1, pp. 883–888. IEEE (2017)
5. Bousmalis, K., Silberman, N., Dohan, D., Erhan, D., Krishnan, D.: Unsupervised pixel-level domain adaptation with generative adversarial networks. In: Proceedings of the IEEE Conference on Computer Vision and Pattern Recognition, pp. 3722–3731 (2017)
6. Bukhari, S.S., Dengel, A.: Visual appearance based document classification methods: Performance evaluation and benchmarking. In: 2015 13th International Conference on Document Analysis and Recognition (ICDAR), pp. 981–985. IEEE (2015)
7. Chen, S., He, Y., Sun, J., Naoi, S.: Structured document classification by matching local salient features. In: Proceedings of the 21st International Conference on Pattern Recognition (ICPR2012), pp. 653–656. IEEE (2012)
8. Chen, X., Duan, Y., Houthooft, R., Schulman, J., Sutskever, I., Abbeel, P.: Infogan: interpretable representation learning by information maximizing generative adversarial nets. In: Advances in Neural Information Processing Systems, pp. 2172–2180 (2016)
9. Das, A., Roy, S., Bhattacharya, U., Parui, S.K.: Document image classification with intra-domain transfer learning and stacked generalization of deep convolutional neural networks. In: 2018 24th International Conference on Pattern Recognition (ICPR), pp. 3180–3185. IEEE (2018)
10. Deng, J., Dong, W., Socher, R., Li, L.J., Li, K., Fei-Fei, L.: Imagenet: a large-scale hierarchical image database. In: 2009 IEEE Conference on Computer Vision and Pattern Recognition, pp. 248–255. IEEE (2009)

11. Diem, M., Kleber, F., Fiel, S., Grüning, T., Gatos, B.: cbad: ICDAR 2017 competition on baseline detection. In: 2017 14th IAPR International Conference on Document Analysis and Recognition (ICDAR), vol. 1, pp. 1355–1360. IEEE (2017)
12. Eaton-Rosen, Z., Bragman, F., Ourselin, S., Cardoso, M.J.: Improving data augmentation for medical image segmentation (2018)
13. Gattal, A., Abbas, F., Laouar, M.R.: Automatic parameter tuning of k-means algorithm for document binarization. In: Proceedings of the 7th International Conference on Software Engineering and New Technologies, pp. 1–4 (2018)
14. Gidaris, S., Singh, P., Komodakis, N.: Unsupervised representation learning by predicting image rotations. arXiv preprint arXiv:1803.07728 (2018)
15. Goodfellow, I., et al.: Generative adversarial nets. In: Advances in Neural Information Processing Systems, pp. 2672–2680 (2014)
16. Harley, A.W., Ufkes, A., Derpanis, K.G.: Evaluation of deep convolutional nets for document image classification and retrieval. In: 2015 13th International Conference on Document Analysis and Recognition (ICDAR), pp. 991–995. IEEE (2015)
17. Hinton, G.E., Osindero, S., Teh, Y.W.: A fast learning algorithm for deep belief nets. Neural Comput. 18(7), 1527–1554 (2006)
18. Isola, P., Zhu, J.Y., Zhou, T., Efros, A.A.: Image-to-image translation with conditional adversarial networks. In: Proceedings of the IEEE Conference on Computer Vision and Pattern Recognition, pp. 1125–1134 (2017)
19. Ji, B., Chen, T.: Generative adversarial network for handwritten text. arXiv preprint arXiv:1907.11845 (2019)
20. Kanezaki, A.: Unsupervised image segmentation by backpropagation. In: 2018 IEEE International Conference on Acoustics, Speech and Signal Processing (ICASSP), pp. 1543–1547. IEEE (2018)
21. Kumar, J., Doermann, D.: Unsupervised classification of structurally similar document images. In: 2013 12th International Conference on Document Analysis and Recognition, pp. 1225–1229. IEEE (2013)
22. Long, J., Shelhamer, E., Darrell, T.: Fully convolutional networks for semantic segmentation. In: Proceedings of the IEEE Conference on Computer Vision and Pattern Recognition, pp. 3431–3440 (2015)
23. Maroñas, J., Paredes, R., Ramos, D.: Generative models for deep learning with very scarce data. In: Vera-Rodriguez, R., Fierrez, J., Morales, A. (eds.) CIARP 2018. LNCS, vol. 11401, pp. 20–28. Springer, Cham (2019). https://doi.org/10.1007/978-3-030-13469-3_3
24. Ntirogiannis, K., Gatos, B., Pratikakis, I.: ICFHR 2014 competition on handwritten document image binarization (h-dibco 2014). In: 2014 14th International Conference on Frontiers in Handwriting Recognition, pp. 809–813. IEEE (2014)
25. Pratikakis, I., Zagoris, K., Barlas, G., Gatos, B.: ICDAR 2017 competition on document image binarization (dibco 2017). In: 2017 14th IAPR International Conference on Document Analysis and Recognition (ICDAR), vol. 1, pp. 1395–1403. IEEE (2017)
26. Radford, A., Metz, L., Chintala, S.: Unsupervised representation learning with deep convolutional generative adversarial networks. arXiv preprint arXiv:1511.06434 (2015)
27. Ronneberger, O., Fischer, P., Brox, T.: U-Net: convolutional networks for biomedical image segmentation. In: Navab, N., Hornegger, J., Wells, W.M., Frangi, A.F. (eds.) MICCAI 2015. LNCS, vol. 9351, pp. 234–241. Springer, Cham (2015). https://doi.org/10.1007/978-3-319-24574-4_28

28. Saddami, K., Afrah, P., Mutiawani, V., Arnia, F.: A new adaptive thresholding technique for binarizing ancient document. In: 2018 Indonesian Association for Pattern Recognition International Conference (INAPR), pp. 57–61. IEEE (2018)

29. Schomaker, L.: Lifelong learning for text retrieval and recognition in historical handwritten document collections. arXiv preprint arXiv:1912.05156 (2019)

30. Simistira, F., et al.: ICDAR 2017 competition on layout analysis for challenging medieval manuscripts. In: 2017 14th IAPR International Conference on Document Analysis and Recognition (ICDAR), vol. 1, pp. 1361–1370. IEEE (2017)

31. Tensmeyer, C.A.: Deep learning for document image analysis (2019)

32. Wei, H., Chen, K., Seuret, M., Würsch, M., Liwicki, M., Ingold, R.: Divadiawi- a web-based interface for semi-automatic labeling of historical document images. Digital Humanities (2015)

33. Xia, X., Kulis, B.: W-net: A deep model for fully unsupervised image segmentation. arXiv preprint arXiv:1711.08506 (2017)

A Two-Stage Unsupervised Deep Learning Framework for Degradation Removal in Ancient Documents

Milad Omrani Tamrin$^{(\boxtimes)}$, Mohammed El-Amine Ech-Cherif, and Mohamed Cheriet

École de technologie supérieure, 1100 Notre-Dame St W, Montreal, Qc, Canada
{milad.omrani-tamrin.2,mohammed-el-amine.ech-cherif.1}@ens.etsmtl.ca,
mohamed.cheriet@etsmtl.ca

Abstract. Processing historical documents is a complicated task in computer vision due to the presence of degradation, which decreases the performance of Machine Learning models. Recently, Deep Learning (DL) models have achieved state-of-the-art accomplishments in processing historical documents. However, these performances do not match the results obtained in other computer vision tasks, and the reason is that such models require large datasets to perform well. In the case of historical documents, only small datasets are available, making it hard for DL models to capture the degradation. In this paper, we propose a framework to overcome issues by following a two-stage approach. Stage-I is devoted to data augmentation. A Generative Adversarial Network (GAN), trained on degraded documents, generates synthesized new training document images. In stage-II, the document images generated in stage-I, are improved using an inverse problem model with a deep neural network structure. Our approach enhances the quality of the generated document images and removes degradation. Our results show that the proposed framework is well suited for binarization tasks. Our model was trained on the 2014 and 2016 DIBCO datasets and tested on the 2018 DIBCO dataset. The obtained results are promising and competitive with the state-of-the-art.

Keywords: Historical documents · Degradation · Low-scale data set · Generative adversarial networks · Restoration

1 Introduction

Motivated by discovering hidden information in ancient manuscripts, the analysis of historical documents is considered an important and active research area in image processing/understanding, which has been the subject of much recent research. In traditional applications of historical document image processing, input data distributions are assumed to be noise-free, whereas due to various degradations such as shading, non-uniform shapes, bleed-through background,

© Springer Nature Switzerland AG 2021
A. Del Bimbo et al. (Eds.): ICPR 2020 Workshops, LNCS 12667, pp. 292–303, 2021.
https://doi.org/10.1007/978-3-030-68787-8_21

and warping impacts in some corrupted images need to be removed and are considered as a pre-processing step [9]. Numerous techniques have been put forward to deal with naturally degraded images during the past few decades, and promising results have been obtained [5]. Deep learning models and mainly convolutional neural networks have recently outperformed traditional image processing techniques on numerous tasks ranging from computer vision, speech recognition, and times series forecasting. The latter models' tremendous success is due mainly to their reliance on computed or learned features from an extensive collection of images rather than handcrafted features obtained from the raw image pixels. Moreover, in both supervised and unsupervised learning settings, convolutional neural networks must be trained on massive data sets to achieve a better generalization error on unseen data. For image processing tasks, data augmentation is customarily and successfully used to provide arbitrarily large data sets for training convolutional neural networks. It is important to note that data augmentation must operate on clean images, i.e., not corrupted by degradation. We do not have much data for the deep network to capture the degradation process. The degradation will also damage the generated data and, therefore, does not improve the model's accuracy [11]. For the ancient image analysis tasks, data augmentation must not be restricted to only elementary geometric transformations. Instead, it requires geared towards reproducing the artifacts that the old document has been subjected to, such as ageing, spilled ink, stamps hindering some essential parts of the image, etc. [8]. The latter task requires advanced mathematical modelling and is beyond the scope of the present work. To overcome the lack of dataset in ancient manuscripts, GAN [7] provides a new perspective of synthesizing documents. We aim to leverage the deep learning paradigm to extract binarized images from the generated historical documents using the recently developed deep image prior [19], as shown in Fig. 1. This paper proposes a two-stage method. The first stage aims to generate realistic-looking high-quality documents by training the state-of-the-art generative models, Deep

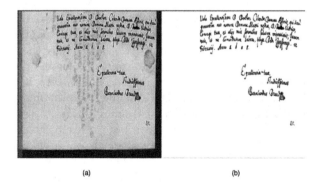

(a)   (b)

Fig. 1. Restored degraded document designed by cleaning foreground from noisy background. a) original degraded document b) Restored image using proposed neural network based approach with an inverse function

Convolutional GAN (DC-GAN), on the DIBCO datasets. In the second stage, we adapt a deep image prior to the generated images, to produce binarized images to be evaluated on the 2016 version of DIBCO datasets. The contribution of this paper is three-fold:

- We propose a modified DC-GAN structure to synthesize more realistic data from ancient document images. The model generates high-resolution images.
- We adapt deep image prior to the generated images and develop a new loss function to perform image binarization.
- We validate the binarized images on the DIBCO datasets and we obtain competitive results in the 2014 and 2016 versions.

Section 2 presents in generative models and depth restoration using deep neural networks. Section 3 describes how we will compare them. Finally, we will review in Sect. 4, the results regarding the different measurements are discussed.

2   Related Work

Several methods have proposed to generate historical documents, while the corruption process in the case of large-scale damage becomes a complicated task to in-paint the lost area. Here we review some related works on augmenting historical documents. A Deep Learning algorithm [7] is proposed to generate an artificial dataset. Recently, GANs have become more interesting for synthesizing documents images. By having vanilla GAN, many approaches were introduced to synthesize document images such as GAN-CLS [17], where the proposed method consists of two neural networks. Generator G generates fake images, where the Discriminator D plays a discriminating role between G output and real images, including an auxiliary condition on text description $\varphi(t)$. However, a significant problem of such a method for document image augmentation would be a lack of substantial training data. The model requires a large number of images, including their text descriptions. Another version of GAN related to synthesis data for digital documents is [2] that the author proposed a style-GAN to synthesize alphabets that could predict the missed alphabets. However, the input needs labels, which are time-consuming and complex tasks. Despite the argument that generative models could be an advantage to overcome limited datasets, such a model can also increase damaged images' resolution. However, it is necessary to add a technique that can understand the available samples' underlying characteristics by considering the low quality of training images, as shown in Fig. 2. For multiple decades, inverse problems have been the subject of many studies in image restoration. Their success heavily depends on designing an excellent prior term to uncover the degraded images. The prior is usually hand-crafted based on specific observations made on a dataset. Creating a prior is often a difficult task as it is hard to model the degradation distribution. In the context of DL, the prior is learned from training a ConvNet on a vast dataset [3]. Most of the proposed methods using deep learning models only perform as good as the available datasets. The solution is tied up to the image space. In [19],

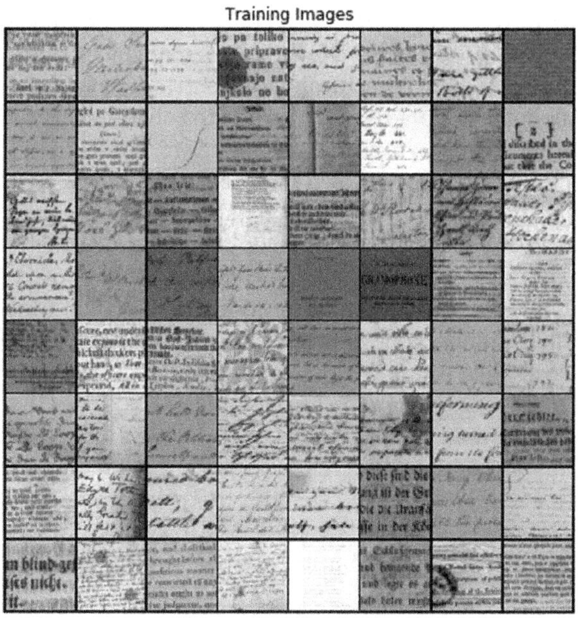

Training Images

Fig. 2. Training samples from DIBCO degraded dataset [15]

the authors have shown that the structure of a ConvNet contains a great deal of information, and a prior can be learned within the weights of the architecture. In other words, exploring ConvNet weights' space can result in recovering a clean image from a degraded image without the need to have a considerable dataset. Moreover, Processing Document Image Binarization (DIB) in historical image documents suffers in different challenges due to the nature of the old manuscripts that leads to degraded image either by faded or stains ink, bleed-through, document ages, documents quality and many other factors that may affect the historical documents. Therefore, the degradation manuscripts increase the challenging binarization process task since it requires classifying the foreground from background pixels as a pre-processing stage. That being said, the initial methods [13] used for classifying document image pixels (foreground vs background) are based on different single and multiple threshold values.

3   Work Methodology

3.1   Stage *I* - Data Augmentation Framework

In this section, we will introduce DC-GAN, and provide technical information regarding the generative model.

Deep Convlutional GAN (DC-GAN). As of the original GAN's general idea, in Deep Convolutions GAN (DC-GAN), the augmentation process is similar to the unique GAN but specifically concentrates on deep fully-connected networks. The model uses an adversarial game to solve generalization tasks. The generator is liable to create synthetic instances from random noises, and the discriminator tries to distinguish between fake and real images. By this adversarial process, the generator attempts to improve its weights and also generate images. The Convolutional-transpose layers try to do the feature extraction task by finding the correlated areas of images. The authors in [16] proposed that DC-GAN precisely fits for unsupervised-learning, whereas the original idea of GAN more relies on the public domain. Following the Eq. 1 in DCGAN, where the G utilizes the transposed technique to apply up-sampling of image size and allow to transfer the random noises into the shape of the input images. In $D(x)$, the ConvNet tries to find the correlated area of images. $G(z)$ represents real data; the $D(x)$ is also used to distinguish the difference between generated images versus real data using a classifier. The x is the samples of images from the actual dataset, and also the distribution of data is represented by $P_{data(x)}$. z is also a sample from the generator with the distribution of $P(z)$.

$$\min_{G} \max_{D} V(G, D) = \mathbb{E}_{\mathbf{x} \sim P_{\text{data}}(\mathbf{x})}[\log(D(\mathbf{x}))] + \mathbb{E}_{\mathbf{z} \sim P_{\text{noise}}(\mathbf{z})}[\log(1 - D(G(\mathbf{z})))]$$

(1)

The objective of training consists of two processes. In the first step, the discriminator updates parameters by maximizing the expected log-likelihood, and in the second step, while the discriminator parameters are updated, the generator generates fake images. The architecture used is given in Table 1. Hence, the input size of each image is $(3 \times 128 \times 128)$, the learning rate is considered 0.0002, batch-size is 256, and the number of epochs is 25k. To evaluate the performance of the generation effect of modified DC-GAN, we perform a quantities evaluation index called the Frechet Inception Distance network (FID) [10].

Table 1. Architecture of generative model used

Summary of DC-GAN		
Layer(type)	Output	Connected to
$input_1$ layer	None, 128, 512	
Lambda layer	512, $eps = 1e-05$	$input_1$
$input_2$ layer	512, $eps = 1e-05$	$input_2$, lambda
Gan model	None, 0, 1	$input_1$, lambda
yFake	None, 1	gan(1, 0)
yReal	None, 1	gan(1, 1)
Total Sample: 200	6 layers	Nb epochs: 25k

3.2 Stage *II* Convolutional Neural Network-Based Document Binarization

Several deep learning models have achieved state-of-the-art performance on binarization for degraded document analysis and printed machinery text [4,20]. In our training, to get promising results from generative models, the first step is that the enhancement task is performed to improve the quality of degraded document images. However, for this process, it is necessary to train a learning model that requires many data. Indeed, there is a lack of big datasets to train a learning model when it comes to historical documents. To overcome the limitation, we explore a way that can allow us to enhance the quality of our images, using inverse problems. Inverse problems have been widely studied in document images but without promising results. Previously, the problem was formulated, and the goal was to look for the prior (inverse image).

In our approach, we will use the structure of a neural network proposed in [19]. Convolutional networks have become a popular tool for image generation and restoration. Generally, their excellent performance is credited to their ability to learn realistic image priors from many example images. In this stage, we adapt and extend the original deep image prior method to historical documents. We show that the structure of a generator ConvNet is sufficient to capture any information about the degradation of historical documents without any learning involved. To do so, we define a ConvNet architecture (U-Net) that is untrained. The network is then used as handcrafted prior to performing the text's binarization from the background and hence removing the degradation.

In image restoration problems the goal is to recover the original image x having a corrupted image x_0.

Such problems are often formulated as an optimization task:

$$\min_{x} E(x; x_0) + R(x) \tag{2}$$

where $E(x; x_0)$ is a data term and $R(x)$ is an image prior.

The data term $E(x; x_0)$ is usually easy to design for a wide range of problems, such as super-resolution, denoising, inpainting, while image prior $R(x)$ is a challenging one. Today's trend is to capture the prior $R(x)$ with a ConvNet by training it using a large number of examples.

It is noticed, that for a surjective $g : \theta \mapsto x$ the following procedure, in theory, is equivalent to 2:

$$\min_{\theta} E(g(\theta); x_0) + R(g(\theta))$$

In practice, g dramatically changes how the image space is searched by an optimization method. Furthermore, by selecting a "good" (possibly injective) mapping g, we could get rid of the prior term. We define $g(\theta)$ as $f_\theta(z)$, where f is a ConvNet (U-Net) with parameters θ and z is a fixed input, leading to the formulation:

$$\min_{\theta} E(f_\theta(z); x_0)$$

Here, the network f_θ is initialized randomly and input is filled with noise and fixed. Figure 3 depicts the learning of the proposed networks. Moreover, the reduction of losses for training and validations proves that the model has improved and eliminate the noises from generated images.

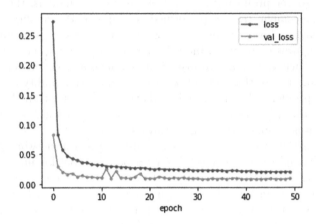

Fig. 3. Training and validation Loss functions error getting minimized as the training epochs increase.

In other words, instead of searching for the answer in the image space we now search for it in the space of the neural network's weights. We emphasize that only a degraded document image x_0 is used in the binarization process. The architecture is shown in Fig. 4. The whole process is presented in Algorithm 1.

Algorithm 1: Deep GAN Perior

---

for number of training **do**
    for n steps **do**
        sample $\left\{x^{(i)}\right\}_{i=1}^{i=m} \sim P_{data}$ a real sample
        sample $\left\{z^{(i)}\right\}_{i=1}^{i=m} \sim P_z$ a restored sample
        update the discriminator by ascending its stochastic gradient
    end for
    sample $\left\{z^{(i)}\right\}_{i=1}^{i=m} \sim P_z$ a restored sample
    Update the generator by ascending its stochastic gradient
end for
initialize generated document $z^{(i)}$
take $x^{(i)}$ min by $\arg\min_\theta E(f_\theta(z))\hat{x}^{(i)}$
apply the gradient
result $x^* = f_{\theta^*}(z^{(i)})$

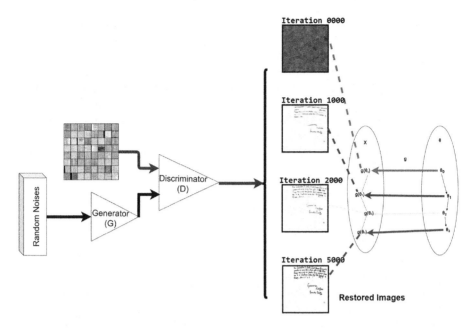

Fig. 4. The proposed framework in two-fold: Stage-I on the left generates new synthetic images using DC-GAN, and stage-II on the right, removes degradation and perform binarization from generated images.

3.3   Datasets

To train and validate our developed methods, we used the most common image binarization datasets in handwriting documents, namely 2014 H-DIBCO [16] (Document Image Binarization Competition), 2016 H-DIBCO [17] and 2018 H-DIBCO [18], organized by ICFHR (Interna-tional Conference on Frontiers in Handwriting Recognition) 2014, ICFHR 2016 and CFHR 2018 respectively. These benchmark datasets have been extensively used to train and validate the results of binarization algorithms in historical handwritten documents. The 2014 and 2016 H-DIBCO datasets are used to train our models, and the 2018 H-DIBCO is used to validate our results.

4   Result and Analysis

To evaluate our method, we adopt the benchmark historical handwritten dataset DIBCO described in Sect. 3.3. Moreover, we have tested the results for denoised images to understand the effectiveness of the proposed model. The document images in the dataset suffer from degradation. Furthermore, to further assess the performance of the method, we employ the four commonly used metrics to evaluate competitors in the DIBCO contest, namely F-Measure (FM), pseud-oFMeasure (Fps), PSNR, and Distance Reciprocal Distortion (DRD) [12].

The model learns well the general idea of historical document augmentation that can be noted in Fig. 5. By having the degraded samples, it is clear that the new documents have been enhanced, rather than using original generator methods. To evaluate the synthesized images in the recognition accuracy, we apply FID to measure the quality of generated images. FID computes the KL-divergence between real images distributions and generated image distributions. Table 2 shows the FID implies that both distributions are close to the real images.

Table 2. FID evaluation on generated distribution over real images distributions

Model	FID-5k	FID-20k
Real images	9.33	7.4
DC-GAN	36.73	6.45

Furthermore, the proposed method's output could remove degradation and increase the accuracy of CNN, resulting in better classifications in document analysis. The encouraging results we obtained motivate more the effectiveness of data augmentation and the challenge of limited data and degraded in ancient documents taken from the basic GAN. A consequence of underlying GAN leads us to get more in-depth by using deep convolutional networks in the generator. Simultaneously, we were not convinced that we would get the same results from the underlying GAN. Our goal was to improve the quality of augmented document images. During this process, it was noted that DC-GAN provided better performance in the use of basic GAN. To also include, the PyTorch [14] framework was used during the discoveries.

Table 3. FM, Fps, PSNR and DRD evaluation and comparison with DIBCO 2018 winners

Method	FM	Fps	PSNR	DRD
Adak et al. [1]	73.45	75.94	14.62	26.24
Gattal et al. [6]	64.52	68.29	13.57	16.67
Saddami et al. [18]	46.35	51.39	11.79	24.56
Proposed method	**83.08**	**88.46**	**17.04**	**5.09**

The results obtained in this research paper are attributed to the design of good generative models and adapting newly discovered inverse-problem algorithms based on ConvNets. We constructed two new custom DC-GANs architecture. These architectures' choice seems to work best because very deep networks are known to learn more features. In our paper, this seemed to be accurate and helped us get excellent results. Due to our efforts, we could generate realistic-looking synthetic document images by training our proposed DC-GANs. The

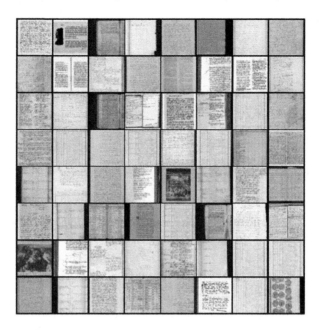

Fig. 5. Samples generated by our proposed method from the degraded documents augmentation by Stage-I

generator presents different transformations such as cropping to capture the documents' characters and resize the samples to normalize the data to meet the requirements for synthesizing high-quality images. Furthermore, to improve the augmentation task with unlabeled data, we alter the G and D networks for 128 * 128 size, including the extra Conv and pooling layers. To perform efficient binarization, we adapted and extended the original deep image prior algorithm to the problem. The unique deep image prior was developed to work on generated images. However, to the best of our knowledge, no one intended to work with ancient historical documents. The performance of previously developed state-of-the-art algorithms in binarization heavily relies on the data. Table 3 shows either state-of-the-art results or competitive results with the best binarization algorithms. The metrics shown in Table 3 are FM, Fps, PSNR and DRD. Our method outperforms all the algorithms that were used in the DIBCO 2018 competition. In this work, we showed that the space of a ConvNet contains valuable information about clustering the degraded ancient documents into two clusters, both background and foreground. As shown in Fig. 6, the proposed method shows promising results with removing noise from degraded document images.

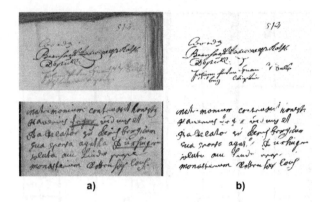

Fig. 6. a) samples generated by our proposed DC-GAN b) binarized images produced by our method.

5   Conclusion

In this paper, a combined deep generative - image binarization model has been implemented and trained on degraded documents datasets. Our algorithm consists of two main steps. At first, an augmentation task is performed on unlabeled data to generate new synthetic samples for training. The second step is to remove the noise from generated images by taking the generators' minimum error and removing the degradations. Experimental results have shown that the method was able to generate new realistic historical image documents. We performed binarization on the 2018 DIBCO dataset to validate our approach. The obtained results demonstrate that our method gets very close results to the 2018 DIBCO contest winner and vastly surpasses the other participants. Despite competitive results, there is room to improve our model by exploring different ConvNet architectures. We believe that the choice of the structure in the binarization task profoundly impacts our method's performance. In future work, we will explore other ConvNet architectures as hyper-parameter model selection.

Acknowledgement. The authors thank the NSERC Discovery held by Prof. Cheriet for their financial support.

References

1. Adak, C., Chaudhuri, B.B., Blumenstein, M.: A study on idiosyncratic handwriting with impact on writer identification. In: 2018 16th International Conference on Frontiers in Handwriting Recognition (ICFHR), pp. 193–198. IEEE (2018)
2. Azadi, S., Fisher, M., Kim, V.G., Wang, Z., Shechtman, E., Darrell, T.: Multi-content GAN for few-shot font style transfer. In: Proceedings of the IEEE Conference on Computer Vision and Pattern Recognition, pp. 7564–7573 (2018)

3. Bui, Q.A., Mollard, D., Tabbone, S.: Automatic synthetic document image generation using generative adversarial networks: application in mobile-captured document analysis. In: 2019 International Conference on Document Analysis and Recognition (ICDAR), pp. 393–400. IEEE (2019)
4. Calvo-Zaragoza, J., Gallego, A.J.: A selectional auto-encoder approach for document image binarization. Pattern Recogn. **86**, 37–47 (2019)
5. Dumpala, V., Kurupathi, S.R., Bukhari, S.S., Dengel, A.: Removal of historical document degradations using conditional GANs. In: ICPRAM, pp. 145–154 (2019)
6. Gattal, A., Abbas, F., Laouar, M.R.: Automatic parameter tuning of k-means algorithm for document binarization. In: Proceedings of the 7th International Conference on Software Engineering and New Technologies, pp. 1–4 (2018)
7. Goodfellow, I., et al.: Generative adversarial nets. In: Advances in Neural Information Processing Systems, pp. 2672–2680 (2014)
8. He, K., Zhang, X., Ren, S., Sun, J.: Deep residual learning for image recognition. In: Proceedings of the IEEE Conference on Computer Vision and Pattern Recognition, pp. 770–778 (2016)
9. Hedjam, R., Cheriet, M.: Historical document image restoration using multispectral imaging system. Pattern Recogn. **46**(8), 2297–2312 (2013)
10. Heusel, M., Ramsauer, H., Unterthiner, T., Nessler, B., Hochreiter, S.: GANs trained by a two time-scale update rule converge to a local nash equilibrium. In: Advances in Neural Information Processing Systems, pp. 6626–6637 (2017)
11. LeCun, Y., Bengio, Y., Hinton, G.: Deep learning. Nature **521**(7553), 436–444 (2015)
12. Lu, H., Kot, A.C., Shi, Y.Q.: Distance-reciprocal distortion measure for binary document images. IEEE Signal Process. Lett. **11**(2), 228–231 (2004)
13. Otsu, N.: A threshold selection method from gray-level histograms. IEEE Trans. Syst. Man Cybern. **9**(1), 62–66 (1979)
14. Paszke, A., et al.: Automatic differentiation in PyTorch (2017)
15. Pratikakis, I., Zagori, K., Kaddas, P., Gatos, B.: ICFHR 2018 competition on handwritten document image binarization (H-DIBCO 2018). In: 2018 16th International Conference on Frontiers in Handwriting Recognition (ICFHR), pp. 489–493 (2018). https://doi.org/10.1109/ICFHR-2018.2018.00091
16. Radford, A., Metz, L., Chintala, S.: Unsupervised representation learning with deep convolutional generative adversarial networks. arXiv preprint arXiv:1511.06434 (2015)
17. Reed, S., Akata, Z., Yan, X., Logeswaran, L., Schiele, B., Lee, H.: Generative adversarial text to image synthesis. arXiv preprint arXiv:1605.05396 (2016)
18. Saddami, K., Afrah, P., Mutiawani, V., Arnia, F.: A new adaptive thresholding technique for binarizing ancient document. In: 2018 Indonesian Association for Pattern Recognition International Conference (INAPR), pp. 57–61. IEEE (2018)
19. Ulyanov, D., Vedaldi, A., Lempitsky, V.: Deep image prior. In: Proceedings of the IEEE Conference on Computer Vision and Pattern Recognition, pp. 9446–9454 (2018)
20. Vo, Q.N., Kim, S.H., Yang, H.J., Lee, G.: Binarization of degraded document images based on hierarchical deep supervised network. Pattern Recogn. **74**, 568–586 (2018)

Recommender System for Digital Storytelling: A Novel Approach to Enhance Cultural Heritage

Mario Casillo[1], Dajana Conte[2] (ID), Marco Lombardi[1](✉) (ID), Domenico Santaniello[1] (ID), and Carmine Valentino[1,2]

[1] DIIN, University of Salerno, Fisciano, Italy
{mcasillo,malombardi,dsantaniello,cvalentino}@unisa.it
[2] DIPMAT, University of Salerno, Fisciano, Italy
dajconte@unisa.it

Abstract. Italy is characterized by a significant artistic and cultural heritage. In this scenario, it is possible and necessary to implement strategies for cultural heritage enhancement. This vision has become increasingly feasible due to the introduction of systems based on new technologies, particularly those based on intensive use of Information and Communication Technologies (ICT). This approach has allowed the development of applications to build adaptive cultural paths usable by different types of users. In addition to the technological dimension, a fundamental role is played by methodologies that convey information content innovatively and effectively.

The objective of this paper is to propose a Recommender approach that aims at the enhancement of Italian Cultural Heritage. In this way, everyone could have the opportunity to know or deepen their knowledge of the cultural sites that are most suited to them, which will be presented through the narrative technique of Digital Storytelling. The Recommender methodology introduced has been tested through an experimental campaign, obtaining promising results.

Keywords: Digital storytelling · E-tourism · Recommender system

1 Introduction

The Italian vast artistic and cultural heritage allows a full knowledge of it to a limited number of people. Thus, the support of modern technologies, in the field of cultural tourism, can play a role of primary importance.

The goal is to move from traditional cultural tourism to tourism 2.0 [1]. It consists of the integration of technologies related to the Future Internet [2], and in particular, the technologies of the Internet of Things (IoT) [3] and the Internet of Service (IoS) [4], to make the touristic experience digital [5]. Such integration plays a key role, for example, in the development of the concept of the smart city. In this scenario, a citizen can acquire information and suggestions through applications designed for this purpose [6]. This paradigm is made possible by the interconnection between smart objects capable of processing and transferring information (typical in the IoT concept).

© Springer Nature Switzerland AG 2021
A. Del Bimbo et al. (Eds.): ICPR 2020 Workshops, LNCS 12667, pp. 304–317, 2021.
https://doi.org/10.1007/978-3-030-68787-8_22

However, only data acquisition is not enough. Moreover, their quantity makes their management very difficult. Therefore, after the first phase of data collection, a tool capable of analyzing and filtering information is essential. Such a tool is defined as a Recommender System (RS), which brings a considerable capacity to manage Big Data [7, 8]. The RS allows, moreover, to calculate the affinities between users and services to be suggested. Subsequently, these affinities are improved through contextual information [9] that allows adapting the forecasts provided by RS to the specific situation in which the user finds himself.

The context can be defined as "any information useful to characterize the situation of an entity that can affect the way users interact with systems" [10]. The context, defined through contextual information, will be introduced through the Context Dimension Tree (CDT) [11]. The presentation of the results provided through the Digital Storytelling technique will allow better user involvement in the world of next-generation cultural tourism.

This article is structured as follows. In Sect. 2, the Recommender Systems will be described, and the CDT and Digital Storytelling models will also be presented. In Sect. 3, the proposed Recommender Approach will be presented. Section 4 will deal with a case study. Conclusions will be presented in Sect. 5.

2 Background

This section deals with introducing the technologies used in tourism 2.0. These range from recommender systems, context awareness, and presentation techniques such as Digital Storytelling. The last part of the section will be dedicated to the presentation of the factoring to singular values, which will provide the theoretical basis for the presentation of the recommendation approach developed.

2.1 Recommender Systems

The Recommender System [12] is a data analysis and filtering means, which provides support to the user in choosing the most suitable services. The system and the user interaction through the transaction phase, which usually consists of rating assignments. The rating could take several forms, even if the most common are numerical (e.g., 1–5 score) or ordinary (very agree, agree, neutral, disagree, very disagree). From a formal point of view, it represents a domain application of the Cartesian product of user sets and items. The main feature of the rating function (or utility function) is that not all the images of the domain pairs are known. Therefore, a key feature of a Recommender System is predicting the tastes and preferences of users [13]. Therefore, it can be inferred that each RS has its modus operandi for rating forecasting and data analysis and filtering; which implies the possibility of classifying them based on these factors obtaining different recommendation methodologies, such as [12, 14]:

- Content-Based RS: a method based on the construction of profiles for items and users that numerically describe their main features. The data is acquired and transformed into numerical information contained in vectors of the same vector space. The prediction of the user's liking for an item is calculated through the Cosine Similarity [12]. These techniques do not require too much information to assess user preferences, but tend to suggest the same item types to the user;

- Collaborative Filtering (CF) RS: techniques based on the concept of sharing opinions. These opinions can be useful and therefore obtained through the calculation of the similarity between users and items. This kind of approach is named Memory-Based CF and consists of creating user groups (User-Based) or items (Item-Based) defined Neighborhood [14]. This approach is easy to implement and finds different types of items than the Content-Based procedure. It has, however, poor adaptability to large datasets. In fact, the systems that best approach the management of a large number of data are Model-Based Collaborative Filtering, which stores the known ratings within the rating matrix. This matrix associates each row to a user and each column to an item. The Model-Based procedures aim to identify the numerical information characterizing the defined matrix and process it to obtain the rating forecasts. The information described takes the name of the latent factors of the model [14]. The acquisition of numerical information is made through matrix factoring techniques. In particular, one of the most widespread is the Singular Value Decomposition (SVD). The last described procedures, as already said, present a high level of adaptability to large datasets, and can obtain reliable rating forecasts even in the presence of very scattered matrices. However, they suffer from the Cold Start problem, which consists of not predicting the tastes of a user just entered the system or the possible predictions of items not rated by any user;
- Hybrid RS: methods based on combining different recommendation techniques. In particular, Content-Based and Collaborative Filtering are the most familiar techniques. The implementation methods can include [12]:
  - the construction of a single model recommendation having the properties of both techniques;
  - the use of one technique in support of the other;
  - the implementation of the two techniques independently and the comparison or union of the results obtained.

Before-mentioned recommendation strategies succeed in overcoming the limitations of the techniques that compose them but at the cost of a significant increase in the model's complexity.

The use of Recommender Systems in the management of Big Data in support of artistic and cultural heritage is a technique already widely used, aiming to support users in visiting a museum [15–17]. A further example is reported in [18], which, through the use of tags, manages to improve the experience of a user visiting the Vatican Museums.

Singular Value Decomposition
Considering the rating matrix associated with a system of m users and n items. The singular value decomposition [19, 20] allows decomposing the given matrix in the product of three matrices:

$$R = UDV^T \tag{1}$$

Where the matrices $U \in R^{m \times m}$ and $V \in R^{n \times n}$ are invertible, square, and orthogonal. In particular, the orthogonality properties are described in (2) and (3), where I_m and I_n denote the identity matrice of dimension m and n, respectively (Fig. 1).

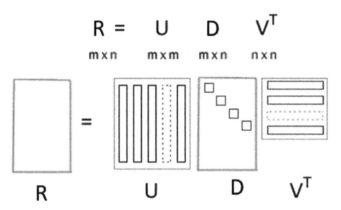

Fig. 1. Graphic representation of SVD

$$U^T = U^{-1}, \qquad U^T U = I_m = UU^T \tag{2}$$

$$V^T = V^{-1}, \qquad V^T V = I_n = VV^T \tag{3}$$

The defined matrices U and V are called matrices of left singular value vectors and right singular value vectors. Moreover, the matrix D in (1) is a diagonal matrix containing the square roots of eigenvalues of matrices RR^T and $R^T R$. The diagonal elements σ_i, $i = 1, \ldots, p = \min\{m, n\}$ have the property described in (5). They are called the singular value of ratings matrix R.

$$D = diag\left(\sigma_1, \sigma_2, \ldots, \sigma_{p-1}, \sigma_p\right) \in R^{m \times n} \tag{4}$$

$$\sigma_1 \geq \sigma_2 \geq \ldots \geq \sigma_{p-1} \geq \sigma_p \geq 0 \tag{5}$$

For application purposes, the Eckart-Young Theorem [20] is essential. It allows us to approximate the rating matrix with a low-rank matrix. This technique is diffused in the application field and, it has several applications [21, 22].

Before presenting the theorem, we define the matrices:

- $U_k \in R^{m \times k}$ obtained from matrix U without the last m-k columns;
- $V_k \in R^{n \times k}$ obtained from matrix V without the last n-k columns;
- $D_k \in R^{k \times k}$ obtained from matrix D without the last m-k rows and the last n-k columns.

Where $k \leq r(R) \leq p = \min\{m, n\}$.

Theorem 2.1. Let the rating matrix R of rank r, let $k \leq r$ and let the matrix $R_k = U_k D_k V_k^T \in R^{m \times n}$ obtained from the product of the previously defined matrices, then

$$\min_{r(B)=k} ||R - B||_F^2 = ||R - R_k||_F^2 = \sum_{i=k+1}^{p} \sigma_i^2 \qquad (6)$$

$$\min_{r(B)=k} ||R - B||_F^2 = ||R - R_k||_F^2 = \sum_{i=k+1}^{p} \sigma_i^2 \qquad (7)$$

The estimates of the applications obtained through (6) and (7) are good ones thanks to property (5). Lastly, we underline that the matrices U_k and V_k consist of orthogonal columns:

$$U_k^T U_k = I_k \qquad (8)$$

$$V_k^T V_k = I_k \qquad (9)$$

Where I_k is the identity matrix of dimension k.

2.2   Context-Awareness

Each rating forecast generated by a Recommendation System considers only the user's general preferences in relation to an item. However, such a ranking is limiting. For example, if a user had to choose between a museum and an archaeological site on a rainy day, they would undoubtedly choose indoor activities beyond their preferences. In fact, a RS needs additional information to improve the rating forecast to be performed.

Such information is called contextual information, representing a means to identify the user's contingent situation and adapt the choices to each possible situation [23]. In this way, the single user or the single item can be represented through a multitude of possible cases as if in each contextual representation, they represented similar but different individuals.

In general, the utility function of a context-aware recommendation system is a $U \times I \times C$ domain application [24]. The U and I set represent the user and item set while the C set is made up of the possible contexts considered. The elements of set C are defined through the contextual information that is collected. These can be collected [12]:

- Explicitly, e.g., through questions asked to the user;
- Implicitly, through mobile devices or changes in the user's environmental conditions;
- Through statistical or Data Mining techniques.

The contextual information has also been classified according to the type of information they report. In the following, we report such classification [24]:

- Individual Context: contextual information associated with users or items. They are divided into Natural, Human, Artificial, and Group of Entities;
- Location Context: refers to the physical or digital coordinates where the user's activity takes place or where an item is located;

- Time Context: refers to the physical time linked to the activity of the elements of the system;
- Activity Context: refers to the activities performed by the elements of the system and can serve as a basis for possible future activities;
- Relational Context: refers to the contextual information associated with the interactions between the system elements (user-user, user-item, item-item).

Once defined and acquired the contextual information, the problem of being able to identify the specific Context arises. In this Context, the Context Dimension Tree is exploited.

Context Dimension Tree
As mentioned above, the contextual information analysis for the construction of the specific context is performed by Context Dimension Tree (CDT) [11, 25].

The Context Dimension Tree <r, N, A> is a tree, which is represented by a non-oriented, connected, and acyclic graph. The root of the tree is r, N represents the set of nodes and A the set of arcs.

The set of nodes of a CDT can be divided as follows:

- Dimension nodes, graphically represented by black nodes, which represent the possible contextual dimensions;
- Concept nodes are graphically represented by white nodes, which are the children of dimension nodes and represent a specific aspect. In other words, the values that dimension nodes can assume;
- Parameters, graphically represented by white rectangles, which are the children of concept nodes and further specify the associated information.

Figure 2 shows a generic Context Dimension Tree in a graphic form. The purpose of the CDT is to represent the possible contextual information that can be acquired and determine the specific context to be evaluated [26]. Therefore, its peculiar function is to schematize and identify the context [27, 28]. In this way, it is possible to associate the single case values further to improve the rating forecasts of the Recommender System.

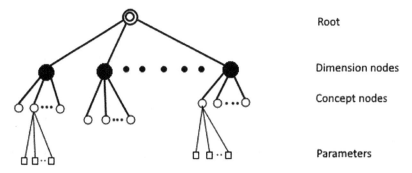

Fig. 2. Generic context dimension tree structure

2.3 Digital Storytelling

Storytelling is defined as a learning technique based on "telling" a story with the aim of [29]:

- transmit a message;
- capture the public's attention;
- stimulate in those who listen to a dramatic question.

The combination of Storytelling with modern multimedia allowed us to present content more effectively. The combination of Storytelling and multimedia content, obtained through new technologies, allowed the arising of Digital Storytelling (DS) [13]. The DS may take different forms depending on the purpose and the field of application. In particular, the different storytelling models that a Digital Storytelling content can assume are [25]:

- Linear Storytelling: the narrative form is the traditional format, where the user's role is that of the standard viewer. The linearity is found in the immutability of the storyline;
- Non-Linear Storytelling: the storyline is disjointed into sections with multiple possibilities for assembly. In this context, the audience becomes a co-author of the story and influences the order of the story.
- Adaptive Storytelling: such a structure exploits a communicative strategy, which involves the user through adaptability. A fundamental step is to maintain narrative consistency for any possible user conditioning on the story;
- Social/Collaborative Storytelling: through this structure, the narrative experience, besides aiming to convey the intrinsic message, becomes a means of social interaction for the audience that is constantly stimulated for the construction of the story itself;
- Mobile Storytelling: the goal is to build an engaging story for the user through the use of available technologies provided by mobile devices (such as geolocation) combined with the contextual information acquired. In this way the story is structured on each user to make the narrative experience more engaging;
- Game Storytelling: the main feature of this structure is the game, which develops according to the choices or specific skills acquired by the player during the experience.

The possibility of involving and making the user experience unique has been studied in depth. To this end, seven elements have been established to maximize the effectiveness of the DS [30]. Most importantly, it is suggested to expose personal or real stories (Point of View) to convey a message or teaching to the audience (Dramatic Question) so that the story is thoroughly engaging (Emotional Content). The narration could be more effective if done through a narrating voice (The Gift Of Your Voice) and an adequate background soundtrack (The Power Of Soundtrack). It is also essential that every part of the story is balanced (Economy) with specific attention to the rhythm of the narration (Pacing).

3   The Proposed Approach

This work aims to improve the experience of a tourist by designing an innovative Recommender System that uses contextual parameters to suggest adaptive content. Moreover, multimedia content will be able to arouse the user's active involvement through the use of the main storytelling methodologies.

As shown in Fig. 3, the architecture of the proposed system is divided into three layers.

- Data Layer. The data acquire a new focus, becoming a key factor for the proposed system. The first phase (fetch phase) consists of collecting the data that will be processed by the next layer.
- Elaboration Layer. The core of the system has the task of processing the data to provide reliable recommendations to users. The proposed research work is more focused on this module, and its operation will be described in detail. This module can use context information (location, time, mood, etc.) to improve recommendations.
- Presentation Layer. During the last phase (execute phase), the contents to be recommended are presented to the user. In this regard, storytelling is one of the most efficient approaches to building comprehensible and engaging storytelling.

3.1   Recommendation Module

Many approaches based on singular value decomposition work on the rating matrix which is sparse. Therefore, it has many zero values that act as unknown ratings. For this reason, the rating matrix can be reworked in a specific way and after factored according to Theorem 2.1.

In particular, when the matrices U_k, D_k, V_k described in the previous section are obtained, we can calculate the following matrices:

$$\hat{P} = U_k \sqrt{D_k} \in R^{m \times k} \tag{10}$$

Obviously, it is obtained

$$R_k = U_k D_k V_k^T = \hat{P}\hat{Q} \tag{11}$$

From (10) and (11) we deduce that the matrix $\hat{P}$ columns and the matrix $\hat{Q}$ row are orthogonal vector systems. Indeed:

$$\widehat{P^T}\hat{P} = \left(U_k \sqrt{D_k}\right)^T \left(U_k \sqrt{D_k}\right) = \sqrt{D_k^T} U_k^T U_k \sqrt{D_k} \tag{12}$$

From (8) since D_k is a diagonal matrix therefore $D_k^T = D_k$, we have:

$$\hat{P}^T \hat{P} = D_k \tag{13}$$

which means that matrix $\hat{P}$ columns are a orthogonal vectors system.

Working in the same way on $\hat{Q}$ we obtain:

$$\widehat{\hat{Q}\hat{Q}^T} = \left(\sqrt{D_k}V_k^T\right)\left(\sqrt{D_k}V_k^T\right)^T = \sqrt{D_k}V_k^T V_k\sqrt{D_k^T} \tag{14}$$

From (9) and $D_k^T = D_k$ we deduce

$$\sqrt{D_k}V_k^T V_k\sqrt{D_k^T} \tag{15}$$

Such properties of orthogonality will be pivotal for the methods that we are showing.

Let the input matrices $P \in R^{m \times k}$ and $Q \in R^{k \times n}$ that contain the features of m users and n item collected on k categories of interest. From the properties shown we require that the rank of input matrices P and Q is equal to k.

$$r(P) = k = r(Q) \tag{16}$$

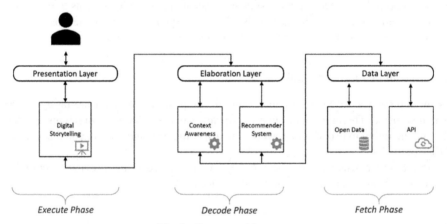

Fig. 3. System architecture

The hypothesis introduced requests semantically that the k categories of interest used to build the users and items profiles are chosen correctly. Therefore, the hypothesis is not limiting. From hypothesis (15), the columns of matrix P constitute a system of linearly independent vectors. Applying the orthogonalization method of Gram-Schmidt, it is possible to obtain a system of an orthogonal vector from the columns of matrix P. The same procedure can be applied on the rows of the input matrix Q. In this way, we obtain a system of orthogonal vectors.

The Algorithm 1 describes the orthogonalization procedure.

Algorithm 1: Gram-Schmidt orthogonalization
1: Input: matrix $A = (a_1, \dots, a_l) \in R^{s \times l} : s \leq l$
2: $w_1 \leftarrow a_1$
3: **For** $i = 2, \dots, l$ **do**
4:     $w_i \leftarrow a_i - \sum_{h=1}^{i-1} \frac{<a_i, w_h>}{<w_h, w_h>} w_h$
5: Output: $\bar{A} = (w_1, \dots, w_l) \in R^{s \times l}$

In this way, through the Gram-Schmidt orthogonalization, we obtain the matrices $\bar{P} \in R^{m \times k}$ and $\bar{Q} \in R^{k \times n}$ satisfying the orthogonality properties requests to matrices $\hat{P}$ and $\hat{Q}$ and described at the beginning of Section.

The rating forecast matrix $\bar{R}$ is obtained from the product

$$\bar{R} = \bar{P}\bar{Q} \in R^{m \times n} \tag{17}$$

4 Experimental Results

This section shows the analyses conducted and the results of the experimental campaigns. In this first preliminary phase, the recommendation form, developed according to the proposed approach, has been tested. To effectively test this Recommendation Module, which is one of the main modules of the presented framework, two experimental campaigns were conducted. The first campaign concerned a numerical test using a known dataset (MovieLens100k) and a second experimental campaign that concerned the use of a real cultural heritage scenario.

In the first experimental campaign the MovieLens100k [31] database was adopted. This database contains 80000 ratings for the training phase and 100000 rating for testing one. Each of 983 users rated at least 20 of the 1682 movies. The user's profiles are having been constructed through the means of the known ratings. They have been divided by the k categories of the movies. The items profiles have been taken from the database itself. Indeed, there is a matrix that classifies each item for the categories in which the movie falls. Therefore, each component of the item profiles is 1 or 0. This approach does not valorize the proposed method, but we have to work in this way in order to obtain numerical tests. The errors that we have considered are:

- Mean Absolute Error:

$$MAE = \sum_{(i,j) \in N} \frac{|\hat{r}_{ij} - r_{ij}|}{|N|}$$

- Root Mean Squared Error:

$$RMSE = \sqrt{\sum_{(i,j) \in N} \frac{\left(\hat{r}_{ij} - r_{ij}\right)^2}{|N|}}$$

Where N is the set of the pairs (i, j) for which the numerical test is carried out and $\hat{r}_{i,j}$ is the rating forecast of pair (i, j).

In Table 1 there are the results of the tests on the database MovieLens100k.

Table 1. Experimental results of RS on MovieLens100k database.

Method	Performance
MAE	0.7846
RMSE	0.9691

The obtained results show that the proposed approach gives promising results. Moreover the recommender method has a theoretical support structure in order to calculate ratings forecasts.

A further experimental campaign was conducted in order to test the system designed in a real scenario, involving 50 users with heterogeneous characteristics. It was proposed that these users interact with a prototype developed ad hoc, which contains several multimedia contents related to the archaeological park of Paestum, located in southern Italy. The developed prototype is able to recommend the multimedia contents according to the proposed methodology. After the interaction with the prototype, a questionnaire was submitted to the participants to evaluate different aspects:

A. Presentation
B. Reliability
C. Recommendation
D. Performance
E. Usability

Each section of the questionnaire, based on the Likert scale, presented two statements to which five possible answers were associated: I totally disagree - TD, I disagree - D, undecided - U, I agree - A, I totally agree - TA. The answers have been summarised in Table 1. The results of the questionnaire are shown in Table 2 and, in graphic shape, in Fig. 4.

Table 2. Questionnaire answer

Section	Answer				
	TD	D	U	A	TA
A	2	3	1	13	31
B	0	2	2	14	32
C	1	2	1	8	38
D	0	1	2	10	37
E	1	3	4	12	30

From the experimental results, it can be seen that the users have positively evaluated section C and section D, representing the Recommendation and the Performance of the product system.

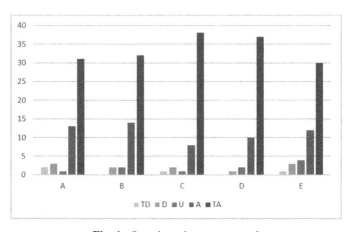

Fig. 4. Questionnaire answer trend

5   Conclusion and Future Works

In this article, a novel approach for the recommendation in the Cultural Heritage field has been introduced. For this purpose, the Recommender Systems, Context Awareness and Digital Storytelling were covered. Besides, the factoring to singular values was presented. The latter was used to develop a novel Content-Based recommendation method that exploits the properties and advantages of matrix factoring. In this way, the proposed approach achieved better rating forecasting results than the previously developed method. According to the results obtained, there is a need to test the proposed methodology with already affirmed recommendation models, such as Collaborative Filtering. Furthermore, future developments include the introduction of contextual information within the proposed model to obtain a more performing model.

References

1. Colace, F., et al.: How to describe cultural heritage resources in the web 2.0 era? In: Proceedings - 11th International Conference on Signal-Image Technology and Internet-Based Systems, SITIS 2015 (2016). https://doi.org/10.1109/sitis.2015.50
2. Atzori, L., Iera, A., Morabito, G.: The internet of things: a survey. Comput. Networks **54**(15), 2787–2805 (2010). https://doi.org/10.1016/j.comnet.2010.05.010
3. Ashton, K.: That 'internet of things' thing. RFID J. **22**(7), 97–114 (2009)
4. Armbrust, M., et al.: A view of cloud computing. Commun. ACM **53**(4), 50–58 (2010). https://doi.org/10.1145/1721654.1721672
5. D'aniello, G., Gaeta, M., Reformat, M.Z.: Collective perception in smart tourism destinations with rough sets. In: 2017 3rd IEEE International Conference on Cybernetics, CYBCONF 2017 - Proceedings, pp. 1–6 (2017). https://doi.org/10.1109/cybconf.2017.7985765
6. Colace, F., De Santo, M., Lombardi, M., Santaniello, D.: CHARS: a cultural heritage adaptive recommender system. In: Proceedings of the 1st ACM International Workshop on Technology Enablers and Innovative Applications for Smart Cities and Communities – TESCA 2019, pp. 58–61 (2019). https://doi.org/10.1145/3364544.3364830
7. Tole, A.A.: Big data challenges. Database Syst. J. **4**(3), 31–40 (2013)
8. Boyd, D., Crawford, K.: Critical questions for big data. Inf. Commun. Soc. **15**(5), 662–679 (2012). https://doi.org/10.1080/1369118X.2012.678878
9. Carratù, M., Dello Iacono, S., Ferro, M., Paciello, V., Pietrosanto, A.: Test platform for data fusion application in indoor positioning. In: Di Francia, G., et al. (eds.) AISEM 2019. LNEE, vol. 629, pp. 329–333. Springer, Cham (2020). https://doi.org/10.1007/978-3-030-37558-4_50
10. Abowd, G.D., Dey, A.K., Brown, P.J., Davies, N., Smith, M., Steggles, P.: Towards a better understanding of context and context-awareness. In: Gellersen, H.-W. (ed.) HUC 1999. LNCS, vol. 1707, pp. 304–307. Springer, Heidelberg (1999). https://doi.org/10.1007/3-540-48157-5_29
11. Bolchini, C., Curino, C., Schreiber, F.A., Tanca, L.: Context integration for mobile data tailoring. In: SEBD 2006 - Proceedings of the 14th Italian Symposium on Advanced Databases Systems (2006). https://doi.org/10.1109/mdm.2006.52
12. Ricci, F., Rokach, L., Shapira, B.: Introduction to recommender systems handbook. In: Ricci, F., Rokach, L., Shapira, B., Kantor, P.B. (eds.) Recommender Systems Handbook. LNCS, pp. 1–35. Springer, Boston, MA (2011). https://doi.org/10.1007/978-0-387-85820-3_1
13. Cutolo, A., et al.: An Ontology-based recommender system in e-commerce. In: 2nd International Workshop on Recommender Systems meet Big Data & Semantic Technologies (co-located with ACM RecSys 2013) (2013)
14. Koren, Y., Bell, R., Volinsky, C.: Matrix factorization techniques for recommender systems. Computer (Long. Beach. Calif) (2009). https://doi.org/10.1109/mc.2009.263
15. Pavlidis, G.: Recommender systems, cultural heritage applications, and the way forward. J. Cult. Heritage (2019). https://doi.org/10.1016/j.culher.2018.06.003
16. Amato, F., et al.: Big data meets digital cultural heritage: design and implementation of SCRABS, a smart context-aware browsing assistant for cultural environments. J. Comput. Cult. Herit. (2017). https://doi.org/10.1145/3012286
17. Colace, F., De Santo, M., Lombardi, M., Mosca, R., Santaniello, D.: A multilayer approach for recommending contextual learning paths. J. Internet Serv. Inf. Secur. **2**(May), 91–102 (2020). https://doi.org/10.22667/JISIS.2020.05.31.091
18. Basile, P., et al.: Augmenting a content-based recommender system with tags for cultural heritage personalization. Pers. Access Cult. Herit. PATCH (2008)

19. Symeonidis, P., Zioupos, A.: Matrix and tensor factorization techniques for recommender systems (2016)
20. Golub, G.H.: Matrix Computations. 4th edn. (2013)
21. Conte, D., Lubich, C.: An error analysis of the multi-configuration time-dependent Hartree method of quantum dynamics. ESAIM Math. Model. Numer. Anal. (2010). https://doi.org/10.1051/m2an/2010018
22. Conte, D.: Dynamical low-rank approximation to the solution of parabolic differential equations. Appl. Numer. Math. **156**, 377–384 (2020). https://doi.org/10.1016/j.apnum.2020.05.011
23. Colace, F., De Santo, M., Lombardi, M., Pascale, F., Santaniello, D., Tucker, A.: A multilevel graph approach for predicting bicycle usage in london area. In: Yang, X.-S., Sherratt, S., Dey, N., Joshi, A. (eds.) Fourth International Congress on Information and Communication Technology. AISC, vol. 1027, pp. 353–362. Springer, Singapore (2020). https://doi.org/10.1007/978-981-32-9343-4_28
24. Villegas, N.M., Sánchez, C., Díaz-Cely, J., Tamura, G.: Characterizing context-aware recommender systems: a systematic literature review. Knowl.-Based Syst. (2018). https://doi.org/10.1016/j.knosys.2017.11.003
25. Casillo, M., Colace, F., De Santo, M., Lemma, S., Lombardi, M.: CAT: a context aware teller for supporting tourist experiences. Int. J. Comput. Sci. Eng. (2019). https://doi.org/10.1504/ijcse.2019.103255
26. Colace, F., Lombardi, M., Pascale, F., Santaniello, D.: A multilevel graph representation for big data interpretation in real scenarios. In: Proceedings - 2018 3rd International Conference on System Reliability and Safety, ICSRS 2018, pp. 40–47 (2019). https://doi.org/10.1109/icsrs.2018.8688834
27. Colace, F., Lombardi, M., Pascale, F., Santaniello, D.: A multi-level approach for forecasting critical events in smart cities. In: Proceedings - DMSVIVA 2018: 24th International DMS Conference on Visualization and Visual Languages (2018). https://doi.org/10.18293/dmsviva2018-002
28. Colace, F., Khan, M., Lombardi, M., Santaniello, D.: A multigraph approach for supporting computer network monitoring systems. In: Yang, X.-S., Sherratt, S., Dey, N., Joshi, A. (eds.) Proceedings of Fifth International Congress on Information and Communication Technology. AISC, vol. 1184, pp. 470–477. Springer, Singapore (2021). https://doi.org/10.1007/978-981-15-5859-7_46
29. Alexander, B., Levine, A.: Web 2.0 storytelling: emergence of a new genre. Educ. Rev. (2008)
30. Lambert, J., Hessler, B.: Digital Storytelling: Capturing Lives, Creating Community. Routledge (2018)
31. Harper, F.M., Konstan, J.A.: The MovieLens datasets. ACM Trans. Interact. Intell. Syst. **5**(4), 1–19 (2016). https://doi.org/10.1145/2827872

A Contextual Approach for Coastal Tourism and Cultural Heritage Enhancing

Fabio Clarizia, Massimo De Santo, Marco Lombardi⬥, Rosalba Mosca⬥,
and Domenico Santaniello[✉] ⬥

DIIN, University of Salerno, Fisciano, Italy
{fclarizia,desanto,malombardi,rmosca,dsantaniello}@unisa.it

Abstract. In the panorama of Italian coastal tourism, there are many unique and unexplored places. These places, which suffer from the lack of government investment, present the need to be promoted through low consumption systems and widely used: distributed applications.

The present work aims to develop innovative solutions to support citizens and tourists to offer advanced services, highly customizable, able to allow, through the use of new technologies, a more engaging, stimulating, and attractive use of information than the current forms. The developed system is based on graph-based formalisms such as Context Dimension Tree and Bayesian Networks, representing the context through its main components and react to it anticipating users' needs. Through the development of a mobile app, it was analyzed a case study applied in the area of Amalfi Coast (in Italy). Finally, an experimental campaign was conducted with promising results.

Keywords: E-tourism · Coastal tourism · Context awareness · Cultural heritage · Recommender system

1 Introduction

Nowadays, Italian coasts represent one of the most characteristic and priceless tourist places globally, i.e., offering users an important cultural heritage. Unfortunately, not all sites receive the attention or financial support necessary to bring out their uniqueness. Thanks to the advent of new technologies and the smart cities phenomenon, these places could finally be protected and promoted. In fact, the adoption of Future Internet (FI) technology and its most challenging components, such as the Internet of Things (IoT) [1] and the Internet of Services (IoS) [2], can provide the foundation for progress towards unified platforms that offer a variety of advanced services. Besides, the constant use of mobile devices to form interactive and participatory sensor networks, which allow users to collect, analyze and share local knowledge, can contribute to developing the smart city paradigm where the citizen is called to play an active role [3, 4]. One of the sectors that could potentially benefit the most is tourism. In such a scenario, places and objects such as sculptures, buildings, etc. can be brought into contact with users in a completely new and stimulating way [5]. In particular, data, which represents a significant added value,

© Springer Nature Switzerland AG 2021
A. Del Bimbo et al. (Eds.): ICPR 2020 Workshops, LNCS 12667, pp. 318–325, 2021.
https://doi.org/10.1007/978-3-030-68787-8_23

can be processed to enrich further the system's ability to relate man and machine. In this regard, one of the main problems is to model the awareness of the context. This problem can be solved through the Context Dimension Tree: a graph formalism representing all possible contexts [6, 7]. The next step is to predict the possible scenarios to model the proposals to each user's needs. This further problem can be addressed through the use of Bayesian Networks [8]. Bayesian networks represent graph formalisms able to predict specific events when some variables (in our case, contextual variables) change [9].

A modern system, able to take advantage of context analysis, needs it to understand what the user is doing [10]. This objective is achieved by analyzing data coming from reality or from the services he is using at that moment [11, 12], from augmented reality services [13, 14] or technologies aimed at predicting needs [15, 16].

These technologies have also been used in tourism to valorize Cultural Heritage [17, 18]. One of the main challenges is to find the available information [19], filter it avoiding the overload of information [20], and process it by combining it with the interests, preferences, and context of the user [21].

In this scenario, it could be useful a platform able to build custom paths, acquiring contextual information from the environment [22] in order to provide the tourist with tailored support through a chatbot able to maintain a logical discourse with the tourist [23].

This paper intends to propose a system based on a "Content/API Economy Platform", characterized by a strong awareness of the context. The designed system allows the content-generating actors (Institutions such as Museums, Communities or companies, and individuals) and the content user actors (the Institutions themselves, the service companies and, above all, the end-users) to operate through a platform-broker that, through the automatic composition (orchestration) of services, is able to activate in a controlled way they access and consumption of the information contained in the Knowledge Base. In fact, the operating modes include the entire life cycle of the Knowledge Base that provides for the collection, storage, classification, and availability of the contents accessible through simple mobile applications oriented to provide tourists with richer visiting experiences [24].

In particular, through the identification and processing of the context of use in which the user operates, it is therefore essential to define flexible methods, i.e., to dynamically recommend data and services that best meet users' situational needs. When necessary, this approach can tailor the information extracted to offer the user what may be useful at a given time.

2 System Architecture

As highlighted above, we want to propose a system for the automatic selection of services adaptive to the context and its users' needs.

The characteristics of the proposed architecture (Fig. 1) mainly concern the information content that is available to end-users through the orchestration of services, proposing three different points of view:

- Representation of the Context;
- Data Management and Organization;
- Inferential Motors.

2.1 Context Representation

First of all, it is intended to convey to different categories of users, at a specific time, useful information in a given context; in practice, it is intended to create a system with a high degree of Context-Awareness. Knowledge of the context in which the user finds himself allows, in fact, to offer a wide range of services that can help the user during daily, work or private life, managing the time and resources at disposal, revealing what is around and satisfying their needs. The real-time knowledge of the context in which the user finds himself, through its representation in the form of graphs, allows, therefore, to offer highly personalized services ("tailored") able to take into account countless aspects as well as, for example, the mood of the user through an analysis of Affective Computing. For this reason, the application fields can be the most diverse: cultural heritage, tourism, e-learning, etc.

Context Awareness must be understood as a set of technical features able to give added value to services in different application segments. Context-Aware Computing applications can exploit, in our case, these features to present context information to the user or to propose an appropriate selection of actions [25]. In order to obtain a better representation of the various features, therefore, context representation formalities will be adopted, able to define, in detail, the needs of the user in the environment in which he is acting, through an approach such as: Where, Why, When, How. Everything will be declined through the state-of-the-art technologies present in the sector.

2.2 Data Management and Representation

In this scenario, therefore, data represent the key to building and enabling innovative services; therefore, we intend to create a Knowledge Base (KB) to collect, process and manage information in real-time. In this regard, as Knowledge Management Systems (KOS), we refer to some well-known schemes such as Taxonomies, Thesauri, or other types of vocabularies that, together with Ontologies, represent useful tools that allow modeling the reality of interest in concepts and relations between concepts. The resulting advantages are many: the use of Ontologies, for example, allows to fix a series of key concepts and definitions related to a given domain, which can be shared, providing the correct terminologies (collaborative knowledge sharing). Moreover, an ontology allows complete reuse of the knowledge encoded in it also within other ontologies or for their completion (non-redundancy of information) [26]. Electronic computers' interpretation enables the automatic treatment of knowledge, with considerable benefits (Semantic Web).

2.3 Inferential Engines

Finally, the system, designed to be in continuous operation, will have to continuously collect data from various sources and process them immediately to provide accurate services according to users and events. These, detected and analyzed, will have to be translated into facts associated with specific semantic values: it is necessary, therefore, to use an inferential engine able to conclude by applying some rules on the reported facts.

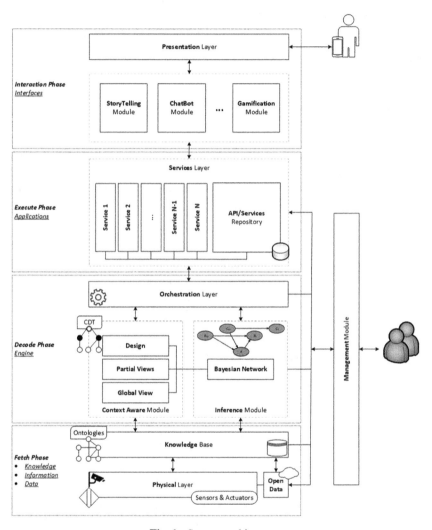

Fig. 1. System architecture

3   Experimental Results

In order to provide a validation of the proposed methodology, a prototype was developed. The prototype is implemented through a hybrid mobile app and a server-side component implementation. The developed App is designed to support tourists (users) visiting Campania's coastal area (South of Italy Region). Only some user preferences and interests were considered in the first phase of methodology validation, and only the main services and points of interest have been identified. The experimental phase involved 60 volunteers aged between 21 and 55 who were unknown from the study's main purpose. The prototype was installed on the mobile device of each participant, and after an interaction phase, the system proposes a questionnaire covering several sections:

A. Presentation
B. Usability
C. Performance
D. Recommendation
E. Reliability.

Each section presents two assertions associated with five possible answers according to the Likert scale: I totally disagree - TD, I disagree - D, undecided - U, I agree - A, I totally agree - TA. The answers to the questionnaire have been collected in Table 1.

Table 1. Questionnaire answers

Section	Answer				
	TD	D	U	A	TA
A	0	16	22	53	29
B	5	0	24	50	41
C	6	8	12	58	36
D	4	0	8	62	46
E	6	7	13	60	34

Table 1 shows that the users agree or strongly agree that the system provides a satisfying and reliable recommendation and contextual information and appropriate services on the site and its points of interest, meets the tourist's needs and experiences. Therefore, users show an excellent appreciation for the app: they appreciated the contents and services proposed in general.

Also, further analysis was conducted involving a smaller number of participants to evaluate the system's ability to recommend. In the first experimental phase, three pathways (P1, P2, and P3) and two activities (A1 and A2) were selected to be recommended to users. This experimental phase was divided into three steps. In the first phase, the users respond to an aptitude test. According to these tests, the users were divided into macro-groups for aptitude similarity. Subsequently, a training set was created, consisting of about 75% of the participants belonging to each macro-group. In the second phase, the training set users were able to experience the system's suggestions and interact with it. In this phase, the system could learn about the system. In the third and last phase, the users belonging to the test set group have brought to experiment with the prototype's suggestions and evaluate if the type of path or activity suggested by the system was inherent to the context presented. The results were collected in the form of a confusion matrix in Table 2.

Table 2. Confusion matrix

		Reference				
		P1	P2	P3	A1	A2
Prediction	P1	58	8	2	7	1
	P2	7	39	9	4	5
	P3	0	6	45	5	7
	A1	8	5	4	40	1
	A2	0	6	3	4	51

Overall Accuracy : 71,69%

According to Table 2, the overall accuracy of the system is higher than 71%. This result is very encouraging and could improve over time, based on the increase of experimental data available (Fig. 2).

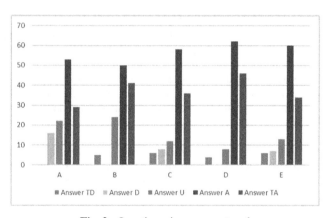

Fig. 2. Questionnaire answers trend

4 Conclusion and Future Works

This paper aimed to introduce a framework that can support tourists during each phase of the travel experience in the coastal area south of Italy. The system was designed to provide highly customizable and tailored services, making a tailored and unique experience. The innovation of the recommender system presented lies in the use of a high degree of context-awareness.

The proposed architecture could be used in several contexts and applications. The experimental results show that the system is able to recommend a high degree of reliability with results. In addition, the experimental campaign shows users positive feedback in-service presentation, usability, and performance shown. Future developments include improvements to the developed prototype and enlargement of the experimental campaign.

References

1. Ashton, K.: That 'Internet of Things' thing. RFID J. **22**(7), 97–114 (2009)
2. Armbrust, M., et al.: A view of cloud computing. Commun. ACM **53**(4), 50–58 (2010). https://doi.org/10.1145/1721654.1721672
3. Annunziata, G., Colace, F., De Santo, M., Lemma, S., Lombardi, M.: Appoggiomarino: a context aware app for e-citizenship. In: ICEIS 2016 - Proceedings of 18th International Conference on Enterprise Information System, vol. 2, pp. 273–281 (2016)
4. Colace, F., Lombardi, M., Pascale, F., Santaniello, D.: A multilevel graph representation for big data interpretation in real scenarios. In: Proceedings - 2018 3rd International Conference on System Reliability and Safety, ICSRS 2018, pp. 40–47 (2019). https://doi.org/10.1109/ICSRS.2018.8688834
5. Amato, F., et al.: Big data meets digital cultural heritage: design and implementation of SCRABS, a smart context-aware browsing assistant for cultural environments. J. Comput. Cult. Herit. (2017). https://doi.org/10.1145/3012286
6. Schreiber, F.A., Bolchini, C., Curino, C.A., Quintarelli, E., Tanca, L.: Context information for knowledge reshaping. Int. J. Web Eng. Technol. **5**, 88–103 (2009). https://doi.org/10.1504/ijwet.2009.025015
7. Colace, F., Khan, M., Lombardi, M., Santaniello, D.: A multigraph approach for supporting computer network monitoring systems. In: Yang, X.-S., Sherratt, S., Dey, N., Joshi, A. (eds.) Proceedings of Fifth International Congress on Information and Communication Technology. AISC, vol. 1184, pp. 470–477. Springer, Singapore (2021). https://doi.org/10.1007/978-981-15-5859-7_46
8. Colace, F., Lombardi, M., Pascale, F., Santaniello, D.: A multi-level approach for forecasting critical events in smart cities. In: Proceedings - DMSVIVA 2018: 24th International DMS Conference on Visualization and Visual Languages (2018). https://doi.org/10.18293/DMSVIVA2018-002
9. Colace, F., De Santo, M., Lombardi, M., Mosca, R., Santaniello, D.: A multilayer approach for recommending contextual learning paths. J. Internet Serv. Inf. Secur. **10**(2), 91–102 (2020). https://doi.org/10.22667/JISIS.2020.05.31.091
10. Dey, A.K.: Understanding and using context. Pers. Ubiquitous Comput. **5**(1), 4–7 (2001). https://doi.org/10.1007/s007790170019
11. Schilit, B., Adams, N., Want, R.: Context-aware computing applications. In: 1994 First Workshop on Mobile Computing Systems and Applications, pp. 85–90 (1994). https://doi.org/10.1109/WMCSA.1994.16
12. Flores, O., Rayle, L.: How cities use regulation for innovation: the case of Uber, Lyft and Sidecar in San Francisco. Transp. Res. Procedia **25**, 3756–3768 (2017). https://doi.org/10.1016/j.trpro.2017.05.232
13. Rauschnabel, P.A., Rossmann, A., tom Dieck, M.C.: An adoption framework for mobile augmented reality games: the case of Pokémon Go. Comput. Hum. Behav. **76**, 276–286 (2017). https://doi.org/10.1016/j.chb.2017.07.030

14. Thakur, S.: Personalization for Google now. In: Proceedings of the 10th ACM Conference on Recommender Systems, p. 3 (2016). https://doi.org/10.1145/2959100.2959192
15. Li, D., Chen, X., Zhang, Z., Huang, K.: Learning deep context-aware features over body and latent parts for person re-identification. In: 2017 IEEE Conference on Computer Vision and Pattern Recognition (CVPR), pp. 7398–7407 (2017). https://doi.org/10.1109/CVPR.201 7.782
16. Kepuska, V., Bohouta, G.: Next-generation of virtual personal assistants (Microsoft Cortana, Apple Siri, Amazon Alexa and Google Home). In: 2018 IEEE 8th Annual Computing and Communication Workshop and Conference (CCWC), pp. 99–103 (2018). https://doi.org/10. 1109/CCWC.2018.8301638
17. Logesh, R., Subramaniyaswamy, V.: Exploring hybrid recommender systems for personalized travel applications. In: Mallick, P.K., Balas, V.E., Bhoi, A.K., Zobaa, A.F. (eds.) Cognitive Informatics and Soft Computing. AISC, vol. 768, pp. 535–544. Springer, Singapore (2019). https://doi.org/10.1007/978-981-13-0617-4_52
18. Lu, J., Wu, D., Mao, M., Wang, W., Zhang, G.: Recommender system application developments: a survey. Decis. Support Syst. **74**, 12–32 (2015). https://doi.org/10.1016/j.dss.2015. 03.008
19. Cheverst, K., Davies, N., Mitchell, K., Friday, A., Efstratiou, C.: Developing a context-aware electronic tourist guide. In: Proceedings of the SIGCHI Conference on Human Factors in Computing Systems - CHI 2000, pp. 17–24 (2000). https://doi.org/10.1145/332040.332047
20. Gavalas, D., Konstantopoulos, C., Mastakas, K., Pantziou, G.: Mobile recommender systems in tourism. J. Netw. Comput. Appl. **39**, 319–333 (2014). https://doi.org/10.1016/j.jnca.2013. 04.006
21. Colace, F., et al.: How to describe cultural heritage resources in the web 2.0 Era?. In: Proceedings - 11th International Conference on Signal-Image Technology and Internet-Based Systems, SITIS 2015 (2016). https://doi.org/10.1109/SITIS.2015.50
22. Colace, F., De Santo, M., Lombardi, M., Pascale, F., Santaniello, D., Tucker, A.: A multilevel graph approach for predicting bicycle usage in London area. In: Yang, X.-S., Sherratt, S., Dey, N., Joshi, A. (eds.) Fourth International Congress on Information and Communication Technology. AISC, vol. 1027, pp. 353–362. Springer, Singapore (2020). https://doi.org/10. 1007/978-981-32-9343-4_28
23. Colace, F., De Santo, M., Lombardi, M., Santaniello, D.: CHARS: a cultural heritage adaptive recommender system. In: Proceedings of the 1st ACM International Workshop on Technology Enablers and Innovative Applications for Smart Cities and Communities – TESCA 2019, pp. 58–61 (2019). https://doi.org/10.1145/3364544.3364830
24. Ioannidis, Y., El Raheb, K., Toli, E., Katifori, A., Boile, M., Mazura, M.: One object many stories: Introducing ICT in museums and collections through digital storytelling. In: Proceedings of the DigitalHeritage 2013 - Federating the 19th Int'l VSMM, 10th Eurographics GCH, and 2nd UNESCO Memory of the World Conferences, Plus Special Sessions fromCAA, Arqueologica 2.0 et al. (2013). https://doi.org/10.1109/DigitalHeritage.2013.6743772
25. Raverdy, P.G., Riva, O., De La Chapelle, A., Chibout, R., Issarny, V.: Efficient context-aware service discovery in multi-protocol pervasive environments. In: Proceedings - IEEE International Conference on Mobile Data Management (2006). https://doi.org/10.1109/MDM.200 6.78
26. Chang, M., D'Aniello, G., Gaeta, M., Orciuoli, F., Sampson, D., Simonelli, C.: Building ontology-driven tutoring models for intelligent tutoring systems using data mining. IEEE Access **8**, 48151–48162 (2020). https://doi.org/10.1109/ACCESS.2020.2979281

A Comparison of Character-Based Neural Machine Translations Techniques Applied to Spelling Normalization

Miguel Domingo[✉] and Francisco Casacuberta

PRHLT Research Center, Universitat Politècnica de València, Valencia, Spain
{midobal,fcn}@prhlt.upv.es

Abstract. The lack of spelling conventions and the natural evolution of human language create a linguistic barrier inherent in historical documents. This barrier has always been a concern for scholars in humanities. In order to tackle this problem, spelling normalization aims to adapt a document's orthography to modern standards. In this work, we evaluate several character-based neural machine translation normalization approaches—using modern documents to enrich the neural models. We evaluated these approaches on several datasets from different languages and time periods, reaching the conclusion that each approach is better suited for a different set of documents.

1 Introduction

Due to the lack of spelling conventions and the nature of human language, orthography in historical texts changes depending on the author and time period. For instance, as Laing [22] pointed out, the data in *LALME* (Linguistic Atlas of Late Medieval English) indicate 45 different forms recorded for the pronoun *it*, 64 for the pronoun *she* and more than 500 for the preposition *through*. This linguistic variation has always been a concern for scholars in humanities [3].

Since historical documents are an important part of our cultural heritage, interest in their effective natural language processing is on the rise [3]. However, the aforementioned linguistic problems suppose an additional challenge. In order to solve these problems, spelling normalization aims to achieve an orthography consistency by adapting a document's spelling to modern standards. Figure 1 shows an example of normalizing the spelling of a text.

In this work, we evaluate several normalization approaches based on different character-based neural machine translation (NMT) techniques. The rest of this document is structured as follows: Sect. 2 introduces the related work. Then, in Sect. 3 we present the different character-based NMT techniques and normalization approaches. Section 4 describes the experiments conducted in order to assess our proposal. The results of those experiments are presented and discussed in Sect. 5. Finally, in Sect. 6, conclusions are drawn.

© Springer Nature Switzerland AG 2021
A. Del Bimbo et al. (Eds.): ICPR 2020 Workshops, LNCS 12667, pp. 326–338, 2021.
https://doi.org/10.1007/978-3-030-68787-8_24

¿Cómo estays, Rozinante, tan delgado?   ¿Cómo estáis, Rocinante, tan delgado?
Porque nunca se come, y se trabaja.   Porque nunca se come, y se trabaja.
Pues ¿qué es de la ceuada y de la paja?   Pues ¿qué es de la cebada y de la paja?
No me dexa mi amo ni vn bocado.   No me deja mi amo ni un bocado.

Fig. 1. Example of adapting a document's spelling to modern standards. Characters that need to be adapted are denoted in red. Its modern versions are denoted in teal. Example extracted from *El Quijote* [13]. (Color figure online)

2 Related Work

Some approaches to spelling normalization include creating an interactive tool that includes spell checking techniques to assist the user in detecting spelling variations [2]. A combination of a weighted finite-state transducer, combined with a modern lexicon, a phonological transcriber and a set of rules [31]. A combination of a list of historical words, a list of modern words and character-based statistical machine translation (SMT) [36]. A multi-task learning approach using a deep bi-LSTM applied at a character level [4]. The application of a token/segment-level character-based SMT approach to normalize historical and user-created words [26]. The use of rule-based MT, character-based SMT (CBSMT) and character-based NMT (CBNMT) [21]. Domingo and Casacuberta [10] evaluated word-based and character-based MT approaches, finding character-based to be more suitable for this task and that SMT systems outperformed NMT systems. Tang et al. [42], however, compared many different neural architectures and reported that the NMT models are much better than SMT models in terms of CER. Hämäläinen et al. [16] evaluated SMT, NMT, an edit-distance approach, and a rule-based finite state transducer, and advocated for a combination of these approaches to make use of their individual strengths. Finally, Domingo and Casacuberta [11] proposed a method for enriching neural system using modern documents.

Character-based MT strikes to be a solution in MT to reduce the training vocabulary by dividing words into a sequence of characters, and treating each character as if it were a basic unit. Although it was already being researched in SMT [27,43], its interest has increased with NMT. Some approaches to CBNMT consist in using hierarchical NMT [23], a character level decoder [7], a character level encoder [9] or, for alphabets in which words are composed by fewer characters, by constructing an NMT system that takes advantage of that alphabet [8].

3 Normalization Approaches

In this section, we present the different normalization approaches under study— which are based in several CBNMT techniques—and the CBSMT approach which is used as an additional baseline.

Given a source sentence $\mathbf{x}$, MT aims to find the most likely translation $\hat{\mathbf{y}}$ [5]:

$$\hat{\mathbf{y}} = \arg \max_{\mathbf{y}} \; Pr(\mathbf{y} \mid \mathbf{x}) \tag{1}$$

3.1 Character-Based SMT

CBSMT computes Eq. (1) at a character level, using models that rely on a log-linear combination of different models [29]: namely, phrase-based alignment models, reordering models and language models; among others [20,46].

Since CBSMT approaches are still part of the state of the art for some tasks [16,21,42], we used a CBSMT approach as an additional baseline—we considered as baseline the quality of the original document with respect to its ground truth version, in which the spelling has already been normalized. To that end, considering the document's language as the source language and its normalized version as the target language, we split words into character and applied conventional SMT.

3.2 Character-Based NMT

CBNMT models Eq. (1) with a neural network. Its most frequent architecture is based on an encoder-decoder (although others architectures are possible), featuring recurrent networks [1,40], convolutional networks [14] or attention mechanisms [44]. At the encoding state, the source sentence is projected into a distributed representation. Then, at the decoding step, the decoder generates its most likely translation—word by word—using a beam search method [40]. The model parameters are typically estimated jointly on large parallel corpora, via stochastic gradient descent [34,35]. Finally, at decoding time, the system obtains the most likely translation by means of a beam search method.

CBNMT works at a character level: words are split into a sequence of characters and each character is treated as a basic unit. There are different approaches to CBNMT, some of which combine character level strategies with sub-word level strategies. In this work, we made our normalization approaches using the following CBNMT techniques:

- **CBNMT**: This technique uses a character level strategy. Words from both the source and the target are split into characters.
- **SubChar**: This technique combines a sub-word level and a character level strategies. Source words are split into sub-words and target words into characters.
- **CharSub**: This technique combines a character level and a sub-word level strategy. Source words are split into characters and target words into sub-words.

For working at a sub-word level, we use Byte Pair Encoding [37]. This algorithm is a standard in NMT. Based on the intuition that various word classes are translatable via smaller units than words, this technique aims at encoding rare and unknown words as sequences of sub-words units.

Normalization Approaches. For each CBNMT technique (see Sect. 3.2), we propose a different normalization approach. Considering the document's language as the source language and its normalized version as the target language, each approach follows a CBNMT strategy. Source and target words are split into either characters or sub-words (depending of the technique) and, then, conventional NMT is applied to train the normalization system.

Additionally, considering how the scarce availability of parallel training data is a frequent problem when working with historical documents [4]—specially for NMT approaches, which need an abundant quantity of parallel training data. Thus, we propose additional normalization approaches (one for each CBNMT) based on Domingo and Casacuberta [11]'s proposal for enriching normalization models using modern documents to generate synthetic data with which to increase the training data. To achieve this, we follow these steps:

1. We train a CBSMT system—since SMT is less affected by the problem of scarce availability of training data—using the normalized version of the training dataset as source and the original version as target, and following the *cbnmt* technique (i.e., splitting all words into characters).
2. We use this system to translate the modern documents, obtaining a new version of the documents which, hopefully, is able to capture the same orthography inconsistencies that the original documents have. This new version, together with the original modern document, conform a synthetic parallel data which can be used as additional training data.
3. We combine the synthetic data with the training dataset, replicating several times the training dataset in order to match the size of the synthetic data and avoid overfitting [6].
4. We use the resulting dataset to train the enriched CBNMT normalization system.

4   Experiments

In this section, we describe the experimental conditions arranged in order to assess our proposal: MT systems, corpora and evaluation metrics.

4.1   Systems

NMT systems were built using `OpenNMT-py` [18]. We used long short-term memory units [15], with all model dimensions set to 512. We trained the system using Adam [17] with a fixed learning rate of 0.0002 [45] and a batch size of 60. We applied label smoothing of 0.1 [41]. At the inference time, we used a beam search with a beam size of 6.

The CBSMT systems used for enriching approaches were trained with `Moses` [19]. Following the standard procedure, we used `SRILM` [39] to estimate a 5-gram language model—smoothed with the improved KneserNey method—and optimized the weights of the log-lineal model with MERT [28].

As baseline, we considered the quality of the original document with respect to its ground truth version, in which the spelling has already been normalized. Additionally, taking into account that CBSMT approaches are still part of the state of the art for some tasks [16, 21, 42], we used a CBSMT approach as an additional baseline. This approach uses the CBSMT models trained for the enriched CBNMT approaches.

4.2 Corpora

In order to asses our proposal, we made use of the following corpora:

Entremeses y Comedias [13]: A 17th century Spanish collection of comedies by Miguel de Cervantes. It is composed of 16 plays, 8 of which have a very short length.

Quijote [13]: The 17th century Spanish two-volumes novel by Miguel de Cervantes.

Bohorič [25]: A collection of 18th century Slovene texts written in the old Bohorič alphabet.

Gaj [25]: A collection of 19th century Slovene texts written in the Gaj alphabet.

Table 1 shows the corpora statistics. As we can see, the size of the corpora is small. Thus, the need of profiting from modern documents to increase the training data. To that respect, we selected half a million sentences from Open-Subtitles [24]—a collection of movie subtitles in different languages—to use them as monolingual data to enrich the neural systems.

Table 1. Corpora statistics. $|S|$ stands for number of sentences, $|T|$ for number of tokens, $|V|$ for size of the vocabulary and $|W|$ for the number of words whose spelling does not match modern standards. M denotes millions and K thousand. *Modern documents* is the monolingual data used to enrich the neural systems.

		Entremeses y Comedias	Quijote	Bohorič	Gaj
Train	$|S|$	35.6K	48.0K	3.6K	13.0K
	$|T|$	250.0/244.0K	436.0/428.0K	61.2/61.0K	198.2/197.6K
	$|V|$	19.0/18.0K	24.4/23.3K	14.3/10.9K	34.5/30.7K
	$|W|$	52.4K	97.5K	33.0K	32.7K
Development	$|S|$	2.0K	2.0K	447	1.6K
	$|T|$	13.7/13.6K	19.0/18.0K	7.1/7.1K	25.7/25.6K
	$|V|$	3.0/3.0K	3.2/3.2K	2.9/2.5K	8.2/7.7K
	$|W|$	1.9K	4.5K	3.8K	4.5K
Test	$|S|$	2.0K	2.0K	448	1.6K
	$|T|$	15.0/13.3K	18.0/18.0K	7.3/7.3K	26.3/26.2K
	$|V|$	2.7/2.6K	3.2/3.2K	3.0/2.6K	8.4/8.0K
	$|W|$	3.3K	3.8K	3.8K	4.8K
Modern documents	$|S|$	500.0K	500.0K	500.0K	500.0K
	$|T|$	3.5M	3.5M	3.0M	3.0M
	$|V|$	67.3K	67.3K	84.7K	84.7K

4.3   Metrics

We made use of the following well-known metrics in order to compare our different strategies:

Character Error Rate (CER): number of character edit operations (insertion, substitution and deletion), normalized by the number of characters in the final translation.

Translation Error Rate (TER) [38]: number of word edit operations (insertion, substitution, deletion and swapping), normalized by the number of words in the final translation.

BiLingual Evaluation Understudy (BLEU) [30]: geometric average of the modified n-gram precision, multiplied by a brevity factor.

In order to ensure consistency with BLEU scores, we used `sacreBLEU` [32]. Additionally, in order to determine whether two systems presented statistically significant differences, we applied approximate randomization tests [33] with $10,000$ repetitions and using a p-value of 0.05.

5   Results

Table 2 presents the results of our experimental session. As baseline, we assessed the spelling differences of the original documents with respect to their normalized version. Additionally, since CBSMT approaches are still part of the state of the art for some tasks [16, 21, 42], we used a CBSMT approach as a second baseline.

Table 2. Experimental results. Baseline system corresponds to considering the original document as the document to which the spelling has been normalized to match modern standards. All results are significantly different between all systems except those denoted with † and ‡ (respectively). Best results are denoted in **bold**.

System	Entremeses y Comedias			Quijote			Bohorič			Gaj		
	CER [↓]	TER [↓]	BLEU [↑]	CER [↓]	TER [↓]	BLEU [↑]	CER [↓]	TER [↓]	BLEU [↑]	CER [↓]	TER [↓]	BLEU [↑]
Baseline	8.1	28.0	47.0	7.9	19.5	59.4	21.7	49.0	18.0	3.5	12.3	72.6
CBSMT	1.3	4.4	91.7	2.5	3.0†	94.4†	2.4	8.7	80.4	1.4	5.1	88.3
CBNMT	1.7†	12.0	82.7	2.7	4.3†	93.3‡	29.4	39.5	48.7	31.5‡	36.9	53.1
SubChar	23.3	32.8	54.1	2.2†	3.7	93.8‡	36.7	47.7	39.4	32.7	37.3	52.4
CharSub	5.8	18.2	75.2	3.7	5.8	89.8	67.9	83.8	5.3	37.2	48.1	36.3
Enriched CBNMT	1.7†	13.3	79.4†	2.2†	4.0†	93.2‡	28.6	38.3	49.5	30.5	35.4†	54.9†
Enriched SubChar	37.8	35.8	59.3	2.3†	3.3†	94.9†	29.5	36.9	51.5	31.5‡	35.9†	54.3†
Enriched CharSub	3.8	15.2	78.9†	2.3†	4.1†	93.0‡	27.5	39.6	47.2	29.4	37.2	52.3

With a few exceptions, all approaches successfully improved the baseline according to all metrics. Those exceptions include all approaches using *Bohorič* and *Gaj*—this behavior was already noticed by Domingo and Casacuberta [10] and is most likely related to the small size of the corpora and the nature of Slovene—and the SubChar approaches with *Entremeses y Comedias*.

From all the proposed approaches, CBNMT yielded the best results in all cases except with *El Quijote*, for which the best results were achieved using the SubChar approach. While this last approach yielded improvements for *El Quijote*, results were slightly worse for *Gaj*, considerably worse for *Bohorič* and significantly worse for *Entremeses y Comedias*. The CharSub approach yielded the worst results in all cases. These results, however, behave differently for each task: while they are only slightly worse than CBNMT's result for *El Quijote*, they are significantly worse for *Bohorič*. This shows that not all approaches are equally suited for each task.

Profiting from modern documents to enrich the neural systems improved results in all cases, except for a few exceptions in which they were not significantly different. In the cases of *Bohorič* and *Gaj*, however, these improvements were still worse than the baseline. None the less, results demonstrate how profiting from modern documents successfully improve the neural systems. In a future work, we shall investigate further methods for profiting from these documents.

All in all, except for *El Quijote*—for which the enriched SubChar approached yielded results as good as or better than the CBSMT approach—the CBSMT approach yielded the best results in all cases and according to all metrics. These results are coherent with other results reported in the literature [11,16,42].

5.1   In-depth Comparison

In this section, we study the behavior of each normalization approach when normalizing a sentence from each dataset.

Figure 2 shows an example from *Entremeses y Comedias*. In this case, the normalization only affects two characters. The CBSMT approach is able to successfully normalized those characters. However, it introduces an error (it normalizes the word *Salid* as *Salí*).

Both the CBNMT and the enriched CBNMT approaches behave as the CBSMT approach: they successfully normalized the words *O* and *moço*, but introduce an error normalizing the word *Salid*.

The SubChar approach successfully normalizes the word *moço* but makes a great mistake normalizing the word *O*. Additionally, it fails at normalizing the word *Salid*—it makes the same mistake as the previous approaches–and adds a new word between *Salid* and *fuera*. Moreover, both this extra word and the error normalizing *O* correspond to made-up words. This phenomenon has been observed on other tasks [12] and it is most likely due to an incorrect segmentation of a word via the sub-word algorithm used in this approach (see Sect. 3.2). The enriched version of this approach solves this problem. However, part of the sentence (*Salí fuera;*) is gone. This is a known miss-behavior of neural systems in MT.

Finally, the CharSub approach is able to successfully normalize the words *O* and *moço* but fails at normalizing *Salid*—confusing that word with *allí*.

Original: ¡O mal logrado moço! Salid fuera;
Normalized: ¡Oh mal logrado mozo! Salid fuera;

CBSMT: ¡Oh mal logrado mozo! Salí fuera;

CBNMT: ¡Oh mal logrado mozo! Salí fuera;
Enriched CBNMT: ¡Oh mal logrado mozo! Salí fuera;

SubChar: gueso mal logrado mozo Salí guesto fuera;
Enriched SubChar: ¡Oh mal logrado mozo! ‿‿‿‿ ‿‿‿‿‿

CharSub: ¡Oh mal logrado mozo! allí fuera;
Enriched CharSub: ¡Oh mal logrado mozo! Salí fuera;

Fig. 2. Example of modernizing a sentence from *Entremeses y Comedias* with all the different approaches. ‿ denotes a character that has been removed as part of its normalization. Unnormalized characters that should have been normalized and wrongly normalized characters are denoted in red. Characters which were successfully normalized are denoted in teal. (Color figure online)

Its enriched version improves that error, but it still is not able to make the correct normalization.

Original: "Para esso se yo vn buen remedio", dixo el del Bosque;
Normalized: "Para es‿o sé yo un buen remedio", dijo el del Bosque;

CBSMT: "Para es‿o sé yo un buen remedio", dijo el del Bosque;

CBNMT: "Para es‿o sé yo un buen remedio", dijo el del Bosque;
Enriched CBNMT: "Para es‿o se yo un buen remedio", dijo el del Bosque;

SubChar: "Para es‿o se yo un buen remedio", dijo el del Bosque;
Enriched SubChar: "Para es‿o sé yo un buen remedio", dijo el del Bosque;

CharSub: "Para es‿o se yo un buen remedio", dijo el del Bosque;
Enriched CharSub: "Para es‿o se yo un buen remedio", dijo el del Bosque;

Fig. 3. Example of modernizing a sentence from *El Quijote* with all the different approaches. ‿ denotes a character that has been removed as part of its normalization. Unnormalized characters that should have been normalized and wrongly normalized characters are denoted in red. Characters which were successfully normalized are denoted in teal. (Color figure online)

In the example from *El Quijote* (see Fig. 3), there are four characters that need to be normalized. In this case, the CBSMT, CBNMT and Enriched SubChar approaches are able to successfully normalized the whole sentence. The other approaches, however, fail to normalize the word *se* with all of them leaving the original word unnormalized. It is worth noting how, despite that the enriched CBNMT approach offered results equal or better than the CBNMT approached, in this case its normalized is slightly worse.

Original: vadljajo ali lófajo, de bi svédili, kdo jim je kriv te nefrezhe.
Normalized: vadljajo ali losajo, da bi izvedeli, kdo jim je kriv te nesreč_e.

CBSMT: vadljajo ali losajo, da bi izvedeli, kdo jim je kriv te nesreč_e.

CBNMT: vadljajo ali losajo, da bi _zvedili, kdo jim je kriv te nesreč_e.
Enriched CBNMT: vadljajo ali losajo, da bi _zvedili, kdo jim je kriv te nesreč_e.

SubChar: vadol ali lozoja, da bi _zvedili, kdo jim je kriv te nesreč_e.
Enriched SubChar: vadljajo ali losajo, da bi _zvedili, kdo jim je kriv te nesreč_e.

CharSub: ugaali ddobra, da bi jim je v va držala.
Enriched CharSub: valjo ali jokajo, da bi _zvedili, kdo jim je kri te nesreč_e.

Fig. 4. Example of modernizing a sentence from *Bohorič* with all the different approaches. _ denotes a character that has been removed as part of its normalization. Unnormalized characters that should have been normalized and wrongly normalized characters are denoted in red. Characters which were successfully normalized are denoted in teal. (Color figure online)

In the example from *Bohorič* (see Fig. 4), ten characters from four words need to be normalized. As with the previous dataset, the CBSMT approach successfully normalizes the sentence.

Both CBNMT approaches successfully normalized three of the words and make a mistake with two of the characters of one word: one of the, which did not exist in the original word, is still missing and the other one is left unnormalized.

The SubChar approach behaves similarly to the CBNMT approaches—it makes the same mistakes normalizing the word *svédili*—but makes additional mistakes normalizing the words *vadljajo* and *lófajo*. The enriched version of this approach does not suffer from this additional mistakes, but it is still unable to normalize the word *svédili* correctly.

Finally, the CharSub approach suffers from a combination of the two phenomenon mentioned in the example from *Entremeses y Comedias*: the generation of made-up words and the disappearance of part of the sentence. The enriched version solves these problems, but behaves similarly to the SubChar approach (making different mistakes in the normalization of the words *vadljajo* and *lófajo*).

The last example comes from *Gaj* (see Fig. 5). In this case, five characters (two of which need to be removed) from three words are affected by the normalization. All the normalization approaches successfully normalized all words except *beračevati*. The SubChar approach correctly normalizes two out of three characters but changes a character that did not have to be modified. The

Original: mislili so povsod, de nihče iz zlate vasí beračevati ne more.
Normalized: mislili so povsod, da nihče iz zlate vasi berači‿ti ne more.

CBSMT: mislili so povsod, da nihče iz zlate vasi bračevati ne more.

CBNMT: mislili so povsod, da nihče iz zlate vasi bračevati ne more.
Enriched CBNMT: mislili so povsod, da nihče iz zlate vasi bračevati ne more.

SubChar: mislili so povsod, da nihče iz zlate vasi berača‿te ne more.
Enriched SubChar: mislili so povsod, da nihče iz zlate vasi beračevati ne more.

CharSub: mislili so povsod, da nihče iz zlate vasi varovati ne more.
Enriched CharSub: mislili so povsod, da nihče iz zlate vasi beračevati ne more.

Fig. 5. Example of modernizing a sentence from *Gaj* with all the different approaches. ‿ denotes a character that has been removed as part of its normalization. Unnormalized characters that should have been normalized and wrongly normalized characters are denoted in red. Characters which were successfully normalized are denoted in teal. (Color figure online)

CharSub approach replaces the word with *varovati* (which has the same suffix but a different meaning). Finally, the rest of the approaches leave the word unnormalized.

In general, the examples show how the CBSMT approach makes less mistake normalizing and how enriching the neural models using synthetic data from modern documents improve the normalizations generated by each approach.

6   Conclusions and Future Work

In this work, we evaluated different CBNMT normalization approaches, some of which their neural models were enriched using modern documents. We tested our proposal in different datasets, and reached the conclusion that not all approaches are equally suited for each task.

Additionally, while these approaches successfully improved the baseline—except for a few exceptions—CBSMT systems yielded the best results for three our of the four tasks. We believe that this is mostly due to the scarce availability of parallel training data when working with historical documents [4].

As a future work, we would like to further research the use of modern documents to enrich the neural systems. In this work, we used a previously known method in order to assess the different CBNMT approaches under the same circumstances. We should further investigate new methods such as using a data selection approach to find the most suitable data for each corpus.

Acknowledgments. The research leading to these results has received funding from the European Union through *Programa Operativo del Fondo Europeo de Desarrollo Regional (FEDER)* from Comunitat Valenciana (2014–2020) under project IDIFEDER/2018/025; from Ministerio de Economía y Competitividad under project

PGC2018-096212-B-C31; and from Generalitat Valenciana (GVA) under project PROMETEO/2019/121.We gratefully acknowledge the support of NVIDIA Corporation with the donation of a GPU used for part of this research.

References

1. Bahdanau, D., Cho, K., Bengio, Y.: Neural machine translation by jointly learning to align and translate. arXiv:1409.0473 (2015)
2. Baron, A., Rayson, P.: VARD2: a tool for dealing with spelling variation in historical corpora. In: Postgraduate Conference in Corpus Linguistics (2008)
3. Bollmann, M.: Normalization of historical texts with neural network models. Ph.D. thesis, Sprachwissenschaftliches Institut, Ruhr-Universität (2018)
4. Bollmann, M., Søgaard, A.: Improving historical spelling normalization with bidirectional LSTMs and multi-task learning. In: Proceedings of the International Conference on the Computational Linguistics, pp. 131–139 (2016)
5. Brown, P.F., Pietra, V.J.D., Pietra, S.A.D., Mercer, R.L.: The mathematics of statistical machine translation: parameter estimation. Comput. Linguist. **19**(2), 263–311 (1993)
6. Chatterjee, R., Farajian, M.A., Negri, M., Turchi, M., Srivastava, A., Pal, S.: Multisource neural automatic post-editing: FBK's participation in the WMT 2017 APE shared task. In: Proceedings of the Second Conference on Machine Translation, pp. 630–638 (2017)
7. Chung, J., Cho, K., Bengio, Y.: A character-level decoder without explicit segmentation for neural machine translation. In: Proceedings of the Annual Meeting of the Association for Computational Linguistics, pp. 1693–1703 (2016)
8. Costa-Jussà, M.R., Aldón, D., Fonollosa, J.A.: Chinese-Spanish neural machine translation enhanced with character and word bitmap fonts. Mach. Transl. **31**, 35–47 (2017)
9. Costa-Jussà, M.R., Fonollosa, J.A.: Character-based neural machine translation. In: Proceedings of the Annual Meeting of the Association for Computational Linguistics, pp. 357–361 (2016)
10. Domingo, M., Casacuberta, F.: Spelling normalization of historical documents by using a machine translation approach. In: Proceedings of the Annual Conference of the European Association for Machine Translation, pp. 129–137 (2018)
11. Domingo, M., Casacuberta, F.: Enriching character-based neural machine translation with modern documents for achieving an orthography consistency in historical documents. In: Cristani, M., Prati, A., Lanz, O., Messelodi, S., Sebe, N. (eds.) ICIAP 2019. LNCS, vol. 11808, pp. 59–69. Springer, Cham (2019). https://doi.org/10.1007/978-3-030-30754-7_7
12. Domingo, M., et al.: A user study of the incremental learning in NMT. In: Proceedings of the European Association for Machine Translation, pp. 319–328 (2020)
13. Jehle, F.: Works of Miguel de Cervantes in Old- and Modern-Spelling. Indiana University Purdue University, Fort Wayne (2001)
14. Gehring, J., Auli, M., Grangier, D., Yarats, D., Dauphin, Y.N.: Convolutional sequence to sequence learning. arXiv:1705.03122 (2017)
15. Gers, F.A., Schmidhuber, J., Cummins, F.: Learning to forget: continual prediction with LSTM. Neural Comput. **12**(10), 2451–2471 (2000)

16. Hämäläinen, M., Säily, T., Rueter, J., Tiedemann, J., Mäkelä, E.: Normalizing early English letters to present-day English spelling. In: Proceedings of the Workshop on Computational Linguistics for Cultural Heritage, Social Sciences, Humanities and Literature, pp. 87–96 (2018)
17. Kingma, D.P., Ba, J.: Adam: a method for stochastic optimization. arXiv preprint arXiv:1412.6980 (2014)
18. Klein, G., Kim, Y., Deng, Y., Senellart, J., Rush, A.M.: OpenNMT: open-source toolkit for neural machine translation. In: Proceedings of the Association for Computational Linguistics: System Demonstration, pp. 67–72 (2017)
19. Koehn, P., et al.: Moses: open source toolkit for statistical machine translation. In: Proceedings of the Annual Meeting of the Association for Computational Linguistics, pp. 177–180 (2007)
20. Koehn, P., Och, F.J., Marcu, D.: Statistical phrase-based translation. In: Proceedings of the Conference of the North American Chapter of the Association for Computational Linguistics on Human Language Technology, pp. 48–54 (2003)
21. Korchagina, N.: Normalizing medieval German texts: from rules to deep learning. In: Proceedings of the Nordic Conference on Computational Linguistics Workshop on Processing Historical Language, pp. 12–17 (2017)
22. Laing, M.: The linguistic analysis of medieval vernacular texts: two projects at Edinburgh. In: Rissanen, M., Kytd, M., Wright, S. (eds.) Corpora Across the Centuries: Proceedings of the First International Colloquium on English Diachronic Corpora, vol. 25427, pp. 121–141. St Catharine's College, Cambridge (1993)
23. Ling, W., Trancoso, I., Dyer, C., Black, A.W.: Character-based neural machine translation. arXiv preprint arXiv:1511.04586 (2015)
24. Lison, P., Tiedemann, J.: Opensubtitles 2016: extracting large parallel corpora from movie and tv subtitles. In: Proceedings of the International Conference on Language Resources Association, pp. 923–929 (2016)
25. Ljubešić, N., Zupan, K., Fišer, D., Erjavec, T.: Dataset of normalised Slovene text KonvNormSl 1.0. Slovenian language resource repository CLARIN. SI (2016). http://hdl.handle.net/11356/1068
26. Ljubešic, N., Zupan, K., Fišer, D., Erjavec, T.: Normalising Slovene data: historical texts vs. user-generated content. In: Proceedings of the Conference on Natural Language Processing, pp. 146–155 (2016)
27. Nakov, P., Tiedemann, J.: Combining word-level and character-level models for machine translation between closely-related languages. In: Proceedings of the Annual Meeting of the Association for Computational Linguistics, pp. 301–305 (2012)
28. Och, F.J.: Minimum error rate training in statistical machine translation. In: Proceedings of the Annual Meeting of the Association for Computational Linguistics, pp. 160–167 (2003)
29. Och, F.J., Ney, H.: Discriminative training and maximum entropy models for statistical machine translation. In: Proceedings of the Annual Meeting of the Association for Computational Linguistics, pp. 295–302 (2002)
30. Papineni, K., Roukos, S., Ward, T., Zhu, W.J.: BLEU: a method for automatic evaluation of machine translation. In: Proceedings of the Annual Meeting of the Association for Computational Linguistics, pp. 311–318 (2002)
31. Porta, J., Sancho, J.L., Gómez, J.: Edit transducers for spelling variation in old Spanish. In: Proceedings of the Workshop on Computational Historical Linguistics, pp. 70–79 (2013)
32. Post, M.: A call for clarity in reporting BLEU scores. In: Proceedings of the Third Conference on Machine Translation, pp. 186–191 (2018)

33. Riezler, S., Maxwell, J.T.: On some pitfalls in automatic evaluation and significance testing for MT. In: Proceedings of the Workshop on Intrinsic and Extrinsic Evaluation Measures for Machine Translation and/or Summarization, pp. 57–64 (2005)
34. Robbins, H., Monro, S.: A stochastic approximation method. Ann. Math. Stat. **22**, 400–407 (1951)
35. Rumelhart, D.E., Hinton, G.E., Williams, R.J.: Learning representations by back-propagating errors. Nature **323**(6088), 533–536 (1986)
36. Scherrer, Y., Erjavec, T.: Modernizing historical Slovene words with character-based SMT. In: Proceedings of the Workshop on Balto-Slavic Natural Language Processing, pp. 58–62 (2013)
37. Sennrich, R., Haddow, B., Birch, A.: Neural machine translation of rare words with subword units. In: Proceedings of the Annual Meeting of the Association for Computational Linguistics, pp. 1715–1725 (2016)
38. Snover, M., Dorr, B., Schwartz, R., Micciulla, L., Makhoul, J.: A study of translation edit rate with targeted human annotation. In: Proceedings of the Association for Machine Translation in the Americas, pp. 223–231 (2006)
39. Stolcke, A.: SRILM - an extensible language modeling toolkit. In: Proceedings of the International Conference on Spoken Language Processing, pp. 257–286 (2002)
40. Sutskever, I., Vinyals, O., Le, Q.V.: Sequence to sequence learning with neural networks. In: Proceedings of the Advances in Neural Information Processing Systems, vol. 27, pp. 3104–3112 (2014)
41. Szegedy, C., et al.: Going deeper with convolutions. In: Proceedings of the IEEE Conference on Computer Vision and Pattern Recognition, pp. 1–9 (2015)
42. Tang, G., Cap, F., Pettersson, E., Nivre, J.: An evaluation of neural machine translation models on historical spelling normalization. In: Proceedings of the International Conference on Computational Linguistics, pp. 1320–1331 (2018)
43. Tiedemann, J.: Character-based PSMT for closely related languages. In: Proceedings of the Annual Conference of the European Association for Machine Translation, pp. 12–19 (2009)
44. Vaswani, A., et al.: Attention is all you need. In: Advances in Neural Information Processing Systems, pp. 5998–6008 (2017)
45. Wu, Y., et al.: Google's neural machine translation system: bridging the gap between human and machine translation. arXiv:1609.08144 (2016)
46. Zens, R., Och, F.J., Ney, H.: Phrase-based statistical machine translation. In: Jarke, M., Lakemeyer, G., Koehler, J. (eds.) KI 2002. LNCS (LNAI), vol. 2479, pp. 18–32. Springer, Heidelberg (2002). https://doi.org/10.1007/3-540-45751-8_2

Weakly Supervised Bounding Box Extraction for Unlabeled Data in Table Detection

Arash Samari[1(✉)], Andrew Piper[2], Alison Hedley[2], and Mohamed Cheriet[1]

[1] Ecole De Technologie Supérieure, Montreal, Canada
arash.samari.1@etsmtl.net, mohamed.cheriet@etsmtl.ca
[2] McGill University, Montreal, Canada
andrew.piper@mcgill.ca, afhedley@gmail.com

Abstract. The organization and presentation of data in tabular format became an essential strategy of scientific communication and remains fundamental to the transmission of knowledge today. The use of automated detection to identify typographical elements such as tables and diagrams in digitized historical print offers a promising approach for future research. Most of the table detection tasks are using existing off-the-shelf methods for their detection algorithm. However, datasets that are used for evaluation are not challenging enough due to the lack of quantity and diversity. To have a better comparison between proposed methods we introduce the NAS dataset in this paper for historical digitized images. Tables in historic scientific documents vary widely in their characteristics. They also appear alongside visually similar items, such as maps, diagrams, and illustrations. We address these challenges with a multi-phase procedure, outlined in this article, evaluated using two datasets, ECCO (https://www.gale.com/primary-sources/eighteenth-century-collections-online) and NAS (https://beta.synchromedia.ca/vok-visibility-of-knowledge). In our approach, we utilized the Gabor filter [1] to prepare our dataset for algorithmic detection with Faster-RCNN [2]. This method detects tables against all categories of visual information. Due to the limitation in labeled data, particularly for object detection, we developed a new method, namely, weakly supervision bounding box extraction, to extract bounding boxes automatically for our training set in an innovative way. Then a pseudo-labeling technique is used to create a more general model, via a three-step process of bounding box extraction and labeling.

Keywords: Weakly supervision bounding box extraction · Faster-RCNN · Pseudo-labeling · Gabor filter · Distance transform

1 Introduction

In the context of object detection in digitized documents, similar to many other machine learning applications, learning that generalizes well to unseen data is a

© Springer Nature Switzerland AG 2021
A. Del Bimbo et al. (Eds.): ICPR 2020 Workshops, LNCS 12667, pp. 339–352, 2021.
https://doi.org/10.1007/978-3-030-68787-8_25

significant dilemma that we need to address. Moreover, to have a fair comparison between other methods, we should have a dataset with enough data and various classes to make our proposed methodology more challenging. Historical documents can be a suitable example of this family of datasets. Recently, preserving and analyzing historical documents in digital format has become an important task for historians. Most of these documents are degraded and have complex and/or unusual structures, requiring novel or custom detection methods. Detecting typographical features of interest to historians not only provides researchers with more targeted searching capability when accessing collections. It can also facilitate the large-scale study of bibliographic or textual changes over time [3]. In this paper, first we focus on information tables, a visual feature that appears frequently in historical scientific print documents. Then we propose a method that performs bounding box extraction via weakly supervision.

Historians of science have long emphasized the importance of visual evidence for the communication of scientific proof. Tables provided a new way for scientists to structure information in digestible ways, aiding the speed and reliability of communicating information as well as establishing new protocols of correlational thinking. While we think of tables as natural to any scientific communication today, this process of the typographic organization of knowledge was both varied and historically complex. The ability to detect and study tables at large scale can help us better understand the origins and evolution of this key form of scientific communication.

Identifying tables in historical scientific print involves addressing some unique challenges. Tables are commonly structured as matrices of cells with a row-column structure, but there is some variation in their layout; this is particularly true of tables in historical print. Additionally, tables appear amidst a number of other visual conventions that share typographic features. These can include diagrams, maps illustrations, and ornamental items such as headpieces.

In developing a novel approach to table detection that addresses these challenge areas, we build on a number of recent advancements in machine learning-based approaches [4] to image detection. The advent of deep convolutional neural networks has generated new possibilities for object detection tasks, including table detection in documents. We used a CNN-based model for table detection, making several customisations. To boost reliability and accuracy, we trained our model with a dataset that consisted of multiple classes in addition to the table class, because the number of pages with tables in our historical dataset is relatively small. Our general model also had to be able to account for multiple table formats, including tables with and without ruling lines.

For example, in the [5], they used Faster Recurrent Convolutional Neural Network (Faster-RCNN) [2] as their table detector algorithm and train and evaluate their results on UNLV dataset [6]. The UNLV dataset contains only 427 document images with tables, which raises questions regarding its generalizability. If we use the proposed model by [5] on dataset which consist of different classes we will get a considerable number of false detected table (FP) because the model trained just based on table images.

The main contribution of this paper is proposing a method that produces enough labeled data and extracts bounding boxes from a limited available ground truth in hand. This way of training overcomes the problem of manual labeling and extracting bounding boxes of big datasets. To this end, we propose three phases of training. First, we train on a small subset that contains the ground-truth bounding box labels. Then, in the second phase, we apply our weakly supervision bounding box extraction that is using false positive detected samples from phase. Finally, we use the trained model from phase 2 to produce more (pseudo) labels and perform bounding box extraction for table detection on a much larger dataset.

This article is organized as follows: Sect. 2 surveys existing work in the field of table detection. Section 3 outline of proposed methodology, notably the technique of "Weakly supervised bounding box extraction" and prepossessing. Section 4 describes our experiments with this method and our results; Sect. 5 summarizes our conclusions to date and describes next steps.

2 Related Work

There is a considerable body of existing research on table detection. Most approaches to this task cannot accommodate the identification of tables with different structures or formats. In other words, generalization is the most challenging problem in table detection.

We can divide existing research on table detection into two categories: the first one depends on deep learning methods and the second is based on layout analysis. [7] uses components and structural features of tables to detect them. [8] proposed one of the first methods for analysing tables, the T-Recs recognition system. This method detects tables by extracting word bounding boxes and segmenting them by bottom-up clustering. T-Recs depends heavily on word bounding boxes. [9] detects tables by recognizing column and row line separators and classifying them by SVM classifier. This method is suitable only for tables with ruling lines. [10] proposed one of the first method for spotting tables in PDF files by detecting and merging multi-lines with more than one text segment. However, this method cannot be used for multi-column documents. [11] localize tables in PDF files by using visual separators and geometric content layout information. It detects tables with or without ruling lines. [12] recognize tables based on computing an optimal partitioning of a document into some number of tables. This approach does not depend on ruling lines, headers, etc. Rather, the table quality measures is defined based on the correlation of white space and vertical connected component analysis. [13] used Hidden Markov Models (HMMs) in a different way to analyse document images. This approach computes feature vectors of white spaces between texts by using HMMs.

[14] extracts the size of text blocks and then compares their heights with the average height in the page. This approach can detect tables based on predefined rules. [15] finds regions as tables based on intersection between horizontal and vertical lines. Although this is an effective method, it entirely depends on the presence of ruling lines and a specific table structure.

Recent research has produced promising results in table detection by improving applications of deep learning algorithms specially in computer vision tasks. One well known algorithm in detection tasks is Faster-RCNN [2]. [16] uses a data-driven system that does not need heuristics to detect tables and their structures. This method detects columns, rows, and cell positions by carrying out Faster-RCNN on the ICDAR 2013 dataset [17]. Gilani [5] uses Faster-RCNN on the UNLV dataset [6]. While this method is good for detecting tables with different structures, it is limited by its small training sample set, which contains only 427 table images. It also lacks some of the image classes pertinent to our historical dataset, such as ornamental items and diagrams, and so cannot be generalized as our model.

3   Proposed Method and Dataset

Building on existing approaches, we optimized our model with samples of false detection, as well as true detection, and measures to reduce the cost of labeling and extracting boxes. We used Faster-RCNN [2] as our detection algorithm, which is the third generation of RCNN [18] based models. RCNN are "Rich feature hierarchies for accurate object detection and semantic segmentation" that use a selective search to propose regions of interest that can be classified by a Convolutional Neural Network (CNN). This process is very time-consuming; to improve efficiency of RCNN based algorithms, Girshick introduced the Fast-RCNN [19], which decreases the computational costs of detection tasks by implementing the Region of Interest Pooling technique. In the end, by replacing Region Proposal Network (RPN) instead of selective search in Faster-RCNN, Girschick introduced the ultimate version of RCNN based model. Faster-RCNN is a well-known and exemplary model for detecting natural scene images; hence we need to prepare our dataset before implementing it. In Faster-RCNN, a feature map is extracted from a pre-trained model based on natural scene images.

For training Faster-RCNN, we required labelled data and bounding boxes for each typographical element. The most prevalent datasets that are applied for table detection tasks are as follows:

- Marmot [20]: contains 2000 Chinese and English documents. It also consists of different page layouts like one-column and two columns as well as various types of tables;
- UNLV [6]: contains 427 document images in different subjects such as newspapers, business letters etc.;
- ICDAR 2013 [17]: contains 128 documents that were used for analysing document images. It involves different domains of table competition tasks like table structure recognition, table location and their combination.

As mentioned in Sect. 1, our historical dataset contains a variety of table structures and visual objects similar to tables. To date, no table detection tasks have been undertaken with respect to historical documents. To evaluate our model, we used two new datasets that are drawn from collections of historical documents relevant to the history of scientific knowledge:

- ECCO: contains 32 million document images drawn from the Eighteenth-Century Collections Online database, which consist of over 200,000 documents published in the British Isles in the eighteenth century (INSERT CITATION). This dataset represents documents from a number of different genres printed over the course of one century in a single geographic region.
- NAS: contains 2 million document images drawn from the proceedings of five national academy of sciences (France, Sweden, Russia, Germany, and Britain) from 1666 to 1916. This resource provides documents from multiple languages and time periods that all belong to a related textual domain of scientific communication.

Because these datasets contain documents with different typographic conventions from different time periods and multiple kinds of visual representation, they pose significantly greater challenges than previous datasets. We present some examples in Fig. 1.

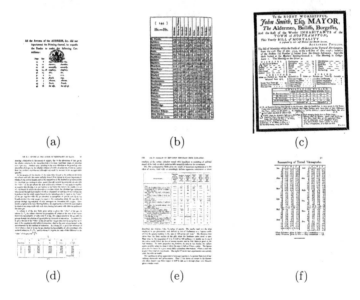

(a)   (b)   (c)

(d)   (e)   (f)

Fig. 1. a, b and c are samples of table documents from ECCO. d, e and f are samples of table documents from NAS.

3.1   Preprocessing

As mentioned above, the pre-trained model in Faster-RCNN is based on natural scene images. To make the images in our dataset comprehensible for Faster-RCNN, we transformed them to more closely resemble natural images. We used two well-known image processing applications for transforming images, Distance

transform [21] and the Gabor filter [1]. The first method, distance transformation, gives us a blurred version of the initial image, changing intensities in the
foreground so that they are more easily distinguished from the background. The
transformed images can aid object recognition by facilitating machine intuition
about the place of white background, text, and typographical elements. In [5],
the author compute the distance between background and foreground by merging three different types of distance transforms such as Euclidean, Linear and
Max distance transform. Figure 2 represents the distance transformed of d, e
and f images from Fig. 1.

(a)   (b)   (c)

Fig. 2. Results of Distance transformed on images d, c and f from Fig. 1.

Like distance transformation, the second method we used to convert document image files to natural images, the Gabor filter [1], separates contents from
background to make an image more comprehensible to a machine. The Gabor
filter is used to analyze the texture of images. Figure 3 displays some images
transformed with the Gabor filter. It is a sinusoidal signal that detects frequency
of images in a particular direction. Extracting image features involves convolving
a set of Gabor filters with different directions to the image. This filter consist of
imaginary and real parts which are in orthogonal orientations. Equation (1) is
demonstrating Gabor filter function and its variables:

$$g(x, y; \lambda, \theta, \psi, \sigma, \gamma) = e^{-\frac{x'^2 + \gamma^2 y'^2}{2\sigma^2} + 2\pi i \frac{x'}{\lambda} + \psi i} \tag{1}$$

where λ = wavelength, θ = orientation of the normal, σ = standard deviation
of the Gaussian, ψ = phase offset, γ = spatial aspect ratio, $x' = x cos\theta + y sin\theta$,
$y' = -x sin\theta + y cos\theta$ [1].

Training Approach. Our approach to training was unusual in that it used two
classes. Most work in table detection uses relatively small datasets and trains
only on one class. However, historical documents such as those in our dataset
contain a wide array of image objects and a very unbalanced distribution of
each classes. Because of the unbalanced distribution of each class, we deemed it
more useful to train Faster-RCNN based on a no-table class (i.e. pages without

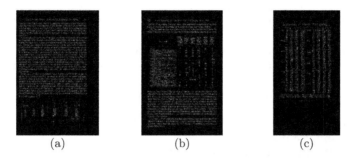

(a)   (b)   (c)

Fig. 3. Results of Gabor filter on images d, c and f from Fig. 1.

any tables) as well as the table class. Many images in our dataset belong to the non-table category (see Fig. 4 for examples). The use of two classes prevents our model from overfitting on recognizing tables, and, consequently, decreasing the false positive rate.

(a)   (b)   (c)

Fig. 4. Images without any table (no-table).

To develop a reliable model for predicting tables in new images, we needed to train our model with an adequately large set of labeled data with bounding boxes. To acquire this data manually was not ideal, given the high cost involved. We developed an approach that would mitigate manual labour.

The difficulty of generating training sets for our model can be divided into two parts: extracting bounding boxes, and labelling for table and no-table classes. To automate bounding box extraction, we developed a new procedure that we call "Weakly supervised bounding box extraction". This innovative technique makes productive use of false positives which represented by the Algorithm 1.

We began with two mini-subsets of table and no-table items that lacked bounding boxes. We had these two mini-subsets labeled manually using Amazon Mechanical Turk. Three workers classified each document image with either the table or no-table label depending on whether the image contained any table items. Labels assigned by at least 2/3 workers to a given image became ground truth data. This process gave us the necessary training dataset comprised of images from two classes with their labels and bounding boxes.

Algorithm 1. The weakly supervised bounding box extraction model

---

//Inputs:
table_images ← list of images that contain at least one table
table_bboxes ← dictionary that maps each image to its corresponding bounding boxes

notable_images ← list of images that contain no table

//Pre-Processing:
for *image in table_images* **do**
   image ← *Gabor_Preprocess(image)*
end for
for *image in notable_images* **do**
   image ← *Gabor_Preprocess(image)*
end for

//Train on images with tables:
model ← *FasterRCNN.train(*
      table_images,
      {*table_bboxes,* "*TABLE*"})

//Extract bounding boxes for images without tables:
notable_bboxes ← *model.evaluate(*
      images = notable_images)

//Train on images with tables and notables:
model ← *FasterRCNN.train(*
      table_images ∪ *notable_images,*
      {*table_bboxes,* "*TABLE*"} ∪
      {*notable_bboxes,* "*NOTABLE*"})

//Output weakly supervised trained checkpoint:
return model

At the first step, we manually extracted bounding boxes around some table images. Then we trained our model based on the table mini-subset. The weight was based merely on tables. Then we applied the theory of weakly supervised bounding box extraction, which supposes that if we train our model based on Label 1 and we get a test on images which belong to Label 2, we will expect to receive a lot of samples which have been wrongly detected as Label 1 (i.e. a high rate of false positive). Because the model is just trained on one class, it is overfitted to detect the defined class. But here we optimized the first proposed model by using detected bounding boxes around an undefined class and changing their wrongly detected labels to their actual labels. In this experiment, the second class acquires the label of no-table; it contains text and any typographical elements that do not belong to the table class. The proportion of no-table class items is much greater than the table class in historical scientific books and documents. As a result, automatically extracting bounding boxes around the undefined, no-table class decreases the costs of bounding box extraction. These extracted bounding boxes are not very accurate but they are relatively acceptable boxes around text (no-table class). It is because of this relative extraction that we call the technique weakly supervised bounding box extraction.

This process gave us the necessary training dataset comprised of images from two classes with their labels and bounding boxes.

In the next phase of training, we associated the table and no-table labels with bounding boxes using the Pseudo Labeling technique, a semi-supervised learning approach. Pseudo Labeling consists of three main steps which are demonstrated in Fig. 5.

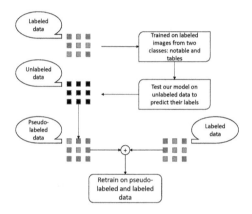

Fig. 5. Pseudo-labeling approach pipeline.

The first phase of Pseudo Labeling uses the weakly supervised bounding box extraction technique already described. The second involves giving table and non-table images to our model to predict them. We called the resulting subset "Pseudo-Labelled Data." In the third phase, we gathered labelled data from Phase 1 and pseudo-labelled data from Phase 2 in one subset that we used to train our model.

4 Experiment and Results

In this section, after introducing the NAS and ECCO datasets, we first compare different image transformations techniques. Then, using the processed data, we apply our three-phase training approach and report the table detection results on these datasets.

- **NAS:**
  Our model training used images from the NAS subset altered using the Gabor filter and distance transformation. Then we compared the results of these two models on a mini-subset containing 500 distance transformed and 500 Gabor

Table 1. Comparison results of table detection with Faster-RCNN on mini-subset with 500 distance transformed and 500 Gabor images of NAS dataset.

Transformation	Precision	Recall
Distance transform	76.77	85.03
Gabor filter	88.21	92.63

images. The proportion of the table class is 20% and the no-table is 80%. The following Table 1 represent the results.

We extracted bounding boxes around 922 table images and trained our algorithm based on them (Model A). We then tested Model A with 922 no-tables. As we expected, the result is overfitted on detecting tables; our Model (A) detected 879 tables from 922 no-tables, and there were a lot of false positive (FP) samples. To increase the accuracy, we decided to define two labels for table and no-table, determining that all images that do not contain tables would fall in the no-table class. We used weakly supervised bounding box extraction to put boxes around texts from 879 false positive tables and 43 true positive notables. Then we re-assigned false positive table items to the no-table class, creating a new mini-subset for a new training process. This mini-subset has 922 tables and 922 no-tables. In order to resolve the overfitting problem, we trained the algorithm based on this two labeled mini-subset (Model B). The next step was to generalize the model. We used pseudo labeling method to have more labeled images; after testing Model B on 1600 random images, we receive 576 tables and 1024 no-tables, calling this the NAS Final Subset. Then we trained the algorithm with the final subset (Model C). The steps of training, from A to C, are demonstrated in the Table 2. At the end, we tested our model (model C) on bigger subset of NAS which consist of 2705 tables and 11607 no-tables. Table 3 represents the test results of this subset on our proposed model (model C) compared to the Faster-RCNN base model (model A) which has been trained on the "table" class without utilizing the weakly supervision bounding box extraction. It can be observed detected tables with our proposed idea in Fig. 6.

Table 2. Different steps of training our algorithm with different subsets of NAS.

Model	Tables	Notables
Model A	922	0
Model B	922	922
Model C	1498	1946

Table 3. Results of model C and A on the final subset of NAS

Method	Precision	Recall
Faster-RCNN (2 labels + weakly supervision bbox)	81.19	86.44
Faster-RCNN (1 label)	54.2	93.66

– **ECCO:**
  For the ECCO dataset, as for the NAS data, we trained our model with the Gabor filter and distance-transformed images. Then we compared the results of these two models on mini-subset containing 500 distance transformed and 500 Gabor images. The proportion of table is 20% and no-table is 80%. The results are represented in Table 4.

Table 4. Comparison results of table detection with Faster-RCNN on mini-subset with 500 distance transformed and 500 Gabor images of ECCO dataset.

Transformation	Precision	Recall
Distance transform	71.77	80.03
Gabor filter	82.21	87.63

In the first step, we extracted 785 bounding boxes around table images and trained our algorithm based on them (model A). In the second step, we tested Model A with 785 no-tables. As we expected, the result is overfitted on detecting tables; our model (A) detected 768 tables from 785 no-tables and included false positive samples. As before, we used the weakly supervised bounding box extraction technique to obtain bounding boxes around 768 false positive tables and 17 true positive no-tables. Then, we changed the labels of these false positive tables to no-table and created a new mini-subset for training. This mini-subset has 785 tables and 785 no-tables. In order to resolve the overfitting problem, we trained the algorithm based on the two labeled mini-subsets (model B). To generalize the model, we used the pseudo labeling

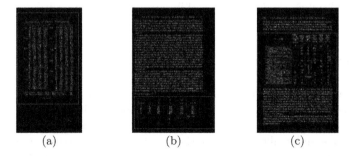

(a)   (b)   (c)

Fig. 6. True detected tables on images d, c and f from Fig. 1.

method to produce more labeled images. After testing Model B on 1124 random images, we were left with 437 tables and 687 no-table items. To further generalize the dataset for training, we added 437 tables and 687 no-tables to our mini-subset, calling this the ECCO Final Subset. The steps of training from A to C are demonstrated in the Table 5. Finally, we tested our model (model C) on a bigger subset of NAS which consisted of 1230 tables and 5289 notables. Results of testing this subset on our proposed model (model C), versus the Faster-RCNN base model (model A) trained solely on "table" class without utilizing weakly supervision bounding box extraction, are represented in the Table 6.

Table 5. Different steps of training our algorithm with different subsets of ECCO.

Model	Tables	Notables
Model A	785	0
Model B	785	785
Model C	1222	1472

Table 6. Results of model C and A on the final subset of ECCO

Method	Precision	Recall
Faster-RCNN (2 labels + weakly supervision bbox	77.15	71.46)
Faster-RCNN (1 label)	47.36	88.79)

From the comparison between our proposed method (model C) and the Faster-RCNN base model (model A) in Tables 3, 6, it can be observed that for model A, the precision is very low because of the high rate of false positive. Therefore, adding another label (no-table) along with using a weakly supervised bounding box extraction help to significantly improve the precision of the detection algorithm. It can also be observed from Table 3 and Table 6 that the precision and recall from the ECCO dataset is lower than that of the NAS dataset. The main reason is the particularly wide range of table structures in the ECCO data compared to NAS.

5   Conclusion

There are not many comprehensive and challenging datasets in the domain of object detection tasks for the use case of table detection in document images. To address this issue, first, we introduced two new datasets. These datasets are more comprehensive and challenging since they contain various structures of tables as well as a different type of classes. In this article, we used Faster-RCNN as the state-of-the-art detection algorithm. The essential requirement for training on Faster-RCNN is to have enough labeled data, i.e., bounding boxes around typographical elements. To overcome the problem of shortage of labeled data on the proposed new datasets, we used our Weakly supervised bounding box extraction based on Faster-RCNN that by having a limited number of labeled images of one class, introduces a 3-step training procedure to produce labeled data and bounding boxes around their typographical elements. This model generalizes against different classes and accommodates various table structures. The innovative concept of Weakly supervised bounding box extraction technique used in this procedure, is particularly useful for limiting the manual cost of tedious bounding box labeling process. Future work on this project will involve making NAS dataset accessible to the public.

Acknowledgment. The authors thank the NSERC Discovery held by Prof. Cheriet for their financial support.

References

1. Lee, T.S.: Image representation using 2D Gabor wavelets. IEEE Trans. Pattern Anal. Mach. Intell. **18**(10), 959–971 (1996)
2. Ren, S., He, K., Girshick, R., Sun, J.: Faster R-CNN: towards real-time object detection with region proposal networks. In: Advances in Neural Information Processing Systems, pp. 91–99 (2015)
3. Piper, A., Wellmon, C., Cheriet, M.: The page image: towards a visual history of digital documents. Book History **23**(1), 365–397 (2020)
4. Michie, D., Spiegelhalter, D.J., Taylor, C.C., et al.: Machine learning. Neural Stat. Classif. **13**(1994), 1–298 (1994)
5. Gilani, A., Qasim, S.R., Malik, I., Shafait, F.: Table detection using deep learning. In: 2017 14th IAPR International Conference on Document Analysis and Recognition (ICDAR), vol. 1, pp. 771–776. IEEE (2017)
6. Shahab, A., Shafait, F., Kieninger, T., Dengel, A.: An open approach towards the benchmarking of table structure recognition systems. In: Proceedings of the 9th IAPR International Workshop on Document Analysis Systems, pp. 113–120 (2010)
7. Pyreddy, P., Croft, W.B.: TINTIN: a system for retrieval in text tables. In: Proceedings of the Second ACM International Conference on Digital Libraries, pp. 193–200 (1997)
8. Kieninger, T., Dengel, A.: Applying the T-Recs table recognition system to the business letter domain. In: Proceedings of Sixth International Conference on Document Analysis and Recognition, pp. 518–522. IEEE (2001)
9. Kasar, T., Barlas, P., Adam, S., Chatelain, C., Paquet, T.: Learning to detect tables in scanned document images using line information. In: 2013 12th International Conference on Document Analysis and Recognition, pp. 1185–1189. IEEE (2013)
10. Yildiz, B., Kaiser, K., Miksch, S.: pdf2table: a method to extract table information from pdf files. In: IICAI, pp. 1773–1785 (2005)
11. Fang, J., Gao, L., Bai, K., Qiu, R., Tao, X., Tang, Z.: A table detection method for multipage pdf documents via visual seperators and tabular structures. In: 2011 International Conference on Document Analysis and Recognition, pp. 779–783. IEEE (2011)

12. Hu, J., Kashi, R.S., Lopresti, D.P., Wilfong, G.: Medium-independent table detection. In: Document Recognition and Retrieval VII, vol. 3967, pp. 291–302. International Society for Optics and Photonics (1999)
13. e Silva, A.C.: Learning rich hidden Markov models in document analysis: table location. In: 2009 10th International Conference on Document Analysis and Recognition, pp. 843–847. IEEE (2009)
14. Tran, D.N., Tran, T.A., Oh, A., Kim, S.H., Na, I.S.: Table detection from document image using vertical arrangement of text blocks. Int. J. Contents 11(4), 77–85 (2015)
15. Gatos, B., Danatsas, D., Pratikakis, I., Perantonis, S.J.: Automatic table detection in document images. In: Singh, S., Singh, M., Apte, C., Perner, P. (eds.) ICAPR 2005. LNCS, vol. 3686, pp. 609–618. Springer, Heidelberg (2005). https://doi.org/10.1007/11551188_67
16. Schreiber, S., Agne, S., Wolf, I., Dengel, A., Ahmed, S.: DeepDeSRT: deep learning for detection and structure recognition of tables in document images. In: 2017 14th IAPR International Conference on Document Analysis and Recognition (ICDAR), vol. 1, pp. 1162–1167. IEEE (2017)
17. Göbel, M., Hassan, T., Oro, E., Orsi, G.: ICDAR 2013 table competition. In: 2013 12th International Conference on Document Analysis and Recognition, pp. 1449–1453. IEEE (2013)
18. Girshick, R., Donahue, J., Darrell, T., Malik, J.: Rich feature hierarchies for accurate object detection and semantic segmentation. In: Proceedings of the IEEE Conference on Computer Vision and Pattern Recognition, pp. 580–587 (2014)
19. Girshick, R.: Fast R-CNN. In: Proceedings of the IEEE International Conference on Computer Vision, pp. 1440–1448 (2015)
20. Fang, J., Tao, X., Tang, Z., Qiu, R., Liu, Y.: Dataset, ground-truth and performance metrics for table detection evaluation. In: 2012 10th IAPR International Workshop on Document Analysis Systems, pp. 445–449. IEEE (2012)
21. Breu, H., Gil, J., Kirkpatrick, D., Werman, M.: Linear time euclidean distance transform algorithms. IEEE Trans. Pattern Anal. Mach. Intell. 17(5), 529–533 (1995)

Underground Archaeology: Photogrammetry and Terrestrial Laser Scanning of the Hypogeum of Crispia Salvia (Marsala, Italy)

Davide Tanasi$^{(\boxtimes)}$ ⓘ, Stephan Hassam ⓘ, and Kaitlyn Kingsland ⓘ

Department of History, Institute for Digital Exploration (IDEx), University of South Florida,
4202 E Fowler Ave, SOC 107, Tampa, FL 33620, USA
{dtanasi,shassam,kkingsland}@usf.edu

Abstract. The convergence of issues such as safety, lighting, and physical accessibility with problems of archaeological conservation make underground contexts particularly difficult to study, preserve, and make accessible to the public. The Hypogeum of Crispia Salvia at Marsala (Italy) is a particularly apt case study as the frescoed burial site, unique in all of Sicily, is now built over by an apartment complex that can only be accessed through scheduled tours. The authors, in partnership with the local archaeological authorities, harnessing the power of machine learning, created a digital model of this underground burial space using terrestrial laser scanning and digital photogrammetry. This is part of a larger ongoing effort to re-document important subterranean heritage sites of Sicily in order to make them accessible to both researchers and the public, increasingly important in a historic moment where even local mobility is limited due to a global pandemic.

Keywords: Roman Lilybaeum · Hypogeum · Photogrammetry · Terrestrial laser scanning · Sicily

1 Introduction

In recent years, as part of the "Archaeology of Sicily in 3D" project, the University of South Florida's Institute for Digital Exploration (www.usfidex.com) has begun 3D scanning hypogeal (i.e. subterranean) sites, among others, to make them more accessible to researchers and the public while putting no burden on local cultural heritage management institutions and to develop a methodology that addresses the many challenges of doing research in an underground context. While Structure from Motion (SfM), also known as digital photogrammetry, and Terrestrial Laser Scanning (TLS) have been used a great deal in archaeological projects to date, this contribution aims to further demonstrate the viability of photogrammetry for recording and disseminating difficult-to-access sites, specifically subterranean contexts on the island of Sicily. Though Sicily can boast of many important archaeological sites, the institutions that maintain them must also manage extensive areas, including hypogeal sites that pose different issues of preservation and access. The development over the past decade of increasingly potent digital tools

© Springer Nature Switzerland AG 2021
A. Del Bimbo et al. (Eds.): ICPR 2020 Workshops, LNCS 12667, pp. 353–367, 2021.
https://doi.org/10.1007/978-3-030-68787-8_27

for archaeological documentation have provided archaeologists with a new kit of tools to perform archaeological data recording [1], but considering the difficulties inherent in working in underground environments, these tools must be tested for their ability to satisfy the requirements of archaeological documentation. The underground nature of these contexts in Sicily makes it difficult to collect data using traditional methods of pen and paper; coupled with high humidity and heat and lack of proper illumination, both researchers and the public cannot enjoy these sites at leisure. The Hypogeum of Crispia Salvia provides further issues, as it is located underneath a private apartment complex and requires special appointments to visit. Due to its relatively recent discovery, the site is also poorly represented in the scientific literature, and its digital publication will allow it to be more easily accessed and incorporated into archaeological and art historical research.

After a brief summary of the advances of machine learning for digital archaeology, and a short review of digital tools in underground sites, the hypogeum and its archaeological and art historical significance is introduced. The digital archaeological methods are then explained and discussed in light of recent advancements in methods and ongoing archaeological investigations to bring light to the underground heritage of Classical Sicily. The case study of the Hypogeum of Crispia Salvia in Marsala (ancient Lilybaeum) is an example of how digital tools, particularly digital photogrammetry and terrestrial laser scanning, can contribute to the cultural heritage management of inaccessible sites while further valorizing them for public and scholarly use.

1.1 Machine Learning and Advances in Archaeological Practice

Machine learning and pattern recognition have sparked a sort of digital revolution in archaeology. It was recognized early on that archaeological methods of knowledge production were mechanical in nature and could be automated [1, 2] in some way or another with a variety of techniques. New means of analysis began to be generated for glass [3] and ceramic [4] objects, incorporating machine learning to improve these tools as they were exposed to more data. Such techniques have continued to be developed to exploit advances in computer science and the availability of technology to automatize the painstaking work of creating typologies for ceramics [5, 6] and classifying them [7]. Pattern recognition technologies also led to break-throughs in conservation, developing tools for restaurateurs to use on damaged objects [8], ceramics [9], frescoes [10], mosaics [11], sculptures [12], and buildings [13]. These technologies have even made improvements tackling some issues of subjective analysis when it comes to color determination [14].

Perhaps the most influential tools, however, have come in the form of 3D capturing technologies themselves, which have allowed archaeologists in all fields of study to improve the speed and accuracy of their documentation methods. Whether in the field of architecture [15], ceramic analysis [4], or landscape archaeology [16], the ability to capture new data sets with comparatively little investment has shaken up what was previously thought possible in archaeology. No technical solution has been quite as influential as the development of SfM technologies, or photogrammetry, whose algorithms have allowed archaeologists to create high fidelity 3D models of archaeological subjects of inquiry from the level of objects to that of landscapes [17].

1.2 Digital Methods for Hypogeal Contexts

The development of SfM and TLS as archaeological tools has been extensively covered elsewhere ([18, 19], see [20] for discussion in Mediterranean contexts, see [21] for TLS). Other scholars have established best practices and guidelines for digitization of archaeological sites [22]. The improvement of SfM algorithms over the past decade have made digital photogrammetry an extremely low-cost and easy-to-use tool for archaeological data recording [17]. However, a short discussion of the use of the technologies in an underground context is warranted, considering its relatively rare usage in these contexts. There have been some attempts at the digitization of hypogeal contexts in the Mediterranean, the earliest of which consist of studies on Late Roman catacombs, including the University of Austria's Domitilla Catacomb Project (START) and the consortium of European universities and research units that comprised Project Rovina. Both projects were able to successfully digitize catacombal complexes in Rome, but the focus of these projects was on the technology rather than the study of the catacombs themselves and the final products thus far, pertaining to the catacombs, consist of YouTube videos and some basic plans (see [23] for further discussion).

1.3 Digital Methods for Hypogeal Contexts in Sicily

There have been a few projects with the express focus of recording hypogeal complexes for dissemination. These efforts include a series of projects headed through the Sicilian branch of the Pontifical Commission of Sacred Archaeology and partner universities. These consisted of using TLS to map two catacombs at Syracuse, the catacombs of San Giovanni for a revalorization of the site for public audiences [24–26] and the catacombs of Santa Lucia [23, 27, 28] to document the site in conjunction with excavations [29]. The methods used at these sites were further developed by including digital photogrammetry and using a new TLS scanner in the site of the hypogeum of Crispia Salvia.

2   Materials

The frescoed tomb of Crispia Salvia was discovered in 1994 in a now densely populated area of Marsala in western Sicily during the construction of a private apartment complex (Figs. 1, 2 and 3). It is currently a unique hypogeum in Sicily. The site's name comes from an inscription naming a certain Crispia Salvia, the only one of the six inhumation burials having a name attributed to it within the burial chamber. The Latin inscription, found opposite the entryway of the hypogeum, is dated to the 2nd century AD based on its syntax and the funerary frescoes [30]. The only documentation that exists of the site is a singular plan drawn during the salvage excavations of the site (Fig. 2). Despite the lack of contextualized finds, the inscription provides important iconographic evidence and the decoration of the tomb is evidence of a lively local funerary iconography and painter's workshops that demonstrate precedents for future decorative motifs in a local Sicilian paleo-Christian style [31].

Marsala (Lylibaeum)
Hypogeum of
Crispia Salvia

Fig. 1. Plan of Marsala with indication of the location of the
Hypogeum of Crispia Salvia.

Fig. 2. Modern apartment
complex built above the
Hypogeum of Crispia Salvia.

Fig. 3. Entrance stair shaft to the Hypogeum of Crispia Salvia, located in the basement of the apartment complex.

2.1 The Hypogeum

A hypogeum can be characterized as compact private or semi-private burial chamber, built by a family or small group, as opposed to the large sprawling public catacombs known in Rome and Syracuse [32]. The hypogeum is accessed by a dromos, or entrance, consisting of a series of stairs that are excavated into the rock (Fig. 4). It consists of six tombs in an approximately 5 m by 5 m quadrangular chamber located roughly 3 m underground. The ground is covered with a layer of mortar. In the center there is a small rise of mortar where an altar was placed, visible in the original plan only, most likely as a focus for burial rites that would take place in the honor of the dead. The rites likely consisted of an annual sacred meal in honor of the dead and shared with them. This is evidenced by small cavities adjacent to the tombs through which one could pour milk and honey or wine for the deceased. Four of the tombs are rectangular while the other two are *arcosolia* tombs. Though the *arcosolia* (Tombs 1 and 6) no longer show any traces of decoration, the walls above the rest of the tombs are decorated with extremely well-preserved frescoes. The inscription and iconography of the tombs point to a 2nd century date, but the hypogeum was likely used much later, after the onset of Christianity due to the existence of the *arcosolia* to the sides of the entrance [33]. The two *arcosolia* are hypothesized to be much later additions to the hypogeum as this form of tomb was not popular until 4th century CE. The fact that Tomb 1 is excavated partially outside of the original area of the hypogeum reinforces this notion.

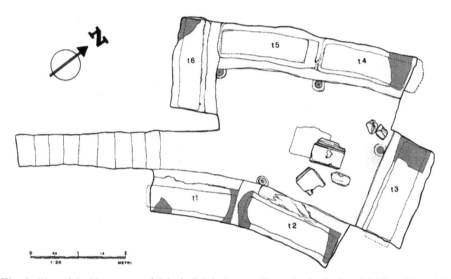

Fig. 4. Plan of the Hypogeum of Crispia Salvia (source Parco Archeologico di Lilibeo-Marsala).

2.2 The Inscription

The most revealing tomb and the namesake for the site belonged to a woman named Crispia Salvia. Her name is given on a formulaic inscription consisting of a terracotta tile nailed into a niche above Tomb 3 (Fig. 5). The slab was broken by looters *ab antiquo*, but its recovered fragments are now in the local museum. Painted in red, the inscription includes the name of the deceased, the name of the dedicant, and the number of years lived with the conclusory formula *libenti animo*. Crispia Salvia was 45 years old when she died and had been married to her husband for 15 of those years. The inscription mentions the name of two important *gentes* from this part of the island, the *gens Crispius* and *gens*

Salvius. The name *Crispius* is attested by various domestic utensils bearing the stamp *C.A. Crispi* and in the city of Segesta, possibly meaning that the family had strong ties to the area, which would explain the rich decoration of the tomb. The *Salvii* are recorded in funerary inscriptions elsewhere in Lilybaeum and was likely another important family in the area [30]. Whatever the case may be, the decoration of the tomb is indeed rich, and the reason that the Hypogeum of Crispia Salvia is such an important site.

2.3 The Frescoes

The research value of the Crispia Salvia complex lies in its frescoes, which are rarely featured in the academic literature (see [30, 33–35] for exceptions), likely due to the fact that it is largely inaccessible. Three of the four walls bear frescoes above the four original tombs[1]. The southeastern wall bears a fresco depicting a funerary banquet and a line of dancers, each holding the person in front with his left arm, advancing towards a flute player with a background of red flowers referencing a paradisiacal garden, a common theme in Roman catacombs [36]. As an ensemble, the frescoes attest a rich local repertoire of painting motifs that could be found in both pagan and Christian tombs [31].

Tomb 1, an *arcosolium* and therefore likely a later addition, has no traces of fresco. The southern wall above Tomb 2 has five male figures that walk towards the right, each with a hand on the shoulder of the man in front, all marching towards a sitting flutist on a background of red flowers. The shorter walls of the niche in which the tomb is placed also bear decorations. On the north wall above the tomb is a banquet scene, in which the same five male figures sit around a horseshoe shaped table drinking wine from glass goblets. In the center is a *trapeza*, or alter, with a glass of wine on top of it (Fig. 6 and 13) [30, 34].

Tomb 3 in the northeastern part of the wall, apart from the aforementioned terracotta tile with a Latin inscription painted in red, has decoration consisting of two winged figures on the frontal wall, off-center towards the east, in order to leave space for the slab bearing the inscription. The wall is otherwise decorated with red flowers throughout. Each winged figure holds a garland of red flowers from which fall ribbons and green clothes. On the side walls of the niche in which the tomb is placed are a male peacock with a female peacock on the opposite wall surrounded by 10 pomegranates. Both are sitting on a kalathos or basket full of flowers or fruit.

On the western wall are two more rectangular tombs excavated into the rock and two quadrangular niches per wall. One wall has decorations rich in flowers and garlands (Fig. 10), reminiscent of those used in the predominantly Christian catacombs of Vigna Cassia in Syracuse [37]. On the other side is a dove flying away from a basket full of flowers. There are two peacocks that are symmetrically opposed that are holding up garlands, with a *kalathos* flanked by two garlands with festoons [30].

---

[1] It is possible that the fourth wall also contained decorations that were destroyed by the construction of Tomb 6 (southwestern wall of the hypogeum).

Fig. 5. Digital reassembly of the two portions of the inscription (on the left that in display at the Museo Archeologico Baglio Anselmi of Marsala, on the right that still *in situ*).

Fig. 6. Frescoes decorating the walls of Tomb 2 (license Creative Commons).

3   Methods

In Summer 2018, a team of University of South Florida's Institute for Digital Exploration (IDEx), in partnership with the Parco Archeologico di Lilibeo-Marsala carried out the virtualization of the Hypogeum of Crispia Salvia. As with traditional pen and paper methods of recording, digital scans can be used in conjunction with one another to improve results and cover some of the limitations of each method. Here, digital photogrammetry was employed for photorealistic accuracy of the model and as the primary method for dissemination to the public. TLS was used in order to provide highly accurate geometric information of the site for research and documentation purposes. Both of these methods were carried out over the course of a single day.

For the TLS, a Leica BLK 360 was chosen to capture the site for its ability to register scans in real time using its proprietary Autodesk ReCap Pro mobile application on a 2017, 10.5-in. iPad Air that runs it via the BLK's internal WiFi. This scanner was chosen due to its small size and portability combined with its high level of accuracy, up to six millimeters at 10 m range with a 60-m range. The compactness of the scanner and its wide capturing arc was ideal for the hypogeum's underground environment and the site's fairly restricted space (Fig. 7). The Leica BLK 360 was able to capture the site with minimal holes in 12 scans. The scans covered the entirety of the site while the scanning itself was taking place. Upon completion of data collection and on-site automatic processing, the Autodesk ReCap project with the registered and processed scans were imported into the Autodesk ReCap Pro (version 5.0.2.41) desktop application for further examination. Manual evaluation of the point cloud verified the accuracy of the on-site registration and manual cleaning of the point cloud where stray points and bad data were removed. After manual cleaning, the finalized point cloud was exported as an E57 file from the Autodesk software for future use.

Fig. 7. Leica BLK 360 scanning in a hypogeal context.

Fig. 8. Digital photogrammetry in a hypogeal context.

For the photogrammetry, a total of 397 images were taken onsite at 4000 x 6000 resolution using a Nikon D3400 (Fig. 8). A floodlight was used in order to illuminate the walls in concordance with the camera. A total of 397 images were taken on site over a short period. These images were brought into Agisoft Metashape Professional 1.4.4 for processing. Agisoft Metashape was chosen as it is a reliable processing software for cultural heritage applications [38]. Following the workflow for Metashape, images were aligned. After manual inspection that they were aligned properly, a dense cloud was created, and the model was cleaned manually of any outlier data. Finally, the mesh and the texture were built. The final mesh was exported as an OBJ file with a 4000 × 4000 JPEG texture file for dissemination and potential use in other programs. The original exported OBJ file was then decimated using Geomagic Wrap 2015 to make it an appropriate size for uploading it to Sketchfab to make it publicly available online.

Animations of the mesh were created with Blender 2.79b and Bentley Pointools (version 10.00) for public outreach. The animation files of the point cloud and the mesh were edited into a single video using Adobe Premiere Pro CC 2019 and exported as an MP4 for upload to YouTube and other social media accounts and was provided to IDEx's partners in Sicily to be used for their purposes.

3.1 Results

The final result of the project was a complete 3D model of the interior of the hypogeum. The primary objectives, however, of capturing the overall geometry of the space and photorealistic representations of their decorations was achieved, creating a digital surrogate of the tomb with which the layout, frescoes, and other less tangible aspects of the original hypogeum can be visualized [39]. Updated plan and section views of the complex were generated to better understand its spatial and volumetric development (Figs. 9, 10, 11 and 12) as well as detailed digital replicas of the frescoes for public outreach and conservation purposes (Figs. 13, 12 and 14).

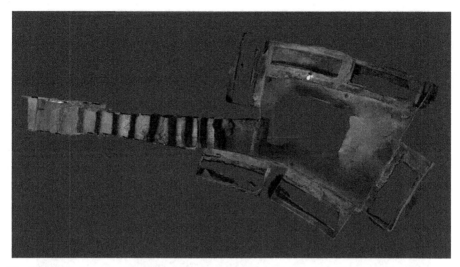

Fig. 9. Updated planar view of the Hypogeum of Crispia Salvia generated from the photogrammetric model.

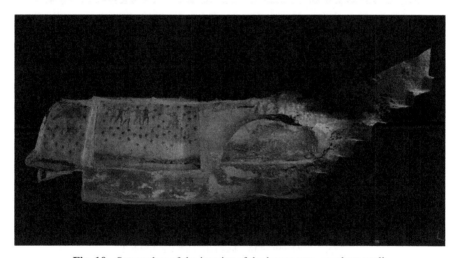

Fig. 10. Screenshot of the interior of the hypogeum, southern wall.

The completed.OBJ and texture files were uploaded to Sketchfab for dissemination to the public and IDEx's global partners (https://skfb.ly/6VQZY). The animations created were incorporated into an exhibition by the Parco Archeologico di Lilibeo. The video animation for public engagement is available on the IDEx YouTube channel (https://youtu.be/zqYC0euMwyM).

Fig. 11. Screenshot of the northern wall of the 3D model of the hypogeum.

Fig. 12. Screenshot of the interior of the eastern wall of the 3d model of the hypogeum.

Fig. 13. Detail of the decoration above Tomb 2.

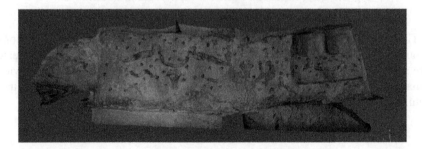

Fig. 14. Tomb 5 (left) and Tomb 6 (right) and the northern wall of the hypogeum.

3.2 Discussion

The nearly complete digital surrogate of the Hypogeum of Crispia Salvia has the potential to serve many purposes, providing both the public and researchers with an accessible and accurate version of the underground complex. The first objective of the project, to make it more accessible to the public, has been achieved. The local museum that manages the site, part of the Parco Archeologico di Lilibeo, is now able to display one of its prominent yet hidden sites to the public. The necessity of having to organize short visits is a barrier to entry for the public, and many with disabilities are not able to navigate the steep and narrow staircase to visit it at all. The 3D model now can act as a stand in for the private tour, and hopefully will increase awareness of the site, while preserving it and not draining the local museum's limited resources. Additionally, the model is VR capable, allowing individuals a further degree of immersion, rather than simply looking at a 2D screen. This immersion can help foster the important feeling of "enchantment" surrounding archaeology [40].

Not only is accessibility provided by this digital surrogate important for the general public, it is also helpful to researchers. They are in fact able to extract plans from the 3D model, examine the frescoes in detail and at their leisure, and even view the site in VR to ask new questions. The model's high level of accuracy can provide researchers with the ability to measure different parts of the site that may not be as easy or even possible in the physical space. The old plan has been supplemented by a new plan that can be extrapolated from the point cloud of the TLS scanning. Due to the size and density of the point cloud, the TLS data is currently unavailable via an online 3D viewer. This is the purpose of the animations which showcase the point cloud to the public in an accurate and representative way. The integration of the mesh into the animation shows the transformation and differences between the two methods—the point cloud which captures the geometry of the site better than the mesh while the mesh captures the color better than the point cloud. The newfound accessibility of the important site will hopefully lead to its increasing incorporation into wider academic narratives on the development of funerary iconography in Sicily and the wider Mediterranean [35].

Additionally, accessibility has become more of a significant topic of discussion due to recent events. While this site is able to gain increased visibility in general, further emphasis can be placed on digitization as it facilitates digital exploration of sites that cannot be visited by the public. At the time of writing, the COVID-19 pandemic has virtually shut down both domestic and international travel, as well as physical museums and cultural heritage institutions [41, 42]. Sites and museums with completed or ongoing digitization efforts have been a feature for understanding the scope of accessibility and engagement possible for a global public [43]. Online interactions with cultural heritage institutions increased during the lockdown in Italy [44], with visitors increasingly becoming digital guests that engage with museums through the virtual. Collections and sites that have been ~~already~~ digitized in 3D, allowing users to manipulate them and provide a better amount of engagement than simple 2D images and virtual reality experiences can allow people to enter the space digitally. Not only has the pandemic led to a new importance of digitization and digital engagement, but it has also posed similar issues for researchers. Researchers who were unable to travel to their sites are able to study the digitized surrogates with virtually the same accuracy of being there using these 3D models. With the digital Hypogeum of Crispia Salvia, visitors and researchers researchers can still access the site and engage with it in virtual form without compromising public and personal health and safety.

Even before the exponential growth of the use of digital photogrammetry, the production of archaeological data occurred at a much faster rate than it could be analyzed, creating a need for faster analytical tools. With the generation of 3D and online data that previously only existed in rare or hard to find publications, including the case study of Crispia Salvia, there is a great deal of potential for digital photogrammetric data, among other types of 3D data, to be incorporated into automatized analyses of their contents. As mentioned above, the analytical potential of the site lies largely in the site of Crispia Salvia's frescoes. Machine learning and pattern recognition technologies on frescoes have focused largely on the virtual anastylosis of disparate fresco pieces [10], and the relative completeness of the major motifs in the frescoes could be useful as a contribution to a control dataset for the reconstruction of less complete frescoes found in other hypogeal contexts. Automatic recognition of motifs using contour analysis within the fresco could also contribute to art-historical analyses of localized stylistic variations and repertoires, as has been attempted for mosaics [45].

4 Conclusion

Underground contexts are particularly hard to visit, much less work in. This project used digital tools to not only redocument the Hypogeum of Crispia Salvia but to show that it is possible to do so in a short time with tools that have wide-ranging applications. The point cloud and photogrammetry of this difficult to access site demonstrates that the poor lighting and confined space of the underground complex was not an insurmountable obstacle to the project. This case study proves the merits of digital methods for the documentation and valorization of a specific type of cultural heritage that is largely inaccessible to the public. The products of the project have already been incorporated into exhibitions by the local museum. Scholars also have access to a holistic view of the Hypogeum of Crispia Salvia's digital surrogate that previously had to be extrapolated from simple photographs and a single plan. Future research and applications into the creation of virtual reality platforms and engagement with the public in digital storytelling methods would provide the public with an immersive and educational understanding of the hypogeum as well as the history of Crispia Salvia herself. With the point cloud and digital photogrammetry, researchers can continue the study of the site, despite current limitations in travel. Further integration of the digital surrogate into a web-based tour of the site with its history and context would be beneficial to public dissemination and engagement, especially in a world increasingly reliant on digital technologies.

Acknowledgements. Special thanks must be given to Anna Maria Parrinello and Maria Grazia Griffo, senior officers of the Parco Archeologico di Lilibeo, for the support and to Roberto Miccichè and Filippo Pisciotta for providing material for lighting the hypogeum and their assistance in the arduous task of keeping stable light conditions in the hypogeum while taking pictures for the photogrammetry.

References

1. Barceló, J. A.: Computational intelligence in archaeology. State of the art. In: Making History Interactive. Computer Applications and Quantitative Methods in Archaeology (CAA). Proceedings of the 37th International Conference, pp. 11–21. Williamsburg, Virginia, United States of America, Archaeopress (2010)
2. Barceló, J.A.: Visual analysis in archaeology. An artificial intelligence approach. In: Elewa, A.M.T. (ed.) Morphometrics for Nonmorphometricians. Lecture Notes in Earth Sciences, vol. 124, 93–156. Springer, Heidelberg (2010). https://doi.org/10.1007/978-3-540-95853-6_5
3. van der Maaten, L.: Computer vision and machine learning in archaeology. In: Proceedings of Computer Applications and Quantitative Methods in Archaeology, pp. 112–130 (2006)
4. Karasik, A., Smilansky, U.: 3D scanning technology as a standard archaeological tool for pottery analysis: practice and theory. J. Archaeol. Sci. **35**(5), 1148–1168 (2014). https://doi.org/10.1016/j.jas.2007.08.008
5. Hörr, C., Lindinger, E., Brunnett, G.: Machine learning based typology development in archaeology. J. Comput. Cult. Heritage **7**(1), 1–23 (2014). https://doi.org/10.1145/2533988
6. Wilczek, J., Monna, F., Barral, P., Burlet, L., Chateau, C., Navarro, N.: Morphometrics of second iron age ceramics-strengths, weaknesses, and comparison with traditional typology. J. Archaeol. Sci. **50**, 39–50 (2014). https://doi.org/10.1016/j.jas.2014.05.033
7. Bickler, S. H.: Machine Learning Identification and Classification of Historic Ceramics. Archaeology 20 (2018)
8. Stanco, F., Tanasi, D., Giovanni, G.: Digital reconstruction of fragmented glass plate photographs: the case of archaeological photography. Commun. Appl. Indust. Math. **2**(1), 1–11 (2011). https://doi.org/10.1685/journal.caim.361
9. Kotoula, E.: Semiautomatic fragments matching and virtual reconstruction: a case study on ceramics. Int. J. Conserv. Sci. **7**(1), 71–86 (2016)
10. Barra, P., Barra, S., Nappi, M., Narducci, F.: SAFFO: a SIFT based approach for digital anastylosis for fresco reconstruction. Pattern Recogn. Lett. **138**, 123–129 (2020). https://doi.org/10.1016/j.patrec.2020.07.008
11. Gabellone, F., Chiffi, M., Tanasi, D., Decker, M.: Integrated technologies for Indirect Documentation, Conservation and Engagement of the Roman mosaics of Piazza Armerina (Enna, Italy). In: Cicalò, E. (ed) Proceedings of the 2nd International and Interdisciplinary Conference on Image and Imagination, IMG 2019. Advances in Intelligent Systems and Computing, vol. 1140, pp. 1016–1028. Springer (2020)
12. Stanco, F., Tanasi, D., Allegra, D., Milotta, L.F.M., Lamagna, G., Monterosso, G.: Virtual anastylosis of greek sculpture as museum policy for public outreach and cognitive accessibility. J. Electron. Imaging **26**(1), 1–12 (2017). https://doi.org/10.1117/1.JEI.26.1.011025
13. Bennoui-Ladraa, B., Chennaoui, Y.: Use of photogrammetry for digital surveying, documentation and communication of the cultural heritage. Example regarding virtual reconstruction of the access doors for the nameless temple of Tipasa (Algeria). Stud. Digit. Heritage **2**(2), 121–137 (2018). https://doi.org/10.14434/sdh.v2i2.24496
14. Milotta, F.L.M., et al.: Challenges in automatic munsell color profiling for cultural heritage. Pattern Recogn. Lett. **131**, 135–141 (2020). https://doi.org/10.1016/j.patrec.2019.12.008
15. Allegra, D., Gallo, G., Inzerillo, L., Milotta, F. L. M., Santagata, C., Stanco, F.: Low cost handheld 3D scanning for architectural elements acquisition. In: Proceedings of the Conference on Smart Tools and Applications in Computer Graphics, Genova, Italy, pp. 127–131 (2016)
16. Berquist, S., et al.: A new aerial photogrammetric survey method for recording inaccessible rock art. Digit. Appl. Archaeol. Cult. Heritage **8**, 46–56 (2018). https://doi.org/10.1016/j.daach.2018.03.001

17. Magnani, M., Douglass, M., Schroder, W., Reeves, J., Braun, D.R.: The digital revolution to come: photogrammetry in archaeological practice. Am. Antiq. **85**(4), 737–760 (2020). https://doi.org/10.1017/aaq.2020.59
18. Tanasi, D.: The digital (within) archaeology. Aanalysis of a phenomenon. Historian **82**(1), 22–36 (2020). https://doi.org/10.1080/00182370.2020.1723968
19. Green, S., Bevan, A., Shapland, M.: A comparative assessment of structure from motion methods for archaeological research. J. Archaeol. Sci. **46**, 173–181 (2014). https://doi.org/10.1016/j.jas.2014.02.030
20. Olson, B.R., Placchetti, R.A.: A discussion of the analytical benefits of image based modeling in archaeology. Visions of substance: 3D imaging in Mediterranean archaeology, pp. 17–25 (2015)
21. Lercari, N.: Terrestrial Laser Scanning in the Age of Sensing, p. 33. Springer, Cham (2016). https://doi.org/10.1007/978-3-319-40658-91
22. Sapirstein, P., Murray, S.: Establishing best practices for photogrammetric recording during archaeological fieldwork. J. Field Archaeol. **42**(4), 337–350 (2017). https://doi.org/10.1080/00934690.2017.1338513
23. Tanasi, D., Gradante, I., Hassam, S.: Best practices for 3d digital recording and global sharing of catacombs from late roman Sicily. Stud. Digit. Heritage **3**(1), 60–82 (2019). https://doi.org/10.14434/sdh.v3i1.25290
24. Bonacini, E., D'Agostino, G., Galizia, M., Santagati, C., Sgarlata, M.: The catacombs of san Giovanni in Syracuse: surveying, digital enhancement and revitalization of an archaeological landmark. In: Ioannides, M., Fritsch, D., Leissner, J., Davies, R., Remondino, F., Caffo, R. (eds.) EuroMed 2012. LNCS, vol. 7616, pp. 396–403. Springer, Heidelberg (2012). https://doi.org/10.1007/978-3-642-34234-9_40
25. Bonacini, E., D'Agostino, G., Galizia, M., Santagati, C., Sgarlata, M.: Hidden cultural landscapes: survey and digital enhancement of the catacombs of san giovanni in syracuse. In: Heritage Architecture and Design Focus on Conservation Regen- eration Innovation Le Vie Dei Mercanti, XI Forum Internazionale Di Studi. pp. 267–71. La Scuola di Pitagora (2013)
26. Santagati, C.: Metodologie digitali per il rilievo e la valorizzazione del patrimonio culturale ipogeo. Virtual Archaeol. Rev. **5**(10), 82–92 (2014)
27. Gradante, I., Sgarlata, M., Tanasi, D.: 3d digital technologies to record excavation data: the case of the catacombs of st. lucy (siracusa, sicily). In: 8th International congress on archaeology, computer graphics, cultural heritage and innovation, pp. 71–77. Editorial Universitat Polit'ecnica de Val'encia (2016)
28. Gradante, I., Tanasi, D.: 3d digital technologies for architectural analysis. The case of the 'pagan shrine'in the catacombs of santa lucia (siracusa, sicily). Archeologia e Calcolatori **28**(2), 581–586 (2017)
29. Gradante, I., Tanasi, D.: Nuove indagini archeologiche nella regione c del cimitero di santa lucia a siracusa. In: Sgarlata, M., Tanasi, D. (eds.) Koimeis: Recent Excavations in the Siracusan and Maltese catacombs, pp. 31–62. Parnassos Press, Sioux City, Iowa (2016)
30. Giglio, R.: Lilibeo: l'ipogeo dipinto di Crispia Salvia. Accademia nazionale di scienze lettere e arti (1996)
31. Mazzei, B.: Funerary painting and sculpture: tangency and divergence in the for- mation process of early christian repertoire. Antiquit´e Tardive **19**, 79–94 (2011). https://doi.org/10.1484/J.AT.1.3005
32. Toynbee, J.M.C.: Death and burial in the Roman world. Cornell University Press, Ithica (1971)
33. Giglio, R.: La necropoli di lilibeo alla luce delle recenti scoperte. In: Se cerchi la tua strada verso Itaca . . . Omaggio a Lina Di Stefano, pp. 101–114 (2016).
34. Dunbabin, K.M.: The Roman Banquet: Images of Conviviality. Cambridge University Press, Cambridge (2003)

35. Giglio, R.: La cristianizzazione di lilibeo attraverso le recenti scoperte archeologiche. In: Bonacasa Carra, R.M., Vitale, E. (eds.) La cristianizzazione in Italia fra tardo antico e medioevo. Atti del IX Congresso Nazionale di Archeologia Cristiana (Agrigento, 20–25 Novembre 2004), pp. 20–25 (2004)

36. Bellia, A.: Affigurazioni musicali nell'Ipogeo di Crispia Salvia a Lilibeo (Marsala). Philomusica on-line **7**(2), 75–82 (2008). https://doi.org/10.6092/1826-9001.7.381

37. Stevenson, J.: The Catacombs: Life and Death in Early Christianity. Thomas Nelson Publishers, Nashville (1978)

38. Kingsland, K.: Comparative analysis of digital photogrammetry software for cultural heritage. Digit. Appl. Archaeol. Cult. Heritage **18** (2020). https://doi.org/10.1016/j.daach.2020.e00157

39. Rabinowitz, A.: The work of archaeology in the age of digital surrogacy. In: Olson, B.R., Caraher, W.R. (eds.) Visions of Substance: 3D Imaging in Mediterranean Archaeology, pp. 27–42. The Digital Press at the University of North Dakota, Fargo (2015)

40. Perry, S.: The enchantment of the archaeological record. Eur. J. Archaeol. **22**(3), 354–371 (2019). https://doi.org/10.1017/eaa.2019.24

41. Christiansen, K.: The met and the covid crisis. Museum Manage. Curatorship **35**(3), 221–224 (2020). https://doi.org/10.1080/09647775.2020.1762362

42. Potts, T.: The j. paul getty museum during the coronavirus crisis. Museum Manage. Curatorship **35**(3), 217–220 (2020). https://doi.org/10.1080/09647775.2020.1762360

43. Iguman, S.: If visitors won't go to Heritage, Heritage must go to visitors. In: Digitization of Heritage in time of Corona, pp. 165–172. Universita' degli Studi di Bergamo (2020)

44. Agostino, D., Arnaboldi, M., Lampis, A.: Italian state museums during the COVID-19 crisis: from onsite closure to online openness. Museum Manage. Curatorship **35**(4), 362–372 (2020). https://doi.org/10.1080/09647775.2020.1790029

45. Ioniță, S., Țurcanu-Caruțiu, D.: Automation of the expertise of the roman mosaic arts in constanta: analytical and statistical models for a fuzzy inference-based system. In: Daniela Turcanu-Carutiu (ed) Heritage. IntechOpen (2020). https://doi.org/10.5772/intechopen.92679

PRAConBE - Pattern Recognition and Automation in Construction and the Built Environment

Preface

The PRAConBE workshop covers a topic that is rapidly gaining attention in the recent years, with a continually increasing number of research papers, research groups, projects and applications in various subfields of applying pattern recognition-related methods to automating different facets of the construction and renovation process. The architecture, engineering and construction industry, an economic sector of significant importance (annual revenues of approx. US $10 trillion, or about 6% of global GDP), is expected to be radically transformed by digitalizing ever more aspects of the construction model, thereby boosting productivity, managing complexity and enhancing worksite safety and quality. Pattern recognition is central to this process of transformation, with computer vision, signal & image processing, machine learning applications increasingly finding uses of great impact to the field. At the same time, as novel problems arise corresponding to new applications in automating construction, the need for novel models and methods of pattern recognition is becoming ever-more urgent, in a process that is revitalizing and beneficial for both pattern recognition as a research field, as well as the construction industry. We have welcomed contributions of papers targeting the workshop scope, which includes the following topics: Pattern recognition for construction planning, Structural asset detection, Vision and Perception, Process simulation models, Defect & Crack detection, Automated construction progress assessment, Energy efficiency estimation, Scan-to-BIM and Scan-vs-BIM, Augmented & Mixed reality, Automatic demand response flexibility estimation, Uses of UAVs and Pattern Recognition in construction, Decision support systems, Management of constructed facilities, Energy efficiency estimation, Robot vision for construction applications, Robot path and motion planning in construction sites, Robot multimodal perception in construction, Human robot interaction and safety issues in construction sites.

The review process followed was single blind peer review, performed by the members of the workshop program committee. Regarding the number of reviews per paper, submissions each received 1 to 2 reviews (5 papers with one review, 6 papers with two reviews). A total of 11 papers were submitted, out of which 9 papers were accepted. All papers were full papers, each spanning 12–15 pages length.

November 2020   Giorgos Sfikas

Organization

Workshop Chairs

Giorgos Sfikas	University of Ioannina, Greece
Athanasios Tsakiris	CERTH/ITI, Greece
Dimitrios Giakoumis	CERTH/ITI, Greece
Dimosthenis Ioannidis	CERTH/ITI, Greece
Dimitrios Tzovaras	CERTH/ITI, Greece

Invited Speaker

Frèdèric Boschè	University of Edinburgh, UK

Program Committee

Dimitriou Nikolaos	CERTH/ITI, Greece
Kargakos Andreas	CERTH/ITI, Greece
Kostavelis Ioannis	CERTH/ITI, Greece
Krinidis Stelios	CERTH/ITI, Greece
Malassiotis Sotiris	CERTH/ITI, Greece
Mariolis Ioannis	CERTH/ITI, Greece
Peleka Georgia	CERTH/ITI, Greece
Skartados Evangelos	CERTH/ITI, Greece
Stavropoulos Georgios	CERTH/ITI, Greece
Topalidou-Kyniazopoulou Angeliki	CERTH/ITI, Greece
Vasileiadis Manolis	CERTH/ITI, Greece

Automatic MEP Component Detection with Deep Learning

John Kufuor, Dibya D. Mohanty$^{(\boxtimes)}$ ⓘ, Enrique Valero ⓘ,
and Frédéric Bosché ⓘ

School of Engineering, The University of Edinburgh, Edinburgh, UK
{s1512601,d.mohanty,e.valero,f.bosche}@ed.ac.uk

Abstract. Scan-to-BIM systems convert image and point cloud data into accurate 3D models of buildings. Research on Scan-to-BIM has largely focused on the automated identification of structural components. However, design and maintenance projects require information on a range of other assets including mechanical, electrical, and plumbing (MEP) components. This paper presents a deep learning solution that locates and labels MEP components in 360° images and phone images, specifically sockets, switches and radiators. The classification and location data generated by this solution could add useful context to BIM models. The system developed for this project uses transfer learning to retrain a Faster Region-based Convolutional Neural Network (Faster R-CNN) for the MEP use case. The performance of the neural network across image formats is investigated. A dataset of 249 360° images and 326 phone images was built to train the deep learning model. The Faster R-CNN achieved high precision and comparatively low recall across all image formats.

Keywords: Scan-to-BIM · MEP · Radiators · Sockets · Switches · Convolutional Neural Network · Deep learning

1 Introduction

In Scan-to-BIM research, work on automating object detection has mostly focused on large structural components such as floors, ceilings, and walls, or openings such as doors and windows [5,27,32]. However, the effective maintenance of buildings and other structures requires BIM models that contain many other details including mechanical, electrical and plumbing (MEP) components. In fact, MEP assets account for a large share of building maintenance costs [1]. They, thus, constitute important information to collect for maintenance and renovation. Therefore, there is a clear need to develop Scan-to-BIM technology that extends current capability to MEP components.

Detecting MEP components presents a set of unique challenges. They are generally much smaller than structural components which makes it difficult for object detection models to identify them [23]. MEP assets also have a

© Springer Nature Switzerland AG 2021
A. Del Bimbo et al. (Eds.): ICPR 2020 Workshops, LNCS 12667, pp. 373–388, 2021.
https://doi.org/10.1007/978-3-030-68787-8_28

greater range of variation within classes than structural components do; therefore, an MEP detector must learn more feature patterns. For example, different brands of radiators will have slightly different markings, valve designs and other characteristics.

Recent developments in deep learning have led to impressive results in the detection of many classes of small objects [23,24]. If successful, the application of deep learning to detect MEP components in photographic and point cloud data will support their integration into Scan-to-BIM frameworks and ultimately deliver more detailed BIM models.

This paper describes work on using deep learning models to detect MEP components in images, specifically sockets, switches and radiators. In addition, the performance of the object detection neural networks across different image formats, specifically 360° images and standard images collected by mobile phones, is interrogated. One of the main challenges of training deep learning models for MEP detection is that building a large dataset is a time-intensive process. If it was possible for models trained on one image format to infer detections on another this would create the opportunity to aggregate larger cross-format datasets. In addition, this cross-format functionality would make the models useful in a wider variety of settings.

2   Related Work

2.1   Mathematical Algorithms

The automatic identification and positioning of MEP components in building interior spaces is a field that has received limited research attention. Methods that have been developed usually only detect a single class of object, e.g. pipes.

Regarding electrical components, researchers have experimented with various techniques for detecting sockets. [12] propose a method that finds the holes of sockets in input images using a feature detector algorithm, then applies a geometric equation to group them into coherent sets. A 3D position of the outlet is then determined using a mathematical algorithm called a planar Perspective-n-Point solver. [29] detect a specific variant of orange on white electrical outlets in images using a colour thresholding technique and geometric filtering. Finally, [15] identify the features of a socket in an image using Gaussian filters and contrast limited adaptive histogram equalisation (CLAHE), then apply thresholding to extract the outlet boxes.

[10] detect ceiling lights in laser scan data. The ceiling of the interior space is segmented using a Random Sample Consensus (RANSAC) algorithm. Then the ceiling point cloud is converted into an image by the application of nearest neighbour rasterisation. A Harris corner detector function finds the fluorescent lights in the image and a Hough transform algorithm identifies the circular form of the standard light bulbs.

In the field of plumbing, much of the object detection research has focused on pipes. [9] propose a method for identifying pipes in cluttered 3D point clouds. Assuming that the curvature of a pipe spool would differ from the surrounding clutter, they filter the point cloud for clusters of points that had a cylindrical shape. Then, using the Bag-of-Features method – a computer vision technique where features are aggregated into a histogram – they compare each potential pipe object to what was present in a 3D CAD file of the scene. The clusters with the highest similarity are registered as being accurate representations of as-built pipe spools.

[36] also apply a curvature-based algorithm to point cloud data in order to detect pipelines. Their system uses region growth to segment the point cloud. Then segments are classified as pipelines based on whether 30 randomly selected points fit a curvature requirement. Alternative research detects pipes in laser scans of interior spaces by applying the Hough transform algorithm to slices of the point cloud [2,6]. [11] proposed a point cloud MEP detection method that begins with a multi-level feature extraction of each 3D point, including variables such as the curvature and roughness, followed by the development of potential pipe segments from promising 'seed' points.

It is also notable that automated pipe detection in point cloud data is a functionality that a number of commercial software packages already offer.

More recently, [1] built a system that detected multiple classes of MEP components including extinguishers, sockets and switches. First, the system extracts orthoimages of walls from point clouds of interiors spaces. Then these orthoimages are separated into their geometric and colour components. Colour-based detection algorithms are applied to the colour images, and geometric detection algorithms are applied to the depth images. Finally, objects are recognised and positioned based on the consensus between the two results.

2.2   Machine Learning

Machine learning, where computer models learn how to perform tasks from experience, has also been employed in research on MEP detection [30].

[20] use a random forest classifier – a type of machine learning classifier – together with a sliding window on orthophotos of walls to detect sockets and light switches.

[17] developed a framework for detecting a range of objects in point cloud data, including MEP assets such as valves and spotlights. Primitive shapes, such as pipes and planes, are identified using a support vector machine (SVM) which is another type of machine learning classifier. Large primitives, such as walls, are assumed to be background elements and discarded. Then, the remaining points are clustered using their Euclidean distance. Clusters that passed a linearity filter undergoes a detailed matching process comparing them to components in a pre-made 3D object library. If the alignment between a cluster and a target component exceeds a threshold, the cluster is deemed to be a detected instance of the target.

[21] extracted visual features from images using a 'Histogram of Oriented Gradients' and used them to train a SVM to detect radiators. Based on whether the radiator was present or not present their system could evaluate the progress of installation works.

Alternative data sources, such as thermal imaging have also been used. [19] identify light fixtures and display monitors by applying a machine learning clustering model to a thermal point cloud.

2.3 Deep Learning

Deep learning models have outperformed conventional computer vision systems when applied to industry-standard object classification and detection benchmarks such as the Pascal VOC challenge and the MS COCO challenge [13]. In these challenges, models are tasked to detect a wide array of common objects such as cars, humans, chairs and clocks in 100,000 s of images [25]. Based on the widely documented success of deep learning in computer vision solutions, applying deep learning technology to the MEP use case should produce significantly better results than prior attempts.

There are already many positive case studies of the application of object detection deep learning models to construction and asset management problems. [3] developed a deep learning model that semantically segmented furniture in laser scans of interior spaces. [7] used a neural network to detect structural elements such as beams and columns in the S3DIS point cloud data set. These successes offer further motivation to investigate the application of deep learning to MEP asset detection.

3 Methodology

3.1 Dataset

Building a large, diverse dataset is the most critical step in any successful deep learning project. By providing a large quantity and variety of examples for the model to learn from, a robust dataset ensures the model will perform well when applied to a range of real-world cases [31]. Currently, there are no open-source image databases focused on MEP assets in interior spaces. Therefore, one of the main objectives of this project was to build a small MEP dataset that could be used to train models using transfer learning.

In fact, we built one dataset composed of two sub-datasets. A Ricoh Theta V 360° camera was used to capture the RGB images that make up the 360° sub-dataset. And a selection of mobile phones (including the Pixel 2, Galaxy S8, and iPhone5s) was used to collect samples for the standard image sub-dataset. A variety of lighting conditions, camera angles and levels of occlusion are represented in the data. The images were collected from different residential and educational (University) buildings in UK. The dataset contains radiators of different model, shape and size, Type-G sockets of different types (single and double sockets) and styles, and switches of different styles. Figure 1 shows the variety of the data in each category. This diversity ensures that models trained on the dataset will generalise well to a range of realistic cases.

The images gathered for the dataset were large and this presented a problem (360° images = 5376 × 2688; standard images = 4272 × 2848 − 1600 × 739).

Fig. 1. Sample images from dataset

Training the deep learning model on such massive images would be very computationally expensive so they had to be scaled down to a reasonable input size. This process makes sockets, switches and radiators that are already small with respect to the image harder for a model to detect [13]. The amount of detail in the images that the model can use to make decisions is compressed.

To address this issue, the dataset images were segmented into 'tiles' as shown in Fig. 2. Thus, the MEP objects were made larger with respect to their images and the scaled down inputs. Each 360° image was divided into six tiles and each standard image was divided into four tiles. Then the tiles that contained sockets, switches and radiators were selected for use in the corresponding sub-datasets.

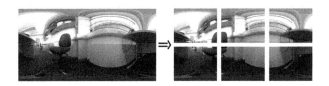

Fig. 2. Tiling

Using a Python program, 80% of images were randomly assigned to the training portion of each sub-dataset, and the remaining 20% were assigned to validation. The sockets, switches and radiators in the images were labelled using the open-source tool LabelImg. Finally, the completed dataset of images and labels was uploaded to Google Drive where it could be accessed from a remote server and used to train models.

3.2   Model Training and Validation

The deep learning model chosen for this research is one with the Faster Region-based Convolutional Neural Network (Faster R-CNN) meta-architecture that uses Neural Architecture Search Net (NASNet) as a feature extractor and was previously trained on the Microsoft Common Objects in Context (COCO) detection dataset. Faster R-CNN has achieved state-of-the-art accuracy on industry standard benchmarks [33].

Model parameters and training process settings were defined in a configuration file before the training began. These included variables such as the input image size the model would accept, the number of training steps that should occur and the location of the dataset files.

During each validation trial, the values of loss, average recall (AR) and average precision (AP) were saved in log files. Once training was complete, the data was used to analyse the model's learning progress, as shown in Sect. 4.

During the model development process it was observed that growth in performance usually stagnated in the 10,000 to 20,000 training step range. This stagnation signalled that overfitting was occurring and that the model was learning feature patterns that were useful when applied to the training data but did not generalise to new validation data. Thus, the training process for all of the experimental models was stopped at 20,000 steps in order to deliver the highest performance models using the least possible computational resources.

3.3   Dataset Augmentation

Dataset augmentation was used to increase the size of the dataset and thereby improve model performance. Horizontal flip was randomly applied to the images with a 50% probability. Patch Gaussian, was also implemented. This method adds a square of Gaussian noise to a random location on the input image [26]. The square was applied with a 50% probability at random sizes between 300 $pixels^2$ and 600 $pixels^2$ with a random standard deviation between 0.1 and 1.

4   Experiments and Results

4.1   Dataset

A total of 249 360° images were collected and labelled. When segmented into six tiles as described in Sect. 3.1, this image base expanded to 1,494 images. 105 of these contained radiators and were selected for the radiator sub-dataset. The 80/20 split resulted in 84 training examples and 21 validation images. 224 images contained sockets and were selected for the socket sub-dataset, with 179 training images and 45 validation images.

326 landscape phone camera images were captured. After being cut into four tiles as described in Sect. 3.1, the standard image set expanded to 1,304 images. The result was a radiator sub-dataset of 97 images, a socket sub-dataset of 190 images and a switch sub-dataset of 76 images.

4.2   Measuring Performance

Measuring the Average Precision (AP) and Average Recall (AR) is a common strategy for evaluating the performance of object detection neural networks [13,18,34]. During each validation step, these metrics are calculated by comparing the detections the model made on the validation images to the labelled reality.

The AP of an object class is the area under the precision-recall curve. AP is defined according to the Intersection over Union (IoU) threshold that was used. For example, mAP@0.5 is the mAP when 0.5 is the IoU threshold for a positive detection.

AR is the maximum recall given a defined number of detections per image, averaged over a range of IoU thresholds, specifically $IoU = 0.5$ to $IoU = 0.95$ with a step of 0.5 [8,16]. For example, AR@100 is the average recall at a maximum of 100 detections per image. Since all the images in our dataset contain more than one and less than ten MEP assets AR@10 is used in the experimental analysis.

K-fold cross-validation was used to verify the accuracy of the results. This strategy is standard practice in leading-edge object detection research [28,38]. For the following experiments $K = 3$ was used and images were allocated to training and validation at an 80%/20% split.

4.3   360° Image MEP Detector

As shown in Table 1, the maximum AP@0.5 achieved by the Faster R-CNN when trained on the 360° radiator sub-dataset was 0.897. This means that at peak precision an average of 89.7% of the model's detections were accurate.

The AR@10 of the radiator model reached a maximum of 0.728, as seen in Table 2. This metric indicates that, on average, 72.8% of the radiators in the validation images were detected.

The socket model had higher performance in terms of precision with an AP@0.5 of 0.939 but lower recall with an AR@10 of 0.698.

Comparing these values of recall with the relatively high precision, it is evident that although most of the Faster R-CNN's predictions were accurate there were a high number of false negatives where radiators and sockets of interest were missed entirely.

Table 1. Peak AP@0.5 of 360° models

Class	Fold 0	Fold 1	Fold 2	Average
Radiator	0.884	0.960	0.892	0.897
Socket	0.929	0.936	0.951	0.939

Table 2. Peak AR@10 of 360° models

Class	Fold 0	Fold 1	Fold 2	Average
Radiator	0.719	0.735	0.730	0.728
Socket	0.693	0.706	0.694	0.698

4.4   Standard Image MEP Detector

Training the Faster R-CNN on standard images yielded improved accuracy. The peak AP@0.5 of the standard image radiator model was 0.995, as seen in Table 3. Therefore, the fraction of the detections the model made that were accurate was higher. This could be due to more frequent true-positive detections, fewer false-positive detections, or both. The maximum AR@10 exhibited during validation was 0.886, as shown in Table 4. This is evident that the Faster R-CNN was able to identify and locate a greater proportion of the ground-truth radiators when trained with standard images.

The precision and recall of the socket models was also higher than those trained with 360° images with a maximum AP@0.5 of 0.977 and a peak AR@10 of 0.762.

Table 3. Peak AP@0.5 of standard image models

Class	Fold 0	Fold 1	Fold 2	Average
Radiator	0.985	1.000	1.000	0.995
Socket	0.978	0.963	0.989	0.977
Switch	0.980	1.00	0.965	0.982

Table 4. Peak AR@10 of standard image models

Class	Fold 0	Fold 1	Fold 2	Average
Radiator	0.929	0.855	0.873	0.886
Socket	0.770	0.725	0.791	0.762
Switch	0.844	0.906	0.822	0.857

This improved performance could be the result of a number of factors. The number of training samples collected for the standard image sub-datasets was lower than that gathered for the 360° sub-datasets, therefore the jump in model accuracy must have been a result of the content of the images as opposed to their quantity.

The standard image data may have presented a less diverse range of examples to study and therefore fewer patterns for the model to learn, resulting in improved validation results [35]. The increased accuracy could also be because the randomly selected validation testing examples were too similar to the training examples. This is likely judging from the unrealistically high AP results recorded in some of the experiments. In fact, an AP of 1 which would normally be judged as anomalous was observed when training the radiator models on two of the folds. More K-fold trials could have been used to ensure that training-validation splits that proved too easy for the model did not overly skew the results.

Another explanation is that even though the 360° camera had high pixel resolution, the level of detail in the images was low because the pixels were stretc.hed over a 360° frame [4]. The phone cameras captured a much smaller field of view. Therefore, even if their pixel resolution was lower than the 360° camera a higher level of detail could be achieved for objects of interest. This could explain the superior performance of the models trained on standard images.

The switch models also exhibited strong performance with an AP@0.5 of 0.982 and an AR@10 of 0.857. As was the case for the 360° models, precision was higher than recall in all of the standard model experiments.

4.5   Cross-Format Testing

Proving that MEP detection models trained with this methodology can deliver high performance across different image formats would make them useful in a wider range of settings. For the sake of repeatability and fair comparison all the models used for the following cross-format experimentation had the exact same 20,000 steps of training time. The previously explored Peak AP models all had different amounts of training because peak AP was achieved at different stages in the training process for each fold.

It is expected that cross-format functionality should be possible between 360° and standard images because the only major difference between the two formats is the level of distortion created by the 360° camera. The Ricoh Theta V camera used for this research employs two fisheye lenses on the front and back. Fisheye lenses make use of barrel distortion, where object scale decreases with distance from the optical centre, to capture an extended field of view seen in Fig. 3 [22].

The distortion that the 360° model encounters during training could potentially help it to fare better when faced with 'simpler' image samples. There is evidence that intentionally applying optical distortion to training images for augmentation purposes can improve precision. For example, [39] used different lens distortions, including barrel distortion, to augment image training data for their Deep Image neural network and achieved state of the art classification accuracy.

In support of this theory, testing the 360° radiator model on 360° images and standard images yielded similar results. As shown in Table 5, the AP was only 0.001 lower when the model was applied to standard images.

However, as seen in Table 6, the 360° socket model exhibited significantly lower accuracy when tested with standard images.

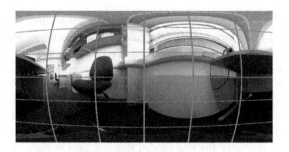

Fig. 3. Barrel distortion

Table 5. AP@0.5 results of testing the 360° radiator model on 360° images and standard images

	360° images	Standard images
Fold 0	0.794	0.874
Fold 1	0.943	0.822
Fold 2	0.847	0.885
Average	0.861	0.860

Occlusion may have played a significant role in this drop in performance. 31% of the sockets in the standard image dataset are only partially visible in the image tile (note that a fully visible socket with a plug is still considered partially visible), while only 2% of the sockets in the 360° images were partially hidden. As research has demonstrated, objects that are only partially visible are harder for a model to recognise because they offer fewer visual features [14]. The 360° socket model was not prepared to handle a high incidence of occluded objects.

Table 6. AP@0.5 results of testing the 360° socket model on 360° images and standard images

	360° images	Standard images
Fold 0	0.920	0.661
Fold 1	0.918	0.609
Fold 2	0.941	0.651
Average	0.926	0.640

To verify whether occlusion was actually hindering the performance of the 360° models on the standard images, the 360° models were tested on the uncropped standard images. In their uncropped format all of the sockets in the images were fully visible. As explained in Sect. 3.1, using uncropped images came with the disadvantage that the MEP assets would be smaller with respect to the images and therefore harder to detect in the feature map. Despite this handicap, the performance of the 360° models on the uncropped standard images was much higher. As shown in Table 7, AP on standard image sockets rose 21% to 0.773.

Interestingly, testing on uncropped standard images also improved the cross-format performance of the radiator 360° model. As shown in Table 8, AP increased 10% to 0.949. This improvement can similarly be attributed to the fact that most of the radiators are fully visible in the 360° training data and uncropped standard images, but not in the standard image cropped tiles.

Therefore, it can be concluded that the high occurrence of occlusion in the tiled image examples hindered model performance. This indicates that in future research on the use of neural networks for MEP detection, models should be developed with occlusion invariance so that they can better handle such cases. This could be achieved through further diversification of the training data to ensure that the proportion of occluded objects is similar to what is expected in the testing and real-world samples. There are also many examples in published research of deep learning object detection architectures that have been designed to handle occlusion using techniques that could be applied to the MEP context [37].

Table 7. AP@0.5 results of testing the 360° socket model on standard images and uncropped standard images

	Standard images	Uncropped standard images
Fold 0	0.661	0.788
Fold 1	0.609	0.731
Fold 2	0.651	0.801
Average	0.640	0.773

Table 8. AP@0.5 results of testing the 360° radiator model on standard images and uncropped standard images

	Standard images	Uncropped standard images
Fold 0	0.874	0.950
Fold 1	0.822	0.951
Fold 2	0.885	0.946
Average	0.860	0.949

The standard image models fared much worse when tested on 360° images. As shown in Table 9, AP was 34% lower when the standard image radiator model was applied to 360° images. Similarly, Table 10 shows that AP was 43% lower when the socket model was applied to 360° images. This supports the theory that the barrel distortion of the 360° images better prepares the 360° models to handle standard images with less optical distortion but hampers the performance of the standard image models when they are tested on 360° images.

Table 9. AP@0.5 results of testing the standard image radiator model on standard images and 360° images

	Standard images	360 images
Fold 0	0.976	0.615
Fold 1	0.984	0.660
Fold 2	0.996	0.649
Average	0.985	0.641

Table 10. AP@0.5 results of testing the standard image socket model on standard images and 360° images

	Standard images	360 images
Fold 0	0.973	0.595
Fold 1	0.960	0.539
Fold 2	0.988	0.531
Average	0.974	0.555

Based on these results, it can be concluded that in future applications of Faster R-CNN to cross-format object detection, models trained on the format with the most distortion will likely perform the best when applied to other formats.

5   Conclusion

5.1   Summary and Limitations

This paper aimed to investigate the usefulness of deep learning neural networks in detecting sockets, radiators and switches in images. A dataset of 360° images and standard phone images was built and used to retrain an existing Faster R-CNN model. Then, an analysis of the deep learning model performance in and across these formats was carried out to explore how best to apply the Faster R-CNN for this use case. The results proved that neural networks can be an effective tool for detecting MEP assets and thereby add value to Scan-to-BIM frameworks.

As discussed in Sect. 4, the Faster R-CNN exhibited high precision and comparatively low recall when trained on both the 360° images and standard images. This indicates that most of the model's predictions were accurate, but there were many false negatives i.e. sockets and radiators that were overlooked. Strategies to overcome this challenge are discussed in the following sub-section.

The primary limitations faced in this research have been high computational demand, and a limited dataset. Training multiple models to cross-validate each experiment was a time intensive process. In further research that builds upon this project, the existing setup could be scaled to make use of a cluster of dedicated GPU or TPU servers. This would facilitate the execution of more detailed experiments exploring a wider range of model configurations.

The dataset for this project did not achieve the scale of industry-standard datasets which usually have millions of object instancess [25]. Also, the standard image sub-datasets did not have sufficient differentiation between the training and validation images which resulted in anomalously high validation results. Therefore, this project can only give a limited view of the accuracy that could be achieved in the practical application of Faster R-CNN to detecting MEP components. However, the observations that have been made on the model's precision-recall relationship and cross-format performance in this use case can be applied to future work backed by more resources.

5.2 Future Research

There are many promising methodologies outside the scope of this paper that could be investigated to support the integration of MEP object detection into other processes, such as scan-to-BIM.

The cross-validation experiments detailed in Sect. 4.5 evidenced that occlusion can significantly hinders model performance. One technique that could be investigated for addressing this issue is the use of overlapping tiles as opposed to the discrete ones used in this project. Using an overlapping tile system as shown in Fig. 4, would mean that even if an MEP asset was not fully visible in one tile it would be more likely to appear fully in another. The detections from the overlapping images could then be combined to yield improved overall performance. This is preferable to the discrete tile system where, if one tile contains a portion of an asset, then none of the other tiles can provide a full view of that asset.

Another area of research that should be explored is the combination of detection data from multiple images of an interior space linked through photogrammetric reconstruction. Gathering the classification and location data for all the MEP components in a room using detection models applied to overlapping images and merging this information with 3D photogrammetric data would be useful to improve overall detection performance, as well as to support subsequent processes, for example to automatically insert those assets into BIM models generated through Scan-to-BIM processes.

(a) Discrete tile system   (b) Overlapping tile system

Fig. 4. Comparison of tiling methods

Acknowledgements. This work was conducted as part of the BIMERR project has received funding from the European Commission's Horizon 2020 research and innovation programme under grant agreement No 820621. The views and opinions expressed in this article are those of the authors and do not necessarily reflect any official policy or position of the European Commission.

References

1. Adán, A., Quintana, B., Prieto, S.A., Bosché, F.: Scan-to-BIM for 'secondary' building components. Adv. Eng. Inf. **37**, 119–138 (2018)
2. Ahmed, M.F., Haas, C.T., Haas, R.: Automatic detection of cylindrical objects in built facilities. J. Comput. Civ. Eng. **28**(3), 04014009 (2014)
3. Babacan, K., Chen, L., Sohn, G.: Semantic segmentation of indoor point clouds using convolutional neural network. ISPRS Annals Photogramm. Remote Sens. Spat. Inf. Sci. **4**, 101–108 (2017)
4. Barazzetti, L., Previtali, M., Roncoroni, F.: Can we use low-cost 360 degree cameras to create accurate 3D models? Int. Arch. Photogramm. Remote Sens. Spat. Inf. Sci. **42**(2), 69–75 (2018)
5. Bassier, M., Vergauwen, M., Van Genechten, B.: Automated classification of heritage buildings for as-built BIM using machine learning techniques. In: ISPRS Annals of the Photogrammetry, Remote Sensing and Spatial Information Sciences, vol. 4, pp. 25–30. Copernicus GmbH (2017)
6. Bosché, F., Ahmed, M., Turkan, Y., Haas, C.T., Haas, R.: The value of integrating Scan-to-BIM and Scan-vs-BIM techniques for construction monitoring using laser scanning and BIM: the case of cylindrical MEP components. Autom. Constr. **49**, 201–213 (2015)
7. Chen, J., Kira, Z., Cho, Y.K.: Deep learning approach to point cloud scene understanding for automated scan to 3D reconstruction. J. Comput. Civ. Eng. **33**(4), 04019027 (2019)
8. COCO Dataset: Detection Evaluation (2019). http://cocodataset.org/#detection-eval
9. Czerniawski, T., Nahangi, M., Haas, C., Walbridge, S.: Pipe spool recognition in cluttered point clouds using a curvature-based shape descriptor. Autom. Constr. **71**(2), 346–358 (2016)
10. Díaz-Vilariño, L., González-Jorge, H., Martínez-Sánchez, J., Lorenzo, H.: Automatic LiDAR-based lighting inventory in buildings. Meas. J. Int. Meas. Conf. **73**, 544–550 (2015). https://doi.org/10.1016/j.measurement.2015.06.009

11. Dimitrov, A., Golparvar-Fard, M.: Segmentation of building point cloud models including detailed architectural/structural features and MEP systems. Autom. Constr. **51**, 32–45 (2015)
12. Eruhimov, V., Meeussen, W.: Outlet detection and pose estimation for robot continuous operation. In: 2011 IEEE/RSJ International Conference on Intelligent Robots and Systems, pp. 2941–2946. Institute of Electrical and Electronics Engineers (IEEE), December 2011
13. Fan, Q., Brown, L., Smith, J.: A closer look at Faster R-CNN for vehicle detection. In: IEEE Intelligent Vehicles Symposium, Proceedings, pp. 124–129. Institute of Electrical and Electronics Engineers Inc., August 2016
14. Gao, T., Packer, B., Koller, D.: A segmentation-aware object detection model with occlusion handling. In: CVPR 2011, pp. 1361–1368. IEEE (2011)
15. Hamledari, H., McCabe, B., Davari, S.: Automated computer vision-based detection of components of under-construction indoor partitions. Autom. Constr. **74**, 78–94 (2017)
16. Hosang, J., Benenson, R., Dollár, P., Schiele, B.: What makes for effective detection proposals?. Technical report, Max Planck Institute for Informatics (2015)
17. Huang, J., You, S.: Detecting objects in scene point cloud: a combinational approach. In: 2013 International Conference on 3D Vision, pp. 175–182 (2013)
18. Huang, J., et al.: Speed/accuracy trade-offs for modern convolutional object detectors. In: The IEEE Conference on Computer Vision and Pattern Recognition (CVPR), pp. 7310–7311. The IEEE Conference on Computer Vision and Pattern Recognition (CVPR), Long Beach (2017)
19. Kim, P., Chen, J., Cho, Y.K.: Robotic sensing and object recognition from thermal-mapped point clouds. Int. J. Intell. Robot. Appl. **1**(3), 243–254 (2017). https://doi.org/10.1007/s41315-017-0023-9
20. Krispel, U., Evers, H.L., Tamke, M., Viehauser, R., Fellner, D.W.: Automatic Texture and Orthophoto Generation From Registered Panoramic Views. The International Archives of the Photogrammetry, Remote Sensing and Spatial Information Sciences (2015)
21. Kropp, C., Koch, C., König, M.: Interior construction state recognition with 4D BIM registered image sequences. Autom. Constr. **86**, 11–32 (2018)
22. Lee, M., Kim, H., Paik, J.: Correction of barrel distortion in fisheye lens images using image-based estimation of distortion parameters. IEEE Access **7**, 45723–45733 (2019)
23. Li, J., Liang, X., Wei, Y., Xu, T., Feng, J., Yan, S.: Perceptual generative adversarial networks for small object detection. In: 2017 IEEE Conference on Computer Vision and Pattern Recognition (CVPR), pp. 1951–1959 (2017)
24. Liang, Z., Shao, J., Zhang, D., Gao, L.: Small object detection using deep feature pyramid networks. In: Hong, R., Cheng, W.-H., Yamasaki, T., Wang, M., Ngo, C.-W. (eds.) PCM 2018. LNCS, vol. 11166, pp. 554–564. Springer, Cham (2018). https://doi.org/10.1007/978-3-030-00764-5_51
25. Lin, T.-Y., et al.: Microsoft COCO: common objects in context. In: Fleet, D., Pajdla, T., Schiele, B., Tuytelaars, T. (eds.) ECCV 2014. LNCS, vol. 8693, pp. 740–755. Springer, Cham (2014). https://doi.org/10.1007/978-3-319-10602-1_48
26. Lopes, R., Yin, D., Poole, B., Gilmer, J., Cubuk, E.D.: Improving robustness without sacrificing accuracy with patch Gaussian augmentation. ArXiv (2019)
27. Maalek, R., Lichti, D.D., Ruwanpura, J.Y.: Automatic recognition of common structural elements from point clouds for automated progress monitoring and dimensional quality control in reinforced concrete construction. Remote Sens. **11**(9), 1102 (2019)

28. Maji, S., Malik, J.: Object detection using a max-margin Hough transform. In: 2009 IEEE Conference on Computer Vision and Pattern Recognition, pp. 1038–1045. Institute of Electrical and Electronics Engineers (IEEE), March 2009
29. Meeussen, W., et al.: Autonomous door opening and plugging in with a personal robot. In: Proceedings - IEEE International Conference on Robotics and Automation, pp. 729–736 (2010)
30. Michie, D.: "memo" functions and machine learning. Nature **218**(5136), 19–22 (1968)
31. Perez, L., Wang, J.: The effectiveness of data augmentation in image classification using deep learning. ArXiv, December 2017
32. Quintana, B., Prieto, S.A., Adán, A., Bosché, F.: Door detection in 3D coloured point clouds of indoor environments. Autom. Constr. **85**, 146–166 (2018)
33. Ren, S., He, K., Girshick, R., Sun, J.: Faster R-CNN: towards real-time object detection with region proposal networks. IEEE Trans. Pattern Anal. Mach. Intell. **39**, 1137–1149 (2015). https://doi.org/10.1109/TPAMI.2016.2577031
34. Ren, Y., Zhu, C., Xiao, S.: Small object detection in optical remote sensing images via modified faster R-CNN. Appl. Sci. **8**(5), 813 (2018)
35. Shorten, C., Khoshgoftaar, T.M.: A survey on image data augmentation for deep learning. J. Big Data **6**(1), 60 (2019)
36. Son, H., Kim, C., Kim, C.: Fully automated as-built 3d pipeline extraction method from laser-scanned data based on curvature computation. J. Comput. Civ. Eng. **29**(4), B4014003 (2015)
37. Song, L., Gong, D., Li, Z., Liu, C., Liu, W.: Occlusion robust face recognition based on mask learning with pairwise differential Siamese network. In: Proceedings of the IEEE International Conference on Computer Vision, pp. 773–782 (2019)
38. Turcsany, D., Mouton, A., Breckon, T.P.: Improving feature-based object recognition for X-ray baggage security screening using primed visual words. In: Proceedings of the IEEE International Conference on Industrial Technology, pp. 1140–1145 (2013)
39. Wu, R., Yan, S., Shan, Y., Dang, Q., Sun, G.: Deep image: scaling up image recognition. arXiv preprint arXiv:1501.02876 7(8) (2015)

Mixed Reality-Based Dataset Generation for Learning-Based Scan-to-BIM

Parth Bhadaniya[1] , Varun Kumar Reja[1,2](✉) , and Koshy Varghese[1]

[1] Indian Institute of Technology Madras, Chennai 600036, India
varunreja7@gmail.com
[2] University of Technology Sydney, 15 Broadway, Ultimo, NSW 2007, Australia

Abstract. Generating as-is 3D Models is constantly explored for various construction management applications. The industry has been dependent on either manual or semi-automated workflows for the Scan-to-BIM process, which is laborious as well as time taking. Recently machine learning has opened avenues to recognize geometrical elements from point clouds but has not been much used because of the insufficient labeled dataset. This study aims to set up a semi-automated workflow to create labeled data sets which can be used to train ML algorithms for element identification purpose. The study proposes an interactive user interface using a gaming engine within a mixed reality environment. A workflow for fusing as-is spatial information with the AR/VR based information is presented in Unity 3D. A user-friendly UI is then developed and integrated with the VR environment to help the user to choose the category of the component by visualization. This results in the generation of an accurate as-is 3D Model, which does not require much computation or time. The intention is to propose a smooth workflow to generate datasets for learning-based methodologies in a streamlined Scan-to-BIM Process. However, this process requires user domain knowledge and input. The dataset can be continuously increased and improved to get automated results later.

Keywords: Scan-to-BIM · Machine learning · Mixed reality · Data labeling · Object recognition · Gaming engine · Construction 4.0

1 Introduction

Building Information Modelling (BIM) and Digital Twin technologies have transformed the overall scenario of project management. Technological advancements towards data acquisition technologies have created new opportunities for automation in Scan-to-BIM. Laser Scanners & Depth sensor cameras enable us to collect real-time physical data into a digital format called point-cloud. Various commercial/open-sourced tool-sets provide the functionality to work with point clouds to generate the as-is model into the CAD/BIM format. The current workflow in this area consists of various time-consuming and tedious processes with large manual interventions.

Various computational algorithms are proposed and continuously being developed to automate several processes in this area. With the development of Artificial Intelligence

© Springer Nature Switzerland AG 2021
A. Del Bimbo et al. (Eds.): ICPR 2020 Workshops, LNCS 12667, pp. 389–403, 2021.
https://doi.org/10.1007/978-3-030-68787-8_29

(AI), the Integration of Machine learning (ML) & Deep learning (DL) concepts with these algorithms become one of the most promising approaches. Learning-based concepts enable computers to learn without explicit programming. These methods adapt the learning from training datasets consisting of multiple similar instances organized into a featured attribute structure. Currently, neither any established big data sets nor any methodology to generate one is available in the automated BIM generation area. Scan-Net [1] and Stanford Large Scale 3D Indoor Spaces (S3DIS) data [2] are the few available datasets in semantic segmentation & building elements recognition area. Researchers had to use their own generated or openly available small data sets to feed the learning algorithms.

This paper proposes a methodology to produce a training dataset for learning based in the area of – (1) Shape/Pattern recognition & object identification from the segmented point clouds & (2) Automated BIM property allocation, parameter value assignment & identity labeling to a 3D object using its visual & semantic properties. This method introduces the integrated use of Augmented Reality (AR) & Virtual Reality (VR) with interactive interfaces into a hybrid gaming environment to collect feedback data from training operators. Precisely, this paper provides a framework to generate big universal data to be required to feed into the Convolutional Neural Networks (CNNs).

Hence, this paper aims to define a step-wise process for semi-automated data extraction & manual data collection methods & propose a fully automated data integration process to produce the training datasets. The data generation methods are described as an experimented workflow, and data-management procedures are projected as a practicable roadmap.

This paper presents a user interface workflow using Unity3D environment integrated with Google VR enabled Android-based smartphone devices. Collected data is proposed to store in a local/cloud-based data server. The database structure is derived considering typical large varieties in types & parameters of BIM elements. A prototype of this idea is projected in this paper.

The Paper outline contains seven broader sections. The second section discusses automation methods & learning-based approaches in Scan-to-BIM. The third section discusses XRs in constructions using hybrid gaming engines. The fourth section reflects the whole methodology of the proposed idea, and further sections present results, discussions, and conclusions.

2   Automation in Scan-to-BIM

This section focuses on the need for automation & proposed approaches by previous studies in the Scan-to-BIM.

2.1   BIM and Its Applications

Engagement of AEC information with 3D CAD models has shaped the idea of Building Information Modeling. BIM Models are geometry-rich parametric 3D models consisting of a specific level of 2D/3D detailing along with various non-geometrical information. The development of BIM with additional dimensions have enriched the models with information related to time – 4D, Cost – 5D, Sustainability – 6D, Facility Management – 7D, and beyond.

BIM is utilized and accepted widely in the construction domain. Initial applications of BIM consist of design co-ordination, visualization, structural analysis, energy simulation, building performance, lifecycle analysis, activity scheduling, cost estimation, clash detection, facility management & more. However, the extended uses of BIM for project management & construction automation purposes include automated project monitoring, construction error detection, automated schedule modifications & productivity management, safety improvements, IoT as well as robotics integration, and more.

2.2   The Need for Automation

The extended applications of BIM require a simultaneous update about the physical site situation. A digital model is required to be in live sync with the actual updates on the project site – This model is called the As-is model. Figure 1 demonstrates the need for automated Scan-to-BIM into the workflow to find execution errors and project progress by comparing as-is and as-planned model. Thus, the As-is model generation becomes a recurring process, and automation becomes inevitable in this area.

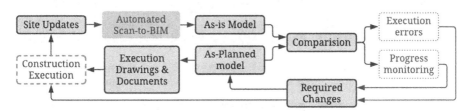

Fig. 1. Need for automated Scan-to-BIM

Automation in Scan-to-BIM requires multiple part process integration. Being a large area of research, studies in this area provide specific explorations in one or more segments at once. Figure 2 describes a conclusive idea of the workflows adopted by several previous studies.

In Fig. 2, which shows the workflow for automated Scan-to-BIM, four significant extents for automation requirements are – (1) Point cloud Registration, (2) Part Segmentation of point clouds, (3) Automated geometry generation, (4) Assignation of BIM Properties.

Some notable approaches in the area consist of an automated volumetric 3D reconstruction approach that was developed using the RANSAC algorithm with Markov clusterization concept with Point Cloud Library (PCL) & Computational Geometry Algorithms Library (CGAL) for plane detection and cloud point segmentation [3]. This approach also includes labeling 3D spaces confined by building elements extracted using the intersection methodology of infinite planes. An automated approach for point cloud segmentation & semantic 3D reconstruction of Structural Building Elements based on local Concavity and Convexity was proposed using the Super-voxel algorithm into edge-preserving segmentation & Region Growing Algorithm into Convexity graph segmentation [4]. A generative process approach to create complex 3D forms was proposed using NURBS based advanced 3D modeling methods [5]. Other similar studies also provide specific solutions in particular segments in the same area.

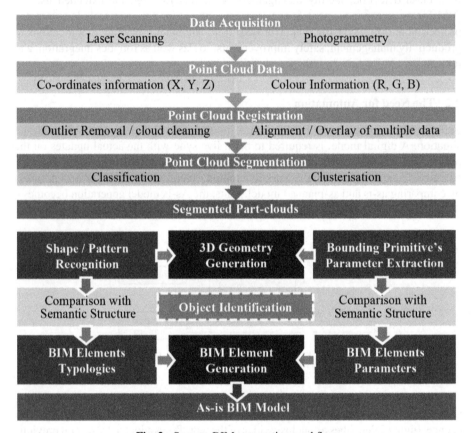

Fig. 2. Scan-to-BIM automation workflow

The development of CNNs & Deep Neural Networks (DNNs) has induced novel area of explorations of emerging ML & DL based algorithms. Learning-based approaches started replacing traditional coding paradigms based on specific logical heuristics.

PointNet and Point++ are the pioneering works using convolutions to derive object features from point semantics [6]. FloorNet is a unified platform based on three different DNNs, including PointNet, which provides floorplan reconstruction workflow using Google Tango [7].

Edges based segmentation was experimented with using Multi-Layer Perceptron (MLP) classifier [8]. SegGCN proposes 3D segmentation using a spherical kernel [9]. The learning-based object detection approach has also been used to verify object categories by comparing it to expected data from digital models [10]. A learning technique was also proposed for classifying ten building material classes [11]. The technique uses material reflectance, surface roughness, and Hue-Saturation (HSV) color values as the features.

A combination of PointNet and Dynamic Graph Convolutional Neural Network (DGCNN) was experimented with using synthetic point cloud data generated from a pre-available BIM model as training inputs to compare learning outputs with point cloud from real scan data [12].

Recently exemplar-based data feeding is explored, where point cloud is trained with deep feature extractor and then region growing, and clustering algorithms are applied for segmentation. Finally, it requires a manual selection of exemplar by the Lasso tool, which is given as an input to the peak finding algorithm for determining positive matches [13].

3   Augmented, Virtual and Mixed Reality

3.1   Introduction to MR as the Emergence of AR and VR

AR and VR technologies enhance visualizations and improve understanding of three-dimensional project data from multiple project perspectives.

Virtual reality replaces actual human surroundings with a virtual 3D environment using a Head Mount Display (HMD). The user perceives himself being a part of the digital environment generated using a set of computer applications. Whereas Augmented Reality contextualizes the digital model into the actual space by overlaying virtual 3D imageries onto real surroundings.

The mixed reality concept is the emergence of AR & VR concepts. It directs the augmentation inside the virtual 3D surroundings by blending real-scale digital models to the actual world objects using an HMD/spectacle with Camera functionality embedded with them. The MR assists in a better understanding of the spatial relationship between digital and real environments.

3.2   AR, VR and MR in AEC

The construction sector is using AR & VR technologies broadly for design visualization purposes since the '90s, but the extended purposes include visualizations for activity sequencing, site planning, safety precautions, and more [14, 15]. MR [16] technologies have also been explored for progress monitoring. VR integration was proposed for 3D reconstruction of archeological conservation for asset creation in gaming environments [17].

3.3   Integration of Gaming Engines in AEC

Gaming engines have been mainly implemented to visualize the design aesthetics and construction process simulations in the AEC sector, which are now also being used for construction monitoring & safety-related demonstrations. A Unity 3D based workflow is proposed for the construction progress monitoring by comparing depth images from the live site and as-designed BIM model [18].

4   MR-Based Data Collection

Figure 3 shows the five broader steps of the methodology proposed. Figure 6 Outlines an overview perspective of the whole methodology.

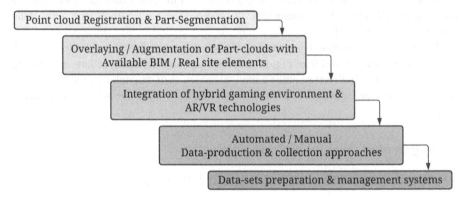

Fig. 3. Broader outline of the methodology

4.1   Point Cloud Registration and Part Segmentation

Laser scanner device & photogrammetry provides scan data as point clouds, which consist of coordinates & color - (X, Y, Z & R, G, B) information. Cloud Compare tool is required to convert the scanner output into.xyz format. A scan data only consists of the points which are visible from the particular device location at the time of the scan performed. To generate a whole data set for a building or space, a multiple scan process needs to be performed & these all data sets are required to be aligned and overlap with one another – This process is known as point cloud registration. Semi-automated point cloud registration can be performed using a cloud-based commercial application named VERCATOR. The registered data set still consists of occluded and cluttered regions – The outlier removal process eliminates unnecessary & meaningless points. A fully registered and pre-cleaned data set will be used as input in a segmentation algorithm. The registered data set points are required to classify into homogeneous regions and need to clusterize meaningfully to further extract building elements from the individual part segments. Figure 4 indicates a detailed overview of pre-processes and segmentation workflow.

Efficient RANSAC ideology using the PCL environment can classify points according to the object wise distribution. However, a certain level of manual intervention is required due to the lack of a perfect algorithm for the segmentation process.

4.2   Overlay and Augmentation

The part clouds are required to be overlaid with the design BIM model or real site elements. The method proposes separate data-feeding opportunities for two different cases based on the availability of design BIM or on-site/off-site implementation:

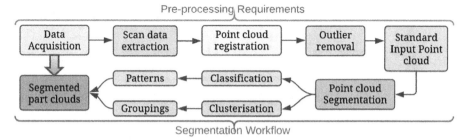

Fig. 4. Pre-processes of Scan-data & Point-cloud Segmentation workflow

Off-Site; if Design BIM is Available. Part segments of the point cloud will be overlaid on the design BIM model in the VR environment. In this case, both – part clouds and bim model will be in VR only. Thus, a headset without a back-side camera can also work.

On-Site; if Design BIM is not Available. Part segments of the point cloud in the VR environment will be augmented onto real site-building elements using AR technologies. Thus, it integrates mixed reality concepts & requires a headset with back-side camera functionality (Fig. 5).

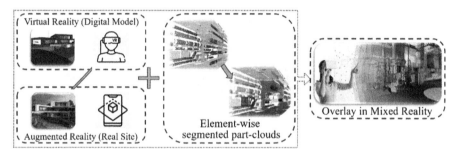

Fig. 5. Integration of mixed reality

4.3 Data Production and Collection

Two types of systems are accumulated into the method.

Automated Extraction: This type of data is extracted from the digitally available information, specifically sourced from (1) Part-cloud parameters and (2) Existing design BIM (if Available). This automated data extraction process is explained in detail in the dataset creation and management section.

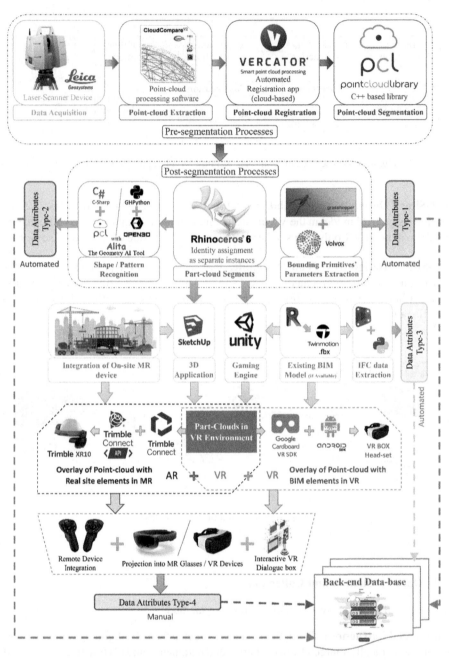

Fig. 6. Overall Process-flow from Scan-data to Database creation

Manual Feeding: This type of data will be input by the feeder person.

Data-Feeding Process

- A feeder person will wear a VR headset or MR headset according to the off-site/on-site input process.
- The feeder will see an overlaid view of segmented part-clouds onto a BIM model or an augmented view blending part-clouds onto real site elements into the VR environment.
- The person can pick individual elements using Bluetooth controller devices connected with the headset.
- Once an element is selected, an interactive dialogue is popped up inside the VR scene and asks the user to feed the required parameters (Fig. 7).

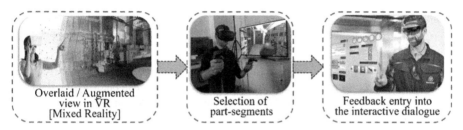

| Overlaid / Augmented view in VR [Mixed Reality] | Selection of part-segments | Feedback entry into the interactive dialogue |

Fig. 7. Data-feeding process-flow

4.4   Hybrid Gaming Engine and AR/VR Integration

Gaming engines provide a better virtual camera movement & orbital rotation of view scenes inside digital models. Hybrid gaming environments provide location-based camera movement, dynamic augmentation, and XR integrations. Many of such environments are developed and available as "free to use" or as proprietary software. Unity3D, Unreal Engine by EPIC games, Cry Engine by Crytek, Lumberyard by Amazon; are a few well-known 3D enabled cross-platform engines. Unity3D amongst them consists of the largest user community & uses open-sourced platforms. Unity3D was found to be a better engine with good accessibility, functional & audio-visual fidelities, and proper documentation of developer and deployment tool-kits [19]. Thus, the method proposes the use of Unity3D in the workflow.

For the 1st Case – Part-Clouds and Design BIM Integration: The design BIM model available as autodesk revit file (.rvt) is converted into autodesk game-ware format (.fbx). The process was performed using the twinmotion link plug-in inside the revit to export the .fbx file with material textures.

The part-clouds are exported as a whole group of separate instances using the volvox plug-in inside the Rhinoceros3D and Grasshopper3D environment. Multiple.xyz files are exported in a defined folder automatically using a script.

The BIM model (.fbx) & part-clouds (.xyz) can be imported as separate assets and overlayed by snapping a key point. A specific package called PCX is required to be used to enable point cloud import functionality into Unity3D. Google VR SDK for Android development will be set build-settings to project overlayed objects into mobile VR devices.

For the 2nd Case – Part-Clouds and Real Site Objects Integration: Part clouds can be imported into the sketchup application, and the model (.skp) needs to be uploaded to the trimble connect cloud. An API development with the Trimble connect is proposed to receive inputs from the trimble XR10 device. Trimble XR10 is a mixed reality visualization device integrated with Microsoft HoloLens.

A set of interactive dialogue boxes are developed using Google VR SDK and Unity3D. The same is also proposed into Trimble XR10 & connect API. Remote input devices are required to be configured & attached using wireless connectivity.

4.5 Data-Set Creation and Management Systems

Variety of Data-Types: As shown in Fig. 6, the four types of data attributes are required to be managed according to the generation and inflow of the data entering the datasets. Data generation from part-segments analysis and design BIM parameter extraction is semi-automated. Computational processes in this sequence are fully automated, yet the interoperability of multiple software requires a basic level of manual interventions. Data collection through feeder inputs is an almost manual process, yet back-end data processing and management are automated processes.

All cloud part-segments will be assigned a unique identity into the Rhinoceros3D environment. Grasshopper3D – a plug-in to Rhinoceros3D & Volvox – a plug-in to Grasshopper3D -are required to find bounding primitives by converting segment clouds into a basic mesh object. Geometrical parameters & types of the bounding primitives can be extracted using analyses panel tool-sets into the grasshopper environment. The output of the analysis provides dimensional limits of Boundary Representative (B-Rep) objects. Thus, the generated data will be 3D semantics of the elements part-cloud, which will be stored into the attributes type-1.

A grasshopper script is required to develop for shape/pattern recognition purposes using C-sharp and GHPython code blocks to integrate the functionalities of PCL & Open3D, respectively. A geometric artificial intelligence (AI) tool called Alita is needed to compare recognized 2D sections of elements with a pre-listed object shape library. The generated data will be 2D geometrical shapes from the list, stored in the attributes type-2.

A dynamo script using python code block functionality can be developed to extract required BIM information from the existing design BIM model. The generated data will be well-structured IFC elements & parameters, stored into the attributes type-3.

The data generated through the feeder inputs contains a basic level of BIM information, including the elements' types and visual parameters. In-case of on-site data feeding, dimensional parameters can be extracted using Trimble XR10 augmented measurement

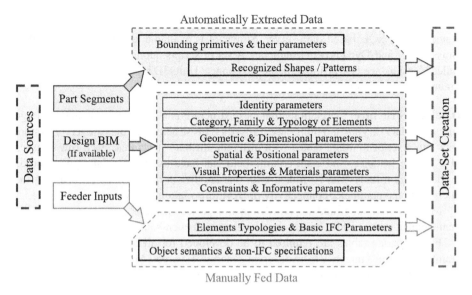

Fig. 8. Varieties of generated data

functionality. The generated data will consist of un-structured IFC information, which will be stored in the attributes type-4.

As shown in Fig. 8, Data-type-1 & 2 can be automatically analyzed from the part-clouds and Type-3 from the BIM model. In contrast, Type-4 is manually fed by an operator.

Data-Flow: Production to Storage: All four types of data are required to be stored in a database. A specific database management system (DBMS) is required to be implemented. a cloud-based data storage & management system - MySQL can be suggested for the purpose.

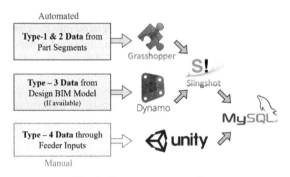

Fig. 9. Data management flow

A pre-developed tool-set called Slingshot is required to connect automatically generated data to SQL based data-server. Slingshot is available as a plug-in into both – Grasshopper and Dynamo environments. A set of scripts, along with a Unity-package called Hanslen, needs to be implemented to connect Unity3D inputs with the SQL server. Figure 9 reflects an overall data management flow.

Database Structure: A relational database structure is a key need to manage a large amount of data varying into multiple data-types. This structure enables the server to store data into a set of multiple tables with different attribute structures. Each row consists of a unique instance, and each column/field can have its specific data-type. records in the different tables can be linked with one another in this structure, enhancing the inter-relational parameter connectivity of BIM information.

MySQL was suggested as DBMS in the project as it is a relational database management system and is widely used by almost all open-sourced projects as a DBMS.

Four separate tables are required to be developed for all four input data types to maintain the data's integrity from different generative sources. Multiple scenarios having typical elements verity were considered to define attributes for all 4 Tables.

- Attributes in the 1st table will broadly involve 2D sectional shapes, edge-curves, best-fit surfaces, color parameters & recurring units in a pattern.
- Attributes in the 2nd table will broadly consist of types of bounding primitives, geometry controlling parameters, the spatial position of center-point, axial arrangement of the object & volume of the B-Rep.
- Attributes in the 3rd table will contain all IFC parameters including instance ID; Category, Family & Type; positional coordinates, dimensional parameters, Material properties, constraints & behaviors.
- Attributes in the 4th table will consist of a selective list of element types, visual parameters, directional parameters & knowledge-based parameters, including constraints and host elements.

A cumulative data-table is needed to be prepared by combining the data from all four tables. This table will be defined as 'Received Data,' and a clone of this table will be generated. A data-cleaning process needs to be integrated into the cloned version of the 'Received Data' table to remove incomplete/meaning-less data instances. All remaining instances will be saved into the final table version called 'Prepared Data' – which is the output dataset.

User Integration: API development can be proposed to directly use this data as an input from the cloud storage to the learning-based algorithms in local/cloud-based integrated development environments (IDE). A specific number of instances with required parameter attributes can be extracted from the output dataset.

All collected data will be stored in terms of numeric or string format in the database. Thus, an ontology is needed to be developed for the storage of geometrical & BIM information. Well-structured documentation will be the key-need to use the generated data efficiently.

5   Results and Discussion

The primary aim of this study is to presents a novel data collection and labeling method, which is based on organized learning. The resulting interactive environment created and the segmented point cloud overlaid onto the BIM model, as viewed in VR integrated with Unity3D, as shown in Fig. 10. This shows that the workflow presented in this paper worked well and adds value to the end-user for a better interactive experience.

Fig. 10. User interface demo

Additionally, this paper proposes to generate the database of the labeled elements using MySQL Database. The dataset structure is derived by considering the types of future needs for user-integration. The cloud-based API will enable upcoming research to utilize prepared datasets or to produce one for the study using a developed structure.

The developing dataset and data-collection method can be enhanced further by adjoining additional functionalities. The dataset structure can be parameterized by allowing the user to create tables & attributes as per the need of their algorithms. The formation of a user community and induce them to contribute their data by performing a few manual set generations requires a management method. Peer-to-peer connectivity through a central server could also be developed for the acknowledged sharing and transparent utilization of the created data. An automated element selection cycle can be proposed using grid-based approaches in computer vision. The feeding process can also be automated further by integrating voice recognition & word filtering techniques. These additions can surely help end-users to have a better experience as well as help in automating the entire process for feeding classified data to learning algorithms.

6 Conclusion

The novel data-collection method developed and demonstrated using interactive VR dialogues into the gaming engines is a key contribution of this study. Smooth workflow for automated data-generation and manual data-collection is derived by aligning the whole process-flow into a defined sequence of the tool-set applications & developed scripts.

The developed dataset resolves the matter raised due to the lack of labeled data for the training of ML or DL based algorithms. However, the dataset requires re-formatting and filtration of collected instances to utilize it further for benchmarking and testing purposes. This seems to be one of the limitations of this study. A matrix is needed to be defined for the performance benchmarking and validation of the generated dataset. This future scope of this research will be taking feedback from the end-users to improve data integrity by adjoining analytical algorithms.

References

1. Dai, A., Chang, A.X., Savva, M., Halber, M., Funkhouser, T., Nießner, M.: ScanNet: richly-annotated 3D reconstructions of indoor scenes. In: Proceedings - 30th IEEE Conference on Computing Vision and Pattern Recognition, CVPR 2017, January 2017, pp. 2432–2443 (2017)
2. Armeni, I., et al.: 3D semantic parsing of large-scale indoor spaces. In: Proceedings of IEEE Computer Society Conference on Computing Vision and Pattern Recognition, December 2016, pp. 1534–1543 (2016)
3. Ochmann, S., Vock, R., Klein, R.: Automatic reconstruction of fully volumetric 3D building models from oriented point clouds. ISPRS J. Photogramm. Remote Sens. 151, 251–262 (2019)
4. Son, H., Kim, C.: Semantic as-built 3D modeling of structural elements of buildings based on local concavity and convexity. Adv. Eng. Informatics 34, 114–124 (2017)
5. Banfi, F., Fai, S., Brumana, R.: BIM automation: advanced modeling generative process for complex structures. ISPRS Ann. Photogramm. Remote Sens. Spat. Inf. Sci. 4(2W2), 9–16 (2017)
6. Qi, C.R., Yi, L., Su, H., Guibas, L.J.: PointNet++: deep hierarchical feature learning on point sets in a metric space. In: Advances Neural Information Processing System, December 2017, pp. 5100–5109 (2017)
7. Liu, C., Wu, J., Furukawa, Y.: FloorNet: a unified framework for floorplan reconstruction from 3D Scans. In: Ferrari, V., Hebert, M., Sminchisescu, C., Weiss, Y. (eds.) ECCV 2018. LNCS, vol. 11210, pp. 203–219. Springer, Cham (2018). https://doi.org/10.1007/978-3-030-01231-1_13
8. Chen, J., Kira, Z., Cho, Y.K.: Deep learning approach to point cloud scene understanding for automated scan to 3D reconstruction. J. Comput. Civ. Eng. 33(4) (2019)
9. Lei, H., Akhtar, N., Mian, A.: SegGCN: Efficient 3D Point Cloud Segmentation With Fuzzy Spherical Kernel, pp. 11608–11617 (2020)
10. Braun, A., Tuttas, S., Borrmann, A., Stilla, U.: Improving progress monitoring by fusing point clouds, semantic data and computer vision. Autom. Constr. 116, 103210 (2020)
11. Yuan, L., Guo, J., Wang, Q.: Automatic classification of common building materials from 3D terrestrial laser scan data. Autom. Constr. 110, 103017 (2020)
12. Ma, J.W., Czerniawski, T., Leite, F.: Semantic segmentation of point clouds of building interiors with deep learning: augmenting training datasets with synthetic BIM-based point clouds. Autom. Constr. 113, 103144 (2020)

13. Zeng, S., Chen, J., Cho, Y.K.: User exemplar-based building element retrieval from raw point clouds using deep point-level features. Autom. Constr. **114**, 103159 (2020)
14. Zollmann, S., Hoppe, C., Kluckner, S., Poglitsch, C., Bischof, H., Reitmayr, G.: Augmented reality for construction site monitoring and documentation. Proc. IEEE **102**(2), 137–154 (2014)
15. Golparvar-Fard, M., Peña-Mora, F., Savarese, S.: Integrated sequential as-built and as-planned representation with D4AR tools in support of decision-making tasks in the AEC/FM industry. J. Constr. Eng. Manag. **137**(12), 1099–1116 (2011)
16. Kopsida, M., Brilakis, I.: Real-time volume-to-plane comparison for mixed reality-based progress monitoring. J. Comput. Civ. Eng. **34**(4), 1–5 (2020)
17. Ferdani, D., Fanini, B., Piccioli, M.C., Carboni, F., Vigliarolo, P.: 3D reconstruction and validation of historical background for immersive VR applications and games: the case study of the Forum of Augustus in Rome. J. Cult. Herit. **43**, 129–143 (2020)
18. Pour Rahimian, F., Seyedzadeh, S., Oliver, S., Rodriguez, S., Dawood, N.: On-demand monitoring of construction projects through a game-like hybrid application of BIM and machine learning. Autom. Constr. **110**, 103012 (2020)
19. Christopoulou, E., Xinogalos, S.: Overview and comparative analysis of game engines for desktop and mobile devices. Int. J. Serious Games **4**(4), 21–36 (2017)

An Augmented Reality-Based Remote Collaboration Platform for Worker Assistance

Georgios Chantziaras(✉), Andreas Triantafyllidis, Aristotelis Papaprodromou, Ioannis Chatzikonstantinou, Dimitrios Giakoumis, Athanasios Tsakiris, Konstantinos Votis, and Dimitrios Tzovaras

Information Technologies Institute, Centre for Research and Technology Hellas, Thessaloniki, Greece
{geochan,atriand,arispapapro,ihatz,dgiakoum,atsakir,kvotis, Dimitrios.Tzovaras}@iti.gr

Abstract. Remote working and collaboration is important towards helping workplaces to become flexible and productive. The significance of remote working has also been highlighted in the COVID-19 pandemic period in which mobility restrictions were enforced. This paper presents the development of an augmented reality platform, aiming to assist workers in remote collaboration and training. The platform consists of two communicating apps intended to be used by a remote supervisor (located e.g., at home) and an on-site worker, and uses intuitive digital annotations that enrich the physical environment of the workplace, thereby facilitating the execution of on-site tasks. The proposed platform was used and evaluated in user trials, demonstrating its usefulness and virtue by assessing its performance, worker satisfaction and task completion time.

Keywords: Augmented reality · HMD · Remote collaboration · Spatial mapping

1 Introduction

Remote working and collaboration, i.e., the ability to work and collaborate from anywhere-anytime, allows for increased autonomy and flexibility for workers and may enhance their productivity [1]. Limitations in mobility which have been enforced during the recent COVID-19 outbreak, served to underline the importance of remote collaboration digital tools, and have bolstered their application in the workplace [2].

Augmented Reality (AR) is an emerging technology that enhances our perception of the real word by overlaying virtual information on top of it. According to Azuma [3] an AR system must combine real and virtual content, be interactive in real time and be registered in 3D. AR applications are pervasive in our everyday lives and cover various domains such as manufacturing, repairs, maintenance and architecture. The rapid adoption of AR technology can facilitate the development of various AR-based collaboration tools.

Remote collaboration and training can be significantly enhanced through the use of immersive technologies such as AR. According to Regenbrecht et al. [4] collaborative

© Springer Nature Switzerland AG 2021
A. Del Bimbo et al. (Eds.): ICPR 2020 Workshops, LNCS 12667, pp. 404–416, 2021.
https://doi.org/10.1007/978-3-030-68787-8_30

AR is defined as an AR system where "multiple users share the same augmented environment" locally or remotely and which enables knowledge transfer between different users. AR-enabled collaboration is a relatively young field of research, although the first achievements date back several decades [5]. Nonetheless, the potential of AR for improvement in collaboration efficiency has been reported [6]. Previous research has shown that AR-enhanced remote collaboration can have a major impact in the construction industry [7]. AR-based training platforms allow instructions and annotations to be attached to real world objects without the need of an on-site expert. As the tasks of assembling, operating or maintaining in the construction industry field become more complex the need to reduce costs and training time is essential. The immersion provided by AR-based systems has shown to significantly reduce training time and costs required by employers [8].

The majority of AR platforms developed for workplaces, have been so far application-specific and limited in integrating both remote collaboration and training capabilities. In this direction, we present an AR-based platform aiming to improve collaboration efficiency, productivity, and training. The platform is based on the marker-less augmented reality technology and it can be used on any environment and workplace from any user equipped with a smartphone, a tablet or a Head-Mounted Display (HMD) as the only required equipment. The platform also uniquely takes advantage of augmented reality-enhanced training, through providing the ability to extract keyframe clips with step-by-step instructions, and store them for future reference. The rest of the paper is organized as follows: Sect. 2 presents related works found in the scientific literature. The proposed system design is described in Sect. 3. Section 4 shows the system development. Preliminary experimental results from user trials are reported in Sect. 5. Concluding remarks are discussed in Sect. 6.

2 Augmented Reality for Training and Collaboration

Piumsomboon et al. [9] report on CoVAR, a remote collaboration Mixed-Reality system that is based on the fusion of Augmented Reality and Augmented Virtuality concepts. A local user's AR HMD is used to map the environment, which is transmitted and presented to the remote user as a 3D environment. Users may interact through eye gaze, head gaze and hand gestures. The proposed system incorporates several collaboration facilitating features such as 3rd person view, awareness cues and collaborative gaze.

Alem et al. [10] report on HandsOnVideo, an AR-enabled remote collaboration system that is based on the use of natural hand. The remote collaborator uses an overhead fixed camera to capture hand motion and transmit it as video feed to the display of the local collaborator. The local collaborator essentially sees the video feed of the remote collaborator's hands superimposed over their viewing field and registered with the environment. Thus the remote collaborator is able to guide the local collaborator through hand gestures that are visible in real-time.

Billinghurst et al. [11] propose a face-to-face collaboration system where users manipulate Tangible User Interface (TUI) elements through an AR interface. The elements reported in the paper are materialized in the form of flat markers that are used for identification and tracking. A 3D representation of the corresponding element is super-imposed on the tracking marker. Authors present a series of applications of the proposed approach.

Barakonyi et al. [12] report on an AR-augmented videoconferencing system. The system aims to facilitate collaborative control of applications through augmentation of input using marker-based tracking. Application content is superimposed over the markers, and the users may manipulate the markers or place them on their workspace. Thus, the user is able to control an application using marker manipulation, in addition to regular mouse-based input.

Vassigh et al. [13] report on the development and testing of a collaborative learning environment with application to building sciences with the aim of integrating simulation technologies with AR for enhanced decision making in architecture, engineering and construction (AEC). Authors present a system application to the design of an architectural building component, where professionals collaborate through the manipulation of blocks in an AR-enhanced tablet interface.

Webel et al. [14] propose a platform for multimodal Augmented Reality-based train-ing of maintenance and assembly skills to improve training in the field of maintenance and assembly operations. They report that the skill level of technicians who trained with the developed training platform was higher than the skill level of those who used traditional training methods.

The innovation of our proposed system compared to the related work is its ability to extract keyframes and a summary of the performed steps that can benefit the remote supervisor by reducing her/his cognitive load during a demonstration. It can also operate at any environment to assist any task without the use of markers or a specific hardware setup and it can be deployed both on a mobile device and on an HMD.

3 System Design

The platform consists of two applications that communicate with each other, one running on the device of the on-site worker and another running on the remote device used by an expert guide. Figure 1 shows the schematic overview of the proposed system.

Both apps connect to a backend manager platform. The remote supervisor receives video feed from the AR HMD of the on-site worker, sharing their first-person view of the workspace. The remote expert guide is able to guide the on-site worker by inserting virtual cues and annotations on his workspace view. Annotations become available in the view of the on-site worker.

Using their credentials, users can log in to the local and remote applications. The on-site user can use a mobile device (smartphone) or a Mixed Reality (MR) HMD, such as the Microsoft Hololens. Through the device's sensors the surrounding environment is scanned. The same application can run on both devices allowing the preferred choice of use depending on the situation and the task at hand.

For example an HMD can be more useful for a task that requires both hands to be free while a tablet could be more suitable for the task of simply inspecting a machine and for simple, one-handed interactions. The on-site worker (Hololens) can select an available remote expert guide from a list and call for assistance using hand gestures or

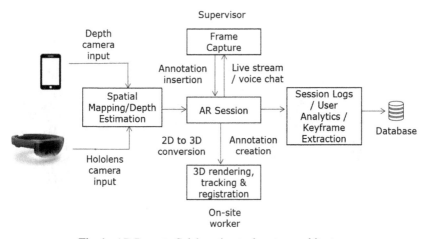

Fig. 1. AR Remote Colaboration tool system architecture

touch screen (mobile). The remote expert (mobile) chooses whether to accept or reject the call.

Once the call is setup the remote expert receives live video view from the on-site worker on his mobile device (Fig. 2). Additionally the two users can communicate through real time voice chat. At any time, the remote expert is able to freeze a specific frame from the live view. The expert can zoom and pan on the frame by using pinching and dragging touch gestures in order to focus on a specific part of the worker's view. Subsequently, the expert can insert annotations on the frozen frame, selecting from an array of available symbols (pointing arrows, 3D models), as well as text. Insertion is intuitively performed through touching a point in the viewing field. Through a 2D screen space to 3D world space coordinates transformation, the annotations are sent to the on-site user and rendered as 3D meshes superimposed on his view of the surroundings. Through an on-screen shortcut, the worker and remote expert may clear all annotations with a single interaction.

For each annotation we extract the relevant keyframes and save a clip of the annotation step. During the session the remote expert can access the list of the previous annotation clips and view the corresponding step in real time. Once the call is terminated we generate a session summary containing every annotation step and upload it to a server.

Those sessions can be accessed at any time from any user thus contributing to knowledge sharing and reducing training costs and time. Thus we combine real time collaboration and training with asynchronous AR-enabled step by step instructions.

Furthermore, a log of the whole session containing timestamps for each action performed is uploaded to the server. The saved logs offer valuable insights concerning the time spent on each screen, the total duration of the call and annotations that are used more frequently.

The platform also incorporates a push notification system that informs the remote supervisor about incoming calls. Through the same system and a web based manager back-end platform scheduled calls can be arranged between different users for a specific date and time.

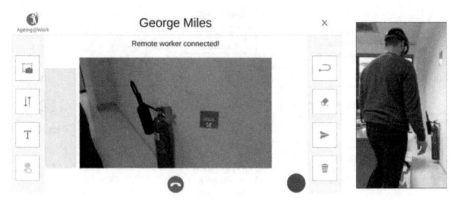

Fig. 2. Remote supervisor app view with live stream from the Hololens camera (left) On-site worker wearing the Hololens (right)

An overview of the remote expert app user interface functionality can be seen in Fig. 3. On the center of the screen the live camera preview of the on-site worker's view is located. On the left panel there are four buttons. The top button is used to capture a frame from the live view. The rest are used for inserting arrow, text and 3D hand annotations respectively. Next to that panel there is the clips preview panel with thumbnails for each recorded action clip. The right panel contains buttons to undo, erase and send annotations or delete the annotations from the on-site user's view. Next to that panel a red button for recording clips is located.

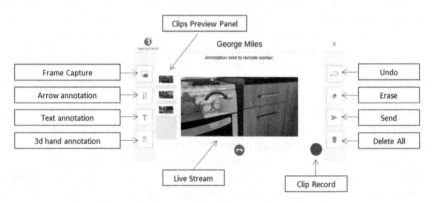

Fig. 3. User interface functionality overview of the guide app

4 Implementation

Both on-site and remote user applications were developed with the Unity3D game engine. Unity3D is ideal for the development of AR applications as it can render 3D meshes on top a device's camera view. The basic component of a Unity application is a scene. The main scene of the on-site app is initially an empty 3D space that consists of a virtual camera that is aligned with the device's physical camera and the camera's live view as a background. The 3D annotations are created as 3D transformations that contain 3D meshes and are continuously tracked as the device moves. The engine offers the ability to build for multiple target platforms so the same core application can be deployed on a mobile device and an HMD. The basic components implemented in the system are presented in Fig. 4 and described below.

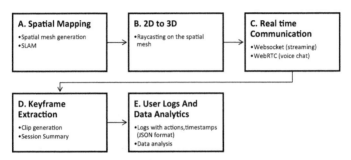

Fig. 4. Impelented modules flow

4.1 Spatial Mapping

The system is based on the markerless augmented reality technology. No previous knowledge of the environment or markers is needed and it can work on any indoor or outdoor space. For the mobile version we implemented the ARCore library that can detect horizontal and vertical planes as well as the ability to reconstruct a spatial mesh of the environment based on the depth camera of the mobile device [15]. Given a 3D point A in the real-world environment and a corresponding 2D point a in the depth image, the value assigned by the Depth API at a is equal to the length of the distance between the camera center C and point A, projected onto the principal axis Z as shown in Fig. 5. This can also be referred as the z-coordinate of A relative to the camera origin C. By assigning a depth value to every point in the camera frame we construct a depth map of the surrounding environment. Through a process called simultaneous localization and mapping, or SLAM, the device understands where it is located relative to the world around it [16]. The app detects and tracks visually distinct feature points in the camera image to compute its orientation and change in location. The visual information is fused with inertial measurements from the device's IMU to estimate the pose (position and orientation) of the camera relative to the world over time. We align the pose of the virtual camera of the 3D scene with the pose of the device's camera in order to render the virtual content from the correct perspective. The rendered virtual image can be overlaid on top of the image obtained from the device's camera, making it appear as if the virtual content is part of the real.

Similarly on the Hololens we used Microsoft's spatial mapping API to detect surfaces. The 6 sensors of the Hololens provide a more detailed spatial map that leads to

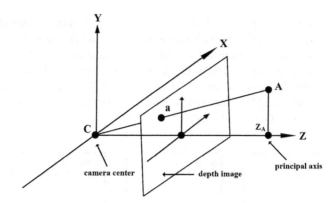

Fig. 5. Projection of a real word point A on the principal axis Z, source: [15]

more precise annotations [17]. The application continuously scans different volumes of the environment in order to receive spatial mapping data. Spatial mapping provides a set of spatial surfaces for the scanned volumes. Those volumes are attached to the HoloLens (they move, but do not rotate, with the HoloLens as it moves through the environment). Each spatial surface is a representation of a real-world surface as a triangle mesh attached to a world-locked spatial coordinate system. During the AR session new data are continuously gathered from the environment through the sensors and the spatial surface is updated. For each new spatial surface acquired a spatial collider component is calculated that will be later used for the mapping of the 2D coordinates in the 3D space.

4.2 Mapping 2D Coordinates in the 3D World

The interaction of the remote expert while inserting annotations is performed on the 2D surface of the tablet. In order to create 3D annotations in the on-site user's view we convert the 2D coordinates of the inserted annotations in the captured frame to 3D world space coordinates. To do so we implement the raycasting method [18]. Raycasting is the process of shooting an invisible ray from a point, in a specified direction to detect whether any colliders lay in the path of the ray. The spatial mesh that is extracted in the spatial mapping process described in the previous section contains a collider component. Each time a frame is captured a virtual camera is stored at the current position and orientation. The virtual camera's projection and world matrix are identical to the device's camera matrices. The ray originates from the virtual camera's position and goes through positions (x,y) pixel coordinates on the screen. The point in 3D world space where the ray intersects with the spatial collider is the origin of the 3d annotation (Fig. 6). Thus the 3D annotations appear in the equivalent positions of their 2D counterparts.

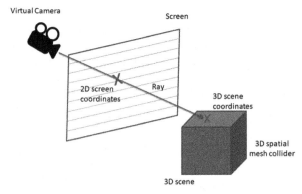

Fig. 6. Ray originating from a virtual camera and intersecting with a 3D collider

4.3   Real Time Communication

In order to achieve a low latency and fast communication between the two users we implemented the Websocket protocol [19]. WebSocket is a computer communications protocol, providing full-duplex communication between a client and a remote server over a single TCP connection. Through WebSocket, servers can pass data to a client without prior client request, allowing for dynamic content updates. We used the websocket connection to stream frames from the on-site application camera to the supervisor. The video stream resolution and aspect ratio depends on the on-site device's camera resolution so the supervisor application dynamically updates the stream preview frame for each call. Apart from the real time video stream the platform offers real time voice chat to facilitate the communication between the users. The voice chat is based on the WebRTC framework [20]. The WebRTC framework combines two different technologies: media capture devices and peer-to-peer connectivity. Media capture devices includes video cameras and microphones. For cameras and microphones, we used the mediaDevices module to capture MediaStreams. The RTCPeerConnection interface handles the peer-to-peer connectivity. This is the central controller for the connection between two clients in the WebRTC communication.

4.4   Keyframe Extraction

A novel feature of the proposed system is the ability to extract keyframe clips of the generated annotations. A 10 s clip of the on-site user's view can be saved for each created annotation. During the call those clips are available for the supervisor to inspect on a separate panel. Once the call is terminated the clips can be uploaded to a knowledge base and be available for future users to watch for training purposes or to assist them during the performance of a task.

4.5   User Logs and Data Analytics

During each user session the system records a log of the performed actions. Each action is defined by its type and a timestamp. The available actions range from user login and call for assistance to the type of annotation created. Based on those logs valuable information can be extracted such as which users had the most call time or what type of annotations are mostly used. Through acquiring and analyzing such quantitative data collections, we are able to examine the usability and efficiency of the platform, and improve its features.

5   Experimental Results

In order to evaluate our system we performed user trials within a laboratory environment. The basic purpose was to test the usability of the system and the collaborative experience of the users, both remote and on-site.

5.1   Experiment Setup

We chose the use of a 3D printer by an untrained worker as experimental task, because of the value and potential of 3D printers in the modern construction industry. This scenario can be adapted to similar cases in the construction and manufacturing domain as it involves the operation of a machine by a worker, input through buttons and panels and the use of different devices. The printer used for this task is the Ultimaker 3 3D printer, a desktop 3D printer with a dual extruder (Fig. 7). This printer uses Polylactic Acid (PLA), a thermoplastic polyester, to extrude the plastic on a build platform where it solidifies. The on-site users were equipped with an Android mobile device equipped with a depth sensing camera with a resolution of 2260×1080 pixels. The remote supervisors where equipped with an Android tablet and were stationed in a separate room away from the laboratory in which the printer resided. The communication was handled through a high speed Wi-Fi connection.

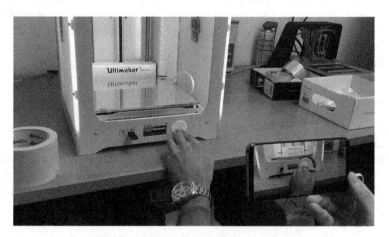

Fig. 7. The Ultimaker 3 3D printer set up

5.2 Participants and Procedure

A total of 8 participants took part in the study, 7 male and 1 female. The mean age of the participants was 25 ($\pm$1.36) years. The participants were asked to perform the task of printing a cube from a usb stick. None of them had used the 3D printer before. The remote guide assisted the on-site user by annotating the usb stick on the table, the usb port on the printer as well as the actions required on the printer input menu (Fig. 8). After the test the users were asked to fill out a questionnaire with questions about the ease of communication during the collaboration session, the usability of the interfaces and the effectiveness of the platform. The questionnaire was based on the System Usability Scale (SUS) [21]. The System Usability Scale (SUS) is an effective tool for assessing the usability of a product such as an application. It consists of a 10-item questionnaire with five response options for respondents; from Strongly agree to Strongly disagree.

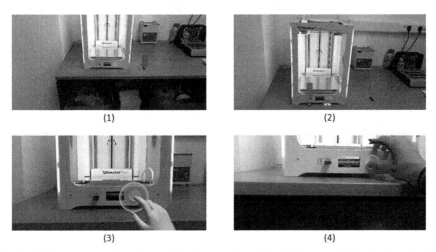

Fig. 8. The basic annotations inserted by the remote guide. (1) Arrow pointing to the usb stick (2) Arrow pointing to the usb port (3) 3D hand animation indicating the button to push (4) rotating arrow indicating the clockwise rotation of the button to select a file

5.3 Results

Every participant was able to complete the task successfully without previous knowledge of using the 3D printer. The average SUS score was 94. According to Bangor et al. [21] any system above 68 can be considered usable. The higher the score the more usable the system is. We can deduct from the score that the AR platform is highly intuitive for the users. The average of positively-worded questions Q1, Q3, Q5, Q7 and Q9 (e.g. questions related to easiness to use and learn) is relatively high while the average of negatively-worded questions Q2, Q4, Q6, Q8 and Q10 (e.g. questions related to complexity and required technical support) is low (Fig. 9). Apart from the questionnaire, quantitative data was collected through the platform's log files. Based on those we were able to measure the mean time required for a user to perform the task compared to the time needed using a traditional manual. The mean execution time was 78 (±15) s. The fastest completion time was 60 s. A separate group of 4 inexperienced users acting as a control group, was asked to perform the same task using only written instructions. Their mean task completion time was 87 (±26) s. We notice a 10% improvement in completion times using our proposed system (Fig. 10).

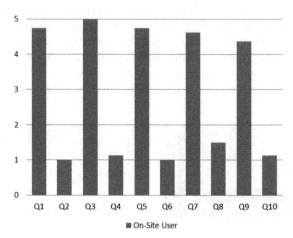

Fig. 9. Average SUS scale rating results from the on-site users (1: strongly disagree, 5: strongly agree) – Q1: I would use this system frequently, Q2: The system is unnecessarily complex, Q3: The system is easy to use, Q4: The support of a technical person is needed, Q5: The functions in this system are well, Q6: Too much inconsistency, Q7: The system is easy to learn, Q8: The system is very cumbersome to use, Q9: I felt very confident using the system, Q10: I needed to learn a lot of things before using

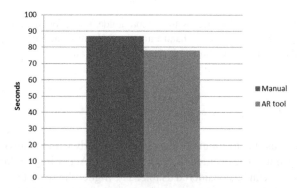

Fig. 10. Mean task completion time using a traditional manual and the AR tool

Regarding the performance of the system, we measured the frame rate of the applications. The on-site app runs at 60 fps with no drops even when multiple annotations are rendered. The average frame rate of the video stream received by the supervisor app is 15 fps over a high speed Wi-Fi connection.

6 Conclusion

In this paper we proposed a novel AR remote collaboration platform for workplaces. The platform primarily aims to facilitate the execution of on-site tasks by inexperienced workers, through the guidance by a remote user, using intuitive digital annotations which enrich the physical environment of the on-site worker. In this context, the platform could be particularly significant during the COVID-19 pandemic period, in which several people, including vulnerable groups such as older people or individuals with a chronic disease, were enforced to work from their home.

In addition to real-time collaboration through AR, the platform offers a novel approach to generating intuitive process documentation, through the automatic extraction of keyframe video clips, that enable highlighting the critical parts of the process at hand. To this end, the platform may contribute to the lifelong training paradigm [22].

Preliminary results from our experimental user study, showed that the platform promotes efficiency in task completion, and it is highly usable. As a next step, we aim to conduct longitudinal studies in real-life working environments, to further assess the effectiveness of the proposed system.

Acknowledgment. This work was funded by the European Union's Horizon 2020 Research and Innovation Programme through Ageing at Work project (under grant agreement no 826299).

References

1. Attaran, M., Attaran, S., Kirkland, D.: The need for digital workplace: increasing workforce productivity in the information age. Int. J. Enterp. Inf. Syst. (IJEIS) **15**(1), 1–23 (2019)
2. Waizenegger, L., McKenna, B., Cai, W., Bendz, T.: An affordance perspective of team collaboration and enforced working from home during COVID-19. Eur. J. Inf. Syst. **29**, 429–442 (2020)
3. Azuma, R.: A survey of augmented reality, tele-operators and virtual environments. Pres.: Teleoper. Virtual Environ. **6**(4), 355–385 (1997)
4. Regenbrecht, H.T., Wagner, M., Baratoff, G.: Magicmeeting: a collaborative tangible augmented reality system. Virtual Real. **6**(3), 151–166 (2002). https://doi.org/10.1007/s10055 0200016
5. Billinghurst, M., Kato, H.: Collaborative augmented reality. Commun. ACM **45**(7), 64–70 (2002)
6. Jalo, H., Pirkkalainen, H., Torro, O., Kärkkäinen, H., Puhto, J., Kankaanpää, T.: How can collaborative augmented reality support operative work in the facility management industry? In: KMIS, pp. 39–49 (2018)
7. El Ammari, K., Hammad, A.: Remote interactive collaboration in facilities management using BIM-based mixed reality. J. Autom. Constr. **107**, 102940 (2019)

8. Martínez, H., Skournetou, D., Hyppölä, J., Laukkanen, S., Heikkilä, A.: Drivers and bottle-necks in the adoption of augmented reality applications. J. Multimed. Theory Appl. 1, 27–44 (2014)
9. Piumsomboon, T., Day, A., Ens, B., Lee, Y., Lee, G., Billinghurst, M.: Exploring enhancements for remote mixed reality collaboration. In: SIGGRAPH Asia 2017 Mobile Graphics Interactive Applications, 27 Nov 2017, pp. 1–5 (2017)
10. Alem, L., Tecchia, F., Huang, W.: HandsOnVideo: towards a gesture based mobile AR system for remote collaboration. In: Alem, L., Huang, W. (eds.) Recent trends of mobile collaborative augmented reality systems, pp. 135–148. Springer, New York (2011). https://doi.org/10.1007/978-1-4419-9845-3_11
11. Billinghurst, M., Kato, H., Poupyrev, I.: Collaboration with tangible augmented reality interfaces. In: HCI international, vol. 1, pp. 5–10 (2001)
12. Barakonyi, I., Fahmy, T., Schmalstieg, D.: Remote collaboration using augmented reality videoconferencing. In: Graphics Interface, vol. 2004, pp. 89–96 (2004)
13. Vassigh, S., Newman, W.E., Behzadan, A., Zhu, Y., Chen, S.C., Graham, S.: Collaborative learning in building sciences enabled by augmented reality. Am. J. Civ. Eng. Archit. 2(2), 83–88 (2014)
14. Webel, S., Bockholt, U., Engelke, T., Peveri, M., Olbrich, M., Preusche, C.: Augmented reality training for assembly and maintenance skills. In: BIO Web of Conferences, vol. 1 (2011). https://doi.org/10.1051/bioconf/20110100097
15. https://developers.google.com/ar/develop/java/depth/overview
16. Cadena, C., et al.: Past, present, and future of simultaneous localization and mapping: toward the robust-perception age. IEEE Trans. Rob. 32(6), 1309–1332 (2016). https://doi.org/10.1109/TRO.2016.2624754
17. Evans, G., Miller, J., Pena, M.I., MacAllister, A., Winer, E.: Evaluating the Microsoft HoloLens through an augmented reality assembly application. Defense + Security (2017)
18. Roth, S.D.: Ray casting for modeling solids. Comput. Graph. Image Process. 18, 109–144 (1982)
19. Wang, V., Salim, F., Moskovits, P.: The Definitive Guide to HTML5 Websocket. Apress, New York (2013)
20. https://www.webrtc.org
21. Bangor, A., Kortum, P., Miller, J.: Determining what individual SUS scores mean: adding an adjective rating scale. Usab. Stud. 4(3), 114–123 (2009). https://doi.org/10.5555/2835587.2835589
22. Lee, M., Morris, P.: Lifelong learning, income inequality and social mobility in Singapore. Int. J. Lifelong Educ. 35(3), 286–312 (2016)

Demand Flexibility Estimation Based on Habitual Behaviour and Motif Detection

George Pavlidis[✉], Apostolos C. Tsolakis, Dimosthenis Ioannidis, and Dimitrios Tzovaras

Information Technologies Institute, Centre for Research and Technology - Hellas, Thessaloniki, Greece
{george.pavlidis,tsolakis,djoannid,Dimitrios.Tzovaras}@iti.gr
https://www.iti.gr

Abstract. Nowadays the demand for energy is becoming higher and higher, and as the share of power supply from renewable sources of energy (RES) begins to rise, exacerbating the problem of load balancing, the need for smart grid management is becoming more urgent. One of such is the demand response technique (DR), which allows operators to make a better distribution of power energy by reducing or shifting electricity usage, thereby improving the overall grid performance and simultaneously rewarding consumers, who play one of the most significant roles at DR. In order for the DR to operate properly, it is essential to know the demand flexibility of each consumer. This paper provides a new approach to determining residential demand flexibility by identifying daily habitual behaviour of each separate house, and observing flexibility motifs in aggregate residential electricity consumption. The proposed method uses both supervised and unsupervised machine learning methods and by combining them acquires the ability to adapt to any new environment. Several tests of this method have been carried out on various datasets, as well as its experimental application in real home installations. Tests were performed both on historical data and in conditions close to real time, with the ability to partially predict Flexibility.

Keywords: Residential demand flexibility · Demand response · Motifs detection · Pattern recognition · RES · Neural network · LSTM

1 Introduction

In the period from 2005 to 2018, the share of renewable energy in Europe has doubled from 9.02% in 2005 to 18.09% in 2018 and the goal of the European Union (EU) is to achieve 20% in its gross final consumption of energy by 2020 [2] and at least 45% and 75% by 2030 2050 respectively [5, 26]. These percentages are even higher in some of the Member State countries. This change, of course, has many positive effects in various areas such as the environment [24] or economics [8],

© Springer Nature Switzerland AG 2021
A. Del Bimbo et al. (Eds.): ICPR 2020 Workshops, LNCS 12667, pp. 417–431, 2021.
https://doi.org/10.1007/978-3-030-68787-8_31

but at the same time the integration of RES in the electric power grid drastically increases, the problem of balancing power, which is necessary for leveling fluctuations in demand/supply mismatches. The establishment of technologies of Smart Grid enabled the development of programs such as Demand Response [28] which takes advantage of consumers' flexibility during high demand periods to reduce or shift this demand. The residential and commercial electricity consumption account for a significant part of total demand, for example, according to a study in this field [30] in the U.S these two sectors account for 73% of the national consumption. By properly managing the demand flexibility, it is possible to reduce the supply/demand mismatch [21] in the grid due to volatility and unpredictability renewable energy sources (RES).

In order to fully understand the energy flexibility's untapped potential, it is necessary to provide a clear definition of demand flexibility. There are many definitions in bibliography such as *flexibility is the capacity to adapt across time, circumstances, intention and focus* [12]. However, the best way to describe demand flexibility in the case of residential demand is as an indicator of how much load can be shifted or reduced within user-specified limits [9]. In other words, how much energy can be saved at a specific time-frame without sacrificing the consumers' comfort. There are many attempts to study and predict demand flexibility in previous and current research, with all methods and technologies proposed can be divided into two major categories depending on how they obtain the needed information about the consumption. The methods for determining the flexibility of the first category require measurements to be taken directly from the devices, while the methods of the second category, the non-intrusive, collect only the total house's consumption [17]. The advantage of the first category approach is the fact that there is accurate knowledge about the consumption of each appliance separately, which allows estimating the flexibility through scheduling of home appliances. There are plenty of studies whose aim is to categorize appliances into flexible and non-flexible and measure the flexibility of each of them [9,13,17]. Using this information it is possible to estimate the demand flexibility with sufficient accuracy. Nevertheless, this approach is not desirable in many cases, since many smart metering devices need to be installed and, at the same, time, this infringes on consumer privacy by monitoring each device 24/7 [17].

Because the installation costs and the privacy of customers are of great importance, disaggregation methods can be used, installing high-frequency meters to read the household's total consumption and then detect the individual signatures and consumption patterns of each device [17]. This approach is-called non-intrusive load monitoring (NILM) [10]. There are several successful attempts of applying this method [22,25]. In order to properly apply NILM techniques, the minimum required sample rate should be about 1.2–2 kHz [10], which is a fairly high rate that in many cases is difficult to achieve. Of course, there are other attempts that exploit lower frequencies, however even these there are examples that convert low frequencies to high ones using Deep Learning [15], but still, the sample rate needed for that remains high. In most cases, sampling is usually done once per minute or even less frequently due to the large amount of data that would have to be transferred and stored. Moreover, training the disaggregation algorithm is a rather difficult task, since in many cases the same devices from different manufacturers may have different signatures, so a large amount of data from different devices is required to achieve decent results. Finally, the Flexibility of each separate house is usually very low and it should be combined with the flexibility of multiple houses in order to perform Demand Response, this is why many researchers try to calculate it directly from the aggregate load of residential buildings [6, 27].

The aim of this paper is to estimate residential demand flexibility without knowledge of the specific household appliances available in the home, by monitoring only total consumption, trying to identify patterns or events that can be characterized as flexible, thus avoiding problems which occurs when observing the flexibility of each appliance. As previous studies have shown [3], it is possible to conclude the habits of occupants by observing only their current consumption. Similar efforts have been made in the past in the industrial sector [18], where the consumption patterns are much clearer and the daily load is almost the same, as the same machines run at the same pace every day. In addition, the variety of different devices is much smaller compared to the residential and commercial sector. The document is structured as follows: Sect. 2 presents the data used for implementing, evaluating and validating the presented work. Section 3 introduces the novel methodology proposed, followed by the evaluation results in Sect. 4. Finally, Sect. 5 concludes the manuscript.

2   Datasets

In order to have more reliable results, many different datasets have been used for this paper. In all of them, the sampling is done once a minute and there are historical data for at least one year. Also, all datasets provide electrical consumption at the aggregate and appliance level. This fact is very useful in order to evaluate the results, since for flexibility evaluation the sum of consumption of appliances which are described as flexible in the bibliography [9, 13, 17] was used as ground truth. The first dataset contains data of house electric power consumption for almost 4 years [1], the second is the Almanac of Minutely Power dataset (AMPds2) [19] which provides 2-year consumption data based on home monitoring from over 20 electricity meters, as well as weather conditions for the same period of time. For both datasets, a washing machine, clothes dryer, dishwasher, and lighting were used as flexible appliances for the evaluation. Finally, experiments were performed with real consumption scenarios in a smart home [4].

3   Method

In this section, the proposed method is introduced. The main idea of this approach is to identify flexibility based on consumption routines of residents and possible patterns of flexible events. The calculation of flexibility is performed in

3 main steps (see also Fig. 1 and Algorithm 1). The first (Sect. 3.1) is to categorize the days of the year into clusters in order to establish some baselines of consumption, since it is reasonable to expect different consumption on a working day and on the weekend, as well as in summer and winter. The second step (Sect. 3.2) is to analyze all days of the past year to find similar motifs and patterns of flexible consumption. And after that the third step (See also Algorithm 3) is to observe if in the course of a day the consumption deviates from the normal levels of the category in which this day belongs, an analysis is made to find a known pattern of flexibility and in case it is identified as such then this consumption is considered flexible.

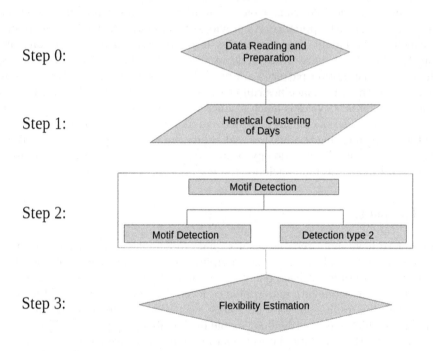

Fig. 1. Flow diagram explaining the process of flexibility estimation

Algorithm 1: Proposed method's main steps

1. Read Historical data   (Step 0)
2. Perform Fast Fourier transformation   (Step 1)
3. Create Clusters   (Step 1)
4. Generate motifs based on historical data   (Step 2)
5. Create time-series of flexible consumption using LSTM   (Step 2)
6. Estimate Flexibility   (Step 3)

In this way, flexibility can be achieved without compromising customer comfort and habits. For example, if a consumer has a habit of using a specific consumption motif (e.g. a washer) in the afternoon, and one day this motif is identified during midday, this will be considered as a flexible event that can be shifted to afternoon.

3.1   Routine Detection

Clustering is one of the most important steps (Step 1) of the introduced methodology since all subsequent processes are based on it. The first thing that needs to be done in order to optimize the results of clustering is to simplify the original time series of each day's power consumption. By using Fast Fourier Transformation the simplification shown in Fig. 2 is achieved. After this transformation, it is easier to group time series into more generalized clusters. The next step is to perform clustering on this simplified time series using Heretical Clustering with Ward variance minimization algorithm [29] for distance calculation. To evaluate the results and determine the appropriate number of clusters, the elbow method was used, which showed a clear presence of 3 to 8 clusters depending on the dataset (Fig. 3). The final step after the establishment of the clusters is to determine which deviation level is considered normal. In this paper, after a process of trial and error the upper and lower bounds was defined as the mean of cluster plus minus standard deviation (Eq. 1).

$$Bounds = \frac{1}{N} \cdot \sum_{i=0}^{N} x_i \pm \sqrt{\frac{1}{N} \cdot \sum_{i=0}^{N} (x_i - \frac{1}{N} \cdot \sum_{i=0}^{N} x_i)^2} \qquad (1)$$

where N is the total number of days in a particular cluster and x_i is the time series of days of this category. Thus, anything higher or lower than these boundaries is considered abnormal consumption and should be analyzed for flexibility.

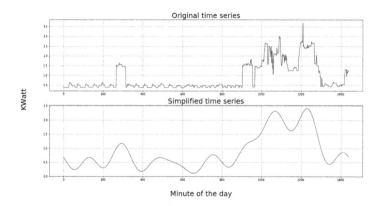

Fig. 2. Example of fast fourier Transformation

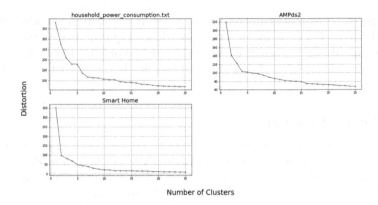

Fig. 3. Elbow method for each dataset

3.2 Flexibility Detection

The aim of this sub-step (Step 2) is to detect motifs and extract hidden patterns in consumption. Once the system has the ability to recognize specific patterns, these patterns can then be correlated with some known events and decide if it is flexible or not. However, the biggest problem is that most known methods for pattern recognition are supervised methods, but because in many cases there is no available information about appliances and their flexibility, these algorithms are difficult to be applied. For this reason, two pattern detection methods were used, one supervised and the other unsupervised. Each of them has advantages and disadvantages, for example, supervised has better accuracy on known data, but low generalization in unknown data, when unsupervised, has lower accuracy, but works better with unknown data. We call the supervised one *flexibility prediction* and the unsupervised one we call *motif detection*.

Motif Detection. The method of sub-step (Step 2.1) takes as input the entire consumption history divided into one-day time series in minutes i.e. 1440 points per time series. The first step is to separate each time series into subsequences. Most existing motif detection algorithms have predefined and fixed length of subsequences [14, 16, 23] and use algorithms such as *sliding window* for the segmentation. A fixed window length, however, greatly limits the correct pattern detection process, as different patterns may have different lengths, and even the same pattern may appear with different lengths or intensities. For this reason, it is applied a segmentation algorithm capable of detecting subsequences of different length. Moving average is used to create a baseline and accepted levels of noise for each time series. Whenever the consumption is higher than that, for some time, this part is stored as a subsequence (Fig. 4). The next steps to be taken are, first, to normalize these subsequences so that they can be represented at the same scale regardless of their length and intensity, and second, to perform dimension reduction to store more generalized patterns and to speed up the process of detection. For these steps the Piecewise Aggregate Approximation (PAA)

[16] representation and the Symbolic Aggregate approXimation (SAX) [14] were used. The PAA helps to represent subsequences in a scaled and reduced way, and SAX mapping these representations to alphabetical symbols, so at the end, each subsequent has its signature with which it can be compared to others.

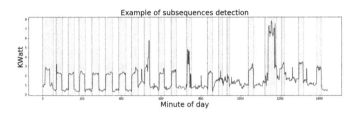

Fig. 4. Example of subsequences detection

The next sub-step (Step 2.2) is to create buckets of random projected signatures. First of all, random projection is performed on SAX representations in order to group signatures with small differentiations, which might occur due to accidental ups and downs. A bucket of each random projection contains all the signatures that produce this projection, which in essence represents a potential pattern. The buckets that contain small amounts of signatures are discarded as they are not repeatable enough to be considered as motifs. For the remaining buckets, a P-profile matrix is calculated. P-profile is a matrix of the probability for each symbol to appear in each position of the signature. Based on this matrix it is possible to calculate the probability that any signature belongs to this set. Table 1 shows an example of p-profile for projection $ab\_bc\_d\_$.

Table 1. P-profile matrix for $ab\_bc\_d\_$.

		Position							
		1st	2nd	3rd	4th	5th	6th	7th	8th
Symbol	a	1.0	0.001	0.25	0.001	0.001	0.60	0.001	0.01
	b	0.001	1.0	0.25	1.0	0.001	0.001	0.001	0.24
	c	0.001	0.001	0.25	0.001	1.0	0.40	0.001	0.30
	d	0.001	0.001	0.25	0.001	0.001	0.001	1.0	0.70

Now, if, for example, there are two segments that have the signatures $ababccdb$ and $abbbcadd$ respectively, and it is needed to examine if either of them belongs in the bucket $ab\_bc\_d\_$, so the probability of each is calculated.

$$Prob(ababccdb\|P) = 1.0 \cdot 1.0 \cdot 0.25 \cdot 1.0 \cdot 1.0 \cdot 0.4 \cdot 1.0 \cdot 0.24 = 0.024 \quad (2)$$

$$Prob(abbbcadd\|P) = 1.0 \cdot 1.0 \cdot 0.25 \cdot 1.0 \cdot 1.0 \cdot 0.6 \cdot 1.0 \cdot 0.7 = 0.105 \qquad (3)$$

As it is seen the first signature has probability 2.4% while the second one 10.05% So from these two segments, the second one fits better in the specific bucket, thus it is possible to say that it follows the specific pattern, with some variations.

So when it is needed to determine if a new subsequence is a pattern, all that needs to be done is to create a SAX signature and then compute the probability for each bucket to belong to it. If all probabilities are small (smaller than a predefined threshold, for example 10 or 20, depending on the amount of data available), then the subsequence is not a pattern, otherwise, it is considered as a pattern of the bucket with the highest probability.

Algorithm 2: *Motif Detection based on Buckets*

1. Create subsequences of day's time series
2. Normalize and reduce dimensionality of subsequences using PAA
3. SAX representation of subsequences
4. Apply random projection of SAX representations
5. Group SAX representations to buckets based on random projection
6. Remove small buckets
7. Create P-profiles for each bucket

Flexibility Prediction. For the supervised machine learning method for flexibility estimation, a Recurrent Neural Network (RNN) was used, more specifically an LSTM (Long Short-Term Memory) which has shown great results in time series analysis and prediction. This choice was made as this type of neural networks have been proved to be very effective in sequence-to-sequence problems [7,11,20], and the goal in this approach is to give to the model a subsequence of total consumption as input, and take a subsequence of potential flexible consumption as a result for the same period of time. This approach can have remarkably accurate results but a low level of generalization, which means that in a different house it will need to be retrained. However, to train such a model, it is necessary to have some prior knowledge of real flexibility, which in many cases may not be available (or well defined). In our experiments, the sum consumption of devices that are considered flexible according to bibliography is used, as actual flexibility. This limitation can be overcome by combining it with the previously presented motif detection approach. If the first method is applied beforehand, then knowledge of real flexibility is gathered, by collecting each time the proposed flexibility is accepted or rejected by the consumer, and then, based on the accepted flexibility, train the LSTM.

Once the neural network returns a time series of potential flexibility, the next step is to check, at a certain point in time, if there is indeed flexibility, which affects the overall consumption. To do so, both total and potential flexible consumption are converted into PAA/SAX representation and compare their signatures. If they have a sufficient degree of similarity then this point in time is considered flexible. Finally, if a whole day need to be analyzed for flexibility, the sliding window algorithm are applied and do this check for each subsequence.

Algorithm 3: *Flexibility Detection*

1. **for** *each subsequence of a day* {
2. {*Sliding Window*}
3. **if** *subsequence is outlier* **then** {
4. {*Higher than upper cluster's bound*}
5. **if** *Similarity* $\geq$ *Similarity_Threshold* **then** {
6. {*Similarity between Total and Lstm predicted flexibility* Consumption}
7. *flexible.append(subsequence)* }}}
8. **for** *each segment* {
9. **if** *Motif* = *True* **then** {
10. {*Motif is detected based on bucket's P-profile probability*}
11. **if** *segment is outlier* **then** {
12. {*Higher than upper cluster's bound*}
13. *flexible.append(subsequence)* }}}
14. **return** *flexible*   {*A time series of flexible consumption*}

4   Results

In this section, the results of the application of this method on different datasets and different ways of its application is presented. Specifically, the difference between the two motif detection methods that were observed in the experiments, the results of evaluation metrics for each dataset, the clusters analysis, and the estimation per hour and case study at the smart house are presented.

Table 2. Evaluation metrics

	MSE	MAE	RMSE
Household_power_consumption [1]	0.80	0.78	0.89
Ampds2 [19]	0.19	0.20	0.43
Ampds2 with forecast [19]	0.63	0.58	0.79

In order to be able to quantify the results and compare them, some metrics (MSE, RMSE, MAE) were calculated using the sum of the consumption of

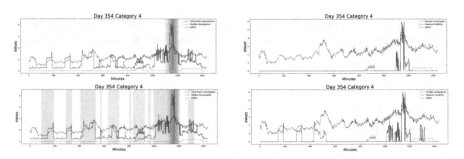

Fig. 5. Example of flexibility detection without (Only Supervised Method)(upper Figures) and with motif buckets (Both Methods) (lower Figures). (Purple: flexibility detected, Green: Motif detected but not consider as flexibility) (Color figure online)

flexible devices as a target flexibility. When analyzing metrics, you need to keep in mind that they show half the truth, since they cannot completely approach zero. Because when a pattern of flexible consumption is identified, this does not directly mean that it will be characterized as flexibility because if it did not exceed the limits of the day class, it is an acceptable consumption that can not be used, for example, in a possible DR request. Thus, in order to have a more complete and comprehensive view of the results, it is also necessary to observe the results in the form of a diagram. The metrics are presented in Table 2 and visual results are shown in Fig. 5.

In data from AMPds2 dataset the flexibility prediction was applied in two different ways, and the results of both ways are presented. The first, as described previously, takes a segment of total consumption as input, and returns a segment of potential flexible consumption for the same period of time. The second one uses a forecast of total consumption as well, it takes the last four hours of total consumption and the next four hours of forecasted total consumption as input and returns potential flexible consumption for the next hour.

More details on how a time series is analysed to detect flexibility can be seen in Fig. 5. As you can see, if only a supervised method is used to identify flexibility, it can find exactly the point in time at which there is flexibility. However, if both methods are used, it was noticed that there are other points of abnormal consumption that could be considered flexible, therefore, there is a greater likelihood of spotting flexible points than those the model has been trained to detect. Another worth mentioning point is around 900th minute of the day, where there is flexible consumption which was detected. Nevertheless, it was not considered as flexibility because it did not exceed the upper level of consumption of the specific day.

In a DR request, it is necessary to know the available flexibility in real-time in order to make the right decision at the right moment. For this reason, the application of proposed method in near real-time conditions was tested, determining flexibility throughout the day. More specifically, the determination is performed every hour. For these tests, a version that is also forecast based was used, so it will be possible to have an estimation of future flexibility. It is expected that the results of these tests will differ from the classical application of the method in only two cases. The first case of differentiation is during the day, the cluster of this day can be incorrectly defined, as there is no information about the whole day, and as a result, segments are considered outliers while in fact, they are not. The second reason, which can lead to different results, is that different Random Projections can be performed throughout the day, which can change which segments are considered part of a particular bucket (motif) and which are not. Although in practice, no big differences are expected.

As it is shown in Fig. 6 the hypotheses that had been made were verified. In this figure is seen the evolution during the day. In each instance, it is shown the consumption until the time of estimation and the forecast of consumption from the moment of estimation until the end of the day. Moreover, the figure shows the cluster of the day, and the cluster's upper bound, the prediction given by the neural network and the final flexibility. There are differences in estimates due to the different categorization, however, the differences are not significant. Moreover, the prediction given by the neural network can be a satisfactory estimation of the next hour. So, it could be said that the proposed method can be applied just as well in real-time.

By analyzing the clusters it is also possible to draw conclusions about the flexibility of the next day. If a simple demand forecast for the next day is available, it won't be detailed enough to be able to detect flexibility, but it will be enough to estimate the cluster of this day. It is possible to draw conclusions about flexibility, as the experiments showed there is a variation in flexibility depending on the cluster (Fig. 7).

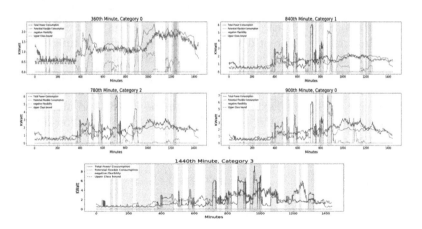

Fig. 6. Flexibility estimation per hour

In the available house where additional tests were performed, there is no information about flexible consumption, which means that it is not possible to

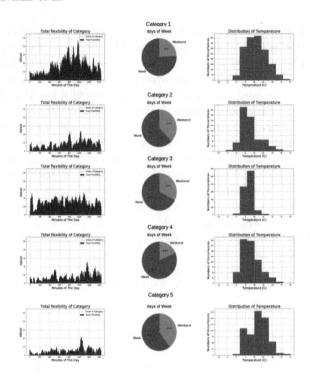

Fig. 7. 1. Total Flexibility per cluster (left) 2. Percentage of weekends per cluster(middle) 3. Distribution of temperature per cluster(right)

calculate metrics such as MSE or MAE, as there are no actual values to compare with the results. In this house there are three sub-meters in three sub-areas of the house. In our tests different devices were active at different times of the day to see what flexibility would be found. The model identified all the abnormal consumption that were added to the total consumption as shown in Fig. 8. Furthermore, consumption patterns were identified to exceed normal consumption levels and were marked as flexible as shown in the Fig. 8. And also vice versa, around 400th minute, as a rule, consumption increases, so the consumption at this point does not considered flexible.

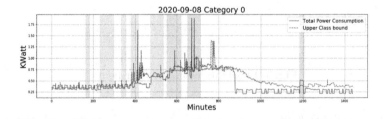

Fig. 8. Flexibility detected at smart home (Purple: flexibility detected)

5   Conclusion

The rapid growth of RES and the increased energy demand have led to new technologies and practices in the field of energy management. An example of such practices, the application of residential DR programs, whose goal is to optimize the balance between energy demand and supply, depends directly on the assessment of residential demand flexibility. In this paper, a new method of residential flexibility estimation is presented, based on analysis of habitual behaviour and identification of repeatable consumption patterns. This method consists of a combination of technologies such as clustering, motif detection and neural networks. It was shown that this method has the ability to identify flexibility with satisfactory accuracy both in a new environment and in an already familiar environment, improving its results as it learns and adapts to new conditions. Moreover, the method has the ability not only to work with historical data but also to combine forecast data with historical. In this way, one of its most important features is achieved, i.e. the ability to adapt to each case and improve the results over time.

For the validation of this method different datasets of residential consumption were used, including also real home experiments. The tests were performed both on a daily basis and per hour, thus approaching the real-time scenario. Despite the fact that the experimental results have been encouraging, it is necessary to conduct additional tests. Ideally, tests should be conducted using the final cost as a benchmark, that can be saved by applying this flexibility assessment method. Such a method of unsupervised flexibility identification is very hard to be evaluated properly, as there is no specific expected result with which the resulted estimation can be compared. So in such cases, the best way to evaluate is to apply it in real conditions and to measure the final goal.

Finally, there is significant room for improvements in this methodology. Example of such enhancements is the deeper analysis of identified patterns so that there is a better understanding of what causes the specific patterns. Additionally, better clustering can be achieved by using additional information such as weather data, daylight hours for each day, the day of the week, the day of the month, etc.

Acknowledgment. This paper has been partially funded by the European Union's Horizon 2020 research and innovation programme under Grant Agreement No 773960 (DELTA project).

References

1. Household electric power consumption. https://www.kaggle.com/uciml/electric-power-consumption-data-set. Accessed 30 Sep 2020
2. Share of renewable energy in gross final energy consumption in Europe – European Environment Agency. https://www.eea.europa.eu/data-and-maps/indicators/renewable-gross-final-energy-consumption-4/assessment-4

3. Abreu, J.M., Pereira, F.C., Ferrão, P.: Using pattern recognition to identify habitual behavior in residential electricity consumption. Energy Build. **49**, 479–487 (2012)

4. Apostolos, C.T.: Design and real-life deployment of a smart Nanogrid: A Greek case study. Accepted for publication PECon **2020**, (2020)

5. European Commission: Communication from the Commission to the Council, the European Parliament, the Council, the European Economic and Social Committee and the Committee of the Regions Energy Roadmap 2050/COM/2011/0885 final/, Brussels (2011). https://eur-lex.europa.eu/legal-content/EN/ALL/?uri=celex%3A52011DC0885#

6. Ayón, X., Gruber, J., Hayes, B., Usaola, J., Prodanovic, M.: An optimal day-ahead load scheduling approach based on the flexibility of aggregate demands. Appl. Energy **198**, 1–11 (2017). https://doi.org/10.1016/j.apenergy.2017.04.038

7. Chiu, C.: State-of-the-art speech recognition with sequence-to-sequence models. In: 2018 IEEE International Conference on Acoustics, Speech and Signal Processing (ICASSP), pp. 4774–4778 (2018)

8. Connolly, D., Lund, H., Mathiesen, B.: Smart energy Europe: the technical and economic impact of one potential 100% renewable energy scenario for the European union. Renew. Sustain. Energy Rev. **60**, 1634–1653 (2016)

9. D'hulst, R., Labeeuw, W., Beusen, B., Claessens, S., Deconinck, G., Vanthournout, K.: Demand response flexibility and flexibility potential of residential smart appliances: experiences from large pilot test in Belgium. Appl. Energy **155**, 79–90 (2015)

10. Esa, N.F., Abdullah, M.P., Hassan, M.Y.: A review disaggregation method in non-intrusive appliance load monitoring. Renew. Sustain. Energy Rev. **66**, 163–173 (2016). https://doi.org/10.1016/j.rser.2016.07.009

11. Gensler, A., Henze, J., Sick, B., Raabe, N.: Deep learning for solar power forecasting - an approach using autoencoder and lstm neural networks. In: 2016 IEEE International Conference on Systems, Man, and Cybernetics (SMC), pp. 002858–002865 (2016)

12. Golden, W., Powell, P.: Towards a definition of flexibility: in search of the holy grail? Omega **28**, 373–384 (2000). https://doi.org/10.1016/S0305-0483(99)00057-2

13. Ji, Y., Rajagopal, R.: Demand and flexibility of residential appliances: An empirical analysis. In: 2017 IEEE Global Conference on Signal and Information Processing (GlobalSIP), pp. 1020–1024 (2017)

14. Lin, J., Keogh, E., Wei, L., Lonardi, S.: Experiencing sax: a novel symbolic representation of time series. Data Min. Knowl. Disc. **15**(2), 107–144 (2007)

15. Liu, G., Gu, J., Zhao, J., Wen, F., Liang, G.: Super resolution perception for smart meter data. Inf. Sci. **526**, 263–273 (2020). https://doi.org/10.1016/j.ins.2020.03.088, http://www.sciencedirect.com/science/article/pii/S0020025520302681

16. Lonardi, J., Patel, P.: Finding motifs in time series. In: Proceedings of the 2nd Workshop on Temporal Data Mining, pp. 53–68 (2002)

17. Lucas, A., Jansen, L., Andreadou, N., Kotsakis, E., Masera, M.: Load flexibility forecast for DR using non-intrusive load monitoring in the residential sector. Energies **12**(14), 2725 (2019)

18. Ludwig, N., Waczowicz, S., Mikut, R., Hagenmeyer, V., Hoffmann, F., Hüllermeier, E.: Mining flexibility patterns in energy time series from industrial processes. In: Proceedings of 27 Workshop Computational Intelligence, Dortmund, pp. 13–32 (2017)

19. Makonin, S., Ellert, B., Bajic, I., Popowich, F.: Electricity, water, and natural gas consumption of a residential house in Canada from 2012 to 2014. Sci. Data **3**, 160037 (2016). https://doi.org/10.1038/sdata.2016.37

20. Marino, D.L., Amarasinghe, K., Manic, M.: Building energy load forecasting using deep neural networks. In: IECON 2016–42nd Annual Conference of the IEEE Industrial Electronics Society, pp. 7046–7051 (2016)

21. Mathiesen, B.V., Lund, H.: Comparative analyses of seven technologies to facilitate the integration of fluctuating renewable energy sources. IET Renew. Power Gener. **3**(2), 190–204 (2009)

22. Mocanu, E., Nguyen, P.H., Gibescu, M.: Energy disaggregation for real-time building flexibility detection. In: 2016 IEEE Power and Energy Society General Meeting (PESGM), pp. 1–5. IEEE (2016)

23. Mueen, A., Keogh, E., Zhu, Q., Cash, S., Westover, B.: Exact discovery of time series motifs. In: Proceedings of the 2009 SIAM international conference on data mining, pp. 473–484. SIAM (2009)

24. Panwar, N., Kaushik, S., Kothari, S.: Role of renewable energy sources in environmental protection: a review. Renew. Sustain. Energy Rev. **15**(3), 1513–1524 (2011)

25. Ponoćko, J., Milanović, J.V.: Forecasting demand flexibility of aggregated residential load using smart meter data. IEEE Trans. Power Syst. **33**(5), 5446–5455 (2018)

26. Resch, G., Panzer, C., Ortner, A., Resch, G.: 2030 res targets for Europe-a brief pre-assessment of feasibility and impacts. Vienna University of technology (2014)

27. Sajjad, M.I.A., Chicco, G., Napoli, R.: Definitions of demand flexibility for aggregate residential loads. IEEE Trans. Smart Grid **7**, 1–1 (2016). https://doi.org/10.1109/TSG.2016.2522961

28. Strbac, G.: Demand side management: benefits and challenges. Energy Policy **36**(12), 4419–4426 (2008)

29. Ward Jr., J.H.: Hierarchical grouping to optimize an objective function. J. Am. Stat. Assoc. **58**(301), 236–244 (1963)

30. Zhao, P., Henze, G.P., Plamp, S., Cushing, V.J.: Evaluation of commercial building HVAC systems as frequency regulation providers. Energy Build. **67**, 225–235 (2013)

Road Tracking in Semi-structured Environments Using Spatial Distribution of Lidar Data

Kosmas Tsiakas$^{(\boxtimes)}$, Ioannis Kostavelis, Dimitrios Giakoumis,
and Dimitrios Tzovaras

Centre for Research and Technology Hellas - Information Technologies Institute
(CERTH / ITI), 6th Km Harilaou -Thermi Road,
57100 Thessaloniki, Greece
{ktsiakas,gkostave,dgiakoum,dimitrios.tzovaras}@iti.gr

Abstract. The future civilian, and professional autonomous vehicles to be realised into the market should apprehend and interpret the road in a manner similar to the human drivers. In structured urban environments where signs, road lanes and markers are well defined and ordered, landmark-based road tracking and localisation has significantly progressed during the last decade with many autonomous vehicles to make their debut into the market. However, in semi-structured and rural environments where traffic infrastructure is deficient, the autonomous driving is hindered by significant challenges. The paper at hand presents a Lidar-based method for road boundaries detection suitable for a service robot operation in rural and semi-structured environments. Organised Lidar data undergo a spatial distribution processing method to isolate road limits in a forward looking horizon ahead of the robot. Stereo SLAM is performed to register subsequent road limits and RANSAC is applied to identify edges that correspond to road segments. In addition, the robot traversable path is estimated and progressively merged with Bézier curves to create a smooth trajectory that respects vehicle kinematics. Experiments have been conducted on data collected from our robot on a semi-structured urban environment, while the method has also been evaluated on KITTI dataset exhibiting remarkable performance.

Keywords: Autonomous vehicles · Road tracking · Spatial distribution · Semi-structured environments

1 Introduction

Autonomous navigation of civilian and construction vehicles in urban environments comprises an active research topic [7]. During the last decades, a plethora of methods have been developed to enable vehicles of future, e.g. public transports [29], private cars [12], or machinery enabled automated guided vehicles (AGVs) [19,25] to drive autonomously in human populated environments. Even

© Springer Nature Switzerland AG 2021
A. Del Bimbo et al. (Eds.): ICPR 2020 Workshops, LNCS 12667, pp. 432–445, 2021.
https://doi.org/10.1007/978-3-030-68787-8_32

if a great amount of significant findings has already been realised and documented [34], the developed solutions address only a fraction of the existing issues and this is due to the fact that the subsequent challenges significantly vary when it comes to different applications and operational environments [3].

In particular, in the field of construction planning, the subsurface applications span across numerous domains including assessment of dense underground utilities in urban areas, e.g. construction of pipelines, electricity cables, communication cables, water and waste network etc. [19]. In this domain, several systems for autonomous scanning of civil constructions with Ground Penetrating Radar (GPR) transported with automated or semi-automated vehicles have been introduced [21, 22]. Even if autonomous driving witnessed intense research endeavours the last decades [27], such machines that target operation in construction sites are still manually driven, on their great majority [31]. This is mainly due to the fact that typical construction sites are not well structured environments, e.g.. roads without lanes and strips, where autonomous vision-based mobility can be facilitated.

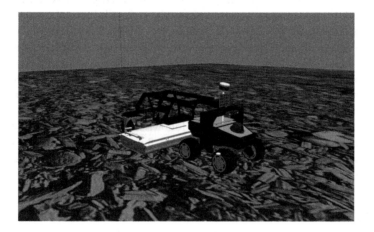

Fig. 1. The model of the surface operating rover towing a GPR antenna with Lidar and stereo vision sytem.

A great challenge and prerequisite for autonomous driving in urban environments is the robust detection of the road boundaries and the traversability [33] estimation on it to enable safe operation of the automated vehicles and construction machines. There has been plenty of research the last decades regarding the task of detecting and tracking the road regions with two main different approaches regarding the type of the sensor used, i.e. vision and Lidar-based methods. There is also a division on the environment that the robot operates on, where it can be a structured urban area, that is probably equipped with lane markings, or unstructured environments with no specific features that delimit the road boundaries. It is important for these methods to satisfy real-time constraints, as the autonomous navigation strongly relies on such systems.

Vision-based methods for road traversability estimation are preferred in structured environments, where the task of detecting the lane markings has been widely studied [2,23,28]. On the other hand, approaches based on Lidar data can be more robust on detecting the road boundaries, as they are not affected by any of the environmental changes mentioned before. Road areas that use lane markings can be detected using the reflective intensity data from Lidar sensors [15,32]. In unstructured areas, segmentation and classification methods are applied to extract the drivable regions [4]. A common assumption made is that the road plane is relatively flatter than non-road areas and as a result it is possible to take advantage of the height differences on the ground. Lane marking detection can also be used as a component of the localisation module for an autonomous car, as presented in [13]. However, these methods are vulnerable to the variations of road and lane texture, weather conditions as well as shadowing effects. Approaches related to switching colour space, vanishing points detection and parallel line extraction are some of the most common that work under specific assumptions.

In our work, we introduce a method for Lidar-based progressive road boundaries detection and their registration through stereo SLAM techniques to define the operational area of a robot in semi-structured urban areas. In our work, with the term semi-structured we refer to those urban regions where marker-lanes and other typical infrastructure signs do not exist, which is the common case in construction sites. The utilised automated vehicle is a surface operating rover that tows a GPR antenna to perform autonomous GPR scanning in construction sites.

The rest of the paper is organised as follows: Sect. 2 provides the state of the art techniques used for road tracking. Section 3 provides details on the proposed method. The conducted experiments and their results are exhibited in Sect. 4, while in Sect. 5 the final conclusions are drawn.

2   Related Work

In general the existing methods for road boundaries detection can be categorised to those exploiting range data (Lidar, Laser scanners) to detect non-uniformities in the measurements and those methods that rely on texture input stemming from RGB cameras. Regarding range-based approaches Ort et al. [30] in their recent work demonstrated a high-accuracy road tracking method as a part of a mapless autonomous driving framework in a rural area with no obstacles around. The navigation relies on topological maps from Open Street Maps and a local perception system that is able to robustly track road boundaries using a 3D Lidar, by calculating the distance signal for each point and thresholding it in the frequency domain. The idea behind this implementation is that the road points in each ring exhibit less variation than the points lying on other areas, such as the grass. They use RANSAC [9] to remove the outliers and the reference trajectory is the average between two boundary splines. However, the performance of this method degrades when outside the road sides solid obstacles exist that do not produce variations in the frequency domain of Lidar measurements. In a similar approach followed in [35], the authors employed Hough transform which has been applied on the road bounds, in order to construct a consistency map and an obstacle map in Bird's Eye View. Their fusion outcome is the final road region, yet with performance limitations due to Hough thresholding sensitivity. Chen et al. [6] presented a novel approach to the detection of traversable road regions and obstacles in off-road scenes using Lidar data. The method initially converts the unordered point cloud into an organised structure, called Lidar-imagery, and creates a histogram by converting the distance values to disparity values. Given the assumption that the area in front of the vehicle is flat, RANSAC is applied to extract the road section and separate both positive and negative obstacles. This way, the road and obstacle detection becomes a 2D classification problem. The authors in [14] tackled the road detection problem using a downward-looking 2D Lidar sensor. Line segmentation applied on the raw data provided the road boundaries. These are tracked using an integrated probabilistic data association filter. Another approach of road detection using high resolution 3D Lidar data is presented in [8]. The initial point cloud data is projected into a 2D reference plane and an upsampling method creates a dense height map. A similarity measure between the height of neighbouring regions is used to determine the road segment from the road edges. A deep learning approach is presented in [5]. The unstructured point cloud is converted into top-view images that feed a fully convolutional neural network, the performance of which significantly depends on the size and variation of the data provided for training.

Considering the camera based methods, a real-time lane detection and tracking approach is presented in [17]. Possible lane markings are detected in the image using an artificial neural network and a particle-filter technique is employed for tracking. Another visual approach presented in [24] used specific steps to extract the road region including i) basic image pre-processing that comprised cropping to the region of interest and grayscale conversion ii) Canny edge detection and Hough transform to detect possible lines iii) road lane modelling by grouping similar lines and extracting an average result. The outcomes of such methods were sensitive to illumination variations. Aiming to surpass this crucial issue Manoharan et al. [26] in their work converted the RGB image into Lab colour space in order to remove shadows and make it invariant from illumination conditions. Then the image is converted back to RGB and Sobel filters are applied for edge detection on the grayscaled image. Hernandez et al. [16] presented a visual approach to road boundary tracking for non-structured areas. They fused the result of a colour-based road detector and a texture line detector with an Unscented Kalman filter to estimate the best road candidate. Deep learning methods for road tracking with RGB image data became also very popular. Almeida et al. [1] simultaneously employed two models, one for road segmentation and one for road line detection. By fusing their result, they achieved a better result than having a single classifier, however still the performance of such approaches heavily relies on the size and variability of data employed for the training of the models.

3   Methodology

In the proposed method, we consider semi-structured environments where the road does not have lane marking and is typically one-way. We seek to model the road free space in order to estimate traversability of the vehicle thus, parked vehicles on the road side that hinder the actual road edges are considered as non-traversable areas and, thus counted in the road limits calculation. To calculate the robot navigation trajectory we employ the detected road limits and position the vehicle in the middle of the detected boundaries respecting also the robot embodiment and kinematics. To further restrict the problem, we assume that the vehicle is already placed on the street since vehicle pull-out refers to a different problem. In order to perform the road area detection a Lidar sensor, namely Velodyne Puck Hi-Res^{TM} tilted towards the ground, so as to exploit as many scan rings as possible, is used. The overall process comprises of specific steps which are outlined as follows:

- Data processing to organise point clouds into scan rings
- Spatial distribution computation on the rings ahead of the robot
- Traversal area detection with gradient descent search to isolate the candidate road limits
- Compute road segments with a two step RANSAC outliers removal processing registered with SLAM transformations
- Detect traversable paths by fitting Bézier curves among the candidate road segments

3.1   Data Pre-processing

The raw data acquired from the Lidar sensor are unstructured and must be re-organised in order to accommodate their processing in a ring-wise manner. The Lidar sensor is placed with a slightly tilted orientation (around 15%) in order to take advantage of more points from the ground region rather than far away areas. This was found to be a decent compromise among the length of forward looking area and the amount of useful rings that can be used for our method. For each point, we calculate its angle $\theta = \arctan(y/x)$ relative to the sensor origin, in order to discard the points that are behind the robot. By keeping the points that belong in the range of $[-\pi, +\pi]$ we can omit points that do not provide any useful information for our task. The remaining data are stored in a structure according to the ring they belong to and sorted by their angle θ, in order to avoid unnecessary computational burden introduced by processing a redundant amount of points. Sub-sampling is also applied to the points of each ring, by defining a fixed step size of S degrees. In our case, we choose S to be equal to $1°$, which means that we acquire a single point per degree, even though the sensor's horizontal angular resolution is higher than that. This remains a free parameter, which should be configured accordingly, depending on the sensor pose and range, as it partially could affect the road tracking process.

3.2   Candidate Road Limits Detection

Our road tracking method relies on the calculation of the spatial distribution among the Lidar rings. It is a metric that can provide useful insights regarding how sparsely or densely the rings are spread in space and how this effect varies around the robot. These variations indicate possible road bounds that will be investigated later on.

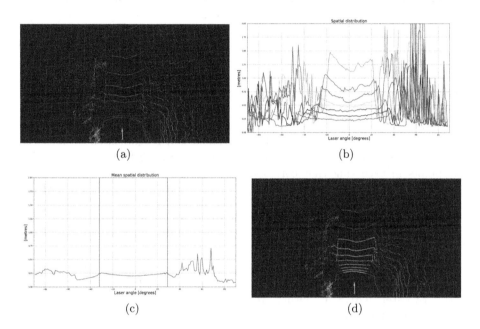

(a)   (b)

(c)   (d)

Fig. 2. a) An instance of Lidar point cloud measurements, b) the spatial distribution between 8 Lidar rings c) the average spatial distribution from b) and the detected road boundaries marked with red lines on vector **Sp** and, d) the corresponding points on the rings that belong to the traversable road area. (Color figure online)

For each new Lidar scan received, the spatial distribution between the rings of the point cloud is calculated. More precisely, starting from the ring closer to the robot, we calculate the euclidean distance d_i between each point $x_{i,r}$ that belongs to the ring r and the respective point that belongs to the next ring with the same θ value $x_{i,r+1}$. Assuming that the number of rings used is N, we end up with $N-1$ distance vectors that outline the relative distances of the subsequent ring points for the search range of horizontal FoV of Lidar (see Fig. 2b). The mean spatial distribution is then calculated for all of the examined rings and the resulting vector **Sp** imprints how the laser beams are reflected from the obstacles existing to the robot's surroundings (see Fig. 2c). It is anticipated that the spatial distribution of the points among the subsequent rings that correspond to the traversable road areas will remain relative constant, while the respective points that correspond to obstacles will have random spatial distribution depending on the obstacles structure. This process is applied to a specific number of rings according to the sensor pose and type. This limitation exists due to the fact that not all of the rings have direct view of the road area, especially in non-flat regions. The number of rings that should be taken into consideration can be easily determined by defining the desired visible area in front of the robot. In our method we employed eight (8) rings which on flat terrain correspond to five (5) m which is considered as adequate space for the robot to manoeuvre when moving in low speed.

Due to the assumption that the robot is already placed centred to the road, we consider that the points in front of the robot's direction (i.e. 0°) belong to the road region. Thus, starting from 0° and searching on both sides of robot's direction, a gradient descent method is applied in order to determine the first local maximum of the mean spatial distribution vector **Sp** that indicates a change in the road traversability, one on the left and one on the right direction. Consequently, in order to determine the candidate road limits, the angle for which the slope in vector **Sp** exhibits a specified threshold is determined, as exhibited in Fig. 2c. After specifying the road limits in the spatial distribution vector **Sp**, the points in each ring that correspond to traversable road area are isolated (see Fig. 2d). The right and left outmost points for each ring correspond to the candidate road limits.

3.3   Road Tracking with SLAM

The so far calculated road limits for each examined Lidar scan are a set of points which are further processed to model the respective road segment. To achieve this a two step RANSAC outliers removal processing step is applied [18]. At the first step, for each side of the road, we execute the RANSAC on the set of outmost points of the segmented Lidar scans in order to discard the outliers. The inliers of this process for each scan are then merged and fitted to a line, using a Total Least Squares approach. The computed line with its parameters describe the road segment for the current measurements of the Lidar. Afterwards, the inliers are transformed to the common reference map frame through a stereo SLAM method. For this we employed a stereo-based visual odometry relying on SURF features tracking to compute incremental robot motion transformations which are then applied to the Lidar scans to formulate a consistent map. The computed robot motion transformations are stored in a pose graph operating at the SLAM back-end which contributes in the mapping optimisation purposes [20]. At the second step, the registered inliers that correspond to the current observed road segment along with past observations that correspond to a certain robot travelled distance undergo an additional RANSAC outlier removal step in order to further adjust and smooth the orientation of the computed road edges.

We found that the second RANSAC repetition after 1m travelled distance of the robot as a decent compromise between computation cost and the ability to capture road wide and sharp curves as well as non-traversable objects existing on the road sides. The outcome of this procedure is the progressive detection and tracking of the road segments ahead the robot.

3.4   Final Trajectory Estimation

After the estimation of the road segments, the trajectory that the robot should follow, in order to remain within road limits so as to serve its construction task (i.e. autonomous GPR scanning), should be computed. In this work we apply a simplified method for the estimation of a reference trajectory, that can be provided to the robot in real-time and ensures safe and smooth navigation that respects the robot kinematic constraints. To this end, once the road boundaries are registered and merged (see Sect. 3.3), a Total Least Squares minimisation criterion is performed to model these data and describe them as a linear parametric equation. The points (x, y) that belong on a line segment $\ell = \langle r, \phi \rangle$ satisfy the equation $r = x\cos\phi + y\sin\phi$, where r is the length and ϕ the inclination angle of the normal. By simply calculating the spatial average of the two line segments, l_{left} and l_{right}, a line equation l_{mid} is obtained that describes the middle of the traversable area in front of the robot. The final trajectory estimation l_{ref} occurs from the accumulation of the l_{mid} lines, that are continuously updated with each new Lidar scan. Then Bézier curves are used to ensure that the resulting path is smooth and suitable for the navigation of the robot. Specifically, a quadratic Bézier curve is applied, where the three control points (p_0, p_1, p_2) are the starting, the intermediate and the ending point of l_{ref} accordingly. Since the reference trajectory is being provided to the robot controller for autonomous navigation, apart from the position of the waypoints, the orientation of each one must also be calculated. Regarding straight segments, the orientation remains constant and the same as the current robot direction. As for curved trajectories, the orientation of each waypoint is calculated with interpolation between the neighbouring waypoints, so as to avoid any abrupt turning manoeuvres that cannot be satisfied by the robot velocity model. This approach facilitates the curvature continuity for the path to be followed including both straight segments and curves.

4   Experimental Evaluation

The performance of the proposed method has been evaluated both with our robot and with the publicly available KITTI Road/Lane Detection dataset [10]. Regarding the first set of experiments, we employed our surface operating rover equipped with a Velodyne Puck Hi-Res^{TM}, as shown in Fig. 1 at a semi-structured environment at premises of CERTH. The specific 16 channel Lidar sensor has a measurement range of 100 m and horizontal angular resolution 0.2°. Figure 3a depicts the region where the road tracking method was assessed. It is

(a)   (b)

Fig. 3. a) Snapshot of the area that the experiment within the premises of CERTH took place. In is an unmarked road with a small curb. b) The result of the road extraction for a distance of 20 m. With blue we display the road boundaries and with green the final trajectory. (Color figure online)

a semi-structured environment with no lane-markings on the road and several arbitrary obstacles around. It is an one-way non-flat road and we accept that the desired reference trajectory is in the middle between the road edges. The covered distance from the slow speed robot corresponded to twenty (20) m and, the road tracking results are graphically illustrated in Fig. 3b. The road edges are shown with a blue line, while the green one represents the calculated reference trajectory.

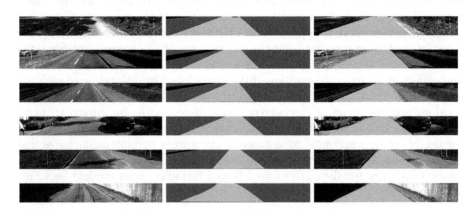

Fig. 4. Road extraction results on the KITTI Road/Lane Detection dataset for urban scenes. From left to right: the original image, the ground truth provided and our method's road extraction result. The road region is denoted with magenta color. (Color figure online)

Regarding the evaluation on the KITTI dataset, we tested our method on two different road scenes: urban marked (UM) and urban unmarked (UU), so as to evaluate the ability of our method to operate in diverse environments. The Lidar sensor used for this dataset recording is different than the one that we used in the previous experiments. Specifically, it is the Velodyne HDL-64E^{TM}, which contains 64 laser channels. We adapted our implementation's parameters accordingly and the first 48 Lidar rings were used for road detection. With this limitation in mind, our method can detect the road boundaries in a distance of twenty-five (25) m, which is also considered as adequate for autonomous vehicles in urban environments. We applied a pixel-level comparison between the manually annotated ground truth images and our method's output, in order to calculate the accuracy for the different frames used from the dataset. In Fig. 4 we present the comparison between our method's result and the provided ground truth for different road scenes. Table 1 summarises these results where it is concluded that in overall the proposed method exhibits accuracy greater than 95% in all examined solutions test cases. The errors correspond to situations where some small objects and road segments anomalies with diameter less than 1m exist on the side of the road limits and in our method are excluded due to the second RANSAC filtering step parameters. Moreover, considering the precision-recall and overall accuracy estimation the conducted experiments are considered credible since the number of pixels that correspond to the road segments are considerable enough when compared to the rest of the image content.

(a)   **(b)**

Fig. 5. a) Snapshot of the road area from the KITTI dataset that was used for evaluation. b) The result of the road extraction for a distance of 35 m. With blue we display the road boundaries and with green the final trajectory. (Color figure online)

Complementary to the per-frame evaluation on the KITTI road dataset, we exhibit the performance of our method on the raw data provided [11]. Figure 5a depicts a selected route that correspond to 35 m travelled distance. By applying our method for autonomous road tracking, it is showcased that the road extraction and the reference trajectory estimation is successful, as illustrated in Fig. 5b.

Table 1. Road extraction results on the KITTI dataset

Scene	Precision	Recall	Accuracy
UM_000008	0.94	0.99	0.97
UM_000020	0.95	0.99	0.98
UM_000047	0.95	0.99	0.98
UU_000001	0.96	0.97	0.97
UU_000056	0.90	0.98	0.97
UU_000090	0.95	0.97	0.97

5   Conclusion

In this work, a Lidar-based method for robust road boundaries detection, suitable for semi-structured environments without the need for prior knowledge of the area has been introduced. We target to address a fraction of autonomous construction machines to increase automation in construction sites where the environment is unstructured. To this end, the road limits extraction is applied with the spatial distribution notion among the Lidar rings, considering that the points lying on traversable areas have a relatively constant distribution, in contrast to other points on surrounding obstacles. Gradient descent search is applied on the mean spatial distribution signal to extract the road boundaries, which are subsequently registered using stereo SLAM techniques and two step RANSAC filtering is applied to remove the outliers and determine the final road edges. Finally, Bézier curves are used to create a smooth traversable trajectory for the robot. The proposed method was evaluated with a surface operating rover in the premises of CERTH and also with the KITTI road detection dataset. In both cases the results confirmed the accuracy and the robustness of the proposed method. In our future work, we plan to extend our method to operate in structured indoors environments (e.g. parking lots) where dedicated navigation policies are required to enable safe autonomous operation.

Acknowledgment. This work has been supported by:

1. The project "ODYSSEAS (Intelligent and Automated Systems for enabling the Design, Simulation and Development of Integrated Processes and Products)" implemented under the "Action for the Strategic Development on the Research and Technological Sector", funded by the Operational Programme "Competitiveness, Entrepreneurship and Innovation" (NSRF 2014–2020) and co-financed by Greece and the European Union, with grant agreement no: MIS 5002462.

2. The EU Horizon 2020 funded project namely: "BADGER (RoBot for Autonomous unDerGround trenchless opERations, mapping and navigation)" under the grant agreement with no: 731968.

References

1. Almeida, T., Lourenço, B., Santos, V.: Road detection based on simultaneous deep learning approaches. Robot. Autonom. Syst. **133**, 103605 (2020). https://doi.org/10.1016/j.robot.2020.103605, http://www.sciencedirect.com/science/article/pii/S0921889020304450
2. Borkar, A., Hayes, M., Smith, M.T., Pankanti, S.: A layered approach to robust lane detection at night. In: 2009 IEEE Workshop on Computational Intelligence in Vehicles and Vehicular Systems, pp. 51–57 (2009)
3. Buehler, M., Iagnemma, K., Singh, S.: The DARPA Urban Challenge: Autonomous Vehicles in City Traffic. Springer, New York (2009)
4. Byun, J., Na, K., Seo, B., Roh, M.: Drivable road detection with 3D point clouds based on the MRF for intelligent vehicle. In: Mejias, L., Corke, P., Roberts, J. (eds.) Field and Service Robotics. STAR, vol. 105, pp. 49–60. Springer, Cham (2015). https://doi.org/10.1007/978-3-319-07488-7_4
5. Caltagirone, L., Scheidegger, S., Svensson, L., Wahde, M.: Fast lidar-based road detection using fully convolutional neural networks. In: 2017 IEEE Intelligent Vehicles Symposium (IV), pp. 1019–1024 (2017)
6. Chen, L., Yang, J., Kong, H.: Lidar-histogram for fast road and obstacle detection. In: 2017 IEEE International Conference on Robotics and Automation (ICRA), pp. 1343–1348 (2017)
7. Fayjie, A.R., Hossain, S., Oualid, D., Lee, D.J.: Driverless car: autonomous driving using deep reinforcement learning in urban environment. In: 2018 15th International Conference on Ubiquitous Robots (UR), pp. 896–901. IEEE (2018)
8. Fernandes, R., Premebida, C., Peixoto, P., Wolf, D., Nunes, U.: Road detection using high resolution lidar. In: 2014 IEEE Vehicle Power and Propulsion Conference (VPPC), pp. 1–6 (2014)
9. Fischler, M.A., Bolles, R.C.: Random sample consensus: a paradigm for model fitting with applications to image analysis and automated cartography. Commun. ACM **24**(6), 381–395, June 1981. https://doi.org/10.1145/358669.358692
10. Fritsch, J., Kuehnl, T., Geiger, A.: A new performance measure and evaluation benchmark for road detection algorithms. In: International Conference on Intelligent Transportation Systems (ITSC) (2013)
11. Geiger, A., Lenz, P., Stiller, C., Urtasun, R.: Vision meets robotics: the kitti dataset. Int. J. Robot. Res. (IJRR) (2013)
12. Geyer, J., et al.: A2d2: Audi autonomous driving dataset. arXiv preprint arXiv:2004.06320 (2020)
13. Ghallabi, F., Nashashibi, F., El-Haj-Shhade, G., Mittet, M.: Lidar-based lane marking detection for vehicle positioning in an HD map. In: 2018 21st International Conference on Intelligent Transportation Systems (ITSC), pp. 2209–2214 (2018)
14. Han, J., Kim, D., Lee, M., Sunwoo, M.: Enhanced road boundary and obstacle detection using a downward-looking lidar sensor. IEEE Trans. Veh. Technol. **61**(3), 971–985 (2012)
15. Hata, A., Wolf, D.: Road marking detection using lidar reflective intensity data and its application to vehicle localization. In: 17th International IEEE Conference on Intelligent Transportation Systems (ITSC), pp. 584–589 (2014)
16. Hernandez, D.E., Blumenthal, S., Prassler, E., Bo, S., Haojie, Z.: Vision-based road boundary tracking system for unstructured roads. In: 2017 IEEE International Conference on Unmanned Systems (ICUS), pp. 66–71 (2017)

17. Kim, Z.: Robust lane detection and tracking in challenging scenarios. IEEE Trans. Intell. Transp. Syst. **9**(1), 16–26 (2008)
18. Kostavelis, I., Gasteratos, A.: Learning spatially semantic representations for cognitive robot navigation. Robot. Autonom. Syst. **61**(12), 1460–1475 (2013)
19. Kouros, G., et al.: 3D underground mapping with a mobile robot and a GPR antenna. In: 2018 IEEE/RSJ International Conference on Intelligent Robots and Systems (IROS), pp. 3218–3224. IEEE (2018)
20. Kouros, G., Psarras, C., Kostavelis, I., Giakoumis, D., Tzovaras, D.: Surface/subsurface mapping with an integrated rover-gpr system: A simulation approach. In: 2018 IEEE International Conference on Simulation, Modeling, and Programming for Autonomous Robots (SIMPAR). pp. 15–22. IEEE (2018)
21. La, H.M., et al.: Autonomous robotic system for high-efficiency non-destructive bridge deck inspection and evaluation. In: 2013 IEEE International Conference on Automation Science and Engineering (CASE), pp. 1053–1058. IEEE (2013)
22. Le, T., Gibb, S., Pham, N., La, H.M., Falk, L., Berendsen, T.: Autonomous robotic system using non-destructive evaluation methods for bridge deck inspection. In: 2017 IEEE International Conference on Robotics and Automation (ICRA), pp. 3672–3677. IEEE (2017)
23. Li, Y., Ding, W., Zhang, X., Ju, Z.: Road detection algorithm for autonomous navigation systems based on dark channel prior and vanishing point in complex road scenes. Robot. Autonom. Syst. **85**, 1–11 (2016). https://doi.org/10.1016/j.robot.2016.08.003, http://www.sciencedirect.com/science/article/pii/S092188901 5301925
24. Low, C.Y., Zamzuri, H., Mazlan, S.A.: Simple robust road lane detection algorithm. In: 2014 5th International Conference on Intelligent and Advanced Systems (ICIAS), pp. 1–4 (2014)
25. Magalhães, A.C., Prado, M., Grassi, V., Wolf, D.F.: Autonomous vehicle navigation in semi-structured urban environment. In: 8th IFAC Symposium on Intelligent Autonomous Vehicles. IFAC Proceedings, vol. 46(10), pp. 42–47 (2013). https://doi.org/10.3182/20130626-3-AU-2035.00051, http://www.sciencedirect.com/science/article/pii/S1474667015349077
26. Manoharan, K., Daniel, P.: A robust approach for lane detection in challenging illumination scenarios. In: 2018 International Conference on Advances in Computing, Communication Control and Networking (ICACCCN). pp. 132–135 (2018)
27. Matthaei, R., et al.: Autonomes Fahren. In: Winner, H., Hakuli, S., Lotz, F., Singer, C. (eds.) Handbuch Fahrerassistenzsysteme. A, pp. 1139–1165. Springer, Wiesbaden (2015). https://doi.org/10.1007/978-3-658-05734-3_61
28. McCall, J.C., Trivedi, M.M.: Video-based lane estimation and tracking for driver assistance: survey, system, and evaluation. IEEE Trans. Intell. Transp. Syst. **7**(1), 20–37 (2006)
29. Meyer, J., Becker, H., Bösch, P.M., Axhausen, K.W.: Autonomous vehicles: the next jump in accessibilities? Res. Transp. Econ. **62**, 80–91 (2017)
30. Ort, T., Paull, L., Rus, D.: Autonomous vehicle navigation in rural environments without detailed prior maps. In: 2018 IEEE International Conference on Robotics and Automation (ICRA), pp. 2040–2047 (2018)
31. Roudari, S.S., Okore-Hanson, T., Hamoush, S., Yi, S.: GPR robotic assisted non-destructive evaluation of concrete structures-20196. In: Waste Management (2020)
32. Thuy, M., León, F.: Lane detection and tracking based on lidar data. Metrol. Meas. Syst. **17**, 311–321 (2010)

33. Tsiogas, E., Kostavelis, I., Giakoumis, D., Tzovaras, D.: V-Disparity based obstacle avoidance for dynamic path planning of a robot-trailer. In: Tzovaras, D., Giakoumis, D., Vincze, M., Argyros, A. (eds.) ICVS 2019. LNCS, vol. 11754, pp. 143–152. Springer, Cham (2019). https://doi.org/10.1007/978-3-030-34995-0_14

34. Wille, J.M., Saust, F., Maurer, M.: Stadtpilot: driving autonomously on braunschweig's inner ring road. In: 2010 IEEE Intelligent Vehicles Symposium, pp. 506–511. IEEE (2010)

35. Xu, F., Chen, L., Lou, J., Ren, M.: A real-time road detection method based on reorganized lidar data. PLoS One **14**(4), 1–17 (04 2019). https://doi.org/10.1371/journal.pone.0215159

Image Segmentation of Bricks in Masonry Wall Using a Fusion of Machine Learning Algorithms

Roland Kajatin$^{(\boxtimes)}$ and Lazaros Nalpantidis

Department of Electrical Engineering, Technical University of Denmark,
Elektrovej 326, 2800 Kgs., Lyngby, Denmark
roland.kajatin@gmail.com, lanalpa@elektro.dtu.dk

Abstract. Autonomous mortar raking requires a computer vision system which is able to provide accurate segmentation masks of close-range images of brick walls. The goal is to detect and ultimately remove the mortar, leaving the bricks intact, thus automating this construction-related task. This paper proposes such a vision system based on the combination of machine learning algorithms. The proposed system fuses the individual segmentation outputs of eight classifiers by means of a weighted voting scheme and then performing a threshold operation to generate the final binary segmentation. A novel feature of this approach is the fusion of several segmentations using a low-cost commercial off-the-shelf hardware setup. The close-range brick wall segmentation capabilities of the system are demonstrated on a total of about 9 million data points.

Keywords: Image segmentation · Construction robotics · Machine learning · Deep learning

1 Introduction

The work presented in this paper focuses on the construction industry domain, the automation of which has gained an increased attention in recent years. The application of computer vision systems at different phases of the lifecycle of civil assets were analyzed in [26]. Such systems are applied during construction, operation, as well as maintenance, and perform operations such as defect detection and condition assessment [13, 26]. From a safety perspective, [14] analyzed the feasibility of a drone based hazard detection system at construction sites. The application of augmented reality in the construction industry is yet another field of interest [25, 27]. Building information modeling has also gained new advances in recent years [1, 2, 15].

This paper focuses on the renovation aspect of the construction industry; more specifically on the renovation of brick walls. During construction of the wall, mortar is used to bind bricks together. Over time, the integrity of the wall

© Springer Nature Switzerland AG 2021
A. Del Bimbo et al. (Eds.): ICPR 2020 Workshops, LNCS 12667, pp. 446–461, 2021.
https://doi.org/10.1007/978-3-030-68787-8_33

might become compromised due to the degradation of the mortar (and bricks). This paper proposes a computer vision system for masonry wall segmentation in order to enable a robotic platform—affixed to the surface of the wall, as shown in Fig. 1—to automatically mill away the mortar from between the bricks without damaging them. By replacing the old mortar with fresh one the integrity of the wall is enhanced, which prolongs the lifetime of the building.

Without the robot, this operation would be carried out by a craftsman who would hold the tool in hand and progressively mill away the mortar. This operation requires the construction of some kind of scaffolding, ensuring the safety of the operator. Furthermore, this process takes time and requires the operator to pay close attention to the edges of the bricks. During the renovation process, it is imperative that only the mortar is milled and the bricks are left unscathed. All these constraints put a burden on the operator. Furthermore, according to [4], prolonged exposure to such mechanical vibrations may lead to disorders in the vascular and neurological systems of the upper limb, called hand-arm vibration syndrome, posing a health risk to operators.

Fig. 1. An example setup of the autonomous mortar raking robot (designed by Robot At Work [18]). It is composed of a modular rail system to which electric motors are attached (blue housing in the image). The end tool is a milling device used to remove the mortar from between the bricks. (Color figure online)

The robotic solution mitigates all of the above problems and harmful effects towards the operators. However, it now becomes a challenge for the robot to *know* where the mortar is. The brick wall has presumably deformed over the years, or was inherently unstructured—depending on the type and uniformity of bricks used. This makes the mortar detection a more general problem. Therefore, the contribution of this paper to enable a robotic platform to perform autonomous mortar raking is summarized as follows:

1. First, a number of image segmentation algorithms are considered and evaluated for the segmentation of close-range images of brick walls using color information and depth from stereo vision.
2. Secondly, a process to fuse the individual segmentation masks is proposed based on the weighted sum and empirically determined threshold operation of said masks.

2   Related Work

Although the application of computer vision systems in the construction industry in general is abundant, the literature on the specific application of masonry (brick) wall segmentation is scarce. Some applications employ laser technology (such as terrestrial laser scanners) to sample the environment [19,22,23], while others rely on 24-bit color images [11,16].

Valero et al. [23] present a technology for automatic fault detection in ashlar masonry walls. They argue that surveying of buildings for condition done by human experts is often unreliable and dependent on the expertise and experience of the operators. Therefore, their proposal uses terrestrial laser scan (TLS) data (precise 3D point cloud), contrary to our approach, together with color information gathered by a DSLR camera. They overlay the color information by generating a color-cloud using structure from motion. Their segmentation of the masonry wall is based on the 2D continuous wavelet transform documented in [22], contrary to our machine learning based classifiers.

Riveiro et al. propose an algorithm for processing laser scanning data using an improved, marker-controlled watershed segmentation in [19]. They used a Riegl terrestrial laser scanner in their case study to sample a point cloud, contrary to our stereo vision based depth calculation. They reduce the dimensionality of the data by using a raster model to lattice the (planar) point cloud of the masonry wall. They fit a plane to the point cloud, and then take the orthogonal projection for each lattice to form a 2D pixel. The intensity value of each pixel is dependent on all the 3D points in the cloud inside the corresponding lattice. While our approach uses ML classifiers, their segmentation of the bricks is done using markers to perform the watershed based segmentation. The markers are derived from geometrical constraints under the assumption that the bricks follow a horizontal course. Using image gradients, the horizontal and vertical mortar channels are found, and connected to form a rough segmentation of the bricks – they call it a wireframe. The inner areas of the found segments in the wireframe serve as the markers for the watershed algorithm, which provides a more accurate segmentation along the edges.

In [16], Oses et al. proposes an automatic, image-based delineation method used in connection with built heritage assessment. Their goal is to assist and speed up the process of determining the degree of protection required for a certain built heritage. Their method converts the input image into a single-channel grayscale one, and then slices it into a number of smaller region of interests (ROIs). These cover the entire image, but are processed independently.

Outliers (i.e. intensity values with a frequency lower than a certain threshold) are removed by inpainting. For each ROI, three modes (i.e. intensity values) are selected based on the histogram of the image. Using an arbitrary neighborhood around these modes, the image is binarized. The blobs in the three binary image are thinned by removing their inner parts. Afterwards, they use the probabilistic Hough transform to detect straight lines in the three images. The detected lines are then fused: colinear lines that are close to each other are connected, and short ones are removed. While our approach uses the color- and depth information to train the models, they construct a series of features using the line segments, which are used to train several classifiers (e.g. SVM, naive Bayes, decision trees, etc.). These classifiers then provide the final segmentation of the bricks.

Similarly to our system, Ibrahim et al. present a machine learning based segmentation algorithm in [11], however, they only use a single model. Their goal is to segment individual brick instances in a 2D image input, both for modern brick walls as well as ancient archaeological sites. Their method can be divided into two steps. During the first step, a convolutional neural network (UNet) is used to generate a grayscale prediction image from the input. Their network is trained on the RGB values of the input image. The second step aims to extract an accurate outline of the bricks using the delineation map obtained in the previous step by applying the inverted distance transform and the H-minima transform. Finally, the watershed algorithm is applied using the H-minima basins as markers for starting points. This last step is helpful in separating touching bricks from each other and correctly drawing an edge in between them. However, in our case, this is not a concern, since the close-range images of the brick wall do not contain touching bricks.

The work presented in this paper aims to add to the body of literature within brick wall segmentation to provide the necessary segmentation for autonomous mortar raking. Contrary to [19,22,23], our approach is based on color and depth information (from stereo vision) using low-cost imaging hardware. Similarly to [11,16], we use machine learning models, however, we take the pixel-wise classification further and propose an algorithm to combine the segmentation masks of several models.

3   Proposed System

The proposed system focuses on providing an accurate segmentation of close-range images of masonry walls. The algorithm involves a number of steps outlined in Fig. 2. Contrary to the approaches of related work presented in Sect. 2, this system is designed to work with close-range (i.e. 100–250 mm from the wall) and cost-effective imaging of small areas of the wall at a time. Therefore, suitable hardware is selected (see Sect. 3.1) and the rest of the system is tailored to work with the available data (see Sect. 3.2).

Fig. 2. Outline of the proposed system for the segmentation of close-range images of masonry walls.

3.1 Hardware

The selected hardware is the Intel RealSense D435 camera [12], which is a compact device ($90 \times 25 \times 25$ mm and 72 g) that houses a depth module and an extra RGB module. The depth module uses assisted stereo vision to calculate the depth. There are two grayscale imagers and an extra infrared projector which projects a static IR pattern to help aid the depth calculation in scenes with inadequate texture. Based on the characteristics of the device presented in [12] and visible dimensions of 54×228 mm of the bricks in the considered use cases, the D435 is able to capture an entire brick along the vertical and horizontal axes at a minimum distance of $r_{\min} = 67.14$ mm and $r_{\min} = 159.46$ mm respectively, using:

$$r_{\min} = d_{\text{target}} \frac{f}{d_{\text{CCD}}}, \tag{1}$$

where d_{target} denotes the dimensions of the brick, f is the focal length of the device, and d_{CCD} denotes the dimensions of the sensor. Furthermore, the single-pixel resolution is expected to be less than 1 mm up to a maximum distance of $r_{\max} = 197.7$ mm from the wall based on:

$$r_{\max} = d_{\text{target}} \frac{f}{p_{\text{res}} d_{\text{CCD}}}, \tag{2}$$

where $p_{\text{res}} = 3$ is the minimum distance between two centroids in pixels (i.e. the minimum distance required to have a well-defined separation between two points in the image).

Depth information is recovered from stereo vision using the epipolar geometry [9]. The two cameras are offset from each other by a baseline of $b = 50.27$ mm. The D435 uses the left imager as the reference. Since the left-most part of the left image is not seen by the right imager, the depth map contains a so-called invalid depth band on the left side. This is given in [12] as:

$$\frac{b}{2z \tan\left(\frac{\text{HFOV}}{2}\right)}, \tag{3}$$

where HFOV is the horizontal field of view of the imagers, and z is the distance from the wall. In the aforementioned working range of the device, (3) yields around 10%–15% of the depth map being invalid. According to [9], the depth is recovered as:

$$z = \frac{bf}{x - x'}, \tag{4}$$

where the term $x - x'$ is called the disparity, and z is the depth value. As the depth is inversely proportional to the disparity, the theoretical minimum depth is bound by the maximum disparity value. By the introduction of an artificial disparity shift (i.e. an artificial decrease in the denominator in (4)), the range of the valid depth calculations can be modified. Using a shift of 86, the depth range is moved to be within approximately 99.83 mm and 246.08 mm, which corresponds to the desired working range of the device.

3.2 Software

The acquired depth map and color image are further processed as outlined in Fig. 2.

Preprocessing. The preprocessing steps convert the raw data from the device into the required format used by each algorithm (detailed in Sect. 3.2). There are four main groups of preprocessing methods used: filtering of the raw depth map, alignment of the depth map with the color frame, color space conversion, and image transformations (e.g. resizing and slicing).

There are a number of filters used to make up for various shortcomings of the depth map, which in turn enhance its overall quality. The spatial noise is corrected with a filter that smooths out variations in the depth map while keeping the integrity of actual edges. This filter is based on a 1D exponential moving average (EMA) calculation controlled by an extra parameter to preserve the integrity of the edges in the depth map. The same filtering principle is also applied in the time domain across consecutive depth maps to reduce temporal noise, which manifests in small variations in the depth values for a static scene. Finally, missing depth values (i.e. holes) in the depth map are filled in using the neighboring left depth value.

Since both the color and the depth information is used by the segmentation algorithms, it is important that the depth values be aligned with the color pixels. The alignment is based on the inverse transformation of pixel coordinates to camera coordinates using the intrinsic parameters of the cameras. Then, the two frames are aligned using their measured extrinsic relation. Regarding the color frames, three input domains are considered for the algorithms: RGB, HSV, and a color and texture based [24] feature sets.

Segmentation. Following the description in Sect. 1, the proposed system is concerned with the accurate segmentation of close-range images of brick walls. The task is interpreted as a pixel-wise classification problem using two distinct classes: mortar and brick.

In total, there are eight classifiers investigated, of which the first one is the k-nearest neighbor (kNN) algorithm [3]. This classifier assigns class allocation based on the majority-class of k nearest neighbors of the data point. The second classifier is the naive Bayes algorithm [28], which applies Bayes' theorem with a (naive) strong assumption of conditional independence between the features.

Another classifier which uses Bayes' theorem is the quadratic discriminant analysis (QDA) [21], which applies a quadratic decision surface to discriminate the different classes. The fourth classifier is the support vector machine (SVM) [7], which separates the classes based on the maximum margin decision boundary solution. The maximum margin refers to the fact that the decision boundary is selected such that it is as far away as possible from the classes. The fifth one is the decision tree classifier [6], which recursively partitions the input space and model each region locally. These regions are connected in a recursive manner. An extension of the decision tree classifiers is the random forest model [5], which fits a number of decision trees and combines their individual outputs using averaging, thus improving the predictive accuracy. Another ensemble classifier is the AdaBoost [10], which iteratively fits classifiers on the data, adjusting the weights of incorrectly classified points at each iteration (i.e. forcing the subsequent classifiers to focus more on difficult examples). Finally, the last classifier is the UNet deep learning model [20], which is a convolutional deep neural network that outputs pixel-wise classification.

Each of these classifiers produces a binary segmentation (i.e. pixel-wise classification) of each preprocessed (as outlined in Sect. 3.2) input image individually. During training, the outputs are used to adjust the parameters of the models, while during inference, the masks are post-processed (see Sect. 3.2) and then combined (see Sect. 3.2) to produce the final binary segmentation mask.

Post-processing. There are two types of post-processing methods applied to each binary mask individually: morphological image processing and connected components analysis, both of which aim to reduce the noise in the output and produce homogeneous (complete) areas for the bricks.

The first method relies on applying morphological operations on the binary mask. The applied morphological operation is the closing operation, which performs a dilation and an erosion in this particular order on the input image. This post-processing step closes the holes inside the brick regions, as well as removes small brick-labeled objects from the frame (which are assumed to be noise due to their small pixel size).

The second method is based on the connected components analysis of the binary mask. Similarly to the morphology, the goal is to remove small patches of foreground objects under the assumption that the bricks are expected to occupy a large portion of the image. The labeling of distinct regions is based on a decision tree approach presented in [8]. The analysis uses 8-connectivity, and produces an output image where connected components are uniquely labeled. The size of each of these components is determined simply by the amount of pixels they occupy. If this area is smaller than a certain threshold, then the corresponding pixels are set to 0 (i.e. background) in the mask. Since the connected components analysis only considers foreground pixels, the same procedure is performed on the inverted mask as well. Although the morphological transformation fills in most of the holes inside the bricks, there could still be some left at this point.

By inverting the image, these small holes are now labeled by this algorithm, and removed due to their area being below the threshold.

Fusion. At the final step, the post-processed masks produced by all considered classifiers are combined to form the final segmentation. The combination logic is based on a weighted voting scheme. First, each classification algorithm is assigned a specific weight based on their performance (see Sect. 4). The weights are assigned by taking the softmax function of the selected performance metrics (average of F1-score and accuracy) of the classifiers.

Let s_i denote the score of the ith classifier, then the weights are given by the softmax function as

$$w_i = \frac{\exp\left(s_i\right)}{\sum_j \exp\left(s_j\right)}, \tag{5}$$

where the denominator is the sum of the exponentials of all the scores. Using the softmax function ensures that the weights sum up to 1, and that their relative importance is guided by the performance of the corresponding classifiers. The binary masks are multiplied by the corresponding weights and then summed up to generate a single mask. Then, a threshold operation is performed to binarize the combined mask and yield the final segmentation.

The value of the threshold is experimentally determined. If the threshold is too large, the final mask will have a high confidence for the labeled brick areas, but these will be smaller in size and less accurate around the edges. If the threshold is too small, then the output will have brick areas with less confidence around the edges. Therefore, it is important to select a threshold which retains the accuracy around the edges, but still has a high confidence on the output brick regions.

4 Experimental Evaluation

The evaluation of the proposed system outlined in Sect. 3 is first performed for each algorithm individually. Once these performance scores are evaluated, the weights are calculated as shown in (5), and the performance of the entire system, using the combined mask, is again evaluated.

The evaluation is based on standard classification metrics. The binary classification problem at hand produces either a positive or a negative output (depending on the class) for each pixel, which means there are four possible scenarios: true negative (TN), false negative (FN), true positive (TP), and false positive (FP). These outcomes are encapsulated into the following metrics which are used for the evaluation: recall, precision, specificity, negative predictive value, F1 score, and accuracy [17].

4.1 Dataset

In order to train and test the machine learning classifiers, a dataset is created in the following manner. The D435 is used to record four video streams of brick walls under various environmental conditions, but only for reddish bricks. In total, 27 static frames are extracted from both the color and the depth streams. The depth frame is preprocessed, according to the description in Sect. 3.2, therefore, it is only necessary to apply the same preprocessing steps during inference, and not during the training. The color and preprocessed depth frames constitute the entire dataset (i.e. four data points for each pixel location). A color frame example from each recording is shown in Fig. 3.

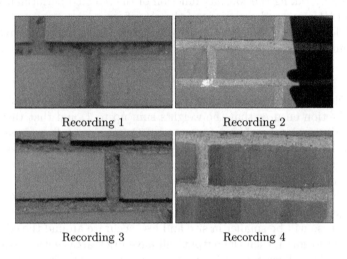

Fig. 3. Example color frames from each of the four recordings. Such color frames, together with the corresponding depth information, constitute the dataset. Note that the four recordings are made under different lighting conditions. In (b), the recording contains a shadow in the right side, while in (d), the bricks have multiple colors.

The dataset is further diversified by three data augmentation processes: flipping the image (i.e. mirroring along either the vertical or horizontal axis), changing the contrast, or adjusting the brightness. These modifications introduce some variance, and noise into the frames, which in turn enable the algorithms to learn parameters which can deal with these factors. These processes also mimic the possible effects of the environmental conditions (e.g. lighting condition), as well as the relative orientation of the camera with respect to the wall. Thanks to the data augmentation step, the number of samples in the dataset is increased to 108 in total. Since each frame has a resolution of 848×480 pixels, the dataset contains almost 44 million data points, each of which is a four-element vector with the corresponding color and depth information.

The ground truth segmentation masks for each training sample are manually created in the next step using Photoshop. These masks represent the perfect segmentations, which are regarded as the 100% accurate outputs. These are used both during the training of the algorithms, as well as during the evaluation to compare the segmentation output with these perfect masks.

The dataset is split into training and test sets at a ratio of four to one. Each split contains examples from each of the four recordings. Therefore, the final training set contains 86 examples, and there are 22 in the test set. The training set is used to train all of the machine learning classifiers, while the test set is used to evaluate them.

Table 1. Evaluation results of the chosen classifiers

Model	Domain	Recall	Precision	Specificity	NPV	F1	Accuracy
kNN	HSV	0.97	0.96	0.87	0.91	0.93	0.94
Naive Bayes	HSV	0.98	0.89	0.65	0.92	0.85	0.90
QDA	RGB	0.98	0.93	0.78	0.93	0.90	0.93
SVM	HSV	0.98	0.95	0.83	0.94	0.92	0.94
Decision tree	HSV	0.97	0.95	0.85	0.91	0.92	0.94
Random Forest	HSV	0.98	0.95	0.86	0.93	0.93	0.95
AdaBoost	RGB	0.96	0.94	0.83	0.87	0.90	0.93
UNet	RGB	0.98	0.95	0.84	0.93	0.92	0.94
Fusion		0.98	0.96	0.87	0.94	0.94	0.95

4.2   Results

The eight machine learning classifiers are evaluated individually in the first step. The metrics are summarized in Table 1. As mentioned above, the F1-score and accuracy metrics are used to determine the weight for each algorithm during the fusion step.

The kNN was set up to use 3 neighbors, uniform weights for each neighborhood, and the Euclidean distance measure. This classifier achieved one of the best results in multiple metrics using the HSV color space. It outperforms all other models in both precision and specificity. High precision means that the kNN tends not to make false positive predictions compared to true positives, while the high specificity score indicates that the model accurately classifies most of the true negatives. Overall, this classifier achieved an F1-score of 0.93 and an accuracy of 0.94 on the test set.

The second model evaluated was the naive Bayes, which performed worst among the eight classifiers. Although it handled the true positive cases well, it struggled with the negatives. A low specificity value of 0.65 indicates that this model made a large amount of false positive predictions compared to the true negatives. It achieved an F1-score of 0.85 and accuracy of 0.9 using the HSV color space. Due to the positioning of the camera close to the wall, a large portion of the image is occupied by the positive class (i.e. bricks). Therefore, even the naive Bayes classifier could achieve acceptable F1-score and accuracy, even though it handled the negative class poorly.

Similarly to the naive Bayes, the QDA classifier shows the same results in terms of predictive capabilities regarding the positive and negative classes, however, it performed better using the RGB color space. This is not surprising, considering that the QDA also uses Bayes' rule internally. Regardless, the overall performance of this classifiers is superior to that of the naive Bayes, with an F1-score of 0.90 and accuracy of 0.93.

The support vector machine classifier was set up with a squared-exponential kernel (i.e. *RBF*), and a regularization parameter of 1, using the HSV color space. Although the SVM achieved high evaluation scores, with an F1-score of 0.92 and accuracy of 0.94, the downside of using it is that there are 5240 support vectors in the trained exponential model for each class, so in total more than 10 thousand. Thus, the model takes a long time to make predictions, since there are a great amount of cross products to be calculated for each input (and each image has more than 400 thousand pixels).

The decision tree classifier, on the other hand, performs similarly to the SVM (using the HSV color space, the F1-scores and accuracy metrics are the same), yet this model is much faster than the SVM model. The decision tree, using the HSV domain, has 875 nodes in total, however, since there are two classes, each split only has two possible outcomes, and the maximum depth is set to 10 during training. So at most, there are 10 decision rules that each input goes through. Thus, the decision tree classifier beats all of the previous classifiers, with the exception of the kNN, simply because it is faster with better F1-score and accuracy.

The random forest model adds a layer of complexity on the decision trees by training 10 of them and having them vote for the most likely outcome. Naturally, there are approximately 10 times as many nodes (i.e. 8598), however the maximum depth of each tree is still 10. So each input pixel goes through 100 decisions altogether. It also makes this classifier slower than the decision tree, yet it achieves a slightly better performance. It has an F1-score of 0.93 and an accuracy of 0.95. Another insight into the random forest is the relative importance of the features calculated as the normalized total reduction of the Gini index by the given features in the whole model. In the case of the HSV-D color space, the importances are: 0.307, 0.500, 0.111, and 0.082. The saturation channel alone corresponds to half of the predictive value of this model. This is a consequence of having a very low saturated mortar as one class and a somewhat saturated brick class. The second most important feature is the hue channel. Although not tested, this value is expected to drop on a multi-colored brick dataset, simply because in the current case, the model is expecting a red brick as input. Finally, not much emphasis is put on the depth input, which might be a result of having the lowest variance within the depth values (i.e. the two planes are close to each other).

The AdaBoost model was set up with a maximum number of 50 estimators, a decision tree-based classifier, and a learning rate of 1. Although this classifier handled the positive cases well, it has the lowest negative predictive value of 0.87. It means that AdaBoost predicted a significant amount of false negatives

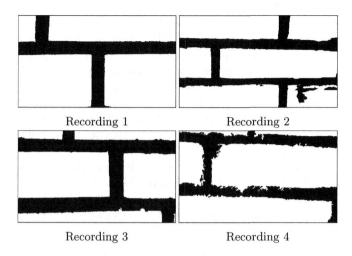

Recording 1   Recording 2

Recording 3   Recording 4

Fig. 4. Binary segmentation masks for the inputs in Fig. 3 created with the final computer vision system, which combines the individual outputs of the eight machine learning based classifiers (see Table 1).

compared to the true negatives. Overall, it achieved an F1-score of 0.90 and accuracy of 0.93 (same as the QDA) using the RGB color space.

Finally, the training of the deep learning UNet model is slightly different from the other classifiers. The same training set was used, however, this model required a longer training process. The learning rate was set to 0.005 initially, and it was reduced by 20% after every four epochs. The reduction of the learning rate should allow the model to gradually close in on the optimal set of weights. Another tweak of the training process has to do with the disproportionate representation of the two classes. Since there are almost three times as many brick examples than mortar, during the evaluation of the loss, if the classes are not represented equally, the model could learn to disregard the errors caused by misclassification of mortar. Therefore, during the calculation of the loss, the contribution of the brick pixels is reduced by 65%, such that it would match the weight of the mortar contribution, which improves the performance of the UNet model. The model was trained over 280 epochs with a batch size of 1 under 168 min. The accuracy of the model using the RGB color space is 0.94 with and F1-score of 0.92, thus it is slightly worse than the random forest, and on par with the kNN classifier.

In order to combine the individual masks, the following weights are assigned to each classifier shown in Table 1 from top to bottom, calculated according to (5): 0.127, 0.119, 0.124, 0.126, 0.126, 0.127, 0.124, and 0.126. The kNN and the random forest classifiers received the highest weights, while the naive Bayes received the lowest weight (0.119). The threshold value used to binarize the combined segmentation mask was determined experimentally by looking at the performance of the entire vision system on the test set. Finally, a value of 140 was used as the threshold, and the combined vision system achieved an

F1-score of 0.94 and accuracy of 0.95 (see Table 1). The system has equally high recall and precision scores, which means that there are not many misclassified pixels in the output. In total, there were almost 9 million data points in the test set. Approximately 3.25% of the predictions were false positive, and 1.44% were false negative. The false positives often have an effect on the accuracy around the edges of the bricks, however, having false positives would only cause the robotic platform to be less thorough during the milling. False negatives, on the other hand, indicate to the robot that there is mortar to be milled, where in reality it is actually brick.

The final segmentations of the four example inputs in Fig. 3 are shown in Fig. 4. Using the combination of classifiers produces the best overall segmentation in all four recordings at the same time. The first and third masks are the most accurate. The system is able to handle the shadows in Fig. 4b, however, it struggles most with the fourth example in Fig. 4d.

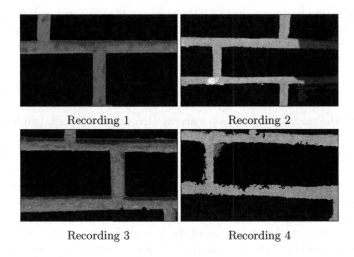

Recording 1   Recording 2

Recording 3   Recording 4

Fig. 5. Overlay of the final segmentation masks shown in Fig. 4 on the inputs shown in Fig. 3. The output masks were inverted to mask out the brick areas, so that the accuracy of the system around the edges of the bricks would be visible.

The masks are overlaid on the example inputs in Fig. 5. These images intend to show the accuracy of the masks around the edges of the bricks. The masks in Fig. 5a and Fig. 5c have a high accuracy at the edges, which would allow the robot to mill most of the mortar away without damaging any of the bricks. The mask in Fig. 5b is also accurate in most areas of the image, except for the lower right side in the shadow. The mask in Fig. 4b has a hole in the brick area at the bottom right corner, however, the opening at the top edge of this brick is narrow. Since the hole does not go through the entire brick area, it is not a mortar channel. Finally, the segmentation overlay in Fig. 5d is the least accurate one. The small protruding false brick classifications could be ignored to some extent by reducing the shape to a more regular rectangular one (assuming the bricks have rectangular shapes). However, the most serious issue is the upper left corner of the large brick in the middle, which is not classified as brick. This would indicate to the robot that there is mortar there, which would mill away the corner of the brick.

5 Conclusion and Discussion

This paper has presented a computer vision system used to produce accurate binary segmentation masks of close-range images of brick walls. The advantages of the presented approach are cost effectiveness (it requires only cheap hardware with stereo vision capabilities, e.g. the Intel RealSense D435), accuracy (achieved by combining the results from a number of classifiers), and flexibility (the system can easily be expanded with additional classifiers). The performance of vision system was evaluated on around 9 million data points with a final F1-score of 0.94 and accuracy of 0.95. The segmentations shown in Fig. 4 are accurate in most cases, with minor issues for areas in the shadow (Fig. 4b) and multi-colored bricks (Fig. 4d).

In order to further enhance the final segmentation, the threshold operation could be modified to be more dynamic. For instance, one could try to find brick shapes (i.e. rectangles) at different gray-levels in the combined mask. It is equivalent to localizing the threshold, instead of using a single global threshold value. In this case, one could train classifiers that work well, for instance, on shadowy areas, and then use a local threshold value (or even a higher local weight) for such parts of the image. Thus, the final mask would be more accurate, using local information for the binarisation process.

The work presented in this paper serves as a proof of concept and thus the evaluation of the system was performed offline. The design and implementation of the requirements for the online adaption of the vision system is left for future work.

Acknowledgment. The authors would like to thank the company Robot At Work for offering their collaboration to solve the mortar raking problem. Furthermore, we thank Rune Hansen, Finn Christensen, and Kasper Laursen from Robot At Work for their support and contribution to the project.

References

1. Adán, A., Quintana, B., Prieto, S., Bosché, F.: An autonomous robotic platform for automatic extraction of detailed semantic models of buildings. Autom. Constr. **109**, 102963 (2020)
2. Adán, A., Quintana, B., Prieto, S.A., Bosché, F.: Scan-to-BIM for 'secondary' building components. Adv. Eng. Inform. **37**, 119–138 (2018)
3. Altman, N.S.: An introduction to kernel and nearest-neighbor nonparametric regression. Am. Stat. **46**(3), 175–185 (1992)

4. Bovenzi, M.: Health effects of mechanical vibration. G Ital. Med. Lav. Ergon. **27**(1), 58–64 (2005)
5. Breiman, L.: Random forests. Mach. Learn. **45**(1), 5–32 (2001). https://doi.org/10.1023/A:1010933404324
6. Breiman, L., Friedman, J., Stone, C.J., Olshen, R.A.: Classification and Regression Trees. CRC Press, Boca Raton (1984)
7. Cortes, C., Vapnik, V.: Support-vector networks. Mach. Learn. **20**(3), 273–297 (1995). https://doi.org/10.1007/BF00994018
8. Grana, C., Borghesani, D., Cucchiara, R.: Optimized block-based connected components labeling with decision trees. IEEE Trans. Image Process. **19**(6), 1596–1609 (2010)
9. Hartley, R., Zisserman, A.: Multiple View Geometry in Computer Vision. Cambridge University Press, Cambridge (2003)
10. Hastie, T., Rosset, S., Zhu, J., Zou, H.: Multi-class AdaBoost. Stat. Interface **2**(3), 349–360 (2009)
11. Ibrahim, Y., Nagy, B., Benedek, C.: CNN-based watershed marker extraction for brick segmentation in masonry walls. In: Karray, F., Campilho, A., Yu, A. (eds.) ICIAR 2019. LNCS, vol. 11662, pp. 332–344. Springer, Cham (2019). https://doi.org/10.1007/978-3-030-27202-9_30
12. Intel Corporation: Intel RealSense D400 Series Product Family Datasheet (2020). https://dev.intelrealsense.com/docs/intel-realsense-d400-series-product-family-datasheet
13. Kapoor, M., Katsanos, E., Thöns, S., Nalpantidis, L., Winkler, J.: Structural integrity management with unmanned aerial vehicles: state-of-the-art review and outlook. In: Sixth International Symposium on Life-Cycle Civil Engineering, IAL-CCE 2018, Ghent, Belgium (2018)
14. Kim, D., Yin, K., Liu, M., Lee, S., Kamat, V.: Feasibility of a drone-based on-site proximity detection in an outdoor construction site. Comput. Civ. Eng. **2017**, 392–400 (2017). https://doi.org/10.1061/9780784480847.049
15. Lu, Y., Wu, Z., Chang, R., Li, Y.: Building information modeling (BIM) for green buildings: a critical review and future directions. Autom. Constr. **83**, 134–148 (2017)
16. Oses, N., Dornaika, F., Moujahid, A.: Image-based delineation and classification of built heritage masonry. Remote Sens. **6**(3), 1863–1889 (2014)
17. Powers, D.M.: Evaluation: from precision, recall and F-measure to ROC, informedness, markedness and correlation. J. Mach. Learn. Technol. **2**, 37–63 (2011)
18. RAW: About Robot At Work (2019). https://robotatwork.com/about-raw/
19. Riveiro, B., Lourenço, P.B., Oliveira, D.V., González-Jorge, H., Arias, P.: Automatic morphologic analysis of quasi-periodic masonry walls from LiDAR. Comput.-Aided Civ. Infrastruct. Eng. **31**(4), 305–319 (2016)
20. Ronneberger, O., Fischer, P., Brox, T.: U-Net: convolutional networks for biomedical image segmentation. In: Navab, N., Hornegger, J., Wells, W.M., Frangi, A.F. (eds.) MICCAI 2015. LNCS, vol. 9351, pp. 234–241. Springer, Cham (2015). https://doi.org/10.1007/978-3-319-24574-4_28
21. Srivastava, S., Gupta, M.R., Frigyik, B.A.: Bayesian quadratic discriminant analysis. J. Mach. Learn. Res. **8**(Jun), 1277–1305 (2007)
22. Valero, E., Bosché, F., Forster, A.: Automatic segmentation of 3D point clouds of rubble masonry walls, and its application to building surveying, repair and maintenance. Autom. Constr. **96**, 29–39 (2018)

23. Valero, E., Forster, A., Bosché, F., Hyslop, E., Wilson, L., Turmel, A.: Automated defect detection and classification in ashlar masonry walls using machine learning. Autom. Constr. **106**, 102846 (2019)
24. Wang, X.Y., Wang, T., Bu, J.: Color image segmentation using pixel wise support vector machine classification. Pattern Recogn. **44**(4), 777–787 (2011)
25. Webster, A., Feiner, S., MacIntyre, B., Massie, W., Krueger, T.: Augmented reality in architectural construction, inspection and renovation. In: Proceedings of the ASCE Third Congress on Computing in Civil Engineering, vol. 1, p. 996 (1996)
26. Xu, S., Wang, J., Wang, X., Shou, W.: Computer vision techniques in construction, operation and maintenance phases of civil assets: a critical review. In: Proceedings of the International Symposium on Automation and Robotics in Construction, ISARC, vol. 36, pp. 672–679. IAARC Publications (2019)
27. Zaher, M., Greenwood, D., Marzouk, M.: Mobile augmented reality applications for construction projects. Constr. Innov. **18**(2), 152–166 (2018)
28. Zhang, H.: Exploring conditions for the optimality of naive Bayes. Int. J. Pattern Recogn. Artif. Intell. **19**(02), 183–198 (2005)

Sentinel-2 and SPOT-7 Images in Machine Learning Frameworks for Super-Resolution

Antigoni Panagiotopoulou[1]([✉]), Lazaros Grammatikopoulos[2], Georgia Kalousi[3], and Eleni Charou[1]

[1] Institute of Informatics and Telecommunications, NCSR Demokritos, Athens, Greece
antigoni27aug@gmail.com, exarou@iit.demokritos.gr
[2] Department of Surveying and Geoinformatics Engineering, University of West Attica, Athens, Greece
lazaros@uniwa.gr
[3] Terra Spatium SA, Athens, Greece
g.kalousi@terraspatium.gr

Abstract. Monitoring construction sites from space using high-resolution (HR) imagery enables remote tracking instead of physically traveling to a site. Thus, valuable resources are saved while recording of the construction site progression at anytime and anywhere in the world is feasible. In the present work Sentinel-2 (S2) images at 10 m (m) are spatially super-resolved per factor 4 by means of deep-learning. Initially, the very-deep super-resolution (VDSR) network is trained with matching pairs of S2 and SPOT-7 images at 2.5 m target resolution. Then, the trained VDSR network, named SPOT7-VDSR, becomes able to increase the resolution of S2 images which are completely unknown to the net. Additionally, the VDSR net technique and bicubic interpolation are applied to increase the resolution of S2. Numerical and visual comparisons are carried out on the area of interest Karditsa, Greece. The current study of super-resolving S2 images is novel in the literature and can prove very useful in application cases where only S2 images are available and not the corresponding SPOT-7 higher-resolution ones. During the present super-resolution (SR) experimentations, the proposed net SPOT7-VDSR outperforms the VDSR net up to 8.24decibel in peak signal to noise ratio (PSNR) and bicubic interpolation up to 16.9% in structural similarity index (SSIM).

Keywords: Deep-learning · Spatial resolution · Super-resolution · Sentinel-2 · SPOT-7 · VDSR · SPOT7-VDSR

1 Introduction

The availability of detailed and precise pieces of information regarding the spatial variation of land cover/land use is a vital factor not only in local ecology and environmental research but also in practical applications such as target detection, pattern classification and construction sites monitoring [1–3]. Satellite images of high spatial resolution are necessary to accomplish the pre-mentioned tasks. Super-resolution (SR) techniques can

© Springer Nature Switzerland AG 2021
A. Del Bimbo et al. (Eds.): ICPR 2020 Workshops, LNCS 12667, pp. 462–476, 2021.
https://doi.org/10.1007/978-3-030-68787-8_34

be applied on remotely sensed (RS) images and increase their spatial resolution beyond the resolution of the image acquisition sensor [4–6]. Basically, the missing details in a low resolution (LR) image can be either reconstructed or learned from other high resolution (HR) images as soon as both LR and HR images have been created via approximately the same resampling process. Deep learning techniques for SR are widely applied in the field of satellite imaging [4, 5, 7–10].

In [11] a new technique for super-resolving the Sentinel-2 (S2) short wave infrared band B11 from 20 to 10 m (m) is presented. Then, the 10 m resolution band is used to detect water basins through the modified normalized difference water index. Three convolutional neural network (CNN) models have been developed in relation to three input combinations. The simplest case does not involve CNN guiding with HR bands. The other two cases resemble pan-sharpening since the CNN is guided either with the near-infrared band B8 or with all the HR 10 m bands B2, B3, B4 and B8. In [12] a SR approach which is based on CNN and is adapted to work with multispectral images is proposed. Spatial features are emphasized and color information is preserved by means of incorporating the intensity hue saturation transform into the CNN models called very deep super-resolution (VDSR) and SRCNN. Synthetic and real experiments of single image SR per factors 2, 3 and 4 are carried out. The testing data are SPOT images and Pleiades images. In [4] the LR Sentinel-2 bands at 20 m and 60 m are super-resolved to 10 m by means of CNN. Two deep network models are developed for separately super-resolving per factors 2 and 6. During net training it is assumed that the transfer of high-frequency information across spectral bands is invariant over a range of scales. Training data consist of S2 images from different geographical locations of the world. Original HR Sentinel-2 images have been downsampled per factors 2 and 6 to acquire the training pairs of input and output images. The proposed networks have generalization ability of super-resolving S2 across different climate zones and land cover types with favorable computational speed and preservation of spectral characteristics. Furthermore, S2 images are used to train shallow and deep CNNs in [13]. The testing data represent three different environments namely boreal forest, tundra and cropland/woodland. Regarding both spatial and temporal extension, the deep CNN performs equally to the shallow CNN or even better, but it is computationally more expensive. With regard to temporal extension, the two different CNNs perform almost equally. According to the experimental results, the best case scenario for spatial resolution enhancement of Landsat is the CNNs training and inference on the same spatial domain.

In [8] the 10 m RGB bands of S2 are super-resolved per factor 2 thus to 5 m. Images of 5 m from the RapidEye satellite, that were captured the same date and of almost the same spectral band, serve as a source for training the network to super-resolve S2 images. Manual and automatic validation of the images took place for avoiding dissimilar zones to be included in the training image pairs. The enhanced deep residual network technique has been utilized after applying modifications to it. Different learning strategies which rely on progressive data resizing are considered. Also, an ultra-dense generative adversarial net (GAN) named udGAN is presented in [14] for SR of remotely sensed images. In udGAN the internal layout of the residual block is reformed into a 2D matrix topology. Improved SR performance is achieved through rich connections that can adapt to the diverse image content. The adversarial learning strategy in combination with the information fusion due to the ultra-dense connections brings more photorealistic results than existing CNN and GAN based SR techniques. In [5] three different types of deep CNNs are developed and applied for SR. The first basic network is called SRDCN and relies on hierarchical architecture for learning the mapping from the LR image to the HR image. The other two networks, named DSRDCN and ESRDCN, are extensions of the SRDCN and are based on residual learning and multi scale, respectively. The proposed networks predominate over custom sparse representation techniques on SR of both multispectral and hyperspectral image data. An improved super-resolution GAN named ISRGAN is presented in [7]. In comparison with SRGAN, the ISRGAN demonstrates greater training stability and better generalization ability across locations and sensors. The experimental data come from two different sensors, namely the Landsat 8 OLI and the Chinese GF1, and cover two different locations in China. Land use classification and ground-object extraction were the SR application cases. Moreover, in [15] a novel technique for SR of S2 images to 2.5 m is proposed. The 10 m and 20 m S2 bands are fused with images of greater spatial resolution from the PlanetScope constellation. Residual CNNs are utilized to simultaneously achieve radiometric normalization and SR. Photointerpretation as well quantitative measures prove that the technique is both accurate and robust.

Monitoring construction sites from space using commercial HR imagery enables the sites to be tracked remotely instead of physically traveling to a site thus saving valuable resources. In addition, the ability to explore areas remotely means you can record the construction site progression at anytime and anywhere in the world. On the other hand, the freely available satellite imagery such as S2 holds a medium resolution (10 m and 20 m for certain bands) which is not detailed enough for applications such as construction sites progress tracking and monitoring. In this work, we aim to increase the spatial resolution of S2 images to the resolution of SPOT-7 satellite imagery (2.5 m) using SR techniques. Specifically, S2 images are SR reconstructed by means of deep-learning techniques. During experiments, the VDSR network [16] is trained with matching pairs of S2 and SPOT-7 images where 2.5 m is the target resolution. The obtained network after training is called SPOT7-VDSR and can perform real prediction by super-resolving S2 images of initial spatial resolution 10 m to the target resolution 2.5 m. Additionally, the VDSR technique and bicubic interpolation are applied for SR of the S2 images. Comparisons of the results from the different techniques are carried out on the area of study which is Karditsa, Greece. The present methodology of super-resolving S2 images is novel in the literature of satellite imaging.

This paper is organized into four sections. In Sect. 2, the procedures and settings of the machine learning (ML) frameworks which are utilized are described. The experimental results are given in Sect. 3 while the conclusions are drawn in Sect. 4.

2   Machine Learning Frameworks for Super-Resolution: Data, Procedures and Settings

The S2 and SPOT-7 data cover the area of Karditsa, Greece on August 2, 2019. Figure 1(a) depicts the SPOT-7 image with spatial resolution 2.5 m and Fig. 1(b) shows the lower

Table 1. Parameter values per training stage

Training stage	Parameter value			
	Epochs number	Learning rate	Last layer learn rate factor	Gradient threshold
1st	3	0.01	20	0.0001
2nd	1	0.001	20	0.0001
3rd	1	0.001	10	0.0001
4th	1	0.1	3	0.0001
5th	2	0.1	1	0.04

resolution S2 image at 10 m. Both above satellite images have resulted from the corresponding original satellite images after radiometric preprocessing. The particular preprocessing is necessary before the data being involved in the ML tasks, so that to avoid inaccurate results caused by radiometric inconsistencies between the different satellite images.

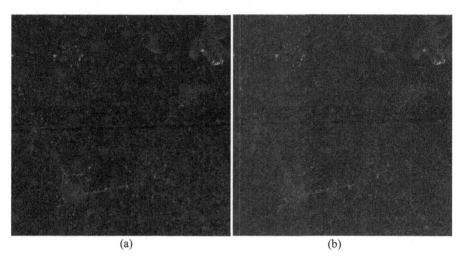

(a)   (b)

Fig. 1. The study area of Karditsa, Greece on August 2, 2019 (a) SPOT-7 image at 2.5 m. (b) Sentinel-2 image at 10 m.

The VDSR network has already been trained on natural images [16]. In fact, multiscale training per factors 2, 3 and 4 has taken place in [16]. For the present work, the VDSR network is re-trained with matching pairs of S2 and SPOT-7 images for single scale SR per factor 4. S2 images of 10m are upsampled via bicubic interpolation to 2.5 m. These images enter the VDSR net. As far as the VDSR net output is concerned, the residual image (SPOT-7 at 2.5 m)-(upsampled S2 at 2.5 m) is presented to it. The re-training input-output pairs consist of spatially or geometrically co-registered S2 and SPOT-7 images. Additionally, the SPOT-7 images have been radiometrically matched to the S2 images. The resulting re-trained VDSR network is named SPOT7-VDSR. The net re-training has been carried out throughout 8 epochs with 31,196 training observations and 3,124 validation observations. The training root mean square error (MSE) equals 369 and the validation root MSE is 362, where the image value range is 0-255. The training parameter values are given in Table 1. Stochastic gradient descent with momentum, equal to 0.9, is the solver during training the network. The mini-batch used for each training iteration has the value 64. The MSE estimator is utilized in the regression layer of the network during re-training.

3   Experimental Results

During experimentation, the SPOT7-VDSR network is asked to increase the resolution of S2 images that are completely unknown to the net, thus images which belong neither to the training set nor to the validation set. Single scale prediction experiments are carried out, namely prediction per factor 4. The MSE estimator is utilized in the regression layer of the network during prediction. The S2 images of 10 m spatial resolution are converted to images of 2.5 m spatial resolution.

The SPOT7-VDSR results are compared with those of the VDSR and of bicubic interpolation, visually and numerically via structural similarity index (SSIM) and peak signal to noise ratio (PSNR). Tests have been carried out with twenty scenes. Some of the image results are presented in Figs. 2, 3, 4, 5, 6, 7 and 8 and all the numerical comparisons are given in Table 2. In Fig. 2, 3, 4, 5, 6, 7 and 8 (a) the result of bicubic interpolation having been applied on the initial S2 image is depicted. The VDSR net output is shown in Fig. 2, 3, 4, 5, 6, 7 and 8 (b) while the SPOT7-VDSR net result is depicted in Fig. 2, 3, 4, 5, 6, 7 and 8 (c). Numerical comparisons of the upsampled S2 images at 2.5 m with the corresponding original SPOT-7 images 2.5 m are carried out. The latter images are depicted in Fig. 2, 3, 4, 5, 6, 7 and 8 (d). The SPOT7-VDSR network outperforms both bicubic interpolation and VDSR network, as mandated by visual inspection and numerical results in the SR scale per factor 4. Actually, as shown in Table 2 for "scene 1721", the proposed net SPOT7-VDSR outperforms the VDSR net up to 8.24 decibel in PSNR and bicubic interpolation up to 16.9% in SSIM. In our work the numerical measures SSIM and PSNR have been calculated on the Luminance component of the images in the Ycbcr color space, as soon as the original SPOT-7 images have been spatially co-registered with the upsampled S2 images. Radiometrical matching of SPOT-7 to S2 Luminance images has also been applied. Ringing effects can be observed on the image results of the VDSR net. This is an expected characteristic of VDSR performance which has been already experimentally observed and concluded by the work in [17].

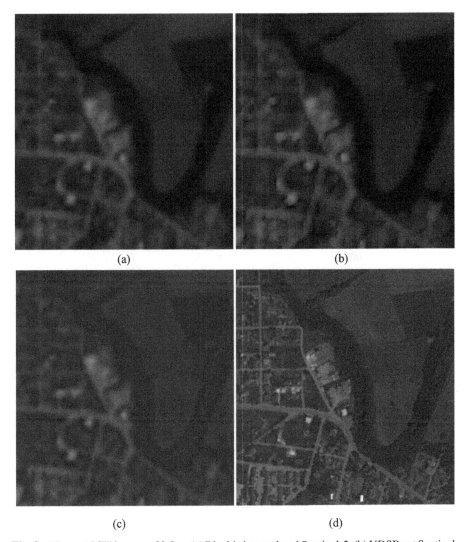

(a)

(b)

(c)

(d)

Fig. 2. "Scene 1567" images of 2.5 m. (a) Bicubic interpolated Sentinel-2. (b) VDSR net Sentinel-2. (c) SPOT7-VDSR net Sentinel-2. (d) SPOT7.

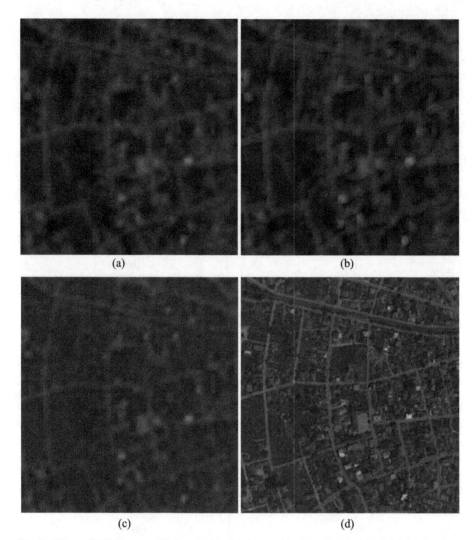

(a)   (b)

(c)   (d)

Fig. 3. "Scene 1568" images of 2.5 m. (a) Bicubic interpolated Sentinel-2. (b) VDSR net Sentinel-2. (c) SPOT7-VDSR net Sentinel-2. (d) SPOT7.

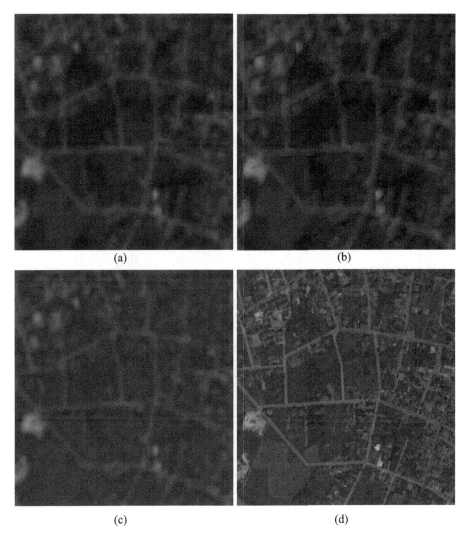

(a)

(b)

(c)

(d)

Fig. 4. "Scene 1569" images of 2.5 m. (a) Bicubic interpolated Sentinel-2. (b) VDSR net Sentinel-2. (c) SPOT7-VDSR net Sentinel-2. (d) SPOT7.

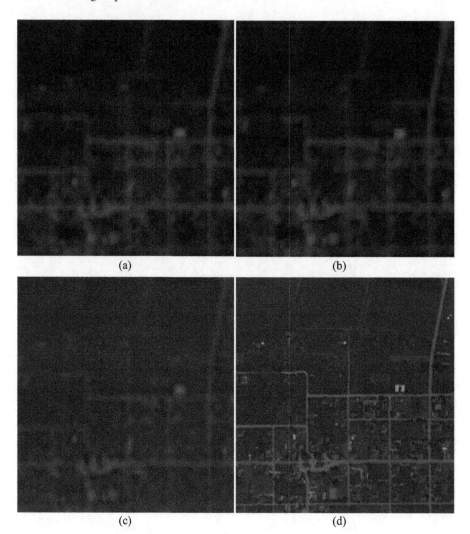

(a)   (b)

(c)   (d)

Fig. 5. "Scene 1660" images of 2.5 m. (a) Bicubic interpolated Sentinel-2. (b) VDSR net Sentinel-2. (c) SPOT7-VDSR net Sentinel-2. (d) SPOT7.

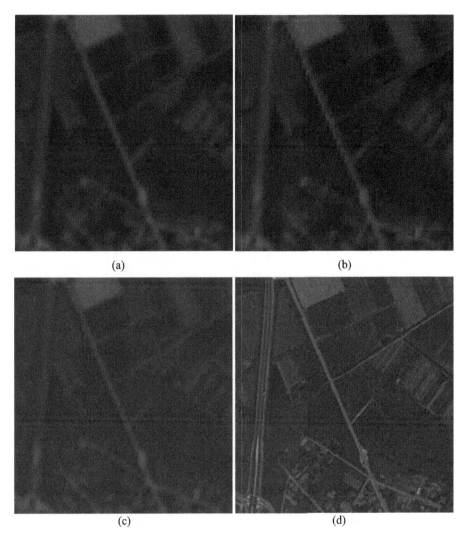

(a)   (b)

(c)   (d)

Fig. 6. "Scene 1868" images of 2.5 m. (a) Bicubic interpolated Sentinel-2. (b) VDSR net Sentinel-2. (c) SPOT7-VDSR net Sentinel-2. (d) SPOT7.

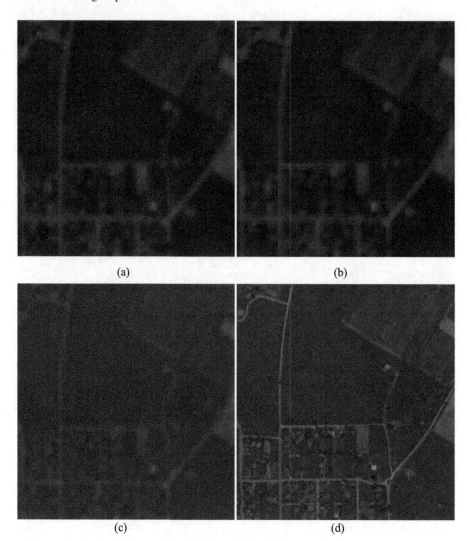

(a)   (b)

(c)   (d)

Fig. 7. "Scene 1883" images of 2.5 m. (a) Bicubic interpolated Sentinel-2. (b) VDSR net Sentinel-2. (c) SPOT7-VDSR net Sentinel-2. (d) SPOT7.

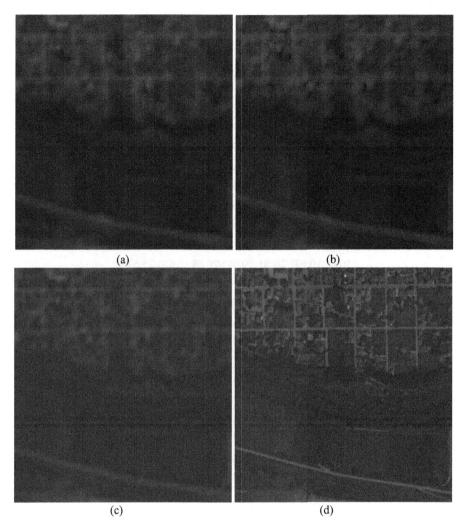

(a)   (b)

(c)   (d)

Fig. 8. "Scene 1721" images of 2.5 m. (a) Bicubic interpolated Sentinel-2. (b) VDSR net Sentinel-2. (c) SPOT7-VDSR net Sentinel-2. (d) SPOT7.

Table 2. Numerical Comparisons (SSIM/PSNR(decibel)) on all tested scenes

Scene	Image origin		
	Bicubic interpolation	VDSR	SPOT7-VDSR
1567	0.812/26.26	0.786/26.26	0.847/30.71
1568	0.761/27.27	0.729/27.44	0.784/31.17
1569	0.680/22.76	0.653/23.04	0.712/26.74
1601	0.464/13.27	0.468/13.40	0.647/15.40
1619	0.632/19.89	0.610/20.23	0.700/22.55
1620	0.711/22.57	0.686/22.90	0.809/27.79
1621	0.701/23.43	0.679/23.75	0.751/26.92
1640	0.775/21.34	0.772/21.66	0.896/26.74
1653	0.692/20.30	0.685/20.58	0.834/25.59
1654	0.767/21.10	0.769/21.39	0.923/27.97
1660	0.800/25.61	0.780/25.91	0.845/32.98
1672	0.696/18.67	0.693/18.93	0.821/22.11
1673	0.723/20.39	0.715/20.69	0.863/25.67
1674	0.776/20.55	0.773/20.89	0.866/24.07
1675	0.618/17.35	0.611/17.59	0.725/19.70
1684	0.794/21.63	0.785/22.02	0.858/24.98
1709	0.679/19.59	0.673/19.86	0.828/24.39
1721	0.740/22.06	0.733/22.32	0.909/30.56
1868	0.875/27.12	0.858/27.45	0.913/33.39
1883	0.879/27.46	0.859/27.86	0.913/34.17

4   Conclusions

In this work a novel study of super-resolving Sentinel-2 images is presented. Deep learning techniques are utilized to execute the SR reconstruction experiments. The multiscale VDSR network is re-trained with matching pairs of Sentinel-2 and SPOT-7 images at 2.5 m and becomes SPOT7-VDSR network. The latter net gains the ability to increase the resolution of Sentinel-2 images from 10 m to 2.5 m. The Sentinel-2 images during prediction are completely unknown to the net. The resulting images are validated against the corresponding original SPOT-7 images. The SPOT7-VDSR net proves superior over both the VDSR net and bicubic interpolation. The entire experimentation procedure which is presented can be very useful in cases where only Sentinel-2 images are available and not the corresponding SPOT-7 higher-resolution ones. Applications such as construction sites progress tracking and monitoring could benefit from this study. For future work, interesting tests could be carried out with image content loss or texture loss as network loss function, since in the current study only pixel loss has been considered.

Acknowledgment. We would like to thank Terra Spatium SA and AIRBUS for providing us with the SPOT-7 data that have been utilized during the present study.

References

1. Yadegari, M., Shamshiri, R.R., Mohamed Shariff, A.R., Balasundram, S.K., Mahns, B.: Using SPOT-7 for nitrogen fertilizer management in oil palm. Agriculture **10**, 1–17 (2020). https://doi.org/10.3390/agriculture10040133
2. Bektas Balcik, F., Karakacan Kuzucu, A.: Determination of land cover/land use using SPOT 7 data with supervised classification methods. In: International Archives of the Photogrammetry, Remote Sensing and Spatial Information Sciences, Copernicus Publications, Turkey, pp. 143–146 (2016). https://doi.org/10.5194/isprs-archives-xlii-2-w1-143-2016
3. Shermeyer, J., Van Etten, A.: The effects of super-resolution on object detection performance in satellite imagery. In: IEEE/CVF Conference on Computer Vision and Pattern Recognition Workshops, USA, pp. 1434–1441. IEEE (2019). https://doi.org/10.1109/cvprw.2019.00184
4. Lanaras, C., Bioucas-Dias, J., Galliani, S., Baltsavias, E., Schindler, K.: Super-resolution of Sentinel-2 images: learning a globally applicable deep neural network. ISPRS J. PHOTOGRAMM **146**, 305–319 (2018). https://doi.org/10.1016/j.isprsjprs.2018.09.018
5. Ran, Q., Xu, X., Zhao, S., Li, W., Du, Q.: Remote sensing images super-resolution with deep convolution networks. Multimed. Tools Appl. **79**, 8985–9001 (2020). https://doi.org/10.1007/s11042-018-7091-1
6. Bratsolis, E., Panagiotopoulou, A., Stefouli, M., Charou, E., Madamopoulos, N., Perantonis, S.: Comparison of optimized mathematical methods in the improvement of raster data and map display resolution of Sentinel-2 images, In: 25th IEEE International Conference on Image Processing, Greece, pp. 2521–2525. IEEE (2018). https://doi.org/10.1109/icip.2018.8451729
7. Xiong, Y., et al.: Improved SRGAN for remote sensing image super-resolution across locations and sensors. Remote Sens. **12**, 1–21 (2020). https://doi.org/10.3390/rs12081263
8. Galar, M., Sesma, R., Ayala, C., Aranda, C.: Super-resolution for Sentinel-2 images. In: International Archives of the Photogrammetry, Remote Sensing and Spatial Information Sciences, Copernicus Publications, Germany, pp. 95–102 (2019). https://doi.org/10.5194/isprs-archives-xlii-2-w16-95-2019
9. Zioga, E., et al.: Spatial resolution enhancement of remote sensing mine images using deep learning techniques. https://arxiv.org/abs/2007.08791 (2020)
10. Xiang Zhu, X., et al.: Deep learning in remote sensing: a comprehensive review and list of resources. IEEE Trans. Geosci. Remote Sens. **5**, 8–36 (2017). https://doi.org/10.1109/mgrs.2017.2762307
11. Gargiulo, M., Mazza, A., Gaetano, R., Ruello, G., Scarpa, G.: A CNN-based fusion method for super-resolution of Sentinel-2 data. In: IEEE International Geoscience and Remote Sensing Symposium, Spain, pp. 4713–4716. IEEE (2018). https://doi.org/10.1109/igarss.2018.8518447
12. Tuna, C., Unal, G., Sertel, E.: Single-frame super resolution of remote-sensing images by convolutional neural networks. Int. J. Remote Sens. **39**, 2463–2479 (2018). https://doi.org/10.1080/01431161.2018.1425561
13. Pouliot, D., Latifovic, R., Pasher, J., Duffe, J.: Landsat super-resolution enhancement using convolution neural networks and Sentinel-2 for training. Remote Sens. **10**, 1–18 (2018). https://doi.org/10.3390/rs10030394

14. Wang, Z., Jiang, K., Yi, P., Han, Z., He, Z.: Ultra-dense GAN for satellite imagery super-resolution. Neurocomputing **398**, 328–337 (2020). https://doi.org/10.1016/j.neucom.2019.03.106

15. Latte, N., Lejeune, P.: PlanetScope radiometric normalization and Sentinel-2 super-resolution (2.5 m): a straightforward spectral-spatial fusion of multi-satellite multi-sensor images using residual convolutional neural network. Remote Sens. **12**, 1–19 (2020). https://doi.org/10.3390/rs12152366

16. Kim, J., Lee, J.K., Lee, K.M.: Accurate image superresolution using very deep convolutional networks. In: Proceedings of 2016 IEEE Conference on Computer Vision and Pattern Recognition, USA, pp. 1646–1654. IEEE (2016). https://doi.org/10.1109/cvpr.2016.182

17. Vint, D., Caterina, G.D., Soraghan, J.J., Lamb, R.A., Humphreys, D.: Evaluation of performance of VDSR super resolution on real and synthetic images. In: Sensor Signal Processing for Defence Conference, United Kingdom, pp. 1–5. IEEE (2019). https://doi.org/10.1109/sspd.2019.8751651

Salient Object Detection with Pretrained Deeplab and k-Means: Application to UAV-Captured Building Imagery

Victor Megir[1], Giorgos Sfikas[1(✉)], Athanasios Mekras[2], Christophoros Nikou[1], Dimosthenis Ioannidis[2], and Dimitrios Tzovaras[2]

[1] Department of Computer Science and Engineering, University of Ioannina, Ioannina, Greece
{megir,sfikas,cnikou}@uoi.gr
[2] Information Technologies Institute, CERTH, 57001 Thessaloniki, Greece
{athmekras,djoannid,Dimitrios.Tzovaras}@iti.gr

Abstract. We present a simple technique that can convert a pretrained segmentation neural network to a salient object detector. We show that the pretrained network can be agnostic to the semantic class of the object of interest, and no further training is required. Experiments were run on UAV-captured aerial imagery of the "smart home" structure located in the premises of the CERTH research center. Further experiments were also run on natural scenes. Our tests validate the usefulness of the proposed technique.

Keywords: Deep features · Deeplab · Salient object detection · Structure detection

1 Introduction

Computer vision and pattern recognition today play a role of steadily increasing importance in various fields of the industry. Constructions, structure surveillance, agricultural productivity applications, autonomous driving are only a few of the fields that benefit from new pattern recognition technology advances. For example, as automotive industry is progressing to fully autonomous vehicle, computer vision is a tool for the development of many intelligent systems and important safety measures. Lane departure warning and lane keeping assistance are two technologies that can identify vehicles entering the current lane and trigger warnings for the driver and activate automatic braking systems to avoid a collision. Similar systems can be used to prevent accidents by detecting and monitoring pedestrians, traffic lights and signs [17]. Another area that takes advantage of those technologies is the agriculture and food industry. Computer vision inspection systems can accelerate the increase in agricultural productivity. Pattern recognition can be applied to detect crop diseases, thus allowing timely intervention. Vision algorithms are being used to classify the healthy food from defective, resulting in faster and more reliable harvest [19].

© Springer Nature Switzerland AG 2021
A. Del Bimbo et al. (Eds.): ICPR 2020 Workshops, LNCS 12667, pp. 477–489, 2021.
https://doi.org/10.1007/978-3-030-68787-8_35

Fig. 1. Sample test images of the *CERTH* dataset.

Applications in construction benefit ever-increasingly by solutions provided by computer vision and pattern recognition. Classification systems can assess video data from construction sites in real-time, preventing defects and mistakes in this industry that can be crucial for both saving resources and human lives. Cameras can track the arrival of materials on a site and compare them to a project schedule. This process can improving efficiency, quality and safety [18]. Remote cameras and unmanned aerial vehicles (UAVs) can offer non-contact solutions to civil infrastructure condition assessment. Aerial survey and inspection of buildings for the purpose of gathering useful information for their assets, such as solar panels or air condition units, can provide a more comprehensive picture of their energy performance. Analyzing those data, can contribute to the development of a framework for energy loss evaluation and building energy efficiency improvement [10]. Accurate detection of structures of interest can help determine properties that are related to auxiliary sensors, like thermographic cameras [8].

Fig. 2. Sample test images of the *Natural* dataset.

With this work we propose a method for salient object detection [2], tested to a setting where the object of interest is a structure. The base component of the method is a convolutional neural network that, pretrained for the task of semantic segmentation. We have used the popular Deeplab network [3], although in principle any off-the-shelf convolution segmentation network could be used in its place. Intermediate convolutional layer results, referred to in the literature as deep features [13] are used as powerful, high-level features. Deep features are in turn clustered, and the centermost cluster is selected as the salient object segment. This technique is shown to be succesfully applied where the object of interest is a building, as well as for a set of natural image scenes. Importantly, no extra training is required for the off-the-shelf base network. Furthermore, we show that our method works even when the base network is competely agnostic to the semantic class of the object of interest.

The paper is structured as follows. In Sect. 2, we briefly review related work. Semantic segmentation using a state-of-the-art neural network is discussed in Sect. 3, and in Sect. 4 we discuss the concept of deep features and how to use them for salient object segmentation. Experimental results, which compare the discussed segmentation methods, are presented in Sect. 5, and close the paper with our conclusions in Sect. 6.

Fig. 3. Deep feature visualizations on images from the CERTH dataset. From left to right column: original image, result with PASCAL VOC20 pretrained weights, result with ADE20k pretrained weights. (Color figure online)

2   Related Work

The idea of using deep features as powerful image cues has been previously employed in a diverse range of computer vision tasks. The simplest variant of deep features is related to creating a holistic image descriptor by computing the activations of one of the network fully connected layers, typically situated on the head of convolutional networks [1]. Convolutional layers have also been used in this regard, creating pixel-level cues out of convolutional layer pointwise activations. This concept has been further extended to concatenating activations of a set of convolutional layers, after being resized and interpolated to a common height and width if required. This type of deep features has been referred to as hypercolumns [9,12,16]. These local cues can then be optionally encoded, with operations as simple as sum pooling leading to powerful image descriptors [16].

Variants of the idea of using deep features with clustering have been previously used as a data processing pipeline component to the end of producing Demand Response potential estimates [8,15]. In [8], deep features are extracted from pretrained Deeplab, and used to create a binarization mask with an infrared input. This idea is demonstrated on a set of synthetic infrared images, created on the basis of infrared image statistics. In [15], the same concept is validated on aligned pairs of colour and real infrared images, captured using a dual camera mounted on a UAV. In both works, in contrast to the present work, two important issues are not covered, which are: a) what is the role and effect of the choice of the dataset used to create the pretrained model weights? b) if the pretrained model has seen the object class of interest during training, how does the proposed deeplab-based technique fare in comparison to using Deeplab output? With the current work, we discuss and attempt to answer these issues.

3   Semantic Segmentation with Deeplab

Semantic segmentation as a task combines two long-standing problems in computer vision, that of image segmentation and image classification. In particular, it is defined as a simultaneous segmentation of the image and classification of each pixel to a semantic category. DeepLab is a state-of-the-art semantic segmentation model designed and open-sourced by Google. The original network components [3], employed and popularized "atrous" convolutional and deconvolutional layers, which act by inserting holes between nonzero filter taps. The final result was refined using a conditional random field model. In this work, we use one of the latest reiterations of the Deeplab, namely Deeplab v3+ [4]. This version of Deeplab uses atrous convolution and an encoder-decoder architecture, plus a refined decoder module to detect object boundaries. The output layer is topped by a pointwise softmax layer, giving class predictions for each pixel.

4   Segmentation Using Deep Features

Deep features are defined as features that are computed as the result of intermediate neural network layers, when fed with the test input on which we need

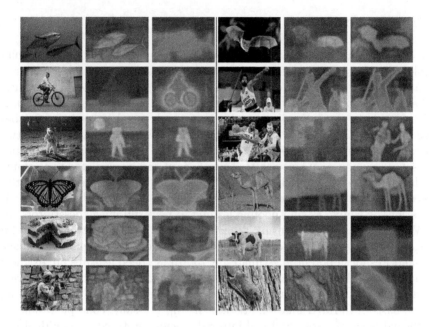

Fig. 4. Deep feature visualizations on images from the Natural dataset. From left to right column: original image, result with PASCAL VOC20 pretrained weights, result with ADE20k pretrained weights. (Color figure online)

to compute features [7,11–13]. In other words, instead of using a feed-forward pass to compute the output of a neural network, which would of course require computation of all intermediate layers, we instead aim to compute the activation or pre-activation of a layer that stands between the input layer and between the network output. Powerful features can be obtained in this manner, after having ensured that the network has been trained on a specific task. In the context of image processing, convolutional neural networks (CNNs) are the norm when neural net-based methods are considered. CNNs comprise three main type of layers that we are interested in with respect to computing deep features: convolutional layers, deconvolutional layers, and dense or fully-connected layers. Dense layers feature a standard number of neurons, sharing no specific topology. On the contrary, convolutional and deconvolutional layers result in feature maps that consist of neurons arranged in an image-like 2D topology. Deep features are relevant to either dense or convolutional/deconvolutional layers, with dense layers leading to holistic descriptors and convolutional/deconvolutional layers leading to localized cues. This stems from the aforementioned topological properties of the neuron set associated with each type of layer. More formally, we can extract deep features from a dense layer in the form of a vector $x \in \Re^D$, where D is the number of layer neurons. On the other hand, deep features from a convolutional or deconvolutional layer come in the form $I \in \Re^{H \times W \times C}$, where H and W are the height and width of the associated feature map, and C is the number of channels resulting from the number of convolutional/deconvolutional layer depth. In other words, we obtain a vector $x \in \Re^C$ for each point $(i,j) \in [1,H] \times [1,W]$ in the feature map I. Note that these local cues can be combined to create a holistic feature using an encoding method [16].

What is of note is the type of deep features obtained as a function of the "distance" of the associated layer from the input and the output layers. Layers that are close to the input tend to produce deep features that are more generic and have little dependence on the training set with the which the network has been trained with. On the contrary, as our choice of layer moves toward the output, features become more and more training set-specific. It is frequently observed that the first convolutional layers after training completes typically correspond to low-level filters such as edge and blob detectors; subsequent layers encode more complex filters such as texture detectors; finally, layers that are situated close to the output act in effect as filters that produce cues with highly semantic content. The content of these features tends to be a close function of the training set characteristics, with filters that can be interpreted as e.g. object part detectors.

In Figs. 3 and 4 we show visualizations of deep features on sets of images (images of a structure, natural scenes). These visualizations were created by applying Principal Component Analysis (PCA) on points $x \in \Re^C$ obtained as deep features by a convolutional feature map. PCA is set to reduce dimension to 3, and each principal component is set to correspond to one of the RGB channels. Two different pretrainings are considered (PASCAL VOC20, ADE20k sets), with both using the same layer to obtain cues ($decoder/decoder\_conv1\_pointwise/Relu : 0$). (Pseudo-)color in these visualizations is perhaps difficult to interpret in absolute terms; however, what is highly interpretable is comparing pseudocolors of one image are to the other. Indeed, areas with similar pseudocolor are perceived by the network also to be similar in content. This rule also applies vice versa, with dissimilar color denoting objects/content that is also dissimilar.

In this work, we use Deeplab after assuming that it has already been trained on a specific set comprising K semantic classes. We aim to exploit the fact that, while the Deeplab output is a point-wise softmax that produces a K-size probability vector, deep features from the same model are more flexible; flexibility here is to be understood in the sense that deep features are not constrained to be tied to one or more of K semantic classes. Our strategy is first to cluster (convolutional) deep features into a set of n_s segments. We use k-means++ as our clustering method, after which we choose the cluster that is situated the most towards the center of the image as the salient object [15]. If the size of the feature map is different to that of the input, we resize the former to match the dimensions of the latter. The rest of the pixels are marked as background.

5 Experiments

Our experiments consist of salient object detection trials, executed on a number of different setups. The setup of the trials is chosen so as to check whether our

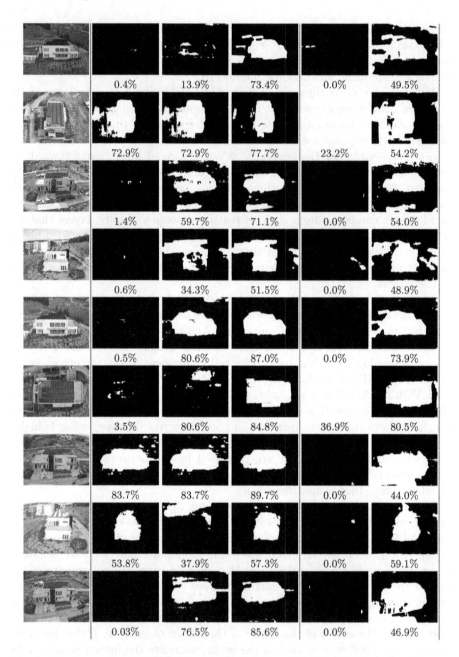

Fig. 5. Results on the *CERTH* dataset. From left to right, in each row the following images are shown: original image, ADE20k result by taking the centermost segment, ADE20k result by taking the estimated building class, ADE20k result by using the proposed method, PASCAL VOC20 result by taking the centermost segment, PASCAL VOC20 result by using the proposed method. Below each row IoU scores are also presented for the corresponding segmentation estimates.

main premise holds under a variability of experimental parameters, which is whether it is beneficial to use Deeplab "as-is", or use the proposed Deeplab deep feature-based technique.

We have compared standard Deeplab segmentation against the proposed technique on two datasets. The first dataset, which we refer to as *CERTH* in this paper, is composed of 18 images of the "smart home" building, found in the premises of the CERTH-ITI institute in Thessaloniki, Greece. All images depict the same structure, captured using a camera mounted on a DJI Unmanned Aerial Vehicle. The second dataset, which we refer to as *Natural*, is made up of 34 images that depict a variety of objects in various different scenes and layouts. We use the *CERTH* dataset as proof-of-concept that our premise is applicable in the context of structure segmentation, while the *Natural* dataset is used to test the method on a different, heterogeneous dataset. Samples of the two datasets can be seen in Fig. 1 and Fig. 2 respectively. All images have been manually annotated with corresponding pixel-level binary masks. In this manner, a ground-truth binarization to 'salient object' and 'background/rest' classes was available for evaluation of salient object segmentation.

Two variants of Deeplab were used, with the difference being in the dataset on which the network was trained at each time. In all cases the Xception architecture was used as the Deeplab backbone [5], employing depthwise separable convolutions. The two training sets used were the PASCAL-VOC20 dataset [6] the ADE20k datasets [21]. These datasets contain a total of 20 and 150 classes (plus background). What is important for our experiments here is that the PASCAL VOC20 dataset does not have a structure or building class, while ADE20k does. This means that a version of Deeplab (or any similar convolutional semantic segmentation network) that is trained on PASCAL VOC20 cannot recognize image areas that correspond to a building or structure correctly.

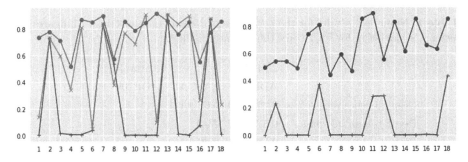

Fig. 6. Plots for results on *CERTH*, using ADE20k (left) and PASCAL VOC20 pretrained models (right). Horizontal axis corresponds to image id (1 to 18), vertical axis corresponds to IoU result (higher is better). Depicted curves are the proposed technique (green curve with circle markers), Deeplab output for ADE20k building class (orange curve with 'x' markers), Deeplab output for the "centermost" class (blue curve with '+' markers) (Color figure online).

The proposed method was compared against simply using the output of Deeplab. In all our experiments, for both pretrained models considered we use the *decoder/decoder_conv1_pointwise/Relu* : 0. We have chosen this layer as it is situated close to the output, therefore it is highly semantically "charged". The Intersection over Union (IoU) metric was used to evaluate each segmentation.

Visual and numerical results for trials over the *CERTH* dataset can be observed in Fig. 5. Two plots comparing results over all *CERTH* dataset considered can be examined in Fig. 6. One observation that is notable is that the proposed technique outperforms vanilla Deeplab, even when the dataset used to create the pretrained model weight is ADE20k, which *does* contain a structure class (this is clearer in the reported statistics of Table 1). As PASCAL VOC20, which does not contain a structure class could not be directly compared in this manner, we have compared our technique against the Deeplab output by considering the Deeplab cluster that is situated the most near the center (this is denoted in Table 1 as "Deeplab centermost class"). Again, the proposed technique outperformed vanilla Deeplab. Commenting on the results between the pretrained model weights that correspond to the two considered datasets, ADE20k fares better than PASCAL VOC20. This is perhaps unsurprising, as ADE20k is considerably larger and contains more semantic classes than PASCAL VOC20.

We have run supplementary trials on the *Natural* dataset, of which visual and numerical results can be examined in Fig. 7. Note that not all classes were detectable by the softmax output when used with PASCAL; (the available classes were 'aeroplane', 'bicycle', 'bird', 'boat', 'bottle', 'bus', 'car', 'cat', 'chair', 'cow', 'diningtable', 'dog', 'horse', 'motorbike', 'person', 'pottedplant', 'sheep', 'sofa', 'train', 'tv', plus background). Despite this fact however, our method could correctly detect object classes that would otherwise be uncategorizable by this version of the Deeplab model. Finally, statistics over results the *CERTH* and *Natural* datasets can be examined in Table 1.

Table 1. Numerical results for the *CERTH* and *Natural* dataset trials. All figures are mean ± st.deviation for IoU scores (higher mean is better).

	CERTH		Natural	
	ADE20k	PASCAL	ADE20k	PASCAL
Deeplab centermost class	0.22 ± 0.4	0.09 ± 0.1	–	–
Deeplab building class	0.57 ± 0.3	*N/A*	–	–
Proposed method	0.78 ± 0.1	0.66 ± 0.2	–	0.70 ± 0.2

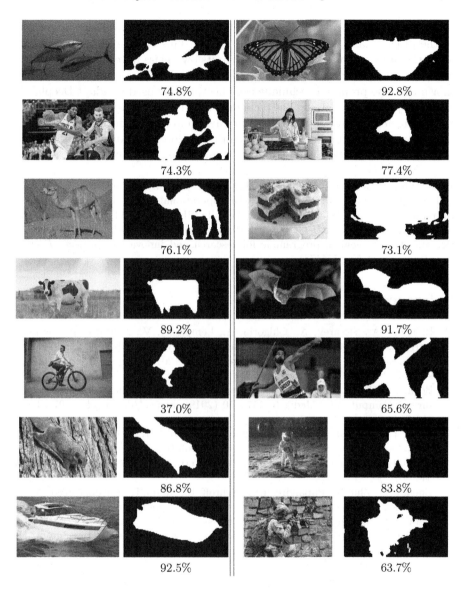

Fig. 7. Results on the *Natural* dataset. From left to right, in each row the following images are shown: original image, PASCAL VOC20 result, IoU score for the result of the current row. Note that objects that would otherwise be undetectable as Deeplab outputs (i.e. softmax classes) are correctly detected (see text for details).

6   Conclusion

We have discussed a simple technique in order to perform salient object segmentation, that is based on a pretrained semantic segmentation network. What we believe that is important here, is that the pretrained network can be agnostic to the object class that we require to detect. This can be an advantage also when the object of interest is an outlier in its own class in terms of appearance, hence the network will normally have a hard time detecting it correctly. We have shown that the proposed technique can effectively be used to adapt Deeplab for salient object segmentation. The technique was tested succesfully on our dataset containing aerial photography of a structure of interest. As future work, we plan to test our method more extensively and to explore and adapt more advanced segmentation techniques (e.g. [14,20]) to apply over deep features.

Acknowledgements. This research has been partially co-financed by the EU and Greek national funds through the Operational Program Competitiveness, Entrepreneurship and Innovation, under the call OPEN INNOVATION IN CULTURE, project *Bessarion* (T6YBΠ-00214). It has also been partially co-financed by the EU's Horizon 2020 framework programme for research and innovation, project *eDREAM* (grant agreement No. 774478).

References

1. Babenko, A., Slesarev, A., Chigorin, A., Lempitsky, V.: Neural codes for image retrieval. In: Fleet, D., Pajdla, T., Schiele, B., Tuytelaars, T. (eds.) ECCV 2014. LNCS, vol. 8689, pp. 584–599. Springer, Cham (2014). https://doi.org/10.1007/978-3-319-10590-1_38
2. Borji, A., Cheng, M.M., Hou, Q., Jiang, H., Li, J.: Salient object detection: a survey. Comput. Vis. Media **5**, 117–150 (2019). https://doi.org/10.1007/s41095-019-0149-9
3. Chen, L.C., Papandreou, G., Kokkinos, I., Murphy, K., Yuille, A.L.: DeepLab: semantic image segmentation with deep convolutional nets, atrous convolution, and fully connected CRFs. IEEE Trans. Pattern Anal. Mach. Intell. **40**(4), 834–848 (2017)
4. Chen, L.C., Zhu, Y., Papandreou, G., Schroff, F., Adam, H.: Encoder-decoder with atrous separable convolution for semantic image segmentation. In: Proceedings of the European Conference on Computer Vision (ECCV), pp. 801–818 (2018)
5. Chollet, F.: Xception: deep learning with depthwise separable convolutions. In: Proceedings of the IEEE Conference on Computer Vision and Pattern Recognition, pp. 1251–1258 (2017)
6. Everingham, M., Van Gool, L., Williams, C.K., Winn, J., Zisserman, A.: The pascal visual object classes (VOC) challenge. Int. J. Comput. Vis. **88**(2), 303–338 (2010). https://doi.org/10.1007/s11263-009-0275-4
7. Goodfellow, I., Bengio, Y., Courville, A., Bengio, Y.: Deep Learning, vol. 1. MIT Press, Cambridge (2016)
8. Sfikas, G., Noula, A., Patacas, J., Ioannidis, D., Tzovaras, D.: Building thermal output determination using visible spectrum and infrared inputs. In: International Conference on Energy and Sustainable Futures (ICESF) (2019)
9. Hariharan, B., Arbeláez, P., Girshick, R., Malik, J.: Hypercolumns for object segmentation and fine-grained localization. In: Proceedings of the IEEE Conference on Computer Vision and Pattern Recognition, pp. 447–456 (2015)

10. Kanellakis, C., Nikolakopoulos, G.: Survey on computer vision for UAVs: current developments and trends. J. Intell. Robot. Syst. **87**(1), 141–168 (2017). https://doi.org/10.1007/s10846-017-0483-z

11. Retsinas, G., Louloudis, G., Stamatopoulos, N., Sfikas, G., Gatos, B.: An alternative deep feature approach to line level keyword spotting. In: Proceedings of the IEEE Conference on Computer Vision and Pattern Recognition, pp. 12658–12666 (2019)

12. Retsinas, G., Sfikas, G., Gatos, B.: Transferable deep features for keyword spotting. In: Multidisciplinary Digital Publishing Institute Proceedings, vol. 2, p. 89 (2018)

13. Retsinas, G., Sfikas, G., Louloudis, G., Stamatopoulos, N., Gatos, B.: Compact deep descriptors for keyword spotting. In: 2018 16th International Conference on Frontiers in Handwriting Recognition (ICFHR), pp. 315–320. IEEE (2018)

14. Sfikas, G., Nikou, C., Galatsanos, N., Heinrich, C.: Majorization-minimization mixture model determination in image segmentation. In: CVPR 2011, pp. 2169–2176. IEEE (2011)

15. Sfikas, G., Patacas, J., Psarros, C., Noula, A., Ioannidis, D., Tzovaras, D.: A deep neural network-based method for the detection and accurate thermography statistics estimation of aerially surveyed structures. In: 19th International Conference on Construction Applications of Virtual Reality (2019)

16. Sfikas, G., Retsinas, G., Gatos, B.: Zoning aggregated hypercolumns for keyword spotting. In: 2016 15th International Conference on Frontiers in Handwriting Recognition (ICFHR), pp. 283–288. IEEE (2016)

17. Stein, G.P., Rushinek, E., Hayun, G., Shashua, A.: A computer vision system on a chip: a case study from the automotive domain. In: 2005 IEEE Computer Society Conference on Computer Vision and Pattern Recognition (CVPR 2005) - Workshops, pp. 130–130 (2005)

18. Tay, J., Shi, P., He, Y., Nath, T.: Application of computer vision in the construction industry. SSRN Electron. J. (2019). https://doi.org/10.2139/ssrn.3487394

19. Tian, H., Wang, T., Liu, Y., Qiao, X., Li, Y.: Computer vision technology in agricultural automation–a review. Inf. Process. Agric. **7**, 1–19 (2019). https://doi.org/10.1016/j.inpa.2019.09.006

20. Uziel, R., Ronen, M., Freifeld, O.: Bayesian adaptive superpixel segmentation. In: Proceedings of the IEEE International Conference on Computer Vision, pp. 8470–8479 (2019)

21. Zhou, B., Zhao, H., Puig, X., Fidler, S., Barriuso, A., Torralba, A.: Scene parsing through ADE20K dataset. In: Proceedings of the IEEE Conference on Computer Vision and Pattern Recognition, pp. 633–641 (2017)

Clutter Slices Approach for Identification-on-the-Fly of Indoor Spaces

Upinder Kaur, Praveen Abbaraju[(⊠)], Harrison McCarty,
and Richard M. Voyles

Purdue University, West Lafayette, IN 47907, USA
{kauru,pabbaraj,mccarth,rvoyles}@purdue.edu

Abstract. Construction spaces are constantly evolving, dynamic environments in need of continuous surveying, inspection, and assessment. Traditional manual inspection of such spaces proves to be an arduous and time-consuming activity. Automation using robotic agents can be an effective solution. Robots, with perception capabilities can autonomously classify and survey indoor construction spaces. In this paper, we present a novel identification-on-the-fly approach for coarse classification of indoor spaces using the unique signature of clutter. Using the context granted by clutter, we recognize common indoor spaces such as corridors, staircases, shared spaces, and restrooms. The proposed clutter slices pipeline achieves a maximum accuracy of 93.6% on the presented clutter slices dataset. This sensor independent approach can be generalized to various domains to equip intelligent autonomous agents in better perceiving their environment.

Keywords: Mobile robots · Identification-on-the-fly · Clutter slices

1 Introduction

Large-scale construction spaces need periodic surveying, inspection, and renovation [3]. Continuous assessment helps to identify the completion status as well as localize problems which may arise [1]. Traditionally, this requires a well-coordinated surveillance activity which consumes enormous man-hours, even resulting in delays and overheads. Further, the inherent complexity of such spaces, in terms of design, inter-connectivity, and scale complicate this already arduous undertaking. Automation of processes in such activities has the potential to greatly reduce the effort required and boost overall productivity, at the same time reducing overhead costs and delays. This need for process automation in the complex and fast-paced world of construction calls for innovation at all levels.

Inspection and surveying of outdoor large-scale construction activities now utilizes satellite imagery and Global Positioning Systems (GPS) based localization [5,15]. While these methods are robust and cost effective solutions for

---

U. Kaur and P. Abbaraju—Equal contribution.

© Springer Nature Switzerland AG 2021
A. Del Bimbo et al. (Eds.): ICPR 2020 Workshops, LNCS 12667, pp. 490–499, 2021.
https://doi.org/10.1007/978-3-030-68787-8_36

outdoor spaces, they prove to be in-effective for indoor spaces. Moreover, indoor GPS-based navigation is not effective for multi-level structures and the signal in itself becomes unreliable [5]. Alternative solutions including WiFi signals and quantum sensors require expensive equipment for implementation [4]. Further, these limitations of expenses, time, and resources for efficient inspection and surveillance is withholding the extensive application of Building Information Modelling (BIM) in construction activities [1,10]. Robotic technologies, such as mobile robots, rovers, and aerial manipulators, are proving to be an efficient automation solution for construction activities [2]. Mobile robots, such as aerial manipulators (UAV) [7] and ground-based manipulators (wheeled and legged) [12] are a cost-effective solution for real-time large scale inspections due to their robust and reliable performance.

Mobile robots with capabilities of perception are proving to be a paradigm shifting technology in inspection and surveillance. Perception sensors such as LiDARs (2D and 3D), stereo cameras, RGB-D cameras, ultrasonic and infrared proximity sensors have been extensively used in robot vision to identify the surrounding of a robot and its subsequent localization [9,14]. This is similar to human perceiving their surroundings through multiple modal sensing. For example, humans use vision and their knowledge base to comprehend the characteristics of a construction site. They also use tactile sensing to provide an understanding over various states and properties of surfaces [12,13]. However, humans have the ability to inherently perform these identification procedures as a secondary task, while performing primary targeted tasks such as reaching a target location, navigating among obstacles, etc. We call this identification-on-the-fly as it enables multi modal perception for intelligent and self-adaptive systems [8]. Extending this methodology to coarse identification and classification of indoor spaces yields systems capable of multi-modal perception and intelligent operation yet efficient, especially for BIM development.

In this paper, the identification-on-the-fly method is used to coarsely identify human-built spaces based on the distribution of clutter. Each space has its own distinct signature. Clutter, the things which occupy space in an indoor environments such as doors, desks, and wall fittings, grant context to a space. The aim of this study is to develop the ability to identify and classify spaces based on this inherent signature. Hence, we present a unique sensor independent approach for classifying indoor spaces based on their inherent signatures. A sensor independent approach allows generalization of this method to numerous avenues and also allows for fast and inexpensive implementations.

In order to develop and validate this approach, we first present the Clutter Slices dataset. This initial dataset is developed with 2D LiDAR scans of indoor areas, such as staircases, washrooms, corridors, and shared spaces; spaces are common to most developments. We then propose the clutter slices pipeline which utilizes commonly used classifiers to train and subsequently test the approach on the collected dataset. Hence, the contributions of this study are as follows:

- The Clutter Slices dataset of common indoor spaces along with the analysis of its distribution. This dataset is publicly available.

- The clutter slices classification pipeline, including widely used classifiers, is presented. The evaluation of this model on the clutter slices dataset is presented as a baseline.
- A new pipeline for clutter slices classification independent of sensor type, including widely used classifiers. The evaluation of this model on the clutter slices dataset is presented as a baseline.
- Performance analysis of the selected classifiers in the proposed pipeline is presented on the clutter slices dataset.

The organization of this paper is as follows: Sect. 2 describes the Identification-on-the-fly approach using clutter slices to decipher the unique signatures of indoor spaces. Further, Sect. 3 presents the Clutter Slices dataset. In this section, we describe the methodology of data collection and the structure of the dataset. Section 4 presents the model and the classification methods used on the Clutter Slices dataset for identification of spaces. Experiments and results are presented in Sect. 5, followed by the conclusion in Sect. 6.

2   Identification-on-the-Fly

Embedding intelligence and self-adaptive features into robots requires them to perform multi-modal tasks, simultaneously, to extract a rich understanding of their environment. Such rich comprehension is based on contextual as well as state information of the environment which is extracted while navigating or interacting with it. Humans, exhibit this quality of multi-modal perception and cognition, which helps them decipher the surroundings in a way that they are even able to navigate unseen environments. Moreover, humans are able to perform such navigation and classification as a secondary task, while the goal of such movement can be varied. Example scenarios would include identification of different areas while navigation, using vision and tactile sensing to understand the current state of a surface or object. Another such example is performing status checks while navigating an unseen construction space. Identification-on-the-fly incorporates this ability of comprehending the unseen environment as an almost intuitive capability (performed as a secondary task) into autonomous robots, thereby taking them one step closer to human-like intelligence.

In this paper, an identification-on-the-fly approach is utilized to address problems associated with coarse identification of human-built indoor spaces while navigating through them. This is accomplished based on an intuitive assumption that each class of space has its own unique signature. Moreover, common spaces exhibit similar patterns as they are built for specific purposes, such as staircases, corridors, etc. Hence, these unique signatures can be generalized throughout indoor spaces to learn and recognize the class of spaces for unseen environments too.

2.1   Indoor Construction Spaces

Indoor construction spaces are unique environments in the sense that they have both static and dynamic elements. While the structure and walls may not change significantly over the course of time, the dynamic objects such as furniture, fittings, etc. can change drastically even over a short period of time. These changes pose a challenge to most autonomous system which rely on precise and real-time mappings. However, the coarse signature of the space remains rather constant. In this study, we leverage the overall signature of a space for coarse classification of the space.

2.2   Clutter-Slices

Clutter is the class of things which add context to a room. A room is primarily just four walls, however, if there are stairs in it then it becomes a staircase. Similarly, if the stairs are replaced by desks, it becomes a working space. Hence, there is inherent information, albeit coarse, in the distribution of objects in a four wall enclosure. Moreover, there is also information in the structure of the placement of the four walls. A corridor and an office, both have four walls but the structure is inherently dissimilar. The clutter-slices method leverages this inherent information in the distribution of objects and the basic structure of the enclosed spaces to classify the human-built environments.

Clutter includes both static (wall fittings, doors, pillars, sinks) and dynamic objects (tables, chairs, table-top equipment, humans, cabinets). These objects occupy the scans with respect to their position in the environment. At different heights, different objects appear on the scan relative to their position in the environment, as illustrated in Fig. 1. Based on the information available from the clutter-slices, different indoor facilities can exhibit unique distributions.

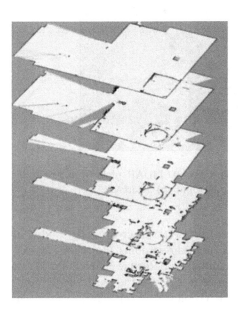

Fig. 1. 2D lidar scans of a room at multiple heights

Clutter slices do not just coarsely map the area, but they also coarsely localize the observer in the scene. The information from clutter slices enables abstraction of details such as the closeness of the observer to ceiling or ground and to the nearby walls. This information can be used to estimate the pose of the observer in the scene and subsequently map their trajectory.

3   Clutter Slices Dataset

Robust identification of construction spaces, especially indoor spaces, needs intelligent models that can comprehend the environment efficiently. The first step in building such models is creating adequate datasets for training. Hence, we present a diverse dataset of real-life indoor spaces. The clutter slices dataset is a collection of scans of common indoor spaces, such as corridors, staircases, restrooms, and large shared spaces (including cafeterias, common areas, and shared working offices), as shown in Fig. 2. This is a fully annotated dataset which enables models to learn the distribution of clutter in such common areas, and thereby contributes to efficient recognition of spaces.

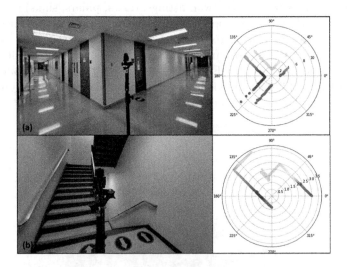

Fig. 2. Images and respective 2D LiDAR plots of indoor spaces with the sensor capturing scans of (a) Corridor and (b) Staircase.

The Clutter Slices dataset was created by taking two-dimensional (2D) LiDAR scans of areas such as restrooms, staircases, shared spaces and corridors around the various buildings of Purdue University. We chose a LiDAR sensor for this data collection as it is one of the most widely used sensors in navigation and mapping in robotic vision. Using this sensor, we measure spatial distribution 270° around a point, as shown in Fig. 2. The maximum range of this sensor is 30 meters. Various positions around the space were used for the data collection to ensure a holistic capture of data. The height of the data collection was varied in steps of 1 m.

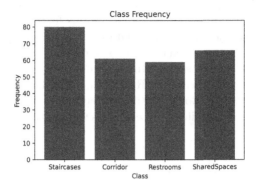

Fig. 3. Frequency distribution of classes of clutter slices dataset

There are four classes in the Clutter Slices dataset: corridors, staircases, restrooms, and large shared spaces. These classes are common to most indoor construction areas and hence are useful for researchers in future work. The distribution of instances of these classes in the dataset are shown in Fig 4. The dataset is publicly available at https://github.com/CRLPurdue/Clutter_Slices [11].

4 Clutter Slices Pipeline

The clutter slices approach with identification-on-the-fly aims to understand inherent patterns in the data, rather than relying on explicit feature engineering. Hence, by just using the distances of clutter around a point, we derive a clutter slice at a fixed height. A stack of these slices would build the clutter signature of the space. However, the goal here is to understand the strength of just a single clutter slice in deriving the class of a space. Therefore, we use a single 2D scan of the space to understand the distribution of clutter and subsequently, classify it.

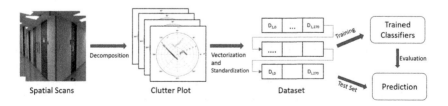

Fig. 4. Flowchart of clutter slices pipeline

In the clutter slices pipeline, the input 2D scan is translated to distances around the point. This allows for use of multiple sensors, as a variety of sensors such as LiDARs, cameras, and infrared sensors can be used to get the distance measurements. These distances are then vectorized as the feature space D_i, wherein $D_i = [D_{i,0}, ..., D_{i,270}]$. The labels for this feature space are defined as y_i where $i \in [0, 3]$ for the clutter slices dataset. The feature space is then scaled using Box-Cox power transformations to standardize the data. The prepared data is then input to the classifiers. In this study, we used six classifiers which are widely used in machine learning: Random Forests, Logistic Regression, Support Vector Machines, AdaBoost, Artificial Neural Network, and Convolutional Neural Network. These classifiers present a baseline on the clutter slices dataset, and prove its effectiveness.

5   Experiments and Results

The validation of the proposed pipeline on the clutter slices dataset using the selected classifiers is presented in this section. We first present the experimental setup, including the hyperparameters selected for the classifiers, and consequently, present the performance in terms of accuracy, precision and recall for the classifiers.

5.1   Experimental Setup

The experiments were conducted with the Clutter Slices dataset using the described pipeline with six classification models. Since this is a multi-class classification task, the dataset was stratified and shuffled, then split into a train and test set with an 80-20 ratio. We followed a five fold cross validation to ensure coverage of the entire dataset. The scikit-learn implementation of Random Forests (RF), Adaboost, Suppport Vector Machine (SVM), and Logistic Regression (LR) were all used [6]. A total of 100 estimators were used for RF with the total depth of 100. In case of Adaboost, the number of estimators used were 200. The polynomial kernel was used for SVM.

The architecture of the artificial neural network (ANN) constitutes of six fully connected dense layers. The number of units in the layers are: 481,364, 256, 125, 50 and 4. The last layer has Softmax activation with rectified linear units (ReLU) activation being used for the previous layers. We also incorporated two dropout layers in this network. The architecture of the convolutional neural network (CNN) comprises of two convolutional layers followed by a MaxPooling layer and three dense, fully-connected layers. The dense layers have 125, 50 and 4 units, respectively. Dropout and input flattening layers were also used in this network. Softmax activation was used at the last layer with ReLU being used in all others. The CNN and the ANN, both used the Adam optimizer with a learning rate of 0.01. The categorical cross-entropy was used as a measure of loss. Both neural network models were trained for 30 epochs with a mini-batch size of 32.

The training and testing was conducted on a computer with 32 GB RAM, NVIDIA GTX 1080 Ti GPU and Intel Core i9 CPU.

Table 1. Accuracy on test set for the Clutter Slices Dataset

Classifiers	Cross validation Accuracy					Overall Accuracy
	1st Fold	2nd Fold	3rd Fold	4th Fold	5th Fold	
RF	0.907	0.88	0.94	0.96	0.94	0.928 ± 0.03
AdaBoost	0.57	0.396	0.53	0.60	0.37	0.495 ± 0.09
SVM	0.83	0.88	0.867	0.924	0.886	0.88 ± 0.03
Logistic Regression	0.759	0.849	0.83	0.79	0.849	0.82 ± 0.035
CNN	0.907	0.905	0.94	0.96	0.96	0.936 ± 0.03
ANN	0.87	0.87	0.925	0.96	0.89	0.90 ± 0.04

5.2 Results

The tests were performed using the Clutter Slices dataset. The accuracy of the six classifiers for each fold, along with the overall accuracy is presented in Table 1. The results indicate that the clutter slices dataset is able to present enough information for recognition of classes, even with just a single scan as input. While random forests, CNN, and ANN models showed more than 90% accuracy, models like SVM and Logistic regression also showed good performance with very little hyper-parameter tuning. The low accuracy of Adaboost can be attributed to over-fitting by the model.

Figure 5 shows the class-wise precision recall curves for the overall performance of the six classifiers. These curves highlight that the models were able to

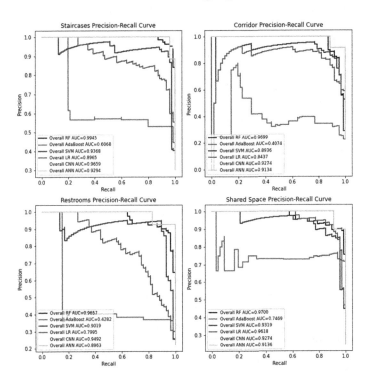

Fig. 5. Overall classifier performance

identify classes Staircases and Shared Spaces without much loss, but Restrooms and Corridors were showing overlap with other classes. The overlap can be intuitively explained as restrooms can have characteristics similar to shared spaces. Nevertheless, despite these challenges, the area-under-the-curve (auc) values prove the performance of these models.

6   Conclusion

In this paper we introduce the identification-on-the-fly approach to imbue human-like intelligence into robotic systems. The proposed clutter slices approach leverages the unique signatures of common indoor spaces for coarse classification. The initial validation of the clutter slices approach is performed on the dataset using 2D LiDAR sensor. Further, we present a scalable pipeline that supports this approach. The pipeline is flexible enough to accommodate varied classifiers. We used some of the widely used classifiers such as random forests, logistic regression, and neural network models to establish a baseline for the dataset. A maximum accuracy of 93.6% was achieved with this approach without significant hyperparameter tuning. The precision-recall plots show the convergence of the models in recognizing the classes of spaces.

The clutter slices approach captures the unique signatures of common indoor spaces and proves the potential of this approach in their coarse classification. Nevertheless, the clutter slices approach is not sensor specific and can be potentially generalized across domains. In the future, this approach of identification-on-the-fly can be an essential tool for perceiving and assessing surroundings of intelligent autonomous agents. Clutter slices is one implementation of the identification-on-the-fly method used for coarse classification of indoor spaces, adding contextual information to the robot perception. However, there are endless opportunities to perform identification-on-the-fly to understand the surrounding while still identifying potential dangers and outcome of future actions.

Acknowledgment. This work was supported, in part, by the Dept. of Energy, the NSF Center for Robots and Sensor for the Human Well-Being (RoSe-HUB) and by the National Science Foundation under grant CNS-1439717 and the USDA under grant 2018-67007-28439. The authors greatly acknowledge the contribution of coffee for the actualization of this work.

References

1. Becerik-Gerber, B., Jazizadeh, F., Li, N., Calis, G.: Application areas and data requirements for BIM-enabled facilities management. J. Constr. Eng. Manag. **138**(3), 431–442 (2012)
2. Bock, T.: Construction robotics. Autonomous Robots **22**, 201–209 (2007). https://doi.org/10.1007/s10514-006-9008-5
3. Jupp, J.: 4D BIM for environmental planning and management. Procedia Eng. **180**, 190–201 (2017)

4. McKinlay, R.: Technology: use or lose our navigation skills. Nature **531**(7596), 573–575 (2016)
5. Ozdenizci, B., Ok, K., Coskun, V., Aydin, M.N.: Development of an indoor navigation system using NFC technology. In: 2011 Fourth International Conference on Information and Computing, pp. 11–14 (2011)
6. Pedregosa, F., et al.: Scikit-learn: machine learning in Python. J. Mach. Learn. Res. **12**, 2825–2830 (2011)
7. Praveen, A., Haoguang, Y., Hyukjun, J., Richard, M.V.: Aerial mobile manipulator system to enable dexterous manipulations with increased precision. In: 2019 IEEE ICRA 2019 workshop on High Accuracy Mobile Manipulation in Challenging Environments. Preprint arXiv:2010.09618 (2019)
8. Praveen, A., Xin, M., Harikrishnan, M., Vishnunandan, L.V., Mo, R., Richard, M.V.: Inspection-on-the-fly using hybrid physical interaction control for aerial manipulators. In: 2020 IEEE International Conference on Intelligent Robots and Systems (IROS). Preprint arXiv:2010.09605 (2020)
9. Su, Z., Zhou, X., Cheng, T., Zhang, H., Xu, B., Chen, W.: Global localization of a mobile robot using lidar and visual features. In: 2017 IEEE International Conference on Robotics and Biomimetics (ROBIO), pp. 2377–2383 (2017)
10. Sun, C., Jiang, S., Skibniewski, M.J., Man, Q., Shen, L.: A literature review of the factors limiting the application of BIM in the construction industry. Technol. Econ. Dev. Econ. **23**(5), 764–779 (2017)
11. Upinder, K., Praveen, A.: Clutter slices dataset. Collaborative Robotics Lab (2020). https://github.com/CRLPurdue/Clutter_Slices
12. Wang, B., Guo, R., Li, B., Han, L., Sun, Y., Wang, M.: Smartguard: an autonomous robotic system for inspecting substation equipment. J. Field Robot. **29**(1), 123–137 (2012)
13. Wang, H., Li, J., Zhou, Y., Fu, M., Yang, S.: Research on the technology of indoor and outdoor integration robot inspection in substation. In: 2019 IEEE 3rd Information Technology, Networking, Electronic and Automation Control Conference (ITNEC), pp. 2366–2369 (2019)
14. Xu, Y., Shmaliy, Y.S., Li, Y., Chen, X., Guo, H.: Indoor INS/LiDAR-based robot localization with improved robustness using cascaded FIR filter. IEEE Access **7**, 34189–34197 (2019)
15. Zhang, F., Duarte, F., Ma, R., Milioris, D., Lin, H., Ratti, C.: Indoor space recognition using deep convolutional neural network: a case study at MIT campus. arXiv preprint arXiv:1610.02414 (2016)

PRRS 2020 - 11th IAPR Workshop on Pattern Recognition in Remote Sensing

Preface

The steady progress in the development of new remote sensing sensors and remote sensing technology has led to ever increasing data, new opportunities, but also new challenges. Thus, need arises to apply the latest methods of machine learning and pattern recognition for automated analysis of remotely sensed data, such as satellite and aerial imagery. One main goal of the PRRS workshops is drawing experts and researchers from the photogrammetry and remote sensing communities to the International Conference on Pattern Recognition (ICPR) and make them aware of the International Association for Pattern Recognition – fostering inter-disciplinary cooperation.

The 2020/2021 edition of PRRS was held online in conjunction with 25th International Conference on Pattern Recognition. The format of the workshop includes a keynote, followed by oral presentations about the accepted papers. 12 manuscripts were submitted to the workshop and reviewed using a single-blind review process by a program committee of international experts. 7 were accepted and all of these were presented as orals at the workshop. This year, the keynote addressed well-known challenges in remote sensing related to limited amount of labels such as continual learning and semi-supervised learning for Earth observation data.

The papers cover a wide range of remote sensing application areas, which include the classification and change detection of land-cover classes, the detection of building footprints and trees, and the estimation of poverty within large geographical regions. The type of data considered by the papers varies from different sensors (optical and radar) to distinct remote sensing platforms (satellites, airborne). In two manuscripts, video and geo-referenced data (i.e., social media) are also analyzed. Overall, the contributions of the 7 accepted papers are in terms of new machine learning frameworks and novel neural network architectures. This includes, for example, novel approaches for data fusion of multiple modalities and for using active learning in semantic segmentation problems. Furthermore, new layers for deep architectures are proposed for the extraction of more informative features. Finally, one of the accepted manuscript releases a new multi-temporal dataset that includes pairs of Sentinel-2 images acquired from 1520 urban areas worldwide.

We take this opportunity to thank the program committee members for their efforts in paper review. We also thank all the authors and the keynote speaker for their contributions, IAPR and the ISPRS working groups II/III and II/6 for their sponsorship. We are grateful to the local organizers of ICPR 2020 for their assistance.

November 2020

Ribana Roscher
Gabriele Cavallaro

Organization

Program Committee Chairs

Gabriele Cavallaro   FZ Jülich, Germany
Ribana Roscher   University of Bonn, Germany
Eckart Michaelsen   Fraunhofer-IOSB, Germany
Jie Shan   Purdue University, USA
Uwe Stilla   Technische Universitaet Muenchen, Germany

Program Committee

Selim Aksoy   Bilkent University, Turkey
John Ball   Mississippi State University, USA
Jón Atli Benediktsson   University of Iceland, Iceland
Lorenzo Bruzzone   University of Trento, Italy
Jocelyn Chanussot   Grenoble Institute of Technology, France
David Clausi   University of Waterloo, Canada
Melba Crawford   Purdue University, USA
Fabio Dells'Acqua   University of Pavia, Italy
Jenny Q. Du   Mississippi State University, USA
Paolo Gamba   University of Pavia, Italy
Surya Durbha   Indian Institute of Technology Bombay, India
Xiangyun Hu   Wuhan University, China
Michael Kampffmeyer   University of Tromsø, Norway
John Kerekes   Rochester Institute of Technology, USA
Sébastien Lefèvre   Universités de Bretagne Sud/IRISA, France
Peijun Li   Peking University, China
Helmut Mayer   Bundeswehr University Munich, Germany
Farid Melgani   University of Trento, Ital
Gabriele Moser   University of Genoa, Italy
Antonio Plaza   University of Extremadura, Italy
Franz Rottensteiner   Leibniz Universität Hannover, Germany
Michael Schmitt   DLR Munich, Germany
Xiaohua Tong   Tongji University, China
Devis Tuia   Wageningen University and Research, Netherlands
Michele Volpi   Swiss Data Science Center, Switzerland
Björn Waske   University of Osnabrueck, Germany
Jan Dirk Wegner   ETH Zurich, Switzerland
Martin Weinmann   Karlsruhe Institute of Technology, Germany
Lexie Yang   Oak Ridge National Laboratoy, USA
Xuezhi Yang   University of Waterloo, Canada
Alper Yilmaz   Ohio State University, USA

Remembering Both the Machine and the Crowd When Sampling Points: Active Learning for Semantic Segmentation of ALS Point Clouds

Michael Kölle[✉], Volker Walter, Stefan Schmohl, and Uwe Soergel

Institute for Photogrammetry, University of Stuttgart, Stuttgart, Germany
{michael.koelle,volker.walter,
stefan.schmohl,uwe.soergel}@ifp.uni-stuttgart.de

Abstract. Supervised Machine Learning systems such as Convolutional Neural Networks (CNNs) are known for their great need for labeled data. However, in case of geospatial data and especially in terms of Airborne Laserscanning (ALS) point clouds, labeled data is rather scarce, hindering the application of such systems. Therefore, we rely on Active Learning (AL) for significantly reducing necessary labels and we aim at gaining a deeper understanding on its working principle for ALS point clouds. Since the key element of AL is sampling of most informative points, we compare different basic sampling strategies and try to further improve them for geospatial data. While AL reduces total labeling effort, the basic issue of experts doing this labor- and therefore cost-intensive task remains. Therefore, we propose to outsource data annotation to the crowd. However, when employing crowdworkers, labeling errors are inevitable. As a remedy, we aim on selecting points, which are easier for interpretation and evaluate the robustness of AL to labeling errors. Applying these strategies for different classifiers, we estimate realistic segmentation results from crowdsourced data solely, only differing in Overall Accuracy by about 3% points compared to results based on completely labeled dataset, which is demonstrated for two different scenes.

Keywords: Active Learning · Crowdsourcing · 3D point clouds · Classification · Labeling · Random Forest · Sparse 3D CNN

1 Introduction

A paramount requirement of supervised Machine Learning (ML) systems is labeled training data. Especially, since the renaissance of neural networks in the form of Convolutional Neural Networks (CNNs) there is an increasing demand for large pools of high-quality training data. In this context, huge effort was put in establishing massive annotated data corpora such as *ImageNet* [7] and *Cifar-10 & Cifar-100* [18]. However, in the context of geospatial data such labeled

© Springer Nature Switzerland AG 2021
A. Del Bimbo et al. (Eds.): ICPR 2020 Workshops, LNCS 12667, pp. 505–520, 2021.
https://doi.org/10.1007/978-3-030-68787-8_37

datasets are rather scarce, which especially applies to 3D point clouds. One publicly available dataset is the *ISPRS Vaihingen 3D Semantic Labeling* benchmark (V3D) [25], which was manually annotated by experts. This annotation process is a highly labor-intensive and therefore costly task.

One method for significantly reducing the necessity of labeled training samples provided by human annotators is Active Learning (AL). The major goal of AL is to maintain the performance of a ML system, while only focusing on a subset of instances from a training pool inhering most information [28]. First AL approaches focused on Support Vector Machines (SVMs) [6], which are well suited for such approaches by design. Ertekin et al. [8] exploited the idea of SVMs of only focusing on points close to the decision boundary by sampling points to be labeled in the vicinity of already learned SVM hyperplanes. More general methods for detecting most informative points focus on the predicted a posteriori probability of a classifier making them more independent of the ML model used. A comprehensive overview of these methods of the pre-Deep Learning era is given by Settles [28]. When using CNNs, Gal and Ghahramani [10] recommend to form Monte Carlo dropout ensembles in order to overcome overestimation of a posteriori probabilities often observed in case of CNNs.

Regardless of the classifier used, AL selection criteria are typically designed for requesting the label of one specific data point per iteration step based on some informativeness measure [28]. However, retraining a classifier each time one individual point is added to the training pool is computationally expensive and will only marginally improve its performance, especially when employing CNNs. Because of this, most commonly batch-mode AL is preferred [15,24]. On the other hand, when adding multiple instances to the training pool based on one classification process, it is very likely that all sampled points are similar in terms of their representation in feature space. In order to increase the diversity of selected samples to boost convergence of the AL process multiple methods have been proposed [16,35].

While using AL for predicting land cover maps from hyperspectral imagery was studied extensively [26,29], only few investigations were conducted on applying AL for the semantic segmentation of Airborne Laserscanning (ALS) point clouds. Hui et al. [14] use a fully automated AL approach for filtering ground points to derive digital terrain models, focusing on a binary segmentation. Li and Pfeifer [19] rely on AL for predicting multiple land cover classes from ALS data by automatic propagation of labels from an initial training dataset without including human annotators. Luo et al. [23] present an approach for semantic segmentation of Mobile Mapping point clouds employing a voxel-based higher order Markov Random Field. Closest related to our method are the findings of Lin et al. [20], who employ the *PointNet++* architecture to ALS point clouds. The authors realize a tile-based approach, where in each iteration step most informative tiles are queried, fully labeled and added to the training pool.

All previously discussed works describe efficient means to reduce the total amount of necessary labels, but these labels are typically still provided by an expert. Our goal is not only to reduce effort of experts but to completely shift and outsource labeling effort to non-experts, namely to the crowd. It is already proven that crowdsourcing is well suited for annotating geospatial data [31,32]. This enables running a fully automated human-in-the-loop [3] pipeline exploiting capabilities of the online crowdsourcing platform *Microworkers* [13] as described by Kölle et al. [17]. Such hybrid intelligence systems were also discussed by Vaughan [30] for combining the individual strengths of both parties.

While in Kölle et al. [17] we mainly concentrated on the performance of the human operator given by the crowd, the emphasis of this work lies on the role of the machine. Therefore, our contributions can be summarized as follows: i) We focus on a deeper understanding of applying AL to geospatial data represented by ALS point clouds. ii) This includes a detailed comparison of different selection strategies provided in literature, which we enhance by different methods for faster convergence. These strategies are applied for both a feature-driven Random Forest (RF) [4] and a data-driven CNN approach. iii) While in literature usually receiving true labels from an oracle is assumed, this hardly holds true for actual labeling of data by experts and is especially unrealistic in case of paid crowdworkers, where labeling errors are inevitable. We therefore test the robustness of our approach, address it using a special sampling strategy and estimate results, which are realistic for the crowd to reach.

2   Methodology

In typical ML scenarios Passive Learning (PL) is applied, where a previously labeled data pool is used for training. In contrast to this, in AL a model is actively involved in establishing such a training dataset. Precisely, after an initial training step the classifier points out instances, which carry most information and are therefore a reasonable addition to the training dataset justifying annotation effort by a human operator. Thus, the inherent hypothesis is that only a small subset of the dataset is required for sufficiently training a classifier.

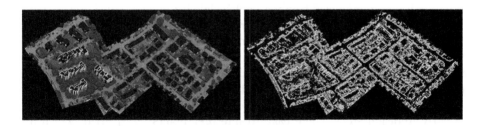

Fig. 1. Visualization of Support Vectors of V3D training dataset (*right*) compared to reference labeling (*left*). (Color figure online)

This is also the idea underlying the SVM. When training such a model, Support Vectors are determined, which define class-separating hyperplanes in feature space. Only these Support Vectors are afterwards used in inference, which means

Fig. 2. Derived pointwise scores of the first iteration step (*left*) and the last iteration step (*right*). Color scale ranges from *dark blue* = low sampling priority to *orange* = high sampling priority. Points missing on the right were selected and added to T. (Color figure online)

that only those instances impact the performance of the trained model. When further pursuing the concept of SVM, we assume that most informative samples are always located in close proximity to the decision boundary. Instances located here are most demanding to classify since they incorporate features of two or more different classes. In context of ALS point clouds, such points naturally are also situated on class borders in object space, so that delineation lines of individual class occurrences can clearly be observed and compared to the reference labeling in Fig. 1. Only 21.68% of provided training points were considered Support Vectors supporting the hypothesis that only a fraction of points needs to be labeled. When used within PL, the SVM utilizes all instances in proximity of the separating hyperplanes until exhaustion of such points.

However, in AL typically significantly fewer labels are required [15,19,24]. Precisely, only a subset of these points closest to the decision boundary is constituted iteratively. In every iteration step only a limited number of points that currently represent most uncertainty and therefore most information (see Sect. 2.2) is drawn from an unlabeled training pool U, labeled by a so-called oracle $\mathcal{O}$ and added to the training pool T. After retraining a classifier C based on expanded T, C becomes much more certain when predicting on points of the remaining training data set $R = U \setminus T$, which are similar to those recently added. Therefore, sampling quasi-duplicates can be limited. Vice versa for our experiments presented in Sect. 3 up to 81.21% of instances selected within the AL procedure are actually Support Vectors. Selection of Non-Support Vectors mainly happens in early iteration steps where easy to interpret points are queried, which are however not included in T so far. The behavior of the AL process can also be traced in Fig. 2, where the model's uncertainty (measured by Eq. 1) of the initial iteration step is compared to that of the last step (30 iteration steps have been conducted). Both results underline that points in close proximity to class boundaries in object space are most complex for automatic interpretation, which persists throughout the complete iteration process. We can also observe that in total the model becomes more confident in its decisions (e.g. points on roofs and vegetation becoming *dark blue*) and the uncertainty margin shrinks to an extent of close to class boundaries.

Based on this conceptional foundation, we now address the main components of AL: i) the employed classifier (Sect. 2.1), ii) the sampling strategy for detecting most informative instances (Sect. 2.2) and iii) the employed oracle (Sect. 2.3).

2.1 Employed Classifiers

For enabling a feature-based RF classifier, a selection of handcrafted geometric and radiometric features is taken from literature [2,5,33] and used within this work (detailed description of features can be found in Haala et al. [12]). All features are computed for each point considering spherical point neighborhoods of 1, 2, 3 and 5 m, so that a multi-scale approach is realized. Employing the RF classifier within the AL scenario is straightforward for its pointwise functionality. We can simply transfer selected points from U to T and use points included in T as individual instances since point neighborhoods were already sufficiently taken into account in the preprocessing, i.e. feature computation. This is a fundamental difference to employing a CNN approach, which we oppose to the RF classifier.

In contrast to applying *PointNet++* as Lin et al. [20], we employ the voxel-based Sparse Convolutional Neural Network (SCNN) [11], transferred for usage on ALS point clouds by Schmohl and Sörgel [27]. Compared to this work, we train slightly shallower networks (4 *U-Net* levels), which are more stable when trained on such few labeled points. The obsolescent need of handcrafted features in Deep Learning is not necessarily advantageous in case of AL, since in every iteration step features need to be relearned or at least refined based on the newly added training points. We therefore also have to include their (non-labeled) surrounding points as input to the network for spatial context. Such points do not directly contribute to the training loss, but assist feature learning/refinement due to their passive presence. However, this is computationally more complex than computing features only one time in advance of the AL loop as for the RF. To reduce training effort, we initialize the network weights and learning rate in each AL iteration step by adopting respective values from the previous one, yielding faster convergence. For each step, we establish an ensemble of 5 differently weight-initialized models.

For dynamic adaption of learning rate and early stopping of the training procedure, a validation dataset is required. In case of AL it is not reasonable to exclude a pre-defined area of the training dataset for this, since the spatial distribution of labeled points in the training set is not known before. Therefore, in each iteration step we randomly pick 20% of points of each class from T and use it to validate our model. Consequently, our validation dataset is more related to the training dataset than in PL, but consists only of most informative points, which are more demanding for classification than conventional validation datasets mitigating this issue.

2.2 Selection Strategies

When applying the trivial strategy of sampling points by randomly picking, it is to be expected that a mixture of both most and low informative points will be selected causing prolonged convergence time of the iteration process. Furthermore, random sampling lacks applicability for highly inhomogeneous class distributions, which are common for ALS point clouds. More directed strategies aim at detecting points where the intrinsic confidence of the model is minimum based on the a posteriori probability $p(c|x)$ that point x belongs to class c. Since strategies such as Least Certainty Sampling and Breaking Ties [28] only consider a fraction of predictive information (provided that multi-class problem is to be solved), we decide to rely on Entropy (E). Points having greatest E are considered to be informative, since E is maximum for an equal distribution of a posteriori probabilities and minimum for one class having a $p(c|x)$ of 1:

$$x_E = \operatorname*{argmax}_x - \sum_c p(c|x) \cdot \log p(c|x) \tag{1}$$

The aforementioned measures can be summarized as *Query-by-Uncertainty* [28]. When applying an ensemble classifier (e.g. RF), uncertainty can additionally be measured as disagreement between different models pursuing the idea of *Query-by-Committee*. This can be achieved by Vote Entropy (*VE*) [1], where we assume to have e ensemble members each predicting a posteriori probabilities for each class placed in $\mathbf{P}_e$. Each member is allowed to vote for one class (the one having highest $p(c|x)$). These votings are then evaluated for each class establishing a new distribution, which is normalized by the number of ensemble members N_e and evaluated using the entropy formula:

$$x_{VE} = \operatorname*{argmax}_x - \sum_c \frac{\sum_e D(\mathbf{P}_e, c)}{N_e} \cdot \log \frac{\sum_e D(\mathbf{P}_e, c)}{N_e}$$

$$\text{where } D(\mathbf{P}_e, c) = \begin{cases} 1, & \text{if } \operatorname{argmax}(\mathbf{P}_e) = c \\ 0, & \text{otherwise} \end{cases} \tag{2}$$

The rationale of *VE* is that the class of one individual instance can be predicted with high confidence as long as most ensemble members vote for this class even if the maximum a posteriori probability is rather low.

For both *VE* and E, we can easily introduce a sampling method yielding a more equal distribution of classes in the created training dataset, which can be accomplished by individual class weighting. Precisely, these weights are calculated dynamically as ratio of the total number of points N_T currently present in T and the number of representatives of each class N_c at iteration step t ($w_c(t) = N_T(t)/N_c(t)$). These weights are then multiplied by the individual score of the respective class (E: $p(c|x)$, *VE*: $\sum_e D(\mathbf{P}_e, c)/N_e$) before inserting into the entropy formula and referred to as wE and wVE respectively.

For efficiency reasons, we aim at selecting and adding multiple points per iteration step to our training dataset according to pool-based AL. Since similar

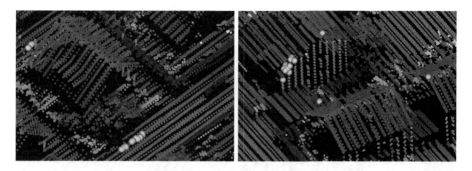

Fig. 3. Subsets of via E sampled points (*cyan*) from two exemplary iteration steps visualized in the training point cloud colorized according to reference data. (Color figure online)

points in feature space yield similar uncertainty scores, sampling quasi-duplicates inhering same information is likely, when only considering this score. In case of ALS point clouds such points typically appear as clusters in object space (see Fig. 3), which is why increasing diversity is related to increasing the distance between sampled points. Consequently, we consider the scores gained by any selection strategy as priority list for creating Diversity in Object Space (*DiOS*). Based on the order in this list, points are transferred from R to T if the distance to all points previously selected within this iteration step is greater than d_{DiOS}. While such methods are commonly realized in feature space [16,34], this procedure directly works in object space, which is of course mainly applicable for geospatial data where an interpretable object space is present.

As a second method we resort to Diversity in Feature Space (*DiFS*) according to Zhdanov [35]. For this we aim at detecting clusters of similar points with regard to their representation in feature space. For focusing on most informative points, we additionally use the score of each instance derived by any of the aforementioned selection strategies as individual weight and combine both measures by running a weighted k-means clustering [21]. Afterwards, from every cluster formed, we sample the same number of instances with the highest scores. In order to reduce computational effort, for this procedure we only consider n_{DiFS} points having highest selection scores since we can assume that points yielding low scores will not improve our model.

Considering our ultimate goal of crowdworkers labeling selected points, we assume that increasing distance to the class boundary is helpful for a better and unambiguous interpretability and helps avoiding weariness of crowdworkers resulting in less labeling errors. As already seen in Fig. 2, in case of geospatial data analysis spatial distance to class boundary is closely related to distance to decision boundary. Therefore, we identify informative points by any of the aforementioned measures and consider neighboring points for labeling instead. Precisely, for Reducing Interpretation Uncertainty (*RIU*) we use a spherical neighborhood of radius d_{RIU} centered in a selected point (seed point) and search within this neighborhood for the lowest score. This point is then presented for labeling instead of the original seed point. This procedure is exemplary visualized for different values of d_{RIU} (i.e. max. distance from the seed point) in Fig. 4 and demonstrates that distance to the class boundary can be efficiently increased.

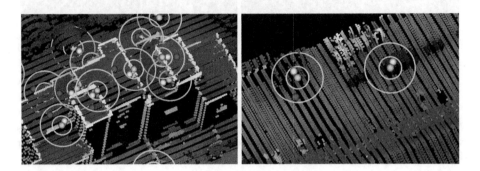

Fig. 4. Increasing distance to decision boundary. Instead of the seed point (*cyan*), we select a point further away from the class border, allowing maximum 3D radii d_{RIU} of 1.5 m (*yellow*) and 4 m (*pink*) indicated by respective circles. (Color figure online)

2.3   Employed Oracle

In the context of the proposed human-in-the-loop pipeline, previous sections focused on the role of the machine for querying most informative points, whereby respective labels are intended to be received from a human annotator. However, in most studies this operator is replaced by an omniscient oracle $\mathcal{O}_O$, which always labels correctly according to the reference data. Especially for paid crowd-sourcing relying on non-experts this assumption is not justified [32]. Lockhart et al. [22] differentiate between two types of erroneous oracles, namely noisy and confused oracles ($\mathcal{O}_N$ and $\mathcal{O}_C$). The noisy oracle behavior $\mathcal{O}_N$ applies both to a human annotator, who has a well understanding of the task but randomly misclassifies some points, and to a crowdworker, who is not paying attention at all and, often observed in crowdsourcing [9], just picks classes randomly. A confused oracle on the other hand misclassifies points by always confusing the same classes (according to some distinct mapping), for instance *Fence/Hedge* vs. *Shrub* or *Roof* vs. *Façade*. This problem occurs especially in AL where focus lies on most informative points, which are situated on or near to class boundaries.

2.4   Datasets

We test our method on two different datasets of individual characteristics. A sub-urban scene featuring single family houses and building blocks is represented by the V3D dataset [25] (visualized in Fig. 1). This point cloud captured in August 2008 incorporates a total of 9 classes (see Table 2). The point density is about $4-8$ pts/m^2. In order to also derive color features the point cloud is colorized by orthogonal projection of corresponding CIR images. As second dataset we rely on an UAV LiDAR point cloud colorized by simultaneously acquired imagery and captured in March 2018 using the same flight mission parameters as in Haala et al. [12], henceforth referred to as Hessigheim 3D (H3D)[1]. The point density is about 800 pts/m^2, but for efficiency reasons, spatial subsampling to a minimum point distance of 0.3 m was applied. The point cloud representing a rural village was manually annotated by the authors using a fine-grained class scheme consisting of 12 classes (see Table 3). For both datasets the initial training set is provided by the crowd as outlined in Kölle et al. [17].

3 Results

3.1 Comparison of Selection Strategies

For evaluating, which strategy for selecting most informative points works best, we apply those presented in Sect. 2.2 on the V3D dataset in combination with the RF classifier using 30 iteration steps and a batch size of 300. We rely on an ensemble of 100 binary decision trees having a maximum depth of 18. The performance throughout the iteration loop is depicted in Fig. 5 (*left*). We want to stress that all our results are obtained after only labeling a small fraction of 1.15% from U. Accuracies within this work are evaluated for a distinct test dataset disjoint to the respective training dataset (i.e. samples are only drawn from U).

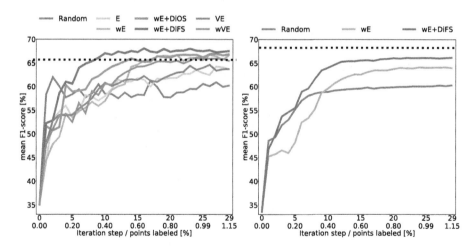

Fig. 5. Comparison of different selection strategies in combination with our RF (*left*) and our SCNN (*right*) classifier applied to the V3D dataset and evaluated according to F1-scores. For reference, the dotted black line depicts the mean F1-score for PL using the completely labeled dataset. (Color figure online)

Although the performance of random sampling rises steeply at first, it soon settles at a mean F1-score of about 60%, since less frequent classes are not

---

[1] Dataset will be made publicly available in early 2021.

selected sufficiently. Later it is outperformed by sampling strategies such as E or VE. These in turn are exceeded by the enhanced strategies by applying individual class weights in each iteration step (wE and wVE), since for every class a sufficient almost equally distributed number of labeled points is obtained. Nevertheless, one disadvantage of these weighting strategies is the resulting comparatively slow (but steady) increase in performance. Motivated by the strong performance gain of random sampling in early iteration steps due to selecting a greater bandwidth of points, we apply both $DiOS$ using an empirically determined value for d_{DiOS} of 5 m and $DiFS$, where we set n_{DiFS} to 10.000 and form 300 clusters (see also Sect. 2.2). We analyze the effect of these two strategies for wE, which has proven to be an efficient sampling strategy regarding the reachable accuracy in the later course of the iteration. Figure 5 (*left*) outlines that both strategies of increasing diversity positively impact the performance of the AL loop.

We want to stress that increasing diversity especially boosts the convergence of the AL loop, which means that less iteration steps are necessary for reaching the same performance of the trained model as if more iteration steps are conducted. For instance, applying $wE + DiFS$ achieves convergence after only 10 iteration steps. At this time, basic wE reaches a mean F1-score of about 10% points less. For reaching an accuracy similar to $wE + DiFS$, wE requires 10 iteration steps more and therefore additional labeling of 3000 points (10 iteration steps and batch size of 300). Relative to $DiFS$, the $DiOS$ strategy performs slightly worse especially in the course of the first few iteration steps, but still outperforms the baseline of pure wE.

3.2   Comparison of Employed Classifiers

For comparing our SCNN classifier to the RF we focus on the selection strategies that have proven to be most effective (wE, $wE + DiFS$), visualized in Fig. 5 (*right*), which is to be interpreted relative to Fig. 5 (*left*). Regarding these two strategies, for both classifiers roughly the same number of iteration steps is necessary for convergence. The performance of SCNN increases more steadily and especially high-frequency oscillations do not occur because in contrast to the RF, each model is only retrained in each iteration step and not trained from scratch again. Although for our best strategy ($wE + DiFS$) both classifiers reach a similar accuracy, that of SCNN rises not as fast as for the RF (after 10 iteration steps mean F1-score for RF: 67% vs. SCNN: 64%). Furthermore, SCNN fails to exceed the accuracy of PL on the completely labeled dataset, which might be due to overfitting regarding the sparsely labeled training dataset. Nevertheless, the difference in Overall Accuracy (OA) between PL and AL is less than 3% points (see Table 2).

3.3   Comparison of Different Oracle Types

All aforementioned results assume an oracle behaving like $\mathcal{O}_O$, which can hardly be observed when working with real crowdworkers. For the more justified assumption of a noisy or a confused oracle we simulate 10%, 30%, 50%

Table 1. Behavior of our confused oracle regarding the V3D dataset.

True label	Powerl	L. Veg	I. Surf	Car	Fence	Roof	Façade	Shrub	Tree
Confused with	Roof	Fence	Façade	I. Surf	Shrub	Façade	Roof	Tree	Shrub

and 100% erroneous labels received in both cases. For the noisy oracle $\mathcal{O}_N$ we randomly use any label (excluding the true one). Regarding the systematically confused mapping of $\mathcal{O}_C$, we apply most observed confusions when employing real crowdworkers as presented in Kölle et al. [17], which are summarized in Table 1.

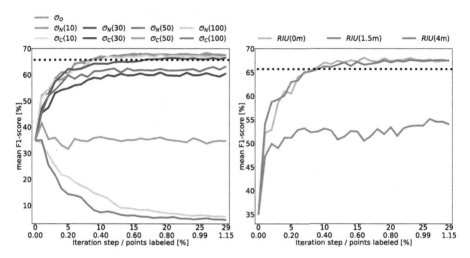

Fig. 6. Comparison of different AL-scenarios when relying on real crowdworkers for the V3D dataset using RF and $wE + DiFS$ (black line represents PL): simulated crowd errors (*left*) and impact of increasing distance to the class border via *RIU* (*right*). (Color figure online)

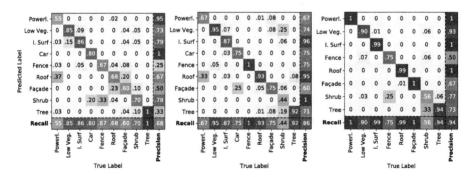

Fig. 7. Comparison of reachable accuracies (normalized confusion matrices) of the crowd when using different values for d_{RIU}. From left to right: $d_{RIU} = 0$ m/1.5 m and 4 m. Accuracies are aggregated via majority vote from 3 acquisitions per point.

This simulation is based on the RF classifier using $wE + DiFS$ with a batch size of 300 for sampling. As visualized in Fig. 6 (*left*), $\mathcal{O}_O$ leads as expected to one of the best performances of the AL loop together with $\mathcal{O}_N(10\%)$ and $\mathcal{O}_C(10\%)$ demonstrating the robustness of our pipeline to a moderate number of labeling errors. All other oracle behaviors naturally diminish accuracies to some extent. Generally it is observable that the confused oracle is especially harmful to the AL loop since systematic false labeling (e.g. according to Table 1) is induced. For instance, the RF performs significantly better when the oracle labels 50% of points randomly false compared to when only 30% of points are labeled systematically false. Other mapping functions of malicious crowdworkers (for instance, labeling all points same or according to any absurd function) are not considered, since such workers can be easily identified using control tasks.

Since our proposed method for minimizing confused labeling (RIU) is only reasonable when the performance of the AL loop can be uphold, we simulate respective AL runs in Fig. 6 (*right*). While increasing the distance to the class border by maximum 1.5 m has no significant impact on the performance of the AL iteration, $d_{RIU} = 4$ m causes the mean F1-score to drop significantly. This is due to selecting less informative samples (i.e. points further away from the class boundary) or that points belonging to a different class than the seed point are selected (see Fig. 4 (*right*) where with $d_{RIU} = 4$ m a street point is selected instead of a car point).

In order to evaluate whether this method helps crowdworkers labeling points, we conducted three crowdsourcing campaigns using the same parameters as for the simulation in Fig. 4 (*right*) and varied $d_{RIU} = 0$ m/1.5 m/4 m. We offered these jobs to the crowd using the *Microworkers* platform as discussed in Kölle et al. [17]. Figure 7 proves our hypothesis that increasing distance to class boundaries is closely tied to label accuracy of crowdworkers. OA was improved from 68% for $d_{RIU} = 0$ m to 86% for 1.5 m and to 94% for 4 m. For $d_{RIU} = 0$ m typical confusion is due to bivalent interpretation possibilities, for instance classes *Roof* vs. *Façade*, *Impervious Surface* vs. *Low Vegetation* and *Shrub* vs. *Fence/Hedge*. Confusion between *Roof* and *Powerline* is mainly caused by the sparsity of the V3D dataset where powerlines are just single points in air difficult for interpretation. Although the labeling accuracy of most classes improves when increasing distance to decision boundary, this does not hold for class *Shrub*, which is either confused with *Low Vegetation* in case of $d_{RIU} = 1.5$ m or *Tree* for $d_{RIU} = 4$ m. This might rather be a problem of misunderstanding of this class and can therefore not be resolved by this strategy.

3.4   Estimation of Reachable Accuracies with Real Crowdworkers

Finally all previous findings are combined in order to estimate the performance of our proposed human-in-the-loop pipeline for our two datasets (Table 2 and 3) and classifiers (Table 2). In each table we compare the respective result of PL on the completely labeled training dataset to AL using $wE + DiFS$, stepwise adding RIU ($d_{RIU} = 1.5$ m, for avoiding $\mathcal{O}_C$) and a noisy oracle $\mathcal{O}_N(10\%)$ (noise assumed to be 10% following Kölle et al. [17] and Fig. 7). Table 2 outlines

Table 2. Comparison of reachable accuracies [%] for different training approaches and assumed oracles using RF and SCNN for the V3D dataset.

Method	F1-score									OA
	Powerl	L. Veg	I. Surf	Car	Fence	Roof	Façade	Shrub	Tree	
RF										
PL	48.39	**83.16**	**91.93**	72.68	14.94	**95.17**	**64.30**	40.60	**80.73**	**84.25**
$wE + DiFS$	61.90	80.53	90.24	**73.12**	**28.58**	94.14	57.08	**43.55**	78.99	82.43
$wE + DiFS + RIU$	67.35	79.37	89.50	70.32	28.53	92.77	60.45	39.62	79.24	81.59
$wE + DiFS + RIU + \mathcal{O}_N$	**68.85**	79.44	90.16	69.43	27.44	92.64	58.06	36.66	77.00	81.17
SCNN										
PL	42.11	**81.40**	**91.11**	72.15	**41.22**	**94.10**	**59.65**	**48.87**	**83.88**	**83.86**
$wE + DiFS$	60.57	79.31	88.59	72.28	24.92	91.21	55.34	43.44	80.16	81.13
$wE + DiFS + RIU$	**63.02**	79.52	89.62	**75.03**	26.33	91.18	54.41	38.45	78.27	80.91
$wE + DiFS + RIU + \mathcal{O}_N$	60.68	78.89	89.48	74.09	22.29	90.64	53.77	39.10	78.54	80.59

Table 3. Comparison of reachable accuracies [%] for different training approaches and assumed oracles using RF for the H3D dataset.

Method	F1-score												OA
	Powerl	L. Veg	I. Surf	Car	U. Fur	Roof	Façade	Shrub	Tree	Gravel	V. Surf	Chim	
PL	30.37	**93.59**	80.23	42.74	**36.71**	**93.80**	**83.03**	**71.11**	**97.84**	32.10	40.93	40.82	**84.85**
$wE + DiFS$	26.10	88.24	81.71	**65.31**	32.97	89.76	77.53	65.33	94.76	**48.65**	**64.06**	**76.22**	83.82
$wE + DiFS + RIU$	32.67	87.88	**85.29**	37.93	34.29	89.65	73.30	61.69	94.40	42.33	57.63	59.81	83.22
$wE + DiFS + RIU + \mathcal{O}_N$	**36.00**	86.70	82.74	38.73	26.90	90.08	73.85	60.96	93.54	48.48	56.14	58.75	82.22

that for the RF, $wE + DiFS$ allows to achieve a segmentation result, which only differs in OA by less than 2% points from PL while only requiring labeling of 1.15% of points from U (assuming unrealistic $\mathcal{O}_O$). When supporting the crowd by RIU, our results still differ less than 3% points from the baseline result of PL or only marginally worse when additionally adding $\mathcal{O}_N$. Compared to our RF classifier, the SCNN yields a slightly bigger loss in OA when applying AL, which is due to the aforementioned overfitting issue. Assuming real crowdworkers (i.e. with RIU and $\mathcal{O}_N$), respective accuracies are less diminished than for the RF.

For the H3D dataset (Table 3) except for n_{DiFS}, which was increased to 100.000 due to the higher point count, all parameters are same as before. Here, sampling and labeling of just 0.59% of U and assuming a realistic crowd oracle only diminishes the OA by less than 3% points. We further observed that under-represented classes such as *Powerline, Gravel, Vertical Surface* and *Chimney* tend to perform better using AL strategies while the accuracies of overrepresented classes decrease marginally. Independent of the dataset, when using AL and considering a real crowd (last row in each table), the impact on classes *Façade, Shrub* and *Urban Furniture* (H3D) is greatest. This is mainly due to the great diversity within these classes. For example, with regard to *Façade* consider any type of façade furniture such as balconies, signs and lamps. Such structures might not be sufficiently sampled by AL and especially by *RIU*.

4 Conclusion

Within this paper we have shown that AL is a well founded approach for crucially reducing labeling effort for semantic segmentation, since annotation is targeted to the most informative 3D points following a similar pattern as the SVM. Basic AL sampling strategies can be purposefully enhanced by means of increasing diversity within one batch when using pool-based AL, thereby further boosting convergence of the iteration. Furthermore, we have proven that even CNN approaches can efficiently work with minimum training datasets. Since our ultimate goal is to shift labeling effort to the crowd, we aim to ease labeling for non-experts using *RIU* in order to avoid systematic errors, for we have demonstrated that especially the confused oracle greatly diminishes the performance of AL. Although *RIU* allows to significantly improve accuracies achieved by the crowd, labeling errors, which are of subjective nature and mainly caused by individual class understanding (e.g. *Tree* vs. *Shrub*), can hardly be avoided.

This work provides an in-depth understanding of the AL part of our proposed hybrid intelligence system where the machine learns solely from the crowd. In order to fully integrate the crowd into the AL loop respective web tools as presented in Kölle et al. [17] are essential. Eventually, we estimate plausible segmentation results for our classifiers (the machine) working together with real human operators (the crowd). We demonstrate that when labeling 1.15% (V3D)/0.59% (H3D) of available training points we can achieve an OA of only about 3% points less compared to PL on the completely labeled training dataset.

References

1. Argamon-Engelson, S., Dagan, I.: Committee-based sample selection for probabilistic classifiers. J. Artif. Intell. Res. **11**, 335–360 (1999)
2. Becker, C., Häni, N., Rosinskaya, E., d'Angelo, E., Strecha, C.: Classification of aerial photogrammetric 3D point clouds. ISPRS Annals IV-1/W1, pp. 3–10 (2017)
3. Branson, S., et al.: Visual recognition with humans in the loop. In: Daniilidis, K., Maragos, P., Paragios, N. (eds.) ECCV 2010. LNCS, vol. 6314, pp. 438–451. Springer, Heidelberg (2010). https://doi.org/10.1007/978-3-642-15561-1_32
4. Breiman, L.: Random forests. Mach. Learn. **45**(1), 5–32 (2001). https://doi.org/10.1023/A:1010933404324
5. Chehata, N., Guo, L., Mallet, C.: Airborne LiDAR feature selection for urban classification using random forests. ISPRS Arch. **38** (2009)
6. Cortes, C., Vapnik, V.: Support-vector networks. Mach. Learn. **20**(3), 273–297 (1995). https://doi.org/10.1007/BF00994018
7. Deng, J., Dong, W., Socher, R., Li, L.J., Li, K., Li, F.F.: ImageNet: a large-scale hierarchical image database. In: CVPR 2009, pp. 248–255 (2009)
8. Ertekin, S., Huang, J., Bottou, L., Giles, L.: Learning on the border: active learning in imbalanced data classification. In: CIKM 2007, pp. 127–136. ACM, New York (2007)
9. Gadiraju, U., Kawase, R., Siehndel, P., Fetahu, B.: Breaking bad: understanding behavior of crowd workers in categorization microtasks. In: HT 2015, pp. 33–38. ACM (2015)

10. Gal, Y., Ghahramani, Z.: Dropout as a Bayesian approximation: representing model uncertainty in deep learning. In: ICML 2016, vol. 48, pp. 1050–1059. PMLR, New York (2016)
11. Graham, B., Engelcke, M., van der Maaten, L.: 3D semantic segmentation with submanifold sparse convolutional networks. In: CVPR 2018, pp. 9224–9232 (2018)
12. Haala, N., Kölle, M., Cramer, M., Laupheimer, D., Mandlburger, G., Glira, P.: hybrid georeferencing, enhancement and classification of ultra-high resolution UAV LiDAR and image point clouds for monitoring applications. ISPRS Annals V-2-2020, pp. 727–734 (2020)
13. Hirth, M., Hoßfeld, T., Tran-Gia, P.: Anatomy of a crowdsourcing platform - using the example of Microworkers.com. In: IMIS 2011, pp. 322–329. IEEE Computer Society, Washington (2011)
14. Hui, Z., et al.: An active learning method for DEM extraction from airborne LiDAR point clouds. IEEE Access 7, 89366–89378 (2019)
15. Kellenberger, B., Marcos, D., Lobry, S., Tuia, D.: Half a percent of labels is enough: efficient animal detection in UAV imagery using deep CNNs and active learning. TRGS 57(12), 9524–9533 (2019)
16. Kirsch, A., van Amersfoort, J., Gal, Y.: BatchBALD: efficient and diverse batch acquisition for deep Bayesian active learning. In: NIPS 2019, pp. 7026–7037. Curran Associates, Inc. (2019)
17. Kölle, M., Walter, V., Schmohl, S., Soergel, U.: Hybrid acquisition of high quality training data for semantic segmentation of 3D point clouds using crowd-based active learning. ISPRS Annals V-2-2020, pp. 501–508 (2020)
18. Krizhevsky, A.: Learning multiple layers of features from tiny images. Technical Report TR-2009, University of Toronto, Toronto (2009)
19. Li, N., Pfeifer, N.: Active learning to extend training data for large area airborne LiDAR classification. ISPRS Archives XLII-2/W13, pp. 1033–1037 (2019)
20. Lin, Y., Vosselman, G., Cao, Y., Yang, M.Y.: Efficient training of semantic point cloud segmentation via active learning. ISPRS Annals V-2-2020, pp. 243–250 (2020)
21. Lloyd, S.P.: Least squares quantization in PCM. IEEE Trans. Inf. Theory 28(2), 129–137 (1982)
22. Lockhart, J., Assefa, S., Balch, T., Veloso, M.: Some people aren't worth listening to: periodically retraining classifiers with feedback from a team of end users. CoRR abs/2004.13152 (2020)
23. Luo, H., et al.: Semantic labeling of mobile lidar point clouds via active learning and higher order MRF. TGRS 56(7), 3631–3644 (2018)
24. Mackowiak, R., Lenz, P., Ghori, O., Diego, F., Lange, O., Rother, C.: CEREALS - cost-effective region-based active learning for semantic segmentation. In: BMVC 2018 (2018)
25. Niemeyer, J., Rottensteiner, F., Soergel, U.: Contextual classification of lidar data and building object detection in urban areas. ISPRS J. 87, 152–165 (2014)
26. Patra, S., Bruzzone, L.: A cluster-assumption based batch mode active learning technique. Pattern Recogn. Lett. 33(9), 1042–1048 (2012)
27. Schmohl, S., Sörgel, U.: Submanifold sparse convolutional networks for semantic segmentation of large-scale ALS point clouds. ISPRS Annals IV-2/W5, pp. 77–84 (2019)
28. Settles, B.: Active learning literature survey. Computer Sciences Technical Report 1648, University of Wisconsin-Madison (2009)
29. Tuia, D., Ratle, F., Pacifici, F., Kanevski, M.F., Emery, W.J.: Active learning methods for remote sensing image classification. TGRS 47(7), 2218–2232 (2009)

30. Vaughan, J.W.: Making better use of the crowd: how crowdsourcing can advance machine learning research. J. Mach. Learn. Res. **18**(193), 1–46 (2018)
31. Walter, V., Kölle, M., Yin, Y.: Evaluation and optimisation of crowd-based collection of trees from 3D point clouds. ISPRS Annals V-4-2020, pp. 49–56 (2020)
32. Walter, V., Soergel, U.: Implementation, results, and problems of paid crowd-based geospatial data collection. PFG **86**, 187–197 (2018). https://doi.org/10.1007/s41064-018-0058-z
33. Weinmann, M., Jutzi, B., Hinz, S., Mallet, C.: Semantic point cloud interpretation based on optimal neighborhoods, relevant features and efficient classifiers. ISPRS J. **105**, 286–304 (2015)
34. Xu, Z., Akella, R., Zhang, Y.: Incorporating diversity and density in active learning for relevance feedback. In: Amati, G., Carpineto, C., Romano, G. (eds.) ECIR 2007. LNCS, vol. 4425, pp. 246–257. Springer, Heidelberg (2007). https://doi.org/10.1007/978-3-540-71496-5_24
35. Zhdanov, F.: Diverse mini-batch active learning. CoRR abs/1901.05954 (2019)

Towards Urban Tree Recognition in Airborne Point Clouds with Deep 3D Single-Shot Detectors

Stefan Schmohl[✉], Michael Kölle, Rudolf Frolow, and Uwe Soergel

University of Stuttgart, Geschwister-Scholl-Str. 24D, 70174 Stuttgart, Germany
{stefan.schmohl,michael.koelle,uwe.soergel}@ifp.uni-stuttgart.de

Abstract. Automatic mapping of individual urban trees is increasingly important to city administration and planing. Although deep learning algorithms are now standard methodology in computer vision, their adaption to individual tree detection in urban areas has hardly been investigated so far. In this work, we propose a deep single-shot object detection network to find urban trees in point clouds from airborne laser scanning. The network consists of a sparse 3D convolutional backbone for feature extraction and a subsequent single-shot region proposal network for the actual detection. It takes as input raw 3D voxel clouds, discretized from the point cloud in preprocessing. Outputs are cylindrical tree objects paired with their detection scores. We train and evaluate the network on the ISPRS Vaihingen 3D Benchmark dataset with custom tree object labels. The general feasibility of our approach is demonstrated. It achieves promising results compared to a traditional 2D baseline using watershed segmentation. We also conduct comparisons with state-of-the-art machine learning methods for semantic point segmentation.

Keywords: Deep learning · Sparse convolutional network · Airborne laser scanning · Vegetation

1 Introduction

Managing urban vegetation is of growing importance for city administrations. High and medium vegetation, e.g. trees and shrubs, have positive effects on local climate and quality of living. However, global warming puts vegetation increasingly under stress and therefore needs more maintenance [3].

Local administrations often use dedicated systems to manage their green spaces, for example to manage watering during particularly dry weather conditions or for hazard prevention. Because trees are of particular concern, they are usually managed in special tree cadasters, containing information like position, height, crown width and species of the individual trees. However, these databases are usually limited to trees on public grounds or along streets. For this reason, an automatic mapping by means of remote sensing is of peculiar interest [18].

© Springer Nature Switzerland AG 2021
A. Del Bimbo et al. (Eds.): ICPR 2020 Workshops, LNCS 12667, pp. 521–535, 2021.
https://doi.org/10.1007/978-3-030-68787-8_38

Tree detection and delineation from airborne laser scanning (ALS) is a well-studied problem in forestry [12]. Arguably, most common approaches leverage a canopy height model (CHM), which is a normalized digital surface model (nDSM) over exclusively tree-covered areas. These height models are derived from point clouds acquired via either ALS or photogrammetry. In such homogeneous scenes, single tree detection can be achieved by searching for local maxima in the nDSM. For delineation, a variety of segmentation methods is used in literature, like for example watershed segmentation or region growing [4, 9, 13, 29].

In urban areas, CHM based methods need to filter out non-tree regions in order to reduce false positives. This can be achieved with vegetation indices from multispectral imagery like NDVI and geometrical features from the point cloud [1, 19, 21, 38, 47]. ALS provides additional features beneficial for vegetation recognition. Laser beams emitted by an ALS sensor are able to partly penetrate higher vegetation such as trees and bushes and to record multiple returning echos, resulting in characteristic representations of vegetation in ALS point clouds [11, 23, 29].

As an alternative to ALS point clouds, other kinds of data have been studied for urban tree detection. For example, [42] separate high-density point clouds from mobile mapping systems (MMS) in tree or non-tree points on the basis of eigenvalue features, followed by separating individual trees using a 2D mean shift segmentation. MMS however can only cover trees seen from street-level and its data impose distinct prerequisites compared to airborne data like ALS. The work of [41] in contrast combines detections by Faster-RCNN deep learning object detectors from both street-level and aerial RGB imagery.

Recent advances in deep learning accelerated progress in many research fields, not least those related to computer vision. Artificial neural networks also proved to be accurate and fast tools for semantic segmentation of large ALS point clouds [33, 43]. Such networks can be used to find all points in a point cloud that belong to trees. Yet, deep learning tends to require large amounts of training data. Generating semantic point labels to train such a deep neural network is a tedious task. An alternative to semantic segmentation is the task of object detection. It may be easier to label relatively few ground truth tree objects in form of bounding circles or cylinders. In addition, object-centered detection networks yield cohesive entities including positions and sizes.

Several well established deep learning algorithms and their variants exist for general 2D object detection [6, 20, 28, 31]. Xie et al. [44] construct a two-phase tree detector. In the first phase, tree proposals are identified in a normalized height model by optimizing a tree-shape approximator. In the second phase, non-tree objects are filtered out by a CNN. Pleşsoianu et al. [25] proposed a single-shot detection network (SSD) [20] to find individual trees. They experiment with varying combinations of input features like RGB and different height representations derived from a DSM. Whilst also implementing a SSD, our method in contrast aims to work more directly on the underlying point cloud, obviating the need to find the optimal height rendering.

Deep learning architectures for 3D object detection can be found mostly in the field of autonomous driving and indoor scene understanding [5,37]. Broadly speaking, such approaches can be divided into 3 groups: a) 2D networks working on projections of the point cloud [2,15,36] b) networks with 2D backbones and a learned projection from a small 3D network at the beginning [16] c) pure 3D networks. In the later case, some works use dense 3D convolution [17,49], which might be to computationally expensive. Several papers utilize PointNet-style [27] backbones [10,26,34,46]. In parallel to the development of this work, sparse convolutional backbones gained increasing popularity in computer vision [30,35,40,45,50], which is a more efficient approach than PointNet [35,45]. Our architecture is most similar to [45], however we omit the learned voxel representation. Furthermore, we use a more complex 3D U-Net backbone [32], but in turn use a simpler region proposal network.

In this work, our contribution is as follows: we propose a deep 3D single-shot detector for tree detection in ALS point clouds. Its backbone is formed by a sparse 3D convolutional network, which obviates the need for 2D projections in pre-processing. A small scale case study on the Vaihingen 3D Semantic Labeling Benchmark dataset with custom tree cylinder labels is used for proof of concept. Besides a watershed segmentation baseline, we further compare our object-level results to point-level state-of-the-art semantic segmentation methods on the original Vaihingen 3D benchmark.

2   Methodology

2.1   Architecture

Feature Extraction Network. To detect individual trees in point clouds, we use a single shot detection network [20] for 3D input. For clarity, we divide the architecture into two main parts: a sparse 3D backbone for feature extraction and a detection head (Fig. 1).

As backbone, we use a 3D submanifold sparse U-Net [7,32] for three-dimensional feature extraction as described previously in [33]. It takes as input voxelized point cloud tiles, which comply to a discrete but sparse form of the point cloud. Per-voxel features are averaged from all respective inlying points. For this work, we chose a sample tile size of $32 \times 32 \times 64$ m and a voxel size of 0.5 m per side [33]. Hence, the network's input shape is $64 \times 64 \times 128$ voxels. The larger size in height ensures that tiles cover the entire vertical data spread at their respective location, therefore obviating vertical tiling. The output are 32 learned features per voxel, which can be used either for a semantic segmentation head like in [33] or, as in this case, a detection head.

Flattening Layers. Between the purely 3D backbone and the region proposal network, three sparse convolutional layers flatten the three-dimensional activations down to two dimensions [45,49]. We achieve this by setting both stride and filter size in z direction to 8 for the first two layers. For the third layer,

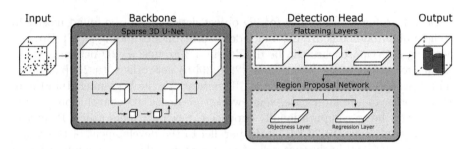

Fig. 1. Proposed network architecture.

the vertical direction is convolved with a stride and size of 4, so that only one channel is left in z. Reducing the height dimension narrows the search space of possible detections by removing vertical redundancy, since multiple trees on top of each other are very unlikely.

In the horizontal directions, stride and filter size are 1 and 3, respectively. The final flattening layer strides by 2 both for x and y, which quarters the number of possible detections to further reduce computational complexity later on.

Thereby, the flattened shape is $32 \times 32 \times 1 \times (5+1) \cdot K$, where the last dimension represents convolutional filter channels and K is the number of default anchor shapes in the region proposal network. We append ReLU non-linearities and batch normalization after each convolutional layer.

Region Proposal Network. The region proposal network finally completes the architecture as a single shot detection network [20]. All layers in this part are standard - i.e. dense - 2D layers. Since the point cloud's horizontal projection is mostly dense in our case, there is no computational benefit gained from using sparse convolution at this stage of the pipeline. Two separate branches of convolutional layers further process the flattened activations in parallel: an objectness layer and a regression layer.

The objectness layer predicts a detection score x_i for each of the K anchor shapes at each of the 32×32 anchor points. The regression layer likewise outputs 5 offsets $\hat{\Delta}_x$, $\hat{\Delta}_y$, $\hat{\Delta}_z$, $\hat{\Delta}_r$, $\hat{\Delta}_h$ for each (cylindrical) anchor.

Tree Shape Encoding. In contrast to standard bounding boxes, we use a cylindrical object definition to better fit the typical tree shape. We follow the usual differential encoding principle [6], however adapted to cylinders instead of bounding boxes. The network's actual regression output are offsets $\hat{\Delta}$ to so called *anchors* or *default boxes/cylinders*. Compared to regressing cylinder parameters directly, this allows us to aid the network by pre-defining default anchor shapes. Also, the exact position of a detection is refined by regressing offsets to the spatial location of the object in the output activation map.

We use $K = 3$ default anchor shapes, defined by pairs of radius r^a and height h^a: (3 m, 8 m), (5 m, 12 m) and (7 m, 16 m). These values are based on the tree size distribution of the ground truth, as shown in Fig. 2. Anchor position x^a and y^a is the location in the output activation map, with z^a set to 0. The actual coordinate and size of a detection in the local sample reference system is then:

$$x = x^a + \hat{\Delta}_x \cdot r^a \qquad y = y^a + \hat{\Delta}_y \cdot r^a \qquad z = z^a + \hat{\Delta}_z \cdot h^a \qquad (1)$$

$$r = \exp(\hat{\Delta}_r) \cdot r^a \qquad h = \exp(\hat{\Delta}_h) \cdot h^a$$

Inversely, when deriving the offset of a ground truth cylinder g to a default anchor for the regression loss during training, we compute:

$$\Delta_x = (x^g - x^a)/r^a \qquad \Delta_y = (y^g - y^a)/r^a \qquad \Delta_z = (z^g - z^a)/h^a \qquad (2)$$

$$\Delta_r = log(r^g/r^a) \qquad \Delta_h = log(h^g/h^a)$$

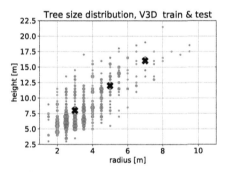

Fig. 2. Tree size distribution in our combined training and testing set, containing 428 individual trees in 170 unique sizes. The trees from the test set inside this distribution leans more towards the smaller sizes, with less outliers in the larger region. Circle area represents frequency. Anchor sizes are marked by three black crosses.

2.2   Training

Training data is augmented by rotating it in $30°$ increments and tiling with an overlap of 30%. Coordinates per tile are reduced, so that $\min(x) = \min(y) = \min(z) = 0$. We use stochastic gradient descent with an initial learning rate of 0.1, which decreases by factor 0.7 every 3 non-improving epochs. Weight decay is set to 10^{-5} and momentum to 0.9. Training is stopped after 8 epochs of stagnating mean average precision (mAP). Although a separate validation set for early stopping is standard practice, we validate on the training set. In preliminary experiments, we noticed no accuracy decline on a separate validation set during long training runs. Because of this, we rather preferred to have a larger training set by not splitting a part of it of into the separate validation set.

Matching Strategy. Before calculating the loss at each training iteration, first one has to determine, which of the $32 \times 32 \times K$ detections are to be considered true positives or false positives, more commonly known in object detection literature as positives and negatives, respectively. For each ground truth tree, we select all detections with an IoU overlap higher than 0.6 as matches and thereby positives. To assist training in early stages, for each ground truth the detection with the highest IoU overlap is also counted as a match. From all other detections, those which do not have any ground truth IoU higher than 0.4 are selected as negative candidates. These values, like most of the hyperparameters in this work, have been empirically determined by an extensive hyperparameter search.

Loss Function. We use a combined loss function similar to works like [20] and [31]. The overall loss (per tile sample) is the weighted sum of an objectness loss L_{obj} and a regression loss L_{reg}.

$$L = \alpha \cdot \frac{1}{N_{pos} + N_{neg}} \cdot L_{obj} + \beta \cdot \frac{1}{5 \cdot N_{pos}} \cdot L_{reg} \tag{3}$$

with N_{pos} beeing the number of positive detections and N_{neg} the number of negative detections. We empirically chose $\alpha = 1$ and $\beta = 3$.

For the objectness loss we opted for the binary cross entropy. Let x_i be the output of the objectness layer for a detection i (at position x^a, y^a and for anchor k), then the loss can be written as:

$$L_{obj} = -p \sum_{i \in Pos}^{N_{pos}} y_i \cdot \log(\sigma(x_i)) - \sum_{i \in Neg}^{N_{neg}} (1 - y_i) \cdot \log(1 - \sigma(x_i)) \tag{4}$$

where σ is the sigmoid function to scale the objectness value to a score between 0 and 1. The ground truth objectness is $y_i = 1$ for positive and $y_i = 0$ for negative candidates. We balance the influence of positive and negative detections on the loss by specifying $p = N_{neg}/N_{pos}$, which is set to 0 for $N_{pos} = 0$.

For regression, smooth L1 loss [6] is used on all positive detections. For $\hat{\Delta}_i$ being the predicted regression offset vector for detection i and Δ_i being the offset of the matching ground truth to the detections default anchor $k(i)$:

$$L_{reg} = \sum_{i \in Pos}^{N_{pos}} \sum_{j \in [x,y,z,r,h]} L1_{smooth}(\hat{\Delta}_{i,j}, \Delta_{i,j}) \tag{5}$$

$$L1_{smooth} = \begin{cases} 0.5 \cdot (\hat{\Delta} - \Delta)^2 & \text{if } |\hat{\Delta} - \Delta| < 1 \\ |\hat{\Delta} - \Delta| - 0.5 & \text{otherwise} \end{cases} \tag{6}$$

2.3   Inference

At inference, we predict detections for each tile individually. Non-maximum supression (NMS) is applied with a maximum allowed IoU overlap of 0.2 and a minimum objectness score of 0.05 to speed up NMS. Then, all detections are transformed into the original coordinate system and merged together. A final NMS removes overlapping trees at former tile borders.

2.4 Baseline

As a baseline, we use a 2D watershed segmentation operating on a nDSM and assisted by other supplementary 2D projections computed from the point cloud using the software opals [24]. The resolution of those 2D feature grids is 1 m.

In pre-processing, the nDSM is firstly smoothed by a Gaussian filter. A binary tree mask is derived by thresholding NDVI > 0.27. Trees are furthermore differentiated from low vegetation by selecting only areas with a minimum of 2 returns per signal. After that, morphological operations are used to filter out outliers and to close obvious gaps in tree borders. The image closing is done with a mask of size 5×5 and afterwards the image opening is performed with a mask of size 3×3.

For each segment from the watershed algorithm, we fit a circle through it's border pixels to derive an estimate of the horizontal center and crown radius. Tree height is obtained by calculating the maximum height of each segment.

3 Data

To our knowledge, there is no appropriately large benchmark dataset available for urban tree detection from ALS data. Therefore, we use the ALS point cloud from the ISPRS Vaihingen 3D Semantic Labeling benchmark dataset (V3D) as data basis for this work [22]. Its training and test subsets comprise 753,876 and 411,722 points, respectively. Point density is about 4–$8 \, \mathrm{pts/m^2}$ and point attributes include intensity, near infrared, red, green, echo number and number of echos, with up to 2 returns per emitted signal. All points have been labeled with one of the following nine classes: *Powerline, Low vegetation, Impervious surfaces, Car, Fence/Hedge, Roof, Facade, Shrub* and *Tree*.

2D tree outlines exist as ground truth in the ISPRS Urban classification and 3D reconstruction benchmark, which only partly covers V3D. In order to take full advantage of the 3D benchmark dataset for our purpose, we decided to generate our own 3D ground truth, which completely covers the semantic point cloud. Using the complete V3D benchmark dataset provides more spatial area to train and test on - which is still very small for deep learning standards - and also allows us to compare our method to other recent state-of-the-art machine learning methods.

To train our network, we manually labeled 269 training trees and 159 trees for testing using the tool described in [39]. Tree sizes delivered by the labeling tool have a resolution of 50 cm. We adhered to the semantic point labels as accurately as it was feasible. Figure 3 shows the training set inside the labeling tool. The overall tree size distribution is shown in Fig. 2. Each ground truth tree is described by 5 parameters: x, y, z, *height* and *radius*.

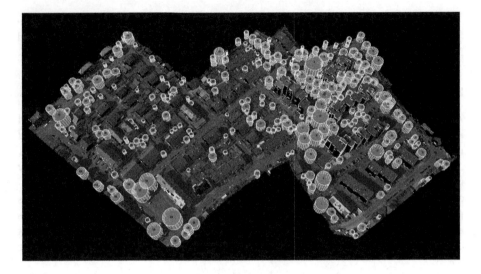

Fig. 3. Training set with ground truth cylinders.

4   Results

4.1   Training

The network trained for about one and a half hours on an Nvidia Titan RTX and finished after 50 epochs. The precision-recall curves for the augmented training set in Fig. 4 indicate that the network accurately finds all trees in the augmented training set, based on the very good average precision (AP) for lower intersection-over-union (IoU) decision thresholds. However, the regressed parameters apparently do not fit as well, as shown by the decline in AP for higher IoU. While we can use almost all anchor points for the objectness loss, the regression loss has only a few positive detections to train on, which might be the reason for its lower performance. Higher weighting of the regression loss, i.e. higher values for β in Eq. 3, did not improve the results.

4.2   Quantitative Assessment

We evaluate the performance of the tree detection network by average precision at three IoU thresholds (0.3, 0.5, 0.7) in Fig. 5. The network does not perform as well on the pure training set compared to the augmented one in Fig. 4. Accuracy drops even more at the test set. The inflection points of the P(R) curves correlate to an objectness score of about 0.995. We will use this threshold for further analysis for a fair recall/precision trade-off.

In order to compare our results to the baseline, the metrics described in [39] are used, namely volumetric correctness, completeness and quality. We also count the number of true positives, false negatives and false positives. For all true positives, we report the RMSE error for position, radius and height.

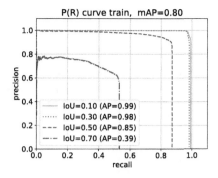

Fig. 4. Precision-recall curve for the augmented training set. IoU values are used as thresholds, to determine if a detection has enough overlap with a ground truth object to be considered correct.

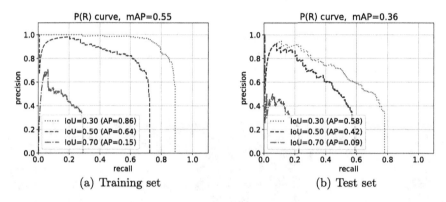

Fig. 5. Precision-recall curves for the pure training set and test set.

Detections are counted as true positives, if they have an (volumetric) overlap to a ground truth object higher than 50%.

As can be seen in Table 1, our method outperforms the baseline in terms of true positives, false negatives and positional RMSE. Yet, it severely falls behind on false positives and height accuracy. This explains the poor values in the volumetric metrics. In practice, height regression could be easily replaced by a height estimation as used for the baseline.

Performance on the test set is overall worse than on the training set for both methods, however even more so for the neural network. This indicates that we have not used enough training data for our model and therefore lack generalization. The quality of true positives (RMSE) keep roughly the same, since the real bottleneck here is the overlap threshold of 50%.

Table 1. Object-based comparison with baseline. RSME are in meters. The values for correctness, completeness and quality refer to [%].

	Training set								
	TP	FP	FN	$RMSE_p$	$RMSE_r$	$RMSE_h$	Corr.	Comp.	Qual.
Baseline	68	**58**	201	1.60	0.62	**0.76**	**48.1**	**40.3**	**28.0**
Ours	**130**	74	**139**	**1.45**	**0.47**	1.41	46.8	35.6	25.3
	Test set								
	TP	FP	FN	$RMSE_p$	$RMSE_r$	$RMSE_h$	Corr.	Comp.	Qual.
Baseline	37	**41**	122	1.50	**0.43**	**0.81**	**37.2**	**31.7**	**20.7**
Ours	**50**	80	**109**	**1.42**	0.47	1.52	23.2	28.9	14.8

4.3   Qualitative Assessment

The previous impression coincides with the qualitative analysis of the tree predictions. Figure 6 shows detections and ground truth together in a top-down view of the test set. There are some pronounced false positives on buildings. It is notable, that these are mostly centered around chimneys. In Fig. 7 one can see some examples for wrongly estimated heights and z-positions.

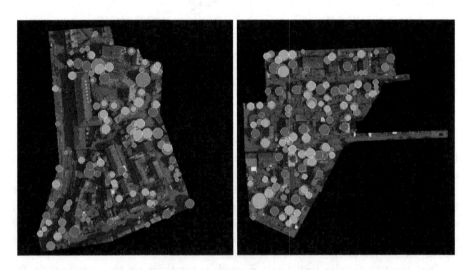

Fig. 6. Test set top-view. Ground truth is in green, predictions are blue. Their horizontal overlap, i.e. true positive area, is in light turquoise. (Color figure online)

On the training set, the detector misses mostly the very small or very large trees (Fig. 8). The former are hardly distinguishable from shrub even for the human interpreters. False positives are only due to the strict overlap threshold, the positions and shape are reasonable in visual quality analysis (only 17 false positives are left at an overlap threshold of 0.3, 3 for 0.1).

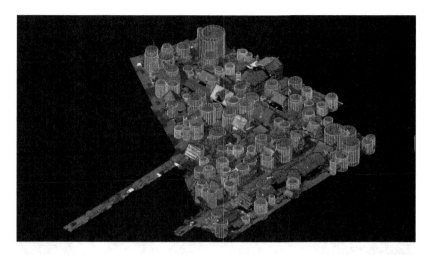

Fig. 7. Test set side-view. Ground truth is in green, predictions are in blue. (Color figure online)

4.4   Comparison with Semantic Segmentation

In Table 2, we compare our results to state-of-the-art methods on the V3D semantic labeling benchmark. For this, we label all points within any tree cylinder as tree points. This allows the computation of precision, recall and F1 for the tree class of the point-wise ground truth of the V3D benchmark. We also include an active learning (AL) approach to the analysis, similar to [14], which is another way to reduce the amount of training samples. In this case, we used 9,156 training points among all classes, corresponding to only 1.15% of the training set.

The row for cylinder ground truth in Table 2 gives a point of reference about the level of accuracy that can be expected from our method in this analysis. Misclassifications here are mainly due to surface points under the actual tree, and to a lesser extent due to shrubs and hedges. Accuracy is similar to those of the semantic classifiers.

In this evaluation, the baseline significantly outperforms our method. On the training set, the detectors precision is still on par with ground truth and baseline. The recall however is lower, partly due to the height problem discussed above. On the test set, the deficit in precision is mostly due to falsely detected houses.

Unsurprisingly, all methods trained on point labels outperform the cylinder-based methods in regards to point-wise labels. However, those were trained on much larger and more costly sets of labels. The active learning variants are on par with those trained on fully labeled data, but still used more labels and are more complex procedures all together. The best overall performance with an F1-score of 84.2% is achieved by a semantic segmentation network using the same backbone as our work [33]. The values for the training set give an indication

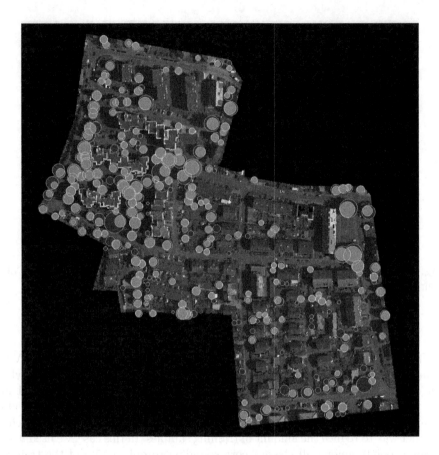

Fig. 8. Training set top-view. Ground truth is in green, predictions are blue. Their horizontal overlap, i.e. true positive area, is in light turquoise. (Color figure online)

Table 2. Comparison to point-wise semantic labels for the V3D tree class. The values for precision, recall and F1-score refer to [%].

	Training set			Test set		
	Precision	Recall	F1	Precision	Recall	F1
Ground truth	77.9	84.9	81.3	76.2	80.1	78.1
Baseline	77.6	67.9	72.4	63.4	56.6	59.8
Ours	78.2	59.0	67.3	45.7	48.9	47.3
Random Forest AL	93.2	90.2	91.7	77.1	81.0	79.0
SSCN AL	92.4	90.0	91.2	76.9	83.7	80.2
Random Forest [8]	**99.3**	**99.4**	**99.3**	75.9	**86.2**	80.1
SSCN [33]	81.7	85.8	83.7	86.7	81.8	**84.2**
ALSNet (PointNet++) [43]	97.3	97.1	97.2	66.6	84.5	74.5
MCNN [48]	–	–	–	**88.3**	77.5	82.6

about how well our method could perform on data that follows a distribution more similar to the training set of this study.

5   Conclusion and Outlook

In this work, we proposed a deep 3D single-shot detector for tree detection in ALS point clouds. A small case study on the Vaihingen 3D dataset demonstrated its general feasibility. Good performance can be achieved for single tree identification. However, we encountered larger issues regarding the regression of the vertical tree shape. While performance on training data is good, the network has problems with generalization and finding trees with lower a-priori probability, i.e. very small or very large ones.

In future work, we expect to solve most of the issues with larger training data. We are currently working on a large urban reference dataset. If this does not improve height regression, this part can be replaced by a more straight forward measurement in the point cloud. Another approach to improve accuracy could be to more closely intertwine the deep learning methodology with problem related priors like the tree shape distribution to reliably detect trees of rarer sizes.

Acknowledgements. The Vaihingen dataset was provided by the German Society for Photogrammetry, Remote Sensing and Geoinformation (DGPF).

References

1. Bulatov, D., Wayand, I., Schilling, H.: Automatic tree-crown detection in challenging scenarios. In: ISPRS Archives, vol. XLI-B3, pp. 575–582 (2016)
2. Chen, X., Ma, H., Wan, J., Li, B., Xia, T.: Multi-view 3D object detection network for autonomous driving. In: CVPR, pp. 6526–6534 (2017)
3. City of Melville Council: Urban forest strategic plan 2017–2036: Plan a: City-controlled plan. Technical report, City of Melville, Perth, Australia (2017)
4. Eysn, L., et al.: A benchmark of lidar-based single tree detection methods using heterogeneous forest data from the alpine space. Forests **6**(5), 1721–1747 (2015)
5. Geiger, A., Lenz, P., Urtasun, R.: Are we ready for autonomous driving? The Kitti vision benchmark suite. In: CVPR, pp. 3354–3361 (2012)
6. Girshick, R.: Fast R-CNN. In: ICCV, pp. 1440–1448 (2015)
7. Graham, B., Engelcke, M., van der Maaten, L.: 3D semantic segmentation with submanifold sparse convolutional networks. In: CVPR, pp. 9224–9232 (2018)
8. Haala, N., Kölle, M., Cramer, M., Laupheimer, D., Mandlburger, G., Glira, P.: Hybrid georeferencing, enhancement and classification of ultra-high resolution UAV lidar and image point clouds for monitoring applications. ISPRS Ann. **V-2-2020**, 727–734 (2020)
9. Hirschmugl, M., Ofner, M., Raggam, J., Schardt, M.: Single tree detection in very high resolution remote sensing data. Remote Sens. Environ. **110**(4), 533–544 (2007). ForestSAT Special Issue
10. Hu, P., Held, D., Ramanan, D.: Learning to optimally segment point clouds. IEEE Robot. Autom. Lett. **5**(2), 875–882 (2020)
11. Höfle, B., Hollaus, M., Hagenauer, J.: Urban vegetation detection using radiometrically calibrated small-footprint full-waveform airborne LiDAR data. ISPRS J. Photogram. Remote Sens. **67**, 134–147 (2012)

12. Kaartinen, H., et al.: An international comparison of individual tree detection and extraction using airborne laser scanning. Remote Sens. **4**(4), 950–974 (2012)
13. Koch, B., Heyder, U., Weinacker, H.: Detection of individual tree crowns in airborne lidar data. Photogram. Eng. Remote Sens. **72**(4), 357–363 (2006)
14. Kölle, M., Walter, V., Schmohl, S., Soergel, U.: Hybrid acquisition of high quality training data for semantic segmentation of 3D point clouds using crowd-based active learning. ISPRS Ann. **V-2-2020**, 501–508 (2020)
15. Ku, J., Mozifian, M., Lee, J., Harakeh, A., Waslander, S.L.: Joint 3D proposal generation and object detection from view aggregation. In: IROS, pp. 1–8 (2018)
16. Lang, A.H., Vora, S., Caesar, H., Zhou, L., Yang, J., Beijbom, O.: Pointpillars: fast encoders for object detection from point clouds. In: CVPR, pp. 12689–12697 (2019)
17. Li, B.: 3D fully convolutional network for vehicle detection in point cloud. In: IROS, pp. 1513–1518 (2017)
18. Li, X., Chen, W.Y., Sanesi, G., Lafortezza, R.: Remote sensing in urban forestry: recent applications and future directions. Remote Sens. **11**(10) (2019)
19. Liew, S.C., Huang, X., Lin, E.S., Shi, C., Yee, A.T.K., Tandon, A.: Integration of tree database derived from satellite imagery and LiDAR point cloud data. ISPRS Arch. **XLII-4/W10**, 105–111 (2018)
20. Liu, W., et al.: SSD: single shot multibox detector. In: Leibe, B., Matas, J., Sebe, N., Welling, M. (eds.) ECCV 2016. LNCS, vol. 9905, pp. 21–37. Springer, Cham (2016). https://doi.org/10.1007/978-3-319-46448-0_2
21. Man, Q., Dong, P., Yang, X., Wu, Q., Han, R.: Automatic extraction of grasses and individual trees in urban areas based on airborne hyperspectral and lidar data. Remote Sens. **12**(17) (2020)
22. Niemeyer, J., Rottensteiner, F., Soergel, U.: Contextual classification of lidar data and building object detection in urban areas. ISPRS J. **87**, 152–165 (2014)
23. Persson, A.: Extraction of individual trees using laser radar data. Technical report, Swedish Defence Research Agency (2001)
24. Pfeifer, N., Mandlburger, G., Otepka, J., Karel, W.: OPALS - a framework for airborne laser scanning data analysis. Comput. Environ. Urban Syst. **45**, 125–136 (2014)
25. Pleoianu, A.I., Stupariu, M.S., andric, I., Pătru-Stupariu, I., Drăguţ L.: Individual tree-crown detection and species classification in very high-resolution remote sensing imagery using a deep learning ensemble model. Remote Sens. **12**(15) (2020)
26. Qi, C.R., Litany, O., He, K., Guibas, L.: Deep Hough voting for 3D object detection in point clouds. In: ICCV, pp. 9276–9285 (2019)
27. Qi, C.R., Yi, L., Su, H., Guibas, L.J.: PointNet++: deep hierarchical feature learning on point sets in a metric space. In: NIPS, pp. 5105–5114 (2017)
28. Redmon, J., Farhadi, A.: YOLOv3: an incremental improvement. CoRR abs/1804.02767 (2018)
29. Reitberger, J.: 3D Segmentierung von Einzelbäumen und Baumartenklasifikation aus Daten flugzeuggetragener Full Waveform Laserscanner. Ph.D. thesis, Fakultät für Bauingenieur- und Vermessungswesen der Technischen Universität München (2010)
30. Ren, M., Pokrovsky, A., Yang, B., Urtasun, R.: SBNet: sparse blocks network for fast inference. In: CVPR, pp. 8711–8720 (2018)
31. Ren, S., He, K., Girshick, R., Sun, J.: Faster R-CNN: towards real-time object detection with region proposal networks. IEEE PAMI **39**(6), 1137–1149 (2017)

32. Ronneberger, O., Fischer, P., Brox, T.: U-Net: convolutional networks for biomedical image segmentation. In: Navab, N., Hornegger, J., Wells, W.M., Frangi, A.F. (eds.) MICCAI 2015. LNCS, vol. 9351, pp. 234–241. Springer, Cham (2015). https://doi.org/10.1007/978-3-319-24574-4_28

33. Schmohl, S., Soergel, U.: Submanifold sparse convolutional networks for semantic segmentation of large-scale ALS point clouds. In: ISPRS Annals, vol. IV-2/W5, pp. 77–84 (2019)

34. Shi, S., Wang, X., Li, H.: PointRCNN: 3D object proposal generation and detection from point cloud. In: CVPR, pp. 770–779 (2019)

35. Shi, S., Wang, Z., Wang, X., Li, H.: From points to parts: 3D object detection from point cloud with part-aware and part-aggregation network. CoRR abs/1907.03670 (2019)

36. Simon, M., Milz, S., Amende, K., Gross, H.-M.: Complex-YOLO: an Euler-region-proposal for real-time 3D object detection on point clouds. In: Leal-Taixé, L., Roth, S. (eds.) ECCV 2018. LNCS, vol. 11129, pp. 197–209. Springer, Cham (2019). https://doi.org/10.1007/978-3-030-11009-3_11

37. Song, S., Lichtenberg, S.P., Xiao, J.: Sun RGB-D: a RGB-D scene understanding benchmark suite. In: CVPR, pp. 567–576 (2015)

38. Wolf (né Straub), B.M., Heipke, C.: Automatic extraction and delineation of single trees from remote sensing data. Mach. Vis. Appl. **18**(5), 317–330 (2007)

39. Walter, V., Kölle, M., Yin, Y.: Evaluation and optimisation of crowd-based collection of trees from 3D point clouds. ISPRS Ann. **V-4-2020**, 49–56 (2020)

40. Wang, D.Z., Posner, I.: Voting for voting in online point cloud object detection. In: Proceedings of Robotics: Science and Systems (2015)

41. Wegner, J.D., Branson, S., Hall, D., Schindler, K., Perona, P.: Cataloging public objects using aerial and street-level images - urban trees. In: CVPR, pp. 6014–6023 (2016)

42. Weinmann, M., Weinmann, M., Mallet, C., Brédif, M.: A classification-segmentation framework for the detection of individual trees in dense mms point cloud data acquired in urban areas. Remote Sens. **9**(3) (2017)

43. Winiwarter, L., Mandlburger, G., Schmohl, S., Pfeifer, N.: Classification of ALS point clouds using end-to-end deep learning. PFG **87**(3), 75–90 (2019)

44. Xie, Y., Bao, H., Shekhar, S., Knight, J.: A timber framework for mining urban tree inventories using remote sensing datasets. In: ICDM, pp. 1344–1349 (2018)

45. Yan, Y., Mao, Y., Li, B.: Second: sparsely embedded convolutional detection. Sensors **18**(10) (2018)

46. Yang, Z., Sun, Y., Liu, S., Shen, X., Jia, J.: STD: sparse-to-dense 3D object detector for point cloud. In: ICCV, pp. 1951–1960 (2019)

47. Zhang, C., Zhou, Y., Qiu, F.: Individual tree segmentation from lidar point clouds for urban forest inventory. Remote Sens. **7**(6), 7892–7913 (2015)

48. Zhao, R., Pang, M., Wang, J.: Classifying airborne lidar point clouds via deep features learned by a multi-scale convolutional neural network. Int. J. Geogr. Inf. Sci. **32**(5), 960–979 (2018)

49. Zhou, Y., Tuzel, O.: VoxelNet: end-to-end learning for point cloud based 3D object detection. In: CVPR, pp. 4490–4499 (2018)

50. Zhu, B., Jiang, Z., Zhou, X., Li, Z., Yu, G.: Class-balanced grouping and sampling for point cloud 3D object detection. CoRR abs/1908.09492 (2019)

Shared-Space Autoencoders with Randomized Skip Connections for Building Footprint Detection with Missing Views

Giannis Ashiotis[1]([✉]), James Oldfield[1,3], Charalambos Chrysostomou[1], Theodoros Christoudias[1,2], and Mihalis A. Nicolaou[1]

[1] Computation-Based Science and Technology Research Center,
The Cyprus Institute, Lefkosia, Cyprus
{g.ashiotis,m.nicolaou}@cyi.ac.cy
[2] Climate and Atmosphere Research Center, The Cyprus Institute,
Lefkosia, Cyprus
[3] School of Electronic Engineering and Computer Science,
Queen Mary University of London, London, UK

Abstract. Recently, a vast amount of satellite data has become available, going beyond standard optical (EO) data to other forms such as synthetic aperture radars (SAR). While more robust, SAR data are often more difficult to interpret, can be of lower resolution, and require intense pre-processing compared to EO data. On the other hand, while more interpretable, EO data often fail under unfavourable lighting, weather, or cloud-cover conditions. To leverage the advantages of both domains, we present a novel autoencoder-based architecture that is able to both (i) fuse multi-spectral optical and radar data in a common shared-space, and (ii) perform image segmentation for building footprint detection under the assumption that one of the data modalities is missing–resembling a situation often encountered under real-world settings. To do so, a novel randomized skip-connection architecture that utilizes autoencoder weight-sharing is designed. We compare the proposed method to baseline approaches relying on network fine-tuning, and established architectures such as UNet. Qualitative and quantitative results show the merits of the proposed method, that outperforms all compared techniques for the task-at-hand.

Keywords: Shared-space · Footprint detection · Missing views

1 Introduction

Deep learning is becoming a necessity for tackling problems that emerge in the analysis of geospatial data [24], as researchers are faced with an ever-increasing volume of data, with sizes exceeding 100 petabytes, and the need to interpret

© Springer Nature Switzerland AG 2021
A. Del Bimbo et al. (Eds.): ICPR 2020 Workshops, LNCS 12667, pp. 536–549, 2021.
https://doi.org/10.1007/978-3-030-68787-8_39

and make predictions in diverse contexts. In this paper, we focus on the problem of detecting building footprints from satellite images and radars. This task carries significant impact, and is a necessary step for a wide range of applications, such as estimating economic factors [17], disaster and crisis response [7,35], human activity monitoring and urban dynamics [9], as well as population density estimation [25][1].

Inspired by the recent `Spacenet`[2] challenge, in this paper we tackle the task of multi-view learning given diverse data from multiple sensors. Concretely, we focus on fusing Synthetic-Aperture Radar (SAR) images, along with their electro-optical (EO) counterparts. Using SAR and EO data in-tandem is a common approach, since these multiple data views are considered to hold complimentary information. Specifically, SAR data are becoming more relevant, as the specific wavelengths used can penetrate clouds (Fig. 1), and can carry significant information even when captured in unfavourable weather conditions - while can also be collected independently of the day-night cycle. However, optical data - although easier to interpret and usually of higher resolution - fail to capture meaningful information when occlusions are present in the optical range, for example when insufficient lighting is present, or when the area is covered with clouds. We adopt the challenging setting where EO data is only available during training, and considered as a missing modality (view) during test-time. This is a realistic assumption inspired from real-world settings, where as aforementioned, EO data are likely to be missing due to conditions at capture time.

Fig. 1. SAR (left) and EO (right) composite from the Rotterdam area, with data collected on the same day by the Sentinel-1 and Sentinel-2 satellites.

---

[1] Human activity monitoring and population density estimation are critical steps for building robust epidemiological models to tackle global events such as pandemics and natural disasters.

[2] https://spacenet.ai/sn6-challenge/.

The straightforward approach towards such a challenging setting is to pre-train a network with the view that is missing at test time, and subsequently *fine-tune* the network using data available both during training and testing - an approach commonly employed in satellite imagery analysis [1,10,28,29]. At the same time, several approaches have been proposed on multi-view learning for satellite imagery for a variety of tasks [18,19,22]. However, these methods are *not* tailored for handling missing modalities at test-time, and are thus unsuitable for the specific setting under consideration. In this light, we propose a novel, multi-view method for building footprint detection that introduces a weight-sharing mechanism for learning a common shared-space where the input modalities are fused. To retain the advantages of skip connections in terms of retaining high-frequency information and facilitate inference with missing modalities, we further propose a novel randomized skip connection mechanism. In summary, the contributions of this work are as follows:

- We propose a segmentation method based on weight-sharing, that enforces a shared latent-space that leverages information from multiple satellite views at train-time. As shown, this facilitates learning more informative representations at test-time given entirely missing views.
- We introduce the concept of randomized skip-connections to *enhance* the shared-space representations, whilst maintaining the benefits of propagating high-frequency information directly to later layers in the network - without circumventing the shared space.
- Through a set of rigorous qualitative and quantitative experiments, we demonstrate how the proposed method outperforms typically used architectures such as UNet [26], as well as other commonly used fine-tuning approaches, in the presence of missing modalities.

The rest of the paper is organized as follows. In Sect. 2, we provide a brief summary of related work in the areas of building footprint detection using SAR, image segmentation, transfer-learning, as well as multi-view fusion. In Sect. 3 we present the proposed methodology, while in Sect. 4 we describe the employed dataset along with the relevant pre-processing steps. Finally, in Sect. 5 we present both qualitative and quantitative results demonstrating the merits of the proposed method.

2   Related Work

Building Detection Using SAR Data. Several works have been proposed for building footprint detection using SAR data. In [33], an approach where SAR data is used to extract lines defined by building faces, which are then used in conjunction with the corresponding optical data. In [32], high resolution images are used to generate Digital Surface Models (DSM) of urban areas using Markovian fusion. In [39], Conditional Random Fields (CRF) were used to detect building footprints on pairs of high-resolution interferometric SAR (InSAR) and orthorectified images. More recently, deep learning approaches such as [27] have been proposed. For a detailed review on deep learning applications on SAR data, the reader is referred to [41,42].

Image Segmentation. The goal of semantic image segmentation is to map an input image to a matrix of class predictions for each pixel. A whole range of modern methods and architectures exploiting the power of deep neural networks have been proposed in the literature, like the Fully Convolutional Networks (FCN) [28], and occasionally even Recurrent Neural Networks (RNN) [36,37], and adversarial losses [16]. But the most prominent architectures used for the purposes of semantic image segmentation are based on the encoder-decoder paradigm. The seminal work of Ronneberger et al. combined in UNet a general-purpose autoencoder-based architecture, with the use of symmetric skip connections, in order to allow for fine-grained details to be recovered in the prediction. SegNet [3] uses a similar encoder-decoder architecture, where the maxpooling indices from the encoding sequence are used in the upsampling procedure. ResNet-DUC [38] is another encoder-decoder based architecture where the encoder part is made up of ResNet [12] blocks while the upsampling is handled by a series of Dense Upsampling Convolutions (DUC). DeepLab [4] makes use of atrous convolutions and atrous spatial pyramid pooling to better handle variations in scale, while it also adds a fully connected Conditional Random Field (CRF) to improve localization performance. FC-DenseNet [30] takes the symmetric skip connections of the UNet and combines them with DenseNet [13] blocks, in which each layer takes input from all the preceding layers in the block. This allows the creation of very deep networks of this kind.

Transfer Learning. By pretraining on comprehensive image datasets such as ImageNet [6], multiple works have achieved state of the art results and/or faster convergence for many segmentation tasks [10,11,15,28], including the SpaceNet baseline model [29]. Recent work [15,29] has also shown that improvements can be gained by pretraining on datasets more closely aligned to the task at hand, such as the Carvana dataset [1]. In attempts to leverage multiple satellite views, the SpaceNet baseline also pretrains the networks on the more informative EO satellite views. We build off such ideas, and propose an approach that models both domains simultaneously at train-time.

Multi-view Fusion. A huge range of different types of image satellite data are readily available [2,5,40]–each providing their own unique benefits and drawbacks. For this reason, many detection and segmentation networks employ techniques to fuse these views to combine the useful features of each. Multi-view satellite fusion methods have been successfully utilized for tasks including crop segmentation [22], target detection [18,19], and a whole host of other application areas [8,20,23].

In contrast to such approaches however, in our case the EO modality is missing at test-time. We thus design our network to leverage both views at train-time to learn a more informative shared representation: inspired from works on coupled and Siamese networks [14,21], we design a weight-sharing scheme to map the two views to a shared representation.

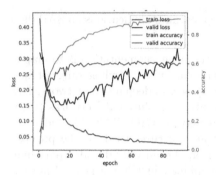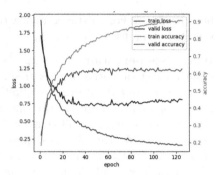

Fig. 2. Learning curves of the models trained with (a) BCE only vs with (b) BCE+DL. As can be seen, including the DL loss leads to better stability, and higher validation accuracy.

3 Methodology

In this section we describe the proposed multi-view shared-space method that facilitates building footprint extraction under missing modalities. We first describe the task at hand in Sect. 3.1. We then detail how we enrich the SAR representations using the EO data available at train time, using a weight-sharing mechanism (Sect. 3.2) and randomized skip-connections (Sect. 3.3). Finally, we detail our choice of loss functions used to train the network in Sect. 3.4. An overview of the proposed method is visualized in Fig. 3.

3.1 Problem Setting

Our goal is to learn a mapping f from satellite image data $\mathcal{X} \in \mathbb{R}^{V \times C \times H \times W}$ (comprised of V views) to its corresponding ground-truth binary mask $\mathbf{Y} \in \mathbb{R}^{H \times W}$, from which we extract its building footprints. In the setting of the SpaceNet challenge we have multiple informative views at train-time, including SAR and EO imagery. However, the EO view is *missing* at test-time, and therefore can only be leveraged during training.

To address this problem, we adopt a UNet [26] as a base segmentation network (as is commonly employed for segmentation of satellite imagery [34]), comprised of an encoder and decoder with symmetric skip connections between these two sub-networks. However, one cannot straight-forwardly pass the entire data tensor $\mathcal{X}$ through such a network at test-time, due to these missing views. We therefore propose accordingly a novel method, building on this UNet architecture, to facilitate learning a shared latent representation of both views that can lead to more accurate mask predictions at test-time, whilst requiring only the SAR data.

Throughout the rest of the paper, we denote view $v \in \{E, S\}$ (denoting the EO and SAR views respectively; both comprised of 4 channels) of our satellite data as $\mathcal{X}^{(v)} \in \mathbb{R}^{C \times H \times W}$, scalars as lower-case Latin letters p, and random variables as lower-case Greek letters ψ.

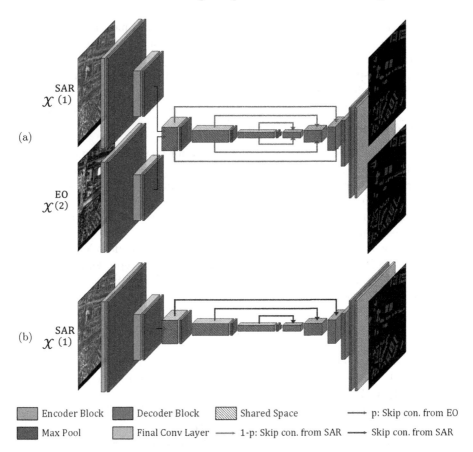

Encoder Block   Decoder Block   Shared Space   ⟶ p: Skip con. from EO

Max Pool   Final Conv Layer   ⟶ 1-p: Skip con. from SAR   ⟶ Skip con. from SAR

Fig. 3. An overview of the proposed method for enforcing a shared space in our segmentation network. During training (a), we first process the two images $\mathcal{X}^{(i)}$ separately with a series of view-specific layers to transform each to a common representation. We then pass these representations from both views through a shared encoder and decoder to generate the corresponding masks predictions, as a means of encouraging the most informative features of both views to be represented in the common encodings. We further enforce the shared-space constraint by introducing stochastic skip connections (shown with red and blue lines) to mix the representations. During testing (b), the available modality (SAR) can be straightforwardly utilized with the respective encoder, while still leveraging information from the missing modality, infused in the shared-space representation obtained during training.

3.2   Enforcing a Shared Space

In order to jointly utilize all views of our satellite data at train-time and learn a shared representation, we make the assumption that they live in the same low-dimensional subspace. To enforce such a shared space, we introduce two siamese *specific* encoders, followed by a final *shared* encoder and decoder. The two specific encoders first map the two separate views to this shared representation, and the single shared encoder and decoder take these common representations and transform them back to image space. By processing both views this way, the common representation extracted from the SAR data can be influenced and enriched by the specific information present in the EO data, without requiring any access to it whatsoever at test-time.

3.3   Randomized Skip Connections

Symmetric skip connections are extremely useful for image transformation tasks that need to retain some semblance of the input image, due to the provided ability for the network to pass low-level image information directly to later layers of the network. In this section, we propose a modification to the skip connection paradigm that not only retains such a desirable property, but jointly encourages shared representations of the multiple satellite views.

Concretely, the representation $\mathcal{D}_i$ at the ith layer in the decoder is concatenated with the $N - i^{\text{th}}$ layer of the shared encoder $\mathcal{E}_{N-i}$'s representations of the multiple views in a stochastic manner. We thus modify the ith activation in the decoder $\mathcal{D}_i$ with a skip connection as

$$\mathcal{D}_i := \left[\psi_i \mathcal{E}_{N-i}^{(S)} + (1 - \psi_i) \mathcal{E}_{N-i}^{(O)}, \, \mathcal{D}_i \right], \tag{1}$$

where $\psi_i \overset{\text{i.i.d.}}{\sim} \text{Bern}(p)$, and $[.,.]$ denotes channel-wise concatenation. At train-time $p \in [0,1]$, and at test-time we fix the parameter $p := 1$ to deterministically pass the only available SAR representations.

We posit that by sending a mixture of representations of both views via the skip connections, we further encourage the shared representations to be generic and retain the informative features from both views in order to best predict the corresponding mask. We show experimentally in Sect. 5.2 the benefit of using such non-deterministic skip connections at train-time. We note that we recover the vanilla skip connection setup when each random variables x_i's 'success' parameter is set to $p = 0$ or $p = 1$.

3.4   Loss Functions

In order to train the network to map input images $\mathcal{X}^{(i)}$ to its binary mask counterpart $\mathbf{Y}$, we impose a typical pixel-wise binary cross-entropy loss, defined as

$$\mathcal{L}_B = \mathbb{E}_{\mathcal{X}^{(i)}, \mathbf{Y}} \left[-\frac{1}{CHW} \sum_{c,h,w} y_{hw} \log f(\mathcal{X}^{(i)})_{chw} \right.$$
$$\left. + (1 - y_{hw}) \log(1 - f(\mathcal{X}^{(i)})_{chw}) \right], \tag{2}$$

where f is the segmentation network, and where we compute the average BCE loss over all spatial and channel dimensions in each image.

We also impose, in addition to this regular BCE loss, the so-called Dice Loss (DL) [31]. This objective more closely encodes our goal of having high

Intersection over Union (IoU) of the predicted and ground-truth masks, and is defined as

$$\mathcal{L}_D = \mathbb{E}_{\mathcal{X}^{(i)}, \mathbf{Y}} \left[1 - \frac{2 \sum_{c,h,w} y_{hw} f(\mathcal{X}^{(i)})_{chw}}{\sum_{c,h,w} y_{hw} + \sum_{c,h,w} f(\mathcal{X}^{(i)})_{chw}} \right]. \tag{3}$$

We find the additional loss term defined in Eq. (3) to increase the stability of the model's training process, along with reducing over-fitting. We show this impact of the two loss terms by plotting the level curves for the model trained with the BCE loss and BCE+DL in Fig. 2a and Fig. 2b respectively. We compute the total loss as an average over both views of the satellite images, so as to facilitate the weight sharing described in Sect. 3.2. This leads to the final combined objective for our segmentation network

$$\mathcal{L} = \lambda_D \mathcal{L}_D + \lambda_B \mathcal{L}_B, \tag{4}$$

where λ_D, λ_B are the weights for the two loss separate loss terms.

4 Data and Data Preprocessing

4.1 Data

For the training and testing of our model we used the publicly available training dataset from the SpaceNet 6 challenge. It consists of 3401 half-meter resolution SAR images (provided by Capella Space) together with their half-meter resolution RGB-NIR counterparts (provided by the Maxar's WorldView 2 satellite) of the city of Rotterdam. The RGB-NIR images were obtained through reconstruction using several other EO images that were also provided in the dataset. In addition, annotations for over 48,000 building footprints were provided, together with look-angle information (north or south facing) for each of the SAR image tiles. It should be noted that although future applications of this technology will be most likely using remote sensing data obtained by satellites, this proof-of-concept dataset was obtained through aerial means.

4.2 Data Preprocessing

Each of the 900 × 900 pixel images was zero-padded to a size of 1024 × 1024 and then normalised/standardised based on values gathered from the whole of the training set (no-data pixels were not taken into account). Also, since SAR images are affected by the direction from which the data was collected (North vs South), they had to be flipped according to their orientation.

The ground truth masks are comprised of two separate channels, one marking the interiors of each of the building footprints and one marking the borders. Using two separate channels allowed to have the border and the interior overlap over a few pixels to facilitate extraction of the polygons from the predicted masks.

5   Experiments and Results

5.1   Training

We randomly selected 20% (680 pairs of images) of the test dataset to use for testing purposes. A further 20% of the remaining test dataset was used for validation during training. The images were preprocessed similarly for all tests. We used a UNet16 as our 'baseline' model, which was firstly trained using the EO data for 150 epochs, and was subsequently trained over a further 50 epochs using the SAR data. All versions of the SS model were trained for 100 epochs using both SAR and EO data, using hyper-parameters $\lambda_D = \lambda_B = 1$ for all experiments. Furthermore, when training our models, the loss was taken to be the average of the separate losses produced by the SAR and EO data. In all cases the Adam optimizer was used with a learning rate of 0.001 and with all the other parameters set to their default value. The batch size was limited to 8 by the capacity of the GPUs used. As mentioned in Sect. 3.3, in the versions of the model using the randomized skip connections, the value of p is randomly chosen as $p \in [0, 1]$ at each occurrence of a skip connection. All models were trained on single nodes of the Cyclone supercomputer of the Cyprus Institute, each featuring dual Intel Xeon Gold 6248 CPUs and quad NVidia V100 GPUs. The training time did not exceed 12 h in any of the experiments.

5.2   Performance Evaluation

The evaluation of the performance of the different models was done using the average pixel-wise intersection-over-union score (IoU) of the prediction versus the ground truth masks and the SpaceNet metric which is the F1 score (harmonic average of precision and recall), where a polygon-wise IoU of a predicted and a ground truth polygon greater than 0.5 is considered to be a true positive.

A summary of the test results is presented in Table 1, where as can be seen, the proposed method outperforms compared approaches. The best results are achieved when utilizing both weight-sharing as well as skip mixing, which is a consistent conclusion with respect to both evaluation metrics employed. Furthermore, in Fig. 4 we present indicative results of our implementation and compare with baseline results using UNet16, along with the ground truth and EO and SAR inputs for each case. In the first two columns, one can see how that our model outperforms UNet16 in detecting more fine-grained details (i.e., small buildings). The fourth column of the figure shows how our model generates considerably less false positives than UNet16. This becomes more apparent in Fig. 5 and Fig. 6, were predictions from all the variants of our model are presented together with predictions from UNet16 and the ground truth. It can be clearly seen that utilizing both weight-sharing *in-tandem* with randomized skip-connections facilitates the detection of smaller buildings, that are often missed in the baseline models. We have also observed that the proposed model is able to detect footprints of complex, large buildings with much better fidelity (e.g., Fig. 6b). To further verify the positive effect of the proposed randomized

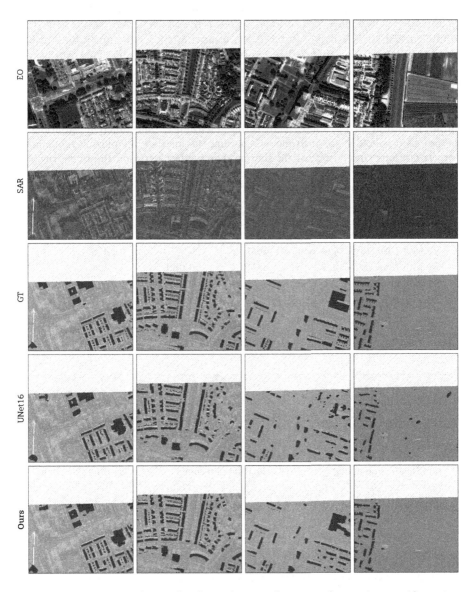

Fig. 4. Different views for 4 tiles from the test datatset, showcasing a wide variety of urban environments. From top to bottom: EO Image, SAR Image, Ground truth, UNet16 mask prediction, Shared Space (ours) mask prediction.

skip-connection architecture, we evaluate a variant of the proposed shared-space architecture where skip connections are entirely removed. As can be seen from results presented in Fig. 5b and Fig. 6b, removing the skip-connections results in segmentation maps that fail to capture fine-grained details. This verifies the successful propagation of high-frequency information through the network layers by employing the randomized skip-connections.

Table 1. Testing Scores for UNet16 (using fine-tuning), and different variations of the proposed shared-space (SS) model, showing the merits of employing randomized skip connections (RSC) and weight sharing. For the last entry on the table, the skip connections originating from non-shared encoder layers were removed. The number of parameters of each model is also presented.

Implementation	No of params	Pixel-wise IoU	SpaceNet metric
UNet16 with fine-tuning	44M	0.596	0.522
SS with UNet skip-conns removed	36M	0.577	0.498
SS with Unet skip-conns	44M	**0.639**	0.592
SS with randomized skip-conns	44M	0.635	0.604
SS with RSC only within the SS	44M	**0.639**	**0.616**

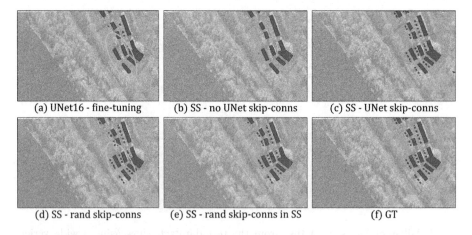

(a) UNet16 - fine-tuning   (b) SS - no UNet skip-conns   (c) SS - UNet skip-conns

(d) SS - rand skip-conns   (e) SS - rand skip-conns in SS   (f) GT

Fig. 5. Predictions from all models together with the ground truth. Yellow circles mark where UNet16 was unable to detect fine details in the image (Color figure online)

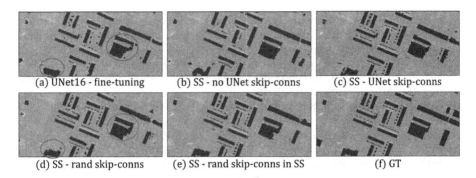

Fig. 6. Predictions from all models together with the ground truth. Our model maintains higher fidelity when predicting complex features like the ones marked by yellow circles (Color figure online)

6   Conclusions

In this work, we presented a novel approach for building footprint detection utilising multiple satellite imagery views, in the challenging setting where only one modality is available at test time. To this end, we presented a novel shared-space autoencoder method that utilizes randomized skip connections to facilitate propagating high-frequency information to the later layers without circumventing the shared-space property. We highlight that the proposed method can be considered as a generic approach to fusion under missing modalities at test-time, and can be readily incorporated into more complex architectures. With a set of rigorous experiments, we presented qualitative and quantitative results that demonstrate the merits of the proposed approach, in comparison to typically employed vanilla UNet architectures as well as other fine-tuning approaches.

References

1. The Carvana masking challenge
2. Spacenet on Amazon web services (AWS). "Datasets" the spacenet catalog (2020). Modified 30 April 2018. Accessed 15 July 2020
3. Badrinarayanan, V., Kendall, A., Cipolla, R.: SegNet: a deep convolutional encoder-decoder architecture for image segmentation. IEEE Trans. Pattern Anal. Mach. Intell. **39**(12), 2481–2495 (2017). https://doi.org/10.1109/tpami.2016.2644615
4. Chen, L.C., Papandreou, G., Kokkinos, I., Murphy, K., Yuille, A.L.: DeepLab: semantic image segmentation with deep convolutional nets, atrous convolution, and fully connected CRFs. IEEE Trans. Pattern Anal. Mach. Intell. **40**(4), 834–848 (2018). https://doi.org/10.1109/tpami.2017.2699184
5. Chiu, M.T., et al.: Agriculture-vision: a large aerial image database for agricultural pattern analysis (2020)
6. Deng, J., Dong, W., Socher, R., Li, L.J., Li, K., Fei-Fei, L.: ImageNet: a large-scale hierarchical image database. In: CVPR 2009 (2009)

7. Dubois, D., Lepage, R.: Object-versus pixel-based building detection for disaster response. In: 2012 11th International Conference on Information Science, Signal Processing and their Applications (ISSPA), pp. 5–10. IEEE (2012)
8. d'Angelo, P., et al.: 3D semantic segmentation from multi-view optical satellite images. In: 2019 IEEE International Geoscience and Remote Sensing Symposium, IGARSS 2019, pp. 5053–5056 (2019)
9. Gavankar, N.L., Ghosh, S.K.: Object based building footprint detection from high resolution multispectral satellite image using k-means clustering algorithm and shape parameters. Geocarto Int. **34**(6), 626–643 (2019)
10. He, K., Girshick, R., Dollar, P.: Rethinking imagenet pre-training. In: 2019 IEEE/CVF International Conference on Computer Vision (ICCV), October 2019. https://doi.org/10.1109/iccv.2019.00502
11. He, K., Gkioxari, G., Dollar, P., Girshick, R.: Mask R-CNN. In: 2017 IEEE International Conference on Computer Vision (ICCV), October 2017. https://doi.org/10.1109/iccv.2017.322
12. He, K., Zhang, X., Ren, S., Sun, J.: Deep residual learning for image recognition. In: Proceedings of the IEEE Conference on Computer Vision and Pattern Recognition, pp. 770–778 (2016)
13. Huang, G., Liu, Z., Van Der Maaten, L., Weinberger, K.Q.: Densely connected convolutional networks. In: Proceedings of the IEEE Conference on Computer Vision and Pattern Recognition, pp. 4700–4708 (2017)
14. Hughes, L.H., Schmitt, M., Mou, L., Wang, Y., Zhu, X.X.: Identifying corresponding patches in SAR and optical images with a pseudo-siamese CNN. IEEE Geosci. Remote Sens. Lett. **15**(5), 784–788 (2018). https://doi.org/10.1109/lgrs.2018.2799232
15. Iglovikov, V., Shvets, A.: TernausNet: U-Net with VGG11 encoder pre-trained on imagenet for image segmentation (2018)
16. Isola, P., Zhu, J.Y., Zhou, T., Efros, A.A.: Image-to-image translation with conditional adversarial networks. In: 2017 IEEE Conference on Computer Vision and Pattern Recognition (CVPR), July 2017. https://doi.org/10.1109/cvpr.2017.632
17. Jean, N., Burke, M., Xie, M., Davis, W.M., Lobell, D.B., Ermon, S.: Combining satellite imagery and machine learning to predict poverty. Science **353**(6301), 790–794 (2016)
18. Kim, J., Kwag, Y.K.: Multi-sensor fusion based target detection using EO/SAR (2014)
19. Kim, S., Song, W.J., Kim, S.H.: Robust ground target detection by SAR and IR sensor fusion using adaboost-based feature selection. Sensors (Basel, Switzerland) **16** (2016)
20. Leotta, M.J., et al.: Urban semantic 3D reconstruction from multiview satellite imagery. In: 2019 IEEE/CVF Conference on Computer Vision and Pattern Recognition Workshops (CVPRW), pp. 1451–1460 (2019)
21. Liu, M.Y., Tuzel, O.: Coupled generative adversarial networks (2016)
22. Pena, J., Boonpook, W., Tan, Y.: Semantic segmentation based remote sensing data fusion on crops detection, July 2019
23. Purri, M., et al.: Material segmentation of multi-view satellite imagery, April 2019
24. Reichstein, M., Camps-Valls, G., Stevens, B., Jung, M., Denzler, J., Carvalhais, N., et al.: Deep learning and process understanding for data-driven earth system science. Nature **566**(7743), 195–204 (2019)
25. Robinson, C., Hohman, F., Dilkina, B.: A deep learning approach for population estimation from satellite imagery. In: Proceedings of the 1st ACM SIGSPATIAL Workshop on Geospatial Humanities, pp. 47–54 (2017)

26. Ronneberger, O., Fischer, P., Brox, T.: U-Net: convolutional networks for biomedical image segmentation. In: Navab, N., Hornegger, J., Wells, W.M., Frangi, A.F. (eds.) MICCAI 2015. LNCS, vol. 9351, pp. 234–241. Springer, Cham (2015). https://doi.org/10.1007/978-3-319-24574-4_28

27. Shahzad, M., Maurer, M., Fraundorfer, F., Wang, Y., Zhu, X.X.: Buildings detection in VHR SAR images using fully convolution neural networks. IEEE Trans. Geosci. Remote Sens. **57**(2), 1100–1116 (2018)

28. Shelhamer, E., Long, J., Darrell, T.: Fully convolutional networks for semantic segmentation. IEEE Trans. Pattern Anal. Mach. Intell. **39**(4), 640–651 (2017). https://doi.org/10.1109/tpami.2016.2572683

29. Shermeyer, J., et al.: SpaceNet 6: multi-sensor all weather mapping dataset (2020)

30. Jégou, S., Drozdzal, M., Vazquez, D., Romero, A., Bengio, Y.: The one hundred layers tiramisu: fully convolutional densenets for semantic segmentation (2017)

31. Sørensen, T.: A Method of Establishing Groups of Equal Amplitude in Plant Sociology Based on Similarity of Species Content and Its Application to Analyses of the Vegetation on Danish Commons. Biologiske skrifter, I kommission hos E. Munksgaard (1948)

32. Tison, C., Tupin, F., Maitre, H.: A fusion scheme for joint retrieval of urban height map and classification from high-resolution interferometric SAR images. IEEE Trans. Geosci. Remote Sens. **45**, 496–505 (2007). https://doi.org/10.1109/TGRS.2006.887006

33. Tupin, F., Roux, M.: Detection of building outlines based on the fusion of SAR and optical features. ISPRS J. Photogram. Remote Sens. **58**(1), 71–82 (2003)

34. Ulmas, P., Liiv, I.: Segmentation of satellite imagery using u-net models for land cover classification (2020)

35. Van Westen, C.: Remote sensing for natural disaster management. Int. Arch. Photogram. Remote Sens. **33**(B7/4; PART 7), 1609–1617 (2000)

36. Visin, F., Kastner, K., Cho, K., Matteucci, M., Courville, A., Bengio, Y.: ReNet: a recurrent neural network based alternative to convolutional networks (2015)

37. Visin, F., et al.: ReSeg: a recurrent neural network-based model for semantic segmentation. In: 2016 IEEE Conference on Computer Vision and Pattern Recognition Workshops (CVPRW), June 2016. https://doi.org/10.1109/cvprw.2016.60

38. Wang, P., et al.: Understanding convolution for semantic segmentation. In: 2018 IEEE Winter Conference on Applications of Computer Vision (WACV), pp. 1451–1460. IEEE (2018)

39. Wegner, J.D., Hänsch, R., Thiele, A., Soergel, U.: Building detection from one orthophoto and high-resolution InSAR data using conditional random fields. IEEE J. Sel. Top. Appl. Earth Obs. Remote Sens. **4**(1), 83–91 (2011). https://doi.org/10.1109/JSTARS.2010.2053521

40. Weir, N., et al.: SpaceNet MVOI: a multi-view overhead imagery dataset. In: 2019 IEEE/CVF International Conference on Computer Vision (ICCV), October 2019. https://doi.org/10.1109/iccv.2019.00108

41. Zhu, X.X., et al.: Deep learning meets SAR. arXiv preprint arXiv:2006.10027 (2020)

42. Zhu, X.X., et al.: Deep learning in remote sensing: a comprehensive review and list of resources. IEEE Geosci. Remote Sens. Mag. **5**(4), 8–36 (2017)

Assessment of CNN-Based Methods for Poverty Estimation from Satellite Images

Robin Jarry[1,2](✉) (iD), Marc Chaumont[2,3] (iD), Laure Berti-Équille[4] (iD),
and Gérard Subsol[2] (iD)

[1] French Foundation for Biodiversity Research (FRB), Montpellier, France
robin.jarry@lirmm.fr
[2] Research-Team ICAR, LIRMM, Univ. Montpellier, CNRS, Montpellier, France
[3] University of Nîmes, Nîmes, France
[4] ESPACE-DEV, Univ. Montpellier, IRD, UA, UG, UR, Montpellier, France

Abstract. One of the major issues in predicting poverty with satellite images is the lack of fine-grained and reliable poverty indicators. To address this problem, various methodologies were proposed recently. Most recent approaches use a proxy (e.g., nighttime light), as an additional information, to mitigate the problem of sparse data. They consist in building and training a CNN with a large set of images, which is then used as a feature extractor. Ultimately, pairs of extracted feature vectors and poverty labels are used to learn a regression model to predict the poverty indicators.

First, we propose a rigorous comparative study of such approaches based on a unified framework and a common set of images. We observed that the geographic displacement on the spatial coordinates of poverty observations degrades the prediction performances of all the methods. Therefore, we present a new methodology combining grid-cell selection and ensembling that improves the poverty prediction to handle coordinate displacement.

1 Introduction

Estimating poverty indicators is essential for the economy and political stability of a nation. These indicators are usually evaluated by surveying the population and asking people many questions. This requires a heavy organization, takes a long time, is sometimes only limited to easily accessible areas, and may be subjective. Therefore, solutions were proposed to estimate poverty at a large scale in an easier and faster way by using observational data, i.e., with no direct interaction with the people.

Satellite images give a quite precise observational overview of the planet. As early as 1980, Welch (1980) monitored urban population and energy utilization patterns from the images of the first Landsat satellites. Since 1999 and 2013 respectively, Landsat 7 and 8 satellite series cover the entire Earth surface with

© Springer Nature Switzerland AG 2021
A. Del Bimbo et al. (Eds.): ICPR 2020 Workshops, LNCS 12667, pp. 550–565, 2021.
https://doi.org/10.1007/978-3-030-68787-8_40

a temporal resolution of 16 days and a spatial resolution of 15 to 30 m depending on the spectral bands (8 for Landsat 7 and 11 for Landsat 8). Since 2014, Sentinel satellite series generate images with a spatial resolution of 10 m. It is then possible to get remote-sensing data with a high time-frequency and a good spatial resolution.

Nevertheless, estimating the local wealth or poverty indicator rather than general value over a country is a very challenging problem. This requires the mapping of the observational data (i.e., the pixel intensity of a satellite image) and the poverty indicator precisely located. In some cases, numerous indicators can be available. For example, in Babenko et al. (2017), 350,000 poverty indicators are collected in two surveys over the city of Mexico or, in Engstrom et al. (2017), 1,300 ground-truth poverty indicators are obtained for a limited 3,500 km^2 area of Sri Lanka. With a large number of indicators, direct supervised training with high-resolution daytime satellite images becomes possible, in particular with Deep-Learning techniques. Unfortunately, the number of such indicators is usually low in most countries, especially in developing ones. For example, only 770 poverty indicators are reported in 2016 for Malawi[1] with an area of more than 118,000 km^2. In 2013, Chandy (2013) reported in general terms that almost two-fifths of the countries do not perform at least one income survey every 5 years. Based on this observation, a direct Machine-Learning approach, processing a set of geolocalized satellite images associated with the corresponding poverty indicators would inevitably lead to over-fitting, and then very bad generalization (e.g., see Ngestrini 2019).

But, in 2016, Jean et al. (2016) proposed an accurate and scalable method based on Deep-Learning to estimate local poverty from satellite imagery, based on sparse socio-economic data. They managed to solve the problem of the limited number of poverty indicators by using a Transfer Learning technique. It consists in training a Convolutional Neural Network (CNN) on one task and then applying the trained CNN to a different but related task. Since this seminal work, many papers have been published with either applying or extending the original algorithm, or propose some variants of Deep-Learning techniques. In particular, Ermon Group[2] at Stanford University proposed different methods to tackle the problem (see Yeh et al. (2020) for their latest results).

The difficulty is then to compare all the available methods as they do not use the same input data and they are not evaluated with the same set of parameters. In this paper, we propose to assess the methods with a common framework in order to analyze their performances, understand the limitations of the available data (both images and indicators), and evaluate whether combining them would improve the results. In Sect. 2, we describe three methods we selected in this line of research. In Sect. 3, we present the common framework to assess fairly the performances of the methods. In Sect. 4, we discuss adapting the methods to improve the performances. Conclusion and future work are presented in Sect. 5.

---

[1] Living Standard Measurements Study, Malawi 2016: https://microdata.worldbank.org/index.php/catalog/2939.

[2] Ermon Group web page: https://cs.stanford.edu/~ermon/website/.

2   Description of the Selected CNN-Based Methods

Transfer Learning emerged recently as an efficient way to deal with a limited number of poverty indicators. For our application, proxy data related to poverty and available in large quantities can be used to train a CNN for classifying satellite images accordingly.

By taking a specific layer of the resulting CNN, we can extract a feature vector that characterizes the input satellite image with respect to its correlation with the corresponding proxy data. As proxy data are chosen to be related to poverty, we can assume that the feature vector is an appropriate representation of poverty in the image.

Finally, we can compute the feature vectors of satellite images at the sparse locations of the limited set of poverty indicators, and perform a regression between the vectors and the poverty indicators. This process can be done efficiently despite a limited number of locations and it can establish a relationship between the satellite images and the poverty indicators.

A major issue is then to select relevant proxy data. Several solutions have been proposed and we review three of them in the following sections.

2.1   Nighttime Light

The concept of using Transfer Learning to estimate poverty from satellite images was proposed in Jean et al. (2016). In this work, the authors used nighttime light values (NLV), which are known, since many years, to be a good proxy for poverty evaluation (see for example, Elvidge et al. (1997), Doll et al. (2000) or Chen and Nordhaus (2011)).

NLV data set is provided by the Earth Observation Group[3] and the corresponding images are extracted from Google Static Map[4], at 2.5 m of resolution.

The authors introduce a CNN architecture to classify daytime satellite images by NLV. Three classes are used for low, medium, and high NLV (Jean et al. 2016, Supplementary Materials). The CNN is based on a VGG-F architecture (Wozniak et al. 2018) and is pre-trained on the ImageNet dataset. Next, the network is fine-tuned on the training data set, which consists of 400,000 (Xie et al. 2016) images, each of them covering a $1\,km^2$ area in Africa.

Perez et al. (2017) is an extension of the previous research based on Landsat images. It shows that despite the lower resolution of Landsat images, the model accuracy is higher than the one of the previous benchmarks.

2.2   Land Use

In Ayush et al. (2020), the authors assume that land use, and specifically the manufactured objects observed in a satellite image emphasize the wealthiness

---

[3] NOAA Earth Observation Group Website: https://ngdc.noaa.gov/eog/.

[4] Google Static Map, getting started Web page: https://developers.google.com/maps/documentation/maps-static/start.

of an area. The authors trained a CNN on a land use detection and classification task, to extract a feature vector related to poverty. As proxy data, they used the xView data set[5] consisting of very high-resolution images (0.3 m) annotated with bounding boxes defined over 10 main classes (building, fixed-wing aircraft, passenger vehicle, truck, railway vehicle, maritime vessel, engineering vehicle, helipad, vehicle lot, construction site) and 60 sub-classes. As the size of the objects in a satellite image may vary (*e.g.*, a truck is much smaller than a building), the network used YoloV3, with DarkNet53 backbone architecture (Redmon and Farhadi 2018), which allows the detection at 3 different scales. This network is pre-trained on ImageNet and fine-tuned on the xView data set. Since it was trained on a detection/classification task, a single satellite image may have several detection results, depending on the number of objects in the image. Thus, the input image may be associated with multiple feature vectors, one for each detection. The authors further explore this additional information by different combinations of the feature vectors.

2.3   Contrastive Spatial Analysis

In Jean et al. (2019), the idea is to be able to cluster homogeneous-looking areas and assume that some clusters will be specific to poor areas. Contrary to the two previous approaches, this method is based on an unsupervised task. A CNN model is trained with the aim of learning a semantic representation of an input image according to the following constraints: (i) If two sub-parts of an image are close spatially, they must have a similar semantic representation (*i.e.*, feature vectors); and (ii) If two sub-parts of an image are far apart, they must have a dissimilar semantic representation.

The data set is a set of image triplets (a, n, d), where a, n, and d are tiles that are sampled randomly from the same image.

More precisely, the *neighbor tile* n is sampled randomly in a given neighborhood of a, the *anchor tile* and d, the *distant tile* is sampled randomly outside of a's neighborhood. The objective is to minimize the following cost function using the CNN:

$$L(t_a, t_n, t_d) = \max\left(0, \|t_a - t_n\|_2 - \|t_a - t_d\|_2 + m\right) \tag{1}$$

where t_a, t_n and t_d are the feature vectors produced by the CNN for the *anchor tile* a, the *neighbor tile* n, and the *distant tile* d respectively. m is the margin to enforce a minimum distance. During the minimization process, if t_n is too far from t_a compared to t_d (using the Euclidean distance), then t_n will be generated to get closer to t_a, and t_d will get more distant from t_a. The equilibrium is obtained when t_d is in the hypersphere with radius $\|t_a - t_n\| + m$. The CNN is a modified version of ResNet-18 taking the three tiles as inputs.

2.4   Regression Step

All the previous methods aim to produce a feature vector representation of a satellite image that should represent poverty to a certain extend. The first app-

---

[5] xView Challenge Website: http://xviewdataset.org/.

roach uses a feature vector that estimates NLV from the satellite images. The second approach uses a feature vector that estimates land use. The third approach uses a feature vector that emphasizes the differences between two satellite images. Throughout the paper, we will name the three methods, *Nighttime Light*, *Land Use*, and *Contrastive* respectively. For each method, a Ridge regression model is trained with the pairs of feature vectors (obtained from the corresponding method) and the poverty indicators. The feature vectors are generated from the images of the sparse locations where some poverty indicators are available. We select the Ridge regression model, that is as close as possible to the methodology exposed in Jean et al. (2016, 2019), and Ayush et al. (2020).

2.5   Comparison Issues

The three methods aforementioned may seem to offer comparable results from the results reported, but as a matter of fact, they differ greatly by the choice of the satellite images, proxy data, and feature vector parameters as we can see in Table 1.

Table 1. Differences between the input data and parameters used in the three methods.

	Nighttime Light	*Contrastive*	*Land Use*
Countries	Uganda, Malawi, Tanzania, Nigeria	Uganda	Uganda
Image source	Google Static Map (DigitalGlobe)	Landsat-7	DigitalGlobe
Resolution	2.5 m	30 m	0.3 m
Spectral bands	3 (RGB)	5 (RGB + 2 additional spectral bands)	3 (RGB)
Feature vector size	4,096	512	10–60

Notice that the images do not share the same resolution and the structures and objects captured in the images do not have the same scale. Moreover, in Jean et al. (2019), the images contain 5 spectral bands, whereas the other methods process standard RGB images.

Experiments reported in Perez et al. (2017) have shown that lower resolution images and additional spectral bands could influence poverty estimation. With this consideration in mind, we can assume that the image resolution and the number of spectral bands are significant features that must be commonly set before any method comparison.

Additionally, the size of the feature vectors generated by the CNN differs for each method. As it is difficult to know the influence of this parameter on the final R^2 score, we set the size to be identical across the different methods, to provide a fair comparison.

3   A Common Framework to Assess the CNN-Based Methods

Our goal is to compare the three methods consistently and fairly with a common framework, to expose their benefits and limitations. Therefore, we decided to use the same satellite image source, the same image dimension and scale, the same regression steps, and the same socio-economic indicators. Doing so, we can compare which approach better emphasizes the poverty and if an unsupervised method, *i.e.*, without proxy data, can outperform *Nighttime Light* or *Land Use* methods.

Before discussing the framework, it is important to notice that the poverty indicators given in the available surveys are artificially moved from their actual position, which may lead to biasing the results.

Surveying operators add a random geographic displacement up to 10 km on latitude and longitude from the location where the socio-economic indicator is evaluated, to protect the anonymity of respondents (see Burgert et al. 2013[6]). In the example given in Fig. 1, the poverty indicators of a village are distributed over a 10 km × 10 km surrounding area. This means that the actual poverty indicator can be significantly different from the reported one in the survey.

3.1   Framework Specifications

We can represent the three methods as the global pipeline shown in Fig. 2. In the common framework we propose, the algorithm operates over a 10 km × 10 km area around a given input location (*i.e.* latitude and longitude coordinates) with a corresponding poverty indicator. It takes as input a 4,000 × 4,000 pixels satellite image centered on the considered location. This ensures that the true indicator location is indeed in the image. Each image is then split into 100 sub-images

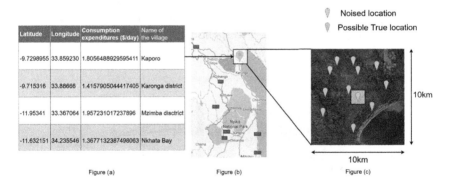

Fig. 1. Geographic displacement procedure performed on LSMS socio-economic surveys.

---

[6] This document shows how Demographic and Health Surveys are modified, and claims that the Living Standards Measurement Study, our survey provider, performs the same anonymization policy.

(of 400 × 400 pixels), each one covering a 1 km × 1 km area according to a regular grid. The sub-images are then processed by a Deep Learning feature extractor specific to a selected method (*Nighttime Light, Land Use, Contrastive*) in order to produce a fixed-size feature vector. Finally, the feature vectors are averaged and sent to a Ridge regressor, which returns the poverty estimation value for the 1 km × 1 km area centered in the input location.

3.2 Data Description

Satellite images are used for both feature extractor training and poverty indicator estimation using regression. Some proxy data are also needed to build *Nighttime Light* and *Land Use* feature vectors.

Satellite Images: Since we want to compare the approaches, the images used to build all the feature extractor and output the socio-economic estimates are provided by the Google Static Map API[7]. The satellite images used are 400 × 400 pixels, covering a 1 km² area (2.5 m resolution) with the classical RGB color channels. For each location in the survey, we use the same type of images to build a larger one that covers a 10 km × 10 km neighboring area.

Proxy Data for *Nighttime Light* Method: As in Jean et al. (2016), we used the 1 km resolution world map of NLV, provided by the Earth Observation Group in 2013[8]. Notice that afterward, the Earth Observation Group has 500 m resolution world maps. Unfortunately, there is no reliable time reference mentioned and associated with Google Static Map images so we assume that 2013 NLV data are roughly consistent with Google Static Map images. Finally, 71,000 daytime images were randomly selected from the NLV world map in Africa.

Proxy Data for *Land Use* Feature Extractor: The xView dataset image resolution (0.3 m) is much higher than GSM one (2.5 m), which prevents us from using the object detection methodology based on xView dataset. We then adapted the idea and use a global land use classifier which outputs a single value instead of a set of feature vectors corresponding to each detected object.

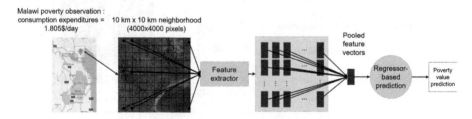

Fig. 2. Canonical pipeline for poverty prediction over 1 km² areas.

---

[7] Google Static Map getting started web page: https://developers.google.com/maps/documentation/maps-static/start.

[8] *Nighttime Light* world map: https://www.ngdc.noaa.gov/eog/dmsp/downloadV4composites.html.

We used land use labels provided in the Eurosat data set (Helber et al. 2018). It consists of almost 30,000 satellite images of European places, labeled into 10 classes: sea lake, river, residential, permanent crop, pasture, industrial, highway, herbaceous vegetation, forest, and annual crop. The authors provided a GeoTIFF data set[9], including the locations of all images, we simply used these locations and downloaded the corresponding Google Static Map API images.

Proxy Data for *Contrastive* Feature Extractor: Since it is an unsupervised method, no proxy data is required. Therefore, we used the poverty indicator location to generate 4,000 × 4,000, images with 2.5 m resolution. Then, for each image, we randomly sample 100 anchor, neighbor, and distant image triplets, with the same size, area coverage, and channel as introduced earlier. We set the neighborhood size to 400 pixels, so the central pixel of each neighbor image (resp. distant image) is less (resp. more) than 400 pixels away from the anchor image. The overall process generates 77,000 triplets.

Poverty Indicators: We used the poverty indicators from LSMS surveys[10]. We focus on the 2016 Malawi survey and consider the natural logarithm of the consumption expenditures as the poverty indicator. Note that the surveys are designed in two steps. The country is divided into clusters, and then, several households are surveyed within each cluster. In the resulting survey, only the clusters coordinates are reported (and randomly displaced for anonymization purposes, as explained earlier). In our experiments, we use the 770 clusters provided by the survey to train and test the poverty prediction models at the cluster level.

3.3 Metrics and Evaluation Goal

Performances of CNNs: We use the accuracy metric for assessing the classification task which allows us to compute feature vectors in *Nighttime Light* and *Land Use*. It is defined as follows:

$$A = \frac{1}{N} \sum_{i=1}^{N} \delta(y_i, \hat{y}_i) \tag{2}$$

with $y = (y_i)_{i \in \{1,...,N\}}$ (resp. $\hat{y} = (\hat{y}_i)_{i \in \{1,...,N\}}$) the true (resp. predicted) NLV value or land use, N the number of predictions, and δ the Kronecker delta. Since *Contrastive* does not make any prediction, we can not use accuracy to measure its quality performance.

Performances of the Ridge Regressor: We consider $y = (y_i)_{i \in \{1,...,N\}}$ (resp. $\hat{y} = (\hat{y}_i)_{i \in \{1,...,N\}}$) as the true (resp. predicted) poverty indicator and N be the

---

[9] GeoTIFF data set provided by Helber et al. (2018): https://github.com/phelber/EuroSAT.

[10] Living Standard Measurements Study, Malawi 2016: https://microdata.worldbank.org/index.php/catalog/2939.

number of predictions. Similarly to previous work, we used the R^2 score, also called coefficient of determination, defined as follows:

$$R^2 = 1 - \frac{\sum_{i=1}^{N}(y_i - \hat{y}_i)^2}{\sum_{i=1}^{N}(\bar{y} - y_i)^2}. \tag{3}$$

R^2 aims to measure the mean squared error (numerator) over the variance (denominator). As a universal and classical metric, it corresponds to the amount of variance explained by the model.

Cross-Validation: The usual train/test splitting process leads to too small data sets impacting the quality of the learning and decreasing the performances. The sparsity of poverty indicators causes some differences between training and testing data distributions. Therefore, the results obtained from a given train/test split can be very different from the ones obtained with other train/test splits. To avoid this problem, we use 10-fold cross-validation and average the scores.

3.4   Implementation

We ran our experiments using a workstation with 32 Gb, Intel Xeon 3.6 GHz 12 cores, and a NVIDIA Quadro GV100 graphic card. We used the Python TensorFlow 2.x library.

The three CNNs are based on the VGG16 architecture, followed by a fully connected layer (used to extract the features) and ended with the classification layer. The VGG16 architecture is pre-trained on ImageNet. We used stochastic gradient descent as optimizer.

All the image pixel values are scaled from 0 to 1 and a horizontal and vertical flip is randomly applied during the training phase as data-augmentation. At the end of each epoch, a validation step is done. The feature extractors are generated with the weights that optimize the validation accuracy when available (*Nighttime Light* and *Land Use*) or the validation loss (*Contrastive*). The training phase ran for 100 epochs and lasts for 18 h for *Nighttime Light*, 13 h for *Land Use*, and 3 h for *Contrastive*.

The feature vectors generated by the feature extractors have $d = 512$ dimensions. We use the Ridge regression with regularization parameters α chosen among the values $\{10^{-4}, 10^{-3}, \ldots, 10^5\}$.

3.5   Results

Table 2 gives R^2 scores which can be considered as baseline results. The first column contains the results obtained when only the feature vector corresponding to the anonymized position is used for regression (without considering the 10 km × 10 km neighborhood). The second column contains the results obtained when all the feature vectors corresponding to an input image in the 10 km × 10 km neighborhood are averaged. Regardless of the feature extractor, we can observe across the methods that there is a significant difference between the R^2 score when all the positions are considered compared to the score obtained with a single feature vector from the anonymized position. The gain ranges from $+0.04$ to $+0.09$. Note that the R^2 values for the three state-of-the-art approaches are similar, with 0.47, 0.46, and 0.45. Nevertheless, the R^2 standard deviation remains high and prevents a fair ranking of the approaches.

Table 2. R^2 scores of the three poverty prediction methods, evaluated on the test data set (10-folds cross-validation).

	Anonymized position	All positions	α
Nighttime Light	0.404 ± 0.07	0.449 ± 0.09	10^2
Land Use	0.383 ± 0.08	$\mathbf{0.47 \pm 0.08}$	10^3
Contrastive	0.385 ± 0.07	0.462 ± 0.08	10^2

4   How to Improve the Results?

Let us investigate two ways to ameliorate the methods' prediction. The first proposition consists in handling the spatial perturbation of the coordinates. The second approach consists in combining the three approaches.

4.1   Handling the Geographic Perturbation

The random perturbation injected in the spatial coordinates of the surveyed poverty indicators may directly affect the prediction results. Therefore, we propose a 2-step method with two variants each, adapting the following step of the framework exposed in Sect. 3.1: For each position in the survey, **(1)** We consider all the $10 \, \text{km} \times 10 \, \text{km}$ neighboring areas for feature extraction, and **(2)** We average the resulting feature vectors.

On the one hand, the first step allows capturing the true position of the poverty indicator. On the other hand, it captures also the 99 false positions of the poverty indicator, perturbing the most important information. The second step reduces drastically the amount of information. The resulting average feature vector is a summarized representation of the $10 \, \text{km} \times 10 \, \text{km}$ neighborhood in which all the specific features are omitted.

Adaptation of Step (1) with Grid-Cell Selection: Instead of considering all the $10 \, \text{km} \times 10 \, \text{km}$ neighboring areas for each position in the survey, we select specific cells in the grid of the neighborhood. The selection is based on the inhabitant number from WorldPop[11] and NLV. More precisely, we keep the cells that correspond to: (a) The n most populated places, and (b) The n highest NLV, with n varying in $\{1, 5, 10, 20, 40, 60, 80\}$.

---

[11] WorldPop: https://www.worldpop.org/geodata/summary?id=123.

After this first adaptation, we exclude "no mans' land" areas where there is no plausible position for a poverty indicator. Then, the feature extractors process only the selected cells and return n feature vectors per position in the survey.

Adaptation of Step (2) Without Averaging the Feature Vectors: For each position in the survey: (a) We average the n feature vectors and compare with the case where (b) The n feature vectors are used for regression. In the latter case, the n feature vectors are annotated with the poverty indicator collected at the corresponding position in the survey. Doing so, we ensure that the specific features captured in all the feature vectors are processed by the regression model.

4.2   Combining the Approaches

There is a large body of research on ensembling methods in the literature. As a starting point, we investigate two simple and straightforward ways of combining the approaches illustrated, in Fig. 3. Future work will explore and test other ensembling methods.

Given the entire grid ($10\,\text{km} \times 10\,\text{km}$ area), a feature extractor outputs one vector for each cell. Please note that some cells may not be processed because of the grid-cell selection, depending on their respective inhabitant number (1a) or NLV (1b). Given a grid-cell, *i.e.*, a sub-image of 400×400 pixels that covers a $1\,\text{km}^2$ area, each of the three feature extractors returns a feature vector. Then, the three feature vectors are either averaged (*Ensembling Averaged*) or concatenated (*Ensembling Concatenated*).

4.3   Experiments and Analysis

Performances of Feature Extractors: The CNNs are used to extract features from images. Therefore, their respective accuracy values are not used to determine whether or not they are good classifiers. However, the accuracy metric can

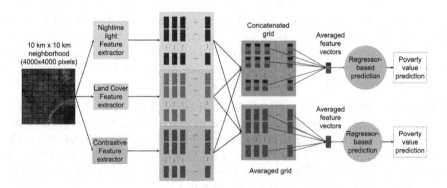

Fig. 3. Ensembling pipeline. Similar to Fig. 2, with an intermediate step of either concatenation or averaging, represented by the gray grids. Note that the previous adaptation (1) and (2) are not shown, for the sake of clarity.

be used as an indirect measure to indicate the degree of consistency between the features generated by the CNNs, according to the classification problem (only for *Nighttime Light* and *Land Use* approaches). *Nighttime Light* reaches 64% of accuracy on the validation data set, whereas *Land Use* reaches 97%. As mentioned earlier, instead of the accuracy measure, we use the R^2 score for evaluating *Contrastive*'s performance on the poverty prediction task.

Discussion on Grid-Cell Selection: We can notice that the two grid-cell selection approaches have similar results, essentially because there is an overlap between the cells selected by each method.

When selecting the grid-cells, either based on the population criterion, or the NLV criterion, the average R^2 score increases up to +0.05 compared to the score obtained when using all the feature vectors. The highest increase is obtained with the population criterion. Each approach benefits from the population-based grid-cell selection. Only *Nighttime Light* benefits from NLV-based grid-cell selection. Compared to the results obtained by averaging all the feature vectors, all the approaches give an average R^2 above 0.48. At this stage, we can say that our grid-cell selection method slightly improves the results. By selecting the most likely true positions of the indicators in the survey, we add the geographical context. However, when considering the same proportion of geographical context, random grid-cell selection is still less efficient than population-based grid-cell selection or NLV-based grid-cell selection, from +0.06 to +0.1. This suggests naturally that capturing the true position improves the prediction of the model.

Discussion on Averaging or Not the Feature Vectors: With the same grid-cell selection, averaging the selected feature vectors leads to the best results and should be recommended. In Table 3, the same grid selection is applied for both columns 3 and 6, but the selected feature vectors are averaged (column 3) and the selected feature vectors are all processed (column 6) by the regression

Table 3. R^2 scores for different grid-cell selection (column) and feature extractors (row). Best $R^2 = 0.502$ is obtained with the ensembling method by concatenation, with NLV-based grid-cell selection ($n = 20$).

	R^2 of SOTA methods		R^2 of our methods handling geographic perturbation			
	Single anonymized position	Averaging across all positions	Population-based grid-cell selection $n = 20$ and averaging	NLV-based grid-cell selection $n = 20$ and averaging	Random grid-cell selection $n = 20$ and averaging	Population-based grid-cell selection $n = 20$ and not averaging
Nighttime Light	0.404 ± 0.07	0.449 ± 0.09	$\mathbf{0.496 \pm 0.09}$	$\mathbf{0.487 \pm 0.08}$	$\mathbf{0.411 \pm 0.07}$	$\mathbf{0.379 \pm 0.08}$
Land Use	0.383 ± 0.08	$\mathbf{0.47 \pm 0.08}$	0.483 ± 0.08	0.466 ± 0.08	0.403 ± 0.05	0.35 ± 0.07
Contrastive	0.385 ± 0.07	0.462 ± 0.08	0.486 ± 0.04	0.464 ± 0.06	0.388 ± 0.05	0.313 ± 0.04
Ensembling Concatenated	0.44 ± 0.08	0.48 ± 0.09	0.491 ± 0.07	$\mathbf{0.502 \pm 0.08}$	0.429 ± 0.07	$\mathbf{0.387 \pm 0.07}$
Ensembling Averaged	0.41 ± 0.08	0.47 ± 0.09	$\mathbf{0.494 \pm 0.07}$	0.487 ± 0.07	0.422 ± 0.05	0.378 ± 0.07

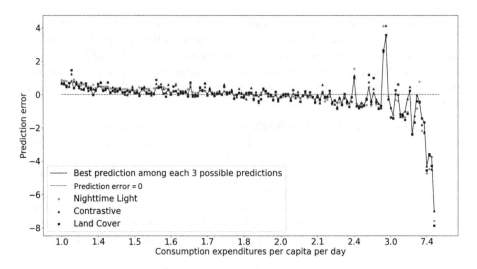

Fig. 4. Prediction error of the three feature extractors for one of the test fold with respect to the poverty level. The prediction is obtained by averaging all the feature vectors for a given position and applying the learnt regression model. Black line connects the best predictions among the three predictions for each test sample. Note that the X-axis is not linear.

model. We can notice that averaging increases the R^2 score up to $+0.15$. The correct cell (correct position) with the correct poverty value may be masked by the 20 other feature vectors. This probably explains the poor performance of this approach.

Discussion on the Ensembling Approaches: Combining the approaches by concatenation or averaging always improves the average R^2 score by $+0.01$ approximately. The best results are obtained with NLV-based grid-cell selection, with an average R^2 reaching 0.50. However, the improvement is negligible. For example, when using the population-based grid-cell selection, there is no improvement compared to *Nighttime Light* alone.

Next, we investigate whether an ensembling approach combining the three methods can significantly improve the results. For several test folds and all the ground truth data in each test fold, we compare the relative prediction error made by *Nighttime Light*, *Land Cover*, and *Contrastive* (shown in Fig. 4, for one particular test fold). Then, for each ground truth observations, we select the prediction with the smallest prediction error. We average the R^2 score obtained with the best prediction over the test folds, and obtain $R^2 = 0.6$. This score is significantly higher than all the other results presented in Table 3. Thus, there is room for improvement by ensembling the methods.

Additionally, in Fig. 4, we observe that, regardless of the feature extractor, the three approaches are slightly over-estimating the richness when the poverty is extreme, and give more erroneous predictions when the poverty is above

2.4\$/day. This can be explained by a fewer number of poverty indicators that are greater than 2.4\$/day in the learning set.

5   Conclusion and Future Work

By providing a fair comparison between three state-of-the-art models for poverty prediction, we present several insightful results: (1) Such models produce similar results on the same framework. (2) The spatial perturbation injected in the coordinates of poverty indicators is a key issue that reduces significantly the prediction power of the models. By handling the spatial perturbation of the coordinates, our grid-cell selection method shows better performances and motivates future work to ameliorate the entire process. (3) Using anonymized coordinates from the surveys implies poverty prediction at a $10\,km \times 10\,km$ scale (which can still capture the true position) rather than $1\,km \times 1\,km$ scale. However, it prevents the use of very high-resolution images available today. Covering a $100\,km^2$ area with high-resolution images would necessitate very large images ($4,000 \times 4,000$ with $2.5\,m$ resolution) that cannot be directly processed by a CNN. We believe that this opens several new research directions to handle noise and high-resolution images for CNN-based prediction models. (4) We showed that our combination of the three considered methods does not augment drastically the quality performance. However, we experience that choosing the best prediction among the three methods leads to $R^2 = 0.6$. Thus, we claim that there exists a combination of the three methods that can give significant improvement of the R^2 score. As it is a choice on the prediction strategy, we believe that other or more sophisticated ensembling methods can be even more efficient. (5) Finally, the small size of the data set causes some differences and discrepancies between the training and testing data sets, which are reflected by high standard deviation values during the cross-validation.

To pursue this work, we aim to propose a combination method that can reach higher R^2 scores, eventually using multi-spectral imagery to estimate poverty indicators as other work in the literature. Using the fair benchmark for poverty prediction we proposed, we plan to explore the benefits of multi-spectral images compared to natural RGB images. Finally, other deep learning architectures may be more likely to give a better feature representation of images. Therefore, one of our goals will be to test and find an optimal architecture.

Acknowledgment. This research was partly funded by the PARSEC group, funded by the Belmont Forum as part of its Collaborative Research Action (CRA) on Science-Driven e-Infrastructures Innovation (SEI) and the synthesis centre CESAB of the French Foundation for Research on Biodiversity. This work was also partly funded by the French ANR project MPA-POVERTY.

References

Ayush, K., Uzkent, B., Burke, M., Lobell, D., Ermon, S.: Generating interpretable poverty maps using object detection in satellite images. In: Bessiere, C. (ed.) Proceedings of the Twenty-Ninth International Joint Conference on Artificial Intelligence, IJCAI-20, pp. 4410–4416. International Joint Conferences on Artificial Intelligence Organization. Special track on AI for CompSust and Human Well-Being (2020)

Babenko, B., Hersh, J., Newhouse, D., Ramakrishnan, A., Swartz, T.: Poverty mapping using convolutional neural networks trained on high and medium resolution satellite images, with an application in Mexico. In: NIPS 2017 Workshop on Machine Learning for the Developing World (2017)

Burgert, C.R., Colston, J., Roy, T., Zachary, B.: Geographic displacement procedure and georeferenced data release policy for the demographic and health surveys. DHS Spatial Analysis Reports No. 7. ICF International, Calverton (2013)

Chandy, L.: Counting the poor: methods, problems and solutions behind the $1.25 a day global poverty estimates. Working Paper No. 337682, Development Initiatives & Brooking Institution (2013). http://devinit.org/wp-content/uploads/2013/09/Counting-the-poor11.pdf

Chen, X., Nordhaus, W.D.: Using luminosity data as a proxy for economic statistics. Proc. Natl. Acad. Sci. **108**(21), 8589–8594 (2011)

Doll, C.N.H., Muller, J.-P., Elvidge, C.D.: Night-time imagery as a tool for global mapping of socioeconomic parameters and greenhouse gas emissions. Ambio **29**(3), 157–162 (2000)

Elvidge, C., Baugh, K., Kihn, E., Kroehl, H.W., Davis, E., Davis, C.: Relation between satellite observed visible-near infrared emissions, population, economic activity and electric power consumption. Int. J. Remote Sens. **18**, 1373–1379 (1997)

Engstrom, R., Hersh, J., Newhouse, D.: Poverty from space: using high-resolution satellite imagery for estimating economic well-being. Policy Research Working Paper No. 8284, World Bank, Washington, DC (2017). https://openknowledge.worldbank.org/handle/10986/29075. License: CC BY 3.0 IGO

Helber, P., Bischke, B., Dengel, A., Borth, D.: Introducing EuroSAT: a novel dataset and deep learning benchmark for land use and land cover classification. In: 2018 IEEE International Geoscience and Remote Sensing Symposium, IGARSS 2018, pp. 204–207. IEEE (2018)

Jean, N., Burke, M., Xie, M., Davis, W.M., Lobell, D.B., Ermon, S.: Combining satellite imagery and machine learning to predict poverty. Science **353**(6301), 790–794 (2016)

Jean, N., Wang, S., Samar, A., Azzari, G., Lobell, D., Ermon, S.: Tile2vec: unsupervised representation learning for spatially distributed data. In: AAAI-19/IAAI-19/EAAI-20 Proceedings, pp. 3967–3974. AAAI Technical Track: Machine Learning (2019)

Ngestrini, R.: Predicting poverty of a region from satellite imagery using CNNs. Master's thesis, Department of Information and Computing Science, Utrecht University (2019). http://dspace.library.uu.nl/handle/1874/376648

Perez, A., Yeh, C., Azzari, G., Burke, M., Lobell, D., Ermon, S.: Poverty prediction with public landsat 7 satellite imagery and machine learning. In: NIPS 2017, Workshop on Machine Learning for the Developing World (2017)

Redmon, J., Farhadi, A.: Yolov3: an incremental improvement (2018). CoRR, abs/1804.02767

Welch, R.: Monitoring urban population and energy utilization patterns from satellite data. Remote Sens. Env. **9**(1), 1–9 (1980)

Wozniak, P., Afrisal, H., Esparza, R., Kwolek, B.: Scene recognition for indoor localization of mobile robots using deep CNN. In: Chmielewski, L., Kozera, R., Orłowski, A., Wojciechowski, K., Bruckstein, A., Petkov, N. (eds.) ICCVG 2018. LNCS, vol. 11114, pp. 137–147. Springer, Cham (2018). https://doi.org/10.1007/978-3-030-00692-1_13

Xie, M., Jean, N., Burke, M., Lobell, D., Ermon, S.: Transfer learning from deep features for remote sensing and poverty mapping. In: 30th AAAI Conference on Artificial Intelligence (2016)

Yeh, C., et al.: Using publicly available satellite imagery and deep learning to understand economic well-being in Africa. Nat. Commun. **11**(1), 2583 (2020)

Using a Binary Diffractive Optical Element to Increase the Imaging System Depth of Field in UAV Remote Sensing Tasks

Pavel G. Serafimovich[1]([✉]) [iD], Alexey P. Dzyuba[2], Artem V. Nikonorov[1,3] [iD], and Nikolay L. Kazanskiy[1,3] [iD]

[1] IPSI RAS – Branch of the FSRC "Crystallography and Photonics" RAS, Molodogvardeyskaya st. 151, Samara 443001, Russia
pavel.serafimovich@gmail.com
[2] ITMO University, Kronverksky av. 49, St. Petersburg 197101, Russia
[3] Samara National Research University, Moskovskoe Shosse 34A, Samara 443086, Russia

Abstract. Using an example of a real-world data set, it is shown that the accuracy of the image detector based on a YOLOv3 neural network does not deteriorate when using only one nonblurred color channel. The binary diffractive optical element was calculated, which allows increasing the imaging system depth of field by several times. This is achieved by using different color channels for various defocus values. A comparison of the MTF curves of the original and apodized imaging systems for a given minimum acceptable value of image contrast is presented. This approach allows us to create novel remote sensing imaging systems with an increased depth of field.

Keywords: Imaging system · Extended depth of field · Diffractive optical element

1 Introduction

The development of neural networks has significantly advanced methods for many tasks in the field of computer vision, in particular, object detection [1–5]. This problem arises in a variety of applications related to the processing of video data from unmanned vehicles, drones, robots, as well as video surveillance data, among many others. The problem has two parts. First, it is the classification of the object, i.e. defining the categories of all instances of objects present in the scene. The values of the reliability of this classification are also determined. Secondly, it is the localization of the object, i.e. calculation of coordinates of rectangles, which limits found objects in the scene. A number of factors make it difficult to solve the problem of object detection. For example, different scales of the detected object. Also, objects can be rotated relative to the camera, i.e. their orientation will not be frontal. Scene lighting conditions can vary significantly due to weather conditions or artificial lighting. Here we will consider an example house number detection task to show the effect of the proposed approach which could be

© Springer Nature Switzerland AG 2021
A. Del Bimbo et al. (Eds.): ICPR 2020 Workshops, LNCS 12667, pp. 566–577, 2021.
https://doi.org/10.1007/978-3-030-68787-8_41

further extended to other drone-based remote sensing tasks, like person or car tracking, street incidents detection, and so on [34]. Optical systems are known to be sensitive to defocusing and chromatic aberration. An increase in the depth of field of the optical system makes it possible to weaken this sensitivity and its negative consequences in blurring defocused images. However, a simple increase in the depth of field (DOF) by reducing the pupil or numerical aperture of the system leads to deterioration in resolution. One way to increase DOF without degrading resolution is to "encode" the wavefront, which is actually a phase apodization of the pupil of the lens [5–7]. As a rule, apodization is accompanied not only by positive effects (an increase in DOF and a decrease in the size of the focal spot) but also by a significant change in the structure of the point scattering function (PSF) and the growth of side lobes that worsen the image properties. Apodization is widely used in focusing [8–10] and scanning [11–14] optical systems, as well as in microscopes to increase contrast [15–17], as well as in various applications for resolving two nearby radiation sources [18, 19]. In imaging systems, the use of apodization requires additional, as a rule, a digital decoding operation [20–26]. Despite the development of various decoding methods, including neural networks [27–29], when optimizing the apodizing function, it is desirable to maintain a compromise between increasing DOF and PSF distortion. Our proposed binary diffractive element is an addition to existing objectives. Thus, this solution is simpler than optical elements for increasing the depth of focus, proposed, for example, in [30, 31].

In the task of images detecting, specific requirements can be imposed on the imaging system. In particular, in this paper, it is shown that for a relatively reliable classification of the image, it is sufficient to have a focused image in only one color channel. This observation is based on the study of only one data set. However, it logically follows from the very specifics of the task, in which the structure of the object is important, not its color.

2   Radially Symmetric Binary Phase Apodization

For a long-focus lens (focal length of the order of several hundred millimeters), the focus variations are insignificant compared to the focus depth, which is estimated by the formula:

$$DOF \approx \frac{\lambda}{NA^2}, \tag{1}$$

where λ is the illumination wavelength. Thus, the depth of field increases with decreasing numerical aperture, i.e. either with an increase in focal length, or a decrease in the radius of the lens (or aperture). However, in this case, the resolution will also deteriorate, which is also inversely proportional to the numerical aperture of the system:

$$RES = \frac{\lambda}{2NA}. \tag{2}$$

Phase apodization of the lens pupil (in contrast to reducing aperture) allows you to increase the depth of field without compromising resolution. However, in this case, the point spread function (PSF) is significantly different from the delta function. Visually, the image becomes very blurry, although it does not change when defocusing. To restore the image, an additional deconvolution operation is required.

The amplitude S in the focal plane of the imaging system can be written as follows:

$$S(r, z) = 2 \int_0^1 P(\rho)J_0(r\rho) \exp(iz\rho^2/2)\rho d\rho \tag{3}$$

where $P(\rho)$ is the pupil function, r and z are the normalized radial and axial coordinates:

$$r = \frac{2\pi R \sin \alpha}{\lambda}, \quad z = \frac{2\pi Z \sin^2(\alpha/2)}{\lambda}. \tag{4}$$

Here $\sin\alpha$ is a numerical aperture, and R and Z denote the radial and axial coordinates. Along the optical axis, the amplitude of the light field is written as follows:

$$S(0, z) = 2 \int_0^1 P(\rho) \exp(iz\rho^2/2)\rho d\rho = \int_0^1 Q(t) \exp(izt/2)dt \tag{5}$$

We assume that $P(\rho)$ is a real function. This assumption is justified, because we consider binary phase elements, where the phase takes the values 0 and π, therefore the amplitude is 1 or -1. In this case, you can write the following ratio:

$$S^*(0, z) = \int_0^1 Q^*(t) \exp(izt/2)dt = \int_0^1 Q(t) \exp(i(-z)t/2)dt = S(0, -z) \tag{6}$$

3   Calculation of Binary Diffractive Optical Element

Binary diffractive optical elements introduce significant chromatic aberrations of the imaging system. As a rule, the compensation of these aberrations requires additional efforts in optimizing the optical element. In this work, chromatic aberration used to optimize PSF separately for each color channel in order to increase DOF. For this, the phase apodization of the aperture using a radially symmetric (ring) binary phase element is used.

The binary diffractive optical element (DOE) is made of silica $n = 1.46$, has an outer radius $r_0 = 1.1$ mm, r stands for the radius of the inner zone (see Fig. 1), h is the height of the ring. The focal distance of the imaging system is $f = 4.6$ mm. The optimized parameters are h and r. Three wavelengths of the illuminating light are $\lambda = 460$ nm, 550 nm, 640 nm, sensor pixel size is 1.2 μm.

Fig. 1. Ring-shaped binary DOE. The outer radius r0 is fixed. The inner radius r and the height of the ring h (not shown in the figure) are optimization parameters.

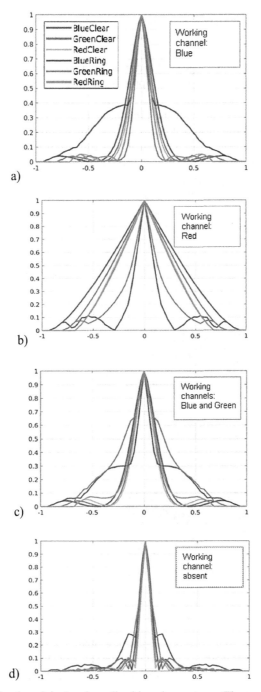

Fig. 2. MTF plots for the original and apodized imaging systems. These graphs are calculated for various defocus values. The imaging system is focused at a distance of 1.2 m from the lens. (a), (b), (c) and (d) show MTF at distances of 9.0, 1.2, 0.65, 0.44 m, respectively.

When optimizing this element, the value of the maximum resolvable frequency is set (in fractions of the cutoff frequency, 0.5 was set) and the value of the minimum allowable contrast at this frequency (20% was set). Increasing the depth of field is performed in the range of 0.7–9 m. This range is sliced into 7 planes. Optimization was carried out on a grid of optimized parameters. The optimal values are $h = 3.0pi$ (0.0014 mm) and $r = 0.73$ mm.

Figure 2 shows MTF plots for the original and apodized imaging systems. These graphs are calculated for various defocus values. We assume that the imaging system (aperture 1.8 mm) is focused at a distance of 1.2 m from the lens. Figures 2a, b, c, and d show MTF at distances of 9.0, 1.2, 0.65, 0.44 m, respectively. A comparison of MTF plots for the initial and apodized imaging systems allows us to conclude that in the apodized system the depth of field is increased by several times.

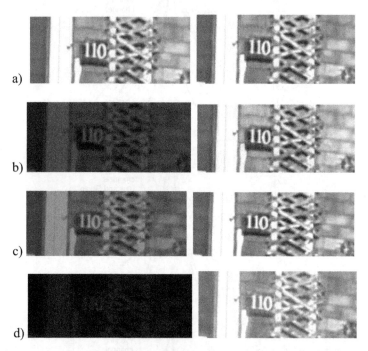

a)

b)

c)

d)

Fig. 3. The content of each of the color channels of the image from the training dataset. (a) original image and its grayscale representation, color channels red (b), green ©, and blue (d) and their grayscale representation (Color figure online)

Figure 3 shows the content of each of the color channels of the image from the training dataset. Figure 3a demonstrates the original image and its grayscale representation. Figures 3b, c and d show color channels red (b), green (c) and blue (d) and their grayscale representation, respectively.

Our image detection experiments were carried out on a fully simulated system. The blurred image after propagation through the imaging system is modeled as a convolution of true image and the PSF and is given by

$$g = h \mathbf{e} f, \tag{7}$$

where g denotes the blurred image, f is the true image, h is PSF. There is no noise additive here because we assume that the images in the real-world SVHN dataset are already quite noisy.

Figure 4 shows the image of the object at a distance of 0.65 m after propagation through the imaging system. Green and blue color channels are "working channels" at this distance. The red channel is blurred. Figure 4a represents the color image. Figures 4b, c and d show their grayscale representation of color channels red (b), green (c) and blue (d).

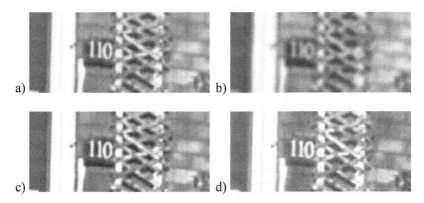

Fig. 4. The image of the object at distance 0.65 m after propagation through the imaging system. a represents the color image. b, c and d show their grayscale representation of color channels red (b), green (c) and blue (d). (Color figure online)

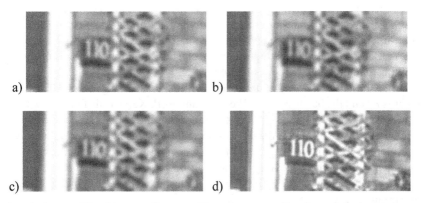

Fig. 5. The image of the object at a distance of 9 m after propagation through the imaging system. Figure 4a represents the color image. Figures 4b, c and d show their grayscale representation of color channels red (b), green (c) and blue (d). (Color figure online)

Figure 5 shows the image of the object at distance of 9 m after propagation through the imaging system. The blue color channel is the "working channel" at this distance. The Red and green color channels are blurred. Figure 5a represents the color image. Figures 5b, c and d show their grayscale representation of color channels red (b), green (c) and blue (d).

4 Detecting Images of House Numbers

There are two types of deep learning methods for object detection. First, these are two-stage detectors. At the first stage, such detectors build a network of regional proposals. At the second stage, on the basis of these proposals, objects are classified and localized. An example of such a detector is Faster R-CNN (Region-based Convolutional Neural Networks) [4]. Two-stage detectors provide state-of-the-art accuracy but are not the fastest.

Secondly, one-stage detectors are being developed. One-stage detectors solve the object detection problem as a regression problem. These methods calculate class probabilities and bounding box coordinates simultaneously. Compared to two-stage detectors, these methods show lower accuracy but are faster. Examples of single-stage detectors are SSD (Single Shot MultiBox Detector) and YOLO (You Only Look Once).

Redmon et al. proposed the YOLO image detector in 2016 [5]. This method is for real-time image processing. YOLO is the development of GoogleNet. In this method, the neural network divides the image into regions and predicts the bounding box and confidence for each region. YOLO splits the image into a grid of $N \times N$ cells, with each cell predicting only one object. Confidence is expressed as a fixed number of boundary blocks, each with its own probability.

The algorithm detects one object per grid cell, regardless of the number of boxes, using a non-maximum suppression algorithm. Typically, YOLO uses ImageNet to pre-train the parameters and then uses the datasets required for a specific task. YOLO has several versions, in particular, versions YOLOv2 and YOLOv3, which, by modifying the network architecture, have increased the detection accuracy, while maintaining a high detection rate. At the heart of YOLOv3 [32] is the architecture of the Darknet, which has 53 layers trained using the ImageNet dataset. An additional 53 layers were added to this architecture for object detection tasks, and this model was trained using the Pascal VOC dataset. Using residual connections and upsampling, the architecture performs detection at three different scales from specific layers of the structure. This improves the efficiency of the YOLOv3 model in detecting small objects, but at the same time results in slower processing than previous versions of YOLO.

To train the network, we use Adam solver with a fixed learning rate of 0.0001. Epochs number is 80 and the batch size is 4. We use framework Keras with Tensorflow backend and an RTX 2080 Ti graphics card. As training data for YOLO net, the Street View House Numbers (SVHN) [33] dataset is selected. SVHN is a real-world image dataset for developing machine learning and object recognition algorithms with the minimal requirement on data preprocessing and formatting. This data set contains about 33000 images for training and about 13000 images for testing. The YOLO model was trained on the training part of the original dataset.

Figures 6 and 7 show hard to detect instances of the test dataset. Figure 6 demonstrates cases of the complex orientation of detected objects. For two samples from the test dataset, Figs. 6a and 6b represent the original image, Figs. 6c and 6d show the original annotation, Figs. 6e and 6f show the detection result. It can be seen from the figure that the model coped well with the detection. At the same time, the confidence for the figures on the left picture was 99%, 78% and 79%, for the right picture - 98%, 99% and 98%. Figure 7 demonstrates cases of complex lighting and background. Similar to Fig. 6, Figs. 7a and 7b represent the original image, Figs. 7c and 7d show the original annotation, Figs. 7e and 7f show the detection result. It can be seen from the figure that the model coped well with the detection. At the same time, the confidence for the figures on the left picture was 78%, 75% and 99%, for the right picture - 55%, 58% and 84%.

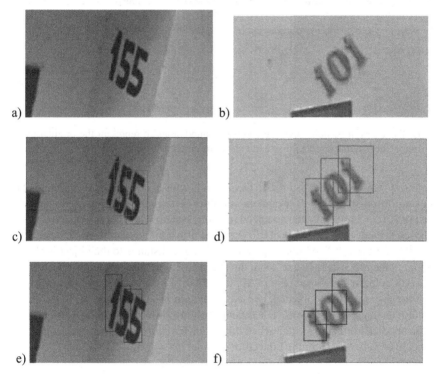

Fig. 6. The cases of the complex orientation of detected objects, a and b represent the original image, c and d show the original annotation, e and f show the detection result.

The calculated model was evaluated on several modifications of the test part of the dataset. These modifications were various combinations of the object distance ranges for unapodized and apodized imaging systems. The measured metric was detection precision mAP at IoU 0.5 (AP50). Table 1 gives a summary of the results. For unapodized imaging system and all images in the focal plane, the model showed AP50 = 59.8% (second column). The third column shows the result (AP50 = 46.2%) for the unapodized

Fig. 7. The cases of complex lighting and background. a and b represent the original image, c and d show the original annotation, e and f show the detection result.

imaging system when the distance to the object is chosen at random in the range of 0.7–9 m (uniform distribution of a random variable). The fourth column demonstrates the result (AP50 = 54.3%) for the apodized imaging system when the distance to the object is chosen at random in the range of 0.7–9 m. The fifth column represents the result (AP50 = 59.8%) for the apodized imaging system when the distance to the object is chosen at random in the range of 0.7–1 m. Here the green and blue color channels are "working". The sixth column shows the result (AP50 = 52.0%) for the apodized imaging system when the distance to the object is chosen at random in the range of 1–1.4 m. Here the red color channel is "working". The seventh column shows the result (AP50 = 55.8%) for the apodized imaging system when the distance to the object is chosen at random in the range of 1.4–9 m. Here the blue color channel is "working".

Table 1. Detection precision on the test data.

Imaging system type, Distance range, m	Unapod., focal	Unapod., 0.7–9	Apod., 0.7–9	Apod., 0.7–1	Apod., 1–1.4	Apod., 1.4–9
mAP at IoU 0.5, %	59.8	46.2	54.3	59.8	52.0	55.8

Table 1 shows that AP50 values for the apodized imaging system are greater than for the unapodized imaging system for an optimized range of object distances (46.2% and 54.3%, respectively). Thus, it was concluded that one non-blurred color channel is sufficient to significantly improve the precision of detecting images from the SVHN dataset. Given the variety of lighting conditions, color palettes, and image position angles in SVHN, this conclusion can probably be generalized to other similar data sets, where the structure of the object is important for classification, not its color.

5 Conclusions

The binary optical element for phase apodization of the pupil function of the optical system is calculated. This optical element provides an increase in the depth of focus of the optical system through at least one color channel for a certain value on the optical axis. The calculated optical element can be used in machine vision problems for image detection. For example, when using robots in storage facilities. Using the appropriate training data set, the obtained results can be generalized, for example, to the task of monitoring the technical condition of railway rolling stock or the task of classification examination of ships and offshore structures. The considered approach could be further extended to other drone-based remote sensing tasks, like person or car tracking, street incidents detection, and so on.

Acknowledgments. The reported study was funded by the Russian Foundation for Basic Research (RFBR), project 19-29-09054, and 18-07-01390.

References

1. Zou, Z., Shi, Z., Guo, Y., Ye, J.: Object detection in 20 years: a survey (2019). arXiv:1905. 05055v2
2. Alganci, U., Soydas, M., Sertel, E.: Comparative research on deep learning approaches for airplane detection from very high-resolution satellite images. Remote Sens. **12**, 458 (2020)
3. Liu, W., et al.: SSD: single shot multibox detector. In: Leibe, B., Matas, J., Sebe, N., Welling, M. (eds.) ECCV 2016. LNCS, vol. 9905, pp. 21–37. Springer, Cham (2016). https://doi.org/10.1007/978-3-319-46448-0_2
4. Ren, S., He, K., Girshick, R., Sun, J.: Faster R-CNN: towards real-time object detection with region proposal networks. In: Proceedings of the International Conference on Neural Information Processing Systems (NIPS 2015), Montreal, QC, Canada, 7–12 December 2015, pp. 91–99 (2015)
5. Redmon, J., Divvala, S., Girshick, R., Farhadi, A.: You only look once: unified, real-time object detection. In: Proceedings of the IEEE Conference on Computer Vision and Pattern Recognition (CVPR 2016), Las Vegas, NA, USA, 27–30 June 2016, pp. 779–788 (2016)
6. Bagheri, S., Javidi, B.: Extension of depth of field using amplitude and phase modulation of the pupil function. Opt. Lett. **33**(7), 757–759 (2008)
7. Reddy, A.N.K., Khonina, S.N.: Apodization for improving the two-point resolution of coherent optical systems with defect of focus. Appl. Phys. B **124**(12), 1–9 (2018). https://doi.org/10.1007/s00340-018-7101-z
8. Elmalem, S., Giryes, R., Marom, E.: Learned phase coded aperture for the benefit of depth of field extension. Opt. Express **26**(12), 15316–15331 (2018)
9. Sun, C.-C., Liu, C.-K.: Ultrasmall focusing spot with a long depth of focus based on polarization and phase modulation. Opt. Lett. **28**(3), 99–101 (2003)

10. Liu, Z., Flores, A., Wang, M.R., Yang, J.J.: Diffractive infrared lens with extended depth of focus. Opt. Eng. **46**(1–9), 018002 (2007)
11. Khonina, S.N., Ustinov, A.V., Porfirev, A.P.: Dynamic focal shift and extending depth of focus based on the masking of the illuminating beam and using an adjustable axicon. J. Opt. Soc. Am. A **36**(6), 1039–1047 (2019)
12. Reddick, R.C., Warmark, R.J., Ferrel, T.L.: New form of scanning optical microscopy. Phys. Rev. B. **39**, 767–770 (1989)
13. Kowalczyk, M., Zapata-Rodriguez, C.J., Martinez-Corral, M.: Asymmetric apodization in confocal scanning systems. Appl. Opt. **37**(35), 8206–8214 (1998)
14. Hecht, B., et al.: Scanning near-field optical microscopy with aperture probes: fundamentals and applications. J. Chem. Phys. **112**, 7761–7774 (2000)
15. Boruah, B.R., Neil, M.A.A.: Laser scanning confocal microscope with programmable amplitude, phase, and polarization of the illumination beam. Rev. Sci. Instrum. **80**, 013705 (2009)
16. Fürhapter, S., Jesacher, A., Bernet, S., Ritsch-Marte, M.: Spiral phase contrast imaging in microscopy. Opt. Express **13**, 689–694 (2005)
17. Situ, G., Warber, M., Pedrini, G., Osten, W.: Phase contrast enhancement in microscopy using spiral phase filtering. Opt. Commun. **283**, 1273 (2010)
18. Maurer, C., Jesacher, A., Bernet, S., Ritsch-Marte, M.: What spatial light modulators can do for optical microscopy. Laser Photon. Rev. **5**, 81–101 (2011)
19. Grimes, D.N., Thompson, B.J.: Two-point resolution with partially coherent light. J. Opt. Soc. Am. **57**(11), 1330–1334 (1967)
20. Xu, B., Wang, Z., He, J.: Super-resolution imaging via aperture modulation and intensity extrapolation. Sci. Rep. **8**, 15216 (2018)
21. Raveh, I., Mendlovic, D., Zalevsky, Z., Lohmann, A.W.: Digital method for defocus correction: experimental results. Opt. Eng. **38**(10), 1620–1626 (1999)
22. Cathey, W.T., Dowski, E.R.: New paradigm for imaging systems. Appl. Opt. **41**(29), 6080–6092 (2002)
23. Xu, L., Ren, J.S.J., Liu, C., Jia, J.: Deep convolutional neural network for image deconvolution. In: Advances in Neural Information Processing Systems, pp. 1790–1798 (2014)
24. Asif, M.S., Ayremlou, A., Sankaranarayanan, A., Veeraraghavan, A., Baraniuk, R.G.: Flat-Cam: thin, lensless cameras using coded aperture and computation. IEEE Trans. Comput. Imaging **3**(3), 384–397 (2017)
25. Eilertsen, G., Kronander, J., Denes, G., Mantiuk, R., Unger, J.: HDR image reconstruction from a single exposure using deep CNNs. ACM Trans. Graph. (SIGGRAPH Asia) **36**, 6 (2017)
26. Sitzmann, V., et al.: End-to-end optimization of optics and image processing for achromatic extended depth of field and super-resolution imaging. ACM Trans. Graph. **37**(4), Article 114 (2018)
27. Dzyuba, A., Serafimovich, P., Khonina, S., Popov, S.: Application of a neural network for calculating the surface relief of a different level two-zone lens with an increased depth of field. In: Proceedings of SPIE, vol. 11516, pp. 115161A-(8 pp.) (2020)
28. Gharbi, M., Chaurasia, G., Paris, S., Durand, F.: Deep joint demosaicking and denoising. ACM Trans. Graph. **35**, 191 (2016)
29. Rivenson, Y., Göröcs, Z., Günaydin, H., Zhang, Y., Wang, H., Ozcan, A.: Deep learning microscopy. Optica **4**(11), 1437–1443 (2017)
30. Banerji, S., Meem, M., Majumder, A., Sensale-Rodriguez, B., Menon, R.: Diffractive flat lens enables extreme depth-of-focus imaging. arXiv preprint arXiv:1910.07928
31. Romero, L.A., Millán, M.S., Jaroszewicz, Z., Kołodziejczyk, A.: Programmable diffractive optical elements for extending the depth of focus in ophthalmic optics. In: 10th International Symposium on Medical Information Processing and Analysis, vol. 9287, p. 92871E (2019)

32. Redmon, J., Farhadi, A.: YOLOv3: an incremental improvement (2018). arXiv:1804.02767
33. Netzer, Y., Wang, T., Coates, A., Bissacco, A., Wu, B., Ng, A.: 2011 NIPS Workshop on Deep Learning and Unsupervised Feature Learning (2011)
34. Wen, L., et al.: VisDrone-MOT2019: the vision meets drone multiple object tracking challenge results. In: Proceedings of the IEEE International Conference on Computer Vision (ICCV) Workshops (2019)

Self-supervised Pre-training Enhances Change Detection in Sentinel-2 Imagery

Marrit Leenstra[1], Diego Marcos[1] ⓘ, Francesca Bovolo[2] ⓘ,
and Devis Tuia[1,3](✉) ⓘ

[1] Wageningen University, Wageningen, The Netherlands
diego.marcos@wur.nl
[2] Fondazione Bruno Kessler, Trento, Italy
bovolo@fbk.it
[3] Ecole Polytechnique Fédérale de Lausanne, Sion, Switzerland
devis.tuia@epfl.ch

Abstract. While annotated images for change detection using satellite imagery are scarce and costly to obtain, there is a wealth of unlabeled images being generated every day. In order to leverage these data to learn an image representation more adequate for change detection, we explore methods that exploit the temporal consistency of Sentinel-2 times series to obtain a usable self-supervised learning signal. For this, we build and make publicly available (https://zenodo.org/record/4280482) the Sentinel-2 Multitemporal Cities Pairs (S2MTCP) dataset, containing multitemporal image pairs from 1520 urban areas worldwide. We test the results of multiple self-supervised learning methods for pre-training models for change detection and apply it on a public change detection dataset made of Sentinel-2 image pairs (OSCD).

1 Introduction

Large amounts of remote sensing images are produced daily from airborne and spaceborne sensors and can be used to monitor the state of our planet. Among the last generation sensors, the European Copernicus program has launched a series of satellites with multispectral sensors named Sentinel-2 (S2 hereafter). S2 has a revisit time between five days (at the Equator) and 2–3 days at mid-latitudes. With such high revisit rate, change detection, *i.e.* the comparison of images acquired over the same geographical area at different times to identify changes [1], allows for near real-time monitoring of dynamics that are observable though remote sensing, including forest monitoring [2,3], urbanisation mapping [4,5] and disaster monitoring [6,7].

Many change detection methods have been proposed in the literature [8]. They tend to identify changes either by comparing classification maps [9] or by first extracting some kind of index to be thresholded to highlight changes [10]. Recently, deep learning has been considered to learn how to align data spaces, so that changes are better highlighted and easier to detect [11–15].

ⓒ Springer Nature Switzerland AG 2021
A. Del Bimbo et al. (Eds.): ICPR 2020 Workshops, LNCS 12667, pp. 578–590, 2021.
https://doi.org/10.1007/978-3-030-68787-8_42

Despite the success of these approaches, the lack of a relevant and large labeled dataset limits their applicability [16]. In computer vision tasks using natural images, it is common to use models that have been pre-trained on a large dataset for a loosely related task. A different number of bands and image structure limits the usability of these models to S2 imagery. This exacerbates the need for a tailored change detection ground truth, which is often difficult to obtain: especially when change is a rare anomaly (*e.g.* after a disaster), there are no labeled sets to train deep learning models on.

To decrease the amount of supervision, one can revert to models using types of annotation requiring less human effort. One could use exploit the geometry of data manifolds by using semi-supervised models, or change the type of annotations, for example by considering weak supervision, *e.g.* image-level annotations rather than pixel level ones [17] or imprecise labels [18]. These approaches are successful, but still require some level of supervision provided by an annotator.

In this paper, we explore the possibility of reducing this requirement to a minimum. We consider strategies based on *self-supervised learning* [19,20], where a neural network is trained using labels extracted directly from the images themselves. Rather than training the model on the change detection task, we train it on a *pretext task* for which the labels can be extracted from the image pairs directly (*e.g.* relative locations of patches). By doing so, we can pre-train the majority of the weights and then teach the model to recognize changes with a minimal amount of labels. We create a large and global dataset of S2 image pairs, S2MTCP, where we train our self-supervised learning model, before then fine-tuning it on the OSCD change detection dataset [21] for pixel-level change detection. The results show that achieving state of art change detection is possible with such a model pre-trained without labels, opening interesting perspectives on the usage of self-supervised learning in change detection.

2 Methods

In this section, we present our entire pipeline (Sect. 2.1) and then detail the self-supervised pretext tasks used for pre-training (Sect. 2.2).

2.1 Change Detection Pipeline

Let I^1 and I^2 be two multispectral images acquired over the same geographical area at time t^1 and t^2 respectively. We want to pre-train a model on a set of unlabeled images $\{U = (I_u^1, I_u^2)_i\}_{i=1}^N$ such that it can be easily fine-tuned on a small set of labeled image pairs $\{L = (I_c^1, I_c^2)_i\}_{i=1}^M$.

The overall pipeline comprises three phases: first the network is trained on the pretext task (see Sect. 2.2), then the layer with the best features for change detection is manually selected. Finally, these features are used in a second network performing change detection. Figure 1 presents the overview of the methodology.

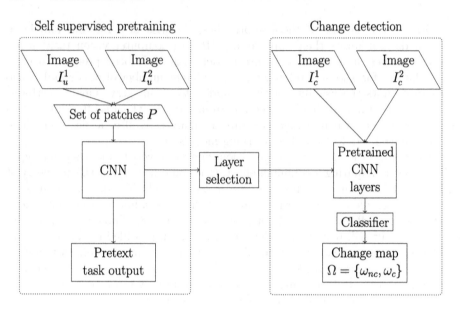

Fig. 1. Overview of the methodology.

Phase 1: Self-supervised Pre-training. Ideally, we would like the change detection network to be able to focus on learning the changed areas. To do so, one would hope that the low level features in the change detection network *align* the two image radiometric spaces, so that the features for I_c^1 and I_c^2 become similar for areas were no changes have occurred.

To facilitate this process, we learn such features using a self-supervised task on a large, unlabeled dataset, U. This task has to be related to the task of change detection so that the learned features become useful. We test two different pretext tasks: (1) discriminate between overlapping and non-overlapping patches and (2) minimizing the difference between overlapping patches in feature space. Both pretext tasks are described in detail in the next Sect. 2.2.

Phase 2: Feature Selection. The deeper layers in the network are likely to be more task-specific, which means that earlier layers might be more suitable for the downstream task [22]. Therefore, we add a feature layer selection step to extract the feature layer that results in the highest change detection performance. Image pairs $(I_c^1, I_c^2)_i$ are passed as input to the network and, at each layer the activation features $\mathbf{f}_{l,i}^1$ and $\mathbf{f}_{l,i}^2$ are extracted. A linear classifier is then trained on top of features extracted from a specific layer l. Performance of each layer is manually compared, and the layer with the highest performance is selected for the change detection task.

Phase 3: Change Detection. The selected layer is used to extract features from the change detection image pairs. We discriminate between unchanged

(ω_{nc}) and changed (ω_c) pixels, based on the assumption that the unchanged pixels result in similar features and the changed pixels yield dissimilar features. Two classifiers are compared for this task: (1) a linear classifier and (2) Change vector analysis (CVA, [8]). The linear classifier is trained in a supervised way on the complete training set L, by minimizing the weighted cross entropy loss. CVA is an unsupervised method and does not require any training. However, note that the classification with CVA is not fully unsupervised as at this stage ground reference maps were used to select the optimal feature layer. However, solutions can be designed to make the selection procedure unsupervised.

2.2 Pretext Tasks for Self-supervision

In self-supervised learning, a pretext task is an auxiliary learning objective on which the model is pre-trained. Although not identical to the final task (self-supervised learning is there to pre-train models when there are not enough labels for the final task), this auxiliary objective is designed such that it helps the model learn features that are expected to be useful on the final task.

Several pretext tasks have been proposed in self-supervised learning literature: for example, [19] predicts relative positions of nearby patches, while [22] rotates patches and predicts such rotation for enforcing invariances. Regardless of the specific implementations, the common denominators are that (1) the pretext labels must be extracted from the images themselves without external supervision and (2) the pretext task must help learn features that are relevant for the real downstream task (in our case detecting changes). In the previous section we discussed the need of the change detection network to learn features that project unchanged pixels pairs in the same part of the feature space (*i.e.* unchanged areas become more similar [10]). To learn features in this direction, we propose two pretext tasks:

1. The first pretext task is defined by a binary classification that requires the network to predict whether or not a patch pair is overlapping. Each training example P_j contains a patch pair $\{(p^1, p^2)_j, y_j\}$. The associated pseudo label equals $y_j = 0$ for spatially overlapping pairs and $y_j = 1$ for spatially non-overlapping ones. The patch pairs are spatially and temporally randomly sampled from the unlabelled image pairs, and equally divided over the two classes. The task is illustrated in Fig. 2a-2c.

   The underlying hypothesis is that sampling p^1 and p^2 randomly from either I_u^1 or I_u^2 learns the model to ignore irrelevant radiometric variations due to acquisition conditions and to focus on relevant spatial similarity/dissimilarity between patches.

   The parameters of the network are optimized by minimizing binary cross-entropy loss, given by

$$L = -(y_j \cdot log(P(y_j)) + (1 - y_j) \cdot log(1 - P(y_j))) \tag{1}$$

   where $P(y_j)$ is the probability of pseudo label y_j given input P_j as calculated by the logistic sigmoid function in the output layer of the network.

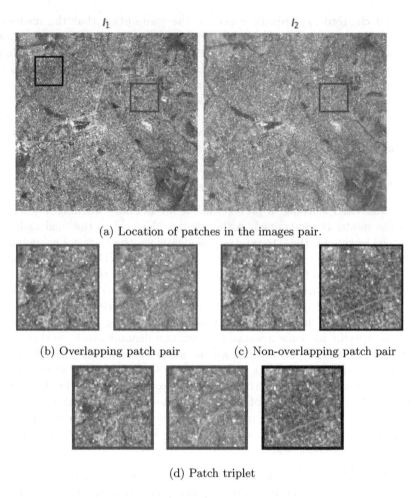

(a) Location of patches in the images pair.

(b) Overlapping patch pair   (c) Non-overlapping patch pair

(d) Patch triplet

Fig. 2. Illustration of the patch sampling strategy for the self-supervised learning tasks. (a) Patches are spatially and temporally randomly sampled in the unlabelled image pair (I_u^1, I_u^2). The colored squares represent the patches locations. (b) Overlapping patch pair (red and green) for pretext Task 1. The associated pseudo label $y_j = 0$. (c) Non-overlapping patch pair (red and blue) for pretext Task 1. The associated pseudo label $y_j = 1$. (d) Patch triplet for pretext Task 2. (Color figure online)

2. The second pretext task aims to learn image representations that project overlapping patches close to each other in the high dimensional feature space and non-overlapping patches far away. The patch sampling strategy is similar to the one of the first pretext task, with patches spatially and temporally randomly sampled in unlabelled image pairs. However, each training example P_j contains one extra patch to form patch triplets $(p^1, p^2, p^3)_j$. Patches p^1 and p^2 are spatially overlapping, while p^3 is not (Fig. 2a and 2d.).

The distance between features extracted from overlapping patches p^1 and p^2 should be close to zero, while the distance between feature extracted from disjoint patches p^1 and p^3 should be larger by a margin m. This can be accomplished by minimizing the triplet margin loss with an additional ℓ_1 loss. The complete loss function is given by

$$L = max(||\mathbf{f}^1 - \mathbf{f}^2||_2 - ||\mathbf{f}^1 - \mathbf{f}^3||_2 + m, 0) + \gamma \cdot |\mathbf{f}^1 - \mathbf{f}^2| \qquad (2)$$

where $\mathbf{f^i}$ is the feature vector for patch p^i and γ is a hyperparameter to balance the triplet loss and the ℓ_1 loss functions.

The network for the first pretext tasks is implemented as a Siamese architecture with three convolutional layers per branch and a fusion layer, as shown in Fig. 3a, while the second one does not require the fusion layer, Fig. 3b.

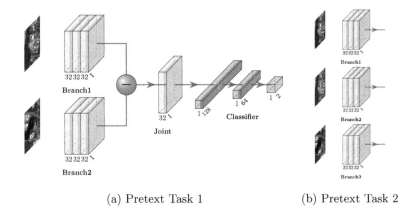

(a) Pretext Task 1   (b) Pretext Task 2

Fig. 3. Schematics of the architecture of the self-supervised CNNs.

3   Data and Setup

3.1   Datasets

Change Detection. For the change detection task, we use the OSCD benchmark dataset [21] with annotated urban changes. It contains 24 S2 image pairs with dense reference labels $\{(I_c^1, I_c^2)_i, \Omega_i\}_{i=1}^{24}$ where $\Omega \in \{\omega_{nc}, \omega_c\}$. Images are approximately 600×600 pixels and contain scenes with different levels of urbanisation. The dataset is originally divided into 14 labeled pairs with freely available ground reference maps. The labels of the remaining 10 test pairs are only available through the DASE data portal (http://dase.grss-ieee.org/) for independent validation. In this work, 12 images are used as training set; we used the two remaining images to evaluate the change maps qualitatively. Quantitative results in the discussion section are computed on the 10 undisclosed images, after upload of the obtained maps to the DASE data portal.

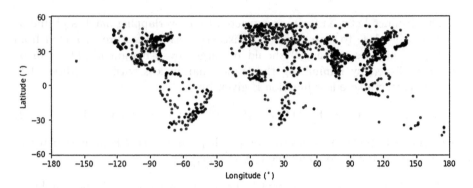

Fig. 4. Location of the cities sampled in the generated S2MTCP dataset.

Sentinel-2 Multitemporal Cities Pairs (S2MTCP) Dataset. A dataset of S2 level 1C image pairs $U = \{(I_u^1, I_u^2)_i\}_{i=1}^N$, was created for self-supervised training. As the scope of this research is limited to urban change detection, the image pairs were focused on urban areas. Locations are selected based on two databases containing central coordinates of major cities in the world [23,24] with more than 200.000 inhabitants.

Image pairs $(I_u^1, I_u^2)_i$ are selected randomly from available S2 images of each location with less than one percent cloud cover. Bands with a spatial resolution smaller than 10 m are resampled to 10 m and images are cropped to approximately 600×600 pixels centered on the selected coordinates. Hence, every image covers approximately $3.6 \, km^2$. According to the Sentinel User Guide [25], level 1C processing includes spatial registration with sub-pixel accuracy. Therefore no image registration is performed.

The S2MTCP dataset contains $N = 1520$ image pairs, spread over all inhabited continents, with the highest concentration of image pairs in North-America, Europe and Asia (Fig. 4). The size of some images is smaller than 600×600 pixels. This is a result of the fact that some coordinates were located close to the edge of a Sentinel tile, the images were then cropped to the tile border. It is available at the URL https://zenodo.org/record/4280482.

3.2 Setup

Self-supervised Pretraining Setup. We use 85% of the S2MTCP dataset U to train the model, and use 10% to validate it. We keep the remaining 5% as a blind test set for numerical evaluation.

The parameters are optimized using the Adam optimization algorithm [26] with the suggested defaults for the hyperparameters ($\beta1 = 0.9$, $\beta2 = 0.999$). The training is stopped when the validation loss does not decrease by 1% in between epochs. We use a fixed learning rate of 0.001 and weight decay (0.0001). The

γ parameter in Eq. (2) is set to 1 experimentally. At each iteration, we sample 5 patch pairs (or triplets for pretext Task 2) from each image to generate 6350 patch pairs per epoch. Data augmentation ($90°$ rotation and horizontal/vertical flips) are applied.

To assess the performance on the pretext tasks, we use the blind test set extracted from U. For pretext Task 1, we assess the success rate in the task itself in percentage, while for Task 2, we consider the value of the loss. We also run the pretext tasks on the 12 images composing OSCD test set to assess domain shifts. Note that no OSCD labels are used at this stage.

Feature Layer Selection Setup. The performance of features $\mathbf{f}_l$ on the change detection task is compared using 3-fold cross validation on the OSCD labeled set. As discussed in Sect. 3.1, the OSCD labeled set contains 12 image pairs $((I_c^1, I_c^2), \Omega)$, hence, we use 4 pairs per fold. We consider features (*i.e.* activation maps) at different levels of the self-supervised model as candidates for the selection. In other words, we retain features $\mathbf{f}_l^{\{1,2\}}$, with $l = [1, ..., 3]$, where l is the depth of the CNN considered (see schematics of Fig. 3) for images I_c^1 and I_c^2, respectively. We use the differences of the corresponding features as inputs for the change detection classifier. For pretext Task 1, we also consider $l = 4$, *i.e.* the substraction layer where $\mathbf{f}_3^1$ and $\mathbf{f}_3^2$ are fused.

The linear classifiers are trained for a maximum of 250 epochs and stopped if the validation loss does not improve for 50 epochs. The same optimizer and augmentation used in the previous step are used. We sample 100 patches pairs per image of the OCSD dataset. To make sure that the results for each experiment (varying layer and pretext task) are comparable, the patches are passed to the classifiers in the same order. Performance is evaluated based on F1-score, sensitivity, specificity and precision.

Change Detection Setup. Two classifiers are compared for the change detection task:

- *Supervised linear classifier*, trained in a supervised way on the OSCD training dataset. This model consists of a single linear layer followed by a softmax activation function returning the probability scores $\{\omega_c, \omega_{nc}\}$. The threshold to obtain the change binary map was set based on the F1-score on the training set.
- *CVA* [27], with detection threshold optimised using either Otsu's method or the triangle method [28].

The CV folds and extracted patches are the same as in the feature layer selection step. Same goes for optimization and augmentation strategies. The learning rate was decreased to 10^{-5}.

4   Results and Discussion

Pretext Tasks Performance. The validation and test results for pretext Task 1 (*i.e.* predicting whether two patches are spatially overlapping) are reported in Table 1. The test accuracy was consistently high in both datasets: in all cases the model was able to correctly predict whether the patches were overlapping in over 97% of the patch pairs. The low number of epochs required to reach this high accuracy indicates the pretext task was easy to solve. Regarding Task 2, the lowest validation loss was reached after 17 epochs and training stopped. The loss on the OSCD dataset was slightly higher than on the S2MTCP dataset (result not shown), as a result of a larger contribution of the triplet loss. We argue that this does not indicate overfitting, but rather a domain gap between the two datasets, since the difference between the validation and test loss on the S2MTCP dataset remains small.

Table 1. Performance on pretext Task 1, expressed in Average Accuracy (%).

Dataset	Data split	Loss	Accuracy
S2MTCP	Validation	0.043	98.93
S2MTCP	Test	0.052	98.28
OSCD	–	0.083	97.67

Selection of Optimal Feature Layer for Change Detection. Table 2 presents the average accuracy over the three folds for change detection performed with features $\mathbf{f}_l$ for layers $l \in [1, 4]$. The features of the second convolutional layer ($l = 2$) perform best in both cases, although the differences are overall small. The performance of the deeper layers in the network trained on pretext task 1 decreases faster than the performance of the ones trained on pretext task 2. It is not surprising that features from deeper layers perform worse on the change detection task, Yosinski et al. [29] have shown that deeper layers of a CNN are specific to the task and dataset used for training, while the first layers are general-purpose. This effect has also been observed when transferring features from a pretext task to the target task in self-supervised learning [30].

Based on these results, the second convolutional layer is selected for the change detection task.

Numerical Results on the OCSD Test Set. As a final step, we compare the results of our self-supervised model with those obtained by fully supervised models on the undisclosed test set on the DASE algorithm testbed data portal (see Sect. 3.1 for details).

The best performance among the self-supervised approaches, top half of Table 3, was achieved by the model pretrained on pretext Task 2 combined with the CVA classifier using the triangle method. This leads to the highest F1-score.

Table 2. Evaluation of features per layer as measured by Average Accuracy (%) on the change detection task by cross validation. $l = [1, 3]$ represents which convolutional layers of the self-supervised model is used. For each pretext task the best performance is highlighted in bold text.

Pretext task	$l = 1$	$l = 2$	$l = 3$	$l = 4$
Pretext task 1	76.06	**77.82**	75.92	74.26
Pretext task 2	78.03	**79.11**	78.19	

Table 3. Comparison between supervised State of Art (S-o-A) and Self supervised models on the undisclosed test set of OCSD. All metrics are expressed in percentage. The best performance as measured by each metric are highlighted in bold text. 'Linear' corresponds to a learned linear classifier for change detection.

	Method		Sensitivity	Specificity	Precision	F1
Self-supervised	Task 1	CVA+Otsu	65.78	86.18	20.60	31.37
	Task 1	CVA+Triangle	41.14	96.11	36.55	38.71
	Task 1	Linear	50.00	96.66	37.98	43.17
	Task 2	CVA+Otsu	**83.85**	81.99	20.24	32.61
	Task 2	CVA+Triangle	52.80	95.76	40.42	**45.79**
	Task 2	Linear	35.37	**97.76**	**46.30**	43.17
S-o-A	Siamese	[21]	**85.63**	85.35	24.16	37.69
	Early fusion	[21]	84.69	88.33	28.34	42.47
	FC-EF	[31]	50.97	**98.51**	**64.42**	56.91
	FC-Siam-Conv	[31]	65.15	95.23	42.39	51.36
	FC-Siam-Diff	[31]	57.99	97.73	57.81	**57.91**

The CVA with the Otsu method has the highest sensitivity (recall, meaning that the most changes are detected), but at the price of a very low precision due to the very high number of false positives; see also the maps in Fig. 5. This is most probably due to the setting of the Otsu threshold, which needs to be very high to favor sensitivity. The learned classifiers ('linear') in Table 3 provide the best results for pretext Task 1 and also the best results in both tasks in terms of specificity, but also show lower sensitivity scores. This results in a slightly lower F1-score for pretext Task 2. Compared with current state of art in the OSCD dataset, the self supervised models perform remarkably well, given its shallow architecture and the fact that they are pre-trained in an unsupervised way.

Finally, Fig. 5 illustrates some change maps for the Beirut image of the OCSD dataset. Looking at the maps, we observe that the CVA detection is accurate on the top right corner, but also that it tends to generate more false positives (in magenta), and, when using the Otsu method, most of the image is predicted as changed. We therefore conclude that Otsu's method is inferior to the other two, which can be both considered usable. Remarkably, the learned classifier reduces

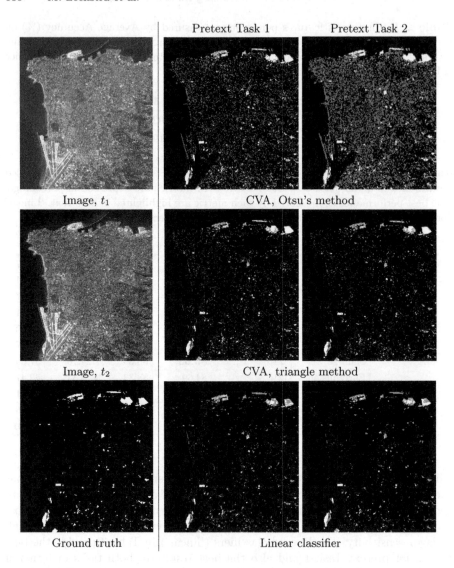

Fig. 5. Example of change detection for the proposed method. True positives are depicted in white, missed changes in green and false positives in magenta. (Color figure online)

the false positive and shows the most visually pleasant results, but at the price of less precise delineation of the change than CVA with the triangle method.

5 Conclusions

In this paper, we explored the possibility of pre-training a convolutional neural network for change detection without labels. We perform such training by forging a pretext task inherent in the data, which aims at learning a feature space where unchanged pixels are close and far from abnormal situations. We use two self-supervised learning approaches and then fine tune the network trained this way to detect changes. Experiments in the benchmark Sentinel-2 OCSD dataset shows that training a model this way can lead to results close to state of the art deep learning change detection. It is available at the URL https://zenodo.org/record/4280482.

References

1. Liu, S., Marinelli, D., Bruzzone, L., Bovolo, F.: A review of change detection in multitemporal hyperspectral images: current techniques, applications, and challenges. IEEE Geosci. Remote Sens. Mag. **7**(2), 140–158 (2019)
2. Verbesselt, J., Hyndman, R., Newnham, G., Culvenor, D.: Detecting trend and seasonal changes in satellite image time series. Remote Sens. Environ. **114**(1), 106–115 (2010)
3. Hamunyela, E., Verbesselt, J., Herold, M.: Using spatial context to improve early detection of deforestation from Landsat time series. Remote Sens. Environ. **172**, 126–138 (2016)
4. Deng, J.S., Wang, K., Hong, Y., Qi, J.G.: Spatio-temporal dynamics and evolution of land use change and landscape pattern in response to rapid urbanization. Landscape Urban Plan. **92**(3–4), 187–198 (2009)
5. Huang, X., Wen, D., Li, J., Qin, R.: Multi-level monitoring of subtle urban changes for the megacities of China using high-resolution multi-view satellite imagery. Remote Sens. Environ. **196**, 56–75 (2017)
6. Brunner, D., Lemoine, G., Bruzzone, L.: Earthquake damage assessment of buildings using VHR optical and SAR imagery. IEEE Trans. Geosci. Remote Sens. **48**(5), 2403–2420 (2010)
7. Longbotham, N., et al.: Multi-modal change detection, application to the detection of flooded areas: outcome of the 2009–2010 data fusion contest. IEEE J. Sel. Top. Appl. Earth Obs. Remote Sens. **5**(1), 331–342 (2012)
8. Bovolo, F., Bruzzone, L.: The time variable in data fusion: a change detection perspective. IEEE Geosci. Remote Sens. Mag. **3**(3), 8–26 (2015)
9. Volpi, M., Tuia, D., Bovolo, F., Kanevski, M., Bruzzone, L.: Supervised change detection in VHR images using contextual information and support vector machines. Int. J. Appl. Earth Obs. Geoinf. **20**, 77–85 (2013)
10. Volpi, M., Camps-Valls, G., Tuia, D.: Spectral alignment of cross-sensor images with automated kernel canonical correlation analysis. ISPRS J. Int. Soc. Photo. Remote Sens. **107**, 50–63 (2015)
11. Lin, Y., Li, S., Fang, L., Ghamisi, P.: Multispectral change detection with bilinear convolutional neural networks. IEEE Geosci. Remote Sens. Lett. (2019)
12. Zhan, Y., Fu, K., Yan, M., Sun, X., Wang, H., Qiu, X.: Change detection based on deep Siamese convolutional network for optical aerial images. IEEE Geosci. Remote Sens. Lett. **14**(10), 1845–1849 (2017)
13. Peng, D., Zhang, Y., Guan, H.: End-to-end change detection for high resolution satellite images using improved UNet++. Remote Sens. **11**(11), 1382 (2019)
14. Mou, L., Bruzzone, L., Zhu, X.X.: Learning spectral-spatialoral features via a recurrent convolutional neural network for change detection in multispectral imagery. IEEE Trans. Geosci. Remote Sens. **57**(2), 924–935 (2019)

15. Saha, S., Bovolo, F., Bruzzone, L.: Unsupervised deep change vector analysis for multiple-change detection in VHR images. IEEE Trans. Geosci. Remote Sens. **57**(6), 3677–3693 (2019)
16. Zhu, X.X., et al.: Deep learning in remote sensing: a comprehensive review and list of resources. IEEE Geosci. Remote Sens. Mag. **5**(4), 8–36 (2017)
17. Kellenberger, B., Marcos, D., Tuia, D.: When a few clicks make all the difference: improving weakly-supervised wildlife detection in UAV images. In: IEEE/CVF Conference on Computer Vision and Pattern Recognition Workshops (CVPRW), Long Beach, CA (2019)
18. Caye Daudt, R., Le Saux, B., Boulch, A., Gousseau, Y.: Guided anisotropic diffusion and iterative learning for weakly supervised change detection. In: Computer Vision and Pattern Recognition Workshops, June 2019
19. Doersch, C., Gupta, A., Efros, A.A.: Unsupervised visual representation learning by context prediction. In: IEEE International Conference on Computer Vision (ICCV), pp. 1422–1430 (2015)
20. Caron, M., Bojanowski, P., Joulin, A., Douze, M.: Deep clustering for unsupervised learning of visual features. In: Ferrari, V., Hebert, M., Sminchisescu, C., Weiss, Y. (eds.) Computer Vision – ECCV 2018. LNCS, vol. 11218, pp. 139–156. Springer, Cham (2018). https://doi.org/10.1007/978-3-030-01264-9_9
21. Daudt, R.C., Le Saux, B., Boulch, A., Gousseau, Y.: Urban change detection for multispectral earth observation using convolutional neural networks. In: IEEE International Geoscience and Remote Sensing Symposium (IGARSS), pp. 2115–2118 (2018)
22. Gidaris, S., Singh, P., Komodakis, N.: Unsupervised representation learning by predicting image rotations. In: International Conference on Learning Representations (ICLR) (2018)
23. Simplemaps: World Cities Database (2019)
24. Geonames: Major cities of the world (2019)
25. Suhet: Sentinel-2 user handbook (2015)
26. Kingma, D.P., Ba, J.: Adam: a method for stochastic optimization. In: International Conference on Learning Representations (ICLR) (2015)
27. Bruzzone, L., Bovolo, F.: A novel framework for the design of change-detection systems for very-high-resolution remote sensing images. Proc. IEEE **101**(3), 609–630 (2013)
28. Rosin, P.L.: Unimodal thresholding. Pattern Recogn. **34**(11), 2083–2096 (2001)
29. Yosinski, J., Clune, J., Bengio, Y., Lipson, H.: How transferable are features in deep neural networks? In: Advances in Neural Information Processing Systems (NIPS), pp. 3320–3328 (2014)
30. Kolesnikov, A., Zhai, X., Beyer, L.: Revisiting self-supervised visual representation learning. In: IEEE Conference on Computer Vision and Pattern Recognition (CVPR) (2019)
31. Daudt, R.C., Le Saux, B., Boulch, A.: Fully convolutional Siamese networks for change detection. In: IEEE International Conference on Image Processing (ICIP), pp. 4063–4067 (2018)

Early and Late Fusion of Multiple Modalities in Sentinel Imagery and Social Media Retrieval

Wei Yao[1], Anastasia Moumtzidou[2], Corneliu Octavian Dumitru[1],
Stelios Andreadis[2(✉)], Ilias Gialampoukidis[2], Stefanos Vrochidis[2],
Mihai Datcu[1], and Ioannis Kompatsiaris[2]

[1] Remote Sensing Technology Institute, German Aerospace Center (DLR),
Cologne, Germany
{Wei.Yao,Corneliu.Dumitru,Mihai.Datcu}@dlr.de
[2] Information Technologies Institute, Centre for Research and Technology Hellas
(CERTH), Thessaloniki, Greece
{moumtzid,andreadisst,heliasgj,stefanos,ikom}@iti.gr

Abstract. Discovering potential concepts and events by analyzing
Earth Observation (EO) data may be supported by fusing other distributed data sources such as non-EO data, for instance, in-situ citizen observations from social media. The retrieval of relevant information
based on a target query or event is critical for operational purposes, for
example, to monitor flood events in urban areas, and crop monitoring for
food security scenarios. To that end, we propose an early-fusion (low-level
features) and late-fusion (high-level concepts) mechanism that combines
the results of two EU-funded projects for information retrieval in Sentinel imagery and social media data sources. In the early fusion part,
the model is based on active learning that effectively merges Sentinel-
1 and Sentinel-2 bands, and assists users to extract patterns. On the
other hand, the late fusion mechanism exploits the context of other geo-
referenced data such as social media retrieval, to further enrich the list
of retrieved Sentinel image patches. Quantitative and qualitative results
show the effectiveness of our proposed approach.

Keywords: Multimodal data fusion · Sentinel imagery retrieval ·
Social media retrieval · Earth Observation · Big data

1 Introduction

The number of Earth Observation (EO) data is increasing rapidly due to the
large number of space missions that were launched during the past years. Moreover, the fact that there are EO data that are freely available to the scientific
community (e.g., data from the Copernicus missions), opens up the horizons
for using them in several applications. Furthermore, the advancements in the
domain of satellite remote sensing helped in producing quick and precise land

© Springer Nature Switzerland AG 2021
A. Del Bimbo et al. (Eds.): ICPR 2020 Workshops, LNCS 12667, pp. 591–606, 2021.
https://doi.org/10.1007/978-3-030-68787-8_43

cover maps that allowed us to identify target categories such as snow, rocks, urban areas, forests, and lakes. We use that to capture the characteristics of the underlying areas, and eventually exploit this information to assist in global monitoring and future planning. One major challenge is the lack of training datasets for building well-performing models using shallow and deep learning models. To that end, an active learning method is proposed. Active learning is a form of supervised machine learning. The learning algorithm is able to interactively interrogate a user (as an information and background knowledge source) to label image patches with the desired outputs. The key idea behind active learning is that a machine learning algorithm can achieve greater accuracy with fewer training labels, if it is allowed to choose the data from which it learns. This operation with the active learning procedure is presented in Fig. 1.

Fig. 1. The active learning concept.

The inclusion of crowdsourced geo-referenced data sources, through the retrieval of social media data, semantically enriches the retrieved results from satellite image content. Twitter is a popular platform, where a set of keywords, locations, and user accounts can be defined to formulate a query in order to obtain relevant information to a concept or event. Such information is integrated with the retrieval of satellite image patches, combining the results from remotely-sensed images with images and text descriptions from citizen observations and user-generated online content.

Our contribution can be summarized as follows:

– Retrieve satellite images using an active learning technique
– Extend satellite image retrieval with social media posts

The paper is organised as follows. Section 2 presents relevant works in multi-modal fusion for the two main fusion strategies. Section 3 presents our proposed methodologies, one based on early fusion of data and the other on late fusion. In Sect. 4, we describe the datasets that we have used, the settings, and also the quantitative and qualitative results. Finally, Sect. 5 concludes our work.

2   Related Work

Over the years, two main strategies for fusing multimodal information have been identified [2]. The first strategy is known as early fusion; it is realized at feature level, where features from multiple modalities are combined into a common feature vector, while the second strategy, known as late fusion, fuses information at the decision level.

In our previous investigation in data fusion [15], the data representation as Bag-of-Words has been discussed, using a clustering of various modalities and an application of Bayesian inference for fusing clusters into image classes. In addition, the work in [4] presents the extraction of different information modalities from the same observation and fusion for enhanced classification. Recently, within the framework of the CANDELA project[1], we implemented the merging of different Sentinel-1 and Sentinel-2 bands [18]. Furthermore, during the Living Planet 2019 Conference[2], a semantic level fusion for Synthetic Aperture Radar (SAR) images has been discussed. By exploiting the specific imaging details and the retrievable semantic categories of TerraSAR-X and Sentinel-1 images, we obtained semantically-fused image classification maps that allow us to differentiate several coastal surface categories [7].

Active learning has important advantages when compared with Shallow Machine Learning or Deep Learning methods, as presented in Table 1.

Table 1. Comparison of different learning schemes

Key performance indicator	Shallow ML	Deep learning	Active learning
Training data volume	Medium (GB)	Very high (PB)	Very small (0.1 KB)
Trained data volume	Large (GB-TB)	Very high (PB)	Large (GB-TB)
No. of classes	Up to 100	Up to 100	Any, user-defined
Classification accuracy	Avg. 85%	Avg. 90%	Avg. 85%
Training speed	Medium (hour)	Slow (days)	Fast (minutes)

Active learning methods include Relevance Feedback and Cascaded Learning, see Algorithm 1. It supports users to search for images of interest in a large repository. A Graphical User Interface (GUI) allows the automatic ranking of the suggested images, which are expected to be grouped in a class of relevance. Visually supported ranking allows enhancing the quality of search results after giving positive and negative examples. During the active learning process, two goals are achieved: 1) learning the targeted image category as accurately and as exhaustively as possible, and 2) minimising the number of iterations in the relevance feedback loop.

---

[1] https://www.candela-h2020.eu/.
[2] https://lps19.esa.int/.

Algorithm 1: Active Learning Algorithm

Data: Sentinel-1, Sentinel-2 image pair with fused feature vectors
Result: semantic annotation stored in DMDB
initialization;
while *user is not satisfied with the annotated results* **do**
 user selects new positive and negative images;
 calculate and show classification result;
 get **relevance feedback** (display ranked boundary images);
 start **cascaded learning** process as follows;
 if *user is satisfied and there is a finer image grid* **then**
  go to the next image grid;
  set constraint on available image patches (only patches within
  previous annotated grid will be taken into account);
  current section becomes this one;
 else
  go back to the beginning of current section;

However, the involvement of social media queries requires multimodal fusion mechanisms that are able to combine textual, visual, and spatiotemporal information. As it is already mentioned, our late-fusion techniques involve fusing information at decision level. This means that initially, each modality is learned separately and then the individual results are combined in order to reach a final common decision. Most of the late-fusion methods for retrieval are, in general, unsupervised techniques that use the document rank and score to calculate the decision. For example, in [19], the authors propose a multimodal knowledge-based technique in order to retrieve videos of a particular event in a large-scale dataset. The authors consider several modalities including speech recognition transcripts, acoustic concept indexing, and visual semantic indexing, which are fused using an event-specific fusion scheme. In [11], the authors describe a system for retrieving medical images. The system considers textual and visual content, separately as well as combined, using advanced encoding and quantisation by combining the results of the modalities in a sequential order. Specifically, the textual modality returns a list of results that is re-ranked based on the visual modality. The work of [9] retrieves text-image pairs, where queries of the same multimodal character are evaluated. Moreover, in [13], the authors combine data from Twitter along with Sentinel-1 images in order to increase the accuracy of the state-of-the-art remote sensing methods related to snow depth estimation. In [1] the authors present a method using social media content to address the problem of flood severity by checking both the text and the image in order to classify articles as flood event-related. Also, the visual features extracted from the images were used to identify people were standing in flooded area. Recently, the EOPEN project[3] has demonstrated the fusion of multiple modalities in the context of EO and non-EO data [8]. Contrary to these approaches, we use a tensor-based late fusion mechanism that aims to complement satellite image search with social media data for related concepts, such as food, flood, city, etc.

3 Methodology

3.1 Early Fusion in Satellite Image Retrieval

Our Early Data Fusion aims at a better understanding of a scene from observations with multiple different sensors. In the particular case of the data fusion in CANDELA, the objective is to obtain a better classification of the Earth's surface structures or objects using Sentinel-1 (S-1) and Sentinel-2 (S-2) observations. The design of the data fusion methods shall exploit the characteristics of the different sensing modalities. Table 2 is summarizing the main aspects of the complementarity of Sentinel-1 and Sentinel-2 observations.

Table 2. The complementarity between Sentinel-1 and Sentinel-2 images.

Criteria	Sentinel-1 (SAR)	Sentinel-2 (multispectral)
Sensor type	Active	Passive
EM spectrum	C-band	Blue to IR (13 bands)
Operation	Day/Night	Day
Dependence on cloud cover	No	Yes
Vegetation signatures	Low sensitivity	Good diversity of classes
Ocean/sea	Waves and currents	Water colour
In-land waters	Low backscatter	Diversity of spectral signatures, water colour
Urban constructions	Strong signatures	Variable depending on may parameters
Soil	Moisture and roughness	Spectral signatures (colour)
Relief	Strong dependence	Moderate dependence
Snow/ice	Classification based on EM properties	Reduced separability, confusion with clouds

Based on these assets, the data fusion was designed using three important paradigms. Firstly, the fusion is performed at the level of image patch features; secondly, the classification is performed by an active machine learning paradigm, and finally, the classifier results are semantic annotations stored in a database.

---

[3] https://eopen-project.eu/.

The early fusion is performed at image feature level, so as to combine the very particular signatures of the scene for the two observation modalities, namely multispectral and SAR imaging. Our feature extractor for Sentinel-1 data is the Adapted Weber Descriptor [5]. Comparing to the original WLD feature, the adapted WLD includes not only local statistics but also local structure information, resulting in an improved performance to characterize SAR signatures by minimizing the noise effect of speckle. The feature extracted from Sentinel-2 is the multi-spectral histogram, since it contains the statistical physical information of the Sentinel-2 multispectral signatures. The two features are concatenated and become a fused descriptor of the Earth's land observed by the two sensors. The classifier is chosen to be an Active Machine Learning tool [3] based on a Support Vector Machine (SVM), allowing the user to select the training samples in an appropriate manner to avoid any contradiction which may occur from the different sensor signatures. The result of the classification is stored into a database as semantic annotation, thus enabling further analyses and the export of the information for integration or a next level of fusion with non-EO data. Figure 2 depicts the software architecture of the Data Fusion module in the back end and in the front end. There are three layers which define a complete process: the platform layer as back-end, the user machine layer as front-end, and the transfer layer via an Internet connection.

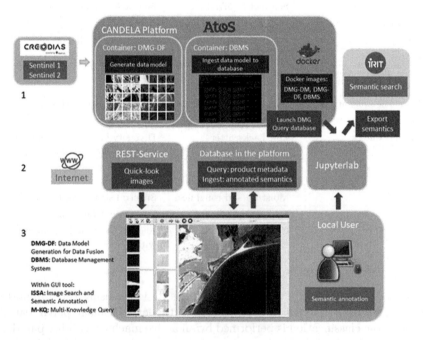

Fig. 2. Architecture of the data fusion module on the platform and front-end.

In the platform layer, Sentinel-1 and Sentinel-2 products are accessed by using the symbolic CreoDIAS[4] links which are provided for the platform. Users start the Data Model Generation for the Data Fusion Docker container and it runs for one Sentinel-1 product and one Sentinel-2 product simultaneously. As a pre-processing step, the two products should be geometrically co-registered. The results (extracted metadata, cropped image patches, and extracted features for the patches) are ingested into the MonetDB[5] database "candela" on the platform. The generated quick-look images are published on the platform to be downloaded by local users via a Representational state transfer (RESTful) service. The Database Management System (DBMS) provides high-speed storage for real-time interactive operation during active learning and data fusion. This is the actionable information of the Data Fusion component. The framework (Fig. 2) provides the following front-end functionalities to the user: **Image Search and Semantic Annotation** (ISSA): image mining, query-by-example, retrieval and adding of semantic annotation to EO image products; **Multi-Knowledge and Query** (M-KQ): multimodal queries based on selected product metadata, image features, and semantic labels; and **System Validation**: supports the evaluation of the retrieval and classification performance. The Data Fusion module evolves from EOLib[6].

In support of the semantic annotations, a hierarchical two-level semantic catalogue has been ingested into the "candela" database, which allows users to select the appropriate label during semantic annotation by using the active learning tool. In the case of Copernicus (e.g., S-1 and S-2), level-1 labels are the most general categories: *Agriculture, Bare Ground, Forest, Transportation, Urban Area*, and *Water Bodies*; while level 2 consists of more detailed labels, concerning each general level, respectively. In addition, because of the diversity of structures in an image, after choosing a specific general-level label, an extra user-defined label annotation function is allowed, so that new land cover or land use cases can be described according to the user's own definition. This is different from a fixed classification system, and particularly useful in the case of evolving land cover patterns, e.g., floods.

3.2 Late-Fusion Approach to Retrieve Relevant Social Media Content

The late-fusion approach retrieves social media posts that are similar to a given tweet by considering its different modalities, i.e., textual information, visual features and concepts, and spatiotemporal information. The late-fusion mechanism consists of the following phases: 1) description of the multimodal query q using a set of modalities; 2) querying the indexing schemes that are used to allow a fast and efficient retrieval for each modality in order to get ranked lists of retrieved items along with the similarity scores of the query tweet q to the available pool

---

[4] https://creodias.eu/.

[5] https://www.monetdb.org/.

[6] http://wiki.services.eoportal.org/tiki-index.php?page=EOLib.

of tweets—these lists are used for creating a 4D tensor; and 3) two-step fusion procedure that initially involves a bi-modal fusion of the retrieved results for each 2D surface of the created tensor, followed by a merging of the produced rankings to get the final list of retrieved tweets (Fig. 3).

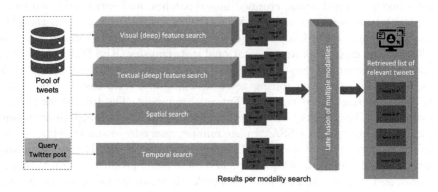

Fig. 3. Late-fusion framework for multimodal retrieval of geo-referenced tweets.

The proposed late-fusion approach fuses the output of four modalities. The algorithm comprises the following steps:

1. Retrieval of N results per modality, which eventually leads to four such lists from unimodal searches.
2. Creation of a fourth-order $\mathbf{L}$ tensor by considering the aforementioned lists. The dimension of the binary tensor $\mathbf{L}$ is (l_1, l_2, l_3, l_4). The value of the single elements results from the following rule:

$$\mathbf{L}_{(\ldots, r_i, \ldots, r_k, \ldots)} = \begin{cases} 1, & \text{if the same element is ordered as } r_i \text{ in list } l_i, \\ & \text{and ordered as } r_k \text{ in list } l_k \\ 0, & \text{otherwise} \end{cases} \tag{1}$$

3. Creation of one 2D tensor surface for each pair of modalities $(i, k), i \leq k$.
4. For each 2D tensor surface, get the list of tweets that are jointly ranked higher by minimising the position in which $\mathbf{L}(i, k) = 1$ (details in [8]).
5. Merging of the rankings to obtain the final list of tweet IDs.

Text similarity between two or more texts is the procedure of computing the similarity in meanings between them. Although there are several approaches that can be used for text similarity that involve text representation as a first step, the one considered in this work is an off-the-shelf text search engine, i.e., the Apache Lucene[7]. Apache Lucene is a full-text search engine that can be used for any application that requires full-text indexing, and searching capability. It is able

---

[7] https://lucerne.apache.org/.

to achieve fast search responses, as it uses a technique known as inverted index and avoids searching the text directly. The representation of the text modality also considers the state-of-art Bidirectional Encoder Representation from Transformers (BERT) algorithm [6], which includes an attention mechanism to learn contextual relations between words in a text. BERT is used to represent each tweet text into a deep representation that allows similarity search.

As far as visual information is concerned, both visual features and visual concepts are taken into consideration. The framework used in both cases, i.e., a deep convolutional neural network (DCNN), is the same, but the vectors used are taken from different layers of the network. Specifically, we used the fine-tuned 22-layer GoogleNet network [16] that was trained on the 345 SIN TRECVID concepts. Regarding the visual features, they are DCNN-based descriptors and are the output of the last pooling layer of the fine-tuned GoogleNet architecture previously described. The dimension of the last pooling layer is 1024 and it is used as a global image representation. The selection of this layer was based on the results of an evaluation analyzing its runtime and quality within the VERGE system [14] that has participated in the Video Browser Showdown in 2018. The visual concept representation is a concatenated single vector with a length of 345 elements, as the output of the aforementioned GoogleNet network.

Fast retrieval of similar visual and textual content is achieved by constructing an inverted file and combining it with Asymmetric Distance Computation [10]. Then, the k-nearest neighbours between the query image and the collection are computed. Temporal metadata also accompany the query tweet q and exist as a *ISODate* datatype inside the MongoDB[8] used for storing the tweets information. The inherent MongoDB sorting functions allow the retrieval of a list of items which are temporally close to the query tweet. Regarding the locations mentioned in a tweet, we extract the corresponding named entities using the BiLSTM-CNNs-CRF [12] model. The bidirectional Long Short-Term Memory part is responsible for encoding, a DCNN for extracting character level features, and a Conditional Random Field for decoding.

4   Experiments

4.1   Datasets Description

For the demonstration and validation of the Data Fusion mechanism in satellite image search we use 33 Sentinel-1 and Sentinel-2 images. The average image size in pixels is 26,400 × 16,600 and 10,980 × 10,980 for Sentinel-1 and Sentinel-2, respectively. These satellite images cover an area of 350,000 km². One band has been considered from Sentinel-1 and four bands at 10 m resolution from Sentinel-2 images. The patch size is 120 × 120 pixels and with one image grid level. For the total number of 340,587 patches, 7,478 samples have been annotated into several semantic labels (see Fig. 6 and Table 3).

---

[8] https://www.mongodb.com/.

Twitter is a suitable social media platform for testing fusion approaches since each tweet comprises several modalities. Specifically, a tweet contains a short text with not more than 140 characters that may contain non-standard terms, sometimes an image that is semantically related to the text, the date and time the tweet was posted, and any named entities of the type "location" that can be extracted from the text. Three datasets were used that include publicly available tweets retrieved via the Twitter Streaming API[9]. The datasets were created by collecting tweets that included the words "alluvione" (i.e., flood in Italian), "food", and "lumi" (i.e., snow in Finnish). The total number of tweets selected in a period of three years for the three datasets are 1,000,383 for floods (IT), 120,666 for food (EN) and 66,175 for snow (FI), respectively. An example collected tweet, that can also be used as a query, is shown in Fig. 4.

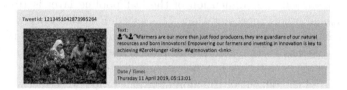

Fig. 4. Query tweet in English language that is related to "food".

4.2   Results

Our final results and examples are presented in Table 3. We observe that the overall classification accuracy is up to 90%, even for a very small training data set and a maximum of three iterations during the active learning stage. Figure 5 and 6 show a visual demonstration of the early fusion result. Five classes are discovered in the scenes of Munich: *Lakes, Mixed Forest, Mixed Urban Areas, Stubble,* and *Grassland.* The S-1 and S-2 images are the inputs for the Data Mining module to be fused, while CORINE land cover 2018 is provided as visual ground truth[10]. Focusing on the urban area, data fusion achieves better results, because the multi-spectral signal together with the radar signal, which generates strong backscattering in the man-made construction areas, helps distinguish the urban signatures.

---

[9] https://developer.twitter.com/en/docs/twitter-api.

[10] http://clc.gios.gov.pl/images/clc_ryciny/clc_classes.png.

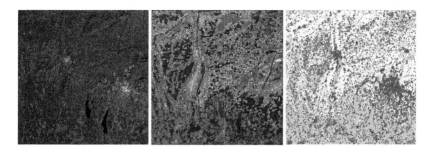

Fig. 5. Munich, Germany as a data fusion example. Left: S-1 image, Middle: S-2 image, Right: CORINE land cover 2018.

Table 3. Examples of the use of the Data Fusion component and overall performances.

Sentinel-1	Sentinel-2	Label	Accuracy
		Mixed Forest	90%
		Beach	80%
		Mixed Urban	90%
		Agriculture	70%
		Land	80%
		Hill	65%
		Low-Density Urban	80%
		Forest Spots	80%

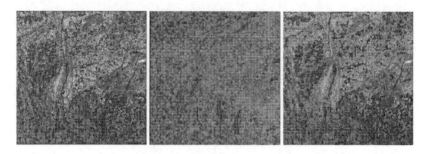

Fig. 6. Left: fusion results combining S-1 and S-2, Middle: classification results of S-1, Right: classification results of S-2.

Table 4. Average precision P@10 and mean Average Precision (mAP) of unimodal and multimodal searches.

Method	Flood, IT (P@10)	Food, EN (P@10)	Snow, FI (P@10)	mAP
Text	1.0	1.0	0.586	0.862
Spatiotemporal data	0.839	0.867	1.0	0.902
Visual features	0.878	1.0	1.0	0.959
Visual concepts	0.638	1.0	1.0	0.879
Multimodal fusion	0.906	1.0	1.0	**0.969**

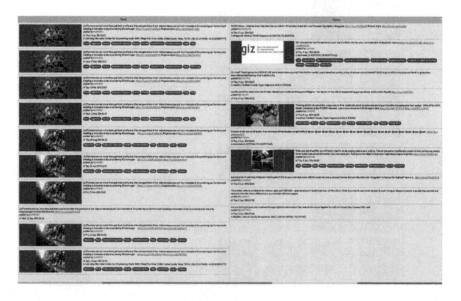

Fig. 7. *Top-10* the retrieved results with unimodal textual and temporal modalities.

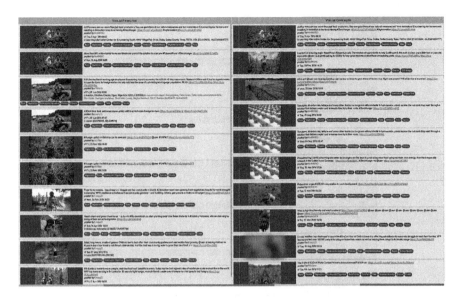

Fig. 8. *Top-10* the retrieved results with unimodal visual feature & concept search.

As far as social media retrieval is concerned, we manually annotate the top-10 retrieved results for each method, and then calculate the average precision for each query and the mean average precision (mAP) for three queries for each method. Table 4 contains the average precision scores for the different similarity methods for each query and the mAP for each method.

We conclude that text modality doesn't perform well when it isn't fused with any other modality. However, in case of tweets, only text and temporal information exist by default, so it is a very important modality to consider. Moreover, time modality has a better mAP compared with text, which can be explained easily, since we consider only the top-10 results. However, it is expected that if we retrieve the top-K results, this score (mAP) will fall for large values of K. Finally, visual features perform very well, since the modality searches for visually similar results using pre-trained models in larger image collections, but they cannot be used disregarding corresponding text. Figure 4 is the example Twitter post query, while Fig. 7 and Fig. 8 provide the top-10 retrieved list of tweets. These lists can be compared to the results of the tensor-based multimodal approach in Fig. 9.

Fig. 9. *Top-10* the retrieved results with multimodal fusion.

5   Conclusion

Active learning with a very small number of training samples allows a detailed verification of images. Thus, the results are trustable, avoiding the plague of training data based biases. Another important asset is the adaptability to user conjectures. The EO image semantics are very different from other definitions in geoscience, as for example cartography. An EO image is capturing the actual reality on ground; a user can discover and understand it immediately, and extract its best meaning, thus enriching the EO semantic catalogue. With CANDELA platform as a back-end solution to support the query and ingestion of information into the remote database "candela" the early data fusion has been verified with various image pairs. The validation results show that the fused results generate more complete classification maps and perform very well even in challenging cases, such as *Beach*. The necessity to design and develop multimodal solutions is apparent also when combining EO with non-EO data, i.e. Twitter content in our case. Our presented method is able to effectively combine textual and visual information from tweets with other associated metadata, providing a search engine that can serve as an extension to satellite image search engines. In future, we plan on running more extensive experiments which involves evaluating the proposed late-fusion algorithm on large datasets that contain a variety of modalities and also testing it on significantly more queries. Finally, further integration and orchestration of EO and non-EO technologies is expected, with additional evaluation that also involves user satisfaction in the context of large-scale exercises in EU-funded projects.

Acknowledgements. This work has been supported by the EC-funded projects CANDELA (H2020-776193) and EOPEN (H2020-776019), and partly by the ASD HGF project. The content of this paper (DLR part) is mainly based on the results presented in the CANDELA Deliverable D2.8 [17].

References

1. Andreadis, S., Bakratsas, M., Giannakeris, P., et al.: Multimedia analysis techniques for flood detection using images, articles and satellite imagery. In: Working Notes Proceedings of the MediaEval 2019 Workshop, Sophia Antipolis, France, 27–30 October 2019. CEUR Workshop Proceedings, vol. 2670. CEUR-WS.org (2019)
2. Atrey, P.K., Hossain, M.A., El Saddik, A., Kankanhalli, M.S.: Multimodal fusion for multimedia analysis: a survey. Multimed. Syst. **16**(6), 345–379 (2010)
3. Blanchart, P., Ferecatu, M., Cui, S., Datcu, M., et al.: Pattern retrieval in large image databases using multiscale coarse-to-fine cascaded active learning. IEEE J. Sel. Top. Appl. Earth Obs. Remote Sens. **7**(4), 1127–1141 (2014)
4. Chaabouni-Chouayakh, H., Datcu, M.: Backscattering and statistical information fusion for urban area mapping using TerraSAR-X data. IEEE J. Sel. Top. Appl. Earth Obs. Remote Sens. **3**(4), 718–730 (2010)
5. Cui, S., Dumitru, C.O., Datcu, M.: Ratio-detector-based feature extraction for very high resolution SAR image patch indexing. IEEE Geosci. Remote Sens. Lett. **10**(5), 1175–1179 (2013)
6. Devlin, J., Chang, M.W., Lee, K., Toutanova, K.: Bert: pre-training of deep bidirectional transformers for language understanding. arXiv:1810.04805 (2018)
7. Dumitru, C.O., Schwarz, G., Datcu, M.: Monitoring of coastal environments using data mining. In: Knowledge Extraction and Semantic Annotation (KESA 2018), pp. 34–39, April 2018
8. Gialampoukidis, I., Moumtzidou, A., Bakratsas, M., Vrochidis, S., Kompatsiaris, I.: A multimodal tensor-based late fusion approach for satellite image search in sentinel 2 images. In: Lokoč, J., et al. (eds.) MMM 2021. LNCS, vol. 12573, pp. 294–306. Springer, Cham (2021). https://doi.org/10.1007/978-3-030-67835-7_25
9. Gialampoukidis, I., Moumtzidou, A., Liparas, D., et al.: Multimedia retrieval based on non-linear graph-based fusion and partial least squares regression. Multimed. Tools Appl. **76**(21), 22383–22403 (2017)

10. Jegou, H., Douze, M., Schmid, C.: Product quantization for nearest neighbor search. IEEE Trans. Pattern Anal. Mach. Intell. **33**(1), 117–128 (2010)
11. Kitanovski, I., Strezoski, G., Dimitrovski, I., Madjarov, G., Loskovska, S.: Multimodal medical image retrieval system. Multimed. Tools Appl. **76**(2), 2955–2978 (2016). https://doi.org/10.1007/s11042-016-3261-1
12. Ma, X., Hovy, E.: End-to-end sequence labeling via bi-directional LSTM-CNNS-CRF. arXiv preprint arXiv:1603.01354 (2016)
13. Mantsis, D.F., Bakratsas, M., Andreadis, S., et al.: Multimodal fusion of sentinel 1 images and social media data for snow depth estimation. IEEE Geosci. Remote Sens. Lett. (2020)
14. Andreadis, S., et al.: VERGE in VBS 2019. In: Kompatsiaris, I., Huet, B., Mezaris, V., Gurrin, C., Cheng, W.-H., Vrochidis, S. (eds.) MMM 2019. LNCS, vol. 11296, pp. 602–608. Springer, Cham (2019). https://doi.org/10.1007/978-3-030-05716-9_53
15. Palubinsks, G., Datcu, M.: Information fusion approach for the data classification: an example for ERS-1/2 InSAR data. Int. J. Remote Sens. **29**(16), 4689–4703 (2008)
16. Pittaras, N., Markatopoulou, F., Mezaris, V., Patras, I.: Comparison of fine-tuning and extension strategies for deep convolutional neural networks. In: Amsaleg, L., Guðmundsson, G., Gurrin, C., Jónsson, B., Satoh, S. (eds.) MMM 2017. LNCS, vol. 10132, pp. 102–114. Springer, Cham (2017). https://doi.org/10.1007/978-3-319-51811-4_9
17. Yao, W., Dumitru, C.O., Datcu, M.: D2.8 data fusion v2, deliverable of the candela project. https://www.candela-h2020.eu/content/data-fusion-v2
18. Yao, W., Dumitru, C.O., Lorenzo, J., Datcu, M.: Data fusion on the candela cloud platform. In: European Geosciences Union (EGU) General Assembly - Big Data and Machine Learning in Geosciences, May 2020
19. Younessian, E., Mitamura, T., Hauptmann, A.: Multimodal knowledge-based analysis in multimedia event detection. In: Proceedings of the 2nd ACM International Conference on Multimedia Retrieval, pp. 1–8 (2012)

RISS 2020 - International Workshop on Research and Innovation for Secure Societies

Workshop on Research and Innovation for Secure Societies (RISS)

High expansion of urban population and recent world events complemented by the alarming increase of the number of threats to infrastructure safety have mobilized Authorities to redesign societal security concepts. Law Enforcement Authorities (LEA) are focusing and aiming consistently their actions at preventing crimes and protecting people, properties and critical infrastructures.

With the accelerated advances of communications and storage technologies, access to critical information acquired from various sensors and sources, e.g., land cameras, satellite data, drones, personal devices, has been significantly eased. Manipulation and processing of such high amount of diverse data is still a steady challenge, and most of the existing solutions involve the use of human resources. However, threats are now at a very large scale, requiring very different security solutions which can make use of interdisciplinary approaches. In this context, computer-assisted or automated technologies are now becoming more and more attractive to substitute expensive human resources in the decisional systems.

Following the first two editions, the 3rd International Workshop on Research & Innovation for Secure Societies – RISS 2020, organized in conjunction with the 25th International Conference on Pattern Recognition (ICPR), focuses on discussing solutions provided by Artificial Intelligence (AI) systems to these challenges.

It aims to bring together researchers from academia and industry, end-users, law-enforcing agencies and citizen groups to share experiences and explore multi- and inter- disciplinary areas where additional research and development are needed, identify possible collaboration and consider the societal impact of such technologies.

Five papers were accepted covering various topics, from video archive investigation, automatic fake news detection, wearable face recognition approaches, to scene understanding for passenger safety and tackling cyberbullying on social media. The accepted articles are proposing contributions, both at application and algorithm level, and brought together practitioners from academia and LEA.

December 2020

Bogdan Ionescu
Tiberio Uricchio
Marian Buric
Răzvan Roman
Vincent Charvillat
Marco Cristani

Organization

General Chairs and Program Committee

Bogdan Ionescu   University Politehnica of Bucharest, Romania
Tiberio Uricchio   University of Florence, Italy
Marian Buric   Protection and Guard Service, Romania
Răzvan Roman   Protection and Guard Service, Romania
Vincent Charvillat   University of Toulouse, France
Marco Cristani   University of Verona, Italy

Additional Reviewers

Mihai-Gabriel Constantin   University Politehnica of Bucharest, Romania
Liviu-Daniel Ştefan   University Politehnica of Bucharest, Romania
Mihai Dogariu   University Politehnica of Bucharest, Romania

SURVANT: An Innovative Semantics-Based Surveillance Video Archives Investigation Assistant

Giuseppe Vella[1]([⊠]), Anastasios Dimou[2], David Gutierrez-Perez[4],
Daniele Toti[5,6], Tommaso Nicoletti[3], Ernesto La Mattina[1], Francesco Grassi[4],
Andrea Ciapetti[6], Michael McElligott[4], Nauman Shahid[4], and Petros Daras[2]

[1] Engineering Ingegneria Informatica S.p.a, Piazzale dell'Agricoltura 24, 00144 Rome, Italy
{giuseppe.vella,ernesto.lamattina}@eng.it
[2] Centre for Research and Technology Hellas, 6th Km Charilaou-Thermi, 57001 Thermi, Greece
{dimou,daras}@iti.gr
[3] Demetrix Srl., Via Ugo La Malfa, 28a/30, 90146 Palermo, Italy
tommaso.nicoletti@demetrix.it
[4] United Technologies Research Centre Ireland, Ltd., Penrose Wharf Business Centre,
Cork City T23 XN53, Ireland
{perezd,grassifr,mcellim,shahidn}@rtx.com
[5] Faculty of Mathematical, Physical and Natural Sciences, Catholic University of the Sacred
Heart, Via Musei 41, 25121 Brescia, Italy
daniele.toti@unicatt.it
[6] Innovation Engineering S.r.l., Via Napoleone Colajanni 4, 00191 Rome, Italy
{d.toti,a.ciapetti}@innen.it

Abstract. SURVANT is an innovative video archive investigation system that aims to drastically reduce the time required to examine large amounts of video content. It can collect the videos relevant to a specific case from heterogeneous repositories in a seamless manner. SURVANT employs Deep Learning technologies to extract inter/intra-camera video analytics, including object recognition, inter/intra-camera tracking, and activity detection. The identified entities are semantically indexed enabling search and retrieval of visual characteristics. Semantic reasoning and inference mechanisms based on visual concepts and spatio-temporal metadata allows users to identify hidden correlations and discard outliers. SURVANT offers the user a unified GIS-based search interface to unearth the required information using natural language query expressions and a plethora of filtering options. An intuitive interface with a relaxed learning curve assists the user to create specific queries and receive accurate results using advanced visual analytics tools. GDPR compliant management of personal data collected from surveillance videos is integrated in the system design.

Keywords: Deep Learning · Inter/intra camera analytics · Spatio-temporal semantic reasoning · Trajectory mining · Complex Query Formulator

© Springer Nature Switzerland AG 2021
A. Del Bimbo et al. (Eds.): ICPR 2020 Workshops, LNCS 12667, pp. 611–626, 2021.
https://doi.org/10.1007/978-3-030-68787-8_44

1 Introduction

The ever-increasing use of video surveillance in multiple business sectors has created new challenges related to the exploitation of surveillance video archives. Performing post-event investigations in archives for large scale camera networks that may comprise multiple sites, complex camera topologies and diverse technologies requires significant human effort. Video analytics are destined to assist in this regard, but in spite of the progress achieved, advanced analytics are still at a relatively nascent stage owing to a number of challenges: (a) large scale processing requirements, (b) support diverse video content with differences in quality, format and extrinsic parameters, (c) inter-camera analytics, (d) effective data visualization and (e) a user-intuitive interface. The need for querying huge amounts of videos from multiple sources and extracting knowledge from them is creating a new demand for tools that can assist investigators to face the challenges in their line of work, streamlining the work of expert law enforcement officers and investigators by automating burdensome processes. Hence an improved situational awareness and search assistance tools to further diminish the possibility of missing evidence due to the huge workload is needed.

The SURVANT system assists investigators to search efficiently and effectively in video archives to contribute towards fighting crime and illicit activities, improving the sense and essence of security for the citizens. Enhancing safety and security, reduction of loss/theft, vandalism prevention, harassment prevention and regulatory compliance are among the main driving applications of surveillance systems. SURVANT provides solutions beyond the industry state-of-the-art to face the challenges identified in the markets targeted.

SURVANT supports video archive investigations via the following elements:

- A modular and scalable system based on microservices and dockerized modules.
- SotA video analysis techniques based on Deep Learning to analyze footages, maintaining an optimal balance between speed and accuracy.
- An inference framework, based on automated reasoning mechanisms, able to combine low-level information and semantic annotations to discover high-level security events and/or investigative hypotheses.
- A large-scale efficient video and image indexing for high-dimensional features and semantically-mapped content (event type and attributes).
- A GIS-based user interface allowing the user to perform complex queries regarding objects and events taking into account time, location and their interconnection.
- Semantics-based query expansion techniques to improve the precision of the search results.
- A privacy-by-design framework for automated video analysis and analytics, compliant with the European legal framework for privacy and data protection. The remainder of the paper is organized as follows. The SURVANT architecture is presented in Sect. 2. Section 3 describes the use-cases used during the system development and experimental. Results are presented in Sect. 4. Final conclusions complete the paper in Sect. 5.

2   SURVANT in a Nutshell

The architecture of SURVANT is a microservice architecture, devised to be modular by nature so that each module is low in coupling and high in cohesion. Each module does one job and communicates with the others to orchestrate all the operations in the best possible way. The *Client layer* contains all the parts of the front-end composed by the dashboard and the main views for operators (investigators and chefs), a control panel for system maintenance and an access point for "superusers".

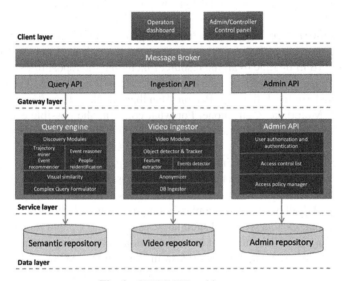

Fig. 1. SURVANT architecture

The UI interacts with the modules within the *Service layer* through the gateway layer that contains a *Message Broker* that dispatches requests to the proper module asynchronously by means of the respective API and validate them against the User Authentication Authority Server (UAAS) and the Microservices *Access Control List* (MACL). UAAS manages the authorization and the authentication of the users on the portal, the MACL manages the authorization of the gateway in relationship with each registered microservice. The *Access Policy Manager* handles the access to all the resources applying a set of pre-defined polices. The *Service Layer* is devoted to computations. It contains the business logic of the core modules like the video modules for the ingestion of footages and the extraction of the events, objects and video features according to which the videos will be anonymized. Moreover, this layer contains the *Query Engine* modules that are dedicated to the querying of all the objects extracted and to enrich and combine them through a geographical, temporal and semantic analysis. The *Data Layer* is the persistence layer of the SURVANT platform, it hosts multifarious storage systems according to each module's needs: a *Video Repository*, an *Admin repository* and an a *Semantic Repository* for storing RDF triples.

2.1 The SURVANT Platform

The SURVANT platform allows the interaction between users and investigation's data and details, such as video footages upload, cameras involved management, notes creation, areas definition, usable semantic relations building, temporal and geo-localized results. The GUI is made up with a web portal that supports multiple users in multiple languages in a collaborative environment with a front-end user interface that allows a user to navigate, create and share information on investigations. The platform is composed of several components that includes the GUI, the different API for the ingestion, the querying and the administration and the gateway to dispatch requests from the different services (see Fig. 1).

The **Administration APIs** give the possibility to an administrator to set up for each authenticated user the authorization rights managed through the **User Authentication and Authorization** module to all the resources including the repositories, the cameras, the investigations, the objects and the events detected in the footages. The objects that can be detected are the following: Person, Handbag, Backpack, Suitcase, Car, Truck, Bus, Bicycle, Motorbike, Cell Phone. For what concerns the possible events that can be detected by the Visual Analytics Components and by the Event reasoner are of three categories: Low-level events (e.g. walking, standing), Group events (e.g. Fighting, chasing), Middle-level events (e.g. Entering a vehicle, e.g. Holding or picking an object). Every resource managed through the GUI has three possible sensitivity levels, i.e. a level of visibility that combined with the three access levels allow the users a granular access to them. The **GUI** allows user to seamlessly interact with underlying services through several macro-phases, that we could summarize as follow: i) Upload footages, ii) create an investigation, iii) collect notes on an investigation, iv) querying on an investigation. Each macro-phase is regulated by a workflow managed by the SURVANT platform that will ensure that every step of the phase is concluded successfully. These workflows imply the interaction between the Operators Dashboard of the Client layer, the Gateway, through the Message broker, listens to the invoked services in the *Service Layer*: the *Query Engine* and the *Video Ingestor* modules.

2.2 Video Analysis for Object Tracking and Event Detecting

The video analysis module of SURVANT is responsible for extracting video analytics that enable content-based retrieval functionalities. The aim of this module is to correctly detect the classes that are useful for users, including Law Enforcement Agencies. Furthermore, it aims to track the objects of interest in order to check which route they followed before/after an event happened. Aim of tracking is to keep the same track identity for every object involved in a security event. Regarding the object detection part, the PVANet [1] architecture has been selected as a baseline. This detection framework follows the common pipeline of CNN (Convolutional Neural Network) feature extraction followed by region proposal and region of interest (RoI) classification. SURVANT improves the baseline by redesigning the feature extraction and region proposal to improve efficiency and performance. Please find more details and results in [2]. Additionally, real-world surveillance data have been collected and annotated. Fine-tuning the object detection network with this data has dramatically improved performance. A "tracking-by-detection" paradigm is used for object tracking, where detections from consecutive frames are connected temporally. As input, the detection results are produced by an object detector. Given a new frame, the tracker associates the already tracked targets and the newly detected objects.

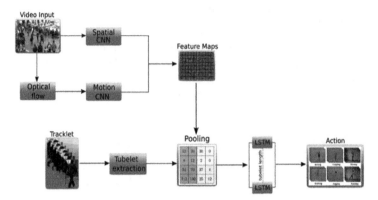

Fig. 2. Pipeline of the proposed scheme.

Object association is performed in multiple steps. The frame to frame association is performed using a smart combination of simple methods (intersection over union and HSV histogram similarity) and LSTM networks modelling the evolution of targets using their appearance, volume, position, velocity and interaction with nearby objects [3]. Tracking results can be improved with tracklet post processing.

Regarding event recognition, a tubelet-based approach was developed. The term tubelet refers to a short sequence of bounding boxes marking a person or an object of interest. These tubelets can be considered as the structural elements of the various actions. The adopted methodology is illustrated in Fig. 2. A two-streams approach is employed for feature extraction. The spatial stream takes as input video RGB frames and captures the appearance of the person as well as cues from the scene, while the second stream, the motion CNN, operates on optical flow input and captures the movement of the person. The event detection module uses an LSTM network to classify each of the extracted tubelets to a specific event.

2.3 The Complex Query Formulator

In a typical investigation, based on a large video collection, the investigator has to search for evidence of criminal activities that may have happened by multiple persons, in multiple locations and time points. To support the search for evidence, SURVANT provides a set of tools for processing and analyzing the raw content, as well as visualizing and gathering evidences.

The videos are analyzed in an offline process, after which the investigator is able to search through the analyzed results using several types of queries. Such types can be text, an image crop, an event, a location, a time point, etc. Most times, however, a more complex type of search is needed for speeding up the investigation time, especially in the first critical hours of the investigation. The Complex Query Formulator (CQF) allows the formation of queries of higher complexity by combining simple query types, identifying the necessary services that need to be queried and interrogating these services to retrieve the relevant information. The main investigation sequences to which the CQF participates are: "Search by Image", "Search by Sentence" and "Geographical Analysis" (see a visual detail in Fig. 3).

Search by Image: The user can obtain investigation results by searching for similarities among the videos related to an investigation. He can select a particular frame of the footage and search for similar people or objects or he can upload an image that he got from other sources and search the object in the video repository.

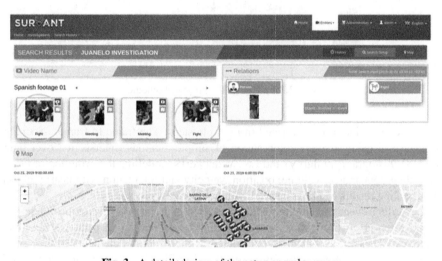

Fig. 3. A detailed view of the setup complex query

Search by Sentence: The investigator can perform an investigation using SURVANT's complex query formulator feature and navigate footages through the bundle of resulting high level events. The user can create through a drag and drop mechanism a list of relations sentence-like composed of objects, events, geographical and temporal coordinates.

Geographical Analysis: Starting from the previous mentioned types of search, objects, suspects, victims or other persons of interest are detected. The investigator can then request the trajectories of the annotated individual(s) and may request to repeat the analysis based on new or refined queries.

2.4   The Indexer: Visual Similarity and People Re-identification

When human investigators are tasked with analyzing large bodies of surveillance camera footage in an effort to identify possible sightings of a suspect, it proves to be highly demanding in terms of time and human resources. Locating possible sightings of a suspect based on similarity to a target image was a key target for SURVANT to automate. The Indexer module takes the bounding boxes and object types reported by the Object Detector for each video frame and constructs a feature vector for the area of frame within the bounding box co-ordinates. This vector is akin to a fingerprint and similar images should have a similar fingerprint. The Indexer stores the feature vector along with metadata (such as frame number, bounding box, time, etc.) in the Indexer Repository. Given a target image, the Indexer constructs a feature vector and compares to the features stored in the Indexer Repository – ranking the results in order of similarity.

Figure 4 describes the person re-identification pipeline. A feature vector is extracted from a query image of a person of interest (blue part at the top of the figure). Next, this vector is compared against catalogued vectors, which are previously computed offline (green part at the bottom of the figure). Finally, a ranked list of identities is obtained by ordering the images by similarity measure.

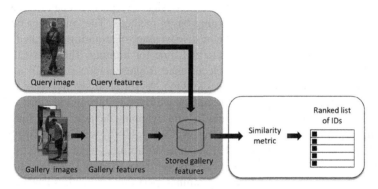

Fig. 4. Person re-identification pipeline

From an architectural point of view, the *Indexer* is composed of three submodules, namely, the *Feature Extractor*, the *Database Ingestor*, and the *Similarity Ranker*. These submodules can be identified in Fig. 4. The *Feature Extractor* performs the computationally intensive task of reading the output of the *Object Detector & Tracker* module and generating feature vectors for each detected object. The *Database Ingestor* stores the feature vectors into a database and provides an internal API for performing queries. The *Similarity Ranker* provides the *Indexer*'s general-purpose, high-performance REST API that is used by the *Complex Query Formulator* as well as provides extensibility capabilities for future modules. The video ingestion pipeline is comprised of a workflow which co-ordinates activity across object detection, feature vector cataloguing, reasoner analysis and anonymization (via targeted blurring) according to object classification and sensitivity level to fine tune the anonymization required according to the privilege level of the person viewing the footage.

The Feature Extractor received the majority of the focus within the Indexer module as its efficiency and quality in constructing a feature vector drives the overall usability of the module. The feature representations are extracted from a Convolutional Neural Network considering the identities as classes and taking the output from the last layer before the softmax layer as the deep features. After initially analyzing an approach using ResNet [4], we subsequently focused our attention on MobileNets [5] due to its improved efficiency. While MobileNets offer an alternative smaller and more efficient network since its feature extraction time is lower, we also want to maximize the performance of a small network to be as accurate as possible. For this purpose, we leveraged network distillation [6] using ResNet-50 as a large model that can act as teacher and MobileNets as a suitable architecture for playing the role of the student network. We further sought to improve the performance of the pipeline in person re-identification in terms of computational cost at test time. Once the deep features have been extracted and assembled into a feature vector then they are stored in the Indexer Repository. To compute similarity between feature vectors we use Euclidian distance – it is simple and can be computed in-situ within the database allowing significant speed improvements over an approach which retrieves all potentially relevant data and computes the similarity externally.

An analysis of different techniques for person re-identification was performed prior to choosing the implemented solution. The considered algorithms can be classified as classical (hand-crafted) and deep learning-based methods. The latter ones outperform significantly the former ones, but with the disadvantage of requiring dedicated hardware (i.e. GPUs), and large amounts of data and time for training. The classical methods evaluated included Local Maximal Occurrence Representation (LOMO) and Cross-view Quadratic Discriminant Analysis (XQDA). As for deep learning-based methods, ResNet [4] and MobileNet [5] were tested, as well as several combinations of both by applying network distillation techniques [6] and swapping the teacher and student roles. For evaluation, Market-1501 [7] and DukeMTMC-reID [8] were used. To summarize the results, classical methods provided much lower accuracy than deep learning-based methods, thus they would be only applicable where there are strong hardware limitations. ResNet-50 and MobileNets showed a similar performance with some differences, while MobileNets described better the features for the Market-1501 dataset, ResNet-50 performed better for the and DukeMTMC-reID dataset.

Market-1501	Rank-1 (%)	mAP (%)	GPU time (ms)
LOMO + XQDA	43.32	22.01	17.25
ResNet-50	64.46	38.95	7.82
MobileNet 1.0 independent	67.37	39.54	1.84
MobileNet 0.25 independent	59.74	34.13	1.63
MobileNet 0.25 distilled from ResNet-50	71.29	45.76	1.63
MobileNet 0.25 distilled from MobileNet 1.0	70.46	45.24	1.63
DukeMTMC-reID	Rank-1 (%)	mAP (%)	GPU time (ms)
LOMO + XQDA [53]	30.75	17.04	17.25
ResNet-50	67.1	44.59	7.82
MobileNet 1.0 independent	57.41	34.86	1.84
MobileNet 0.25 independent	49.69	28.67	1.63

(*continued*)

(continued)

DukeMTMC-reID	Rank-1 (%)	mAP (%)	GPU time (ms)
MobileNet 0.25 distilled from ResNet-50	64.99	42.32	1.63
MobileNet 0.25 distilled from MobileNet 1.0	59.69	38.48	1.63

2.5 The Trajectory Miner

In the field of video-surveillance analysis, the problem of tracking a person of interest given a ground truth image (query), in a large crowded spatiotemporal region is known as "Trajectory Mining" [9]. Several algorithmic challenges have been arising due to absence of information about 1) the length of the true trajectory, 2) the identities of various persons (except for the query), and 3) starting/end point or the position of query in the true trajectory. In particular, the scenario of interest involves m persons moving in a spatial zone and being detected by cameras. Every detection is represented as a tuple (f_i, t_i, s_i), where f_i is the ith frame/detection, t_i is the timestamp and $s_i = (x_i, y_i)$ are the spatial coordinates of the detected person or the camera. This problem via a graph signal processing approach has been tackled, modeling the tuples (f_i, t_i, s_i) as node signals and edge weights as a fusion of visual, spatial and temporal information. The information fusion algorithm can be summarized as follows: **Step 1: Visual Graph.** For every frame f_i a "deep visual signature" $\xi \in \mathbb{R}^p$ from the ResNet50 [4] architecture has been extracted, with dimensionality $p = 2048$. A k_{nn} similarity graph G_ξ [10], where k_{nn} is the number of neighbors, between the features has been obtained using the UMAP (Universal Manifold Approximation and Projection) graph construction algorithm [11]. **Step 2: Spatiotemporal Graph.** k_{nn}-nearest spatial neighbour graph G_s is constructed between the coordinates $s_i = (x_i, y_i)$ using Haversine distance. Denoting $d_{i,j}$ the Haversine distance between coordinates (s_i, s_j), temporal information is fused in the spatial graph using:

$$W_{st}(i, j) = \frac{1}{1 + \exp\left(-10\left(\frac{|t_i - t_j|}{d_{i,j}} - 0.4\right)\right)} W_s(i, j). \tag{1}$$

Assuming an average walking speed of 1.4 m/s [12], the above spatiotemporal weighting scheme allows SURVANT system to decrease the spatial similarity $W_s(i, j)$ between coordinates (s_i, s_j), whose distance cannot be physically traveled in time $|t_i - t_j|$. **Step 3: Fusion of visual and spatial graphs.** To merge the three sources of information into one graph $G = (\mathcal{V}, \mathcal{E}, \text{W})$ the module computes the Hadamard product of the two adjacency matrices $W = W_\xi \circ W_{st}$. The matrix W is still a valid similarity matrix and its entries represent the spatiotemporal similarity in the fused feature space between the tuples (f_i, f_j). **Step 4: Conversion to directed fused graph.** Since a trajectory can only move forward in time, a direction is assigned to each edge such that $e = (v_i, v_j) \notin \mathcal{E}$ if $t_i - t_j > 0$. It is easy to show that the obtained graph G is a directed acyclic graph (DAG). The described algorithm filters out several edges which might lead to false paths, especially those related to poor quality of visual features. In a crowded environment the actual image of a person might be occluded by other people, shadows, objects etc. Thus, the refinement via spatial graph, which is accurate due to the exact knowledge of the spatial coordinates, helps to remove the false edges in the final graph. Once the graph G is constructed, next step is to query the graph for getting the trajectory relevant to a suspect. The investigator uploads the image of a suspect along with its spatial coordinates and timestamp. Let us call this the 'query tuple'. This query tuple after extracting the visual features of the image is represented as:

$$Q = \left(x_q, t_q, \left(sx_q, sy_q\right)\right),$$

where x_q is the image, t_q denotes the timestamp and $\left(sx_q, sy_q\right)$ denote the spatial coordinates of the query q. The goal of the trajectory mining algorithm is to produce a trajectory which involves query tuple. The graph G is a DAG, thus a weighted longest path algorithm can be used to get the trajectory which maximizes the similarity starting from node Q [13] Since the query node is not necessarily the beginning of the trajectory and the end point of the trajectory is not known, the algorithm was run twice, first using Q as starting node, and then reversing the direction of the edges and running the algorithm backwards. Finally, the forward and backward trajectories to obtain the full trajectory have been concatenated. As remarked before, poor visual features quality may affect the knowledge graph construction steps, creating false edges in the graph. In the attempt of maximizing the maximum weighted length, the longest path algorithm may concatenate trajectories which belong to different persons and return a very long trajectory. In order to mitigate this problem, a modification of the algorithm has been proposed so that it maximizes the sum of the edge weights in the path divided by its length. Denoting $p = \left\{e_1, e_2, \ldots, e_{L_p}\right\}$ the forward path starting from query node Q, the algorithm solves the following optimization problem:

$$\arg \max_p \sum_{e \in p} \frac{w_e}{L_p}$$

where w_e is the weight associated to edge e.

2.6   The Reasoner and the Semantic Repository

The event reasoning module is based on an inferential approach to detect high level events using Semantic Web Rules (SWRL). This approach combines all the results collected by the lower level detectors, as entities, such as people and objects, and base events, such as persons running or walking, and their spatial trajectories over time, provided by the trajectory mining algorithm, with a rule based approach to identify potential crimes or high level events, such as pick-pocketing or vandalism. The low-level events and the spatial and temporal information collected from different cameras – including the computed trajectories – are indexed in an optimized semantic datastore, where rules for detecting events are manually defined using SWRL. When these rules are applied to the indexed information, high-level events can be detected. The approach used is based on the standardization effort around the SWRL rule-based language. SWRL is a Semantic Web Rule Language based on a combination of the OWL DL and OWL Lite sub-languages of the OWL Web Ontology Language with the Unary/Binary Datalog

RuleML sub-languages of the Rule Mark-up Language. SWRL includes a high-level abstract syntax for rules in both OWL DL and OWL Lite formalisms. A model-theoretic semantics is given to provide the formal meaning for OWL ontologies including rules written in this syntax. This approach has been successfully used in other domains as well, including law and biomedicine [14–16].

Deduction of the existence of the high-level events is computed using reasoning-based strategies, based on empirical rules, suggested and confirmed by the Madrid Municipal Police involved in the project. The proposed approach is able to recognize crime events like pick-pocketing attempts or street fights in a repository containing low- and middle-level metadata extracted from surveillance videos. The rules and the individuals are evaluated by a semantic reasoner, which infers suspicious events and persons, which can be further inspected by a human officer after the automatic analysis. To define the rules, the output of the Computer Vision algorithms and detectors has been considered as a base. These algorithms analyze the scene and extract information which is stored and indexed in a semantic repository in the ingestion phase, performed after an investigation has been started on the system. The extracted information includes objects like Bus, Car, Motorbike, Handbag and Person. Each object holds information relevant to the detection task, mainly the start and end frame of the object appearance and a collection of statuses for each frame in which it appears. Each frame contains the frame number (for temporal reasoning), position and size of the object (for spatial reasoning), and the low-level action the object is performing in that moment. Some of the low-level detected actions are Standing, Walking and Running for persons, Moving and Stopping for vehicles, etc. In addition, middle-level events, such as Entering or Exiting buildings, Falling or Lying down, Fighting and Graffiti Making are also correctly detected by the analyzers.

The description of objects and events is encoded in a RDF-based ontology, implemented specifically for the SURVANT system, in which each individual can be expressed in RDF-based triple format. In the ingestion phase, the data indexed in the semantic repository can easily reach billions of tuples. One of the implemented features is the ability to summarize the raw temporal data, taking into account only the start and end time of events that can be meaningful for the inference performed by the SWRL rules created manually by the users. In addition, the spatial data of each person can be filtered and summarized, taking into account the position and distance of groups of people that are near enough to potentially interact between each other. The advanced search functionalities provided by the reasoner are able to offer the investigators not only a concise and effective representation of the events detected inside the scene of a crime, but also more high-level abstractions. In particular, if a criminal event, such as a theft or pickpocketing, is reported in one of the roads covered by the video surveillance system, the system should be able to provide investigators with potential "suspicious" situations, combining appropriately several simple basic events. Starting from the position data, and from mid-level events such as "Walking", "Running", "Meeting", high-level events as "potential pickpocketing" or "probable fight" can be recognized by applying rules based on spatial, temporal and empirical criteria defined in behavioral patterns for improving the capability to identify suspicious actions. An example of one of the event "Robbery" is presented in Fig. 5.

Fig. 5. Example of a "Robbery" event as captured by a surveillance camera (images degraded to preserve the privacy of the actors).

"If a person has luggage, another person comes close to him, grabs his luggage, and starts running, and the owner of the luggage runs after him, then there has been a robbery."

One of the most challenging tasks of the event reasoning module has been to find a way to overcome the inherent scalability problems of the reasoning systems, with an innovative approach based on highly parallelized computing. The adoption of the Stardog repository [17] (with embedded reasoning capabilities), the commercial version of Clarks & Parsia Pellet reasoner [18] (previously used), allowed introducing several enhancements in this direction; in particular, the ability to use an in-memory storage for heavy computational scenarios with huge amounts of triples present and the introduction of a high availability and performance clustering, based on Zookeeper and other HA techniques. Stardog is a commercial semantic repository that supports the RDF graph data model, the SPARQL query language, the property graph model and the Gremlin graph traversal language, as well as OWL 2 and user-defined rules for inference and data analytics, distributed by Complexible, an innovative and relatively recent USA company, focused on inference solutions. Stardog reasoning is based on the OWL 2 Direct Semantics Entailment Regime. Stardog performs reasoning in a lazy and late-binding fashion: it does not materialize inferences; but, rather, reasoning is performed at query time according to a given reasoning level. This allows for maximum flexibility while maintaining excellent performance and scalability. After the start of each investigation, when the underlying analyzers have completed the detection process of objects and low-level events, the Reasoner module is invoked by the Vision Service, which signals the presence of data to be ingested in the semantic repository. The reasoner responds immediately with a simple ACK and starts loading the data from a queue, in a typical producer/consumer modality. After having performed deductions and logical consequences from low-level events with the defined set of SWRL rules, the module is directly involved in the SURVANT project pipeline to perform queries on the underlying knowledge base in order to present the aggregated computed results to the investigators in the GUI of the system (see Fig. 6).

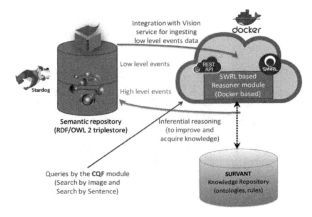

Fig. 6. Interactions between the semantic repository and SURVANT modules.

3 Use Cases

The use cases that have been defined for the SURVANT product are the following:
i) Aggression (Beat and run away), ii) Theft (Pick pocketing), iii) Vandalism (against
parked vehicles, Defacing of buildings, iv) Scene Monitoring (Building monitoring), v)
Missing Person (Vulnerable individual reported missing), vi) People Tracking (Assault
on a Person, Person of Interest Tracking, Detect subsequent criminal behavior). To test
the above use cases the Municipal Police of Madrid has recorded 5 days of videos with
actors that followed specific plots of some possible scenarios that the consortium has
defined for the testing and validation of those use cases. The SURVANT algorithms have
been tested against almost 100 GB of footages.

4 Results

4.1 Video Analysis for Object Tracking and Event Detecting

Object tracking is performed in SURVANT using the track-by-detection paradigm. For
object detection, a modified PVANet model is used that is faster by 15% and smaller
by 79%, producing comparable results to the original PVANet under the same training
procedure. However, the performance was subpar for surveillance footage.

A new dataset was created to cover the needs of the use cases described above,
involving public and challenging real surveillance data. The dataset has almost 430K
samples from the following classes: person, handbag, backpack, suitcase, car, truck, bus,
motorbike, bicycle, cell phone, laptop, and graffiti. The object detection network was
re-trained using the dataset and some augmentation techniques to better simulate the
real situation introducing motion blur.

In order to produce trajectories of objects, SURVANT utilized a DL-based detection
association model using multiple information cues including appearance (see Fig. 7),
position, interaction, volume and velocity. The network was able to give predictions
for batches of images with speed that approximates 1522 FPS and precision of 90%.

Moreover, SURVANT utilized a tracklet association model that was able to identify and connect tracklets of the same person in real time with an accuracy of 91%.

Fig. 7. Example detections on a MET CCTV video by the default PVANet.

Regarding the performance of the event recognition module, a collection of public datasets and surveillance videos were collected and annotated with events of interest for our use cases. The described network described in Sect. 2.2 was trained and tested on separate parts of the dataset and the results are provided in Table 1.

Table 1. Recognition accuracy for different event classes.

Overall accuracy	Average accuracy	Stand	Walk	Run	Fight	Make graffiti	Lie down	Enter building	Get in vehicle
89.37	88.37	77.33	95.06	72.73	81.48	94.12	95.89	95.7	94.68

4.2 Event Reasoning

The experiments on the event reasoning in SURVANT have been carried out using the output of the low-level detectors and of the trajectory miner module. This information was passed to the Stardog-based semantic repository component, where triples were stored and reasoned with. The visual analysis tracks objects frame by frame and identifies low- and middle-level events and actions that each object is performing. This information is then passed to the semantic component, where information is trans-formed to the form of Subject-Predicate-Object triples and stored in the repository. After a video is processed, the reasoning is performed on the stored triples in the datastore and new relations are inferred, containing the detected abnormal events. The performed tests show encouraging results in the recognition of potential suspicious events: on one hand, the system produces some "false positives" in the recognition, but on the other hand the lack of recognition of potentially suspicious events and persons is very rare. The tests have been performed on a relatively small set of surveillance videos (almost 100 GB of files), provided by the Madrid Police; the statistical performance of the reasoner in detecting crimes in real world situations is very encouraging. Often in these videos the crime scene is positioned at the extreme boundaries of the video or even outside of the camera coverage area. In this case it was not feasible for the reasoner to detect the crime correctly. By taking into account this factor and the relatively low quality of the videos recorded and analyzed by the system, a success percentage of 2 detections every 3 crimes (67%) is to be considered very good, as well as the percentage of "false positives", which is around 15%. For each high-level crime type, some rules used by the reasoner perform very well indeed and can be considered already optimized, whereas some other rules are less precise in the detection phase. This may lead towards future refinements of the less performing rules.

4.3 Trajectory Miner

Trajectories of people walking in Cork City, Ireland were simulated as an initial test of the algorithm. The topological graph is obtained from OpenStreetMap XML data [19] and uses $m = 75$ people of the test portion of the publicly available MARS dataset [20] as camera detections. Topological graph consists of $N = 4000$ nodes, representing straight walking roads, which are connected if the corresponding roads are connected. $N_c = 300$ nodes equipped with simulated cameras have been selected. For each person in the dataset, source and destination nodes and a random path between them have been selected. Timestamps are obtained by computing Haversine distance between the nodes and assuming the walking speed to be a Gaussian random variable with mean 1.4 m/s and standard deviation 0.1. Whenever a person, during his trajectory, crosses a camera node, a frame f_i from the corresponding image dataset is used to simulate a detection. The list of the crossed camera nodes is our target trajectory.

As a performance metric, the F-score on the detected nodes was computed in the estimated trajectory as compared to the nodes in the ground truth trajectory. A comparison of our results with simple k_{nn} nearest neighbor search on the visual features as a baseline, with $k_{nn} = 15$ to 100 and a step of 10 has been performed. For most of the cases the performance of our algorithm outperforms k_{nn} algorithms, up to 350% over k_{nn}-15 baseline for class 37. Moreover, for the proposed approach, the standard deviation is much lower as compared to the other algorithms, mainly because of the false positives avoided due to the spatiotemporal refinement of the visual similarity.

5 Conclusions

The SURVANT product that is the main output of the SURVANT project is a fully-customizable, scalable and robust system that is ready to hit the market. SURVANT presents an architecture that is horizontally and vertically scalable. The reliability of its output depends on the positive results that have been produced by SURVANT from a scientific point of view. The adopted CNN was able to give predictions with a precision of 90%. SURVANT utilized a tracklet association model that was able to identify and connect tracklets of the same person in real time with an accuracy of 91%. From the semantic reasoner perspective SURVANT got a success percentage of 2 detections every 3 crimes (67%), as well as a false positive rate around 15%. Thanks to the approach adopted with the trajectory miner, false positives were avoided due to the spatiotemporal refinement of the visual similarity. This work has been supported by the SURVANT project that received funding from the EU Horizon 2020 Fast Track to Innovation (FTI) programme under Grant Agreement No n° 720417.

References

1. Kim, K.H., et al.: PVANET: deep but lightweight neural networks for real-time object detection. arXiv preprint arXiv:1608.08021 (2016)
2. Anastasios, D., et al.: Multi-target detection in CCTV footage for tracking applications using deep learning techniques. In: 2016 IEEE International Conference on Image Processing (ICIP) (2016)
3. Ahmed, E.A.: An improved deep learning architecture for person re-identification. In: Proceedings of the IEEE Conference on Computer Vision and Pattern Recognition, pp. 3908–3916 (2015)
4. He, K., et al.: Deep residual learning for image recognition. In: Proceedings of the IEEE Conference on Computer Vision and Pattern Recognition, pp. 770–778 (2016)
5. Howard, A.G., et al.: MobileNets: efficient convolutional neural networks for mobile vision applications. arXiv preprint arXiv:1704.04861 (2017)
6. Hinton, G., Vinyals, O., Dean, J.: Distilling the knowledge in a neural network. arXiv preprint arXiv:1503.02531 (2015)
7. Zheng, L., et al.: Scalable person re-identification: a benchmark. In: IEEE International Conference on Computer Vision, pp. 1116–1124 (2015)
8. Ristani, E., Solera, F., Zou, R., Cucchiara, R., Tomasi, C.: Performance measures and a data set for multi-target, multi-camera tracking. In: Hua, G., Jégou, H. (eds.) ECCV 2016. LNCS, vol. 9914, pp. 17–35. Springer, Cham (2016). https://doi.org/10.1007/978-3-319-48881-3_2
9. Zheng, Y.: Trajectory data mining: an overview. ACM Trans. Intell. Syst. Technol. (TIST) 6(3), 1–41 (2015)
10. Shuman, D.I., Narang, S.K., Frossard, P., Ortega, A., Vandergheynst, P.: The emerging field of signal processing on graphs: extending high-dimensional data analysis to networks and other irregular domains. IEEE Signal Process. Mag. 30(3), 83–98 (2013)
11. McInnes, L., Healy, J., Melville, J.: Umap: uniform manifold approximation and projection for dimension reduction. arXiv preprint arXiv:1802.03426 (2018)
12. Bohannon, R.W.: Comfortable and maximum walking speed of adults aged 20–79 years: reference values and determinants. Age Ageing 26, 15–19 (1997)
13. Sedgewick, R.: Algorithms. Pearson Education India (2016)
14. Capuano, N., Longhi, A., Salerno, S., Toti, D.: Ontology-driven generation of training paths in the legal domain. Int. J. Emerg. Technol. Learn. (iJET) 10, 14–22 (2015). https://doi.org/10.3991/ijet.v10i7.4609
15. Arosio, G., Bagnara, G., Capuano, N., Fersini, E., Toti, D.: Ontology-driven data acquisition: intelligent support to legal ODR systems. Front. Artif. Intell. Appl. 259, 25–28 (2013). https://doi.org/10.3233/978-1-61499-359-9-25
16. Toti, D.: AQUEOS: a system for question answering over semantic data. In: Proceedings - 2014 International Conference on Intelligent Networking and Collaborative Systems, IEEE INCoS 2014, pp. 716–719 (2014). https://doi.org/10.1109/incos.2014.13
17. Stardog. https://www.stardog.com/
18. Clark & Parsia Pellet reasoner. https://www.w3.org/2001/sw/wiki/Pellet
19. OpenStreetMap contributors: Planet dump. https://planet.osm.org. https://www.openstreetmap.org
20. Zheng, L., et al.: MARS: a video benchmark for large-scale person re-identification. In: Leibe, B., Matas, J., Sebe, N., Welling, M. (eds.) ECCV 2016. LNCS, vol. 9910, pp. 868–884. Springer, Cham (2016). https://doi.org/10.1007/978-3-319-46466-4_52

Automatic Fake News Detection with Pre-trained Transformer Models

Mina Schütz[1,2]($\boxtimes$), Alexander Schindler[2], Melanie Siegel[1], and Kawa Nazemi[1]

[1] Darmstadt University for Applied Sciences, 64295 Darmstadt, Germany
{melanie.siegel,kawa.nazemi}@h-da.de
[2] Austrian Institute of Technology GmbH, 1210 Vienna, Austria
{mina.schuetz,alexander.schindler}@ait.ac.at
http://www.h-da.de
http://www.ait.ac.at

Abstract. The automatic detection of disinformation and misinformation has gained attention during the last years, since fake news has a critical impact on democracy, society, and journalism and digital literacy. In this paper, we present a binary content-based classification approach for detecting fake news automatically, with several recently published pre-trained language models based on the Transformer architecture. The experiments were conducted on the FakeNewsNet dataset with XLNet, BERT, RoBERTa, DistilBERT, and ALBERT and various combinations of hyperparameters. Different preprocessing steps were carried out with only using the body text, the titles and a concatenation of both. It is concluded that Transformers are a promising approach to detect fake news, since they achieve notable results, even without using a large dataset. Our main contribution is the enhancement of fake news' detection accuracy through different models and parametrizations with a reproducible result examination through the conducted experiments. The evaluation shows that already short texts are enough to attain 85% accuracy on the test set. Using the body text and a concatenation of both reach up to 87% accuracy. Lastly, we show that various preprocessing steps, such as removing outliers, do not have a significant impact on the models prediction output.

Keywords: Fake news · Fake news detection · Transformer · BERT · Pre-trained language model

1 Introduction

The increased usage of social media and news consumption over the internet has helped in spreading fake news. Therefore, fake news has already had effects on political processes [17]. Even though a clear definition of the term fake news is not yet decided, automatic fake news detection with machine learning techniques can help users to identify signs of deception easier [22]. On the contrary, expert-based fact-checking needs many resources and is time-consuming, therefore it is an important goal to develop automatic machine learning algorithms

© Springer Nature Switzerland AG 2021
A. Del Bimbo et al. (Eds.): ICPR 2020 Workshops, LNCS 12667, pp. 627–641, 2021.
https://doi.org/10.1007/978-3-030-68787-8_45

[11]. For content-based fake news detection, the Transformer models seem to be a promising approach, which were introduced by Vaswani et al. [40]. Research, using transfer learning, has already outperformed methods, based on state-of-the-art results, in numerous NLP downstream tasks [8,18,21,42]. Due to insufficient comparative results, the goal of this work is to show to which extent pre-trained language models are useful for content-based fake news detection and whether they gain promising results in predicting the classification of body texts and titles of news articles.

The paper is structured as follows. In Sect. 2, we give a brief overview of the definition of fake news. Afterwards, in Sect. 3, we discuss the previous work and state-of-the-art language models, followed by the related work in content-based fake news detection via Transformers. Section 4 describes the methodology, data and preprocessing steps. We illustrate the conducted experiments, results and evaluations in Sect. 5 and 6. We conclude our paper with a summary of the main contributions and give suggestions for future work.

2 Fake News

Usually scientific publications differ in definitions for the term fake news [43]. The intention to create such false news pieces has various reasons. On the one hand, there is a financial motive, where people and companies gain revenue through spreading false articles and generating clicks [15]. Intentions can also be malicious, if the news article is only created to hurt one or more individuals, manipulate public opinion, or spread an ideology [33]. Rubin et al. [29] state that fake articles "[...] may be misleading or even harmful, especially when they are disconnected from their original sources and context." However, Mahid et al. [22] defined it narrower: "Fake news is a news articles that is intentionally and verifiable false." This definition is used by several other publications [7,32]. Some studies have broader definitions of fake news, as Sharma et al. [33]: "A news article or message published and propagated through media, carrying false information regardless the means and motives behind it." This definition integrates fabricated as well as misleading content. Depending on intention and factuality there are many similar concepts of news that fall under the fake news definition: Misinformation (unintentional) [3], disinformation (intentional) [5], satire [17], fabrications [15], clickbait [5], hoaxes [29], rumors [24], propaganda [5]. In this work we define fake news as the following: Fake news is an article which propagates a distorted view of the real world regardless of the intention behind it.

3 State-of-the-Art

There are many promising approaches to detect fake news during the last years. Accordingly, the methods vary from simple (e.g. Naïve Bayes) to more complex methods (e.g. CNN, RNN, and LSTM) resulting in a wide range of prediction outcomes. Several surveys have been published, that give an overview over methods, such as social-context based, content-based and knowledge-based as well as hybrid detection approaches [24,26,33,43]. However, when focusing on content-based classification, Transformer-based models were recently introduced, having results exceeding or outperforming in a wide range of research tasks [39]. The pre-trained models can be fine-tuned with a dataset of a specific NLP task, where the available corpora are often small [39]. Additionally, word embeddings are a significant improvement for language modeling [16]. Embeddings create a numeric representation of the input with additional positional embeddings to represent the position of tokens in a sentence [12]. The standard Transformer architecture consists of an encoder and decoder with self-attention, to capture the context of a word in a sentence [39].

3.1 Transformer and Language Models

There have been several language models already been made publicly available. **ELMo** (Embeddings from Language Models) is bilateral and a deep contextualized word representation, developed to improve word embeddings [25] and to predict the next word in a sentence [10]. Also, ELMo uses both encoder and decoder of the Transformer architecture [13]. However, **ULMFiT** (Universal Language Model Fine-Tuning) uses a multi-layered BiLSTM without the attention-mechanism [10]. Howard and Ruder [14] pre-trained ULMFiT on general data and fine-tuned it on a downstream task, which works well with limited labeled data in multiple languages [14]. **GPT** (Generative Pre-Training Transformer) on the other hand is a multi-layered Transformer decoder [10], which is an extension of the architecture of ELMo and ULMFiT without the LSTM model [27]. However, the second GPT model (GPT-2) has more parameters than the original (over 1.5 billion), which was only released with a smaller version of parameters to the public [12]. Recently the third version (GPT-3) was released [4]. **GROVER** is a semi-supervised left-to-right decoder, which is trained on human-written text.

However, **BERT** is one of the latest innovations in machine learning techniques for NLP and was developed by Google in 2019 [8]. The Transformer "[. . .] is designed to pre-train deep bidirectional representations from unlabeled text by jointly conditioning on both left and right context in all layers" [8]. For pre-training, Devlin et al. [8] constructed a dataset that has over 800 million words. BERT only uses the encoder of the Transformer structure [16] and the Word-Piece embedding model, which has around 30,000 tokens in its vocabulary [8]. The embedding is a combination of multiple tokens, so that fewer vocabulary errors occur [28]. Devlin et al. [8] used two pre-training models. The first one is called Masked Language Modeling (MLM). This means that during training 15% of a sentence is not represented by the original tokens and instead replaced with a "[MASK]" token, so that the model can learn the whole context of the sequence [13]. MLM is used because the masked word would see itself during pre-training, due to the bidirectionality of the model [8]. The second pre-training model is called Next Sentence Prediction (NSP), where the model takes a sentence pair as an input [13].

Liu et al. [21] stated that the BERT model is undertrained and therefore created **RoBERTa** (A Robustly Optimized BERT). Their model has been trained on additional data with a longer period of time and dynamic pre-training during MLM. They gained state-of-the-art results in GLUE, RACE, and SQuAD and improved the results of the original BERT [21]. After the release of RoBERTa, the authors of study [18] published "A Lite BERT" (**ALBERT**) version of BERT. They criticized, that the original BERT has limitations regarding the GPU and TPU memory. The training time for the original model is quite long and therefore they set their goal to reduce parameters in BERT. ALBERT gained state-of-the-art results in the following natural language processing tasks: GLUE, RACE and SQuAD. Their results were even better than the before mentioned RoBERTa, despite having less parameters than the original BERT version [18]. The distilled version of BERT (**DistilBERT**) is another newly developed model with a reduction of the original model size by 40%. The model is 60% faster than the original BERT, which makes it cheaper, while still gaining similar results as BERT [30]. However, **XLNet** uses autoregressive language modeling and outperforms BERT on 20 NLP tasks, such as question answering, natural language inference, and sentiment analysis. Yang et al. [42] stated that BERT has problems with the masking in pre-training and fine-tuning and therefore used a different approach to gain better results. They also used two streams for the attention instead of only one [42].

3.2   Related Work

A few studies have rather applied stance detection than classification of fakeness in an article to provide new information about false articles. Jwa et al. [16] focused on the stance between headlines and texts of articles with the FakeNewsChallenge (FNC-1)[1] dataset. Stance detection describes, whether the text is in favor or against a given object. Jwa et al. [16] tested two approaches with BERT. For the first model they only changed the loss function during fine-tuning, whereas for the second model additional news data was gathered for pre-training. Also, Dulhanty et al. [9] used the FNC-1 dataset, but tested it with RoBERTa. Slovikovskaya [37] used the same dataset but added additional data for stance detection. The author used BERT, XLNet and RoBERTa, whereas the latter gained the best result. Similarly to Jwa et al. [16], Soleimani et al. [38] created two BERT models for evidence retrieval and claim verification based on the data of the FEVER[2] challenge. Another approach on the relation between two titles of fake news was proposed by Yang et al. [41]. They used the data by the WSDM 2019 Classification Challenge on Kaggle[3] with titles in Mandarin.

---

[1] https://github.com/FakeNewsChallenge.

[2] https://fever.ai/.

[3] https://www.kaggle.com/c/fake-news-pair-classification-challenge.

Regarding binary classification, Mao and Liu [23] presented an approach on the 2019 FACT challenge[4] with Spanish data. The data was labeled in *fact* and *counterfact*. The authors said, that their model was overfitting, hence they only had an accuracy of 0.622 as a result. Levi et al. [19] studied the differences between titles and body text of fake news and satire with BERT as a model. Rodriguez and Iglesias [28] compared BERT to two other neural networks with a binary fake news classification. They used the Getting Real About Fake News[5] dataset with additional real news articles. However, Aggarwal et al. [1] tested XGboost, CNN, and BERT with the NewsFN dataset, which is very well balanced into fake and real articles. Their best result was 97.021% Accuracy with the BERT-base-uncased version.

Liu et al. [20] did a multi-classification on short statements with BERT and had an accuracy of 41.58% with additional metadata and 34.51% with statements alone. Antoun et al. [2] used XLNet, RoBERTa and BERT with a dataset from the QICC competition[6] for a binary classification of fake news. Their best model (XLNet) gained an F1-score of 98% accuracy. The second task was a news domain detection, split into six classes: Politics, Business, Sports, Entertainment, Technology, and Education. For this task they used several more models than only the Transformers. RoBERTa gained 94% accuracy, whereas a Bi-LSTM with attention had the same result but an overall better performance. The model was based on word embeddings of ELMo. It has to be mentioned though, that the used dataset only contained 432 articles in total. However, Cruz et al. [6] created a dataset for binary fake news classification for the Filipino language. Additionally, they looked into generalizability across different domains, the influence of pre-training on language models and the effect of attention heads on the prediction output. They used ULMFiT, BERT, and GPT-2 for their experiment, whereas GPT-2 gained the best results with multi-tasking attention heads (96.28% accuracy). The study by Schwarz et al. [31] explored embeddings of multi-lingual Transformers as a framework to detect fake news.

4   Methodology

For this work we used the FakeNewsNet [34–36] dataset, which provides news articles that have a binary classification (*fake* or *real*) and is automatically updated. Since this work presents a content-based approach, only the body text and titles from the dataset were used. As a ground truth Shu et al. [34] used the fact-checking websites PolitiFact and GossipCop. In this work the following Transformer models were used for the experiments: BERT, RoBERTa, ALBERT, DistilBERT, and XLNet.

---

[4] https://www.fing.edu.uy/inco/grupos/pln/fact/.
[5] https://www.kaggle.com/mrisdal/fake-news.
[6] https://www.hbku.edu.qa/en/qicc.

4.1   Data Distribution

At the time of downloading the data, the set contained 21,658 news articles. Since in this work the title and body text are needed, all rows, where one of those features was missing, were deleted. After this process the dataset contained 5,053 fake and 15,998 real articles, which are in total 21,041. The mean length of body text was 3408,728 characters, whereas the titles had a length of 59,106. The longest body text in general contained 100,000 and the title 200 characters. The shortest ones 14 (text) and 2 (title). When comparing fake and real body texts it could be observed that the real body texts mean value is about 300 characters longer, whereas the fake titles are about 7 characters longer than real ones. The cleaned dataset was used for the following preprocessing steps and creation of the different files for the experiments.

4.2   Preprocessing

There were different types of preprocessing steps carried out to test, whether the models have different prediction outcomes based on the article length and other factors. The first step was to delete all titles, which were shorter than 20 and longer than 120 characters. Most of the short titles were rather the website names, the articles were published on. Also, the longer titles were often error messages, which the model should not learn the difference of fake and real articles on. This was discovered by going through a sub-sample of titles manually. The same process was used for the body texts, since many short texts were extracted error messages instead of actual content. Therefore, all body texts with more than 10,000 and less than 1,000 characters were deleted. After going through the dataset manually, it stood out that many of the articles that have been labeled as real were transcripts. Transcripts are conversations or interviews, often from politicians and contain mostly spoken word. Since the dataset contains more real articles than fake ones, it could be a problem for the model to distinguish spoken language and written articles. Based on this examination the second preprocessing step was to remove all articles with more than nineteen colons. The transcripts usually started around 20 colons per body text. All articles contained HTML strings, because the dataset was retrieved by a crawler. It stood out that many fake articles contained *[edit]*, which was the only string that was deleted from the dataset, since there are fewer fake articles and the models should not learn the differences between fake and real based only on this. The last preprocessing step included deleting all non-ASCII signs and digits, to see if this makes any difference when evaluating the experiments. Additionally, the newline tags were deleted for all preprocessed files.

In Table 1 all files, with the various preprocessing steps, are shown. They were split in text only, titles only and the concatenation of titles and text. Depending on the preprocessing steps the smallest dataset has a more balanced distribution than the original data: 3,358 fake and 8,586 real articles, which are in total 11,944. The longest text would be 9,919 and shortest 926 characters long. The titles from 20 up to 120 characters.

Table 1. Preprocessed files.

File no.	Type	Length	Transcript	Edit	ASCII/Digits	Dataset size
1	Text	Yes	Yes	Yes	Yes	11,944
2	Text	Yes	Yes	Yes	No	11,944
3	Text	Yes	Yes	No	No	11,944
4	Text	Yes	No	No	No	12,172
5	Text	No	No	No	No	21,041
6	Title	No	No	No	No	21,041
7	Title	Yes	No	No	No	12,172
8	Title	Yes	No	No	Yes	12,172
9	Both	No	No	No	No	21,041
10	Both	Yes	No	No	No	15,355
11	Both	Yes	Yes	No	No	15,103
12	Both	Yes	Yes	Yes	Yes	15,103

The dataset was split in training set (80%) and test set (20%), which was carried out with a stratified split to balance the classes in both sets. During the implementation of the models, the training set was additionally split into training and validation (10% from training). Depending on the file size and preprocessing steps the classes are more or less balanced (less for the largest dataset). Other standard preprocessing methods, such as removing stop words, punctuation, lemmatization and stemming were not carried out, because the Transformer models need all tokens to understand the context of the sentence. Therefore, valuable information goes missing if the words are cut, deleted or the sentence structure is altered.

5 Experiments

The experiments in this work were carried out five different Transformer models with the PyTorch version of the HuggingFace Transformers library[7] on a GeForce

Table 2. Used Transformer models for the experiments.

Model	Layers	Hidden States	Attention Heads	Parameter
BERT-BASE-CASED	12	768	12	110 Million
ROBERTA-BASE	12	768	12	125 Million
ALBERT-BASE-V2	12	768	12	11 Million
XLNET-BASE	12	768	12	110 Million
DISTILBERT-BASE-CASED	6	768	12	65 Million

[7] https://github.com/huggingface/transformers.

GTX TITAN X as GPU. The used models are also shown in Table 2. They all have the same count of layers except DistilBERT, which is the distilled version of the original BERT model and therefore only has 6 layers instead of 12.

The first experiments were conducted with file no. 1, which is completely preprocessed and only contains body text. This was also used to figure out valuable hyperparameters for the following experiments. The batch size and maximum sequence length was used as recommended by Devlin et al. [8]. After testing different batch sizes, learning rates, warm-up steps, epochs and sequence lengths, the best hyperparameters were used for the other experiments. In this work, we tested the experiments with more than the usual maximum of 5 epochs to gain insight, whether the loss curves change with more epochs and influence the prediction outcomes. First, the different preprocessed body text files were run through the BERT-base-cased model, then the files containing only titles and then the combination of titles and body text. After looking at the results of the BERT-model, the same hyperparameters were used for other Transformer models.

6   Results

As mentioned before, the experiments were split in only body text, only titles and a concatenation of titles and text of the articles. Also, the cased models were used with no lower-casing during tokenization. For only body text, documented in Table 3, the highest accuracy gained was 0.87. For each experiment the best model is highlighted in bold. The first experiment however shows that the models do not work well with a high learning rate, when predicting the labels on this dataset. The best results are gained with RoBERTa, however accuracy values with XLNet are similar. The results show that all models have a good prediction with different hyperparemeters.

For comparison reasons, the maximum sequence lengths have not been changed over 512 tokens, even when the model had a higher sequence length available. Additionally, the results (Table 3) show that the different preprocessing steps have no major impact on the prediction. Although file 5, which is not preprocessed at all, gains the best results with all models, the accuracy and loss are not significantly apart from other experiments. This shows that deleting transcripts, which could be a learned bias during training, has no further impact on the outcome of the models.

However, the results of the titles (Table 4) have a lower accuracy result and higher loss than using the body texts. The highest accuracy was 0.85. Again, RoBERTa and XLNet gained the best results, respectively and show the same behavior as with the body texts and preprocessing.

Lastly, in Table 5 the results of the concatenation of titles and body texts are shown. Again, the highest accuracy value is 0.87, but for this type of experiments the best models were DistilBERT and XLNet. The results are only slightly different for each of the models. Also, the preprocessing did not change the predictions significantly. It is notably though, that the experiments gain the overall best results out of the three different types.

Table 3. Body text only - experiment results.

Model	File	Epoch	Batch	LR	Warm-Up	Max Seq	Val Acc	Test Acc	Loss
BERT	1	5	6	5e−5	0	512	0.82	0.83	0.48
ROBERTA	1	5	6	5e−5	0	512	0.76	0.76	0.56
ALBERT	1	5	6	5e−5	0	512	0.75	0.72	0.60
XLNET	1	5	6	5e−5	0	512	0.77	0.81	0.54
DISTILBERT	1	5	6	5e−5	0	512	**0.85**	**0.86**	**0.19**
BERT	1	15	16	2e−5	100	256	0.85	0.86	0.01
ROBERTA	1	15	16	2e−5	100	256	0.86	0.87	0.02
ALBERT	1	15	16	2e−5	100	256	0.83	0.83	0.03
XLNET	1	15	16	2e−5	100	256	**0.86**	**0.87**	**0.01**
DISTILBERT	1	15	16	2e−5	100	256	0.85	0.86	0.01
BERT	1	10	6	2e−5	100	512	0.85	0.86	0.01
ROBERTA	1	10	6	2e−5	100	512	**0.86**	**0.87**	**0.05**
ALBERT	1	10	6	2e−5	100	512	0.82	0.83	0.17
XLNET	1	10	6	2e−5	100	512	0.86	0.85	0.04
DISTILBERT	1	10	6	2e−5	100	512	0.85	0.85	0.02
BERT	1	10	16	2e−5	0	256	0.85	0.85	0.02
ROBERTA	1	10	16	2e−5	0	256	**0.86**	**0.87**	**0.03**
ALBERT	1	10	16	2e−5	0	256	0.82	0.83	0.07
XLNET	1	10	16	2e−5	0	256	0.86	0.85	0.04
DISTILBERT	1	10	16	2e−5	0	256	0.85	0.87	0.02
BERT	2	10	16	2e−5	0	256	0.84	0.85	0.02
ROBERTA	2	10	16	2e−5	0	256	**0.86**	**0.87**	**0.03**
ALBERT	2	10	16	2e−5	0	256	0.82	0.82	0.14
XLNET	2	10	16	2e−5	0	256	0.86	0.86	0.03
DISTILBERT	2	10	16	2e−5	0	256	0.86	0.85	0.02
BERT	2	10	6	2e−5	0	512	0.85	0.87	0.02
ROBERTA	2	10	6	2e−5	0	512	**0.86**	**0.87**	**0.05**
ALBERT	2	10	6	1e−5	0	512	0.83	0.84	0.08
XLNET	2	10	6	2e−5	0	512	0.83	0.85	0.08
DISTILBERT	2	10	6	2e−5	0	512	0.86	0.85	0.02
BERT	4	10	16	2e−5	0	256	0.84	0.86	0.02
ROBERTA	4	10	16	2e−5	0	256	0.87	0.87	0.04
ALBERT	4	10	16	2e−5	0	256	0.83	0.83	0.08
XLNET	4	10	16	2e−5	0	256	**0.87**	**0.87**	**0.03**
DISTILBERT	4	10	16	2e−5	0	256	0.86	0.85	0.02
BERT	5	10	16	2e−5	0	256	0.87	0.86	0.08
ROBERTA	5	10	16	2e−5	0	256	**0.88**	**0.87**	**0.10**
ALBERT	5	10	16	2e−5	0	256	0.85	0.84	0.17
XLNET	5	10	16	2e−5	0	256	0.87	0.86	0.09
DISTILBERT	5	10	16	2e−5	0	256	0.86	0.86	0.09
BERT	1	10	16	2e−5	0	256	0.87	0.86	0.08
ROBERTA	1	10	16	2e−5	50	256	**0.86**	**0.87**	**0.04**
ALBERT	1	10	16	2e−5	50	256	0.82	0.83	0.05
XLNET	1	10	16	2e−5	50	256	0.86	0.86	0.02
DISTILBERT	1	10	16	2e−5	50	256	0.84	0.85	0.02

Table 4. Title only - experiment results.

Model	File	Epoch	Batch	LR	Warm-up	Max Seq	Val Acc	Test Acc	Loss
BERT	6	5	32	2e−5	0	128	0.84	0.83	0.15
ROBERTA	6	5	32	2e−5	0	128	0.84	0.85	0.26
ALBERT	6	5	32	2e−5	0	128	0.82	0.82	0.01
XLNET	6	5	32	2e−5	0	128	**0.85**	**0.85**	**0.02**
DISTILBERT	6	5	32	2e−5	0	128	0.84	0.84	0.17
BERT	7	5	32	2e−5	0	128	0.84	0.84	0.11
ROBERTA	7	5	32	2e−5	0	128	**0.85**	**0.85**	**0.25**
ALBERT	7	5	32	2e−5	0	128	0.81	0.81	0.20
XLNET	7	5	32	2e−5	0	128	0.84	0.83	0.26
DISTILBERT	7	5	32	2e−5	0	128	0.83	0.85	0.16
BERT	8	5	32	2e−5	0	128	0.83	0.83	0.10
ROBERTA	8	5	32	2e−5	0	128	**0.86**	**0.85**	**0.26**
ALBERT	8	5	32	2e−5	0	128	0.82	0.81	0.18
XLNET	8	5	32	2e−5	0	128	0.83	0.84	0.23
DISTILBERT	8	5	32	2e−5	0	128	0.83	0.83	0.16
BERT	6	10	32	2e−5	0	128	0.84	0.84	0.08
ROBERTA	6	10	32	2e−5	0	128	**0.84**	**0.85**	**0.16**
ALBERT	6	10	32	2e−5	0	128	0.81	0.81	0.08
XLNET	6	10	32	2e−5	0	128	0.85	0.84	0.23
DISTILBERT	6	10	32	2e−5	0	128	0.84	0.84	0.09
BERT	6	30	32	2e−5	0	128	0.84	0.83	0.07
ROBERTA	6	30	32	2e−5	0	128	0.85	0.85	0.08
ALBERT	6	30	32	2e−5	0	128	0.82	0.81	0.06
XLNET	6	30	32	2e−5	0	128	**0.85**	**0.85**	**0.07**
DISTILBERT	6	30	32	2e−5	0	128	0.84	0.85	0.06

To compare these results, we applied some of the methods, which were used in the original paper. The authors of the dataset [34] split the data in PolitiFact and GossipCop articles separately. The best result was 0.723 accuracy with a CNN for GossipCop articles and 0.642 accuracy for PolitiFact with Logistic Regression. For our evaluation we used Gaussian Naive Bayes, Support Vector Machine and Logistic Regression with One Hot Encoding and the default parameters of ScikitLearn, as the original paper has done. We used our former preprocessed files for both types, because we also had to apply standard preprocessing, such as: stemming, lemmatization, removing stop-words and punctuation.

As shown in Table 6, the standard supervised methods seem to have problems with either false positive (FP) or false negative (FN) classification results. The only model that has results closely to the Transformer models are the SVM and LR, but seem to train only on one class. On the contrary it can be seen that

Table 5. Title and body text - experiment results.

Model	File	Epoch	Batch	LR	Warm-up	Max Seq	Val Acc	Test Acc	Loss
BERT	9	10	16	2e−5	0	256	0.87	0.87	0.07
ROBERTA	9	10	16	2e−5	0	256	0.88	0.87	0.09
ALBERT	9	10	16	2e−5	0	256	0.86	0.85	0.10
XLNET	9	10	16	2e−5	0	256	0.87	0.86	0.09
DISTILBERT	9	10	16	2e−5	0	256	**0.87**	**0.87**	**0.08**
BERT	10	10	16	2e−5	0	256	0.87	0.86	0.08
ROBERTA	10	10	16	2e−5	0	256	0.87	0.87	0.09
ALBERT	10	10	16	2e−5	0	256	0.84	0.85	0.09
XLNET	10	10	16	2e−5	0	256	**0.87**	**0.87**	**0.08**
DISTILBERT	10	10	16	2e−5	0	256	0.86	0.86	0.08
BERT	11	10	16	2e−5	0	256	0.87	0.86	0.09
ROBERTA	11	10	16	2e−5	0	256	0.86	0.87	0.09
ALBERT	11	10	16	2e−5	0	256	0.83	0.82	0.13
XLNET	11	10	16	2e−5	0	256	**0.87**	**0.87**	**0.09**
DISTILBERT	11	10	16	2e−5	0	256	0.86	0.86	0.08
BERT	13	10	16	2e−5	0	256	0.87	0.86	0.08
ROBERTA	13	10	16	2e−5	0	256	0.87	0.87	0.10
ALBERT	13	10	16	2e−5	0	256	0.85	0.84	0.09
XLNET	13	10	16	2e−5	0	256	0.87	0.86	0.09
DISTILBERT	13	10	16	2e−5	0	256	**0.87**	**0.86**	**0.08**

Table 6. Comparison of transformer models against a baseline.

Model	File	Type	Accuracy	TN	FP	FN	TP
NB	1	Text	0.299	89	1628	45	627
SVM	1	Text	0.713	1688	29	656	16
LR	1	Text	0.718	1716	1	671	1
XLNET	1	Text	0.86	**1572**	**145**	**201**	**471**
NB	8	Title	0.297	77	1678	32	648
SVM	8	Title	0.707	1711	44	669	11
LR	8	Title	0.720	1753	2	679	1
ROBERTA	8	Title	0.85	**1598**	**157**	**222**	**458**

two experiments[8] with the Transformer models have a more balanced confusion matrix, even though one class has more articles in the dataset. This shows, that those models gain better results overall.

---

[8] XLNet - epochs: 5, batch: 32, LR: 2e−5, warm-up: 0, max seq: 128/RoBERTa: epochs: 10, batch: 6, LR: 2e−5, warm-up: 0, max seq: 512.

Table 7. Sensitivity specific metrics for all models.

Model	File	Type	Precision	Recall	F1
BERT	1	Text	0.84	0.81	0.81
RoBERTa	1	Text	**0.84**	**0.82**	**0.82**
ALBERT	1	Text	0.79	0.78	0.77
DISTILBERT	1	Text	0.84	0.81	0.81
XLNET	1	Text	0.83	0.80	0.80
NB	1	Text	0.47	0.49	0.42
SVM	1	Text	0.53	0.50	0.04
LR	1	Text	0.60	0.50	0.002

Lastly, in Table 7 sensitivity metrics are compared with one experiment on the body text[9]. For each metric the macro-average was chosen, regarding the imbalance of the classes, which shows that Transformers are a better solution for this dataset.

7   Conclusion and Future Work

The results of this work show that a content-based approach can gain promising results for detecting fake news, even without setting hand-engineered features and only titles. Although, literature has shown that some approaches still have better results than the Transformer models. The results of this work are comparable with the current state-of-the-art fake news detection approaches, especially in the field of the newly invented Transformer architectures. Almost all experiments, after the fine-tuning of the hyperparameters, had results over 80% accuracy in the validation and test set without overfitting the data. Therefore, this work shows that Transformer models can also detect fake news based on short statements as well as complete articles. Fake news detection is still underrepresented in the research process. Especially automatic detection, without human intervention, is an open research issue. An important factor for further research is to explore methods of explainable artificial intelligence, to help understanding the difference in fake news concepts and to gain insights into the models and which words have to highest impact to predict the fake and real classes as well as the high accuracy for short titles of news articles and the influence of removing spoken language.

Acknowledgments. This is a revised and enhanced work based on a masterthesis conducted at the Darmstadt University of Applied Sciences in collaboration with the Austrian Institute of Technology (AIT). The Darmstadt University supported this work with the research in Information Science (https://sis.h-da.de/) and the Research Group on Human-Computer Interaction and Visual Analytics (https://vis.h-da.de/).

---

[9] Hyperparameters - epochs: 10, batch size: 16, LR: 2e−5, warm-up: 0, max. seq: 256.

References

1. Aggarwal, A., Chauhan, A., Kumar, D., Mittal, M., Verma, S.: Classification of fake news by fine-tuning deep bidirectional transformers based language model. EAI Endorsed Trans. Scalable Inf. Syst. Online First (2020). https://doi.org/10.4108/eai.13-7-2018.163973
2. Antoun, W., Baly, F., Achour, R., Hussein, A., Hajj, H.: State of the art models for fake news detection tasks. In: 2020 IEEE International Conference on Informatics, IoT, and Enabling Technologies (ICIoT), pp. 519–524 (2020)
3. Bara, G., Backfried, G., Thomas-Aniola, D.: Fake or fact? Theoretical and practical aspects of fake news. In: Bossé, É., Rogova, G.L. (eds.) Information Quality in Information Fusion and Decision Making. IFDS, pp. 181–206. Springer, Cham (2019). https://doi.org/10.1007/978-3-030-03643-0_9
4. Brown, T.B., et al.: Language models are few-shot learners (2020)
5. Campan, A., Cuzzocrea, A., Truta, T.M.: Fighting fake news spread in online social networks: actual trends and future research directions. In: 2017 IEEE International Conference on Big Data (Big Data), pp. 4453–4457 (2017)
6. Cruz, J.C.B., Tan, J.A., Cheng, C.: Localization of fake news detection via multi-task transfer learning. In: Proceedings of The 12th Language Resources and Evaluation Conference, pp. 2596–2604. European Language Resources Association, Marseille, France, May 2020. https://www.aclweb.org/anthology/2020.lrec-1.316
7. Della Vedova, M.L., Tacchini, E., Moret, S., Ballarin, G., DiPierro, M., de Alfaro, L.: Automatic online fake news detection combining content and social signals. In: 2018 22nd Conference of Open Innovations Association (FRUCT), pp. 272–279 (2018)
8. Devlin, J., Chang, M.W., Lee, K., Toutanova, K.: BERT: pre-training of deep bidirectional transformers for language understanding. In: Proceedings of the 2019 Conference of the North American Chapter of the Association for Computational Linguistics: Human Language Technologies, Volume 1 (Long and Short Papers), pp. 4171–4186. Association for Computational Linguistics, Minneapolis, Minnesota, June 2019. https://doi.org/10.18653/v1/N19-1423. https://www.aclweb.org/anthology/N19-1423
9. Dulhanty, C., Deglint, J.L., Daya, I.B., Wong, A.: Taking a stance on fake news: towards automatic disinformation assessment via deep bidirectional transformer language models for stance detection (2019)
10. Ghelanie, S.: From word embeddings to pretrained language models - a new age in NLP - part 2 (2019). https://towardsdatascience.com/from-word-embeddings-to-pretrained-language-models-a-new-age-in-nlp-part-2-e9af9a0bdcd9?gi=bf1f5e22e8e4. Accessed 03 Mar 2020
11. Graves, L.: Understanding the promise and limits of automated fact-checking, February 2018
12. Géron, A.: Hands-on Machine Learning with Scikit-Learn, Keras, and Tensorflow, 2nd edn. O'Reilly Media Inc. (2019)
13. Horev, R.: Bert explained: state of the art language model for NLP, November 2018. https://towardsdatascience.com/bert-explained-state-of-the-art-language-model-for-nlp-f8b21a9b6270. Accessed 05 Nov 2019
14. Howard, J., Ruder, S.: Universal language model fine-tuning for text classification. In: Proceedings of the 56th Annual Meeting of the Association for Computational Linguistics (Volume 1: Long Papers), pp. 328–339. Association for Computational Linguistics, Melbourne, Australia, July 2018. https://doi.org/10.18653/v1/P18-1031. https://www.aclweb.org/anthology/P18-1031

15. Tandoc Jr., E.C., Lim, Z.W., Ling, R.: Defining "fake news". Digit. J. **6**(2), 137–153 (2017). https://doi.org/10.1080/21670811.2017.1360143

16. Jwa, H., Oh, D., Park, K., Kang, J., Lim, H.: exBAKE: automatic fake news detection model based on bidirectional encoder representations from transformers (BERT). Appl. Sci. **9**(19), 4062 (2019). https://doi.org/10.3390/app9194062

17. Khan, S.A., Alkawaz, M.H., Zangana, H.M.: The use and abuse of social media for spreading fake news. In: 2019 IEEE International Conference on Automatic Control and Intelligent Systems (I2CACIS), pp. 145–148 (2019)

18. Lan, Z., Chen, M., Goodman, S., Gimpel, K., Sharma, P., Soricut, R.: ALBERT: a lite BERT for self-supervised learning of language representations (2019)

19. Levi, O., Hosseini, P., Diab, M., Broniatowski, D.: Identifying nuances in fake news vs. satire: using semantic and linguistic cues. In: Proceedings of the Second Workshop on Natural Language Processing for Internet Freedom: Censorship, Disinformation, and Propaganda (2019). https://doi.org/10.18653/v1/d19-5004

20. Liu, C., et al.: A two-stage model based on BERT for short fake news detection. In: Douligeris, C., Karagiannis, D., Apostolou, D. (eds.) KSEM 2019. LNCS (LNAI), vol. 11776, pp. 172–183. Springer, Cham (2019). https://doi.org/10.1007/978-3-030-29563-9_17

21. Liu, Y., et al.: Roberta: a robustly optimized BERT pretraining approach (2019)

22. Mahid, Z.I., Manickam, S., Karuppayah, S.: Fake news on social media: brief review on detection techniques. In: 2018 Fourth International Conference on Advances in Computing, Communication Automation (ICACCA), pp. 1–5 (2018)

23. Mao, J., Liu, W.: Factuality classification using the pre-trained language representation model BERT. In: IberLEF@SEPLN (2019)

24. Oshikawa, R., Qian, J., Wang, W.Y.: A survey on natural language processing for fake news detection (2018)

25. Peters, M.E., et al.: Deep contextualized word representations (2018)

26. Rana, D.P., Agarwal, I., More, A.: A review of techniques to combat the peril of fake news. In: 2018 4th International Conference on Computing Communication and Automation (ICCCA), pp. 1–7 (2018)

27. Rizvi, M.S.Z.: Demystifying BERT: a comprehensive guide to the groundbreaking NLP framework, September 2019. https://www.analyticsvidhya.com/blog/2019/09/demystifying-bert-groundbreaking-nlp-framework/. Accessed 05 Nov 2019

28. Rodríguez, À.I., Iglesias, L.L.: Fake news detection using deep learning (2019)

29. Rubin, V.L., Chen, Y., Conroy, N.J.: Deception detection for news: three types of fakes. In: Proceedings of the 78th ASIS&T Annual Meeting: Information Science with Impact: Research in and for the Community, ASIST 2015. American Society for Information Science, USA (2015). https://doi.org/10.5555/2857070.2857153

30. Sanh, V., Debut, L., Chaumond, J., Wolf, T.: Distilbert, a distilled version of BERT: smaller, faster, cheaper and lighter (2019)

31. Schwarz, S., Theóphilo, A., Rocha, A.: EMET: embeddings from multilingual-encoder transformer for fake news detection. In: 2020 IEEE International Conference on Acoustics, Speech and Signal Processing (ICASSP), ICASSP 2020, pp. 2777–2781 (2020)

32. Shabani, S., Sokhn, M.: Hybrid machine-crowd approach for fake news detection. In: 2018 IEEE 4th International Conference on Collaboration and Internet Computing (CIC), pp. 299–306 (2018)

33. Sharma, K., Qian, F., Jiang, H., Ruchansky, N., Zhang, M., Liu, Y.: Combating fake news: a survey on identification and mitigation techniques. ACM Trans. Intell. Syst. Technol. **37**(4) (2019)

34. Shu, K., Mahudeswaran, D., Wang, S., Lee, D., Liu, H.: FakeNewsNet: a data repository with news content, social context and spatialtemporal information for studying fake news on social media (2018)
35. Shu, K., Sliva, A., Wang, S., Tang, J., Liu, H.: Fake news detection on social media: a data mining perspective. ACM SIGKDD Explor. Newsl. **19**(1), 22–36 (2017)
36. Shu, K., Wang, S., Liu, H.: Exploiting tri-relationship for fake news detection. arXiv preprint arXiv:1712.07709 (2017)
37. Slovikovskaya, V.: Transfer learning from transformers to fake news challenge stance detection (FNC-1) task (2019)
38. Soleimani, A., Monz, C., Worring, M.: Bert for evidence retrieval and claim verification (2019)
39. Uszkoreit, J.: Transformer: a novel neural network architecture for language understanding, August 2017. https://ai.google-blog.com/2017/08/transformer-novel-neural-network.html. Accessed 01 Dec 2019
40. Vaswani, A., et al.: Attention is all you need. In: Guyon, I., et al. (eds.) Advances in Neural Information Processing Systems 30, pp. 5998–6008. Curran Associates, Inc. (2017). http://papers.nips.cc/paper/7181-attention-is-all-you-need.pdf
41. Yang, K.C., Niven, T., Kao, H.Y.: Fake news detection as natural language inference (2019)
42. Yang, Z., Dai, Z., Yang, Y., Carbonell, J., Salakhutdinov, R., Le, Q.V.: XLNET: generalized autoregressive pretraining for language understanding (2019)
43. Zhou, X., Zafarani, R.: A survey of fake news: fundamental theories, detection methods, and opportunities. ACM Comput. Surve. (2020). https://doi.org/10.1145/3395046

A Serverless Architecture for a Wearable Face Recognition Application

Oliviu Matei[1,2]([envelope]) [ORCID], Rudolf Erdei[2], Alexandru Moga[2], and Robert Heb[2]

[1] Technical University of Cluj-Napoca, North University Centre of Baia Mare, Baia Mare, Romania
oliviu.matei@cunbm.utcluj.ro
[2] HOLISUN SRL, Baia Mare, Romania
{rudolf.erdei,alexandru.moga,robert.heb}@holisun.com

Abstract. This article presents an application for face recognition, which takes its video input streamed from smart glasses through an internet connection. The application resides in the cloud and uses serverless technologies. The system has been tested on a database of 1119 individuals and the results show that the classical serverfull architecture is from 1.9 to 8.65 times slower than the serverless method. The advantage of the application resides in its high adaptability, parallelisation and scalability.

Keywords: Augmented Reality · Face recognition · Serverless computing · Serverless architecture

1 Introduction

In the military world, Augmented Reality (AR) has been adopted mainly for training purposes, but recently, due to the advances in the hardware and also software parts, it's starting to be considered for some use cases on the battle field as well. AR can be used for training soldiers in a wider range of combat situations or dangerous settings, as it enables the re-creation and testing of various scenarios without any risk of death or injury. Moreover, it's also cheaper than other traditional methods of military training.

Face recognition is a classic and straightforward application of AR for authorities (emergency responders, security forces) but also for the military and defense industry. From the perspective of an AR program, each recognized entity is nothing more than a unique marker that is shown on the display, so the potential uses for facial recognition combined with AR are already being explored in the research and exploitation fields.

The military has shown interest in any techniques which avoid life risk. Back in 2002, Livingston et al. [15] conclude that many future military operations would occur in urban environments and propose for training and mission management a system based on AR - BARS, consisting of a wearable computer, a wireless network system, and a tracked see-through head-mounted display. They considered as an important step the design and development of a user interface

© Springer Nature Switzerland AG 2021
A. Del Bimbo et al. (Eds.): ICPR 2020 Workshops, LNCS 12667, pp. 642–655, 2021.
https://doi.org/10.1007/978-3-030-68787-8_46

capable of displaying data and processing user inputs. The second step implies the collaboration between the individual BARS systems and users.

Livingston et al. [14] review military benefits and requirements that have led to a series of research efforts in AR and related systems for the military. They consider two components as cornerstones of AR: user interface and human factors.

LaViola et al. [13] examine the use of an AR based adaptive tutoring system for instructing in the wild, in locations where no formal training infrastructure is present, and identify the challenges that arise when developing such a system.

Amaguaña et al. [1] propose an AR system that was developed in Unity-Vuforia. The system simulates a war environment using three-dimensional objects and audiovisual resources to create a real war conflict. The system allows the user to interact with the physical field and the digital objects through virtual controls.

Mitaritonna and Abásolo [19] present the state of art of military systems using AR in the battlefield. One of the main applications identified by the authors is face recognition. However, the current wearable hardware is not capable of doing such complex operations, therefore the video stream needs to be sent further to a central system with enough computational resources to process the video stream and analyse faces.

Ao et al. [2] propose Sprocket, which is a highly configurable, stage-based, scalable, serverless video processing framework that exploits intra-video parallelism to achieve low latency. Sprocket runs on the AWS Lambda[1] serverless cloud infrastructure.

Zhang et al. [23] explore the configuration and implementation schemes of typical video processing functions that are deployed to the serverless platforms. With the gathered data, they and quantify influence on two metrics: execution duration and monetary cost from a developer's perspective.

The current article continues with the requirements of the system in Sect. 2. We capture both functional (Sect. 2.2) and non-functional requirements (Sect. 2.3). Further, Sect. 3 presents the architectural aspects of the system from various perspectives, such as the serverless components (Sect. 3.1), the sequence diagram in Sect. 3.2, respectively the communication modes in Sect. 3.2. The experiments are detailed in Sect. 4 and the conclusions are drawn in Sect. 5.

2   Requirements

The requirements have been defined during several brainstorming sessions [22] with relevant stakeholders, which allowed them to explore various possibilities as well as fully analyze their pros and cons from a user of the system perspective.

In this project, many brainstorming sessions have been used as they generate lots of ideas and allow the integration of various views [12] into the final product. A leader is needed for running the brainstorming session and mitigating the

---

[1] https://aws.amazon.com/lambda/.

various biases and possible conflicts in the group. Every idea is documented such that everyone can see it and potentially build upon it. Finally, a document is prepared comprising the list of requirements and their priority, if it is the case.

The ideas generated by various stakeholders need to be:

- aggregated;
- resolved from conflicting points of views;
- made consistent.

During all these phases, the facilitator has to have in mind the requirements for the application.

2.1   Overview of the AR Face Recognition System Components

The complete Face Recognition consists of three main components that work together in order to provide a complete and seamless service [11]:

- The AR Assistance Client Application - this component will operate on smart glasses, mobile phones or other computing devices;
- The Cloud Platform - a central processing cloud unit, equipped with Melodic, a platform that enables the configuration and deployment of serverless components;
- A Faces source/database - a searchable/queryable source of information about the faces detected in the serverless components.

All these components must coexist at the same time and be configurable, so that the component stack will function correctly and optimally. Entity information about the detected faces must exist in at least one of the connected datasources, in order for the service to return a non-null response.

2.2   Functional Requirements

The functional requirements are structured based on their high-level functionality (e.g. streaming, face recognition, file transfer, recordings, snapshots etc.). Each high-level functionality is split in atomic requirements needed for professional development, testing and validation.

The functional requirements are prioritized based on MoSCoW method [3], which assumes that all requirements are important, but they are prioritized to deliver the most important benefits in terms of value, features and impact. A MoSCoW list has the priorities, namely: Must have, Should have, Could have (and the optional Won't have) requirements but the Should and Could requirements will be the first to be removed from the list if the delivery timescale looks threatened.

The requirements are prioritized according to Tables 1 and 2. The Must requirements are absolutely needed for having a Minimum Viable Product (MVP) or for validating the Melodic platform. The Should requirements are of second priority and are suitable for testing the performance of the Melodic platform and are a step forward into developing a final functional product. The Could requirements are needed for stress tests of the Melodic platform. The Won't requirements will not be implemented because either do not bring added value for validating the Melodic platform, nor are they desired by beneficiaries (e.g. because of security issues - see REQ-7.4).

Table 1. Prioritization of the functional requirements

Req. no.	Requirement specification	Priority level	Rationale
REQ-1.1	Audio streaming	Could	The audio component is not processed by serverless components, but accompanies the video stream in most cases
REQ-1.2	Video streaming	Must	The video stream is, actually, the main object of the whole processing line of the business case
REQ-1.3	Video frame resolution and fps is adjusted automatically based on the bandwidth	Should	It is important for a good quality stream, however, it does not interfere with the stream processing
REQ-2.1	Can detect faces	Must	It is one of the most important requirements and a main functionality
REQ-2.2	Can recognize previously detected faces from an image against various data source	Should	The requirement would prove the quality of the business case for validating the serverless framework
REQ-2.3	The data sources related to faces may vary and can be connected independently to the cloud platform	Could	This is not important for proving the capabilities of the platform, but it might be for having a sound business case
REQ-3.1	A file can be transferred through AR Assistance system	Must	This functionality allows the face recognition to be performed from more sources
REQ-2.4	The system can return meta-data about the recognized face, along with a snapshot containing the detected face	Must	This is the result of the face recognition that will be presented to the user of the system

Table 2. Prioritization of the functional requirements (cont.)

Req. no.	Requirement specification	Priority level	Rationale
REQ-4.1	Snapshots can be performed on a time base	Should	This allows fine tuning of the process and determining the limits of the serverless platform
REQ-4.2	Snapshots are performed automatically by AR Assistance	Must	The snapshots are, actually, frames captured from the stream and constitute the working elements for the serverless component to be analyzed for faces
REQ-4.3	The frequency of the snapshots is adjustable	Could	This allows fine tuning of the process and determining the limits of the serverless platform
REQ-4.4	The snapshots can be forwarded for face recognition	Must	The snapshots are, actually, frames from the video stream and constitute the elements to be analyzed for faces
REQ-5.1	The recording can be stored at a specified location	Should	For backup reasons, the complete stream can be uploaded to a remote server
REQ-5.2	The format of the recording will be chosen so the file size will be as small as possible, preserving resolution and quality, so that the important features will be visible	Could	This would allow the application to be used ubiquitously and seamlessly, even in low internet connectivity areas
REQ-6.1	More than one streams can be processed in parallel	Must	More streams can make the processing even more intensive
REQ-6.2	The maximum number of video streams can be configurable	Could	This allows to determine the limits of serverless platform in specific cases
REQ-7.1	User management by an admin	Must	Needed for the next requirement
REQ-7.2	Authentication of the users	Must	For security reasons, including data protection
REQ-7.3	User profile management	Could	The user profile can be managed also by the admin, who supervises the whole system

2.3   Nonfunctional Requirements

This section presents the non-functional requirements, namely the external interface requirements, the expected performances and the data storage needs in section.

External Interface Requirements. These requirements refer to all hardware and software components used by the business case application.

AR Assistance must run on the following systems and devices:

- ODG R7 HL on Reticle OS, based on Android;
- Epson Moverio BT-300 on Android 5.1;
- Linux and Windows on notebooks;
- Apple mobile phones (6S+) with iOS installed.

AR Assistance should interoperate with the following browsers:

- Desktop PC: Microsoft Edge 12+, Google Chrome 28+, Mozilla Firefox 22+, Safari 11+, Opera 18+, and Vivaldi 1.9+;
- Android: Google Chrome 28+ (enabled by default since 29), Mozilla Firefox 24+, and Opera Mobile 12+.

AR Assistance should inter-operate on the following operating systems: Chrome OS, Firefox OS, Blackberry 10, iOS 11: Mobile Safari/WebKit and Tizen 3.0.

Performance Requirements. The business case software should comply with the performance requirements in Table 3.

Table 3. Performance requirements

Performance	Min	Max
Face recognition time	–	10 s
Number of stream sources	–	5
Reliability, Availability	0,9997	–
Bandwidth	1 MBs	–
Face databases	1	–
Scalability (concurrent streams)	–	10
Scalability (data sources)	–	5

Data Storage Requirements. The system must store at least the figures in Table 4. The data stored in the database refers mostly to metadata related to faces and the corresponding personal information.

Table 4. Data storage requirements

Parameter	Minimum	Maximum
File count	500	5000
File size	50 MB	2,5 GB
Stream count	200	2500
Stream size	360 MB	36. B

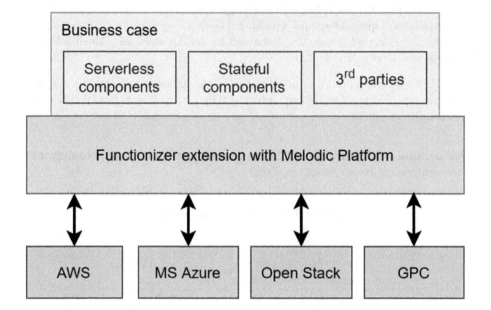

Fig. 1. The software stack of AR Assistance

3   AR Assistance Architecture

The software stack constituting the operating environment for this application is presented in Fig. 1.

3.1   Serverless Architecture

The image/face recognition related modules are very complex, therefore we present only the second level decomposition of AR Assistance architecture related to them [18]. This architecture is depicted in Fig. 2.

The colours of the components have the following meaning:

- The gray components represent the clients (dark grey is the web client and the light grey depicts the wearable client).
- The green components are already serverfull components.

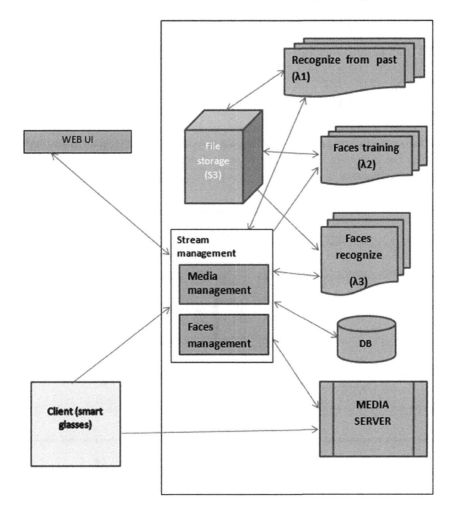

Fig. 2. The serverless architecture of the application

– The ochre components represent cloud side components.

  The architecture consists of:

– 1st tier (the client)
– 2nd tier (the business logic) consisting of:

• Serverful components are deployed in the cloud and refer to:

  * Stream management
  * server (Kurento Media Server [5])
  * Database (DB) (Maria DB)

- Serverless components:
  * 3 lambda functions: Recognize from past, Faces training and Faces recognize
  * 3rd party component for file storage (e.g. Amazon S3 service).

3.2 Sequence Diagram

The sequence diagram for AR Assistance is depicted in Fig. 3. The red life lines are serverfull components (belonging to components living indeterminable), whereas the green life lines belong to serverless components that usually have a very short life-span.

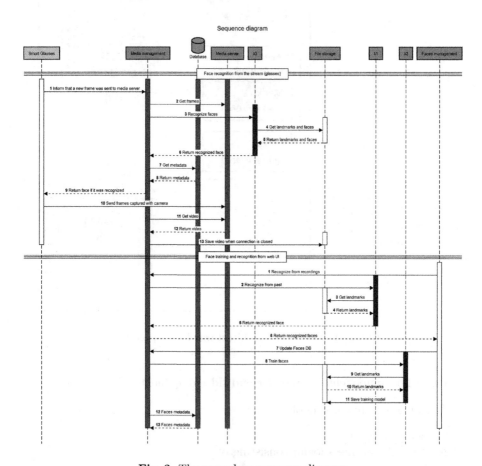

Fig. 3. The serverless sequence diagram

The sequence diagram depicted in Fig. 3 has two lines - online (from the wearable client) and off-line (from the web client), split with a horizontal bar. All use cases start from the client - web for training, respectively wearable for production.

- The wearable client connects to media manager and establishes a communication session. In turn, media manager captures the frames from the Media Server (which is connected to the wearable via WebRTC [9]) and transfers them to λ_3 (for face recognition), which returns the metadata of the recognized person (if it is the case) to Media Manager and from there to the client. For face recognition, λ_3 uses the images stored in File Storage.
- In the same time, the video stream is stored for further detailed processing and historical augmentation.
- Offline, the face recognition can be run on stored and uploaded videos. The action is initiated from the web client.
- However, the face recognition algorithm needs to be trained for running properly. This sequence has been depicted as last one because it is less important in the economy of the application (as it runs less than the former ones).

Communication Modes. The underlying communication mechanisms of the sequence diagram in Fig. 3 are depicted in Fig. 4. The client invokes the 2nd tier by socket connections. The serverless components are called using a specific protocol with an SDK specific for each cloud.

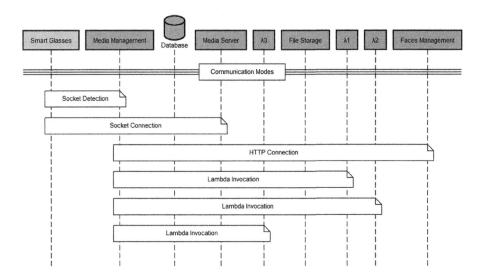

Fig. 4. The communication modes of the serverless approach

AWS Lambda supports synchronous and asynchronous invocation of a Lambda function, called *on-demand invocation* [10]. When the AWS service is used as a trigger, the invocation type is predetermined for each service.

4 Experimental Setup

The system has been tested on various subsets of 14126 images pertaining to 1119 individuals, meaning an average of 12.62 images per person. The benchmark data is from **FERET database** [21]. The FERET database has been used by more than 460 research groups and is managed by the National Institute of Standards and Technology [8]. Please note that the research is focused on comparing the serverless with serverfull architectural approaches on the specific application of face recognition, rather than comparing our recognition methods with existing ones. We are not comparing the recognition rate of the algorithm, so no such data is going to be presented here. In fact, we used the same algorithm for both variants of the system (serverfull and serverless).

We tested the system with four sets of benchmark databases, containing between 250 and the full 1119 individuals. We ran multiple face recognitions on real people in real situations, like:

- Walking (with smart glasses) through a busy company with lots of people passing by, realistic movement and realistic lighting scenarios (fluorescent, LED lighting);
- Walking (with smart glasses) outside buildings, in a populated area, also in various lighting scenarios (sunny, overcast, shade, sunset) that also included high-contrast scenarios;
- Running various previously recorded videos through the face recognition variant (uploadable by web browser) and exporting the detected faces list.

The serverfull approach has been in all cases slower than the serverless architecture because of the high capacity of the latter to parallelize the process and the lack of the large overhead that comes with a classic serverfull approach. Table 5 depicts the size of the benchmarks as number of individuals and the time latency of the serverfull algorithm with respect to the serverless method. Actually, the serverfull approach is between 1.9 and 8.65 s slower than the serverless technique, which can mean a great improvement in terms of resources consumption, parallel requests to the system and lastly but most importantly, the total time needed to get a positive match (time that can be a critical aspect in many scenarios).

Table 5. Serverless vs serverfull face recognition execution times

Benchmark size (individuals)	Time latency
250	1.9
500	3.95
1000	7.8
1119	8.65

5   Conclusions

Based on our research, the advantages of serverless approach consist of:

- The Serverless approach can be more cost effective than renting full underused servers. There is significant research on optimizing the cost function in multi-cloud deployment [6,7,16] which will translate into even better efficiency in the future.
- Serverless architectures are very flexible and very scalable as they use only the needed resources, no extra resources being allocated apriori.
- Serverless components are architecturally simpler and the developer does not have to worry about multi-threading or directly handling HTTP requests in their code.
- The Serverless paradigm is very suitable especially in the context of IoT (Internet of Things) [17,20].

In our tests, the serverless approach was at least two-times more efficient for this application. In the field, this aspect would translate in lower exploitation costs, higher response rate, more clients served at the same time (with the same operational costs), or even the ability to run more complex algorithms that will improve false positive responses.

5.1   Further Developments

The serverless architecture is stable and very scalable, and the results are quite good (but not yet perfect or usable, from a military point of view). However, a reduction of the computation time is needed if the application is to be used in real life scenarios. This can be done either by optimizing the matching algorithm for face recognition (a solution which is highly dependable on the algorithm) or to shift the computational effort partially from the cloud to other nodes, like in the edge-fog-cloud computing paradigm [4].

Acknowledgement. This work has received funding from the Functionizer Eurostars project and the EUs Horizon 2020 research and innovation programme under Grant Agreement No. 731664.

References

1. Amaguaña, F., Collaguazo, B., Tituaña, J., Aguilar, W.G.: Simulation system based on augmented reality for optimization of training tactics on military operations. In: De Paolis, L.T., Bourdot, P. (eds.) AVR 2018. LNCS, vol. 10850, pp. 394–403. Springer, Cham (2018). https://doi.org/10.1007/978-3-319-95270-3_33
2. Ao, L., et al.: Sprocket: a serverless video processing framework. In: Proceedings of the ACM Symposium on Cloud Computing (2018)
3. Bebensee, T., van de Weerd, I., Brinkkemper, S.: Binary priority list for prioritizing software requirements. In: Wieringa, R., Persson, A. (eds.) REFSQ 2010. LNCS, vol. 6182, pp. 67–78. Springer, Heidelberg (2010). https://doi.org/10.1007/978-3-642-14192-8_8

4. Deng, R., et al.: Optimal workload allocation in fog-cloud computing toward balanced delay and power consumption. IEEE Internet of Things J. **3**(6), 1171–1181 (2016)
5. Fernández, L.L., et al.: Kurento: a media server technology for convergent WWW/mobile real-time multimedia communications supporting WebRTC. In: 2013 IEEE 14th International Symposium on A World of Wireless, Mobile and Multimedia Networks (WoWMoM). IEEE (2013)
6. Horn, G., Skrzypek, P.: MELODIC: utility based cross cloud deployment optimisation. In: 2018 32nd International Conference on Advanced Information Networking and Applications Workshops (WAINA), Krakow, pp. 360–367 (2018). https://doi.org/10.1109/WAINA.2018.00112
7. Horn, G., Rózańska, M.: Affine scalarization of two-dimensional utility using the pareto front. In: 2019 IEEE International Conference on Autonomic Computing (ICAC), Umea, Sweden, pp. 147–156 (2019). https://doi.org/10.1109/ICAC.2019.00026
8. Jain, A.K., Li, S.Z.: Handbook of Face Recognition, vol. 1. Springer, New York (2011). https://doi.org/10.1007/978-0-85729-932-1
9. Johnston, A., Yoakum, J., Singh, K.: Taking on webRTC in an enterprise. IEEE Commun. Mag. **51**(4), 48–54 (2013)
10. Kiran, M., Murphy, P., Monga, I., Dugan, J., Baveja, S.S.: Lambda architecture for cost-effective batch and speed big data processing. In: 2015 IEEE International Conference on Big Data (Big Data), pp. 2785–2792. IEEE (2015)
11. Kritikos, K., Skrzypek, P., Moga, A., Matei, O.: Towards the modelling of hybrid cloud applications. In: 2019 IEEE 12th International Conference on Cloud Computing (CLOUD), pp. 291–295. IEEE (2019)
12. Kunifuji, S., Kato, N., Wierzbicki, A.P.: Creativity support in brainstorming. In: Wierzbicki, A.P., Nakamori, Y. (eds.) Creative Environments. SCI, vol. 59, pp. 93–126. Springer, Heidelberg (2007). https://doi.org/10.1007/978-3-540-71562-7_5
13. LaViola, J., et al.: Using AR to tutor military tasks in the wild. In: Proceedings of the Interservice/Industry Training Simulation & Education Conference, Orlando, Florida (2015)
14. Livingston, M.A., et al.: Military applications of augmented reality. In: Furht, B. (ed.) Handbook of Augmented Reality, pp. 671–706. Springer, New York (2011). https://doi.org/10.1007/978-1-4614-0064-6_31
15. Livingston, M.A., et al.: An AR system for military operations in urban terrain. Naval Research Lab Washington DC Advanced Information Technology Branch (2002)
16. Matei, O.: Evolutionary computation: principles and practices. Risoprint (2008)
17. Matei, O., Di Orio, G., Jassbi, J., Barata, J., Cenedese, C.: Collaborative data mining for intelligent home appliances. In: Afsarmanesh, H., Camarinha-Matos, L.M., Lucas Soares, A. (eds.) PRO-VE 2016. IAICT, vol. 480, pp. 313–323. Springer, Cham (2016). https://doi.org/10.1007/978-3-319-45390-3_27
18. Matei, O., Skrzypek, P., Heb, R., Moga, A.: Transition from serverfull to serverless architecture in cloud-based software applications. In: Silhavy, R., Silhavy, P., Prokopova, Z. (eds.) CoMeSySo 2020. AISC, vol. 1294, pp. 304–314. Springer, Cham (2020). https://doi.org/10.1007/978-3-030-63322-6_24
19. Mitaritonna, A., Abásolo, M.J.: Improving situational awareness in military operations using AR (2015)
20. Di Orio, G., et al.: A platform to support the product servitization. Int. J. Adv. Comput. Sci. Appl. IJACSA **7**(2) (2016)

21. Wang, J.-W., Lee, J.-S., Chen, W.-Y.: Face recognition based on projected color space with lighting compensation. IEEE Signal Process. Lett. **18**(10), 567–570 (2011)
22. Yadav, S.B., et al.: Comparison of analysis techniques for information requirement determination. Commun. ACM **31**(9), 1090–1097 (1988)
23. Zhang, M., et al.: Video processing with serverless computing: a measurement study. In: Proceedings of the 29th ACM Workshop on Network and Operating Systems Support for Digital Audio and Video (2019)

RGB-D Railway Platform Monitoring and Scene Understanding for Enhanced Passenger Safety

Marco Wallner[✉], Daniel Steininger, Verena Widhalm,
Matthias Schörghuber, and Csaba Beleznai

AIT Austrian Institute of Technology GmbH, Vienna, Austria
{marco.wallner,daniel.steininger,verena.widhalm,
matthias.schorghuber,csaba.beleznai}@ait.ac.at
https://www.ait.ac.at

Abstract. Automated monitoring and analysis of passenger movement in safety-critical parts of transport infrastructures represent a relevant visual surveillance task. Recent breakthroughs in visual representation learning and spatial sensing opened up new possibilities for detecting and tracking humans and objects within a 3D spatial context. This paper proposes a flexible analysis scheme and a thorough evaluation of various processing pipelines to detect and track humans on a ground plane, calibrated automatically via stereo depth and pedestrian detection. We consider multiple combinations within a set of RGB- and depth-based detection and tracking modalities. We exploit the modular concepts of Meshroom [2] and demonstrate its use as a generic vision processing pipeline and scalable evaluation framework. Furthermore, we introduce a novel open RGB-D railway platform dataset with annotations to support research activities in automated RGB-D surveillance. We present quantitative results for multiple object detection and tracking for various algorithmic combinations on our dataset. Results indicate that the combined use of depth-based spatial information and learned representations yields substantially enhanced detection and tracking accuracies. As demonstrated, these enhancements are especially pronounced in adverse situations when occlusions and objects not captured by learned representations are present.

Keywords: RGB-D visual surveillance · Human detection and tracking · Tracking evaluation · Evaluation framework · Surveillance dataset

1 Introduction

Vision-based robust human detection and tracking are receiving an increasing amount of attention recently. These core technologies are essential enablers for many human-centered applications such as pedestrian safety aspects in autonomous driving [9], public crowd monitoring [32], and human-aware robotics.

© Springer Nature Switzerland AG 2021
A. Del Bimbo et al. (Eds.): ICPR 2020 Workshops, LNCS 12667, pp. 656–671, 2021.
https://doi.org/10.1007/978-3-030-68787-8_47

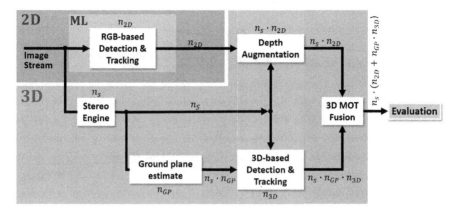

Fig. 1. Our combined 2D and 3D analysis concept exploiting learned representations (ML = machine learning) and cues from spatial data. n_s, n_{GP}, n_{2D} and n_{3D} denote the number of stereo, ground-plane estimation, image-based and depth-based algorithmic methods, along with indication for the number of combinations after each algorithmic module.

With these developments yielding growing algorithmic capabilities, new sets of public benchmarks with added tasks, complexities, and sizes have been proposed. Typical examples for multiple human tracking in RGB images are the MOTChallenge [10] and its recent MOTS [31] extension. The progress in these benchmarks reflects the recent enhancement of discriminative power introduced by representations via deep learning. However, the use of depth data in the form of RGB-D surveillance has received comparatively less attention. This relative scarcity of combined RGB-D analysis is mainly due to the (i) additional need for a depth sensor or stereo configuration, (ii) the increased computational demand when computing stereo depth, and (iii) the need to create a common representation (e.g., a common ground plane) for combining RGB and depth data.

In this paper, we propose a modular RGB-D processing pipeline (see Fig. 1), which allows for the exploration of several RGB-D combined processing schemes. Depth information allows for mapping RGB-based detection results into a 3D space, yielding 3D bounding boxes, which convey size, spatial ordering, and directional information on the ground plane, when being part of a tracking process. Therefore, such information is highly complementary to learned 2D detection results and opens up possibilities to achieve better target separation, segmentation, and occlusion reasoning. In addition, detecting objects from depth data based on geometric cues might yield object proposals that are not captured by learned representations. For example, a box-like object on a platform, when this object type is not part of any class in a training set, will be ignored by learned detectors. This paper introduces the following contributions in the context of RGB-D pedestrian tracking: we present an efficient, sparse-flow based tracking algorithm with an implicit target association step. We present a fusion scheme to

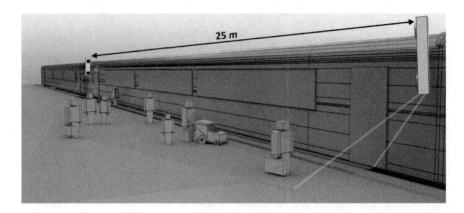

Fig. 2. Our dual stereo-camera configuration mounted on a train, exhibiting partially overlapping field-of-views (stereo-cameras are enlarged for highlighting their location and pose).

combine 2D and depth-based detection results on a common ground plane (see Fig. 2). We present a practically interesting aspect via modularizing algorithmic units within Meshroom [2] and its use as a generic vision processing pipeline and scalable evaluation framework. We use this modular framework to elaborate and evaluate multiple RGB-D detection- and tracking-schemes. Finally, we introduce RailEye3D, a novel RGB-D railway platform dataset[1] along with annotations for benchmarking detection and tracking algorithms, to support research activities in the RGB-D surveillance domain.

2   Related State of the Art

Over the last two decades, pedestrian detection and tracking have received much research interest. Their operational domain has been extended towards increasingly complex scenarios. In this process, the following representations have played a key role:

Appearance: Recent years have demonstrated a marked shift from hand-crafted representations to end-to-end learned recognition concepts employing deep distributed representations. The Integral Channel Features [11], DPM [12], and LDCF [35] detectors represented well-performing detection algorithms using hand-crafted representations. Modern detection schemes based on deep learning have reached great improvements on common benchmarks, however, at the expense of significantly higher computational costs. A representative example for this computing paradigm is the R-CNN framework [37] and its variants [29,40]. Latest representational concepts such as one-stage inference [22,42] of various pedestrian attributes also produce strong performance on common benchmark datasets [8,21,38]. Increasing the data diversity during training [14] reduces the miss rate on difficult (small size, occlusion) data significantly.

---

[1] https://github.com/raileye3d/raileye3d_dataset

Along with the rise of algorithmic capabilities, larger and more complex pedestrian detection datasets have been proposed. The CityPerson [38], the EuroCityPerson [8], and the Wider Pedestrian [34] datasets are relevant benchmarks indicating the progress of appearance-based pedestrian detection.

RGB-D: Information in depth-data inherently offers ways to lower the ambiguity associated with occlusions and depth ordering. The number of related works is significantly fewer than for appearance-based learned representations. Early RGB-D approaches [6] tried to use the depth cue as a segmentation cue in the image space. Approaches with increasing sophistication [17,25] later employed the popular *occupancy map* concept or the voxel space [24] to delineate individual human candidates. The idea of combining the representational strength of learning on combined RGB-D inputs has been proposed by several papers [4,26,41]. Nevertheless, accomplished improvements are rather small.

Only a few datasets for RGB-D human detection exist. The EPFL RGB-D pedestrian dataset [3,26] represent relatively simple indoor (lab, corridor) scenarios. The RGB-D People Dataset [30] is an indoor dataset based on Kinect sensor data, depicting limited variations in its scenes. The Kitti Vision Benchmark Suite [13] also contains an RGB-D pedestrian detection task; nevertheless, for a moving platform. Therefore we think that the proposed RailEye3D dataset fills a missing gap within this research domain.

Multiple Target Tracking: Multiple Object Tracking (MOT) is a crucial step to assign detection results to coherent motion trajectories over time. This fundamental temporal grouping task's relevance is reflected by the vast number of tracking methodologies proposed. For example, the MOT benchmark and its evolutions [18] display significant progress in scenes of increasing complexity. The multiple object tracking task encompasses the critical aspects of data association, motion estimation, and target representation, each impacting the overall quality. Data association has been intensively investigated and often posed as a classical optimization problem [19,27]. Data association has recently been embedded into end-to-end learning schemes, such as predicting future offsets [42] or inferring association states [7]. Another key aspect is the target appearance representation, where learning representations of great discriminative power produced well-performing tracking schemes [33,39]. Accurate target segmentation also substantially contributes to the target representational quality, and it is the main scope of the recent MOTS20 benchmark [31].

3 Proposed Methodologies and Systemic Concept

In this section, we describe our overall processing scheme and its components.

Scalable Processing and Evaluation via Meshroom: Meshroom [2], as the result of an open-source EU project, offers intuitive node-graph-based modular concepts for off-line vision processing. The framework can be used not only for photogrammetry but also for arbitrary algorithmic units in various implementation forms, such as Python and C++. Its ease-of-use and its capability to create and re-configure a large number of algorithmic pipelines allowed us to define a broad set of configuration, detection, tracking, and evaluation components. Following algorithmic blocks have been created: two stereo matching algorithms, multiple 2D and 3D pedestrian detection schemes, a robust-fitting-based ground plane estimation module, multiple tracking methods, a depth augmentation block transforming 2D bounding boxes into 3D by exploiting depth and ground plane information, and a fusion scheme combining multiple 3D observations on the ground plane. A MOT challenge [18] evaluation module was also implemented to evaluate individual workflows. Additionally, modules handling various inputs, parameter configurations, visualizations and format conversions complement the algorithmic units. The Meshroom-based framework also offers internal caching of intermediate results, thus allowing for partial tree updates.

Stereo Camera Setup and Depth Computation: We use a binocular stereo setup with a baseline of 400 mm between the two cameras. The RGB cameras are board-level industrial cameras of 2 Megapixels. During rectification, the images are resampled to 1088×1920 pixels with 8 bit quantization. The stereo matching process outputs disparity data alongside with rectified intensity images, congruent to the disparity image. We integrated two stereo matching methods into our processing pipeline, the S3E [16] and libSGM (based on [15]) techniques. S3E employs a pyramidal implementation of a Census-based stereo matching algorithm, while libSGM combines the Census transform with a semi-global matching step to establish correspondences.

Platform Detection and Automated Ground-Plane Estimation: For all experiment scenarios, we mounted two stereo camera units with largely overlapping field-of-views on the side of a train. The ground plane homography for a given unit is estimated in a fully automated manner. First, during a calibration phase, we determine image regions representing "walkable surfaces" by aggregating the results of a pedestrian detector [36] in the image space and in time. Next, we use a RANSAC-based plane fitting on the depth data to recover the platform's 3D plane parameters. This fitting step is limited to 3D points lying within the previously determined "walkable" areas, and it is also guided by prior knowledge on the camera mounting height, its proximity to the train, and the maximum platform width. This auto-calibration scheme has proved to be successful in all of our scenarios and allowed us to map image-based (denoted as 2D later on) detection results onto a common 3D ground plane. For 3D object detection, such a calibrated ground plane was also a prerequisite for computing an occupancy map representation.

3.1   3D Multi-object Detection and Tracking

To detect human candidates in the depth data, we employ an occupancy map clustering scheme. In the occupancy map, clusters corresponding to humans and compact objects are delineated using a hierarchically-structured tree of learned shape templates [4]. Thus, local grouping within the two-dimensional occupancy map generates consistent object hypotheses and suppresses background clutter and noise. The detection results are tracked with a conventional frame-to-frame tracking scheme. We employ a standard Bayesian filter based multi-target tracking method where data association is performed by the Hungarian algorithm and states are estimated by a Kalman filter. The target states are represented metric coordinates and velocities, given the calibrated ground plane.

3.2   2D Object Detection and Tracking Schemes

FOT/Fast Object Tracker/: We included our own tracking framework called *Fast Object Tracker* (FOT) for the experiments and evaluations. This tracking algorithm has been developed to be detector-agnostic and to exploit run-time optimized sparse optical flow computation for the data association step. Sparse optical flow estimation relies on a high number of local features with distinctive and compact descriptor representations. Matching is performed within a larger temporal neighborhood, resulting in an enhanced discovery of coherently moving object points and suppression of spurious correspondences. For stationary camera setups, background modeling can be computed as an additional hint for identifying potential tracking targets, which along with the sparse-flow computation, is parallelized on the GPU to provide real-time performance even on embedded devices. Our experiments used a pre-trained YOLOv3 [28] detector for generating object proposals to be tracked.

Third-Party Tracking Schemes: In addition to the FOT-tracker, we integrated two recent state-of-the-art tracking schemes employing highly discriminative target representations for re-identification:

TRT-MOT/Towards Realtime MOT/ [33] incorporates an appearance embedding model into a single-shot detector. This integration is performed by formulating the learning task with multiple objectives: anchor classification, bounding box regression, and learning a target-specific embedding. The representational homogeneity and joint optimization for these distinct tasks yield an enhanced detection accuracy and target matching capability.

FairMOT [39] builds upon TRT-MOT, but proposes an anchor-free approach. Multiple nearby anchors in TRT-MOT belonging to the same target might lower the representational specificity, a deficiency removed in FairMOT. Due to this algorithmic enhancement, FairMOT outperforms TRT-MOT in several benchmarks.

3.3   Fusion of MOT Results

The variety of proposed multiple object tracking concepts have increased in recent years. These algorithms often approach the tracking task with different strategies, or rely on different input modalities. The presented fusion scheme's key idea is to conceive a general framework to fuse tracking results independent of their origin. To allow 2D and 3D approaches to be fused, image-based (2D) tracking results are augmented with depth information to create a common 3D bounding box representation.

Depth Estimates: Most recent tracking solutions perform object detection and tracking on a 2D bounding box basis (see Sect. 2). Estimating these objects' depth as the mean of all measurements inside the bounding box leads to wrong results in general as data points, which are part of the background, are used too. The structure of most objects can be exploited to overcome this problem without using semantic segmentation solutions. The objects are most likely located in the middle of the detected bounding box with no holes in their centers. The depth measurements are weighted with a 2D Gaussian kernel centered in the bounding box's middle to exploit this. The $p = 2$ dimensional kernel can be defined in general as

$$f(\mathbf{x}, \mu, \Sigma) = \frac{1}{\sqrt{(2\pi)^p \cdot Det(\Sigma)}} \exp\left(-\frac{1}{2}(\mathbf{x} - \mu)^T \Sigma^{-1}(\mathbf{x} - \mu)\right) \qquad (1)$$

with $\mathbf{x} = (u\ v)^T$, $\mu = (c_u\ c_v)^T$ and $\Sigma = \begin{pmatrix} \sigma_u & 0 \\ 0 & \sigma_v \end{pmatrix}$. c_u and c_v are chosen to be half of the bounding box width and height, σ_u and σ_v to the size of the bounding box. u and v are the column and row indices inside the bounding box. For our use case, this can be simplified with the width and height of the bounding box w_{BB} and h_{BB} to:

$$w(u, v) = \frac{1}{2\pi\sqrt{w_{BB}h_{BB}}} \exp\left(-\left(\frac{\left(u - \frac{w_{BB}}{2}\right)^2}{2w_{BB}^2} + \frac{\left(v - \frac{h_{BB}}{2}\right)^2}{2h_{BB}^2}\right)\right) \qquad (2)$$

As there is not always a valid depth measurement for all pixels, a validity function ϕ is introduced as

$$\phi(u, v) = \begin{cases} 1, & \text{if } d(u, v) \text{ is valid} \\ 0, & \text{otherwise.} \end{cases} \qquad (3)$$

The normalizing weight sum W_i for the ith bounding box can be calculated as

$$W_i = \sum_{u=0}^{w_{BB}-1} \sum_{v=0}^{h_{BB}-1} \phi(u, v) \cdot w(u, v). \qquad (4)$$

With this, the depth $d_{i_{est}}$ is estimated as

$$d_{i_{est}} = \frac{1}{W_i} \sum_{u=0}^{w_{BB}-1} \sum_{v=0}^{h_{BB}-1} \phi(u, v) \cdot w(u, v) \cdot d(u, v). \qquad (5)$$

This calculated distance can be interpreted as the distance to the object's surface facing the camera. With this, the object's 3D volume is estimated to have the same depth as its width. Resulting 3D bounding boxes are finally transformed into a common reference coordinate system (using the estimated platform's plane homography) to allow fusion of multiple camera views.

Fusion Algorithm: Having these multiple tracking results of the same scene as 3D bounding boxes in a common reference frame alleviates the fusion problem. The abstract approach is described in Algorithm 1 and 2. The main idea is to treat the incoming tracker results as tracklets per object. These tracklets are fused into existing tracks (with a new consistent track id) if their current 3D bounding box intersects enough (IoU threshold) or are fully enclosed (i.e., intersection over envelope IoE).

Data: Detection *det*
Result: Track-ID consistent fusion of new observations
if $tracklet\_id = DetectionAlreadyInTrackletHistory(det)$ **then**
$\quad |$ addNewDetectionToTracklet(*det*, *tracklet_id*);
$\quad |$ return;
end
$IoU, IoE, tracklet_id = $ getTrackletWithMostOverlap(*det*);
if $IoU \geq thres$ or $IoE \geq thres$ **then**
$\quad |$ fuseDetectionWithTracklet(*det*, *tracklet_id*);
else
$\quad |$ setupNewTracklet(*det*);
end

Algorithm 1: Fuse new observations (tracklet) with consistent tracks.

Data: Detection *det*, TrackletManager *t_mgr*
Result: True if observations with same tracker ID and track ID already
$\qquad$ contained
if $\exists\, t \in t\_mgr : (track\_ID(t) == track\_ID(det))\;\wedge$
$\qquad\qquad\qquad (tracker\_ID(t) == tracker\_ID(det))$ **then**
$\quad |$ return *true*;
else
$\quad |$ return *false*;
end

Algorithm 2: Check if new observation belongs to existing tracklet.

---

4   The RailEye3D Railway Platform Dataset

Evaluating the performance of multi-object-tracking algorithms requires domain-specific test data. While many available datasets traditionally focus on persons as their main tracking target [8,34,38], few of them provide RGB-D data [3,13,26,30], and none of them consider safety aspects on train platforms as an application setting to the best of our knowledge. Therefore, the RailEye3D stereo dataset was developed to include a diverse set of train-platform scenarios for applications targeting passenger safety and assisting the clearance of train dispatching. Image data is captured by two stereo camera systems mounted on the train's sides (Fig. 2) with partially overlapping fields-of-view, ensuring that

Fig. 3. Sample annotations of the RailEye3D dataset for persons and things.

Fig. 4. Sample frames of the RailEye3D stereo dataset recorded at 10 different railway platforms.

objects occluded in one perspective are still visible in the opposing one. Three representative test sequences were selected for creating annotations of adults and children and selected objects relevant to the scenario, such as wheelchairs, buggies, and backpacks. Every 10th frame of a sequence was annotated to increase annotation efficiency while facilitating a sufficiently precise evaluation of detection and multi-object-tracking methods. Instance and tracking annotations are created manually in two stages using the open-source annotation tool Scalabel [1]. Each object is labeled with a parameter representing its degree of occlusion (0%, 25%, 50%, 75%, 100%), and persons are furthermore assigned a unique ID consistent through all scenes and camera views to enable the evaluation of person tracking and re-identification tasks. The annotations include the position of the safety line defining the area to be cleared before dispatch. The use of stereo cameras additionally provides the opportunity to benchmark algorithms integrating depth cues. Table 1 provides an overview of relevant annotation statistics for each scene.

Table 1. Annotation overview of the RailEye3D dataset

Scene	#Frames	#Annotated	#Persons	#Objects
1	5.505	540	8.707	3.630
2	2.999	300	2.205	1.656
3	3.363	338	4.721	3.951

The selected scenes shown in Fig. 3 include typical scenarios such as people waiting and boarding trains, riding scooters and skateboards, or gathering in groups. Children playing and persons using wheelchairs are represented as well, along with some uncommon situations of luggage left on the platform or objects falling between platform and train. The dataset captures a variety of lighting conditions and environmental context (see Fig. 4).

5   Results and Discussion

Using our presented re-configurable workflow concept, we created and evaluated multiple processing pipelines for the train platform surveillance task.

Selected Methods: The compared stereo engines (see Sect. 3) provided comparable depth data quality. Therefore, for the sake of brevity, we only present results for one (S3E) stereo depth computation technique. The system shown in Fig. 1 is evaluated with the following configurations, where n_s, n_{GP}, n_{2D} and n_{3D} denote the number of stereo, ground-plane estimation, image-based and depth-based algorithmic methods, respectively:

– One stereo engine (S3E): $n_s = 1$
– One platform estimator (disabled masking, see Sect. 3): $n_{GP} = 1$
– Three image-based (2D) detection and tracking algorithms: $n_{2D} = 3$
  • Fast Object Tracker - FOT
  • Towards Realtime MOT - TRT-MOT
  • FairMOT
– One depth-based detection and tracking algorithm: $n_{3D} = 1$

This leads to a fusion of $n = n_s \cdot (n_{2D} + n_{GP} \cdot n_{3D}) = 4$ different MOT results and all their combinations $c = \sum_{k=1}^{n} \binom{n}{k} = 15$ for each scene.

Selected Evaluation Metrics: Our evaluations use established metrics for object detection and tracking (see Table 2), as defined in [5,20], and [23]:

Table 2. Multiple object tracking metric definitions.

IDF1	Global min-cost F1 score
IDP	Global min-cost precision
IDR	Global min-cost recall
Rcll	Number of correct detections over the total number of ground-truth objects
Prcn	Number of correct detections over the total number of detected objects
GT	Sum of tracks in the ground-truth
MT	Number of objects tracked for at least 80% of their lifespan
PT	Number of objects tracked between 20% and 80% of their lifespan
ML	Number of objects tracked less than 20% of their lifespan
FP	Number of detected objects without corresponding ground-truth source
FN	Number of missed detections
IDs	Sum of identity switches of tracked objects
FM	Total number of track fragmentations
MOTA	Incorporates tracking errors including false positives, misses and mismatches
MOTP	Relating the average positional error across all correctly tracked objects

Task Settings: Given on the annotation diversity of our test scenes, we defined two distinct task settings for evaluating algorithmic workflows. The task setting *ALL* covers the detection and tracking of all annotated humans and objects on the platform. The task setting *PEDS* focuses only on humans with at least 25% visibility. These split task definitions help us to characterize the individual workflows in multiple terms. The influence of input data quality such as the depth quality for small, thin or flat objects negatively impacts results in the *ALL* setting. Similarly, objects not covered by learned representations in the *ALL*-Set will likely contribute to high miss rates (FN) or lower tracking rates (ML).

Experiments and Results: We evaluated our algorithmic workflows on 3 different scenes of the proposed dataset (Sect. 4). Evaluation results for the tasks settings *ALL* and *PEDS* are shown in the Tables 3 and 4, respectively. As it can be seen from the tables, for both task settings, the combination between algorithmic modalities lowers the FN rate, increases the number of mostly-tracked (MT) targets, but accumulates the FP rate. However, we observe that most false positives are of transient nature, implying that a human operator monitoring results, can probably easily discard such spurious signals (see Fig. 5).

Experiments in the *ALL* setting (Table 3) clearly indicate the added values of combining depth information with learned representations. Many objects which are not detected by 2D detection schemes, are found by the combined methods, leading to lower FN rates and better MT rates. Such difficult objects, where learned representations are failing and depth-based detection are still yielding valid proposals, are for example pedestrians partially visible or in unusual poses (bending forward), objects not part of learned representations (buggy). On the other hand, learned representations excel in cases when objects are far from the camera and small, or their form is thin (skateboard, luggage, sticks). In such cases depth data contains little evidence for object presence.

Table 3. Individual and combined algorithmic results for the *ALL* setting, covering all object types. (i) "3D Person Detector and Tracker", (ii) "FOT", (iii) "TRT-MOT", and (iv) "FairMOT".

Algorithm	IDF1	IDP	IDR	Rcll	Prcn	GT	MT	PT	ML	FP	FN	IDs	FM	MOTA	MOTP
(i)	45.2%	44.6%	34.0%	18.4%	36.5%	50	0	24	26	3138	7899	394	764	−17.5%	**0.40**
(ii)	45.2%	46.3%	33.0%	32.0%	**71.0%**	50	4	33	13	**1279**	6825	845	654	9.7%	0.28
(iii)	**55.7%**	**55.6%**	41.4%	34.3%	70.8%	50	9	27	14	1427	6544	523	570	14.8%	0.31
(iv)	54.8%	**55.6%**	40.1%	32.4%	70.2%	50	7	28	15	1441	6736	**293**	**499**	15.4%	0.30
(i)+(ii)+(iii)+(iv)	41.7%	31.2%	**46.6%**	**47.2%**	38.3%	50	**13**	30	**7**	7556	**5157**	1055	942	−40.3%	0.31
(i)+(ii)+(iii)	43.0%	33.7%	43.9%	45.5%	43.7%	50	10	31	9	5742	5329	1078	1005	−24.3%	0.31
(i)+(ii)+(iv)	43.7%	34.9%	43.5%	44.3%	44.9%	50	12	28	10	5432	5497	940	904	−19.8%	0.30
(i)+(iii)+(iv)	45.6%	36.2%	45.7%	41.7%	41.7%	50	10	29	11	5721	5660	763	892	−24.6%	0.32
(ii)+(iii)+(iv)	45.3%	36.7%	44.1%	43.1%	45.9%	50	11	31	8	4901	5697	901	697	−17.7%	0.30
(i)+(ii)	43.2%	36.8%	38.8%	41.0%	51.5%	50	5	33	12	3789	5831	1007	1002	−8.1%	0.32
(i)+(iii)	47.9%	40.4%	43.5%	39.2%	47.9%	50	10	27	13	4287	5932	754	943	−10.9%	0.33
(i)+(iv)	48.0%	41.2%	42.8%	36.9%	47.2%	50	7	29	14	4129	6190	518	852	−9.5%	0.32
(ii)+(iii)	48.4%	42.6%	41.7%	40.7%	57.1%	50	9	31	10	2946	5926	894	718	0.2%	0.30
(ii)+(iv)	49.5%	44.5%	41.4%	39.5%	58.8%	50	11	27	12	2730	6092	717	665	4.4%	0.28
(iii)+(iv)	51.7%	46.6%	43.0%	36.5%	55.1%	50	9	28	13	2834	6310	560	578	1.0%	0.31

Table 4. Individual and combined algorithmic results for the *PEDS* setting, considering pedestrians only, with occlusions less than 75%. (i) "3D Person Detector and Tracker", (ii) "FOT", (iii) "TRT-MOT", and (iv) "FairMOT".

Algorithm	IDF1	IDP	IDR	Rcll	Prcn	GT	MT	PT	ML	FP	FN	IDs	FM	MOTA	MOTP
(i)	18.9%	21.0%	17.2%	41.5%	50.7%	46	5	28	13	2627	3742	315	439	−4.4%	0.37
(ii)	12.4%	14.5%	11.1%	50.2%	68.1%	46	4	35	7	1363	3255	822	554	11.6%	0.28
(iii)	27.7%	31.2%	25.1%	55.3%	69.8%	46	11	28	7	1480	2951	497	507	22.9%	0.30
(iv)	26.2%	30.6%	23.0%	52.7%	69.7%	46	8	29	9	1456	3105	291	473	24.3%	0.30
(i)+(ii)+(iii)+(iv)	15.4%	11.5%	23.4%	59.7%	29.3%	46	12	28	6	8695	2682	755	532	−97.4%	0.38
(i)+(ii)+(iii)	16.2%	12.7%	22.6%	60.3%	34.0%	46	10	31	5	7039	2637	748	534	−69.8%	0.38
(i)+(ii)+(iv)	16.9%	13.5%	22.6%	57.8%	34.5%	46	10	31	5	6814	2751	620	532	−62.7%	0.38
(i)+(iii)+(iv)	19.6%	15.7%	25.9%	57.5%	34.8%	46	8	29	9	6850	2901	570	535	−60.3%	0.38
(ii)+(iii)+(iv)	15.3%	12.8%	19.3%	46.8%	31.2%	46	8	30	8	6302	3375	677	530	−73.9%	0.39
(i)+(ii)	17.0%	14.7%	20.3%	56.1%	41.0%	46	4	36	6	4875	2865	723	581	−36.9%	0.38
(i)+(iii)	19.3%	16.5%	23.0%	55.6%	40.0%	46	7	30	9	5235	3018	522	542	−36.1%	0.38
(i)+(iv)	15.1%	27.6%	15.5%	32.3%	42.4%	46	1	19	26	3848	4380	251	346	−29.0%	0.39
(ii)+(iii)	15.3%	14.3%	16.5%	44.3%	38.5%	46	7	30	9	4187	3530	664	541	−41.5%	0.39
(ii)+(iv)	16.9%	16.0%	18.0%	44.6%	39.9%	46	8	28	10	4012	3509	564	505	−34.3%	0.38
(iii)+(iv)	17.8%	17.0%	18.7%	39.4%	36.0%	46	6	23	17	4351	3855	407	424	−39.4%	0.39

Fig. 5. Birds-eye view representations of the platform with critical objects in red and the corresponding fused detection results back-projected into the image. (Color figure online)

The experiments in the *PEDS* setting (Table 4) focus on easier criteria (only humans, mostly visible), where one would assume that both depth- and image-based modalities perform well, even when employed independently. Surprisingly, even in this case, the combination of 2D and 3D modalities significantly improves detection and tracking qualities. We explain this improvement by multiple factors: (i) the combination of weak detection responses in 2D and 3D generates more stable detection responses, yielding recall and tracking stability improvements; (ii) the 3D spatial context, such as depth ordering, introduces advantages when performing multiple object tracking. Occlusion handling, when performed explicitly or by implicit means (i.e., better target separability when modeling the state space in 3D), leads to enhanced tracking stability. In light of all experiment workflows, evaluation results suggest that a combination of 3D pedestrian detection and tracking, combined with the FOT- and FairMOT schemes, generates the best results in both task settings. This combination is indicated by (i)+(ii)+(iii) in the result Tables 3 and 4.

6   Conclusion and Outlook

This paper presents the evaluation for a set of algorithmic combinations in terms of multiple object detection and tracking using RGB-D inputs. Such functionalities play a crucial role in accomplishing automated platform surveillance in transport infrastructures.

We demonstrate a modular processing approach to create and adapt diverse computer vision processing pipelines, a scheme suggesting an impact even beyond the presented scope. We also introduce a novel annotated railway platform dataset, simultaneously recorded by two RGB-D cameras, with largely overlapping fields-of-view. We demonstrate benchmark results on this data using the reconfigurable pipeline. The presented combination of RGB-D modalities achieves high recall and stable track generation for most scene targets. This virtue of the combined algorithmic schemes renders them apt to use in an automated safety monitoring context, where train operators receive real-time situational feedback on potential passenger safety issues in the train's vicinity.

The proposed dataset and the learned failure modes in the experiments imply many future opportunities. The present paper does not exploit the dual-camera setup, as the analysis is only carried out in one view. Auto-calibration and joint processing of the two views will likely mitigate issues related to occluded and small-sized targets. Furthermore, the fusion of multiple tracking results could be formulated as a spatio-temporal graph-based fusion problem.

Acknowledgement. The authors would like to thank both the Federal Ministry for Climate Action, Environment, Energy, Mobility, Innovation and Technology, and the Austrian Research Promotion Agency (FFG) for co-financing the RAIL: EYE3D research project (FFG No. 871520) within the framework of the National Research Development Programme "Mobility of the Future". In addition, we would like to thank our industry partner EYYES GmbH, Martin Prießnitz with the Federal Austrian Railways (ÖBB) for enabling the recordings, and Marlene Glawischnig and Vanessa Klugsberger for support in annotation.

References

1. Scalable open-source web annotation tool. https://scalabel.ai. Accessed 01 Oct 2020
2. AliceVision: Meshroom: A 3D reconstruction software (2018). https://github.com/alicevision/meshroom

3. Bagautdinov, T., Fleuret, F., Fua, P.: Probability occupancy maps for occluded depth images. In: 2015 IEEE Conference on Computer Vision and Pattern Recognition (CVPR), pp. 2829–2837 (2015)
4. Beleznai, C., Steininger, D., Broneder, E.: Human detection in crowded situations by combining stereo depth and deeply-learned models. In: Lu, H. (ed.) ISAIR 2018. SCI, vol. 810, pp. 485–495. Springer, Cham (2020). https://doi.org/10.1007/978-3-030-04946-1_47
5. Bernardin, K., Elbs, A., Stiefelhagen, R.: Multiple object tracking performance metrics and evaluation in a smart room environment. In: Sixth IEEE International Workshop on Visual Surveillance, in Conjunction with ECCV, vol. 90, p. 91 (2006)
6. Bertozzi, M., Binelli, E., Broggi, A., Del Rose, M.: Stereo vision-based approaches for pedestrian detection. In: Proceedings of the 2005 IEEE Computer Society Conference on Computer Vision and Pattern Recognition (CVPR 2005) - Workshops, CVPR 2005, vol. 03, p. 16. IEEE Computer Society, Washington, DC, USA (2005)
7. Brasó, G., Leal-Taixé, L.: Learning a neural solver for multiple object tracking. In: Proceedings of the IEEE ICPR, pp. 6247–6257 (2020)
8. Braun, M., Krebs, S., Flohr, F., Gavrila, D.M.: EuroCity persons: a novel benchmark for person detection in traffic scenes. IEEE Trans. Pattern Anal. Mach. Intell. (2019). https://doi.org/10.1109/TPAMI.2019.2897684
9. Combs, T.S., Sandt, L.S., Clamann, M.P., McDonald, N.C.: Automated vehicles and pedestrian safety: exploring the promise and limits of pedestrian detection. Am. J. Prev. Med. (2019). https://doi.org/10.1016/j.amepre.2018.06.024
10. Dendorfer, P., et al.: MOT20: a benchmark for multi object tracking in crowded scenes. arXiv:2003.09003 [cs], March 2020. http://arxiv.org/abs/1906.04567
11. Dollár, P., Tu, Z., Perona, P., Belongie, S.: Integral channel features. In: Proceedings of the BMVC, pp. 91.1–91.11 (2009)
12. Felzenszwalb, P., Mcallester, D., Ramanan, D.: A discriminatively trained, multiscale, deformable part model. In: IEEE Conference on Computer Vision and Pattern Recognition, CVPR 2008, June 2008
13. Geiger, A., Lenz, P., Stiller, C., Urtasun, R.: The KITTI Vision Benchmark Suite. The KITTI Vision Benchmark Suite (2013)
14. Hasan, I., Liao, S., Li, J., Akram, S.U., Shao, L.: Pedestrian detection: the elephant in the room. arXiv preprint arXiv:2003.08799 (2020)
15. Hirschmüller, H.: Stereo processing by semiglobal matching and mutual information. PAMI (2008). https://doi.org/10.1109/TPAMI.2007.1166
16. Humenberger, M., Engelke, T., Kubinger, W.: A Census-based stereo vision algorithm using modified Semi-Global Matching and plane fitting to improve matching quality. In: 2010 IEEE Computer Society Conference on Computer Vision and Pattern Recognition - Workshops, CVPRW 2010 (2010). https://doi.org/10.1109/CVPRW.2010.5543769
17. Jafari, O.H., Mitzel, D., Leibe, B.: Real-time RGB-D based people detection and Tracking for mobile robots and head-worn cameras. In: Proceedings - IEEE International Conference on Robotics and Automation (2014). https://doi.org/10.1109/ICRA.2014.6907688
18. Leal-Taixé, L., Milan, A., Schindler, K., Cremers, D., Reid, I., Roth, S.: Tracking the trackers: an analysis of the state of the art in multiple object tracking, April 2017. http://arxiv.org/abs/1704.02781
19. Leal-Taixé, L., Pons-Moll, G., Rosenhahn, B.: Everybody needs somebody: modeling social and grouping behavior on a linear programming multiple people tracker. In: Proceedings of the IEEE International Conference on Computer Vision (2011)

20. Li, Y., Huang, C., Nevatia, R.: Learning to associate: hybridboosted multi-target tracker for crowded scene. In: 2009 IEEE Computer Society Conference on Computer Vision and Pattern Recognition Workshops, CVPR Workshops 2009 (2009). https://doi.org/10.1109/CVPRW.2009.5206735

21. Lin, T.-Y., et al.: Microsoft COCO: common objects in context. In: Fleet, D., Pajdla, T., Schiele, B., Tuytelaars, T. (eds.) ECCV 2014. LNCS, vol. 8693, pp. 740–755. Springer, Cham (2015). https://doi.org/10.1007/978-3-319-10602-1_48

22. Liu, W., Hasan, I., Liao, S.: Center and scale prediction: a box-free approach for pedestrian and face detection (2020)

23. Milan, A., Leal-Taixe, L., Reid, I., Roth, S., Schindler, K.: MOT16: a benchmark for multi-object tracking, pp. 1–12 (2016). http://arxiv.org/abs/1603.00831

24. Munaro, M., Basso, F., Menegatti, E.: Tracking people within groups with RGB-D data. In: IEEE International Conference on Intelligent Robots and Systems (2012)

25. Muoñz-Salinas, R., Aguirre, E., García-Silvente, M., Ayesh, A., Góngora, M.: Multi-agent system for people detection and tracking using stereo vision in mobile robots. Robotica (2009). https://doi.org/10.1017/S0263574708005092

26. Ophoff, T., Beeck, K.V., Goedeme, T.: Improving real-time pedestrian detectors with RGB+depth fusion. In: Proceedings of AVSS 2018 - 2018 15th IEEE International Conference on Advanced Video and Signal-Based Surveillance (2019)

27. Pirsiavash, H., Ramanan, D., Fowlkes, C.C.: Globally-optimal greedy algorithms for tracking a variable number of objects. In: Proceedings of the IEEE Computer Society Conference on Computer Vision and Pattern Recognition (2011)

28. Redmon, J., Farhadi, A.: Yolov3: an incremental improvement. arXiv preprint arXiv:1804.02767 (2018)

29. Ren, S., He, K., Girshick, R., Sun, J.: Faster R-CNN: towards real-time object detection with region proposal networks. IEEE Trans. Pattern Anal. Mach. Intell. (2017)

30. Spinello, L., Arras, K.O.: People detection in RGB-D data. In: IEEE International Conference on Intelligent Robots and Systems (2011)

31. Voigtlaender, P., et al.: MOTS: multi-object tracking and segmentation. arXiv: 1902.03604 [cs] (2019)

32. Wang, Q., Gao, J., Lin, W., Li, X.: NWPU-crowd: a large-scale benchmark for crowd counting and localization. IEEE Trans. Pattern Anal. Mach. Intell. 1 (2020)

33. Wang, Z., Zheng, L., Liu, Y., Wang, S.: Towards real-time multi-object tracking, September 2019. http://arxiv.org/abs/1909.12605

34. WiderPed: Wider pedestrian 2019 dataset (2019). https://competitions.codalab.org/competitions/20132

35. Woonhyun, N., Dollár, P., Hee Han, J.: Local decorrelation for improved pedestrian detection. In: NIPS (2014)

36. Wu, Y., Kirillov, A., Massa, F., Lo, W.Y., Girshick, R.: Detectron2 (2019). https://github.com/facebookresearch/detectron2

37. Zhang, S., Benenson, R., Omran, M., Hosang, J., Schiele, B.: How far are we from solving pedestrian detection? In: Proceedings of the IEEE Computer Society Conference on Computer Vision and Pattern Recognition (2016). https://doi.org/10.1109/CVPR.2016.141

38. Zhang, S., Benenson, R., Schiele, B.: CityPersons: a diverse dataset for pedestrian detection (2017)

39. Zhang, Y., Wang, C., Wang, X., Zeng, W., Liu, W.: A simple baseline for multi-object tracking, April 2020. http://arxiv.org/abs/2004.01888

40. Zhou, C., Yuan, J.: Bi-box regression for pedestrian detection and occlusion estimation. In: Ferrari, V., Hebert, M., Sminchisescu, C., Weiss, Y. (eds.) ECCV 2018. LNCS, vol. 11205, pp. 138–154. Springer, Cham (2018). https://doi.org/10.1007/978-3-030-01246-5_9

41. Zhou, K., Paiement, A., Mirmehdi, M.: Detecting humans in RGB-D data with CNNs. In: Proceedings of the 15th IAPR International Conference on Machine Vision Applications, MVA 2017 (2017). https://doi.org/10.23919/MVA.2017.7986862

42. Zhou, X., Koltun, V., Krähenbühl, P.: Tracking objects as points. In: Vedaldi, A., Bischof, H., Brox, T., Frahm, J.-M. (eds.) ECCV 2020. LNCS, vol. 12349, pp. 474–490. Springer, Cham (2020). https://doi.org/10.1007/978-3-030-58548-8_28

A Survey About the Cyberbullying Problem on Social Media by Using Machine Learning Approaches

Carlo Sansone[ORCID] and Giancarlo Sperlí[(✉)][ORCID]

Department of Information Technology and Electrical Engineering (DIETI),
University of Naples "Federico II", Via Claudio 21, 80125 Naples, Italy
{carlo.sansone,giancarlo.sperli}@unina.it

Abstract. The exponential growth of connected devices (i.e. laptops, smartphones or tablets) has radically changed communications means, also making it faster and impersonal by using On-line Social Networks and Instant messaging through several apps. In this paper we discuss about the cyberbullying problem, focusing on the analysis of the state-of-the-art approaches that can be classified in four different tasks (*Binary Classification*, *Role Identification*, *Severity Score Computation* and *Incident prediction*). In particular, the first task aims to predict if a particular action is aggressive or not based on the analysis of different features. In turn, the second and the third task investigate the cyberbullying problem by identifying users' role in the exchanged message or assigning a severity score to a given users or session respectively. Nevertheless, information heterogeneity, due to different multimedia contents (i.e. text, emojis, stickers or gifs), and the use of datasets, which are typically unlabeled or manually labelled, create continuous challenges in addressing the cyberbullying problem.

Keywords: Cyberbullying · Social media · Machine learning · Artificial intelligence

1 Introduction

Nowadays cyberbullying has become an emerging problem affecting children and young adults. It includes uploading of obscene images, unethical hacking into another personal account on a social network, impersonation and verbal harassment. Examples of Cyberbullying effects are the suicide of the 15-years old Phoebe Prince and 14-years old Hannah Smith that committed suicide after being bullied on Facebook[1] and Ask.fm[2]. Recent surveys show that more than half of teenagers have suffered from this problem while 10%–20% experience it regularly[3]. In a survey [21] conducted in 28 countries, 51% reported that the

---

[1] https://facebook.com/.

[2] https://ask.fm/.

[3] http://www.bullyingstatistics.org/category/bullying-statistics.

© Springer Nature Switzerland AG 2021
A. Del Bimbo et al. (Eds.): ICPR 2020 Workshops, LNCS 12667, pp. 672–682, 2021.
https://doi.org/10.1007/978-3-030-68787-8_48

offenders in cyberbullying are classmates of cyberbullied children, having the highest proportion in North America (65%) and the lowest one in the Middle East/Africa (39%). Cyberbullying has some peculiarities that makes it more dangerous with respect to bullying: (i) victims sometimes do not know bully's identity; (ii) the painful actions of a cyberbullying are viral; (iii) it is easier to be cruel hiding behind the technology devices by also avoiding to see the effects of one's actions. Furthermore, it occurs in the cyberspace (i.e. online forum, online social networks and social media platform) introducing new psychological risks and influencing physical well-being [14,15,20]. As described in [17], several factors (i.e. geography, gender, economic and race) can be associated with cyberbullying describing also regulatory actions made in the world to deal with this problem.

Several definition of cyberbullying has been proposed focusing on different point-of-views. Patchin and Hinduja [22] define cyberbullying as voluntary and repeated damage inflicted through textual conversation in the cyberspace. Cyberbullying can be also defined as an aggressive and intentional act conducted repeatedly or over time by an individual or a group in cyberspace through Information and Communication Technologies (e.g. e-mail, mobile phone and social networks) against victims who cannot defend themselves. In particular, it consists of three main features: (i) an act of online aggression; (ii) a power imbalance between involved individuals; and (iii) it is repeated over time. Different ICT technologies (i.e. e-mail, on-line social networks and instant messaging services) [37] have been used by cyberbullies to make their threats, which can take different forms as well as harassment or social exclusion [16] or spreading personal photos or rumors on social media [9].

Furthermore, Kowalski et al. [16] investigated Cyberbullying at work through a user study, composed by 10 questions from the Cyberbullying Behavior Questionnaire, that was provided to 563 workers from five Finnish expert organization and 1.817 Finnish workers. This study showed that the 13% and 17% of enterprise organizations and Finnish workers respectively suffer from cyberbullying every month, also showing symptoms of stress and exhaustion.

In this paper we analyze the state-of-the-art techniques to deal with cyberbullying problem, focusing on several automated tasks and also considering data crawled from social media. In particular, we classified the approaches proposed so far in four categories according to addressed tasks, ranging from cyberbullying prediction until to incident prediction. We further summarize the examined approaches by investigating used features (multimedia, textual, social and content) and the task that they addressed. Finally, we investigate the open issues about cyberbullying problem mainly due to heterogeneity and variability of generated content and and to the difficulty of building data-sets.

The paper is organized as follow. Sect. 2 analyzes state-of-the-art approaches, classifying them in four categories, while Sect. 3 discusses about open-issues of cyberbullying. Finally, some conclusions and future direction has been reported in Sect. 4.

2   Related Works

In the last years several attempts of cyberbullying have happened due to the rapidly diffusion of Online Social Networks (OSNs) that allowed to interconnect people living in different place in the world. In particular, it represents an aggressive phenomena on a person (*victim*), who is affected by embarrassment or depression symptoms that can lead to suicide attempts.

On the other hand, an increasing number of research approaches has been proposed to address cyberbullying problem, as shown in Fig. 1. In particular, Fig. 1 shows the number of papers published between 2013 and 2020 on computer science conference or journal about bullying and cyberbullying topic by performing the following queries:

- TITLE-ABS-KEY(bullying) AND SUBAREA(comp) AND PUBYEAR > 2012;
- TITLE-ABS-KEY(cyberbullying) AND SUBAREA(comp) AND PUBYEAR > 2012.

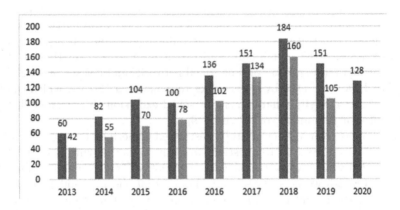

Fig. 1. Number of retrieved papers by performing two queries about *Bullying* and *Cyberbullying* between 2013–2020: i) TITLE-ABS-KEY (bullying) AND SUBJAREA (comp) AND PUBYEAR > 2012, ii) TITLE-ABS-KEY (cyberbullying) AND SUBJAREA(comp) AND PUBYEAR > 2012

Nevertheless, awareness continues to be insufficient though different actions (i.e. school buddies, promotional videos) promoted to deal with this problem. Hosseinmardi et al. [10] analyzed how node's topological properties on interaction graphs are correlated with user behavior on OSNs. Furthermore the same authors [11] compared users behaviors over different social network to analyze how negative user behavior varies across to different venue finding that ASK is more negative due to the anonymity of the authors of the questions.

As shown in Fig. 2, the cyberbullying problem has been investigated from different point of views as *binary classification, role identification, severity* score computation and *incident* prediction.

Cyberbullying

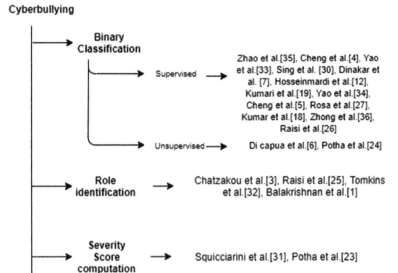

Fig. 2. Classification of cyberbullying approaches according to the addressed task.

In the first task each message published on OSN can be classified as aggressive or not. According to [8,28], cyberbullying detection approaches can be classified in two categories: supervised [27,35] and unsupervised [6,24].

The majority of approaches relies on designing of specialized features for supervised learning, as shown in Fig. 3. It is possible to classify the used features into five categories: i) textual, related to statistical analysis of content information (e.g. n-gram, part-of-speech tagging, text length), ii) social, representing information about users' relationships (e.g. following, followers or friendships) or the related statistics; iii) user, corresponding to user's profiles and demographic information or personality traits that can be computed on the basis of the *MRC Physiolinguistic database*[4] and/or the most used words/expression in Facebook [29]; iv) emotional, corresponding to sentiment information; v) word embedding, representing semantic information.

Zhao et al. [35] proposed a representation learning method, namely *Semantic-Enhanced Marginalized Denoising Auto-Encoder* (smSDA), relying on semantic knowledge, word embedding techniques and sparsity constraints to unveil hidden feature from text message for cyberbullying detection. Cheng et al. [4] proposed a hierarchical attention network relying on two levels in terms of word and comment level for cyberbullying detection predicting also the interval of time between

---

[4] http://websites.psychology.uwa.edu.au/school/MRCDatabase/mrc2.html.

Messages

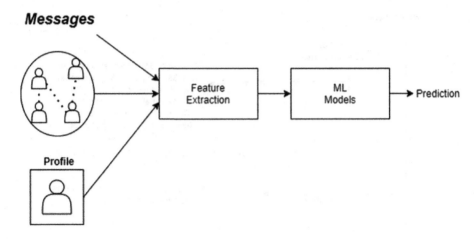

Fig. 3. Overview about the majority of approaches for cyberbullying prediction.

two adjacent comments. The complexity of cyberbullying behavior has been analyzed in [33] in which the authors proposed an algorithm based on hypothesis testing problem to reduce the dimension of the features for the classification problem. Disparity in cyberbullying detection performance based on the network centrality of the potential victim has been analyzed in [30] in which the authors proposed also a post-processing technique based on Equalized Odds to counter this disparity. Dinakar et al. [7] built the knowledge base *BullySpace* by analyzing several subject matter concerning cyberbullying. On top of this space, the authors developed a reasoning technique, called *AnalogySPace*, to analyze messages in OSNs. In [12] a first approach has been proposed to identify cyberbullying activities over images in Instagram combining visual and textual features, that are inferred by images and the related comments respectively. Kumar et al. [19] proposed a unified representation of text and images together in conjunction wit a single-layer Convolutional Neural Network model to identify the bullying comment. A cyberbullying detection framework, named *CONcISE* has been proposed in [34] using a sequential hypotesis testing to reduce the number of features with the aim to raise alerts after identifying a number of detection on Instagram media sessions. Another framework, called *XBully*, has been proposed in [5] for cyberbullying detection: it models multi-modal social network data as an heterogeneous network aiming to learn node embedding representations upon it. Furthermore, deep learning approaches for cyberbullying detection has been investigated in [27] in which three different architecture based on a Convolutional Neural Network and Long-Short Term Memory has been implemented as well as tree text representation model have been trained. In [18], the authors discussed a survey about cyberbullying by using soft computing with the aim to investigate findings of research approaches.

Zhong et al. [36] analyzed images and caption to unveil different features (i.e. Bag of ords, offensive score, LDA) for cyberbullying detection. Raisi et al. [26]

proposed an approach based on co-trained ensembles of embedding models to deal with cyberbullying detection.

In turn, unsupervised methods rely on clustering or pattern matching methodologies. In [6], the authors designed a machine learning model based on Growing Hierarchical SOMs, that combines semantic and syntactic features, for clustering bully traces logs. Furthermore, Potha and Maragoudakis [24] deals with the cyberbullying problem as time series aiming at identifying bullying patterns based on analysis of predator questions. In particular, they transformed cyberbullying data in strings sequences using Symbolic Aggregate approXimation (SAX) to unveil, thus, temporal patterns or slight variations in the predators' strategy.

The second task concerns the ability to automatically detect roles that users assume in OSN according to the analysis of user's profile, personality traits or its behavior on OSNs. Chatzakou et al. [3] have been designed a methodology for identifying bullies and aggressors from normal users in Twitter by combining text, users and network attributes. Raisi and Huang [25] propose a supervised method using social structures to infer user roles (*bullies* and *victim*) on the basis of a vocabulary provided by experts. The methodology computes a score to be bully or victim for each user by increasing also the vocabulary with words that could be indicators of bullying. In [32], the authors designed a socio-linguistic model, that incorporates uncertainty for better generalization, with the aim to identify participant roles, discovering latent text categories and detecting cyberbullying content in messages. Balakrishnan et al. [1] analyzed how users' psychological features (i.e. personalities, emotions), computed through Big Five and Dark Triad models, can be used for classifying tweets into four categories: bully, aggressor, spammer and normal.

The third task has the aim to assign a severity score for identifying cyberbullying activities. Cyberbullying identification as severity score of messages and/or senders has been investigated by [31] that proposed detection and classification of events occurring after a cyberbullying incident. A time series-based approach has been designed by Potha et al. [23] to model attack sequence as numeric labels, representing predator's posts using a sliding window, for computing the severity of a future question of a predator.

Finally, the fourth task concerns the prediction of cyberbullying incidents by using different features and multi-modal analysis. Hosseinmardi et al. [13] developed a prediction model by combining content analysis of images and caption with temporal and social content behavior to prevent occurrences of cyberbullying incidents.

In conclusion, different tools has been developed to prevent and increase awareness on cyberbullying. An example is *Conectado* [2] a video game designed on one hand to support professionals to increase emotional engagement of their classes and on the other hand to raise awareness on cyberbullying through experience and emotions.

Table 1 summarizes the approaches proposed in literature.

Table 1. Synthesis of the discussed approaches according to used features and addressed tasks.

Approaches	Features							TASK				
	Textual			Multimedia	Social	User	Emotional	Binary classification		Role identification	Severity score	Prediction
	Word	N-gram	Deep Learning					Unsupervised	Supervised			
Di Capua et al. [6]		✓			✓		✓	✓				
Potha et al. [24]		✓						✓				
Zhao and Kezhi [35]			✓	✓					✓			
Cheng et al. [4]			✓						✓			
Yao et al. [33]	✓				✓				✓			
Singh et al. [30]	✓				✓				✓			
Dinakar et al. [7]	✓				✓				✓			
Hosseinmardi et al. [12]	✓			✓					✓			
Kumari et al. [19]		✓	✓						✓			
Yao et al. [34]	✓								✓			
Cheng et al. [5]			✓	✓					✓			
Rosa et al. [27]			✓						✓			
Chatzakou et al. [3]	✓			✓	✓	✓			✓			
Zhong et al. [36]	✓		✓	✓					✓			
Raisi and Huang [25]	✓									✓		
Tomkins et al. [32]		✓								✓		
Balakrishan et al. [1]	✓				✓	✓	✓			✓	✓	
Squicciarini et al. [31]					✓	✓	✓				✓	
Potha and Maragoudakis [23]		✓										
Hosseinmardi et al. [13]		✓		✓								✓

3   Open Issues

As discussed in Sect. 2, different approaches have been designed to address the examined problem, mainly focused on the classification problem. The majority of them are mainly focused on the analysis of textual information or social aspects. Someones aim to model user's session, represented as the interaction between bully and victim, that can involved several actors.

Nevertheless, few of them analyze multimedia contents in messages, mainly related to images that are shared on social networks. Therefore, analyzing content heterogeneity is one of the main challenges in dealing with the cyberbullying problem. Furthermore, the temporal variability of these contents – as well as in content, type and shape – makes it difficult to analyze them to support cyberbullying detection system.

Finally, another challenge concerns the data set identification for the cyberbullying analysis, that are classified into manually labeled and unlabeled. An example of the first category is *Formspring*[5], a question-answer based site, containing information about user's biography, location and questions and answers published on its profile. Using Amazon's Mechanical Turk service each pair of question-answer has been labeled by three workers to identify if it contains cyberbullying with the related bullied words and to assign a severity score from 0 (no bullying) to 10 (bullying) providing also the time needed to label this pair.

Furthermore, perverted-justice.com dataset[6] is composed by dialogues between predators and victims in which all questions are labeled by a numeric class according to the predator's intention (i.e., i) activities, ii) personal information, iii) compliment, iv) relationship, v) reframing, vi) communicative desensitization vii) isolation and viii) approach).

Instagram dataset[7] based on the well-known social media is composed by 25K users and 3, 165K unique media sessions. Furthermore, 2, 218 media sessions, including images (having at least 15 comments) and their associated comments, has been also labeled for cyberbullying. Furthermore, Vine dataset (see Footnote 7), an entertainment network, is composed by 972 videos with all comments.

In turn, the second category is composed by large collection of raw text as well as Myspace data, including profiles and the related "wall" posts for 127,974 users, Formspring dataset, containing questions and answers for 18,554 users, ASk (see Footnote 7), composed by 110 profiles with related pair of question answer, and Instagram, including 118 profiles with the related comments on their media (Table 2).

---

[5] https://www.kaggle.com/swetaagrawal/formspring-data-for-cyberbullying-detection.

[6] https://www.chatcoder.com/drupal/index.php.

[7] http://www.cucybersafety.org/home/cyberbullying-detection-project/dataset.

Table 2. Datset characterization

Dataset	Labeled	Unlabeled
Formspring	✓	
Perverted-justice	✓	
Instagram	✓	
Vine	✓	
ASK		✓
Instagram		✓
MySpace		✓
Formspring		✓

4 Conclusions

In the last years, cyberbullying arose as a novel problem both at school and work domain, in which cyberbullies make their threats through instant messaging and On-line Social Networks by spreading rumors and personal or inappropriate photos about a victim.

We analyzed the proposed approaches about the cyberbullying problem, also classifying them in four tasks according to the objective of the analysis. In particular, the first task aims to predict if an action is aggressive or not based on textual, social, user-related, emotional and semantic features. An analysis about user roles in cyberbullying actions has been investigated in the second tasks. In turn, the third category aims to assign a severity score for identifying aggressive actions. Finally, the fourth task concerns the prediction of cyberbullying accidents by using different features and multi-modal analysis.

Finally, we discussed about the open issues in dealing with the cyberbullying problem mainly due to the data heterogeneity and dataset, that are often manually labeled or unlabeled.

Acknowledgement. This work is supported by the Italian Ministry of Education, University and Research (MIUR) within the PRIN2017 - BullyBuster - A framework for bullying and cyberbullying action detection by computer vision and artificial intelligence methods and algorithms (CUP: F74I19000370001).

References

1. Balakrishnan, V., Khan, S., Arabnia, H.R.: Improving cyberbullying detection using Twitter users' psychological features and machine learning. Comput. Secur. 101710 (2020)
2. Calvo-Morata, A., Rotaru, D.C., Alonso-Fernández, C., Freire, M., Martínez-Ortiz, I., Fernández-Manjón, B.: Validation of a cyberbullying serious game using game analytics. IEEE Trans. Learn. Technol. (2018)
3. Chatzakou, D., et al.: Detecting cyberbullying and cyberaggression in social media. ACM Trans. Web (TWEB) **13**(3), 1–51 (2019)

4. Cheng, L., Guo, R., Silva, Y., Hall, D., Liu, H.: Hierarchical attention networks for cyberbullying detection on the Instagram social network. In: Proceedings of the 2019 SIAM International Conference on Data Mining, pp. 235–243. SIAM (2019)
5. Cheng, L., Li, J., Silva, Y.N., Hall, D.L., Liu, H.: XBully: cyberbullying detection within a multi-modal context. In: Proceedings of the Twelfth ACM International Conference on Web Search and Data Mining, pp. 339–347 (2019)
6. Di Capua, M., Di Nardo, E., Petrosino, A.: Unsupervised cyber bullying detection in social networks. In: 2016 23rd International Conference on Pattern Recognition (ICPR), pp. 432–437, December 2016. https://doi.org/10.1109/ICPR.2016.7899672
7. Dinakar, K., Jones, B., Havasi, C., Lieberman, H., Picard, R.: Common sense reasoning for detection, prevention, and mitigation of cyberbullying. ACM Trans. Interact. Intell. Syst. (TiiS) 2(3), 18 (2012)
8. Farag, N., El-Seoud, S.A., McKee, G., Hassan, G.: Bullying hurts: a survey on non-supervised techniques for cyber-bullying detection. In: Proceedings of the 2019 8th International Conference on Software and Information Engineering, pp. 85–90 (2019)
9. Farley, S., Coyne, I., D'Cruz, P.: Cyberbullying at work: understanding the influence of technology (2018)
10. Hosseinmardi, H., Ghasemianlangroodi, A., Han, R., Lv, Q., Mishra, S.: Towards understanding cyberbullying behavior in a semi-anonymous social network. In: 2014 IEEE/ACM International Conference on Advances in Social Networks Analysis and Mining (ASONAM 2014), pp. 244–252. IEEE (2014)
11. Hosseinmardi, H., et al.: A comparison of common users across Instagram and Ask.fm to better understand cyberbullying. In: 2014 IEEE Fourth International Conference on Big Data and Cloud Computing, pp. 355–362. IEEE (2014)
12. Hosseinmardi, H., Mattson, S.A., Rafiq, R.I., Han, R., Lv, Q., Mishra, S.: Detection of cyberbullying incidents on the Instagram social network. In: Association for the Advancement of Artificial Intelligence (2015)
13. Hosseinmardi, H., Rafiq, R.I., Han, R., Lv, Q., Mishra, S.: Prediction of cyberbullying incidents in a media-based social network. In: 2016 IEEE/ACM International Conference on Advances in Social Networks Analysis and Mining (ASONAM), pp. 186–192. IEEE (2016)
14. Juvonen, J., Gross, E.F.: Extending the school grounds?-bullying experiences in cyberspace. J. Sch. Health 78(9), 496–505 (2008)
15. Katzer, C., Fetchenhauer, D., Belschak, F.: Cyberbullying: who are the victims? A comparison of victimization in internet chatrooms and victimization in school. J. Media Psychol. 21(1), 25–36 (2009)
16. Kowalski, R.M., Toth, A., Morgan, M.: Bullying and cyberbullying in adulthood and the workplace. J. Soc. Psychol. 158(1), 64–81 (2018)
17. Kshetri, N., Voas, J.: Thoughts on cyberbullying. Computer 52(4), 64–68 (2019)
18. Kumar, A., Sachdeva, N.: Cyberbullying detection on social multimedia using soft computing techniques: a meta-analysis. Multimed. Tools Appl. 78(17), 23973–24010 (2019). https://doi.org/10.1007/s11042-019-7234-z
19. Kumari, K., Singh, J.P., Dwivedi, Y.K., Rana, N.P.: Towards cyberbullying-free social media in smart cities: a unified multi-modal approach. Soft Comput. 1–12 (2019)
20. Li, Q.: New bottle but old wine: a research of cyberbullying in schools. Comput. Hum. Behav. 23(4), 1777–1791 (2007)
21. Newall, M.: Cyberbullying: A Global Advisor Survey. Ipsos (2018)

22. Patchin, J.W., Hinduja, S.: Bullies move beyond the schoolyard: a preliminary look at cyberbullying. Youth Violence Juvenile Justice **4**(2), 148–169 (2006)
23. Potha, N., Maragoudakis, M.: Time series forecasting in cyberbullying data. In: Iliadis, L., Jayne, C. (eds.) EANN 2015. CCIS, vol. 517, pp. 289–303. Springer, Cham (2015). https://doi.org/10.1007/978-3-319-23983-5_27
24. Potha, N., Maragoudakis, M., Lyras, D.: A biology-inspired, data mining framework for extracting patterns in sexual cyberbullying data. Knowl.-Based Syst. **96**, 134–155 (2016)
25. Raisi, E., Huang, B.: Cyberbullying detection with weakly supervised machine learning. In: Proceedings of the 2017 IEEE/ACM International Conference on Advances in Social Networks Analysis and Mining 2017, pp. 409–416 (2017)
26. Raisi, E., Huang, B.: Weakly supervised cyberbullying detection using co-trained ensembles of embedding models. In: 2018 IEEE/ACM International Conference on Advances in Social Networks Analysis and Mining (ASONAM), pp. 479–486. IEEE (2018)
27. Rosa, H., Matos, D., Ribeiro, R., Coheur, L., Carvalho, J.P.: A "deeper" look at detecting cyberbullying in social networks. In: 2018 International Joint Conference on Neural Networks (IJCNN), pp. 1–8, July 2018. https://doi.org/10.1109/IJCNN.2018.8489211
28. Salawu, S., He, Y., Lumsden, J.: Approaches to automated detection of cyberbullying: a survey. IEEE Trans. Affect. Comput. (2017)
29. Schwartz, H.A., et al.: Personality, gender, and age in the language of social media: the open-vocabulary approach. PLoS ONE **8**(9), e73791 (2013)
30. Singh, V.K., Hofenbitzer, C.: Fairness across network positions in cyberbullying detection algorithms. In: Proceedings of the 2019 IEEE/ACM International Conference on Advances in Social Networks Analysis and Mining, pp. 557–559 (2019)
31. Squicciarini, A., Rajtmajer, S., Liu, Y., Griffin, C.: Identification and characterization of cyberbullying dynamics in an online social network. In: Proceedings of the 2015 IEEE/ACM International Conference on Advances in Social Networks Analysis and Mining 2015, pp. 280–285 (2015)
32. Tomkins, S., Getoor, L., Chen, Y., Zhang, Y.: A socio-linguistic model for cyberbullying detection. In: 2018 IEEE/ACM International Conference on Advances in Social Networks Analysis and Mining (ASONAM), pp. 53–60. IEEE (2018)
33. Yao, M., Chelmis, C., Zois, D.: Cyberbullying detection on Instagram with optimal online feature selection. In: 2018 IEEE/ACM International Conference on Advances in Social Networks Analysis and Mining (ASONAM), pp. 401–408, August 2018. https://doi.org/10.1109/ASONAM.2018.8508329
34. Yao, M., Chelmis, C., Zois, D.S.: Cyberbullying ends here: towards robust detection of cyberbullying in social media. In: The World Wide Web Conference, pp. 3427–3433 (2019)
35. Zhao, R., Mao, K.: Cyberbullying detection based on semantic-enhanced marginalized denoising auto-encoder. IEEE Trans. Affect. Comput. **8**(3), 328–339 (2016)
36. Zhong, H., et al.: Content-driven detection of cyberbullying on the Instagram social network. In: Proceedings of the Twenty-Fifth International Joint Conference on Artificial Intelligence, pp. 3952–3958 (2016)
37. Zych, I., Ortega-Ruiz, R., Del Rey, R.: Systematic review of theoretical studies on bullying and cyberbullying: facts, knowledge, prevention, and intervention. Aggress. Violent Behav. **23**, 1–21 (2015)

Author Index

Printed in the United States
By Bookmasters